Governing America

Governing America

THE REVIVAL OF POLITICAL HISTORY

Julian E. Zelizer

PRINCETON UNIVERSITY PRESS

Princeton and Oxford

Published by Princeton University Press, 41 William Street, Princeton, New Jersey 08540
In the United Kingdom: Princeton University Press, 6 Oxford Street, Woodstock, Oxfordshire OX20 1TW

press.princeton.edu

Library of Congress Cataloging-in-Publication Data
Zelizer, Julian E.
Governing America : The revival of political history / Julian E. Zelizer.
p. cm.
Includes bibliographical references and index.
ISBN 978-0-691-15073-4 (hardcover : alk. paper)
1. United States—Politics and government. 2. Political culture—United States—History. I. Title.
E183.Z45 2011
306.20973—dc23
2011029788

British Library Cataloging-in-Publication Data is available

This book has been composed in Minion Pro

Printed on acid-free paper. ∞

Printed in the United States of America
10 9 8 7 6 5 4 3 2 1

In honor of my mentors at Brandeis University

and The Johns Hopkins University

Contents

ACKNOWLEDGMENTS ix

Governing America: An Introduction 1

PART I
Thinking about the Field 9

ONE
Beyond the Presidential Synthesis: Reordering Political Time 11

TWO
Clio's Lost Tribe: Public Policy History Since 1978 41

THREE
History and Political Science: Together Again? 60

FOUR
Rethinking the History of American Conservatism 68

FIVE
What Political Science Can Learn from the New Political History 90

PART II
Paying for Government: Taxes, Money, and Fiscal Restraint 105

SIX
The Uneasy Relationship: Democracy, Taxation, and State-Building Since the New Deal 107

SEVEN
The Forgotten Legacy of the New Deal: Fiscal Conservatism and the Roosevelt Administration, 1933–1938 124

EIGHT
"Where Is the Money Coming From?" The Reconstruction of Social Security Finance 153

NINE
Paying for Medicare: Benefits, Budgets, and Wilbur Mills's Policy Legacy 168

PART III
The Rules of the Game: The Politics of Process 193

TEN
Seeds of Cynicism: The Struggle Over Campaign Finance, 1956–1974 195

ELEVEN
Bridging State and Society: The Origins of 1970s Congressional Reform 221

TWELVE
Without Restraint: Scandal and Politics in America 232

THIRTEEN
Seizing Power: Conservatives and Congress Since the 1970s 259

FOURTEEN
How Conservatives Learned to Stop Worrying and Love Presidential Power 290

PART IV
Politics and Policy: The Case of National Security 307

FIFTEEN
Congress and the Politics of Troop Withdrawal, 1966–1973 309

SIXTEEN
Détente and Domestic Politics 321

SEVENTEEN
Conservatives, Carter, and the Politics of National Security 335

NOTES 351

INDEX 399

Acknowledgments

I would like to thank my editor Clara Platter, who has been enthusiastic about this book since our lunch at Prospect House to discuss the idea. Chuck Myers has done a great job with the manuscript since Clara's departure. Scott Moyers, my literary agent, who is now the publisher at Penguin, helped to negotiate a deal that would make this possible. I would also like to thank Kety McCoach, my assistant at Princeton, who retyped all of these articles and book chapters that appear in the following pages. Over the years, many colleagues have read the pieces in this book and graciously provided me with comments. Numerous foundations and institutions have also given me financial support to conduct the research that resulted in the work found in these pages. The essays have been copyedited so that there are some minor changes from how they originally appeared.

The book is dedicated to all academic mentors at Brandeis University, including JoAnne Brown, Gordon Fellman, David Hackett Fischer, Louis Galambos, Morton Keller, James Kloppenberg, Sidney Milkis, J.G.A. Pocock, Dorothy Ross, and Ronald Walters, who helped guide me as I embarked on this project. Their training at a time when specializing in political history was not the smartest professional move meant the world to me. They inspired me to continue moving forward. I hope they are all proud of the outcome. In addition, I would like to thank the many scholars at other institutions who supported me in this endeavor.

Finally, the two readers of the manuscript provided outstanding suggestions for revision.

The essays in this volume have been copyedited since they were originally published. References are in the format in which they originally appeared.

Governing America

Governing America: An Introduction

In the spring of 1995, I attended a session at the Organization of American Historians Conference at the Washington Hilton, which focused on the state of political history. When I walked toward the conference room I expected to find a small crowd, and one with little hope for the future.

At the time, the political history field seemed bleak. Senior practitioners, who, for at least two decades, felt that their work had been relegated to the academic dustbin, were demoralized and pessimistic. Graduate students such as myself entered the profession with a sense of trepidation, concerned about how our interests would be received in the academy.

When I entered the meeting room, I was surprised. The panelists spoke to an overflow crowd. The room was filled to capacity. Attendees were standing along the walls, and even outside the door in the hallway peering in. During the discussion, a generational debate opened up. While some of the older panelists and attendees expressed the predictable laments about the demise of the field since the 1960s, younger voices insisted that in fact we were on the cusp of a new era. They pointed to new scholarship that was starting to reenvision how historians wrote about politics by bringing back issues such as public policy and government institutions while integrating these subjects into broader narratives that dealt with social and cultural forces.

It was clear to everyone in the room that something was happening. The electric atmosphere suggested that change might be taking place after decades when U.S. political history had suffered professionally. As it turned out, the younger generation was right.

The problems for political history had begun toward the end of the 1960s, when a new generation of scholars entering the profession developed a stinging critique of political history as it had been practiced by legendary figures such as Arthur Schlesinger Jr. and Richard Hofstadter.

Shaped by the conflicts of the 1960s over civil rights and Vietnam, the scholarly arm of the New Left had argued that political history, as it had been practiced since the founding of the profession in the 1880s, revolved around a narrow group of political elites who did not reflect the experiences of the nation. In the minds of rebellious graduate students, the presidential synthesis had produced a skewed narrative of the American political tradition that ignored intense conflicts over class, race, ethnicity, and gender that had shaped the nation since its founding. The differences separating most presidents were indeed minor, they said, but for them that was a reason to look elsewhere to really explore the national tensions beneath Washington's surface. Claims about a liberal consensus that dampened serious divisions, they said, resulted from only looking at a narrow segment of the nation as opposed to accurately capturing the inherent character of the citizenry.

The social and cultural history revolution that followed in the next two decades pushed scholars to broaden their canvas to emphasize the study of American history from the "bottom up" and at the local level, focusing on questions like class formation and gender relations rather than political leaders, public policy, or government institutions. Whereas older historians had also understood the impact of social movements on politics, this literature relied on more quantitative precision to assure representative case studies and delved much deeper into local archives to unpack their stories.[1]

French scholarship had an important influence on the rise of social history and the decentering of political history. The *Annales* school shifted the attention of historians toward the *longue durée*: big demographic, geographic, and socioeconomic changes that impacted ideational and institutional structures rather than the specific actions of political leaders at given points in time.[2] The school, according to one scholar, treated political historians "with disparagement or even contempt . . . [political history] carries something of the aura of excommunication by the pope."[3] American social and cultural historians drew on these analytic methods as they turned their attention to similar kinds of issues within the United States, such as the formation of the middle class, the process of urbanization, or the evolution of race relations.

Social and cultural historians produced a wealth of knowledge about the formation of the nation from the bottom up. Instead of finding a country that shared some kind of ideological consensus and lacked the kind of social conflict that characterized Europe, these historians found a nation ridden with tensions over race, gender, and ethnicity. Some of the most vibrant scholarship took place in the field of labor history. Scholars examined the demise of a society where workers had maintained strong control of the shop floor in the nineteenth century to one where management and owners maintained much stronger control. Workers organized in response to the need for protecting certain kinds of wage guarantees and the desire to seek more autonomy in their communities. Cultural historians, who began to thrive in the late 1980s, were interested in studying the construction of ideas. Influenced by anthropology and literary studies, they also looked into the questions of whether cultural media such as films or television were hegemonic forces that shaped social identity or whether Americans brought their own interpretation and meaning to these experiences.[4]

And then, slowly, almost imperceptibly, history writing began to change. During his presidential address to the Organization of American Historians in 1986, "The Pertinence of Political History," published in the *Journal of American History*, historian William Leuchtenburg made an unexpected prediction amidst these historiographical trends. Leuchtenburg, whose own work focused on the politics of the New Deal, anticipated that the situation was about to change. Understanding this was an unconventional perspective, to say the least, he wrote, "When someone tells you, as I am about to tell you, that the historian's next frontier is political history, there would appear to be only one sensible response: You have got to be kidding."[5]

To defend his position, Leuchtenburg highlighted slightly more optimistic developments than other political historians of his time. First, there was a group of political scientists, such as Theda Skocpol and Stephen Skowronek, who were writing about the state. Practitioners of "American Political Development" (APD) designed an approach to studying politics that was fundamentally historical. Focusing on the development of institutions, they were interested in the structural constraints faced by policymakers. Some of the analytic strategies for the new political history emanated from the social sciences. These scholars were writing about how the foundational structure of American institutions shaped the evolution of national politics. They were particularly interested in the limits of change given the power of institutional structures to constrain policies. Second, there were some social and cultural historians who started to find their way back to politics, broadly defined, in response to a feeling that the field of American history had become too specialized and fragmented. There was no sense of what held all the pieces of American history together.[6]

It turned out that Leuchtenburg's prediction was correct. When he delivered his presidential address, announcing the return of political history, Leuchtenburg had a lot of evidence to show that political history was, once again, in vogue. Since the early 1990s, the field of American Political History has returned to the forefront of the profession, but not the same political history of the past. The field, once marginalized, has been remade, and in vibrant fashion. There were many reasons that a new generation of scholars turned to political history. Many had concluded that politics had been downplayed so much that huge areas of American history had been left out of the literature. Like all scholarly cycles, they saw a huge hole that existed in the literature and moved to fill it. Social and cultural historians, they said, ironically had made it more difficult to evaluate the structures of power within which different social groups and grassroots movements existed. Furthermore, graduate students who entered into the profession in the 1990s had come of age during Ronald Reagan's presidency in the 1980s, when they saw the impact that a shift in control of political power could have on the nation. As more historians developed an interest in writing about the twentieth century, particularly the decades since the New Deal, it was simply impossible to ignore the role of the state.

The new political historians have offered fresh and original approaches and interpretations about U.S. political history. They have punctured the myth that there was any kind of consensus that shaped political debate in any period, while simultaneously revealing how average citizens had a profound impact on national politics as a result of mass movements. Others have returned to their focus on political elites, from presidents to legislators to intellectuals, but they have done so by situating them within particular institutional contexts. They have shown how the structure of institutions shaped what political elites could or could not do at the same time that they have broadened the range of political elites who they include in their studies. The new political historians have challenged conventional assumptions about political development, such as the nineteenth century being a period when the federal government was absent from public life. They have taken a period thought to be stable and consensual, such as the decades between the New Deal and the 1970s, and shown them to be riddled with tensions and contradictions. Even those scholars who have returned to the subject of the presidency—the centerpiece of political history before the 1960s—have tackled the subject through analyses that avoid presenting the chief executive as a free-floating leader who embodied the spirit of the era. Influenced by the findings of the previous generation of political historians, the new political history has provided rich narratives full of conflict, tension, and contingency, shedding many of the assumptions of previous eras.

In developing my own research, I had to make significant choices about how to organize my narratives and where to focus my questions. Over the past fifteen years, I decided to emphasize three themes in an effort to develop fresh narratives about the political past: policy, political institutions, and electoral politics.

Focusing on policy has been attractive because it has helped me to break free from traditional time frames used in political history, ranging from presidential centered accounts, to the cycles of liberalism and conservatism, to the modernization schema that claimed the turn of the century to be the watershed moment in American political evolution.

While those older frameworks have much to offer, I was eager to experiment with other ways of organizing political time and testing to see whether the existing scholarship had missed watershed turning points or historical patterns. Policy history does not fit into most existing chronological structures. Indeed, different policies have different timelines, something that makes the subject enormously challenging. As historians delve into different policy sectors, they have begun to perceive more complex chronological structures of political history than previous historians have suggested.

Policy history has also allowed me to incorporate a more diverse group of actors into narratives than previous generations of historians have been able to do. The tensions between scholars who study elite politics and grassroots politics quickly dissipates when policy is made the center of inquiry. After all, policies are crafted by government officials in alliance with, and in response to, other social and political actors. Federal, state, and local policies influence—and are reshaped by—all types of social actors and institutions.

I have tried to understand how policy communities have played such an important role in Washington. Policy communities consist of party officials, leaders and experts from umbrella interest group associations, staff members of the executive and congressional branch, bureaucrats and administrators, university professors, independent specialists, editors and writers of the specialized policy media and think tanks. These communities work across institutional lines and create some kind of consistency in the fragmented political system over time. They attempt to sell their ideas to powerful elected officials in the White House and in Congress.

Recent work in policy history has started to accomplish what many scholars had been talking about in abstract theory for years: breaking down the once-rigid barriers between state and society through the use of policy as the object of study and not locating scholarship in any single social realm. Policy likewise has encouraged historians to examine institutions that are often overlooked by historians, such as the mass news media, local government, and the non-profit sector.

The second organizational theme of my research has been political institutions, with a particular focus on Congress. My interest in institutions grew out of the excellent work by historical political scientists in the field of American Political Development who were looking at how institutions constrained and shaped American politics. I found the study of institutions to be an exciting way to think about the political past and to situate political leaders in some type of organizational context.

My goal has been to show how the clash of our democracy has centered on a competition between multiple institutions, organizations, and political actors who have been constantly contesting the formation of policy and vying for power. The problem with some earlier work was that it was so focused on presidents or the "people" (vaguely defined) that their work missed other critical actors whose inclusion provides very different perspectives about how political history operated.

Most important to my writing on institutions has been bringing Congress back into political history. Congress offers an opportunity to break down the division between state and society, to reorganize our chronology of politics, and to see the close intersection between politics and policy. Unfortunately, one of the biggest oversights in the literature on political history had been Congress. Overshadowed by presidents and social movements, legislators had remained ghosts in America's historical imagination other than as a regressive foil to liberalism. When Congress appeared in a few academic books, it was treated as an archaic institution that functions as either a roadblock or a rubber stamp to proposals that emanate from the executive branch or from mass social movements. Congressmen received shallow treatment, if they were even mentioned. Presenting congressional members as caricatures who merely supported or opposed presidential initiatives, these histories described uninteresting, provincial politicians who were concerned exclusively with securing support from the strongest interest in their constituency. They provided little systematic treatment of how Congress as an institution operated within the corporate reconstruction of American politics. When writing about federal government, practitioners of American Political Development and the organizational synthesis tended to concentrate on the expansion of the administrative state with its bureaucracies and expertise. Congress seemed to them a premodern relic, interesting only for its gradual loss of power and an occasional decision to expand its administrative base. The persistent influence of Congress contradicted the teleology of their story of modernization.[7]

Congress is a large, diffuse institution, which makes it difficult to craft a narrative to describe it. I have incorporated the history of Congress into larger narratives of politics through two main strategies. The first has been to focus on particular powerful legislators such as Wilbur Mills to tell the story of the institution. Another has been to focus on how Congress works, using the legislative process, and how it has changed, as a way to understand the evolution and structure of the institution.

My work has documented how Congress has been an active force in national politics as opposed to the traditional depiction of a passive institution whose members usually react to the pressure bearing down on them. Although Congress is extraordinarily sensitive to democratic pressure, the members of Congress have also been able to initiate their own policy proposals, develop their own agenda and interest, and form their own distinct institutional identity.

Finally, in recent years I have been organizing more of my research around the rather traditional themes of campaigns, elections, and partisan strategy. In doing so, I have attempted to bridge the interests of newer and older generations. While using policy and political institutions as a framework for analyzing politics, I have attempted to situate our studies within the basic contours of our democratic system: electoral competition.

The dismissal of "old-fashioned" political history, which has had fruitful results by pushing historians to think of a broader constellation of causal forces in politics and broadening the number of actors who were included in narratives, simultaneously relegated certain key elements of our democratic system—including elections and partisan competition—to the sidelines. To fully understand how policies and institutions have evolved, I have found it essential to analyze their relationship to the electoral competition that Americans undertake every two years.

Electoral politics also allows a window into different policy areas and how they intersected. Instead of looking at one issue, a focus on elections forces historians to see the political landscape as historical actors did and in the same time, one punctuated by regular elections. Many of the most interesting sources of friction in the nation's political history have derived from the clash between different policies as politicians tried to sell their agendas to voters and to maintain political support for their programs. The relationship between different policies often influenced the formation of each other, and the tensions between different policies have impacted the strengths and weaknesses of politicians in the electoral sphere. Historians, as the people they study, must be attuned to that political reality, even as they study policy formation, state-building, and social movements that stretch well beyond election cycles.

The following essays constitute my efforts to participate in the rebuilding of the important field of U.S. political history. The book is divided into four thematic sections. The first covers one of the ongoing concerns in my career, the historiography of political history. In addition to writing about specific moments and leaders in American politics, I have been continually fascinated with the intellectual underpinnings of the field and the multiple analytic foundations upon which it is built. The feelings about political history—both those that have objected to it and those that have supported it—are so intense that they often lack a sophisticated understanding of the actual origins and development of the field. By offering such an analysis, I have hoped to make the new work on political history even stronger.

The second section turns to the theme that shaped the first stage of my writing, the challenges imposed by fiscal constraint in American politics. Much of the early literature on the American state claimed that the United States was a "laggard" compared to comparable Western European democracies. To explain why the United States developed social welfare programs so much later than other countries, and often much more meager in size, scholars emphasized the weakness of the social democratic tradition in this country as well as the tensions over race and gender. In contrast, my work looked at fiscal challenges that I believed were equally as central and caused problems even when social democratic sentiment was strong. At the same time, seeking to move beyond the literature about American Exceptionalism, I used the issue of taxes and budgets to look at how policymakers were able to use innovative fiscal strategies to build programs within the constraints that they faced, such as Social Security and Medicare.

The next phase of my writing, the focus of the third section, revolved around the impact of the political process. In my work on the evolution of Congress I saw how the political process, and the changes that occurred within that process, often defined political eras. By ignoring the process, historians had tended to overlook essential elements in politics. Legislators and other policymakers depended on their mastery of the process to advance their goals and sometimes fought for substantive changes in the political process when reform came to be seen as crucial to overcoming a political coalition. My studies on process pushed me further toward understanding the centrality, as political scientists were writing about, of institutional design in politics. It also brought me further into the relationship between state and society.

Finally, the last section looks at the scholarship that moved me toward the intersection between policy and politics. While much of my earlier work was concerned with examining the autonomous spaces and defining cultures that shaped policymakers in Washington, by the most recent phase of my writing, expanding on some of the issues I looked at in my work on congressional reform, I was particularly concerned with reconnecting the state to its electoral underpinnings. I specifically chose the issue of national security—a policy domain that has been furthest removed from domestic politics—to highlight how these connections worked. Doing so enabled me to bring some standard topics in political history that had been downplayed in recent scholarship, such as elections and partisan strategy, back into our narrative about the state.

My hope is that through this work I have and will continue to advance the new political history and to promote a style of analysis that scholars, students, and general readers can continue to grapple with and advance in the coming decades.

PART I

Thinking about the Field

The essays in this section focus on historiography, mapping the development of political history since the founding of the historical profession in the 1880s. Too often scholars have depicted a flat portrait of how the field evolved by contrasting "old-fashioned" political history from the period before the 1970s, which focused primarily on presidents, to the new era of political history broadly defined that encompasses institutions, political culture, and social movements.

Yet political history had a more complex and multifaceted history than conventional wisdom suggests. The essays in this section move readers through the various periods in the growth of this field and together show how each era offered multiple contributions to studying this subject. For example, "Clio's Lost Tribe" reveals how a generation of scholars working in the 1970s and 1980s responded to the criticism leveled by social and cultural historians, and through policy history began the process of reworking the field. By looking back more carefully at the different ways in which U.S. political history has been written, we can better understand the analytic layers on which current work is built.

These essays also attempt to rethink how we categorize and periodize political time. Traditionally, there have been two conventional strategies to organize our narratives. One has revolved around the presidency and the other around ideological cycles in American politics. As I argue in "Beyond the Presidential Synthesis," the research of the past decade has suggested that historians must push to establish new frameworks. For instance, some historians have been taking a much longer view, tracing the expansion of the federal government back to the nineteenth century. The literature on Congress, moreover, suggests that the particularities of how that institution developed don't mesh at all with the structure of presidential administrations. Indeed, this helps to explain the bitter clash that takes place between the White House and Capitol Hill over the direction of policy.

Finally, the essays stress the interdisciplinarity of political history. The field of American political history traditionally has thrived from its conversations and collaborations with other disciplines. The field offers a model for how to make interdisciplinary scholarship a reality rather than an aspiration. Political historians have relied on other disciplines for analytic questions, methodological debates, as well as to connect historical research to other parts of the academy. With all the changes that have taken place in the practice of political history since the founding of the profession in the 1880s, interdisciplinarity has remained an enduring feature of the work.

When Charles Beard published *An Economic Interpretation of the United States* in 1913, he blended history and economics to explain the origins of the Constitution. He established an enduring tradition of cross-disciplinary research that has continued through today. During the 1950s, Richard Hofstadter turned to psychology and sociology in his classic work *The Age of Reform* (1955) to explain why farmers and middle-class Americans mobilized politically at the turn of the twentieth century. Liberal historians such as Arthur Schlesinger Jr. embraced political science arguments about pluralism to explain how conflict worked in the nation's political system. More recently, as I argue in "Political History and Political Science" as well as "What Political Science Can Learn from the New Political History," younger historians have tapped into a wide range of disciplines, from anthropology to institutional political science, as they have reinvigorated the field. The interdisciplinary character of the field has proven to be an important source of strength that has helped to push scholars when political history seemed stuck in the intellectual mud.

In "Rethinking the History of American Conservatism," I draw on these analytic findings to challenge the prevailing framework that has shaped most of the literature on American conservatism. Through new periodization and interdisciplinary analysis, it is possible to fundamentally rethink the claims of one of the most vibrant and voluminous bodies of work in the new political history and raise new questions that will advance the scholarship.

ONE

Beyond the Presidential Synthesis: Reordering Political Time

In 1948, the historian Thomas Cochran attacked the "presidential synthesis," the prevailing framework that had structured most narratives about the history of the United States.* Cochran (1948) pleaded with colleagues to broaden their analysis beyond Washington, DC, in order to examine the larger social and economic forces that shaped history, as well as developments at the local level. In most areas of history, Cochran's plea would be answered as social, cultural, and economic historians reconstructed our understanding of the past. Even political historians, who found themselves at the margins of the profession after the 1960s, developed complex interpretations of the revolutionary period and nineteenth century that were not centered exclusively on the presidency. But for post–World War II political history, the presidency remained dominant. The last major synthesis of postwar politics continued to place the presidency at the forefront of its story. Not only did presidential administrations mark political time, but the power of the presidency was itself a major theme.

The rise and fall of the presidency from Franklin Roosevelt to Richard Nixon was the central story of a newly formulated liberal presidential synthesis. Whereas historians had often explained politics through presidential administrations as a matter of convenience and familiarity, now the expanding role of the presidency became a central story. Organized around the four- to eight-year time frames of presidential administrations, mainstream historical narratives centered on the rapid expansion of presidential power after the New Deal. The executive branch, in these accounts, was the engine for liberal domestic and international policy. The creation of the national security state during the Cold War accelerated this trend, as did the growth of domestic programs in the 1960s. Even the Supreme Court was said to reflect the president who appointed its justices (Burns, 1965, p. 316). Just as important, the president was able to

*This essay originally appeared in *A Companion to Post–1945 America*, eds. Jean-Christophe Agnew and Roy Rosenzweig (Oxford: Blackwell Publishers, 2002), 345–70.

dominate television in a fashion that was difficult for other politicians. While the presidency came under fire during Nixon's administration, and Watergate-era reforms in the mid-1970s triggered a resurgence of congressional power in areas such as war-making, historians argued that these reforms were unable to tame presidential power. It was in 1973 that historian Arthur Schlesinger Jr. coined the phrase that would forever identify this understanding of political history, when he published his landmark book about the "Imperial Presidency."

Shortly after the liberal presidential synthesis crystallized in the 1960s, historians turned away from the study of government elites and institutions. There were few individuals who conducted archival research on the history of postwar political elites, other than those who were developing the existing framework. The recentness of the postwar period also constrained the historical vision of historians. The two generations who have written about postwar politics came of age in a culture that emphasized the presidency, both liberals who exalted Franklin Roosevelt's legacy in the 1950s and the New Left scholars who were disillusioned by President Lyndon Johnson. As a result, the synthesis remained in place and was incorporated into almost every textbook account of modern American history.

Just as historians turned away from political history, political scientists discovered crucial weaknesses in the presidential-centered history. In almost every subfield of political science, scholars found that the power of the presidency remained limited after World War II. In many political science analyses of policymaking, the president appeared as an official who faced enormous institutional constraints. In fact, exaggerated perceptions of executive power often bred frustration as presidents, and those who voted for them, discovered that the policymaking influence of the chief executive remained limited. In this context, Franklin Roosevelt seemed like more of an aberration than a norm. Furthermore, political scientists depicted a policymaking process that did not revolve around individual presidential administrations. This political science research made it clear that the liberal presidential synthesis—both its four- to eight-year time frames for organizing political history and its emphasis on the expansion of presidential power—needed to be thoroughly reexamined by historians. But given the lack of interest in political elites within the historical profession, mainstream historians have never incorporated the findings of political scientists, resulting in a serious disjunction between historical research and that of political science. The liberal presidential synthesis lingered within the historical profession, more through intellectual inertia than any active defense of the argument.

This disjunction is particularly pertinent today, as historians seek to bring politics back into history. They must avoid blending social and cultural history with outdated narratives about political elites. Traditional political history, largely defined by the liberal presidential synthesis, must be reconceptualized by recognizing and incorporating the findings of political science. This essay begins by restating the basic narrative of the liberal presidential synthesis to revisit the important findings of the last generation of postwar political historians. These works, while providing a much richer understanding of each individual, have downplayed institutional questions about the evolution of the office over time. The essay then examines how political scientists since the 1960s have argued that presidential-centered history does not offer the best way to capture the second half of twentieth-century politics. To move beyond the presidential synthesis, it will be necessary to reorder what political scientist Stephen Skowronek (1993) called political time. Fortunately, an exciting body of interdisciplinary research has offered a solid foundation for historians who want to develop new strategies for writing about government elites and institutions. In the end, a revitalized approach to political history will provide a much richer understanding of the presidency itself.

The Master Narrative

The liberal presidential synthesis flourished in the 1960s, the last time that politics was central to the historical profession. The synthesis presented three views about the presidency: the president was an engine of liberal policy; the presidency had grown in power over the course of the twentieth century; and the president was the prime mover in national politics since the New Deal. Characterized as "liberal historians," this generation of historians had ardently supported Franklin Roosevelt's New Deal agenda. Many of them, including Arthur Schlesinger Jr. and William Leuchtenburg, had even advised Democratic politicians and were members of Americans for Democratic Action, an organization that promoted anticommunism and a progressive domestic agenda. While some of this generation stood farther to the left than others, they all praised Roosevelt for having ushered the nation through its two worst crises without resorting to totalitarianism or socialism. In their view, Roosevelt successfully built federal politics that were grounded in consensual liberal values of individualism and property rights. Their work relied heavily on political scientist Louis Hartz's (1955) argument that liberalism had been the consensual American value since the founding of the nation. Although he had overreached with his court-packing scheme, liberal historians boasted that Roosevelt had tamed the conservative Supreme Court while dragging along a reluctant Congress. On the international front, Roosevelt had forcefully responded to fascism over the opposition of an isolationist Congress. Franklin Roosevelt, in this worldview, embodied the best American politics had to offer (Schlesinger, 1959; Leuchtenburg, 1963). His policies and leadership affirmed that the presidency was now the central institution in contemporary American politics.

Roosevelt's administration served as the linchpin for subsequent accounts about the expansion of presidential power. The growth of presidential power and the triumph of liberalism went hand in hand. Roosevelt's presence in national life was overwhelming. In the 1930s and 1940s, the president had dominated national life in unprecedented style, winning four consecutive elections and achieving an intimate personal connection with citizens. According to Richard Hofstadter (1955), Roosevelt freed the reform tradition from irrational myths that had influenced populism and progressivism. While his cousin Theodore had elevated the importance of the presidency at the turn of the century, liberal historians agreed it was Franklin who brought the office into its modern form. His fireside chats on radio, for instance, embodied the unprecedented contact he achieved with the electorate. Liberal historians also pointed to key organizational changes Roosevelt had implemented. Even though Congress watered down much of his reorganization proposal by the time it passed in 1939, the president increased the independence of his office with respect to the parties, Congress, Supreme Court, and the rest of the executive branch. But it was during World War II that Roosevelt's impact became undeniable. Defying congressional isolationism, Roosevelt harnessed presidential power to bring the nation into the war against fascism. By overcoming congressional resistance, historians credited Roosevelt for directing the defeat of totalitarianism and crafting a response to Stalinist communism.

Roosevelt's administration set the stage for historical analysis of presidential administrations after World War II. When liberal historians wrote about postwar political history, they presented a succession of presidents who preserved the spirit of New Deal politics (Goldman, 1956; Schlesinger, 1965; Hamby, 1973, 1985; Leuchtenburg, 1983). Although presidential administrations traditionally had been used as the framework through which to organize political time, now the expanding power of the office itself became a crucial focus of scholarly research. Until the 1970s, liberal historians found support from the political science professional (although many scholars straddled both intellectual worlds at this time). Before 1960, political scientists such as Clinton Rossiter (1956) and Edward Corwin (1957) had focused on the constitutional sources of presidential power. In his landmark book, Richard Neustadt (1960) claimed that there were limits to formal power but that skilled presidents could be successful through persuasion. In both cases, the scholarship focused on the preeminent power of the presidency within the political system.

James MacGregor Burns best expressed the spirit of this research with his book, *Presidential Government: The Crucible of Leadership* (1965). Samuel Huntington asserted that "If Congress legislates, it subordinates itself to the President; if it refuses to legislate, it alienates itself from public opinion. Congress can assert its power or it can pass laws; but it cannot do both" (1965, p. 6; see also Polsby, 1964; Fisher, 1972). These scholars were convinced that the public agreed (Rossiter, 1956). Conservative scholars, through a critical analysis, acknowledged that Congress had declined in power since the New Deal. James Burnham (1959) warned that the ideology of "democratism" had shaped twentieth-century politics. Burnham explained that this ideology favored popular sovereignty, as expressed through the president, rather than intermediary institutions such as Congress and the rule of law. Twentieth-century U.S. politics, he added, had also privileged bureaucratic over democratic power.

Importantly, the New Left, even while criticizing Schlesinger Jr. and his colleagues, adhered to presidential-centered political history. They attacked the liberal presidential synthesis on its own terms, simply interpreting the inhabitants of that office as being less virtuous in their goals. Rather than using the office to protect average citizens, the New Left emphasized that twentieth-century presidents had maintained an unholy alliance with corporate America (Williams, 1959, 1961; Kolko, 1976, 1985; Matusow, 1985). Since conservatives did not have a major impact within the profession during these formative decades, their understanding of these issues remained underdeveloped.

Political historians, working within the liberal presidential synthesis, have stressed that foreign policy was the key arena where presidents usurped constitutional power. The first major expansion of presidential power after Roosevelt occurred between 1947 and 1949. Although Harry Truman did not achieve the prominence of his predecessor, the Cold War necessitated a further extension of presidential influence since the decentralized Congress could not deal with complicated and sensitive foreign policy issues. The process began with the creation in 1947 of the National Security Council, a small group that centralized military decision-making power in the White House. Truman's subsequent entrance into the Korean War without a congressional declaration of war proved even more decisive. With the decline of isolationism in these years and the expansion of the military budget, historians suggested that little stood in the way of presidential decisions. Presidents would frequently enter foreign conflicts over the next two decades without receiving formal approval from Congress. Until Vietnam, this process was seen as positive since the presidents universally championed Cold War internationalism. Without a strong presidency, historians suggested, foreign policy would have fallen victim to an isolationist Congress. When recounting efforts to constrain presidential power, historians conveyed a tone of disapproval (Patterson, 1967; Porter, 1980).

Although Eisenhower at first seemed an unlikely fit within the synthesis, given his mild demeanor and his initial criticism of the strong presidency, research soon showed this was not the case. Ideologically, Eisenhower forced his party to accept the presidential-centered New Deal state and Cold War internationalism. Just as important, Eisenhower did not reverse the organizational reforms that had strengthened the presidency. Despite his initial opposition to Roosevelt's expansion of the office, he ended up following the same path. For instance, in response to Senator Joseph McCarthy's attacks on executive branch personnel, Eisenhower brought in more officials under the protective privileges enjoyed by the president. Under his leadership, moreover, the size of the presidential staff grew dramatically.

While initial scholarship depicted Eisenhower as a weak leader, archival research revealed that this perception was incorrect (J. Barber, 1992). Political scientist Fred Greenstein (1982) and historian Robert Griffith (1982) both found that behind the scenes, Eisenhower maintained a strong hold on decision-making. In what he called the "hidden-hand presidency," Greenstein presented

Eisenhower as an effective decision-maker who maintained control over his cabinet. In foreign policy, historians Blanche Weisen Cook (1981) and Robert Divine (1981) claimed that Eisenhower had significantly advanced the Cold War by improving relations with the Soviet Union while simultaneously launching covert operations in smaller nations such as Iran, Vietnam, and Guatemala. Later archival research revealed that the allegedly "bumbling" Eisenhower was quite shrewd in crafting his relationship with the mass media (Allen, 1993). By 1990, the noted historian Stephen Ambrose confidently proclaimed that Dwight Eisenhower had been "one of the outstanding leaders of the Western world in this century" (1990, p. 11).

While the 1940s and 1950s witnessed the incremental growth of presidential power, the 1960s brought the second "big bang" (the first being the combined impact of the New Deal and World War II). "The imperial Presidency, born in the 1940s and 1950s to save the outer world from perdition," Schlesinger wrote, "thus began in the 1960s and 1970s to find nurture at home" (1973, p. 212). John Kennedy began by shifting the agenda to a more aggressive Cold War posture and launching new domestic initiatives on poverty, education, healthcare, civil rights, and the economy. In the same fashion that Eisenhower dominated public opinion because of his military service and affable personality, Kennedy enchanted the nation through his charisma and royalty-like stature. Although liberals and the New Left acknowledged that Kennedy accomplished little in domestic policy, he was credited with elevating the issues that dominated the rest of the decade. Moreover, historians pointed to his seminal confrontations with the Soviet Union, particularly the Cuban Missile Crisis of 1962, and his acceleration of U.S. military participation in Vietnam.

If anyone doubted the centrality of the presidency under Kennedy, those feelings evaporated with Lyndon Johnson, whose larger-than-life persona seemed to overwhelm national life. "Johnson left huge footprints wherever he stopped," the historian Bruce Schulman has written, "overwhelming nearly everyone who crossed his path and achieving more than nearly any other American politician" (1995, p. 2). Since Republican presidential candidate Barry Goldwater had attacked the presidency as excessively strong, James Burns believed that Goldwater's decisive defeat in 1964 was a "historic validation both of the interlaced purpose of American domestic and foreign policy and the role of the Presidency in achieving that purpose." Burns concluded that "the power and paradox of the Presidency have reached a new peak in the administration of Lyndon B. Johnson . . . More than ever the White House is a command post for economic, political, diplomatic, and military combat" (1965, pp. 277, 312–13). After winning the 1964 election, Johnson intensified the war in Vietnam through the Gulf of Tonkin Resolution, which allowed him to send more troops into the region without obtaining a congressional declaration of war. At the same time, Johnson's Great Society included important legislation such as Medicare and the Voting Rights Act. While Vietnam was disastrous to the War on Poverty, mainstream accounts stressed that Johnson was his own worst enemy. It was Johnson's brashness and decision to expand the Vietnam War that undermined his own agenda. Revealingly, student activists of the period condemned "Johnson's War," highlighting the grip that the presidency held on the public psyche. It seemed, explained Godfrey Hodgson, that liberals in the 1950s and 1960s had placed an impossible "burden on the institution on which the consensus had counted to carry out that program, and to which everyone turned to put things right when it became apparent that they were going wrong: the presidency" (1976, p. 492).

The liberal presidential synthesis culminated with Richard Nixon's downfall in 1974. Until the 1970s, liberal historians had presented the expansion of presidential power as a positive development. But Nixon revealed the dangerous side of Roosevelt's legacy. Suddenly, the cost of excessive presidential power became evident. Whereas the Imperial Presidency had facilitated unprecedented innovations in domestic policies and Cold War internationalism, Nixon revealed that the office could easily be used toward malicious ends. It was during these years that books and articles began to note the darker side of presidential power (see, for example, Reedy, 1970). Nixon began his presidency by reorganizing the executive branch so that he could circumvent the federal bureaucracy; he used informal channels to assert the type of control that eluded earlier presidents (Nathan, 1975; Patterson, 1996). As the Watergate investigations later revealed, the president carried these activities much further than anyone ever imagined. Nixon had used the FBI and IRS to investigate opponents, his staff broke into opposition headquarters, and his administration exchanged favorable policy decisions for large campaign contributions. Nixon's secret war in Cambodia and his impoundment of budgetary spending offered the strongest evidence that the office had become too powerful. The constitutional separation of power had almost vanished, as the president was dominant. Schlesinger opened his landmark book with an apology of sorts: "It must be said that historians and political scientists, this writer among them, contributed to the rise of the presidential mystique" (1973, p. ix). Watergate encouraged scholars—who still privileged the president as the main storyline in political history—to look back in time at how previous presidents had abused their own power (Pyle, 1974; Theoharis, 1971, 1978). Lyndon Johnson, for example, became a favorite target of these works, with scholars depicting a ruthless and tyrannical Texan who had committed equally disgraceful abuses through his political career (Caro, 1982, 1990). The only difference between the two presidents, some books suggested, was that Congress caught Nixon.

President Nixon inspired Congress to reclaim its constitutional power. In response to Nixon's abuses, Congress increased its strength through the War Power Act, oversight laws, the legislative veto, and budget reform (Sundquist, 1981; Fisher, 1998; Mann, 2001). The War Powers Act of 1973 granted Congress improved authority to terminate war, while the Congressional Budget and Impoundment Act of 1974 limited presidential impoundments and centralized the legislative budget-making process. Although Nixon resigned before Congress could remove him from office, the House Judiciary Committee's impeachment proceedings represented the ultimate reassertion of congressional power. Furthermore, the Ethics in Government Act of 1978, which created the Office of the Independent Prosecutor to investigate potential wrongdoing by the executive branch, indicated that Congress had institutionally weakened the presidency. At the same time that Congress reasserted its power, the Warren Court completed a two-decade campaign that elevated the Supreme Court as an extremely powerful force in shaping policy. By Congress and the Supreme Court both acting more assertively, it seemed that the Imperial Presidency had been tamed. If anything, the reversal had gone too far. One scholar warned regarding the president's power to enter into foreign war after 1973: "While we cannot have rules which permit a stamp of constitutional approval on what Roosevelt felt was necessary, neither can our democracy survive by adopting rules which assume that every president is a Nixon" (Redlich, 1981, p. 294).

It soon became clear in updated versions of the liberal presidential synthesis, however, that the office remained strong despite Watergate. For instance, Schlesinger posited that congressional resurgence had been more of a blip than a transformation: "The indestructibility of the Presidency was demonstrated in the very years when political scientists were pronouncing presidential government as illusion . . . Whatever else may be said about Ronald Reagan, he quickly showed that the reports of the death of the Presidency were greatly exaggerated" (1986, pp. 288, 293). Although presidential power did not return to the condition of the Roosevelt or Johnson years, it remained the preeminent political force. During the 1980s, Reagan demonstrated that the office could be used as a political battering ram. As a public official, Reagan's direct connection to citizens seemed to rival that of Franklin Roosevelt. Continuing along the path that started after World War II, Reagan's administration turned to covert warfare to pursue its Cold War agenda, over the explicit opposition of Congress. He also reorganized the Office of Management and Budget so that it could be used to curtail domestic programs such as environmental regulation (Hays, 1987). Furthermore, changes in the political process seemed to favor the president. The primacy of television as the medium of political communication, along with the decline of political parties, made presidents more prominent. Party reforms in the 1970s weakened the influence of parties in the candidate-selection process. Now the president carried his message directly to the people (Shafer, 1983). Jimmy Carter proved this to be true during the 1976 campaign, when he traveled around the country to meet with news reporters rather than party bosses.

The liberal presidential synthesis, as outlined here, has proved to be remarkably durable. Liberals and New Left historians could at least agree on the expanding power of the presidency. Social and cultural historians, less interested in politics, drew on this synthesis since it was the most comprehensive and compelling account that was available. By organizing American political history around each successive administration and focusing on the expanding size of presidential power, our understanding of "traditional political history" has been shaped by this school of research. Shortly after the 2000 presidential election, popular historian Michael Beschloss published a piece for the *New York Times*, "The End of the Imperial Presidency," that repeated the 1960s traditional narrative of modern U.S. history without qualification. He wrote: "The grand age of presidential power began in the 1930s with Franklin Roosevelt and started to decline in the early 1970s with Richard Nixon. Although presidential power has been slipping for some time, whoever was elected the 43rd president would have been the first leader to govern fully out of the wake of the imperial age" (2000, p. 27; see also Leuchtenburg, 2001). A glimpse at most high school or college textbooks (in an age when many textbooks pay little attention to politics) reveals the staying power of this narrative. Texts still rely on the presidential synthesis when dealing with government elites and institutions (see, for example, Blum et al., 1989; Brinkley and Fitzpatrick, 1997; Goldfield et al., 1998; Gillon and Matson, 2001). Presidents in these texts are usually depicted as free-floating individuals picking and choosing from among the policies they want to promote. Individual presidents set the agenda and dictate the themes of government. Even while admitting that presidents lost many key battles, the liberal presidential synthesis has devoted little rigorous analysis to the forces that constrained the president. Just as important, they present the president's agenda at the center of these battles.

The soundness of the liberal presidential synthesis was not evaluated because political history—defined as the study of political elites and government institutions—became unpopular with the baby boom generation in the 1970s and 1980s (Leuchtenburg, 1986; Leff, 1995). This generation criticized "traditional" political history as elitist and irrelevant, claiming that the actions of political leaders did not reflect the experience of most Americans. Moreover, they claimed that true power rested in social relations. In this intellectual context, the social history revolution swept through the profession, and emphasized history from the "bottom up." When historians wrote about politics, they focused on grassroots social movements, contestations over race, ethnicity, class, and gender, and the social impact of policies. The "new political historians" of the 1970s focused on quantifying voting behavior in the nineteenth century (Kleppner, 1970; P. Baker, 1993).

As a result of the "bottom-up" focus in the mainstream historical profession, the history of postwar political elites was locked into the liberal presidential synthesis. For the next generation, "traditional" political history would be defined as presidential-centered history with an emphasis on the expanding power of the office.

Assessing Individual Presidents

Before examining what political scientists have said about presidential power, it is important to discuss the voluminous literature on individual presidencies. While these seminal historical works have greatly advanced our understanding of each individual president, and most of these books actually offer evidence that the policymaking process was more complex than the liberal presidential synthesis indicates, they have not produced a new framework for understanding the history of government elites and institutions. Each administration is treated as distinct in these books, while the presidents themselves are presented as the prime movers in elite politics. Other actors enter the story briefly only as they impact the administration being studied. Rarely are external forces given sustained analysis.

Focusing on each president, rather than on the evolution of the presidency, presidential history since the 1960s has centered on gauging whether individuals were "strong" or "weak" leaders and if they were "liberal" or "conservative." Historiographical debates, for example, have focused on whether Truman was an ineffective "closet conservative" or a true heir to Roosevelt, who pushed forward New Deal liberalism (Hamby, 1973, 1989; McCullough, 1992; Ferrell, 1996). Kennedy has been a popular subject. Critics have asserted that Kennedy attempted to protect corporate interests and ward off radical changes in civil rights (Heath, 1975; Miroff, 1976; Shank, 1980; Parmet, 1983). Sympathetic accounts insist that Kennedy was truly committed to the liberal agenda and that he accomplished a great deal, even though he often found himself frustrated by conservative opponents (Schlesinger, 1965; Bernstein, 1991; Reeves, 1993). A similar view shaped the first scholarly assessment of Carter's presidency (Fink and Graham, 1998).

With Eisenhower, the focus of presidential history moved in the opposite direction. Scholars have tried to show the conservative bent of the president, particularly in his battles with Democrats over the budget, to counteract claims that he was nothing more than a Republican New Dealer (Morgan, 1990). In contrast to those who stressed comparisons with Franklin Roosevelt, Ambrose traced the conservatism of the 1980s directly back to Eisenhower, particularly with respect to defense, the budget, and anticommunism (Ambrose, 1990).

Research on Lyndon Johnson and Richard Nixon has been less concerned with their forcefulness as leaders, instead focusing exclusively on the underlying nature of their agenda. Studies about President Johnson have weighed his commitment to the Great Society against his enthusiasm or ambivalence about Vietnam (Sherrill, 1967; VanDeMark, 1991; Bernstein, 1996; Dallek, 1998). His 1968 decision to cut "butter" (Great Society) in favor of "guns" (Vietnam) haunts his legacy. Some studies, for example, suggest that he was dragged into the war by national military ideologies and interests despite strong reservations (Dallek, 1998). Others argue that from the start Johnson chose war over viable negotiation (Logevall, 1999). A few scholars have been interested in locating the origins of Johnson's commitment to the poor and African Americans (Kearns, 1976).

Most work on Richard Nixon has probed the details of Watergate (Kutler, 1990). Given that the crisis was so traumatic, scholars set out to determine the details of Nixon's wrongdoing, often to determine whether his actions were exceptional or rooted in the structure of political institutions (Schudson, 1992).

But studies eventually turned to other aspects of Nixon's administration besides Watergate (Ambrose, 1987). Recent historiographical debates on Nixon have addressed his policy contributions as president. Revisionists such as historian Joan Hoff (1994) have asserted that Nixon was an innovator in domestic policy, as evidenced in the new federalism, affirmative action, welfare reform, and Social Security indexation. On the international front, Nixon has been credited with helping to improve relations with both China and the Soviet Union.

Research on individual presidencies has thus fit easily within the liberal presidential synthesis. Presidents established the agenda (even though they could not always pass desired legislation), they were the focus of political history, and political time was organized around each administration. Institutions such as Congress, the courts, interest groups, and the media have not been studied in as much depth, nor have they been integrated into the organization of scholarly narratives. Nonpresidential institutions appear as the supporting cast to the leads of a movie; otherwise, they are treated as outliers and roadblocks.

Political Science and the Presidency

Because of the "bottom-up" direction taken by historians since the 1970s, the profession has paid little attention to how political scientists have analyzed the presidency. While political scientists are not in the business of writing historical narratives, their work has collectively poked holes in popular historical accounts of government elites. At a minimum, political scientists have proved the need for substantial archival research to test existing interpretations of postwar elites. If those findings complicate our understanding of the past, there will be a need to reconceptualize the order and structure of political history. This is an enormous challenge given the familiarity of the existing framework and the fact that popular conceptions of politics revolve around presidents.

Since the 1960s, almost every subfield in political science has greatly qualified the power of the postwar presidency. The shift in emphasis arrived like a thunderbolt with Walter Dean Burnham's (1970) realignment synthesis. Burnham argued that America's political parties had been nonprogrammatic and politically timid. As a result, the nation usually experienced incremental politics. However, incremental politics could not handle major changes in the economic and social system such as a depression. The results, Burnham explained, were realigning periods that were ideologically volatile and transformative. Building on the work of V. O. Key and E. E. Schattschneider, Burnham claimed that during "critical elections" in 1800, 1828, 1860, 1896, and 1932, the governing party switched hands as a result of changed voting behavior. The new alignment favored a cluster of policies that seemed to meet the needs of the new voting majority. The arrangement usually dominated national politics for several decades, until the next realignment, with little major change taking place in between. What was most striking about the twentieth century,

Burnham concluded, was the decline of partisan participation and identification which made realignments more unlikely. Historical political scientists, and a handful of Progressive-era historians, quickly incorporated this synthesis into their work (Ladd and Hadley, 1975; McCormick, 1981; Sinclair, 1982).

Political scientists who focused on policy analysis were likewise aware of the power Congress and the federal bureaucracy exerted, often independent of presidential desire. During the 1970s, Theodore Marmor (1973), Martha Derthick (1979), and James Sundquist (1968) were among those who developed multicausal accounts of policy development. Derthick argued that experts in the Social Security Administration played the key role in building Social Security between 1935 and 1972. Marmor believed that committee chairmen such as Wilbur Mills (D-AR) played an important role in the formation of Medicare, while Sundquist found that much of the Great Society was promoted by congressional Democrats in the 1950s.

Policy analysts were not alone. Within the American Political Science Association, behavioralist scholars examined congressional leadership through participant observation. They found that Congress played a seminal role in policymaking. Richard Fenno (1973), Randall Ripley (1969), and John Manley (1970) were among those interested in how institutional norms shaped the behavior of individual legislators. These books, particularly those focusing on the revenue committees, demonstrated that committee chairmen retained a tight grip on policymaking between the 1940s and 1970s. While Congress as an institution appeared fragmented, chaotic, and decentralized, the books portrayed committee chairmen as exercising enormous influence in policymaking. Arguing that the postwar Congress had initiated many key policies such as environmental protection, Gary Orfield (1975) criticized colleagues who dismissed Congress as "unresponsive." He warned that "it often turns out that the author uncritically assumes either that the President's program actually reflects national needs, or that Congress should respond to the author's own implicit or explicit beliefs about what the primary national needs are. In fact, these goals espoused by the critics may have little or no relationship to the desires of local or national public constituency" (1975, p. 20). In a recent book emphasizing the active role of congressional entrepreneurs, political scientist David Mayhew noted: "it is a fair question whether the 1930s, at least as an epic legislative era, should not be labeled 'the age of Wagner' [referring to Senator Robert Wagner of New York] as much as it is 'the age of Roosevelt' . . . one reading of the significance of the 1932 election might be: It produced a president who would sign Wagner's bills" (2000, pp. 212–13).

Studies about policy implementation, most notably the scholarship of Aaron Wildavsky and Jeffrey Pressman (1984), stressed how the success or failure of policies was only determined after they went into effect at the state and local levels. Political development, in this view, must place substantial emphasis on the implementation stage of policymaking. Here, presidents usually were far less important than when they were making broad proposals. Theodore Lowi

(1969) had also lamented that Congress delegated authority to administrative agencies, which were then "captured" by powerful interest groups. It was in those organizations, Lowi argued, where true power rested.

During the 1980s, political scientists continued to decenter the presidency. Scholarship on agenda-setting, for example, revealed that no single player maintained strong control over the policy agenda (Kingdon, 1984; Polsby, 1984; Baumgartner and Jones, 1993). Instead, their work posited that a myriad of policymakers, inside and outside elected office, promoted issues over long periods of time. Kingdon wrote about the "policy primeval soup" where "many ideas float around, bumping into one another, encountering new ideas, and forming combinations and recombinations" (1984, p. 209). In this analysis, policy communities pushed for, and reconfigured, programs until "focusing events" created a window of opportunity to enact legislation. Policy communities extended well beyond the executive branch. In this model of policymaking, no single institution or policymaker exercised singular control. While vigorous presidential support could create a decisive window of opportunity, other factors had similar effects, including crises, scandals, and strong policy entrepreneurs. During the period that he called policy "incubation," Nelson Polsby explained:

> Demand for innovation is built slowly, and specific plans or proposals are typically the work of people relatively far in social, temporal, and sometimes physical distance from ultimate decision-makers: experts and researchers working in universities or in quasi-academic settings, or technical staff employees of interest groups, government agencies, or congressional committees. Innovations pass through a stage of *incubation*, where political actors—senators, congressmen, lobbyists, or other promoters—take the idea up, reshape it, adapt it to their political needs, publicize it, and put it into the ongoing culture of decision-makers. This culture endures in Washington and in national politics, maintaining an interest in various subject areas from generation to generation and assimilating new participants as they drift into town with the tides of electoral politics. (1984, p. 153)

A dynamic group of political scientists and sociologists in the 1980s developed the subfield of American Political Development. While historians ignored political elites, social scientists embraced political history. Led by Stephen Skowronek, Richard Bensel, Ira Katznelson, and Theda Skocpol, these scholars examined how institutions shaped politics over long stretches of time and how new policies reconfigured politics. Concurring that the presidency had significantly expanded its power over the twentieth century, their research simultaneously showed that other institutions maintained a strong hold on the policymaking process. Skowronek's (1982) pathbreaking book on the Progressive Era revealed that when the administrative state was created at the turn of the century, Congress and the courts built mechanisms into new programs so that they would maintain power. The result, Skowronek said, was a jerry-built state where Congress, parties, and the courts competed with presidents over control of the policy.

In her work, Skocpol (1992, 1995) found that all political actors, including presidents, were constrained by the institutions within which they operated. Through the concept of policy feedback, Skocpol and others revealed how preexisting policies shaped politics. Focusing on policy retrenchment, rather than expansion, Paul Pierson (1994) concluded that Reagan failed to eliminate key domestic programs because they had created powerful constituencies. Budgetary scholars Eugene Steuerle (1996) and Eric Patashnik (2000) showed that precommitted policies, namely Social Security and Medicare, constituted such a large portion of the budget by the 1980s and 1990s that few politicians could produce dramatic changes in the allocation of federal budgeting. Their work built on the foundation laid by Aaron Wildavsky (1964), whose book stressed the incremental nature of federal budgeting. Through his theory of incrementalism, Wildavsky contended that there were only minor departures each year from the previous budget. Legislators, under pressure from entrenched interests who supported programs, built on the base of the preexisting budget. As a result of incremental politics, there was little dramatic change from year to year in the direction of federal spending despite the rhetoric of campaigns.

Even in the subfield of presidential studies, political scientists challenged the power of the "modern" office. Analyzing the constraints that faced the president has a long tradition in this subfield. In his classic treatise, Richard Neustadt (1960) had warned that the public's expectations of the president were far greater than the resources available to them. Even modern presidents had to overcome an array of external forces if they were to achieve their objectives. Reflecting the optimism of an earlier era, Neustadt believed that individuals could nonetheless overcome these constraints if they were skilled at the power of persuasion. By 2000, Paul Light, initially a strong proponent of the presidential-centered analysis of policymaking, admitted that: "The prevailing wisdom today is that this presidency-centered vision of policy making was an inappropriate reading of both constitutional intent and legislative reality . . . To expect the president's agenda to remain dominant year after year is to ignore the normal ebb and flow of power built into the very fiber of the federal system" (2000, pp. 109–10; for an earlier argument along these lines, see McConnell, 1967).

Political scientists shifted their attention to the institutional environment that constrained the modern presidency (Shapiro et al., 2000). Tracing the roots of presidential *weakness* back to the New Deal, Sidney Milkis contended that after Roosevelt severed ties between the presidency and the parties, the strength of the office diminished because it lacked a stable base of popular support: "The modern executive that arose from the ashes of traditional parties was hardly imperial, as scholars and pundits frequently asserted by the end of Richard Nixon's ill-fated reign. Put simply, 'modern' presidents bask in the honors of the more powerful and prominent office that emerged from the New Deal, but find themselves navigating a treacherous and lonely path, subject to a volatile political process that makes popular and enduring achievement unlikely" (1993, p. ix; see also Milkis, 1999).

In the subfield of presidential studies, two books were decisive in changing the direction of scholarship. Building on the work of Mark Peterson (1990) and George Edwards (1989), Charles Jones argued that the system of separated power continued to hold sway after the New Deal—the president was never as strong as some scholars had suggested: "The American presidency carries a burden of lofty expectations that are simply not warranted by the political or constitutional basis of the office . . . The natural inclination is to make the president responsible for policies and political events that no one can claim a legitimate right to control. Presidents are well advised to resist this invitation to assume a position of power as though it conveyed authority" (1994, p. 281; see also Edwards, 1996). Congress, according to Jones, played an enormous role in shaping the agenda and legislating. Based on extensive historical analysis, Jones found that most presidents defined their agenda through proposals that had gestated for many years. Presidents also were forced to contend with the economic and institutional context they inherited when they crafted their proposals. The book shattered many myths. He rebutted the assumption that high presidential approval ratings translated into legislative success. Truman, for example, had the highest number of proposals enacted in 1946 and 1947, when his popularity was extremely low; Eisenhower, who enjoyed tremendous approval ratings until 1956, experienced a lower rate of passing important legislation than any postwar president (Jones, 1994, pp. 128–29). Through these and other examples, Jones demonstrated how presidents were usually frustrated when they discovered that their power was so limited. Rather than a lament, the book celebrated the separation of power and claimed that it resulted in effective government. He added to Mayhew's (1991) findings that divided government worked effectively in terms of legislative production.

The second major publication in presidential studies during the 1990s came from Stephen Skowronek (1993). Presidents, Skowronek argued, amassed power not just through institutional strength but also through their authority. According to Skowronek, every president since George Washington had gained authority based on his relationship to the established political regime of his time. For example, Truman, Eisenhower, Kennedy, Johnson, Nixon, and Carter all had different relationships to the regime which had been created during the New Deal. Their relationship to the established political regime dictated their success or failure. Skowronek identified four types of presidential leaders: those who practiced the politics of *reconstruction* by creating new regimes and abandoning old commitments; those who practiced the politics of *articulation* by being faithful to the established regime but attempting to make its agenda more relevant to contemporary issues; those who practiced the politics of *disjunction* by remaining affiliated to the established regime while simultaneously insisting that its ideology and interests were no longer useful to the problems of the day; and those who practiced the politics of *preemption* by becoming opposition leaders in resilient regimes. Roosevelt, in this scheme, established a regime around certain policies, ideas, interests, and coalitions that lasted until the 1980s. Except for the few presidents who established a new regime, such as Thomas Jefferson or Franklin Roosevelt, Skowronek claimed that most presidents became frustrated when they discovered it was difficult to move beyond inherited agendas. "Power," Lyndon Johnson once lamented, "The only power I've got is nuclear . . . and I can't use that" (cited in Skowronek, 1993, p. 341). While each president attempted to break free from the past to some extent, few presidents amassed the authority needed to succeed. Moreover, Skowronek argued that the possibility of creating new regimes diminished during the twentieth century as preexisting commitments and thickening institutions left presidents with less room to innovate. Although some scholars still claimed that the president had exceptional influence, they targeted specific stages in the policymaking process. In particular, many continued to argue that presidents wielded unusual power in agenda-setting (McKay, 1989). After that stage of the process, most works agree that the president must share power.

Political science scholarship shows that political historians must seriously modify the presidential-centered synthesis if they are to provide an accurate account of the policymaking process. These subfields of political science have demonstrated that the president remained one player in a larger universe of political actors and that those who held the office confronted significant constraints on their behavior. Just as important, political scientists showed that the policymaking process extended far beyond the timeframe of any specific administration. Indeed, some of the most effective presidents had a strong sense of history, improving their ability to pass legislation if they understood their own place in larger policy streams that had unfolded over decades (May and Neustadt, 1986).

Reorganizing Political Time

If we are to take political scientists seriously, historians will have to recognize political time during the postwar period and downplay the presidency as the central storyline of synthetic narratives. Skowronek defined "political time" as the "historical medium through which authority structures have recurred" (1993, p. 30). While he focused on the presidency, Skowronek's concept of political time offers a useful starting point for contemplating the chronology of politics. Reordering political time is essential. This type of dramatic reconceptualization will most likely become easier with greater historical perspective. There are several models—which I will call the revised organizational synthesis, political process, political culture, historical institutionalism, political regimes, policy history, and economic eras—that already offer methods to tackle this challenge.

One possibility originates with a group of maverick historians who continued to study politics in spite of the social history revolution. Their work, labeled the "organizational synthesis," directly challenged the presidential-centered understanding of elites. Given the popularity of social and cultural history, few organizational historians found their work published in the *Journal of American History* or the *American Historical Review*, nor was this view reflected in textbooks. Therefore, while the organizational synthesis dates back several decades, its findings have not yet been incorporated into mainstream historical narratives in the same fashion as the presidential synthesis. Building on modernization theory from the social sciences, organizational historians such as Samuel Hays (1957), Robert Wiebe (1967), Alfred Chandler (1977), and Louis Galambos (1970, 1976, 1983) argued that the major force driving change in the twentieth century was the evolution of large-scale national institutions such as the corporation, the professions, and the administrative state. When writing about the federal government, they concentrated on the expansion of the administrative state with its bureaucracies and expert staff. Proponents of the organizational synthesis downplayed the differences between presidential administrations in any single century. Instead, they stressed large-scale structural shifts that occurred when political institutions were transformed. In their view, the structural changes that distinguished nineteenth-century from twentieth-century politics were far more important than any differences between specific administrations. Their analysis did not ignore the presidency but looked at the office in a more complex light. Indeed, the executive branch was still central as the area of government most sympathetic to working with modern economic institutions. Revisionists attempted to bring home this point by highlighting similarities between Hoover's and Roosevelt's economic policies. Collapsing the alleged differences between the two administrations, the organizational synthesis aimed to prove that all modern presidents shared certain concerns and relied on common solutions to problems of political economy (Hawley, 1979; W. Barber, 1985). By undermining the perception that the New Deal constituted a "big bang" in politics, this work provided some of the most stimulating scholarship of the last two decades. However, there were problems extending the organizational synthesis to the postwar period. Since the synthesis emphasized the centrality of the years between 1880 and 1920, they downplayed changes later in the century. Moreover, critics felt that the synthesis did not acknowledge historical contingency or resistance to modernization (Balogh, 1991b; Brinkley, 1984).

Nonetheless, some scholars brought the organizational synthesis into the modern era, while avoiding the air of inevitability that characterized initial scholarship. In fact, the best research has applied the framework to the second half of the century, when the nation confronted a series of crises and internal upheavals. Extending the organizational synthesis to the postwar period forced historians to develop a more complex analysis. In his work on civil rights, Hugh Graham (1990) showed how the civil rights bureaucracy played a pivotal role in the creation and implementation of affirmative action during the late 1960s, as opposed to the grassroots movement that dominated the first part of the decade. Samuel Hays (1987) discovered that both popular culture and scientific and legal experts were instrumental in shaping environmental policy after 1955. Brian Balogh (1991a), in a book overflowing with contingency and crisis, carefully traced how professional administrators within the state attempted to build a sizable domestic nuclear power program despite lacking external demand. The result of this history was a policy that rested on an extremely unstable foundation. With its attention to bureaucracy, experts, and interest-group politics, the revised organizational synthesis has offered an extremely compelling narrative through which to construct American history since World War II that captures the full range of participants.

A second possibility would be to organize political time around changes in the political process. This approach is related to the organizational synthesis in that it emphasizes fundamental shifts in institutional structure. Studying the process has been a successful strategy for those who focus on earlier periods in political history. Most notably, nineteenth-century historians broke with the presidential synthesis by focusing on landmark changes in the way that politics operated. Joel Silbey (1991), for example, has argued that the decades between 1838 and 1893 were marked by continuity based on the primacy of parties (see also J. Baker, 1983; Shafer, 1993; Altschuler and Blumin, 2000; Kornbluh, 2000). Their work marked political time around the evolution of the democratic process. A related approach toward the nineteenth and early twentieth centuries has centered on the relationship between gender and politics. Led by Paula Baker (1984) and Molly Ladd Taylor (1994), these works looked at the existence of two gendered political worlds in the nineteenth century: one male-centered partisan world of electoral politics with voting and party events, and the other female political world that revolved around voluntary associations and social welfare initiatives. By the end of World War I, they argue, these worlds collapsed. In these accounts, individual presidential administrations fade into a larger historical story as attention shifts to the underlying rules that defined political participation at both the elite and mass levels.

A similar process-centered framework could be used for the postwar period. Based on initial scholarship, we already have sketches of seminal moments during which the political process changed. For example, some political scientists have suggested that after the 1970s, criminal investigation, legal prosecution, and scandal became the dominant modes of conducting political warfare as the importance of elections declined (Ginsberg and Shefter, 1990; Garment, 1991). It would be useful to understand how policymaking and public participation differed in each era, or if the differences were as great as these scholars suggest. In my work (Zelizer, 2004), I highlight changes in Congress during the 1970s when the insulated, committee-based system was replaced by a more porous, scandal-ridden, and partisan-based process. The political impact of changes in the institutional structure of the news media and journalistic ethics, moreover, is an issue that has received scant attention from historians. We will also learn about how presidential strategies were shaped by the evolving process, and how the process impacted the nation's unfolding policy agenda. Another compelling thesis has been put forth by social historians who claim that between the 1960s and 1980s, grassroots social movements played an unprecedented role in shaping the agenda (Chafe, 1998; Wittner, 1998). Although their work has taught us a great deal about the social movements themselves, we know little about the connections between activists and policy outcomes, as well as how grassroots movements turned into interest groups.

Baker's and Ladd Taylor's work on gender is rooted in the third strategy for reorganizing political time: studies on political culture. This scholarship is rooted in cultural studies and anthropology rather than political science. The focus of this research has been to examine how language, discourses, ideology, and symbols shaped all political action in a given period. Resembling studies on political process, scholars of political culture marked political time around key shifts in American's ideological perception about the underlying rules and questions of politics (Kelley, 1989; Sklar, 1995). While examining America's revolutionary period—one of the few eras where political history continued to thrive after the 1970s—landmark studies about culture offered bold analyses of the ideologies and discourses that united the colonists. These linked the founders to European traditions dating back to the Renaissance (Bailyn, 1967; Wood, 1969; Pocock, 1975; McCoy, 1980; Appleby, 1984; Kloppenberg, 1987). Daniel Rodgers's (1998) book on the Progressive Era revealed that political ideas about government expansion originated from around the globe, as an international community of experts in Europe responded to the dilemmas of industrialism.

Looking at the political culture of the postwar period, an intriguing question has been how New Deal liberalism declined as a shared ideology and when a new style of conservatism replaced it. The nature of this shift, and the continuities between the eras, are ripe for archival research. There were also deep divisions within the new conservatism that need to be explored (Dionne, 1991). Equally important have been findings of how older ideologies, such as fiscal conservatism, continued to limit domestic and foreign policy (Hogan, 1998; Zelizer, 2000b). But historians are finding a richer story than the familiar ideological competition between conservatism and liberalism. One group of scholars has shown how a psychological-based political culture triumphed in the 1950s and 1960s (Herman, 1995; Scott, 1997). In this view, psychological rhetoric played a pivotal role in debates over policies ranging from Cold War strategy to race relations. An enormous amount of work remains to be completed on the political culture(s) that shaped political actors and citizens. In the end, by looking at the "larger picture," studies on political culture enable historians to integrate presidents with other elites and non-elites.

Historical institutionalism has offered the fourth compelling model, by using the concept of political regimes. These political scientists have argued that regimes defined politics over long stretches of time. Grounded in Burnham's realignment synthesis, they characterize regimes as a complex, albeit distinct, array of legislative coalitions, presidential administrations, grassroots movements, political discourses, and policy clusters. Regimes situate presidents in a much larger constellation of political actors and forces. One of the most notable by-products of this approach has been a resurgence of scholarly investigation of congressional history. Recent research has shown that Congress played a strong role in the development of postwar policies, ranging from small business regulation, taxation, to foreign affairs (Bean, 1996; Hogan, 1998; Zelizer, 1998; Johnson, 1998–99; Friedberg, 2000). The power of the presidency in relation to the regime, as well as the constraints the president faced as a result of it, become much clearer in this scheme. Scholars have started to study when and why political regimes emerge, collapse, and are replaced by new ones. Thus far, one of the most elaborate versions of this approach has focused on the rise and fall of the New Deal regime (Gerstle and Fraser, 1989; Plotke, 1996). W. Elliot Brownlee (1996), moreover, traced the evolution of tax regimes between 1941 and 1986 that revolved around high progressive rates and extensive tax loopholes.

Building on the institutionalist approach, legal historians have been reminding historians that law has remained integral to politics throughout the twentieth century. This is a fifth avenue toward a new chronology of postwar American history. Some legal scholars have recently argued that seminal changes in law served as the foundation for the modern state. The most important change that has been examined thus far took place in the late 1930s as the Supreme Court legitimated New Deal institutions and policies. The decision culminated shifts in legal thinking that had been taking place since the Progressive Era (Horwitz, 1994; Ackerman, 1998). Focusing on labor policy, Christopher Tomlins (1985) and Karen Orren (1991) have both looked at important developments in law which reconstructed the relationship between business, government, and organized labor during the 1930s. Moreover, Lucas Powe Jr. (2000) has traced how the Supreme Court under Chief Justice Earl Warren exerted a powerful influence on the 1960s political agenda. But these works are limited in number. Except for civil rights, postwar historians downplayed the law.

Policy history is the sixth strategy for organizing the postwar period. Policy history is a subfield that emerged in the late 1970s largely as a way to apply historical methods to practical policy debates and to reconstruct political history without focusing exclusively on elites (Zelizer, 2000a). In this subfield, it became clear that policies had a life of their own which revolved around the stages of the policymaking process: agenda-setting, legislation, and implementation. These stages usually outlasted any specific presidential administration and did not fit neatly into the standard chronology of political history. Social Security, for example, only became central to American domestic policy between 1950 and 1954, not during the New Deal or 1960s. Unlike many domestic programs, Social Security experienced its period of greatest expansion during the "conservative" decades of the 1970s and 1980s (Berkowitz, 1991). Policy offers an exciting opportunity to break free from traditional conceptions of political time. By focusing on policy, rather than the president, it forces the historian to consider a much larger number of actors and to consider alternative timeframes for their narratives. Delving into the implementation of housing policies in Detroit, for instance, social historian Thomas Sugrue (1996) deftly illustrated how policies were reconfigured around local racial struggles. Since many policies have lasted over the course of the entire postwar period, this style of political history also allows scholars to perceive the larger continuities that shaped that period. It simultaneously provides an avenue for historians to contribute to contemporary policy debates.

The policy history framework does pose challenges. Most important, it will produce a more fragmented account of the postwar period. Policy history requires research into unwieldy communities of policymakers, including policy experts, think tanks, academics, bureaucrats, and congressional committees (see, for example, Balogh, 1991a; Berkowitz, 1995). Nonetheless, the fragmentation must be seen as virtue, not a vice. As the modern state has become more complex, it makes sense that its history will be more multifaceted. In my first book (1998), I focused on the influence of a tax policy community that promoted moderate Keynesian economic policy and contributory social insurance. The community, which lasted from the 1950s through the mid-1970s, was not tied to a particular administration and its membership extended far beyond the executive branch.

Finally, economic historians have brought their own distinct approach to the table. They have shown that economic eras have been pivotal to politics. For example, the period of economic growth between the 1940s and the 1960s sustained the expansion of federal policies, as policymakers found themselves with extra revenue: citizens were automatically brought into higher tax brackets as a result of rising income. Policymakers were thus able to increase benefits without raising taxes. This expanding economy, moreover, dulled sharp class conflict over political economy (Collins, 2000). In his synthesis of the postwar period, James Patterson (1996) added that economic growth created rising expectations that were eventually shattered in the 1970s. These expectations shaped the contours of American political debate. Inflation and stagflation in the 1970s, on the other hand, fundamentally transformed the politics of the next two decades (Bernstein and Adler, 1994). Robert Collins (1996), for example, showed how developments in international monetary policy had a devastating effect on the War on Poverty in the late 1960s by forcing Johnson to take unfavorable actions toward his most favored programs. This type of periodization, based on economic conditions rather than presidential administrations, effectively captures broad continuities that span decades.

There are of course tensions between the different approaches to reorganizing political time. For example, while the regime approach has stressed institutional structure, scholars of the economy have been more concerned with the market context within which politicians and citizens operate. Scholars of political culture, moreover, often come into conflict with the political process literature, which stresses self-interest and institutional rules. But these tensions are healthy. Careful research will help us understand the complex relationship that existed between regimes and the economic context within which they operated, while students of political culture will strengthen their work by relating political culture(s) to a specific institutional and political infrastructure. Historians, who tend to relish multicausal explanations of the past, should be excited, rather than fearful, about the tensions between competing approaches.

These alternative frameworks are only a few of the ways that historians can reorder political time during the postwar period. All of them place greater emphasis on the policymaking process, institutional and economic contexts, and cultural boundaries than the liberal presidential synthesis. This fundamental shift in emphasis is a major intellectual change. In the coming years, as we begin to see the postwar period in greater historical perspective, other frameworks will emerge. We can assume that the president will not appear to be as imperial as once was thought and that there will be a fundamental reorganization of the postwar chronology. Far from abandoning the presidency, this approach will require a new generation of historical investigations that situate the office in its proper social, cultural, economic, and institutional contexts. It is likely that our historical understanding of the presidency itself will become much stronger as a result of this new presentation of time.

Toward a New Political History

As historians seek to revitalize and reconceptualize political history, they need to avoid blending social and cultural history with outdated narratives about political elites. At the center of this project will be a new understanding of the postwar presidency that integrates the research of political scientists. This does not mean that the president should be ignored, nor should the enormous power of the office be downplayed. Rather, we need to better understand how presidents grappled with the environment they inherited. As scholars examine the past through new eyes, narratives on politics will become more fragmented, textured, and multicausal as historians discover interrelated storylines as the state expanded its scope and its infrastructure. Since the postwar period remains historically unconstructed, this project promises unexpected turns and will produce exciting new conceptions of the path that links our past to the future.

References

Ackerman, Bruce. 1998. *We The People: Transformations*, vol. 2. Cambridge, MA: Belknap Press of Harvard University Press.

Allen, Craig. 1993. *Eisenhower and the Mass Media: Peace, Prosperity, and Prime-Time TV*. Chapel Hill: University of North Carolina Press.

Altschuler, Glenn C., and Stuart M. Blumin. 2000. *Rude Republic: Americans and Their Politics in the Nineteenth Century*. Princeton, NJ: Princeton University Press.

Ambrose, Stephen E. 1987. *The Education of a Politician*. New York: Simon & Schuster.

———. 1990. *Eisenhower Soldier and President: The Renowned One-Volume Life*. New York: Touchstone.

Appleby, Joyce. 1984. *Capitalism and a New Social Order*. New York: New York University Press.

Bailyn, Bernard. 1967. *The Ideological Origins of the American Revolution*. Cambridge, MA: Belknap Press of Harvard University Press.

Baker, Jean. 1983. *Affairs of Party: The Political Culture of Northern Democrats in the Mid-Nineteenth Century*. Ithaca, NY: Cornell University Press.

Baker, Paula. 1984. The domestication of politics: women and American political society, 1780–1920." *American Historical Review* 89 (1984): 620–47.

———. 1993. A reply to Byron E. Shafer: Social Science in Political History. *Journal of Policy History* 5: 480–84.

Balogh, Brian. 1991a. *Chain Reaction: Expert Debate and Public Participation in American Commercial Nuclear Power, 1945–1975*. Cambridge: Cambridge University Press.

———. 1991b. Reorganizing the organizational synthesis: federal-professional relations in modern America." *Studies in American Political Development* 5: 119–72.

Barber, James D. 1992. *The Presidential Character*, 4th ed. Upper Saddle River, NJ: Prentice Hall.

Barber, William J. 1985. *From New Era to New Deal: Herbert Hoover, the Economists, and American Economic Policy, 1921–1933*. Cambridge: Cambridge University Press.

Baumgartner, Frank R., and Bryan D. Jones. 1993. *Agendas and Instability in American Politics*. Chicago: University of Chicago Press.

Bean, Jonathan J. 1996. *Beyond the Broker State: Federal Policies Toward Small Business, 1936–1961*. Chapel Hill: University of North Carolina Press.

Berkowitz, Edward D. 1991. *America's Welfare State: From Roosevelt to Reagan*. Baltimore: Johns Hopkins University Press.

———. 1995. *Mr. Social Security: The Life of Wilbur Cohen*. Lawrence: University Press of Kansas.

Bernstein, Irving. 1991. *Promises Kept: John F. Kennedy's New Frontier*. New York: Oxford University Press.

———. 1996. *Guns Or Butter: The Presidency of Lyndon Johnson*. New York: Oxford University Press.

Bernstein, Michael A., and David E. Adler, eds. 1994. *Understanding American Economic Decline*. Cambridge: Cambridge University Press.

Beschloss, Michael. 2000. The end of the imperial presidency. *New York Times*, December 18, p. 27.

Blum, John M., William S. McFeely, Edmund S. Morgan, Arthur M. Schlesinger Jr., Kenneth M. Stampp, and C. Vann Woodward. 1989. *The National Experience: A History of the United States, Part II*, 7th ed. New York: Harcourt Brace Jovanovich.

Brinkley, Alan. 1984. Writing the history of contemporary America: dilemmas and challenges. *Daedalus* 113: 121–41.

Brinkley, Alan, and Ellen Fitzpatrick. 1997. *America in Modern Times*. New York: McGraw Hill.

Brownlee, W. Elliot. 1996. *Federal Taxation in America: A History*. Cambridge: Cambridge University Press.

Burnham, James. 1959. *Congress and the American Tradition*. Chicago: Regnery.

Burnham, Walter Dean. 1970. *Critical Elections and the Mainsprings of American Politics*. New York: W.W. Norton.

Burns, James MacGregor. 1965. *Presidential Government: The Crucible of Leadership*. Boston: Houghton Mifflin.

Caro, Robert A. 1982. *The Years of Lyndon Johnson*. New York: Alfred A. Knopf.

———. 1990. *Means of Ascent: The Lyndon Johnson Years*. New York: Alfred A. Knopf.

Chafe, William H. 1998. *The Unfinished Journey: America Since World War II*, 4th ed. New York: Oxford University Press.

Chandler, Alfred D. 1977. *The Visible Hand: The Managerial Revolution in American Business*. Cambridge, MA: Belknap Press of Harvard University Press.

Cochran, Thomas C. 1948. The "presidential synthesis" in American history. *American Historical Review* 53: 748–59.

Collins, Robert M. 1996. The economic crisis of 1968 and the waning of the "American century." *American Historical Review* 101: 396–422.

———. 2000. *More: The Politics of Economic Growth in Postwar America*. New York: Oxford University Press.

Cook, Blanche Weisen. 1981. *The Declassified Eisenhower: A Divided Legacy*. New York: Doubleday.

Corwin, Edward. 1957. *The President and Powers*. New York: New York University Press.

Dallek, Robert. 1998. *Flawed Giant: Lyndon Johnson and His Times, 1961–1973*. New York: Oxford University Press.

Derthick, Martha 1979. *Policymaking for Social Security*. Washington, DC: Brookings Institution.

Dionne, E. J. 1991. *Why Americans Hate Politics*. New York: Touchstone.

Divine, Robert A. 1981. *Eisenhower and the Cold War*. New York: Oxford University Press.

Edwards, III, George C. 1989. *At the Margins: Presidential Leadership of Congress*. New Haven, CT: Yale University Press.

———. 1996. Who influences whom? The president, Congress, and the media. *American Political Science Review* 93: 327–44.

Fenno, Richard F. 1973. *Congressmen in Committees*. Boston: Little, Brown.

Ferrell, Robert H. 1996. *Harry S. Truman: A Life*. Columbia: University of Missouri Press.

Fink, Gary M., and Hugh Davis Graham, eds. 1998. *The Carter Presidency: Policy Choices in the Post–New Deal Era*. Lawrence: University Press of Kansas.

Fisher, Louis. 1972. *President and Congress: Power and Policy*. New York: Free Press.

———. 1998. *The Politics of Shared Power: Congress and the Executive*, 4th ed. College Station: Texas A&M University Press.

Friedberg, Aaron L. 2000. *In the Shadow of the Garrison State: America's Anti-Statism and Its Cold War Grand Strategy*. Princeton, NJ: Princeton University Press.

Galambos, Louis. 1970. The emerging organizational synthesis in modern American history. *Business History Review* 44: 279–90.

———. 1976. *America At Middle Age: A New History of the United States in the Twentieth Century*. New York: McGraw Hill.

———. 1983. Technology, political economy, and professionalization. *Business History Review* 57: 471–93.

Garment, Suzanne. 1991. *Scandal: The Culture of Mistrust in American Politics.* New York: Random House.

Gerstle, Gary, and Steven Fraser, eds. 1989. *The Rise and Fall of the New Deal Order, 1930–1980.* Princeton, NJ: Princeton University Press.

Gillon, Steve M., and Cathy D. Matson. 2001. *The American Experiment: A History of the United States.* Boston: Houghton Mifflin.

Ginsberg, Benjamin, and Martin Shefter. 1990. *Politics By Other Means: The Declining Importance of Elections in America.* New York: Basic Books.

Goldfield, David, Carl Abbot, Virginia De John Anderson, Jo Anne Argersinger, Peter H. Argersinger, William Barney, and Robert Weir. 1998. *The American Journey: A History of the United States.* Upper Saddle River, NJ: Prentice Hall.

Goldman, Eric. 1956. *The Crucial Decade: America, 1945–1955.* New York: Alfred A. Knopf.

Graham, Hugh Davis. 1990. *The Civil Rights Era: Origins and Development of National Policy.* New York: Oxford University Press.

Greenstein, Fred I. 1982. *The Hidden Hand Presidency: Eisenhower as Leader.* New York: Basic Books.

Griffith, Robert. 1982. Dwight D. Eisenhower and the corporate commonwealth. *American Historical Review* 87: 87–122.

Hamby, Alonzo. 1973. *Beyond the New Deal: Harry S. Truman and American Liberalism, 1945–1953.* New York: Columbia University Press.

———. 1985. *Liberalism and Its Challengers: F.D.R. to Reagan.* New York: Oxford University Press.

———. 1989. The mind and character of Harry S. Truman. In *The Truman Presidency*, ed. Michael Lacey. Cambridge: Cambridge University Press and Washington, DC: Woodrow Wilson Center Press.

Hartz, Louis. 1955. *The Liberal Tradition in America.* New York: Harcourt Brace and World.

Hawley, Ellis. 1979. *The Great War and a Search for a Modern Order: A History of the American People and Their Institutions, 1917–1933.* Boston: St. Martin's.

Hays, Samuel P. 1957. *The Response to Industrialism, 1885–1914.* Chicago: University of Chicago Press.

Hays, Samuel P., in collaboration with Barbara D. Hays. 1987. *Beauty, Health, and Permanence: Environmental Politics in the United States, 1955–1985.* Cambridge: Cambridge University Press.

Heath, Jim F. 1975. *Decade of Disillusionment: The Kennedy-Johnson Years.* Bloomington: Indiana University Press.

Herman, Ellen. 1995. *Romance of American Psychology: Political Culture in the Age of Experts.* Berkeley: University of California Press.

Hodgson, Godfrey. 1976. *America in Our Time. From World War II to Nixon: What Happened and Why.* New York: Vintage.

Hoff, Joan. 1994. *Nixon Reconsidered.* New York: Basic Books.

Hofstadter, Richard. 1955. *The Age of Reform: From Bryan to F.D.R.* New York: Vintage.

Hogan, Michael J. 1998. *A Cross of Iron: Harry S. Truman and the Origins of the National Security State.* Cambridge: Cambridge University Press.

Horwitz, Morton J. 1994. *The Transformation of American Law 1870–1960: The Crisis of Legal Orthodoxy.* Cambridge, MA: Belknap Press of Harvard University Press.

Huntington, Samuel P. 1965. "Congressional Responses in the Twentieth Century." In *The Congress and America's Future*, ed. David B. Truman. New York: Prentice Hall.

Johnson, Robert David. 1998–99. The Government Operations Committee and foreign policy during the Cold War. *Political Science Quarterly* 113: 645–71.

Jones, Charles O. 1994. *The Presidency in a Separated System*. Washington, DC: Brookings.

Kearns, Doris. 1976. *Lyndon Johnson and the American Dream*. New York: Harper & Row.

Kelley, Robert. 1989. The interplay of American political culture and public policy: the Sacramento River as a case study. *Journal of Policy History* 1: 1–23.

Kingdon, John W. 1984. *Agendas, Alternatives, and Public Policies*. Glenview, IL: Scott, Foresman.

Kleppner, Paul. 1970. *The Cross of Culture: A Social Analysis of Midwestern Politics, 1850–1900*. New York: Free Press.

Kloppenberg, James T. 1987. The virtues of liberalism: Christianity, Republicanism, and ethics in early American political discourse. *Journal of American History* 74: 9–33.

Kolko, Gabriel. 1976. *Main Currents in Modern American History*. New York: Harper & Row.

———. 1985. *The Triumph of Conservatism: A Re-Interpretation of American History, 1900–1916*, reissue ed. New York: Free Press.

Kornbluh, Mark L. 2000. *Why America Stopped Voting: The Decline of Participatory Democracy and the Emergence of Modern American Politics*. New York: New York University Press.

Kutler, Stanley I. 1990. *The Wars of Watergate: The Last Crisis of Richard Nixon*. New York: Alfred A. Knopf.

Ladd Jr., Everett Carll, and Charles D. Hadley. 1975. *Transformations of the American Party System: Political Coalitions from the New Deal to the 1970s*. New York: W.W. Norton.

Ladd Taylor, Molly. 1994. *Mother-Work: Women, Child Welfare, and the State, 1890–1930*. Urbana: University of Illinois Press.

Leff, Mark H. 1995. Revisioning U.S. political history. *American Historical Review* 100: 829–53.

Leuchtenburg, William E. 1963. *Franklin D. Roosevelt and the New Deal*. New York: Harper & Row.

———. 1983. *In the Shadow of FDR: From Harry Truman to Ronald Reagan*. Ithaca, NY: Cornell University Press.

———. 1986. The pertinence of political history: reflections on the significance of the state of America. *Journal of American History* 73: 585–600.

———. 2001. The twentieth-century presidency. In *Perspectives on Modern America: Making Sense of the Twentieth Century*, ed. Harvey Sitkoff. New York: Oxford University Press, 9–32.

Light, Paul C. 2000. Domestic policy making. *Presidential Studies Quarterly* 30: 109–32.

Logevall, Fredrik. 1999. *Choosing War: The Lost Chance for Peace and the Escalation of War in Vietnam*. Berkeley: University of California Press.

Lowi, Theodore J. 1969. *The End of Liberalism: Ideology, Policy, and the Crisis of Public Authority*. New York: W.W. Norton.

McConnell, Grant. 1967. *The Modern Presidency*. New York: St. Martin's.

McCormick, Richard L. 1981. *From Realignment to Reform: Political Change in New York State, 1893–1910*. Ithaca, NY: Cornell University Press.

McCoy, Drew R. 1980. *The Elusive Republic: Political Economy in Jeffersonian America*. Chapel Hill: University of North Carolina Press.

McCullough, David. 1992. *Truman*. New York: Simon & Schuster.

McKay, David. 1989. *Domestic Policy and Ideology: Presidents and the American State, 1964–1987*. Cambridge: Cambridge University Press.

Manley, John. 1970. *The Politics of Finance: The House Committee on Ways and Means*. Boston: Little, Brown.

Mann, Robert. 2001. *A Grand Delusion: America's Descent into Vietnam*. New York: Perseus.

Marmor, Theodore R. 1973. *The Politics of Medicare*. Chicago: Aldine.

Matusow, Allen J. 1985. *The Unraveling of America: A History of Liberalism in the 1960s*. New York: Harper Torchbooks.

May, Ernest R., and Richard E. Neustadt. 1986. *Thinking in Time: The Uses of History for Decision Makers*. New York: Free Press.

Mayhew, David R. 1991. *Divided We Govern: Party Control, Lawmaking, and Investigation, 1946–1990*. New Haven, CT: Yale University Press.

———. 2000. *American's Congress: Actions in the Public Sphere, James Madison through Newt Gingrich*. New Haven, CT: Yale University Press.

Milkis, Sidney M. 1993. *The President and the Parties: The Transformation of the American Party System Since the New Deal*. New York: Oxford University Press.

———. 1999. *Political Parties and Constitutional Government: Remaking American Democracy*. Baltimore: Johns Hopkins University Press.

Miroff, Bruce. 1976. *Pragmatic Illusions: The Presidential Politics of John F. Kennedy*. New York: McKay.

Morgan, Iwan W. 1990. *Eisenhower Versus "The Spenders": The Eisenhower Administration, the Democrats, and the Budget, 1953–1960*. New York: St. Martin's.

Nathan, Richard P. 1975. *The Plot that Failed: Nixon and the Administrative Presidency*. New York: Wiley.

Neustadt, Richard E. 1960. *Presidential Power: The Politics of Leadership*. New York: Wiley.

Orfield, Gary. 1975. *Congressional Power: Congress and Social Change*. New York: Harcourt Brace.

Orren, Karen. 1991. *Belated Feudalism: Labor, the Law, and Liberal Development in the United States*. Cambridge: Cambridge University Press.

Parmet, Herbert S. 1983. *The Presidency of John F. Kennedy*. New York: Dial Press.

Patashnik, Eric M. 2000. Budgeting more, Deciding less. *Public Interest* 138: 65–78.

Patterson, James T. 1967. *Congressional Conservatism and the New Deal: The Growth of the Conservative Coalition in Congress, 1933–1939*. Lexington: University of Kentucky Press.

———. 1996. *Grand Expectations: The United States, 1945–1975*. New York: Oxford University Press.

Peterson, Mark. 1990. *Legislating Together: The White House and Capitol Hill from Eisenhower to Reagan*. Cambridge, MA: Belknap Press of Harvard University Press.

Pierson, Paul. 1994. *Dismantling the Welfare State? Reagan, Thatcher, and the Politics of Retrenchment*. Cambridge: Cambridge University Press.

Plotke, David. 1996. *Building a Democratic Political Order: Reshaping American Liberalism in the 1930s and 1940s.* Cambridge: Cambridge University Press.
Pocock, J.G.A. 1975. *The Machiavellian Moment.* Princeton, NJ: Princeton University Press.
Polsby, Nelson W. 1964. *Congress and the Presidency.* Englewood Cliffs, NJ: Prentice Hall.
———. 1984. *Political Innovation in America: The Politics of Policy Initiation.* New Haven, CT: Yale University Press.
Porter, David L. 1980. *Congress and the Waning of the New Deal.* Port Washington: National University Publications.
Powe Jr., Lucas A. 2000. *The Warren Court and American Politics.* Cambridge, MA: Belknap Press of Harvard University Press.
Pyle, Christopher H. 1974. Military surveillance of civilian politics, 1967–1970. PhD diss., Columbia University.
Redlich, Dean Norman. 1981. Concluding observations: the constitutional dimension. In *The Tethered Presidency: Congressional Restraints on Executive Power*, ed. Thomas M. Franck. New York: New York University Press.
Reedy, George E. 1970. *The Twilight of the Presidency.* New York: World Publishing.
Reeves, Richard. 1993. *President Kennedy: Profile of Power.* New York: Simon & Schuster.
Ripley, Randall B. 1969. *Majority Party Leadership in Congress.* Boston: Little, Brown.
Rodgers, Daniel. 1998. *Atlantic Crossings: Social Politics in a Progressive Age.* Cambridge, MA: Belknap Press of Harvard University Press.
Rossiter, Clinton. 1956. *The American Presidency.* New York: Harcourt Brace.
Schlesinger Jr., Arthur M. 1959. *The Age of Roosevelt: The Coming of the New Deal.* Boston: Houghton Mifflin.
———. 1965. *A Thousand Days.* Boston: Houghton Mifflin.
———. 1973. *The Imperial Presidency.* Boston: Houghton Mifflin.
———. 1986. *The Cycles of American History.* Boston: Houghton Mifflin.
Schudson, Michael. 1992. *Watergate in the American Memory: How We Remember, Forget, and Reconstruct the Past.* New York: Basic Books.
Schulman, Bruce J. 1995. *Lyndon B. Johnson and American Liberalism: A Brief Biography With Documents.* Boston: Bedford Books.
Scott, Daryl M. 1997. *Contempt and Pity: Social Policy and the Image of the Damaged Black Psyche, 1880–1996.* Chapel Hill: University of North Carolina Press.
Shafer, Byron E. 1983. *Quiet Revolution: The Struggle for the Democratic Party and the Shaping of Post-Reform Politics.* New York: Russell Sage Foundation.
———. 1993. Political eras in political history: a review essay. *Journal of Policy History* 5: 461–74.
Shank, Alan. 1980. *Presidential Policy Leadership, Kennedy, and Social Welfare.* Lanham, MD: University Press.
Shapiro, Robert Y., Martha Joynt Kumar, and Lawrence R. Jacobs, eds. 2000. *Presidential Power: Forging the Presidency for the Twenty-First Century.* New York: Columbia University Press.
Sherrill, Robert. 1967. *The Accidental President.* New York: Pyramid Books.
Silbey, Joel H. 1991. *The American Political Nation, 1838–1893.* Stanford, CA: Stanford University Press.

Sinclair, Barbara. 1982. *Congressional Realignment, 1925–1978*. Austin: University of Texas Press.

Sklar, Kathryn Kish. 1995. *Florence Kelley and the Nation's Work: The Rise of Women's Political Culture, 1830–1900*. New Haven, CT: Yale University Press.

Skocpol, Theda. 1992. *Protecting Soldiers and Mothers: The Political Origins of Social Policy in the United States*. Cambridge, MA: Belknap Press of Harvard University Press.

———. 1995. *Social Policy in the United States: Future Possibilities in Historical Perspective*. Princeton, NJ: Princeton University Press.

Skowronek, Stephen. 1982. *Building a New American State: The Expansion of National Administrative Capacities, 1877–1920*. Cambridge: Cambridge University Press.

———. 1993. *The Politics Presidents Make: Leadership from John Adams to George Bush*. Cambridge, MA: Belknap Press of Harvard University Press.

Steuerle, C. Eugene. 1996, Financing the American state at the turn of the century. In *Funding the Modern American State, 1941–1995: The Rise and Fall of the Era of Easy Finance, 1941–1995*. Cambridge: Cambridge University Press and Washington, DC: Woodrow Wilson Center Press, 409–44.

Sugrue, Thomas J. 1996. *The Origins of the Urban Crisis*. Princeton, NJ: Princeton University Press.

Sundquist, James L. 1968. *Politics and Policy: The Eisenhower, Kennedy, and Johnson Years*. Washington, DC: Brookings.

———. 1981. *The Decline and Resurgence of Congress*. Washington, DC: Brookings.

Theoharis, Athan. 1971. *Seeds of Repression: Harry S. Truman and the Origins of McCarthyism*. Chicago: Quadrangle Books.

———. 1978. *Spying on Americans: Political Surveillance from Hoover to the Huston Plan*. Philadelphia: Temple University Press.

Tomlins, Christopher L. 1985. *The State and the Unions: Labor Relations, Law, and the Organized Labor Movement in America, 1880–1960*. Cambridge: Cambridge University Press.

VanDeMark, Brian. 1991. *Into the Quagmire: Lyndon Johnson and the Escalation of the Vietnam War*. New York: Oxford University Press.

Wiebe, Robert H. 1967. *The Search for Order, 1887–1920*. New York: Hill and Wang.

Wildavsky, Aaron. 1964. *The Politics of the Budgetary Process*. Boston: Little Brown.

Wildavsky, Aaron, and Jeffrey Pressman. 1984. *Implementation: How Great Expectations in Washington Are Dashed in Oakland: Or, Why It's Amazing that Federal Programs Work At All, This Being a Saga of the Economic Development Administration As Told By Two Sympathetic Observers Who Seek to Build Morals on a Foundation of Ruined Hopes*. Berkeley: University of California Press.

Williams, William A. 1959. *The Tragedy of American Diplomacy*. Cleveland: World Publishers.

———. 1961. *The Contours of American History*. Cleveland, OH: World Publishers.

Wittner, Lawrence S. 1998. *The Struggle Against the Bomb: Resisting the Bomb—A History of the World Nuclear Disarmament Movement, 1954–1970*. Stanford, CA: Stanford University Press.

Wood, Gordon. 1969. *The Creation of the American Republic*. Chapel Hill: University of North Carolina Press.

Zelizer, Julian E. 1998. *Taxing America: Wilbur D. Mills, Congress, and the State, 1945–1975*. Cambridge: Cambridge University Press.

———. 2000a. Clio's Lost Tribe: public policy history since 1978. *Journal of Policy History* 12: 369–94.

———. 2000b. The forgotten legacy of the New Deal: fiscal conservatism and the Roosevelt administration, 1933–1938. *Presidential Studies Quarterly* 30: 331–58.

———. 2004. *On Capitol Hill: The Struggle to Reform Congress and its Consequences, 1945–2000*. New York: Cambridge University Press.

TWO

Clio's Lost Tribe: Public Policy History Since 1978

Policy history has straddled two disciplines—history and policy analysis—neither of which has taken it very seriously.[1] What unites those who study policy history is not that they are "policy historians," but that they organize their analysis and narrative around the around the emergence, passage, and implementation of policy.[*] Rather than being a subfield, as the historian Paula Baker recently argued, policy history has resembled area studies programs.[2] Policy history became an interdisciplinary arena for scholars from many different fields to interact. While founders hoped that policies would become an end in themselves, rather than something used to understand other issues, scholarship since 1978 has shown that the two are not mutually exclusive. In fact, some of the most innovative scholarship has come from social or political historians who have used policy to understand larger historical phenomena. In the process, the work provided a much richer understanding of how policymaking evolved.

As we enter the twenty-first century, however, the future of policy history remains unclear. Some practitioners believe that they have reached a critical turning point. As a result of increasingly innovative and bountiful scholarship, successful conferences, and organizational momentum, they claim that policy history is on the cusp of becoming a major subfield. Others are more pessimistic, pointing to chronic problems plaguing the field. Only a handful of history departments have developed policy programs. The *American Historical Review* and the *Journal of American History* rarely publish anything having to do with policy. Nor has a professional association or annual conference been established. Policy schools and scholars have moved decisively away from historical analysis after a brief period of flirtation. Far too often, policy analysts admit that they perceive historians as scholars who "just tell stories."

* This essay originally appeared in *Journal of Policy History* 12 (2000): 369–94.

This history of policy history reveals that its practitioners have always faced the perplexing task of having to satisfy two audiences, each with different types of assumptions, interests, and questions.[3] Unfortunately, in response to this challenge, many scholars chose to retreat from the nonhistorical world. Although there have been several works that explain why historians should take policy and politics seriously, few have attempted to systematically justify the value of their scholarship to policymakers.[4] Synthesizing ten years of scholarship from the *Journal of Policy History*, I argue that five central categories of historical research have emerged: Institutional and Cultural Persistence, Lost Alternatives, Historical Correctives, Political Culture, and Process Evolution. These categories of research offer work that is distinct from the emphasis of mainstream policy analysts and can provide guidance to policymakers without becoming advocates. By situating recent research within these categories, and explaining their analytic value, I will show why historians should be speaking with greater authority in the world of governance.

Professional Development

Policy has never occupied a central role in the work of historians of the United States. At the height of "traditional" political history in the 1950s and 1960s, policies were only studied by scholars such as Arthur Schlesinger Jr. and William Leuchtenburg as a vehicle to understand presidencies.[5] They paid little sustained attention to the policy process itself or to policies as they evolved over time. There are exceptions to this rule. Scholars from the New Left focused on political economy, discovering the influence of big business in shaping economic regulation, as opposed to well-intentioned liberals, during the Progressive Era.[6] But these radicals were not in the mainstream of their profession, still dominated by New Deal liberals who found these arguments anathema to their understanding of the past. There were other historians who wrote about education and welfare policy.[7] But the most prominent political historians only dealt briefly with policy as they focused on presidential administrations and the evolution of liberalism. The status of policy history only worsened in the 1970s as the professional underwent an intellectual revolution. A younger generation of historians who entered graduate school in the 1960s rejected the study of government institutions and political leaders as elitist and unrepresentative.[8] Instead, they focused on social history from "the bottom up." Even the "new political historians" of that decade, as they called themselves, concentrated primarily on quantitative historical analyses of voting behavior. These historians were interested in discovering whether ethnicity or class determined voters' partisan allegiance. Policies were of little interest.[9]

There were, however, two alternate routes through which policy analysis survived at the margins of the historical profession. One was the public history movement that began in the 1970s. Amidst a severe job crisis that left thousands of PhDs and graduate students unemployed, some unemployed scholars turned to public history as a means of applying their knowledge in nonacademic settings. While in the 1990s the popular conception of public historians centered on museums and archives, the use of historical analysis in policymaking stood at the core of these initial efforts. The movement stemmed from a populist hope of bringing history to the general public. Part of public history's success stemmed from the fact that it did not start from scratch. Rather, it provided recognition of what many historians had been doing since the founding of the profession in government agencies, archival institutions, historical societies and tourist sites, and museums.[10] World War II had produced a boom in public history employment when the military services hired historians for practical purposes. The army, for example, opened up historical divisions in each major command and service. Army leaders also started a history branch for the general staff. These historians were directed to produce studies on the U.S. experience in World War I since the army was determined to avoid the problems that beset that effort.[11] While many historians left for the academy after 1945, many of the offices stayed in operation.

In the 1970s, public historians finally loosened the stranglehold that university scholars had maintained on the profession since its founding in the late nineteenth century.[12] The movement developed institutional muscle as various universities established comprehensive public history graduate programs starting in 1976. The University of California at Santa Barbara created an especially prestigious program under the direction of Robert Kelley, an eminent political historian. The Rockefeller Foundation provided a three-year grant to fund these efforts. For this program, Kelley and his colleagues reconceptualized graduate education in history to include internships, courses in other disciplines, and community-center research.[13]

In addition to new graduate programs, public historians formed a national association, the National Council for Public History, and founded a journal called *The Public Historian*. The National Coordinating Committee for the Promotion of History, another association that was founded in 1977, aimed to link scholars with those outside the academy. In light of these developments, Peter Stearns and Joel Tarr, co-directors of Carnegie Mellon's applied history and social science program, promised that if public history departed from "the discipline's narcissism, the result can revive a key discipline: It can also provide a broader range of data and a surer sense of values to the public policy arena. A born-again group of historians is busy making sure that our own past can serve these needs."[14] The first pages of the premier issue of *The Public Historian* expressed forcefully the practical aspirations of this movement:

> Other disciplines, economics, political science, and sociology, have made the transition from academy to public arenas easily and without compromise. Since historians have traditionally occupied a halfway house between social sciences and the humanities, they have tended to

> stay close to the academy. This was especially true with the increasing professionalization of history that took place after the turn of the twentieth century. This was symbolized by the fact that the gifted amateur (such as Theodore Roosevelt, who had been president of the American Historical Association) was now excluded from the discipline. Increasingly the academy, rather than historical society or public arena, became the habitat of the historian, who literally retreated into the proverbial ivory tower. The triumph of the professional was complete, and so was his isolation.[15]

The institutionalization of public history, as historian Peter Novick has argued, took place within an era of heightened skepticism toward the traditional professional claims that historians produced "unbiased" objective scholarship. Critics doubted that scholars hired by public or private institutions could avoid pressure from sponsors to shape their research. When advising policymakers, critics asked, what could historians offer other than propaganda for partisan objectives? But public historians, who created a code of ethics in response to this dilemma, responded that they could, in fact, produce analytic scholarship. Their defense grew out of a new professional consciousness. Unlike many senior scholars, they insisted that all historians were biased to some degree and, like colleagues in the universities, they would strive to obtain the best possible account of the past within the constraints faced by all scholars.[16] Otis Graham Jr. from the University of North Carolina, insisted that "only in degree and in type, but not in kind, does the academic historian experience a different set of corrupting pressures than the friends of Clio who work outside." Another public historian, Barbara Benson Kohn, told readers of *The Public Historian*, "the unblemished scholar-historian who speaks freely, objectively, truthfully, and purely to an audience entirely of his own choosing was dismissed long ago as a fantasy."[17]

While all professional historians have continued to grapple with the ideological dilemma of objectivity, public historians have faced the problem more acutely than any other type of scholar since the institutional context within which they work raises the issue directly. This discomfort with this dilemma would cause many policy historians to be excessively defensive when speaking about why their work mattered to policymakers in practical terms. Regardless, public history offered historians interested in policy with a viable outlet through which to pursue their work.

While public historians advised policymakers outside the academy, a few scholars in the university were not dissuaded by the topic's marginal status. Although sympathetic to the goals of public historians, particularly the notion of making history valuable to those outside the academy, these scholars were firmly rooted in the academy and disseminated their research in university presses and scholarly journals. Some focused on poverty, criminal, and mental health policies as a means of understanding social class relations.[18] Meanwhile, diplomatic, and some legal, historians pursued their traditional interest in policy seemingly immune from the social history revolution taking place around them. Finally, a small group of historians produced the "organizational synthesis." Building on modernization theory, organizational historians argued that the major force driving change in the twentieth century was the evolution of national institutions such as the administrative state.[19]

Many of these university historians gathered at the Harvard University Business School in November 1978 for a Rockefeller Foundation-funded conference organized by Thomas McCraw from Harvard and Morton Keller from Brandeis University. McCraw, who attended to most of the logistics while Keller was a guest scholar at Oxford University, received funding from the Rockefeller Foundation. The effort started with the intention of bringing together historians, lawyers, and political scientists who shared a common interest in regulation. At that time, James Q. Wilson and Paul MacAvoy ran a popular seminar on regulation that generated much of the interest in this project.[20] But the conference ended up being important to broader scholarship since it marked the first "self-conscious discussion" of policy history as a distinct subfield of either history or the policy sciences.[21] While there were several historians who dealt with policies on welfare, technology, science, and economic regulation, the organizers explained, "in each of these cases, the public policy theme is subsumed within the framework of the substantive area of inquiry. There tends to be relatively little concern with the history of the public policy process *per se*."[22] McCraw and Keller hoped this conference could change that. Attendees included distinguished senior and younger scholars such as Edward Berkowitz, Louis Galambos, Ernest May, Robert Kelley, Ellis Hawley, Otis Graham, James Q. Wilson, and Graham Allison (Dean of Harvard's Kennedy School of Government). The organizers agreed that policy history should be an interdisciplinary project and that the research should help policymakers in the "real world." They also wanted the study of policy to overcome the fragmentation of historical scholarship.

At the Harvard conference, two core issues produced the most vigorous debate. Participants disagreed on the basic definition of policy history. One faction defined policy as the coercive power of the state. Another faction promoted a more liberal understanding of policy that encompassed "all institutional programs" impacting significant portions of the population.

Adhering to the new emphasis in the historical profession, this definition blended public and private sources of power.[23] When the participants failed to reach a consensus, they decided that the tension between the public and private elements of policy might itself constitute a central question for policy historians to examine. The second controversy involved methodology. Rejecting the suggestion of a small minority, participants concluded that policy historians should not define themselves by adopting a social scientific model of analysis (which they viewed as ahistorical). Rather, policy historians should define themselves around a common set of issues, including the distinction between the public and private realms, the role of professionals in policymaking, the role of crisis in policy development, how changes in process influenced policy, the impact of institutional structure on policies, the relation between government and nongovernmental actors, the changing definition of policy over time, and the relation of policies to "contemporaneous" intellectual assumptions.[24] One of the biggest opportunities for policy history, all of the participants agreed, was to evaluate policies by determining if policymakers and policy users realized their goals during the implementation process. When the conference ended, the participants promised to build momentum for this subfield through book reviews, research articles, and further meetings.

There was ample reason to believe that history could be integral to policymakers. The policy analysis profession was just emerging as a field independent from political science and public administration. During the 1960s and 1970s, more than a dozen universities, such as Harvard, Berkeley, Princeton, Minnesota, Duke, and Michigan, formed graduate programs to train students in quantitative economic analysis rather than traditional management principles.[25]

Increased funding for policy analysis arrived from government agencies under the Johnson and Nixon administrations as well as from foundations such as Ford. At the same time, think tanks were proliferating at a rapid pace.[26] In May 1979, fifteen representatives from leading policy schools and think tanks formed the Association for Policy Analysis and Management at Duke University, which published the *Journal of Policy Analysis and Management*, held an annual conference, and granted publication awards. First operated by Duke University, in 1993 the association hired a full-time executive director, whose office was located in Washington, DC.[27] Given the inchoate state of the policy analysis discipline in 1978, some historians believed they could be integrated into this field even though the initial emphasis was placed on the quantitative economic analysis.

Between 1978 and 1984, the hopes of policy historians seemed to be realized. The Harvard Business School, under the direction of Morton Keller and Thomas McCraw, organized two subsequent conferences, in 1979 and 1980, focusing on "Innovation and Public Policy" and "The Regulation of Industrial Society."[28] In other initiatives, historians brought history directly to policymakers. In 1979, McCraw conducted a historical seminar for the Federal Trade Commission. At the University of the District of Columbia, Steven Diner directed an institute that provided city officials and the local media with historical analysis on issues such as public education. Other scholars, such as J. Morgan Kousser, testified in court cases. Meanwhile, History and Public Policy programs were founded by Carnegie Mellon University and the University of Houston. These programs included traditional training in historiography as well as quantitative policy courses and internships in the field. The pages of *The Public Historian* were filling up with essays that explained the value of historical analysis to policymaking.[29] Many pieces were written by social historians, particularly urban specialists. While social historians had moved away from government institutions and political elites, they were interested in public policies that affected the poor. *The Journal of Social History* frequently published essays on policy under the editorships of Andrew Achenbaum and Peter Stearns.[30] The Russell Sage Foundation sponsored a conference in Mount Kisco, New York, that brought together several leading social historians and policymakers to examine how historical research could assist policymakers. David Rothman and Stanton Wheeler organized the conference and published the papers as a book.[31] Herbert Gutman, for example, showed how erroneous historical assumptions about the black family had shaped policymaking.[32] The conference raised an early-warning sign as many participants expressed intense frustration. Participants were skeptical that policymakers and scholars could find any consensus about the role of history in policy analysis. Nonetheless, through the event and publication, scholars were at least grappling with these issues. Finally, historians published several important books on modern social and economic policy.[33] If policy historians needed any more signs of encouragement, they received it when Thomas McCraw's 1984 history of the twentieth-century regulatory policy, *Prophets of Regulation*, won the Pulitzer Prize in History.[34]

There was also support for historical analysis among eminent policy scholars between 1978 and 1985. Political scientist Richard Neustadt, for example, taught a course with historian Ernest May at Harvard's Kennedy School of Government entitled "Uses of History." May had published a widely acclaimed book on the misuse of history in policymaking.[35] Both scholars practiced what they preached, each having worked for different parts of the government earlier in their careers—Neustadt for Presidents Kennedy and Johnson and May for the Joint Chiefs of Staff. The course exposed high-level government officials to the utility of historical analysis. The NEH provided funding for May and Neustadt to produce historical case studies for use in graduate classes. Similar courses were launched at Carnegie Mellon, SUNY–Stony Brook and Albany, the University of Chicago, the University of North Carolina–Chapel Hill, and the RAND Graduate Institute.[36] Moreover, the period witnessed the publication of well-reviewed books by social scientists that relied on historical analysis, including Gilbert Steiner's *The Children's Cause*, Henry Aaron's *Politics and the Professors*, Martha Derthick's *Policymaking for Social Security*, Robert and Rosemary Steven's *Welfare Medicine in America*, and Derthick and Paul Quirk's *The Politics of Deregulation*.[37]

Those who were pursuing policy history were not alone in breaking from traditional categories of academic scholarship. The 1970s and 1980s constituted a vibrant era when many historians were becoming involved in innovative interdisciplinary programs that were organized around issues that had previously been ignored or relegated to secondary status. Growing out of the conflicts of the 1960s, the most prominent programs were Women's, Black, and Ethnic Studies, all of which were tied to political movements.[38] These programs integrated scholars with every different methodological approach who focused on a similar topic. In many respects, the evolving policy history movement mirrored these efforts.

But policy historians still lacked a journal, association, annual conference, or the sense that the subfield had arrived. In 1983, a young scholar named Donald Critchlow approached senior historian Ellis Hawley at the Organization of American Historians Convention in Cincinnati, Ohio, to discuss strategies for taking the subfield to a new level. Unlike Hawley, Critchlow had not attended the Harvard Conference. His belief that a subfield did not yet exist indicated that the agenda of the 1978 conference had not been entirely fulfilled. Critchlow was working as an assistant professor of History at the University of Notre Dame, after receiving his doctorate degree at the University of California at Berkeley and completing a book on the Brookings Institution.[39] The following year, while Critchlow was a fellow at the Woodrow Wilson Center, he continued to have conversations with Hawley and sociologist Theda Skocpol about ideas for advancing the subfield.

In the end, Critchlow decided that the best way to solidify the subfield would be through a national conference. Besides offering an alternative to organizational and economic theory, he hoped to bring "coherence to a field whose rapid growth threatens to leave it without a fulcrum."[40] The conference, which was held in October 1985 at Notre Dame, drew scholars from history, political science, and economics. Several papers from the conference were published as a book by the Penn State Press.[41] The preface, written by historian Robert Kelley, argued that one of the major contributions of policy historians was to understand the evolution of the policy process: "Whatever the method, the field should be marked by a *systematic* study of the policy process over time. This should be the distinguishing characteristic of policy history, as the essays in this volume show." Their work offered an alternative to popular social scientific models that depended on the assumption of rational political actors who based every decision on electoral needs.[42] Another project to emerge from Notre Dame was an undergraduate reader on poverty and public policy in modern America. Dorsey Press published the book in 1989.[43]

Despite their accomplishments, the conferees failed to articulate a clear argument about why historical analysis offered policymakers something better than standard economics or political science. Such an argument is crucial to the development of any subfield. All professions, as sociologist Andrew Abbot has argued, need to maintain a desired, secret expertise if they are to obtain and maintain jurisdiction over a particular form of work. Without doing so, they fail to establish themselves amidst interprofessional competition for jurisdiction.[44] There were scattered attempts in the 1980s to build such an argument beyond the vague claims that history matters. David Mock, for example, said that historians were particularly useful to policy evaluation since they could track unintended consequences of policy by comparing the intentions of policymakers with what unfolded.[45] Edward Berkowitz, moreover, wrote that historians could discern systematic patterns in the history of issues that were at the center of the policymaking agenda.[46]

The boldest argument came in 1986 from Harvard University's Ernest May and Richard Neustadt.[47] Based on experiences in their graduate course, May and Neustadt offered several reasons why history mattered to policymakers. Grounded in the practical ethos of the emerging subfield, the book provided an extremely explicit argument for the functional utility of history: "Our primary concern remains with those who try to govern, as they exercise authority through choices large and small. Our focus, to repeat, is on the uses they make of history or fail to make but could, and how they might do better for themselves in their own terms."[48] They posited three ways in which policymakers could use history. First, historical analysis could help policymakers evaluate historical analogies in order to avoid decisions that are based on false comparisons with the past. Second, May and Neustadt argued, historical analysis could help policymakers locate their decision in longer "time-streams" that situated current problems within an ongoing continuum, thereby improving predictions about the future. Finally, the duo claimed that historical analysis could provide a richer explanation of the people, issues, and organizations involved in a debate and thereby improve a policymaker's chances of success in negotiations. According to this logic, a politician would find more success in working with the Social Security Administration if he or she knew how that federal agency had operated and responded to issues in the past.[49] In essence, one reviewer noted, Neustadt and May's advice is that decision-makers use history during policymaking so that they do not have to end up later asking: "How could we have been so mistaken."[50] *Thinking in Time* soon became the standard text in historical policy classes around the country. Andrew Achenbaum called it the "best primer available for teaching nonhistorians how to incorporate insights from the past into the decision-making process."[51]

In 1987, Donald Critchlow announced the formation of a new journal, the *Journal of Policy History*, to be published by the Penn State Press. Critchlow secured commitments from prestigious scholars in political science, sociology, and history. Peri Arnold, a colleague of Critchlow in the political science department, agreed to serve as co-editor.[52] The journal, which published its first issue in 1989, gradually expanded its subscription and submission base, attracting work from leading names across disciplines, and from junior and senior scholars. By the late 1990s it had become the premier forum for policy historians. Besides the journal, many outstanding books on policy were published during the late 1980s and 1990s by historians such as Brian Balogh, Molly Ladd-Taylor, Sonya Michel, Edward Berkowitz, Linda Gordon, and Hugh Graham. The increased sophistication of the new research was dramatic. Policy history did not entail myopic technocratic narratives about individual policies, as some feared it would. Instead, scholars examined policies by situating them in their political, social, cultural, and economic contexts.

Within the social sciences, moreover, the new historical institutionalism created another source of momentum for this field. Starting with the publication of Stephen Skowronek's *Building a New American State* (1982) and the multi-authored *Bringing the State Back In* (1985), social scientists began using historical data to examine how institutions structured politics over long periods of time and how policies reconfigured politics.[53] These scholars included

Skowronek, Theda Skocpol, Karren Orren, Rogers Smith, Martin Shefter, Margaret Weir, and Eldon Eisenach. The historical social sciences were institutionalized in 1988 through the creation of the History and Politics Section of the American Political Science Association. The section, which organized panels for APSA's annual conference and published a newsletter, had more than five hundred members by 1995.[54] In addition, the journal *Studies in American Political Development* (founded in 1986) offered another important publication outlet for the historical institutionalists. Using policies as a tool to understand institutions, these scholars traced the historical development of public welfare, social insurance, and industrial regulation. Many also published in, and served on the editorial board of, the *Journal of Policy History*. Even some rational choice political scientists turned to historical institutions.[55]

If the story ended at this point, one might expect policy history to have experienced scholarly success. Yet policy history did not achieve anywhere near the influence founders seemed poised to obtain. Most troublesome was the fact that neither of the major host disciplines, history or the policy sciences, seriously embraced their scholarship. Despite dramatic advances in research and two successful conferences, policy history still lurks in the disciplinary shadows. At the tenth anniversary celebration of the *Journal of Policy History*, Ellis Hawley lamented that "the work done, I think we would have to agree, has not taken the profession by storm, leading to new programs in our most prestigious universities or broad professional receptivity to its integrating and cutting-edge claims. It has not, so far as I can tell, had much indispensable and hence routine members of the policy sciences community."[56]

During the 1980s and 1990s, historians had turned decisively away from politics and toward cultural studies. While social historians had maintained a modicum of interest in policy as it affected ethnic or class relations, most cultural historians were more interested in postmodern interpretations of popular culture. With a few notable exceptions, most cultural historians dismissed policy history for adopting the structuralist orientation they hoped to overturn.[57] Policy history was particularly irrelevant to cultural historians since most policy historians were grounding their work in the institutionalism of the social sciences. Toward the end of the century, social and cultural historians took over the leadership in most departments. Many of them have not displayed much interest in appointing historians who focus on political institutions and policy. Upon their retirement, for example, diplomatic historians, until recently, had not been replaced at Northwestern University, UCLA, the University of Iowa, or the University of Texas.[58] To make matters worse for policy historians, the profession entered into another severe job crisis in the 1990s due to budgetary cutbacks in state education. In such a dismal labor market, where thousands of graduate students competed for a handful of jobs, few dared to focus their research on a subject that many senior colleagues (including those on hiring and tenure committees) openly disdained. Only one department, at Bowling Green University, constructed its graduate program around policy history.

History outside the academy offered marginally better results. The public history movement continued to expand rapidly as the number of graduate programs grew in universities and membership in public history associations rose.[59] Just as important, a larger number of federal agencies established historical offices.[60] With the job crisis of the 1990s, public history again was a new source of employment for unemployed students. Policy history continues to be one part of this government agency/public history mix. Indeed, the FBI placed an advertisement for a historian whose duties would include "presenting the FBI Director and other authorities with accurate responses to historical questions; maintaining liaison with outside historical and archival organizations; researching, writing and publishing officially approved FBI books; preparing oral presentations on FBI history; and performing other duties as necessary."[61]

But public history programs have increasingly focused on training students to work for cultural organizations, corporations, and multimedia firms. Public history students have chosen to enter more lucrative fields than policy. Some of the best history students still avoid public history employment and research since it lacks the prestige of university employment.[62] In hiring and tenure decisions, it is well known that administrators only consider scholarly monographs and give little professional credit for historical research that is presented in policy reports or "cultural resource" studies.[63] Other scholars shied away from the public realm as a result of controversial cases, such as *Equal Employment Opportunity Commission v. Sears, Roebuck & Company*, when scholarship was used to support causes the author opposed. These controversies revealed how historical research was often used for very different purposes than the author intended once the work was injected into contemporary policy debates. In 1999, moreover, several prominent historians received harsh criticism from scholars and citizens outside the discipline for having presented, what they charged was, inconsistent and misleading analysis that was intended to be used for clearly partisan purposes during the impeachment of President Clinton.[64]

As public historians began turning away from government, policy analysts focused almost exclusively on quantitative economic analysis. Within public policy schools, history fell out of the curriculum with a few exceptions. The Rockefeller College of Public Affairs at SUNY–Albany, for example, decided to end a required history course since students needed to learn more "practical" skills for the job market. As in academics, jobs became more scarce in the public sector, which pushed students to train in more marketable economics and quantitative skills. Some policy analysts were openly hostile to historical research, perceiving it to be little more than telling stories. After reading Otis Graham's manuscript about the history of industrial policy, for example, one nonhistorian reader called the editor to complain, "Graham proposes that more historians join the policy process, but the truth is that they are entirely unprepared."[65] To make matters worse, quantitative analysis was marginalized within the historical profession during the 1980s. After a period in the 1970s when quantitative analysis was popular among political and social historians, the profession abandoned number-crunching in favor of the techniques of linguistic studies and anthropology. As a result of this decision, younger scholars obtained meager intellectual training in the methods of policy analysis, thereby intensifying the linguistic division that separated the two worlds of policy scholarship.

Even though historical institutionalism thrived within the social sciences, it has proven to be different than policy history. Historical institutionalists are still driven by abstract models and theory. Downplaying narrative and human agency, they rely on limited archival research to demonstrate larger theories rather than having the archives shape the argument of the work. Policy historians, moreover, tend to place institutions in much broader context to draw the connections among political institutions, popular culture, social development, and mass movements. Like political historians of the 1960s, historical institutionalists have been more interested in how policies can help explain institutions rather than understanding the history of the policies as an end in itself. Thus, even with many similarities, divisions exist between the two approaches.

Finally, policy historians were themselves to blame for failing to pursue many of the goals that had inspired founders of the subfield. Most important, policy historians lost much of their practical spirit. Policy historians had hoped to contribute to the world of policymaking as much as to the historical and political science disciplines. But as the years progressed, most scholars who wrote policy history targeted colleagues within their respective fields. Their work focused almost exclusively on historiographical debates without bothering to explain the implications for contemporary policy. There have been few sequels to May and Neustadt's treatise about why history matters to policymakers. Nor have there been many works that attempt to synthesize recent scholarship and explain how the findings might enhance public debate on major issues.[66] As Hugh Graham lamented in 1993, "The development of policy history has been anemic and the case made for it has remained largely abstract."[67] This failure is ironic since there is now so much more research on which to base those claims than existed back in the 1970s. In many respects, those who wrote about policy history failed to answer the formative questions raised in 1978 about what distinguished their work. Revealingly, a majority of individuals who have produced the leading works in this area do not categorize or identify themselves as policy historians. Instead, they tend to perceive themselves as social, cultural, or political historians who are studying policy. Such a lack of identity is debilitating to the development of an intellectual field.

Many policy historians have avoided making any defense on ideological grounds, fearful that their work would be perceived as propaganda or they would be forced to make predictions their research could not support. Even the editor of the *Journal of Policy History* insisted: "The aim of policy history is to provide a context for answering such questions. Policy history seeks to edify and not to specifically instruct. Prescriptions are best left to policymakers actively involved in contemporary problems, and not to historians—those physicians of the buried. Historians of policy history, however, can provide careful dissections of past policies"[68] Likewise, historian Andrew Achenbaum warned of intrinsic differences between the type of scholarship his colleagues wrote and what policy analysts wanted. "Current policy analysis," Achenbaum stated, "almost by definition, is work-in-progress; it focuses on a contemporary 'problem' and offers an admittedly incomplete diagnosis and prognosis. Historians, by contrast, are trained to write a 'product,' which has integrity of its own regardless of its practical usefulness."[69]

Policy historians now look back at a checkered history. On the one hand, policy history has made significant advances since the 1970s. Notwithstanding the lack of a disciplinary home, policy history research has become more sophisticated and bountiful than ever before. At the same time, practitioners have lost some of the ethos that guided them in the early years, namely, that their work would aim to contribute to policy analysis. Increasingly, they have withdrawn into the shelter of professionalism while failing to provide basic guidance about how their work might be used. To make matters worse, policy historians were unable to convince their colleagues in history and policy departments that they had a special expertise which entitled them to claim any jurisdiction over policy issues.

The Arguments Policy Historians Make

Ultimately, policy historians will have to make a stronger case for the value of their research to policymaking. While the contribution of public historians who work directly for policymakers has been examined, I focus on an area that has been neglected: the scholarship of university professors. Drawing from the abundance of scholarship written since 1978, I have identified several distinct categories of historical research that could be valuable to policy analysis and to other historians. These do not constitute the full range of possibilities, but they offer a starting point for discussion. Since 1978, policy historians have produced five categories of research that I call: Institutional and Cultural Persistence, Lost Alternatives, Historical Correctives, Political Culture, and Process Evolution. Even though these are each distinct, most scholars can fit their work into various of these categories.

Historical research has shown how certain institutional structures and cultural assumptions continue to shape policymaking over extremely long periods. Institutional and cultural persistence is both a historical and ahistorical argument. On the one hand, this research traces how certain conditions persist over time. On the other hand, it contends that in some respects the present is not that different from the past. By showing specific links between the past and the present, this research can provide policymakers with strategies for success. Explanations of how conditions stifled or supported previous initiatives can be instructive to those who design new proposals. The research offers a systematic response to Santayana's famous warning that those who don't remember the past are condemned to repeat it.

Michael Katz's work has been particularly influential in this regard. *The Undeserving Poor* showed how a discourse about the poor has shaped welfare debates since the early nineteenth century. According to Katz, the distinction between the "deserving" and the "undeserving" poor has been a staple of political debates throughout most of the nation's history. While emphasizing the "moral" failures of those in need, the discourse downplayed questions of power, politics, and equality. Katz ended his introduction by explicitly linking the book to his own political activism: "To transcend this historic division in the way we talk about public issues, to pull poverty away from family and toward power, requires surmounting the strongest conventions in Americans' social vocabulary. I offer this book as a modest toehold for the struggle."[70] Stressing institutional persistence rather than political discourse, Sven Steinmo compared this history of tax policy in the United States, Sweden, and Great Britain. He argued that the design of each nation's political institutions (separation of power, parliamentary government, etc.) determines what type of tax regime a nation adopts.[71] In another institutionalist work, Stephen Skowronek examined how the institutional tension between the nineteenth-century court and party system and the twentieth-century executive bureaucracies resulted in a jerry-built administrative state. Each interest inserted itself into new programs and agencies, such as budgeting and civil service, thereby guaranteeing ongoing conflict.

Gender and race have played an important role in this category. Indeed, one of the most vibrant areas of policy history has focused on how cultural notions of gender influenced social insurance and welfare policies. Linda Gordon, for example, has argued that a shared consensus over the legitimacy of single-wage-earning families produced a bifurcated welfare state that left poor single women to rely on stigmatized welfare benefits while men received pensions that were not considered to be government assistance. Gordon ended her work by writing that contemporary welfare problems "derived more from historical constraints—on the ability to foresee future social and economic developments and on the range of political possibility—and above all from the political exclusion of those with the greatest need to be included: the poor."[72] Other scholars have argued that southern legislators strove to protect the racial hierarchies which defined their region. As a result, Congress created generous social insurance programs that excluded those jobs which employed the greatest number of African Americans. Jill Quadagno also has contended that racism undermined the War on Poverty.[73] In these kinds of work, persistent racism and sexism define the terms over which welfare policy is designed.

But this scholarship is not just about how persistent institutions and cultural beliefs constrain policymaking. In acknowledging the role of human agency, this research occasionally points to how policy entrepreneurs and political groups have succeeded in overcoming obstacles and offer a guide to policymakers who seek to overcome these same cultural and institutional obstacles. Theda Skocpol, for example, has demonstrated how during the Progressive Era middle-class women organized and lobbied effectively within a federalist system to obtain programs to protect mothers and children. She suggested that these women offer a road map for policymakers. "Hopeful scenarios for contemporary American social politics will become more likely, it seems to me, if feminists can learn to recapitulate in contemporary ways some of the best ideas and methods once used by the proponents of maternalist social policies." Skocpol wrote: "Feminists must work in organizations and networks that tie them to others in very different social circumstances. They must also articulate values and political goals that speak to the well-being of all American families. If feminists can find better ways to do these things, organized women will again be at the forefront of the development of social provision in the United States."[74] Studying a very different policy domain, Amy Sue Bix claimed that grassroots activism after World War II was able to undermine the traditional authority of doctors and scientists, resulting in federal funding to fight breast cancer and AIDS.[75] In his biography of Social Security policymaker Wilbur Cohen, Edward Berkowitz showed how a policy entrepreneur worked through bureaucratic politics to expand federal welfare despite America's anti-statist traditions and fragmented political institutions.[76]

In the second category of research, Lost Alternatives, historians use the past to show viable policy alternatives that once succeeded.[77] Policy analysts, who are concerned with practical proposals rather than unworkable theories, can find much value in this scholarship. Of course, in some cases the conditions surrounding past alternatives have changed too drastically for them to be viable in the present. But in other cases, key conditions are still in place so past alternatives might be reconstructed. This is particularly true when one considers the aforementioned persistence arguments. In the long run, policy conditions are often not that much different from those in the past. At other times, these studies offer a warning since particular conditions under which past alternatives succeeded are no longer in existence. The alternatives also provide a clearer perspective of the parameters that define current policymaking.

Historian Hugh Graham has provided an excellent example of Lost Alternatives. Graham showed that until 1969, civil rights policy—as embodied in the Civil Rights Act of 1964—was grounded in popular twentieth-century ideals of individualism, universalism, the timelessness of equal rights, negative government protection for rights (meaning the government should take action after it found an individual was being denied his or her rights), and the centrality of national protection for rights. As civil rights policy departed from these ideals after 1969, Graham argued, programs became less popular.[78] He wrote: "Although proponents of affirmative action were remarkably successful in the 1970s and 1980s in expanding their program base in government and the private economy, by the 1990s they were losing the battle of public opinion. Most Americans supported the nondiscrimination-plus-outreach of soft affirmative action but opposed the preferences of hard affirmative action."[79] Implicit in his analysis is a road map for civil rights policies to become more popular by reverting to the model of the pre-1969 era. Martha Derthick, in her work on federal-state relations, claimed that a different system of federalism existed before the 1960s. Until that time, she explained, the federal government respected the autonomy of local communities even when enacting social programs. After the 1960s, however, the federal government started creating more specific guidelines that required the states to enact protections for specific social groups. The role of place and community, Derthick concluded, was replaced by individuals who were categorized by special ethnicity, race, or gender. The article pointed to an earlier model of federalism that respected the autonomy of local communities while allowing for a more expansive federal government than in the nineteenth century.[80] Others have found lost alternatives in the history of other countries. Helene Silverberg, for instance, has shown why abortion politics has been less polarized in European nations than in the United States.[81]

The third category, Historical Correctives, builds on May and Neustadt's argument that the task of the historian is to evaluate the historical assumptions and analogies used by policymakers. Research in this category constitutes more than simply correcting the historical record for its own sake, although that has been part of the project.[82] Assumptions about history constantly influence politics, even though policymakers are often not aware of their influence. Immediately after World War II, for example, policymakers based many of their arguments about price controls on the post–World War I experience.[83] The power of analogies was extremely apparent in 1999, when the Holocaust loomed large over decisions about what America should do in Kosovo. Policy historians, more than any other scholars, are able to perceive the underlying historical assumptions that shape policy debates and to challenge misperceptions. By doing so, policy historians can sometimes undermine or buttress the basis of policy positions.

There have been numerous contributions to this category. In his recent prize-winning work, Thomas Sugrue challenged the assumption that urban decline began after the War on Poverty and after the riots shook cities such as Detroit and Newark. Instead, Sugrue contended that cities were eroding by the late 1940s as a result of racial discrimination in housing and employment. Sugrue hoped to undermine policymakers who claim that federal welfare programs, radical civil rights activism, and a culture of poverty were to blame for urban decay. Rather, his new chronological framework emphasized the impact of racism.[84] David Beito's study of fraternal societies between 1900 and 1930 contested the assumption that government welfare policies that distinguish the "deserving" from "undeserving" poor reflect white middle-class biases against the poor. In contrast, Beito showed how similar distinctions were made by African Americans and the working class when they provided aid to the needy. Beito thus lent support to such distinctions by showing that they reflect mainstream values, not social-class interests.[85] Christopher Howard offered one of the most striking examples of this research. He showed how most debates over social policy rest on the assumption that government assistance means direct federal expenditures. Instead, Howard looked at the development of the welfare state by considering tax loopholes as a form of government assistance. In doing so, he showed that federal spending in the United States has been much more extensive than is usually assumed and that the majority of benefits go to those who are not poor.[86] Edwin Amenta complemented this finding by revealing that the United States, contrary to the conventional wisdom about its "laggard" welfare state, led the world in spending on social provision programs during the 1930s.[87] Timothy Minchin challenged the assumption that civil rights initiatives have not positively changed race relations since 1969. Through his study of southern industries, Minchin claimed that federal policy has resulted in racial integration.[88]

The next category is Political Culture. One scholar defined political culture as "the underlying assumptions and rules that govern behavior in the political system . . . the political ideals and operating norms of a polity . . . the manifestation in aggregate form of the psychological and subjective dimensions of politics . . . the product of both the collective history of a political system and the life histories of the members of the system."[89] This has been one area of policy history where the work of cultural historians had a positive impact on reconceptualizing the policy process. In showing repeatedly how political culture influenced policymaking, historical research offers a counterpoint to policy analysts who assume all actors are rational.[90] This category of research provides a different understanding of the policy process that is fundamentally at odds with what most policy schools teach. For policy historians, the rational choice model fell short. Historians believed it important for scholars to understand the political culture that established the framework for debate and the larger mindset within which policymakers operate. Robert Kelley argued that the policy sciences depiction of human nature is "mechanical" and "simplistic." With their greater perspective, he said, policy historians would provide a much richer understanding of the ideological context within which policy debates take place, particularly the "shaping influence upon policy of political culture."[91] The evidence that political culture matters has been plentiful. In his landmark book on environmentalism, Samuel Hays showed how post–World War II middle-class values influenced success of environmental policies.[92] Donald Critchlow, moreover, found that family planning policy encountered much more success in the 1960s and 1970s, partially as a result of changing cultural norms on sexuality.[93] Policy historians attempt to delineate how political culture influences policy. Marc Eisner, for example, has traced how ideas about antitrust entered into the executive branch through experts who gained key positions in bureaucracies.[94] In his seminal book on public life in the nineteenth century, Morton Keller showed how persistent cultural traditions of localism and anti-statism constrained political responses to industrialism.[95] The evidence accumulated by this research serves as a warning to policymakers who embrace mainstream, social scientific policy analysis and fail to seriously factor the influence of ideas and culture into their strategies.

The final category of historical research is Process Evaluation. Scholars who write about the evolution of the policy process itself have fulfilled one of the main goals of the policy history subdiscipline. While the immediate utility of this research is often more difficult to discern, it offers those seeking to change the policy process—a wrenching challenge given the tenacity of institutions—a better sense of how this has been accomplished in the past. This research also reveals how the power of politicians often rests on the process through which policies are constructed. One of the best examples comes from Brian Balogh, who showed how the classic iron triangle model of policymaking, which stresses interest-group demand, does not explain policymaking for much of the post–World War II period. Rather, through his study of commercial nuclear power policy, Balogh found that policies were created by professional administrators working within the American state, despite the fact that there was little external demand for the programs they created. Federal administrators then tried to secure interest-group support only after starting their programs. After detailing how commercial nuclear programs became extraordinarily unpopular among the citizenry, the book ends on a note that speaks directly to government administrators. Balogh suggested that the history of nuclear policy shows why administrators have lost their influence. His hope is that history will lead them to seek greater participation in the policy process as programs are created.[96]

All five categories of research—Institutional and Cultural Persistence, Lost Alternatives, Historical Correctives, Political Culture, and Process Evolution—offer distinct contributions that historians can make to policy analysis. But this list is by no means exhaustive. In the coming years, if they are to succeed in influencing policymakers and informing the media and general public, policy historians must think more systematically about the type of research they produce and explain how history can inform current decisions. This does not require that policy historians become advocates. Rather, the record shows that historians can provide sound analysis that enhances decision-making performance.

Thinking About the Future

There are many signs that the future of policy history will be more successful than its past. In addition to the continued success of the *Journal of Policy History*, there is now an annual conference and a continued discussion about a national association. There have also been signs within the historical profession of more interest in policy, especially among the post–baby boom generation graduate students and professors. The continued vitality of historical institutionalism in the social sciences, moreover, complements the efforts of policy historians. On a different front, historians have even started to appear with greater frequency in the media as commentators on contemporary politics. Michael

Beschloss and Doris Kerns Goodwin are familiar faces on prime-time television. Although few in this group would classify themselves as policy historians, their success reflects a thirst that exists among the public and politicians for historians to provide a nuanced understanding of contemporary politics. Maris Vinovskis, a preeminent historian of education policy, served in various positions within President Clinton's administration.

To secure their place in Washington, DC, and state capitals, however, policy historians will have to embark on a campaign to sell their contributions. To be sure, historians will never be fully comfortable in this role. In the end, they will have to accept that their work may be used only when it serves the needs of political interests.[97] Even in an age where applied history has gained greater acceptance, many scholars are hesitant to claim a practical use for their research. Yet it is clear that careful historical research is valuable for training policymakers, evaluating policies, and informing citizens without being propaganda. This essay has attempted to explain what some of those contributions have been. Should historians fail to defend their own value to politics, policy history will continue to be Clio's lost tribe.

THREE

History and Political Science: Together Again?

There was a period in America when the political science and history disciplines were not that far apart.* Both approaches to analyzing civil society had evolved out of an old Anglo-American tradition where these two subjects, along with philosophy and literature, were all considered in relationship to one another. During the formative years of the American research university, which took place at the turn of the twentieth century, both disciplines shared common founding fathers. A classic example was Charles Beard, whose influence spanned both areas of scholarship.[1] Indeed, it was a breakaway faction of the American Historical Association that formed the American Political Science Association.

After the 1920s, the siblings of political science and history remained in close contact. During the 1950s and 1960s, some of the profession's giants, including Arthur Schlesinger Jr. and Ellis Hawley, wrote their books in a dialogue with political science scholarship about pluralism and American Exceptionalism. They directly responded to the arguments of David Truman, Robert Dahl, Louis Hartz, and others.[2] To be sure, by the 1950s, there were already political historians, including Richard Hofstadter, who had started to turn their attention toward other disciplines, such as psychology.[3] Nonetheless, political historians and political scientists shared a common bond until the 1970s. Even the anti-establishment New Left historians in the 1960s, such as Gabriel Kolko and James Weinstein, made pluralism their central target.[4]

During the 1970s, however, the disciplines went their separate ways. Political science became less historical and historians became less interested in politics. Concern with historical analysis had actually started to wane within political science as early as the 1910s.[5] But the behavioral revolution pushed more mainstream political scientists toward pursuing narrower questions that could be answered through clearly defined data sets. Broad, complex historical

* This essay originally appeared as "Political History and Political Science: Together Again?" in *The Journal of Policy History* 16 (2004): 126–36.

problems seemed less appealing to them given that such issues were usually multifaceted and did not lend themselves to the type of precision that political scientists craved. The triumph of the rational choice approach by the 1980s further pushed historical analysis into the background as scholars tried to flatten their portrait of the individual, and to present a model of politics that would work across time and space. Of course, there were exceptions. Martha Derthick, Hugh Heclo, and James Sundquist wrote books and articles that were rich in historical analysis, as did prominent political theorists.[6] Yet these scholars were not in the mainstream of the profession by the early 1990s.

At the same time that the importance of historical analysis declined among political scientists, historians lost interest in government institutions and public policy after the 1970s. Social and cultural historians focused on studying American life from the "bottom up." To do so, many of them turned to sociology and anthropology for guidance. In this intellectual climate, Clifford Geertz replaced Louis Hartz as the social scientist who historians loved to quote.[7] Importantly, the few remaining political historians in the profession during the 1970s and 1980s, most of whom identified themselves as the "new political history," did continue the dialogue with political science. They drew on realignment theory to explore voting behavior in the nineteenth century.[8] Practitioners of the organizational synthesis, moreover, built on modernization theory, in addition to Parsonian sociology, to explain the rise of national institutions in the twentieth century.[9] Policy history, a subfield that emerged in the 1970s which aimed to apply historical analysis to contemporary public policy problems, maintained close links to policy analysis scholarship.[10]

Regardless, since none of these scholars were in the mainstream of their profession and they were few in number, the conversations between political historians and political scientists dwindled. This was evident from American history textbooks that were written after the 1960s. Most authors presented political topics such as the presidency and Congress in a manner that bore little relationship to the theoretical advances that had been made in political science.[11]

The situation changed in the 1980s and 1990s as the field of American Political Development took hold among political scientists who were not fully engaged by rational choice scholarship and who were interested in using their disciplinary tools to tackle larger questions than the ones that interested their colleagues.[12] The founders of the field included Theda Skocpol, Ira Katznelson, Elizabeth Sanders, Richard Bensel, and Stephen Skowronek.[13] They wrote detailed historical treatments of issues such as Progressive Era civil service reform, the New Deal, sectionalism, economic regulation, class relations in cities, and the relationship between bureaucratic infrastructure and public policy. Besides writing solid works of history, practitioners of American Political Development offered novel concepts for understanding how politics was thoroughly a historical process. For instance, many of them wrote about how new policies restructured the long-term interests of politicians and interest groups. Another contribution of the field was to show how "institutional stickiness" made it difficult to fundamentally restructure government even amid dramatic economic crises, war, and scandal. Borrowing the concept of path dependence from economics, other American Political Development works revealed how the options available to political actors at one point in time were limited because of institutions and programs that were created in earlier periods. This line of argument shows how the options available to individual actors in any given period diminish as institutions mature and thicken.[14] In contrast to older versions of political history that depicted politicians as reacting to the demands of social movements and business interests, American Political Development posited that state officials could develop their own autonomous interests and agendas that were not always rooted in social demand. The field was institutionalized through the History and Politics section of the American Political Science Association and a journal entitled *Studies in American Political Development*. Given the state of politics within the history profession, some of the most prominent political historians by the 1990s tended to be political scientists: there are many historians who would currently agree that Harvard University's Theda Skocpol is today's Arthur Schlesinger.

As history took hold among some talented political scientists, by the 1990s a new generation of institutional political historians had emerged. Seeking to bring politics back into the profession—but to do so in ways that avoided the shortcomings of previous generations—the new institutional political historians produced excellent accounts about issues ranging from the development of the modern administrative state, to the unfolding relationship between law and public policy, to the transformation of intermediary institutions such as interest groups and parties. Brian Balogh, for example, wrote an insightful book about the role of professional administrators in shaping domestic atomic energy policy despite a lack of external demand from citizens or business.[15] Edward Berkowitz wrote several books about the construction of welfare policy and the bureaucrats who were instrumental to shaping those programs.[16] Richard John wrote a path-breaking book about the existence of a significant administrative state in the nineteenth century.[17] I tried my hand at this institutional approach with the history of Wilbur Mills, the Democratic chairman of the House Ways and Means Committee from 1958 to 1974 and his relationship to a tax policy community.[18] Institutional political historians have greatly benefited from analytic concepts put forth in American Political Development, but they have also pushed the boundaries of this scholarship by delving into rich archival sources and incorporating ideas that historians are traditionally more comfortable with. These include the importance of contingency, turning points, and the role of individuals in shaping large-scale changes.

The recent reconvergence of history and political science is an exciting development. For political historians to truly reconceptualize the study of politics, they will need to draw on scholarship in political science to think of fresh approaches and frameworks that move beyond the liberal presidential synthesis. If not, we will be stuck with dated frameworks for understanding politics that were crafted several generations ago. The most obvious connection, of course, is that historians will have to keep interacting with scholars in the field of American Political Development who are currently far ahead in this important research.

When turning to political science, however, historians should not limit themselves to American Political Development. There are political scientists working in many other areas who have much to offer to the new generation of political historians. One such scholarly literature has centered on the policymaking process. When writing political history, this field can help us move beyond the presidential synthesis or alternative narratives that have focused on social movements. Political science scholarship on the policymaking process has unpacked a complex universe of political actors who are often ignored by scholars. This field has broadened the world of politics to include bureaucrats, experts, interest groups, think tanks, activists, staffers, and others who constitute the policy communities and issues networks that shape government. Starting with the landmark work of Hugh Heclo and John Kingdon, these political scientists have offered some insightful arguments about how and why issues enter onto the national agenda, the ways in which those in the political arena interact, why some problems gain attention while others do not, and the different factors that are important in making an issue relevant.[19] They have shown that the evolution and formation of policies does not fit neatly into the cycle of presidential administrations or social movement history. If historians want to move beyond the presidential synthesis from the 1950s to develop a more complex portrait of how Washington works—particularly the intersection between state and society below the level of the U.S. president—the literature on the policymaking process offers several important starting points and conceptual tools.

There are many other areas in political science, some well established and others just emerging, that historians would find extremely useful. Many of these literatures have been examined in the book edited by Ira Katznelson and Helen Milner, which offers a fresh look at the state of the discipline.[20] Given the enthusiasm among historians for studying citizenship, we need to pay much closer attention to the political science literature about civic participation. Over the past ten years or so, this scholarship has been moving in very relevant directions. Most important, political scientists have looked beyond the act of voting to understand how and why citizens try to influence politics. For instance, they have been examining what types of participation seem to catch the eye of public officials, as well as the institutional rules and regulations that foster or stifle different types of citizen participation. Studies about social capital have tried to link increases and decreases in civic participation to broader social and cultural changes, such as suburbanization, commuting, and transformations in the gender composition of the workforce.[21] Finally, there have been efforts to understand more clearly pivotal long-term trends, such as the decline in voting since the nineteenth century and the rise of interest-group pressure. While much of this scholarship is not historical, it offers numerous issues that historians can explore historically through rigorous archival research and presents new strategies to frame our studies.[22]

Another area in political science that historians might find interesting centers on the relationship between race and politics. For the last two decades, historians have been paying close attention to the history of race relations in the United States. Many of our colleagues would be pleased to discover that there are numerous political scientists doing the same thing, only they are applying their research to the study of public opinion, government institutions, and public policy. Scholars such as Michael Dawson and Cathy Cohen have been promoting research that looks at political conflict between nonwhite racial groups as well as the multiple ideologies that influence the politics of race.[23] There has been some outstanding work about how factors ranging from the local media to residential neighborhood environments play an important role in shaping the racial attitudes of whites.[24] Jennifer Hochschild, Robert Lieberman, Rogers Smith, Martin Gilens, and others have been integrating studies of race into analyses of political institutions in the United States.[25] Therefore, this is a booming field from which political historians can create links to the issues that have interested their own profession since the 1960s.[26]

Another field that should be of interest to political historians is international political economy.[27] This is a fruitful area of study since historians have recently been trying to understand how movements, policies, and other phenomena occur on a transnational basis.[28] The field of international political economy, which emerged in the late 1970s, has been focusing on the relationship between domestic government and international relations. Practitioners have covered many important issues, such as how globalization has influenced the evolution of social policies and welfare states. They have also been studying how the structure of government institutions and the preexisting political ideologies of different countries affect the formulation of foreign economic policy and international relations.

Although it might be unexpected that historians could be prodded into writing more on the philosophy of history as a result of political scientists, the fields of Comparative Politics and American Political Development have been putting forth some outstanding work on why history matters as a discipline. As they have sought to bring historical analysis back into their profession, many political scientists have been determined to offer analytic justifications to convince their colleagues about the utility of a historical approach. The best work in this light is the book by Paul Pierson entitled *Politics in Time*.[29] As Pierson explains, the aim of his book is to "flesh out the often-invoked but rarely examined declaration that history matters." With incredible analytic clarity, Pierson offers the types of answers to this complex question that many historians will envy. First, Pierson emphasizes the importance of path dependence, which he defines as "the dynamics of self-reinforcing or positive feedback processes in a political system." Second, he talks about how historical analysis shows the centrality of timing and sequence in political development. In other words, he explains that when things happen matters as much as why they happen or what they were intended to do. Third, he argues that studying politics in time captures the slow-moving and incremental components of political development that many mainstream political scientists often miss by focusing on snapshots instead of the big picture. Sounding a little like the Annals school of history, Pierson reminds his colleagues that it often takes a long time for social or political processes to trigger any monumental change. Finally, urging political scientists to look more closely at institutional development, rather than simply at the effects of institutions, he claims that institutions are difficult to change and, given their tenacity, institutions actually structure and constrain efforts to change them. He explains that institutions do not just adapt functionally to emerging social or individual demands, nor do they necessarily reflect the needs or interests of the dominant political elites. Although historians have traditionally been shy about discussing the philosophy and the analytic strengths of their craft, recent political science offers a unique opportunity to tackle these questions more rigorously than before.[30]

As they reengage their colleagues, historians have contributions that they can offer to political science beyond providing them with more data. One contribution that historians can make is to help unpack and define more carefully the concept of "political institutions." Over the past decade, scholars have been using the term "institutions" pretty much to describe everything, so much that the term sometimes risks losing its meaning and power. Institutions could easily become to political scientists what culture sometimes is in the humanities—an explanation for everything and nothing. While most books provide a few lines to define what institutions are—usually a set of rules, norms, organizations, and procedures that frame political activity—historical research can breathe new life into our understanding of what political institutions are, the different kinds of institutions that exist in political history, and how we should analyze the different components to institutions historically. Just as important, after decades of research about social forces and culture, historians can tackle the crucial problem of defining exactly what are *not* institutions in politics and how these non-institutional forces influence political development. Additionally, historians can try to explain through their narratives the relationship in politics between non-institutions and institutions.

Historians can also contribute to a burgeoning interest among political scientists in institutional change.[31] Thus far, most political scientists have been interested in institutional resilience. They have revealed how institutions constrain behavior and how difficult institutions are to change. In talking about ways that institutional change does not occur that easily, political scientists have tended to focus on what might be called "macro-institutional changes," such as a shift away from a system of separated power, a parliamentary system, or federalism. It is true that fundamental institutional changes of this sort do not happen that often, although historians who have studied revolutionary periods would have a lot to say about this issue. More important, historians can jump into this debate through research on "micro-institutional changes," which are much more common. Within the United States—even though the institutional outlines of American government might seem very similar today to those at the founding—most historians would agree that government institutions are very different in 2003 than they were in 1789. The expansion of suffrage, voting reforms, communication revolutions, the direct election of Senators, changes in campaign finance, bureaucratic and administrative development, the policy infrastructure, the expansion and transformation of the executive branch, the various procedural incarnations of Congress, the opening of information to the public, the evolution of media access to politics, and much more have all revealed that indeed institutional change is not only possible but also is quite common.[32] Furthermore, in the James Madison lecture, the political scientist David Mayhew showed in his discussion of the filibuster that the rules of an institutional environment, even when they are firm on paper, can be unclear to political actors at the time and subject to change, negotiation, and manipulation even though the institutions might seem static.[33] This is exactly the type of nuance that historians are good at capturing. By jumping into this debate, historians could play an important role in shaping the research agenda and discussion as it unfolds.

There are of course disciplinary differences that we must respect and should not abandon. For example, historians will be cautious about political science claims as to the "transportability" of historical analysis.[34] Most evident is the issue of particularity. While Peter Novick has argued that "objectivity" was the single ideal that once defined the history profession,[35] before it lost its ideological identity since the 1960s, particularity has been even more important. In general, historians believe that each moment in history is rather unique since it is produced by a complex mix of forces, individuals, cultures, and institutions that all come together at a single point. Despite the famous mantra about history repeating itself, historians have spent an enormous amount of time showing that, when you get down to the details, each historical moment can only be understood on its own terms. While historians are certainly concerned with common forces that remain influential in many times and places—in the past twenty years there has been a virtual obsession with class, race, and gender—the heart and soul of most books is still in the distinctiveness of the specific stories and personalities a scholar is writing about. What happened in the post–World War II reconstruction of Japan, for instance, might have lessons today for Iraq, but only to a limited extent since postwar Japan is very different from postwar Iraq. This is a rather simple point, but it gets to something at the heart of each disciplinary enterprise. Part of the great power of the new institutionalism in political science is to make a very compelling argument that there are components to analyzing politics in time that can be used across time and space. Part of the great contribution by historians has been to show the uniqueness of each moment in time. While bridges can be built to show how these two viewpoints are not incompatible, neither should either discipline abandon its unique approach in the search for collaboration.

Notwithstanding these differences, historians should look into many areas in political science before turning to the task of reconstructing political history. The new generation of historians would make a serious error to return to the study of politics without understanding what has taken place in this neighboring discipline. Furthermore, historians have much to offer political scientists. By subsequently making full use of our profession's tools—namely, by providing rich, multilayered, archivally based narratives—we could move in a positive direction toward fundamentally reconstructing our collective knowledge of the political past.

FOUR

Rethinking the History of American Conservatism

In 1994, the Columbia historian Alan Brinkley stimulated an intense debate within the historical profession when he published an article in the *American Historical Review* that focused on the history of American conservatism.* Brinkley argued that historians had not devoted sufficient attention to the evolution of conservatism in contemporary politics. Historians, he said, had treated conservatism as a marginal, irrational, or irrelevant force since these arguments were first put forth by liberal consensus historians in the 1950s and 1960s. Most scholarly attention focused on the history of liberalism.[1]

The political bias and intellectual orientation of the profession, Brinkley said, had led historians to ignore the origins of the political transformation that had clearly taken place after the 1970s and that reached a new stage right at the time that the article was published, when conservative Republicans took control of Capitol Hill: "The 'problem' of American conservatism as I have tried to describe it here is, in the end, a problem of historical imagination . . . while historians have displayed impressive powers of imagination in creating empathetic accounts of many once-obscure areas of the past, they have seldom done so in considering the character of conservative lives and ideas." While another member of the roundtable, Leo Ribuffo, argued that Brinkley was not paying sufficient attention to a first wave of scholarship that already existed on the subject, a large number of younger historians concurred with Brinkley's basic assessment of the field.[2]

What followed over the next fourteen years was a burst of innovative scholarly activity on the history of conservatism. The *AHR* published Brinkley's article at the same time that there was an unexpected renaissance taking place in the historical profession with a young generation of graduate students and assistant professors who were interested in revitalizing the field of American political history.[3] Many of them, who were part of the post–baby boom generation and who came of age in the Reagan era, were not invested in the intellectual battles of the 1960s; they were determined to use the history of conservatism as an avenue to write about politics through a method different than their predecessors. They preferred one that avoided the criticism from the New Left that political history only covered elites. (To be sure, some of the scholars who joined in this enterprise were more senior.)

Whereas the first wave of scholarship on conservatism, characterized by books like George Nash's intellectual history of the Right, were interested in discovering a serious conservative tradition in America, the second wave of scholarship focused on the rise of the Right between the early Cold War and the 1980s. Attempting to develop a sophisticated scholarly analysis of the compelling backlash thesis that had been put forth by journalists like Thomas Edsall and Susan Faludi and to capture what followed the "New Deal Order," they sought to explain how conservatives shifted from being a small opposition force, marginalized in a liberal nation, to becoming the dominant political force by the 1980s.[4] In their accounts, the origins of Ronald Reagan's victory in 1980 could be found in the emergence of a true grassroots movement that was built from the bottom up, a movement that transformed the terms of national political debate.

The scholarship was especially concerned with analyzing the motivations behind the conservative movement and examining how the Right was able to gain so much organizational momentum following many decades when it had been in the political wilderness. There was no consensus over where they should center their study, with some asking why average citizens joined local organizations of the New Right and other trying to figure out why the Republican Party banished its moderate Northeastern wing and privileged more conservative arguments and personalities.

Although there were multiple arenas where conservatism took hold, these historians attempted to discern single causal arguments about the specific actors and organizations they were examining. One cohort emphasized the importance of a racial backlash against the Civil Rights Act of 1964, the Voting Rights Act of 1965, and the black power movement. Implicitly or explicitly, race played a central role in defining conservative objectives and in explaining their electoral appeal. Much of this work stressed the South, looking at the shift of formerly Democratic voters into the Republican camp (thus confirming the "Southern Strategy").[5]

But younger Southern historians such as Matthew Lassiter, Kevin Kruse, and Joseph Crespino objected to claims about Southern Exceptionalism while agreeing on the centrality of a racial backlash.[6] Turning away from an emphasis on racial extremists in the South and looking instead at moderate suburban voters in the region, this group found that conservatives in cities such as Atlanta and Charlotte abandoned explicit racial appeals and refocused their attention on issues such as suburban rights, local taxation, neighborhood schooling, and residential zoning. By protecting the structure of suburbs, moderates in fact defended racial stratification because of the multiple barriers that hampered African American mobility. Rejecting the concept of a difference between *de facto* and *de jure* segregation, their work contended that the same kinds of policies that motivated conservatives in the South also influenced them in the North, Midwest, and West.[7] Their findings fit with Thomas Sugrue's work on racial stratification and conservative backlash in Detroit.[8] The suburbs, from which most African Americans were excluded, became neighborhoods that were protected by public policy under the guise of neutral homeowner rights. In an interview, Lassiter explained that "when you look at suburbs and middle class, then you start getting a national story. White suburbs outside Charlotte are reacting the same as white suburbs outside Los Angeles or in New Jersey."[9]

A different cohort of scholars emphasized the importance of anticommunism. Harvard historian Lisa McGirr documented the history of Orange County, California, to understand what stimulated average American men and women in these communities to join local conservative organizations in the 1960s and 1970s. Rather than finding citizens who were on the fringe of American society, she discovered mainstream middle-class suburbanites who were disaffected from the political and cultural arguments they heard from Democrats. There were a number of issues that shaped their politics, according to McGirr. The economic importance of the defense industry and military bases in Orange County fed anticommunist sentiment. Migrants from southern regions of the country, moreover, arrived with culturally conservative beliefs, while libertarians and antigovernment values had deep roots with California natives, especially those involved in small businesses and ranching. Her book shows that anticommunism was the glue that held conservatives together until the 1970s and that, after a period of searching for a new overriding issue following the turmoil over Vietnam, they settled on a style of populist conservatism centered on the protection of communities and families.[10]

Still other scholars have looked at the central role played by evangelical religious leaders who entered the political realm and successfully tapped into vast membership groups in churches. Jerry Falwell, Donald Wildmon, James Dobson, and other leaders created an infrastructure of television shows, publications, and radio shows that were crucial to the Right.[11] When the IRS in 1978 attempted to end the tax exemptions offered to Christian schools, civil rights organizations accused the latter of being primarily white institutions created with the purpose of avoiding racial integration. Thereafter, conservative Christian organizations mobilized politically.[12] They focused on a "pro-family" agenda that criticized feminism, gay activism, and secularized, liberalized cultural norms as eroding the strength of the nuclear family.[13]

There have been many other causal arguments put forth in recent years. Shane Hamilton has stressed economic libertarianism with a book showing how agribusiness took advantage of the technology of trucking to avoid federal regulations and union labor. Agribusiness played an important role in the success of the conservative movement because it brought low-cost food to consumers around the country, thereby reducing demand for unions or federal programs to improve purchasing power.[14] Elizabeth Shermer explained the roots of Senator Barry Goldwater's career by discussing the corporate mobilization of business against organized labor and the government policies that supported unions.[15] A recent article of the *Journal of American History* put the spotlight on anti-environmental sentiment in response to the protection of public lands.[16]

There has also been extensive work on the tactics employed by conservatives that could account for the movement's success. The political scientist Steve Teles explored the campaign by conservative activists to reshape the legal profession. Teles examined how conservatives in the 1970s and 1980s created a network that promoted conservative legal ideas and university courses, and nurtured future justices with a variety of strategies. These included the establishment of philanthropic foundations, the founding of fellowships and professorships, and the formation of professional organizations.[17] Rick Perlstein, a journalist with impeccable skills as a historian, wrote about the small group of activists behind Barry Goldwater's campaign in 1964. Although their candidate lost the election in a landslide, they left behind a vibrant network, and they had established tactical precedents for future campaigns.[18] Jonathan Schoenwald produced an account of how elements of extremist conservatism in the early 1960s were gradually co-opted by the mainstream of the Republican Party.[19] Alice O'Connor's recent work has looked at the philanthropists who funded conservative think tanks and candidates during the 1970s; while Kimberly Phillips-Fein, in her 2009 book, took a longer view and wrote about a small group of businessmen, mostly concerned with fighting against government economic regulations and high rates of taxation, who since the New Deal were instrumental as the money-men of the Right.[20]

Regardless of the motivation behind conservatism, there is agreement among these scholars about the basic story. Namely, there was a backlash against New Deal and Great Society liberalism that enabled conservative activists, who had been slowly coalescing since the early Cold War battles, to produce an important realignment in American politics. Through the Republican Party and its capture of the South, the conservative movement offered a new set of ideas and policies, won control of the White House and Congress (first the Senate from 1981 to 1986 and then both houses for most of the period between 1995 and 2007), and prevented liberalism from rebounding.

The literature on conservatism has been extremely good. Historians have shown how conservatism was able to reshape public debate and generate strong public support in key segments of the country. Whereas initial textbook accounts stressed a handful of individual politicians such as Barry Goldwater, Richard Nixon, and Ronald Reagan and a small group of prominent intellectuals, the new literature has provided the type of finely textured, microsocial analysis of how conservatives created a movement and the apparatus that they built within the GOP. We learned about how the Right generated massive electoral support for their cause by using everything from reading groups to direct mail to big money, in order to create a movement culture similar to those that flourished with populism and civil rights earlier in American history.[21]

Their scholarship revealed the intricate connections that linked political elites inside the state to average citizens. Their methodology overcame the artificial divisions that had divided earlier books on politics and society. As a result of their publications, it became clear that conservatism was not an aberration and not just a reactive, irrational response to the 1960s. Rather, the movement had deep roots in American society and revolved around intensely felt positions on a wide range of questions from race to national security. The pulse of conservatism was mainstream America, not those on the fringes.

The story that emerged from this wave of historiography was incomplete, however, and, in many respects, it created certain misleading impressions of the period. In fact, the scholarship about the rise of the Right and disintegration of liberalism has vastly exaggerated the success of the former and the collapse of the latter. From the perspective of 2011, when conservatives have struggled to contain internal divisions and don't control the White House or Senate, the limits to the rise-of-the-Right narrative are becoming clear.

Conservatives Fragmented

The fragmented nature of the scholarship of conservatism reflects the fragmented nature of conservatism itself. The scholarship on conservatism contended that a certain level of coherence developed among conservatives, making a movement out of otherwise disparate political factions.

Most of the scholarship acknowledged that there were numerous factions within conservatism. This has been an enduring theme since George Nash's path-breaking work on its intellectual history, which was one of the first and best looks at the roots of conservatism.[22]

Yet scholars tried to find the different issues that brought the factions together. In his classic work *Why Americans Hate Politics* (1991), journalist E. J. Dionne argued there was a "fusionist consensus" that created a durable coalition between social traditionalists and free-market conservatives. He highlighted the role of the philosopher Frank Meyer, a former communist who had moved into the conservative camp during World War II and the early Cold War. According to Dionne, Meyer had played an important role by connecting social conservatives concerned with tradition and virtue with libertarian and free-market ideologues who otherwise did not share much common ground. Meyer argued that virtue could only be achieved through participation in private markets rather than through government or social traditions. "Free markets," Dionne explained, "could be compatible with virtue, indeed could promote virtue, and virtue was the only proper end of freedom." Dionne stated that anticommunism turned into the "glue" of the "fusionist consensus." The consensus, he says, "proved durable, providing a philosophical rallying point for conservatives right through the 1980s," even though there were opponents. Through anticommunism, they worked through the Republican Party and publications like William Buckley's *National Review*. Dionne treats Ronald Reagan as a successful president because he was able to keep the contradictions with the movement in check.[23]

In his synthetic account of the conservative movement, Godfrey Hodgson agreed with Dionne. Stagflation, the combination of inflation and unemployment, undermined support of the Democratic coalition. At the same time, Republicans by the 1980s, he wrote, had "hammered out an agenda as broad as it was revolutionary. In foreign policy, they wanted a reassertion of American strength in the world and a showdown with the 'evil empire' of the Soviet Union. In the economy, having replaced Keynes as their guide with Milton Friedman, they counted on new policies, some ideological, some practical and popular—monetarism, supply-side economics, but also tax cuts and deregulation—to unleash the frustrated energies of American business. In the society, they dreamed of reversing what they saw as the dire consequences of decades of permissiveness, itself the legacy of 'secular humanism,' relativism, and liberal license."[24]

The assumption that the movement achieved sufficient coherence to hold the factions together suffused almost all of the monographs about the Right in the 1990s and early 2000s. McGirr depicted strategic movement activists who struggled after the 1960s to find an issue as powerful as anticommunism to hold its factions together. During the 1970s, she argued, activists turned their attention to a series of single issues such as busing, but found that those did not attract the same kind of broad middle-class support as anticommunism. Instead, McGirr claimed that movement activists refashioned a language of populist conservatism by focusing on "moral" concerns that included "the autonomy of communities, the erosion of individualism, the authority of the family, and the place of religion in national life" as well as opposition to local, state, and federal taxes. Even though the language that conservatives used contradicted their own lives in suburban and consumer America, it helped to unite the movement.[25]

But the coherence of conservatism has been exaggerated. The movement was as fragile as the New Deal coalition that it replaced. Like recent work rethinking liberalism before the 1970s or progressivism at the turn of the twentieth century, we are starting to see evidence that conservatism was always an unstable political force and that conservative politics required an ongoing process of building ad hoc factional coalitions on specific issues and in key campaigns. In a recent dissertation, Neil J. Young found that there were substantial theological differences within the "Religious Right" that made it challenging for Catholics, Mormons, and Southern Baptists to agree among themselves.[26] Benjamin Cooper Waterhouse's study found how organized business interests, as expressed through the Business Roundtable and other Washington-based operations, were unable to maintain a unified front in the 1980s on issues such as taxation. Organized business fragmented into an "every man his own lobbyist" structure and different associational groups focused on defending the policy issues that were of particular relevance to their members rather than trying to represent the corporate world as a whole.[27]

The divisions were evident in a number of key political battles. In 1982 and 1983, for instance, social conservatives openly rebelled against the Reagan administration for having failed to take their issues seriously or to appoint movement conservatives into the administration. Between 1986 and 1987, Reagan and allied Republicans came under intense fire from conservatives for agreeing to the Intermediate-Range Nuclear Forces (INF) arms treaty with the Soviet Union. Some of the Right compared the treaty to Munich and lamented that Reagan had abandoned the very causes he had fought for. The president was able to build enough support within the Republican Party and to play off Mikhail Gorbachev's enormous popularity in the United States to marginalize and isolate conservatives like Dan Quayle who did not want to ratify the treaty in the Senate. But it was a struggle.

Divisions in the conservative movement were front and center after Republicans took control of Congress in 1994. Whereas the midterm elections were at first hailed as the completion of the Reagan Revolution, particularly when President Clinton signaled that he had heard the message of voters and would move to the political center, Republicans ran into one political problem after another. Not all Republicans, for example, supported the hard line that House Republicans endorsed toward federal spending in the winter of 1995–96 when they forced a shutdown of the federal government. Gingrich would secretly move to form a centrist pact with President Clinton, realizing, according to Steve Gillon, that "the American public embraced the rhetoric of change but often recoiled from its consequences." The pact never saw the light of day as a result of the partisan wars that consumed the remainder of the decade.[28]

Polarization masked the tensions that existed. Indeed, during the late 1990s, the divisions within the GOP intensified to the point that some House Republicans and movement conservatives staked everything on impeachment of President Clinton as they attacked the moral values they said the president and his actions represented. Senate Republicans, however, voted overwhelmingly to allow the president to continued serving. Many neoconservative intellectuals were deeply frustrated that social conservatives had moved the GOP in this direction. They were also angry with neo-isolationists who refused to support Clinton's use of military force in Bosnia and Kosovo.

The divisions among Republicans became worse when the GOP controlled both branches of government. During George W. Bush's presidency, there were heated divisions over national security in the aftermath of 9/11. While most conservatives were hawkish and embraced the ideology of conservative internationalism, there was an ongoing tension between realists who wanted to limit military operations as they focused on containing terrorist threats and rogue states and neoconservatives in the administration who had more ambitious vision about preemptive war and regime change.

Divisions over the expansion of the federal government that occurred under Bush also resulted in an outpouring of publications in which right-wing thinkers openly criticized Bush and others in the GOP who were supporting the use of government on everything from national security to faith-based initiatives. Many neoconservatives were uncomfortable when Bush courted social conservatives on issues like stem-cell research. Some conservatives, noted the columnist Ryan Sager, "are just now waking up to what their party has become: an echo, not a choice. They are realizing that big-government conservatism is no longer an ill-conceived theory, it is the creed of the Republican Party."[29]

Yet the divisions that were evident in recent years were always part of conservatism, and a new look at the past thirty years will likely find that anticommunism, anti-taxation, and other issues were not as successful at dampening these tensions as scholars have claimed; the same criticism has been made about the New Deal coalition. Rather than a coherent movement that swept through American politics in the 1970s and remained united until internal fragmentation opened up in the early part of the twenty-first century, it would be more useful to think of conservatism as having been constantly fragile and always divided. This would open up our historical accounts to more nuanced interpretations of what occurred. Electoral success has come when politicians were able to temporarily build viable coalitions among the factions who were otherwise at odds.

The scholarship spent so much time looking for *the* explanation to the rise of *the* Right that it missed one of the most interesting stories about the era: the multiple factors that fueled the rise of different segments of the Right and the struggles to keep these different factions together.

The Difficulty of Policy Change

These internal tensions would become more pronounced when conservatives were forced to switch from being an opposition movement to becoming office holders dealing with the challenges of governance. It was one thing for conservatives to demand that the federal government should disappear when they were primarily working on the campaign trail and at the grassroots level, but it was quite another to make this demand when they were the ones in charge of government and significant parts of the coalition were calling for more government.

The election of Republicans turned out to be different than the wholesale triumph of conservative politics and ideas. Conservatives in positions of governance had to contend with the durability of public policy. Social scientists have argued that institutions are "sticky" and, as a result, they are difficult to dismantle. Conservatives started to take hold of power after the New Deal and Great

Society, as well as after the expansion of social regulation during the 1970s, which included federal intervention on the environment, consumer protection, workplace safety, and transportation.[30] From 1975 to 2002, spending on social and economic regulation, Gareth Davies found, tripled.[31]

One of the most important books on the subject came from a leading practitioner of historical institutionalism, Paul Pierson. With his work *Dismantling the Welfare State?* (1994), Pierson published a comparative study of England under Prime Minister Margaret Thatcher and the United States under President Ronald Reagan to analyze the politics and processes of policy retrenchment in the domains of income support, old-age pensions, and housing. While Pierson discovered that there was variation in different policies, his main finding was that, overall, retrenchment was extraordinarily difficult to achieve and that in most cases the results were limited. For example, Pierson showed that on issues such as Social Security, and even welfare, the political costs of extracting benefits from organized groups was very high, while the political benefits were low since the payoff was unclear and the beneficiaries of cuts were not as well defined as the losers. "Social Security's recent history," Pierson wrote, "is easily summarized. Extensive conservative efforts to erode public-pension provision have resulted in marginal change. Reagan administration attempts to go on the offensive against this extensive system of retirement provision collapsed in the face of massive and unified resistance. Increasingly, the administration found itself on the defensive, forced to respond to a policy agenda not of its own choosing. Although some cutbacks resulted from trust-fund pressures, the Social Security program survived—indeed almost flourished—through a decade of budgetary austerity."[32] The rest of government grew as well. As James Patterson wrote, federal spending reached 23.5 percent of GDP in 1983, falling only to 21.2 percent in 1989, which was still higher than in the 1970s. At the same time, the number of federal employees expanded to 3.1 million, from 2.9 million, when Reagan was in office.[33]

In his history of federal education policy since 1965, Gareth Davies discovered a similar dynamic. He dated the origins of "big-government conservatism" to the 1970s when liberal social regulatory programs became entrenched in the bureaucracy and were politically buttressed by the emergence of well-organized interest groups. Davies focuses on federal funding for the Elementary and Secondary Education Act, legislation that Congress passed in 1965. Funding steadily increased in the 1970s, just as the conservative revolution supposedly took hold. A conservative reaction to the Great Society, wrote Davies, "*did* take place, and it would be foolish to claim that the liberal impulse was gaining strength. Still, the case of education politics suggests the difficulty of asserting that these were decades of triumph for the antigovernment right."[34] Many Republicans in the 1970s who initially opposed federal intervention in education, on the grounds that the policy violated localism and states' rights, quickly came to accept these policies and even to champion the spending. After suffering a series of defeats when Richard Nixon and Gerald Ford were presidents, Republicans also realized that there was little political support for overturning these programs. Indeed, their own constituents enjoyed the benefits and often backed the interest-group community that formed in Washington to protect the programs. When Reagan tried to eliminate the Department of Education and restructure education spending in the 1980s, his victories were limited. Even when Reagan achieved some education spending cuts in the early part of the decade, his achievements were overturned almost immediately. By the time that Bush took office in 2001, the transformation of education politics was clear when the president proposed a huge expansion of federal education policy with the No Child Left Behind Act, legislation that imposed strict federal standards on public school education, and penalties for those schools where students failed to test adequately.

Religious conservatives were among the most frustrated constituencies with regard to policy change. Although they would obtain restrictions on abortion, conservatives never were able to criminalize the practice. Revised educational curricula based on creationism achieved temporary victories in states like Kansas but were usually rolled back or blocked by the courts, school boards, or voters. While President Bush would restrict stem-cell research in 2001, his position remained highly unpopular. President Obama moved quickly to reverse his policies with an executive order, while many states had already moved to provide financial and institutional support for stem-cell research. On many issues, polls repeatedly showed high levels of public support for liberal ideas such as health care and gay rights in a supposedly conservative age.

Domestic policies also survived after the 1960s because many conservatives often turned out to be more concerned about where and how the federal government should be used rather than about trying to eliminate government altogether. Notwithstanding their rhetoric about the superiority of markets over government, much of the attention of conservatives centered on promoting domestic priorities for areas where, they said, government was most needed, ranging from the regulation of social behavior to the provision of subsidies to the energy industry. Once in power, conservatives frequently redirected their attention away from retrenchment, which proved to be extremely difficult and politically costly, and toward growing the government pie.

Conservatives experienced similar challenges when dealing with national security. In this case, the challenge for conservatives was not so much policy retrenchment as trying to reverse some of the changes in policy and political thought that had occurred in the aftermath of Vietnam as a result of antiwar pressure. When conservatives promoted a hawkish national security agenda, they instantly encountered the legacy of the 1960s. Before winning the presidency in the 1980 election, Reagan had been a consummate anticommunist warrior. He had opposed every major arms treaty with the Soviet Union that was proposed since the 1940s. Reagan staffed key positions in the national security bureaucracy with neoconservative Democrats and hawkish Republicans who were fundamentally opposed to negotiation with the Soviets. His early rhetoric about an evil empire raised tensions with Soviet leaders, with whom Reagan refused to talk. Working with Secretary of Defense Casper Weinberger, Reagan pushed for a substantial increase in military spending and authorized initiatives to combat communism in Central America, Africa, and the Persian Gulf.

But there were limits to what Reagan could achieve. Notwithstanding the so-called Reagan Revolution, the White House never found a political environment that was hospitable toward an aggressive national security policy. Beyond Hollywood films, public rapport for militarism remained thin. On issues such as fighting anticommunism in Central America, polls consistently revealed that a majority of Americans did not support direct military intervention. Congress, moreover, shackled the White House with a series of amendments (the Boland Amendments) that made it illegal to provide arms to anticommunist forces. Even if there had been strong public support for military intervention, Reagan was limited to the kind of wars the professional army could undertake. Instead of direct military intervention, Reagan relied on anticommunist policies that were covert and provided support through third parties. These policies were administered through the executive branch without public knowledge and usually with limited congressional oversight. Key Republicans such as Wyoming Representative Richard Cheney were also frustrated with congressional reforms in the 1970s that had judicially restrained the kinds of operations that could be conducted by intelligence agencies.

The next Republican president, George H. W. Bush, faced the same environment even as he tried to "rid" the nation of the ghosts of Vietnam by authorizing a major military operation. During Operation Desert Storm in 1991, when U.S. forces pushed Iraqi forces out of Kuwait, the White House was very cognizant that they were undertaking this fight in the post-Vietnam era. Therefore, Bush limited the mission from the start by rejecting advisors who wanted him to remove Saddam Hussein from power. Over the opposition of Secretary of Defense Richard Cheney, moreover, Bush approached the Democratic Congress for a resolution of support, realizing that political support for this operation was and would remain fragile. Finally, the administration depended on air power as the primary weapon through which he conducted his attacks on Hussein's forces.

The problems that Reagan and Bush encountered were evident with George W. Bush, who governed with the benefit of their party controlling the White House and Congress from 2003 to 2007. Like Reagan, Bush discovered that there was little room for radical conservative initiatives. His boldest domestic proposal, privatizing Social Security, fell flat *after* his reelection in 2004. In general, domestic spending significantly increased during his presidency, and it grew with Republican support. While Bush opposed many policies that had been born of liberal presidents and legislators, he pushed forth a massive expansion of Medicare through the prescription drug program. He also signed an expensive agriculture bill in 2002 that continued to overturn a reform in 1996 that had attempted to cut commodity price supports. Bush's major successes in retrenchment involved his ability to prevent programs like the minimum wage from being updated. On foreign policy, neoconservatives were able to push for an expansive agenda that included regime change in Iraq and Afghanistan as well as a large expansion of covert counterterrorism policies. But as the war in Iraq proved unsuccessful in 2005 and the professional military found itself strained to carry out the dual missions, the administration drastically scaled back its military ambitions and turned to diplomacy, including with countries such as North Korea. Once exposed to the public, Bush's counterterrorism methods became a major political liability for the Republicans, which Democrats used to their advantage in elections of 2006 and 2008.

President Bush's biggest domestic victory—the tax cut of 2001—did not find strong support in the electorate, even among many Republicans. This is why the administration had to turn to misinformation, budget gimmicks, and partisan intimidation in Congress to achieve its goals, rather than just making a direct appeal. Jacob Hacker and Paul Pierson have shown that, when pursuing President Bush's tax program, the administration was notably off-center from where public opinion was. A majority of the electorate did not support the regressive nature or the size of the tax plan. The administration understood this. According to Treasury official Michele Davis, in a memo to Secretary of Treasury Paul O'Neill on February 27, 2001: "The public prefers spending on things like health care and education over cutting taxes. It's crucial that your remarks make clear that there is no tradeoff here—that we will boost education spending and set aside Social Security and Medicare surpluses to address the future of those programs, and we will still have an enormous surplus."[35] If President Bush represented the heart of conservatism, then conservatism did not represent the majority of the electorate, according to their findings.

Policy change has thus proved to be much more difficult than conservatives hoped for. Whether they were trying to expand or cut government, conservatives in the White House and Congress did find ways to achieve some of their goals by using new tactics—such as relying on executive power or weakening bureaucracies so that they could not administer programs effectively. But by the time President Bush left office in 2009 and Republicans were out of power, what was remarkable was that, almost three decades since Reagan entered the White House, the basic contours of the American state remained intact, and in certain areas it had grown.

This is not to say that there have not been important policy accomplishments by conservatives. Four areas where conservative policies were successful include gradual retrenchment, taxation, deregulation, and anti-unionization. The first strategy was to gradually weaken policies by subtly changing the objectives of a program, reducing the number of recipients protected by a program, and preventing benefits from being updated, thereby diminishing their value. The second policy change, the one that is likely to have the greatest impact, had to do with income taxation. Starting with the Economic Recovery Tax Act of 1981, Republicans have continually pushed for steep reductions in the income tax system and made it extraordinarily difficult, even in times of war, to call for higher taxes. Three of the biggest tax cuts occurred under President Reagan in 1981 and President George Bush in 2001 and again in 2003. While there have been tax increases during this period that offset some of their effect, the result has been to diminish the fiscal slack that is available to federal policymakers to launch and update programs. The long-term tax cuts would be in the trillions, according to Jacob Hacker and Paul Pierson, leaving elected officials to run "a twenty-first-century government on a mid-twentieth-century tax haul."[36]

The third policy domain where there were huge changes came with economic deregulation. During the 1970s and 1990s, many of the regulatory structures that were put into place in the Progressive and New Deal eras were dismantled. The government deregulated trucking, airlines, energy, telecommunications, and the financial industries.[37] One of the reasons they found success is that many liberals, such as Senator Ted Kennedy and consumer activist Ralph Nader, supported deregulation as well. Whereas conservatives made the argument that markets were inherently more efficient than government, liberal advocates of deregulation argued that existing structures had been captured by the regulated businesses and hurt consumers.

Conservative policies were also important to the declining strength of unions in the American economy. Organized labor, supported by the policies of the Roosevelt administration, had been at the heart of the New Deal coalition. But outside of the public sector, unions experienced a sharp decline in numerical strength and political power after the 1970s. There were different reasons behind this turn of events. The shift of economic power away from the manufacturing sector weakened the sector of the economy where unions had been strongest. Lawsuits against unions for failing to abide by affirmative action policies, moreover, greatly harmed their financial status.[38] Nonetheless, conservative politics targeting unions also helped cripple the movement.[39]

Yet with all the policy accomplishments of conservatives, historians have greatly overlooked their failures, which were just as powerful in shaping the political landscape. Indeed, one can argue that the overall size and substance of the federal government not only remained intact after the 1970s, but had expanded significantly and in ways that pleased liberal politicians and organizations.

In the realm of popular culture, the evidence also suggests that conservatives have not been able to roll back the liberalization of norms and values, even in so-called red states. Textbooks often feature the American Family Association's campaigns for actions like having the chain store 7-Eleven ban pornographic magazines in the 1970s and protesting against television shows like *Three's Company* and *Charlie's Angels*. Yet in 2011, television, movies, radio, and the Internet are filled with the kind of sexuality and humor that, at least rhetorically, conservative activists have tried to stop. According to Benjamin Edelman, subscription rates to online adult entertainment are *higher* in states where residents identify more closely with conservative values on sex, gender, and religion.[40]

The Persistence of Liberalism

The fact is that liberalism survived the rise of conservatism. The historiography on the rise of the Right, like most accounts of the period, rests on the assumption that liberalism was an emasculated political force in the years that followed the infamous Democratic Convention in 1968. The internal conflict over Vietnam as well as over issues such as race had shattered the Democratic Party, according to standard accounts. Many of the books on conservatism treated the Right as if it faced almost no opposition. Liberals were virtually written out of the story. When liberals did appear, the point was to demonstrate how weak they had become. When Democrats succeeded, the scholars said, the victorious politicians tended to be centrists—like Bill Clinton—who embraced conservative ideals and lacked the vibrant grassroots strength that the conservative movement enjoyed. In some respects the recent generation of historians treated liberalism in the same way that Richard Hofstadter and other liberal consensus scholars in the 1950s and 1960s had depicted conservatism—as a marginal, fringe element that was out of touch with mainstream politics.

This argument is incomplete, though. To be sure, conservatism commanded strong support, and the movement entrenched itself in American politics. In certain parts of the country, support for conservative issues ran deep. But there is already substantial evidence to suggest that liberal politicians and organizations remained a vibrant, influential, and dynamic political force as well. The rise of the conservative movement took place against the backdrop of post-1960s liberal politics. This is the only way we can understand what was happening and to understand the intensity of the sentiment among conservatives well into the period when they were supposed to be in control.

Political scientist Jeffrey Berry has documented the vast expansion of public interest organizations that occurred in the 1970s and 1980s, almost all of which tended to fall on the liberal end of the political spectrum. "Liberalism is not dead," Berry wrote, "Indeed, it's thriving . . . Today American liberalism stresses culture, status, life-style, morality, and rights—post materialism."[41] According to Berry, liberal activists involved with issues such as environmentalism, good government, social rights, and consumer protection established well-funded organizations in Washington, DC, and state capitals. They commanded support from a broad number of middle-class Americans. The media provided favorable coverage to their causes and they gained access to top politicians. Berry found that these organizations were pivotal to a shift in policy that occurred after the 1960s toward a set of what he calls non-material issues—such as the treatment of toxic waste, consumer protection, ethics-in-government and more. His book fits nicely with Samuel Hays's classic work on environmentalism, which argued that widespread middle-class support for a clean environment, and the proliferation of Washington-based organizations to lobby for and support this cause, proved to be a huge obstacle to conservatives in the 1980s as they tried to roll back the programs.[42]

Another group of political scientists whose specialty is Congress have studied how most House Democrats, who retained control of the chamber until 1994, moved to the left of the political spectrum. For a time in the 1970s and 1980s, most social scientists had been interested in the death of political parties.[43] But as political scientists watched partisan polarization intensify in Washington and in the electorate, the tone of their research changed. In 1993, David Rhode published *Parties and Leaders in the Postreform House*, which argued that parties were becoming stronger and more ideologically homogenized. Congressional reforms in the 1970s strengthened the Democratic Caucus and weakened committee chairpersons who had often been the source of bipartisan compromise. Demographic changes diminished the presence of moderate voters in either party. Among Democrats, Southerners moved into the GOP and their absence pushed the party to the left (while in the GOP, liberal Republicans diminished in numbers).[44] Sophisticated gerrymandering techniques created safe districts where incumbent representatives could keep their seats by playing to voters who leaned to one side of the political spectrum. Similar dynamics occurred in the Senate (without the gerrymandering) with heightened partisan polarization and vanishing moderates. As a result, Presidents Ronald Reagan and George H. W. Bush were forced to contend with a Congress where Democrats opposed most of their agendas.

Similar arguments have been made with regard to the presidential primary process. Party reforms in the 1970s ensured that primaries would be the mechanism through which candidates were selected. Party conventions no longer played a major function as they had for most of the nineteenth and twentieth centuries. As a result of the reforms, all candidates had to campaign actively before the conventions, and their victory depended on their popularity with primary voters. Social scientists have shown that primary voters tend to come from the far sides of the political spectrum. This meant that in the Democratic primaries, candidates had to take positions and make promises that were satisfactory to the Left wing of the party; Republicans had to do the same with the Right. The primary system gave liberal organizations a fair amount of power in setting the agenda for the campaign. Even "centrist" Democrat Bill Clinton focused on government economic intervention and healthcare reform, as well as social issues like gay rights, which differed from positions he had staked out in the Democratic Leadership Council.

Nor were Democrats always on the losing end of campaigns. While political scientists disagree whether "realigning" elections ever happened, there is relatively strong support for the claim that the United States has not seen that kind of election since 1932.[45] When scholarship turns from the presidency to Congress in the 1970s and 1980s, and even through the presidency of George W. Bush, it immediately becomes evident that Democrats were able to hold their ground. In the House, during the high point of the conservative revolution, Democrats—who were now more liberal as a caucus—retained control of the chamber from 1981 until 1994. Democrats lost control of the Senate in 1980 but regained their majority in 1986. Between 1995 and 2001, the Republican majority was razor thin, thus limiting much of what conservatives could accomplish, given the veto power of the minority in the Senate. Democrats temporarily split control of the Senate in 2001 and 2002 after Vermont Senator Jim Jeffords bolted from the GOP. In 2006, Democrats regained control of Congress. Republicans regained the House in 2010, but not the Senate.

The presidency of Bill Clinton also deserves reconsideration. The conventional wisdom has been that Clinton, who was the first Democrat to serve for a full two terms since Franklin Roosevelt, was a centrist who succeeded only because he compromised with Republicans based on a strategy of triangulation, a strategy in which he attempted to steal away certain issues from conservatives by accepting them as his own. The most famous decision, in this account, is his successful effort to work with the Republican Congress in 1996 to eliminate the federal welfare program (AFDC). And Clinton certainly did try to define a new agenda for the Democratic Party that emphasized conservative arguments about markets—such as reviving the economy with low interest rates and free trade, rather than public spending—as well as the use of military force. His healthcare proposal rejected the single-payer option that had been promoted by Democrats throughout the 1970s.

Yet Clinton, who had launched his political career by working on South Dakota Senator George McGovern's campaign against Richard Nixon in 1972, combined these ideas with key tenets of liberalism, just as did other Democrats who came of professional age in the 1970s. Though he sensed there were immense limits to what liberals could accomplish, given the change in tenor after the 1960s, he did not refrain from supporting the use of government to address domestic problems. He also protected many existing domestic programs from conservative attack. Clinton began his presidency by pushing for an ambitious national healthcare program that would provide coverage to all the uninsured and would control costs. While the measure ultimately failed and was not the single-payer program that many liberals were still demanding, the bill itself was still the most sweeping healthcare proposal to come out of the White House since Medicare. Furthermore, Clinton raised taxes on wealthy Americans in 1993 to curb the deficit, and he implemented several policies to broaden middle-class home ownership. His public service program, AmeriCorps, would attract more volunteers than the Peace Corps. He successfully obtained family-and-medical leave benefits and warded off deep cuts to Medicare and Medicaid. If historians add these important politics to our understanding of his presidency, his ability to end the succession of Republican presidents in 1992 and win re-election in 1996, as well as his skyrocketing popularity ratings toward the end of his term, pose a challenge to scholars who claim that Democrats who embraced an activist vision of government could not win office.

There is even evidence that *losing* Democratic candidates sometimes had a long-term positive impact on liberalism and the Democratic Party, planting the seeds for the revitalization of progressive politics in 2008. The most interesting example of a liberal loser whose campaign had beneficial, albeit unnoticed, effects is Senator McGovern, whose disastrous performance against President Nixon is usually presented as the final nail in the coffin of twentieth-century liberalism. A recent book, *The Liberals' Moment* (2007), by political scientist Bruce Miroff, provided evidence to the contrary. Many of the Democrats who were at the center of the revival of Democratic fortunes in the 1990s and in 2008 (ranging from Clinton to John Podesta) cut their teeth in the 1972 election. More importantly, the campaign also accelerated a series of long-term shifts that brought ideas and voting groups into the Democratic camp that would eventually make the party competitive. First, the campaign shifted power within the party toward college-educated, suburban voters who would increasingly be central to the electorate and the McGovern-forged ties with the feminist, environmental, and gay rights movements. Although the "McGovern vote" was a minority in 1972, the number of educated suburban voters would grow into a sizable part of the electorate by the end of the century. More than 90 percent of Americans over twenty-five years of age had high school diplomas by 2000 (compared to about 50 percent in 1970). When Democrats tapped into these votes, combined with those of new immigrant groups such as Asian Americans and Hispanic Americans, as well as African Americans, McGovern's campaign had opened the Democratic nomination process so that there was a better opportunity to cultivate a powerful demographic basis for the persistence of liberalism even after the weakening of the New Deal coalition.[46] The McGovern campaign also legitimated skepticism toward military intervention, a skepticism that would embolden Democrats to challenge the hawkish rhetoric of conservatives. McGovern's staff familiarized Democratic activists with new types of political tactics that would be used in campaigns during the coming years, such as primary electoral organization and broad-based fundraising. "Despite the landslide defeat," Miroff wrote, "the McGovern campaign bequeathed to the Democrats a talented, youthful cadre of strategists, organizers, and wordsmiths who as they aged would largely shape the evolution of the party over the following decades."[47]

The coalition that started to emerge through the McGovern campaign gained political strength in the 1974 midterm and 1976 congressional elections, which brought into Congress an influx of suburban Democrats—the Watergate Babies—such as California's Henry Waxman, Tennessee's Al Gore Jr., and Colorado's Gary Hart, all of whom came into Congress determined to master the legislative process and willing to challenge some of the ideological orthodoxies of the Democratic Party in order to make the party more appealing in the post-1960s era. Many of them were called "Atari Democrats" because of their interest in promoting investment in the high-technology sector while retaining a commitment to progressive social and environmental ideals.

Recent studies have also begun to examine how grassroots liberal movement politics did not disappear after the 1960s. A recent issue of the *Journal of Contemporary History* contained a number of provocative essays about the 1970s that emphasized the continuation and expansion of liberalism in this decade rather than its contraction. The historian Stephen Tuck, for example, argued that civil rights fragmented and diversified but did not vanish. African American women, for instance, were among those who organized to tackle issues such as welfare rights and crime prevention. African American protest flared in prisons around the treatment of detainees and police misconduct. Tuck also found that African Americans made substantial economic gains in the 1970s as a result of class-action suits against companies, who agreed to sign consent decrees with the federal government ensuring the use of affirmative action in hiring practices. The black middle class expanded as a result. Furthermore, African Americans strengthened their role in electoral politics. The Congressional Black Caucus formed in 1971, quickly becoming a formidable legislative force pushing certain issues involving race onto the agenda of the Democratic Caucus. African American candidates were also very successful throughout the decade, with more than 200 black mayors by 1977.[48] The number of African Americans who held national elected positions increased from 193 in 1965, to 764 in 1970, and again to 1,909 in 1980. African American officials at the local level, argues Thomas Sugrue, used patronage to secure support and distributed public jobs to African Americans. The rising number of African Americans working in agencies made them more responsive and generous toward other African Americans in need.[49]

There were gains for feminism as well. Joshua Zeitz presented the 1970s as a critical decade when new issues related to gender, such as reproduction rights, were deemed to be legitimate issues for political debate. Feminist organizations scored a number of major victories at the exact same time that conservatives were mobilizing and expanding their base. He wrote:

> On the federal level alone, women won passage of Title IX of the Education Amendments Act, which cut off federal funds for educational institutions that discriminated against women; an extension of the Equal Credit Opportunity Act, which forbade lending institutions from discriminating against women; and congressional approval of the Equal Rights Amendment. States modernized their divorce and rape laws, women achieved parity with men on college campuses, and the wage gap continued to close.[50]

There were also major gains, Zeitz noted, in the courts.

Gay rights is another example of an area where liberal activists built a formidable movement infrastructure, placed new issues on the national agenda, obtained broadened rights and cultural recognition for gay Americans, and established influence among elected officials. The gay rights movement thrived at the local level, relying on activists who focused on the issues affecting their particular communities rather than on single national issues and rather than depending on prominent national leaders.[51] During the 1970s and 1980s, gay candidates, many of whom were open about their sexual orientation, won office. State and local government officials became increasingly responsive to gay voters. Two years after Reagan was elected, Wisconsin was the first state to ever prohibit discrimination based on sexual orientation. In Pennsylvania and Oregon, governors established task forces to tackle discrimination against gay workers. During the 1990s, the organization Lambda provided legal assistance groups who challenged conservative initiatives such as Amendment 2 in Colorado, which the courts eventually would rule to be unconstitutional. Gay rights activists extended their agenda to issues like the treatment of the partners of gay employees with regard to benefits.[52]

Guian McKee's study of postwar liberalism in Philadelphia showed how many liberals focused their efforts in local government—mirroring many of the recent studies about conservatism—rather than at the national level. In the 1970s and 1980s, for instance, there were several intergovernmental projects administered by the Philadelphia Model Cities Administration and the Philadelphia Industrial Development Corporation that directed federal funds toward urban renewal projects, not all of which, as conventional accounts argue, resulted in detrimental effects to African Americans. The goal of the programs that McKee examined was to use the money to nurture self-sufficient inner-city communities.[53]

Within the realm of national security, one of the most powerful grassroots forces to emerge after the 1960s was the nuclear-freeze movement. This was a transnational network that claimed millions of people around the globe and was able to organize large-scale protests that were comparable in scale and scope to the anti-war movement or the civil rights movement. The historian Lawrence Wittner showed how the movement commanded the support of powerful figures from the world of science, politics, and entertainment. They were able to design effective, sophisticated strategies for furthering global communication among members. Politicians took this movement seriously. Wittner provides compelling evidence that the movement placed immense political pressure during the 1970s and 1980s for leaders in the United States and the Soviet Union to move away from nuclear confrontation and seek opportunities for negotiation. The movement, and not just heroic leadership by the U.S. president and the Soviet premier, according to Wittner, was responsible for helping to prevent a nuclear war from taking place and for pressuring politicians in the 1980s to take advantage of the opportunities for negotiation. Wittner wrote that "most government officials—and particularly those of the major powers—had no intention of adopting nuclear arms control and disarmament policies. Instead, they grudgingly accepted such policies thanks to the emergence of popular pressure . . . Confronted by a vast wave of popular resistance, they concluded, reluctantly, that compromise had become the price of political survival."[54] In *Arsenal of Democracy*, I found that within the Reagan administration the freeze movement was taken quite seriously and perceived by top advisors as a formidable political opponent to their earlier positions. This was one of the political considerations behind proposing the Strategic Defense Initiative, or "Star Wars," which offered a response to criticism that Reagan was hell-bent for war.[55]

Indeed, one of the most visible manifestations of this interpretative bias has been the recent wave of revisionist literature about Reagan. A series of books, written primarily by journalists and former White House officials, has challenged earlier interpretations of Reagan as a hawk who carelessly brought the world to the brink of nuclear war.[56] The new work depicts Reagan as a strategic actor as well as a nuclear abolitionist. Based on new archival discoveries, they attempt to show that Reagan always wanted to eliminate nuclear weapons and was always determined to negotiate with the Soviet Union to achieve that end. In many of these books, however, post-1960s liberalism is virtually written out of the story. Liberalism is the elephant in the room as readers try to understand why Reagan made the shifts that he did. Many factors have not been discussed, ranging from his old interest in nuclear abolitionism to the role of Mikhail Gorbachev, but the pressure from liberalism is rarely part of the mix. We don't learn about the role of the nuclear-freeze movement, the Democratic Party, congressional leaders, or the national security institutions that he inherited from the 1960s.[57] Without that context, the story is incomplete.

What Comes Next?

We are now at the cusp of a third wave of historical scholarship on modern conservatism. If the first wave (1960s–1970s) centered on the discovery of a handful of elite conservative leaders, and the second wave (1990s–2000s) focused on the rise of the Right from the bottom up, the third wave will have to start developing a historical narrative about the divisions, opposition, struggles, and compromises that conservatives grappled with throughout the postwar period, even when they obtained the highest positions of power. A new look will not downplay the centrality of conservatism in contemporary politics but, just the opposite, provide a better appreciation for how they achieved what they did given the numerous internal and external obstacles they faced.

The first issue has to do with our opening questions. Whereas labor historians of the 1970s were fascinated by the question of "Why no socialism in America?" with the implicit assumption that socialism should have happened, the most recent generation of historians on the Right often started with the assumption of "Why conservatism in Modern America?" as if the puzzle was why conservatism was able to take hold. Part of this bias has to do with the fact that the best scholarship about conservatism has been written by liberals. There are only a few scholarly works, based on archival material and connected to the analytic findings of professional historians, about the history of the Right written by conservatives.[58] But scholarship has shown that there was great depth to the support for conservative causes and politicians before and after the 1960s. Even the literature on the 1960s is shifting from this being the heyday of liberalism to a decade characterized by a civil war between the Right and the Left, with both sides gaining strength and moving in new directions.[59] At the same time, we are starting to see that liberalism was not as stable as we assumed. Two recent works, for instance, have presented the period between the 1930s and the end of the twentieth century as an exception in terms of support for the welfare state and progressive income policies.[60] This is not surprising given that, in the biggest landslides in American politics (1936, 1964, and 1972), almost 40 percent of the electorate backed the opposition. The fragmented institutional configuration of the American government (both the executive-legislative-judicial divide as well as federalism) have always offered multiple points of influence for political positions that were not in control of the national government. Therefore, just as historians are starting to ask tougher questions about why liberalism was able to achieve so much success between the New Deal and the Great Society eras, we must abandon the "why conservatism" question. Accepting that conservatism had deep roots in our polity, we must now examine why conservative politicians had as much trouble as they did before and after the 1970s.

This will naturally lead to the second issue: how conservatism unfolded in a dialectical fashion with liberalism rather than as a replacement *of* liberalism. Doing so would entail a study about how the Right built coalitions, secured elected office, and struggled to govern within the institutional, policy, and ideological context the Left created, and sustained, by liberalism.

In his most recent book, historian Donald Critchlow has approached conservatism through this lens. He traces the rise of the Republican Right since World War II but argues that the New Deal state remained formidable throughout the twentieth century. In a work that argues that conservatism was ultimately triumphant, Critchlow acknowledges that:

> George W. Bush's election in 2000 marked the triumph of the conservative ascendancy. The New Deal political coalition had finally been defeated, but the Bush presidency revealed the enduring strength of the liberal welfare state that had been created under Franklin Roosevelt and expanded under Lyndon Johnson. Bush sought to challenge the liberal order by building and strengthening a disciplined Republican party and by reconfiguring (albeit unsuccessfully) the welfare state to impart new power to faith-based public-interest groups. He introduced proposals to bring minimal privatization to Social Security and new measures to allow greater choice in Medicare. These proposals fell on deaf ears or had little impact, and as a consequence the liberal welfare state endured, a lasting legacy of New Deal liberalism.[61]

The coexistence of activist government and conservatism is the focus of the essays in a collection by Theda Skocpol and Paul Pierson. "After the early 1980s," the editors wrote in *The Transformation of American Politics* (2007),

> Federal government expansion was slowed, even rolled back in some areas. Yet the activist state remains a central new fact of modern American politics . . . contemporary American politics reflects the ongoing

> collision, carried out through these new forms of participation, between the rise of the activist state and the emergence of an invigorated conservatism. Conservatives have certainly not destroyed or fundamentally rolled back big, activist government. They have, however, circumscribed and redirected it, upending many of the assumptions made by liberals.[62]

The essays in *Rightward Bound* stress this theme as well. Bruce Schulman and I presented conservatism in the 1970s as an incomplete revolution, given that "liberalism remained deeply embedded in national politics, popular culture retained the impulses of the 1960s, and social movements opposing conservative values flourished . . . the triumphs of the Right, at the ballot box and broadly across American society, would take place against a backdrop where the achievements of liberalism still mattered."[63]

This will open up a final issue that historians are already starting to examine, namely, the challenges that conservatives faced with the process of governance. As historians move deeper into the 1980s and 1990s, they are starting to research what occurred when conservatives gained control of the levers of political power and undertook the process of moving from being in the opposition to being the decision-makers.[64]

These issues will just be the start. None of this is to say the rise-of-the-Right literature has not offered enormous contributions to our understanding of American politics since the 1940s. In fact, the literature has been extremely sophisticated and has provided a convincing portrait of how conservative political elites and activists coalesced.

Yet certain assumptions about conservatism and the political environment in which it operated have produced an incomplete and sometimes skewed picture. Just as the historiography on progressivism shifted away from the study of motivations and toward issues such as institutional context after the 1980s, the time has come to do the same with conservatism. In his landmark essay challenging historians of progressivism, Daniel Rodgers argued that changing the terms of inquiry would not be to "lose the whole enterprise of historical comprehension. It may be to find it."[65] The same holds true with the history of conservatism. By moving away from our search for the reasons why so many citizens identified with conservatism and by abandoning the sense of inevitability that shapes our current narratives of the Right, historians can start moving closer to the fault lines and transformations that have shaped contemporary politics.

FIVE

What Political Science Can Learn from the New Political History

One of the most exciting developments in recent years for students of American politics has been the growing number of scholars who are interested in and willing to cross the disciplinary divide.* The field of American political development (APD) has offered a meeting point for political scientists, sociologists, and historians whose research focuses on the political evolution of the United States. Although the disciplines approach their subject from very different analytical, and sometimes methodological, perspectives, considerable room has emerged for productive interaction. We should not miss this opportunity.

Whereas historians are very cognizant of the contributions that historically oriented political scientists have offered them, the reverse is not always true. Given that for many decades the field of political history had languished, and APD was in fact an effort to fill the gap that had opened up, it was logical for political scientists and political sociologists to have this bias. But there has been a renaissance in political history during the past ten years, and an extensive body of research has emerged. Although some of the work is not directly applicable to the work of political scientists, there are several key areas and arguments that deserve attention.

This essay begins by examining how political historians have rebuilt their field in recent years. I then turn to three particular aspects of the literature—research on the motivations behind the rise of conservatism, the discovery of the nineteenth-century state, and arguments about the particularities of public policy—all of which are essential starting points for beginning an interdisciplinary dialogue.

The Revitalization of Political History

It is now possible to write about the field of American political history without focusing on a crisis that grips this area of scholarship. This was not realistic just

* This essay originally appeared in *Annual Review of Political Science* 13 (2010): 26–36.

ten years ago, when most senior political historians were spending most of their time lamenting how changes within the profession had marginalized their field (Leuchtenburg, 1986; Silbey, 1999).

Their fears were not irrational. During the 1970s and 1980s, a new generation of historians—shaped by the bitter conflicts of the 1960s, with many of them being former members of the New Left on college campuses—had rejected the traditional historical study of presidents and parties as irrelevant to the lived experience of most Americans and as an approach that exaggerated the possibilities for altering power relations with the United States.

In other words, the changes that resulted from Democrats or Republicans holding office, they said, were minimal. Convinced by the types of arguments made by the sociologist C. Wright Mills about the existence of an entrenched power elite who controlled decision-making, the baby boom generation of historians instead decided to focus the majority of their research attention on recovering the history of forgotten voices from the bottom up and documenting cultural phenomena that seemed much more relevant to the lives of average citizens than who was president. Taking seriously the argument that the personal was political, they examined the ongoing contests over class, race, ethnicity, and gender that had taken place across America. The historian Eric Foner argued in 1990, "The old 'presidential synthesis' is dead (and not lamented)" (Leff, 1995, p. 829).

Political history did not disappear, however. On the margins of the profession (as measured by hiring, book publications, and articles published in prestigious journals), numerous factions of scholars worked hard to reinvent how the field of political history was practiced.

Scholars of the "organizational synthesis" argued that the main story in American political history took place between the 1880s and 1920s with the emergence of national, centralized institutions, namely the corporation, professions, and the administrative state, which replaced the localized and decentralized political economy of the nineteenth century (Hays, 1957; Wiebe, 1967; Galambos, 1970, 1983; Keller, 1977).

Meanwhile, historians of American political culture engaged in a vibrant debate over the ideological origins of the American Revolution, trying to determine whether liberalism, Christianity, or republicanism was the most powerful determinant in shaping the minds and rhetoric of the colonists as they confronted London (Bailyn, 1967; Wood, 1969; Pocock, 1975; Appleby, 1984; Kloppenberg, 1987). There were also social historians, such as Michael Katz, who wrote about how Americans experienced policies such as education and welfare, and how those policies often reified social hierarchies (Katz, 1968). A different strategy for combining social and political history emerged in the 1970s with quantitative historians, who called themselves practitioners of the "new political history." They examined how enfranchised citizens in the nineteenth century reached their decisions about which party to vote for; their work attempted to measure which influence mattered more, economic or cultural background (Kleppner, 1970; Silbey et al., 1978). Finally, there was the advent of policy history in the late 1970s, with historians who were eager to contribute to contemporary debates over governance (Zelizer, 2000, Graham, 1993).

As a result of various factors, which I and others have explored, none of these efforts were able to significantly strengthen the standing of political history within the mainstream of the profession until the late 1990s, as the trend-setting historians still focused squarely on social and cultural history (Jacobs and Zelizer, 2003; Zelizer, 2004; Leff, 1995). Even though exciting scholarship was being produced about politics that moved beyond the old presidential synthesis of the 1940s and 1950s, there was little evidence in the hiring decisions of the top history departments that political history had returned.

But that era of struggle has come to an end. In 2011, the field of American political history is no longer wandering in the academic wilderness; it has emerged at the forefront of the profession, where it has been between the 1880s and 1960s. There are a number of reasons behind this dramatic change of fortune. Within political science, the emergence of the field of APD proved to be instrumental to offering younger historians a professional network through which to develop their scholarship. Just as important, APD offered a series of exciting analytic arguments that led scholars to write political history in fresh ways. For example, arguments about state autonomy stimulated archival interest in the history of bureaucrats and staffers who developed policies based on their own interests and agendas rather than simply in response to social pressure. Many younger historians were also extremely interested in exploring how the structure of political institutions did or did not shape the kinds of alternatives that were available to political actors at all levels of politics in different moments of history. Although historians shied away from overly determinist accounts, the basic argument about institutional design proved to be appealing.

Social and cultural history also unexpectedly offered opportunities for political historians to re-energize their field. Lizabeth Cohen generated excitement through her book on how industrial workers overcame ethnic divisions and made the New Deal by forging a coalition that sustained the Democratic Party (Cohen, 1991). A path-breaking book by the pioneering labor historian David Montgomery explained how, as a result of changes in managerial control on the shop floor within the corporation, coupled with the failure by the American Federation of Labor to achieve a stable place in the Democratic Party during the mid-1910s, workers never gained a strong position in the polity (Montgomery, 1987).

Several senior scholars who specialized in gender and race, who began their careers in the 1960s and 1970s by rebelling against "traditional" political history and writing social history from the bottom up, started to examine the ways in which gendered and racialized cultural conceptions about the workforce shaped areas of public policy like Old Age Insurance and Aid to Families with Dependent Children. They imported from APD the notion that the welfare state constructed in the 1930s had two tiers separating superior programs that were federally administered, provided universal benefits, and were funded through strong and often earmarked revenue sources, from inferior programs that were means tested, administered by state and local government, and funded from general revenue. Two pioneers in the field of gender history, Gordon (1994) and Kessler-Harris (2001), for example, argued that the concept of a household with a single, male wage earner was integral to the structure of Old Age Insurance as well as the tax code. Other historians claimed that the reason why certain occupations were excluded from the privileged "first tier" of the welfare state (primarily domestic and agricultural workers) was that they were jobs with a high percentage of African American workers. Because southern Democrats controlled congressional committees in the 1930s, they argued, a deal was struck to allow for new federal programs as long as they did not allow federal administrators to tamper with race relations in their region (Katznelson, 2005).

The Rise of Conservatism

The past decade has seen a massive proliferation of research on U.S. political history by new political historians who were not so invested in the debates of the 1960s and who are building on the work of political scientists and historians who continued to think about politics even as the subfield struggled.

The first area of research has been to trace the rise of conservatism. In 1994, Alan Brinkley published an article in the *American Historical Review* that lamented how little work had been done on modern American conservatism. He wrote that it would not be "a very controversial claim to say that twentieth century American conservatism has been something of an orphan in historical scholarship" (Brinkley, 1994, p. 409). Historians had focused most of their research on the formation of the New Deal coalition and the evolution of liberalism in the twentieth century. After Brinkley's article, however, a group of post–baby boom political historians (primarily, though, some of the work came from more senior scholars as well) challenged older assumptions about the place of conservatism in contemporary politics. They disputed the claims by the liberal-consensus school of the 1950s and 1960s that conservatism was a marginal force in national political life, promoted primarily by uneducated citizens who stood far outside the mainstream. The conventional wisdom among social scientists of that earlier era had also stipulated that modern conservatism was a political agenda that had been defined and driven by elite actors—from Senator Joseph McCarthy in the early 1950s to Barry Goldwater in the 1960s (and, later work stressed, Ronald Reagan in the 1980s)—who played to the anxieties of Americans.

These claims were harder to justify by the mid-1990s, when the conservative movement had firmly established itself in Washington and state capitals for over a decade. The new scholarship on conservatism painted a very different picture than the previous generation of political historians, who wrote from the perspective of Franklin Roosevelt rather than Ronald Reagan. These historians of conservatism, most of whom were politically to the left, described an energetic political mobilization that had started with activities surrounding Goldwater's campaign in 1964 and accelerated into the 1970s. This work painted the 1970s as a pivotal decade, more so than the 1960s.

In contrast to much of the political science scholarship that focuses on the economic basis of conservative politics (Graetz and Shapiro, 2006; McCarty et al., 2006; Shafer and Johnston, 2006; Bartels, 2008), historians have emphasized nonmaterial motivations that drove the movement, ranging from anxieties about national security to social tensions over race and gender. The conservative movement, according to the historical scholarship, was more diverse and multifaceted than historians originally suspected. McGirr's (2001) book on Orange County, California revealed how many conservative activists were middle-class, suburban Americans, driven by fears of communism and cultural norms, disconnected from the racial animosity that animated many southerners.

In contrast, younger southern historians argued that racial politics remained central to conservatism after the 1960s, but that the political dynamics over these issues did not differ much from those in the north (Kruse, 2005; Lassiter, 2006; Crespino, 2009). These southern specialists put forth a series of arguments about how southern conservatism came to shape national political debate in the post-1964 era. Crespino stressed that southern conservatives responded to civil rights activism by recasting their emphasis toward issues that were not explicitly racial and national in scope, such as schooling and the protection of churches. Kruse focused on how southern resistance to civil rights survived the 1960s through white flight and the accompanying political issues of privatization and tax revolts. Lassiter argues that southern conservatism, like northern conservatism, came to focus on the ideology of "suburban entitlement," which ignored the ways that government was essential to maintain these residential areas and which offered an aggressive defense of policies and rights that were detrimental to most African Americans.

Still other scholars have looked at the central role played by evangelical religious leaders who entered the political realm and successfully tapped into vast membership groups in churches. Jerry Falwell, Donald Wildmon, James Dobson, and other leaders created an infrastructure of television shows, publications, and radio shows that were crucial to the right (Boyer, 2008).

In addition to the motivations behind right-wing activism, there has been important work on the organizational mechanisms and political strategies of the movement, starting with those behind the 1964 Barry Goldwater campaign (Perlstein, 2001). Here, economics has received greater emphasis, but the focus is on the money that went to support the movement, not on economics as the sole motivation that fueled activists. Phillips-Fein (2009) and O'Connor (2008) have written about the donors who funded the think tanks and congressional candidates that pushed the Republican Party away from its liberal northeastern wing and toward the right (Phillips-Fein, more than most historians, does stress the importance of concerns about political economy to conservatives).

The literature on the conservative movement has revealed that right-wing activists often employed tactics from the New Left in the 1960s for very different political objectives. From the use of direct mail for soliciting funds to the mobilization of college students behind conservative causes, the political mechanisms of conservatives and liberals were not as far apart as were their ideas.

Although the scholarship has not resolved many disputes over the motivation behind conservatism, there has been a general consensus that this was not a top-down movement, nor was it confined to Americans on the margins. Nor were the motivations of conservatives entirely economic.

Revisiting the Nineteenth Century

A second important area of scholarship has been to reconceptualize politics in nineteenth-century America. Many political scientists have continued to rely on the conception that the government played a minimal role in American politics in the nineteenth century. One of the founders of APD, Stephen Skowronek, famously argued that the nineteenth century was characterized by a "state of courts and parties" that was replaced by an administrative state following the Progressive Era. Skowronek's formulation became the straw man for many historians who saw a different past, although his actual argument was much more subtle (Skowronek, 1982).

As a result of this interpretation, many political scientists, and historians, have started with the assumption that anti-statist values are deeply rooted in the United States based on the fact that the nation lacked a strong government presence for so long and that our current institutions emerged in response to industrialization and economic crisis. Many have also subscribed to the myth that until the twentieth century we had a laissez-faire economy and that somehow public policy since the Progressive Era has moved the polity away from its natural path.

But scholars have punctured the myths that the nineteenth century was "stateless" and characterized by a laissez-faire economy. As the historian Brian Balogh has recently argued in this important synthesis of the century, the literature on the nineteenth century has undermined the one belief on which liberals and conservatives had been able to agree: that the federal government was not a major force in American life before the Progressive Era (Balogh, 2009). Balogh explains that "Americans sought active governance at the federal level time and again over the course of the nineteenth century. Their efforts produced a variety of mechanisms, from debt assumption to Supreme Court decisions that undercut the health and safety prerogatives of states in the name of interstate commerce" (p. 19).

The new political historians have made a convincing case that government was an important component of the United States long before the Progressive Era started. According to Richard John, recent research about the nineteenth century shares "the conviction that the 'party period' paradigm and the 'courts-and-parties' construct are inadequate interpretative frames through which to view the nineteenth-century political economy . . . they exaggerate the influence on policymaking of party leaders, underestimate the integrity of the judiciary, and neglect the often-vital role in the policy process of administrators, lobbyists, and property owners" (John, 2006, p. 8). John's own monograph revealed that administrative government had been important in the early Republic. His book on the development of the U.S. postal system claimed that the delivery of mail was a huge milestone in the evolution of communication policy, and that the United States developed the capacity to transport mail more effectively than most other comparable countries of that time. The U.S. postal system had five times as many offices as France and many more than Great Britain, British North America, or Russia, just to name a few examples (John, 1995, p. 5).

Legal historians have also been instrumental to this new interpretation of the nineteenth century. By exploring the law, Novak (1996) revealed that government intervention was familiar to most Americans at the local level. He found that legal restrictions established regulations to guide numerous kinds of behavior, from fire ordinances to social norms. He focused on regulations involving public safety, public economy, public space, public morals, and public health to show that the notion of a laissez-faire society was incorrect. Novak wrote that the myth of statelessness in the nineteenth century was "the most notorious fallacy in American historiography" (Novak, 1996, p. 3).

Diplomatic historians, including Herring (2008), have destroyed the notion of an "isolationist" American nineteenth century by cataloguing the vast number of military interventions that took place in this era, ranging from efforts to conquer Native Americans in the West to the wars with Britain and Spain.

Balogh's (2009) recent synthesis provides the most compelling interpretation of the federal government in the nineteenth century. He concludes that Americans did oppose federal intervention when it was direct, but that on many issues—especially promoting economic development and the acquisition of new territory—Americans accepted and sought government intervention as long as it was relatively indirect and hidden from public view. Balogh writes that:

> the mystery of national authority in nineteenth-century America can be resolved once we recognize that although the United States did indeed govern differently than its industrialized counterparts, it did not govern less. Americans did, however, govern less visibly. The key feature that distinguished the United States in the nineteenth century was the preference among its citizens for national governance that was inconspicuous. Americans preferred to use the language of law, the courts, trade policy, fiscal subsidies—supported by indirect taxes—and partnerships

> with nongovernmental partners instead of more overt, bureaucratic and visible interventions into the political economy. (2009, p. 379)

Balogh suggests that the seeds were planted in the nineteenth century for the kind of hidden welfare state that political scientists have explored in the twentieth century (Howard, 1997).

The result of this work is that historians can no longer depict the nineteenth century as a wasteland for federal governance. To be sure, not all historians agree with this assessment. Rauchway (2006) has argued that by international standards, in most of the important areas of public policy, the nation-state in the United States did remain weak. Nonetheless, there is now compelling evidence on the other side of the debate, namely, that the federal government became an integral part of national life and that the roots of the twentieth century could be traced from these decades. There were particular forms of government in the United States. Much of the nation's foreign policy was ad hoc and many of its domestic economic interventions were indirect. Yet government was always there.

The Particularities of Public Policy

The third area where there has been a proliferation of work has been policy history. During the past ten years, historians have responded to the vacuum in scholarship on this subject by writing on numerous areas of public policy, ranging from public works to family planning. These historians have traced policy history by using the chronology of public policy—agenda setting, legislation, and implementation—rather than by focusing on presidential administrations or even familiar eras in American politics. Framing their narrative around public policy has also allowed scholars to bring in a broad range of actors when writing about politics—thus responding to some of the criticism from the social and cultural historians—ranging from citizens who are beneficiaries of programs to the politicians that pass them.

One of the biggest differences between most research in political science, including the field of APD, and the new political history is that APD scholars search for singular theoretical models that can best explain the trajectory of policy in different domains. As Katznelson wrote:

> APD scholars produce model-like stories that shadow actual history at a higher level of abstraction and with more portable goals than can be found in most writing by historians. These deliberately simplified accounts that characterize actors, designate situations, and portray mechanisms linking agents to structures in ways that often privilege categories and variables over people and places with proper names offer suggestive helpmates to historians who are more enclosed in the peculiarities and exclusivities of their distinct periods and locations. Such

> intentionally lean representations selectively portray the attributes of actors . . . and structures . . . in order to specify the configuration of mechanisms that shape both these actors and structures and define the terms of their interconnection. (2003, p. 386)

In short, APD is not doing history for its own sake. Practitioners want models that are transportable. One of the most popular arguments in APD work is that the structure of political institutions has an enormous effect on the kinds of policies we produce. Carpenter (2001) relies on network analysis to explain how agency leaders are able to achieve autonomy from Congress, while Schickler (2001) focuses on the impact of institutional layering in American political development. Although their studies do revolve around specific areas of politics, the claims are meant to offer a means to understand developmental patterns throughout U.S. politics (Schickler, 2001). Pierson (2004) offers one of the most sophisticated analytic arguments about why and how a temporal approach to studying politics is relevant to social scientists.

In contrast, historians shy away from moving beyond their own particular areas of inquiry. The work of the new political history does make generalizations, but usually the scholarship offers institutional or cultural explanations as to why particular areas of policy turned out the way they did. There is an essential comfort with messiness in these books and articles, which acknowledge that there are multiple causal forces at work. Many historians refrain from arguing that the explanation in their story can provide an understanding of the evolution of other kinds of public policy beyond the one being studied.

The causal explanations in the new political history, when dealing with policy history, have thus varied greatly. For example, Milazzo (2006) traces the history of water control policy. Challenging the argument that the environmental movement was primarily responsible for the emergence of this policy, Milazzo explores how pork-barrel politics and a discourse about systems analysis unexpectedly gave rise to policy. Milazzo writes, "Advocates of economic development, missile system designers, and dam-building bureaucrats may not have represented the typical audience at an Earth Day rally . . . In the course of pursuing their own agendas within well-established organizational channels, these ubiquitous actors in the nation's political life took an active interest in water pollution and proceeded to shape how policymakers devised solutions to the problem" (2006, p. 5).

Jacobs (2005) and Klein (2003) place greater weight on political economy when dealing with welfare and fiscal policy. Jacobs argues that policies geared toward boosting consumer demand offered a way for the New Deal coalition to unite working- and middle-class voters between the Progressive Era and the 1970s. "For nearly sixty years," Jacobs writes, "from World War I through the Nixon administration, the question of how much things cost fueled American liberalism. The driving desire to secure mass purchasing power put in place a set of institutions and public policies to promote high wages and low prices"

(Jacobs, 2005, p. 262). Klein found that the power of corporate management within capitalism inscribed inequality into the divided welfare state from its inception (where public policy subsidized benefits such as healthcare that were delivered through collective bargaining rather than directly through the state), since workers were always at a disadvantage in shaping programs like private pensions (Klein, 2003).

In a more recent book, Hamilton (2008) breaks new ground by claiming that technological change—namely, the spread of refrigerated trucking—allowed low-cost consumer goods that undermined the rationale behind New Deal policies. "The most mundane of technologies—highways, refrigerated trailers, and diesel engines, none of which were particularly revolutionary in and of themselves—allowed agribusinesses to materially undermine the New Deal-era political integration of state power, organized labor, and mass consumption within the food economy," writes Hamilton (2008, p. 5). In her research on women who worked outside the home between the 1870s and 1990s, Boris (1994) explored how gender shaped certain areas of work regulation. Smith's (2006) account of the history of public works spending and economic development in the 1930s explored multiple factors behind the development of these policies, including the agendas of administrators, electoral and party-building interests, and the role of social movements in pressuring the president.

This third aspect of the new political history complements recent calls by Hacker and Pierson (2009) to bring policy back into the field of American politics. Through debates about common subject matter and archival documents from these very different perspectives, each side will be able to strengthen and define its respective analytic approach.

Where Are Historians Going from Here?

As a result of the new political history, the past few years have generated an exciting body of scholarship that is beginning to produce new narratives about the political past from the founding through the contemporary period. But the research has only begun.

There are many issues in great need of further exploration, and it is possible to see early signs of new directions. One of the most important topics that must be explored is the history of political economy, a subject that has been allowed to languish for too many decades. With the exceptions of work by a few scholars, such as Jacobs, Klein, Hamilton, and Phillips-Fein, most of the work on political history has focused on questions of welfare, gender, and race. Scholars must turn back to traditional concerns about the relationships between business, labor, and government and their roles in shaping public policy and government institutions. This offers historians a wonderful opportunity to connect with political scientists, not only in APD but also in other subfields, such as political economy.

There has also been insufficient attention to the history of liberalism after the 1960s. Ironically, the voluminous literature on the rise of the right has resulted in downplaying the trajectory of liberalism. The assumption has been that after the famous Democratic Convention of 1968, liberalism imploded and became an insignificant political force.

Yet some scholars are questioning this narrative (Zelizer, 2010). For instance, Tuck (2008) argues that civil rights activism in the cities proliferated after the 1970s, focusing on new concerns such as prison reform and urban electoral politics. Davies (2007) shows that in areas such as federal education, policies solidified their bureaucratic and interest-group base of power in the 1970s. Conservatives willingly or grudgingly came to accept the permanence of these programs and incorporated them into their agenda, giving rise to big-government conservatism. He writes that "the case of education politics suggests the difficulty of asserting that these were decades of triumph for the anti-government right. The limits to its success are illustrated by the ease with which supporters of federal aid, including many conservatives, rebuffed the intended Reagan Revolution in education during the early 1980s" (Davies, 2007, pp. 4–5). Jacobs's new work is examining how, when dealing with energy policy, conservatives in the 1970s ended up expanding a government that they had hoped to curtail (Jacobs, 2008). My book on national security stresses the enormous political obstacles that Ronald Reagan faced in the early 1980s as he promoted a hawkish national security agenda and found that the liberal political forces and institutional legacies of the 1960s remained extraordinarily powerful in constraining presidents (Zelizer, 2010).

The interest in the continued importance of liberal politics is related to another area of growing scholarship: what happened after conservatives rose to power and found themselves in positions of governance (Jacobs and Zelizer, 2010; Critchlow, 2007). There is a new work in progress about the challenges that conservatives faced after they had come to power in the White House and on Capitol Hill. This scholarship is examining the tensions that existed between the rhetoric of conservatives about cutting government and waging war and realities of governing over a sizable and entrenched administrative state. The work is also looking at the challenges posed by deep divisions within the conservative movement once the right lost Democrats as a focus of their attack. Rather than writing about a history of conservatism replacing liberalism, new research will examine the two as political ideologies and political forces that coexisted after the 1970s and were defined in relation to each other.

Political scientists who are interested in institutional persistence as well as social-movement politics will find this scholarship to be of considerable interest, as historians are tackling very similar issues to those with which they are engaged.

The good news is that the scholarship has just begun. But it will be important that historians, along with political scientists, continue to take into account the work of their fellow disciplines, paying close attention to how research findings across the disciplinary borders challenge prevailing assumptions and open up fruitful discussions about the different methodological approaches being used to understand our institutions and policies.

References

Appleby, J. 1984. *Capitalism and a New Social Order: The Republican Vision of the 1790s*. New York: New York University Press.

Bailyn, B. 1967. *The Ideological Origins of the American Revolution*. Cambridge, MA: Belknap Press of Harvard University Press.

Balogh, B. 2009. *A Government Out of Sight: The Mystery of National Authority in Nineteenth-Century America*. New York: Cambridge University Press.

Bartels, L. 2008. *Unequal Democracy: The Political Economy of the New Gilded Age*. Princeton, NJ: Princeton University Press.

Boris, E. 1994. *Home to Work: Motherhood and the Politics of Industrial Homework in the United States*. New York: Cambridge University Press.

Boyer, P. 2008. The evangelical resurgence in 1970s American Protestantism. In *Rightward Bound: Making America Conservative in the 1970s*, eds. B. J. Schulman and J. E. Zelizer, pp. 29–51. Cambridge, MA: Harvard University Press.

Brinkley, A. 1994. The problem of American conservatism. *American Historical Review* 99: 409–29.

Carpenter, D. P. 2001. *The Forging of Bureaucratic Autonomy: Reputations, Networks, and Policy Innovation in Executive Agencies, 1862–1928*. Princeton, NJ: Princeton University Press.

Cohen, L. 1991. *Making a New Deal: Industrial Workers in Chicago, 1919–1939*. New York: Cambridge University Press.

Crespino, J. 2009. *In Search of Another Country: Mississippi and the Conservative Counterrevolution*. Princeton, NJ: Princeton University Press.

Critchlow, D. T. 2007. *The Conservative Ascendancy: How the GOP Right Made Political History*. Cambridge, MA: Harvard University Press.

Davies, G. 2007. *See Government Grow: Education Politics from Johnson to Reagan*. Lawrence: University Press of Kansas.

Galambos, L. 1970. The emerging organization synthesis in modern American history. *Business History Review* 44(3): 279–90.

———. 1983. Technology, political economy, and professionalization. *Business History Review* 57: 471–93.

Gordon, L. 1994. *Pitied But Not Entitled: Single Mothers and the History of Social Welfare*. New York: Free Press.

Graetz, M., and Shapiro, I. 2006. *Death by a Thousand Cuts: The Fight Over Taxing Inherited Wealth*. Princeton, NJ: Princeton University Press.

Graham, H. D. 1993. The stunted career of policy history: a critique and an agenda. *Public Historian* 15: 15–37.

Hacker, J., and Pierson P. 2009. *The theoretical benefits of policy focused analysis*. Presented at Annual Meeting of American Political Science Association, Toronto.

Hamilton, S. 2008. *Trucking Country: The Road to America's Wal-Mart Economy*. Princeton, NJ: Princeton University Press.

Hays, S. P. 1957. *The Response to Industrialism, 1885–1914*. Chicago: University of Chicago Press.

Herring, G. 2008. *From Colony to Superpower: U.S. Foreign Relations Since 1776*. New York: Oxford University Press.

Howard, C. 1997. *The Hidden Welfare State: Tax Expenditures and Social Policy in the United States*. Princeton, NJ: Princeton University Press.

Jacobs, M. 2005. *Pocketbook Politics: Economic Citizenship in Twentieth-Century America*. Princeton, NJ: Princeton University Press.

———. 2008. The conservative struggle in the energy crisis. In *Rightward Bound: Making America Conservative in the 1970s*, eds. Bruce J. Schulman and Julian E. Zelizer, pp. 193–209. Cambridge, MA: Harvard University Press.

Jacobs, M., and Zelizer, J. 2003. Introduction in *The Democratic Experiment: New Directions in American Political History*, pp. 1–19. Princeton, NJ: Princeton University Press.

———. 2010. *The Reagan Revolution*. Boston: Bedford Books.

John, Richard. 1995. *Spreading the News. The American Postal System from Franklin to Morse*. Cambridge, MA: Harvard University Press.

———. 2006. *Ruling Passions: Political Economy in Nineteenth-Century America*. University Park: Pennsylvania State University Press.

Katz, M. 1968. *The Irony of Early School Reform: Educational Innovation in Mid-Nineteenth Century America*. Cambridge, MA: Harvard University Press.

Katznelson, I. 2003. The possibilities of analytic political history. In *The Democratic Experiment: New Directions in American Political History*, ed. M. Jacobs and J. Zelizer, pp. 350–80. Princeton, NJ. Princeton University Press.

———. 2005. *When Affirmative Action Was White: An Untold History of Racial Inequality in Twentieth Century America*. New York: Norton.

Keller, M. 1977. *Affairs of State: Public Life in Late-Nineteenth Century America*. Cambridge, MA: Harvard University Press.

Kessler-Harris, A. 2001. *In Pursuit of Equity: Women, Men, and the Quest for Economic Citizenship in Twentieth Century America*. New York: Oxford University Press.

Klein, J. 2003. *For All These Rights: Business, Labor and the Shaping of America's Public-Private Welfare State*. Princeton, NJ: Princeton University Press.

Kleppner, P. 1970. *The Cross of Culture: A Social Analysis of Midwestern Politics, 1850–1900*. New York: Free Press.

Kloppenberg, J. T. 1987. The virtues of liberalism: Christianity, Republicanism, and ethics in early American political discourse. *Journal of American History* 74: 19–33.

Kruse, K. M. 2005. *White Flight: Atlanta and the Making of Modern Conservatism*. Princeton, NJ: Princeton University Press.

Lassiter, M. D. 2006. *The Silent Majority: Suburban Politics in the Sunbelt South*. Princeton, NJ: Princeton University Press.

Leff, M. 1995. Revisioning U.S. political history. *American Historical Review* 100: 829–53.

Leuchtenburg, W. E. 1986. The pertinence of political history: reflections on the significance of the state in America. *Journal of American History* 73: 585–600.

McCarty, N., Poole, K.T., and Rosenthal, H. 2006. *Polarized America: The Dance of Ideology and Unequal Riches*. Cambridge, MA: MIT Press.

McGirr, L. 2001. *Suburban Warriors: The Origins of the New American Right*. Princeton, NJ: Princeton University Press.

Milazzo, P. C. 2006. *Unlikely Environmentalists: Congress and Clean Water, 1945–1972.* Lawrence: University Press of Kansas.

Montgomery, D. 1987. *The Fall of the House of Labor: The Workplace, the State, and American Labor Activism, 1865–1925.* New York: Cambridge University Press.

Novak, W. J. 1996. *The People's Welfare: Law and Regulation in Nineteenth-Century America.* Chapel Hill: University of North Carolina Press.

O'Connor, A. 2008. Financing the counterrevolution. In *Rightward Bound: Making America Conservative in the 1970s*, eds. B. J. Schulman and J. E. Zelizer, pp. 148–68. Cambridge, MA: Harvard University Press.

Perlstein, R. 2001. *Before the Storm: Barry Goldwater and the Unmaking of the American Consensus.* New York: Hill & Wang.

Phillips-Fein, K. 2009. *Invisible Hands: The Making of the Conservative Movement From the New Deal to Reagan.* New York: Norton.

Pierson, P. 2004. *Politics in Time: History, Institutions, and Social Analysis.* Princeton, NJ: Princeton University Press.

Pocock, J.G.A. 1975. *The Machiavellian Moment: Florentine Political Thought and the Atlantic Republican Tradition.* Princeton, NJ: Princeton University Press.

Rauchway, E. 2006. *Blessed Among Nations: How the World Made America.* New York: Hill & Wang.

Schickler, E. 2001. *Disjointed Pluralism: Institutional Innovation and the Development of the U.S. Congress.* Princeton, NJ: Princeton University Press.

Shafer, B., and Johnston, R. 2006. *The End of Southern Exceptionalism: Class, Race and Partisan Change in the Postwar South.* Cambridge, MA: Harvard University Press.

Silbey, J. H. 1999. The state of American political history at the millennium: the nineteenth century as a test case. *Journal of Policy History* 11:1–30.

Silbey, J. H., Bogue, A. G., and Flanigan, W. H., eds. 1978. *The History of American Political Behavior.* Princeton NJ: Princeton University Press.

Skowronek, S. 1982. *Building a New American State: The Expansion of National Administrative Capacities 1877–1920.* Cambridge: Cambridge University Press.

Smith, J. S. 2006. *Building New Deal Liberalism: The Political Economy of Public Works, 1933–1956.* New York: Cambridge University Press.

Tuck, S. 2008. "We are taking up where the movement of the 1960s left off": the proliferation and power of African American protest during the 1970s. *Journal of Contemporary History* 43 (2008): 637–54.

Wiebe, R. 1967. *The Search for Order, 1877–1920.* New York: Hill & Wang.

Wood, G. S. 1969. *The Creation of the American Republic, 1776–1787.* Chapel Hill: University of North Carolina Press.

Zelizer, J. E. 2000. Clio's lost tribe: public policy history since 1978. *Journal of Policy History* 12: 369–94.

———. 2004. Political history and political science: together again? *Journal of Policy History* 16: 126–36.

———. 2010. *Arsenal of Democracy: The Politics of National Security—From World War II to the War on Terrorism.* New York: Basic Books.

———. 2010. Rethinking the history of American conservatism. *Reviews in American History* 38: 367–92.

PART II

Paying for Government: Taxes, Money, and Fiscal Restraint

Paying for government has been one of the biggest challenges facing elected officials on all sides of the political spectrum. While scholars have focused on a number of obstacles to expanding government in the United States, such as the endurance of localism and the ways in which racial tension undermined efforts to strengthen federal power, fewer historians have written about a more basic challenge that has confronted every president and Congress: raising sufficient revenue to pay for services.

The following essays emphasize the primacy of fiscal concerns in American political history. Matters of taxation have been treated as symbols for broader concerns or as a technical backdrop to the real action. In contrast, the following essays place fiscal policy at the center of governance, revealing how elected officials and policymakers have been profoundly impacted by fiscal imperatives of state-building.

In "The Uneasy Relationship" and "Where Is the Money Coming From?" I show how politicians have struggled to find ways to work around the limitations imposed by the urgency of raising revenue. The long-standing resistance toward paying taxes has been a perennial challenge for policymakers who wanted to expand the scale and scope of government.

Importantly, I have not argued that fiscal restraints always prohibit policy innovation from taking place. Indeed, from the New Deal to the Great Society, as examined in "The Forgotten Legacy of the New Deal" and "Paying for Medicare," I have paid close attention to the strategies through which political entrepreneurs worked around these obstacles and were able to sometimes use federal tax policy—such as in the case of Social Security and Medicare—to build long-term support for programs.

The section cumulatively argues that fiscal policy and political economy must be at the very center of our studies of political history, a perennial challenge that has guided political debate since the founding of the Republic.

SIX

The Uneasy Relationship: Democracy, Taxation, and State-Building Since the New Deal

Most politicians sense that Americans hate taxes.* We are a nation with a long tradition of tax revolts. Yet, despite an abundance of historical studies about state-building in the twentieth century, few have confronted the reality of tax resistance and fiscal constraint. Even research on American anti-statism has emphasized the intellectual history of liberalism and republicanism rather than opposition to federal taxes, the most concrete manifestation of anti-statism. Hostility toward federal taxation has remained extremely strong in all income brackets, ranging from blue-collar workers who were central beneficiaries of New Deal programs to elite financial investors. Resistance to local taxation has ebbed and flowed to a greater extent, since the benefits of taxation have been more apparent to constituents; those taxes have also conformed to the localist ethos.[1]

As a result of tax resistance, and the perception among policymakers that tax resistance is and was strong, state-builders have been handcuffed by fiscal constraint. The Founding Fathers virtually guaranteed that the task of modern state-building would be extremely difficult by locating the power to levy federal taxes in the House of Representatives, where it would be most susceptible to democratic pressure. Revealingly, much of the Progressive Era state growth occurred before the nation had a mass federal income tax in place; tariffs were the principal source of federal revenue, and the federal income tax touched only a small portion of the population after it became permanent in 1913.[2] The next major expansion of the federal government, the New Deal, preceded the creation of a mass income tax. Therefore, the problem of revenue extraction loomed large throughout the twentieth century. In the nineteenth century, federal fiscal capacity was not as important, since the principal form of government intervention revolved around less costly court decisions as well as state

* This essay originally appeared in *The Democratic Experiment: New Directions in American Political History*, eds. Meg Jacobs, William Novak, and Julian E. Zelizer (Princeton, NJ: Princeton University Press, 2003).

and local government.[3] What made fiscal restraint so central after 1933 was the persistence of strong anti-tax sentiment among most segments of society in an era when the federal government achieved more of a presence in society than ever before. Citizens came to expect a large number of federal government services and resisted retrenchment after the Great Depression.[4] Through interest groups—which, as Brian Balogh shows, became the intermediary institution through which most citizens conveyed their demands outside the ballot box—Americans pressured Congress to provide more and more services.[5] The irony was that some of the strongest opposition to federal taxes came from populations who were most dependent on government.[6] Yet this irony was of more interest to academic scholars than politicians, who still needed to extract money for programs from a population that was not comfortable with its own dependencies. The awkward juxtaposition of an antipathy toward taxes with stronger demands for federal services resulted in a deficit-based state. As much as deficits were a product of Keynesian macroeconomic policy, they were likewise a symptom of a democratic dilemma: Americans wanted more federal benefits but did not want to pay for them.

One reason that historians have failed to incorporate popular resentment of taxation into their meta-narratives is because it contradicts a basic tenet of postwar historiography, namely, the harmony between state-building and democracy. In the following pages, I make two arguments. The first is that a fundamental tension has existed between state-building and national resistance to federal taxation. In this respect, democracy has sometimes been at odds with state-building as it comes into conflict with strong anti-tax sentiment. Given that the United States is a democracy, elected officials have had considerable trouble avoiding the opposition to taxes that exists across economic classes. To highlight this tension in the post–New Deal period, this essay examines how politicians have operated under fiscal restraint since the 1930s. My second argument, however, is that fiscal restraint has not been an insurmountable barrier. This is evident with the emergence of the mass income tax and social-insurance tax systems as well as the substantial state presence achieved in all areas of life, ranging from welfare to highway construction.

The construction and maintenance of a viable federal tax system remains an underappreciated development in twentieth-century political history. State-builders were able to overcome the challenges of anti-tax sentiment and fiscal restraint by implementing four principal strategies: building democratic support for taxation in times of war; using earmarked taxes and trust funds; relying on automatic revenue generated by economic growth; and accepting federal deficits. One strategy that policymakers used to raise taxes was to mobilize support to expand the tax system during national crises. Even when there was not a direct military conflict, politicians relied on military rhetoric to overcome anti-statism, as is evident with President Lyndon Johnson's "War" on Poverty.[7] The most striking moment came during World War II, when policymakers sold the mass income tax through a national public relations campaign that promoted taxpaying as the patriotic duty of citizens who were not fighting abroad. Another method involved trust funds and earmarked taxes. These devices were used to create the appearance that taxes would be linked to specific benefits and that programs being funded would be protected from wasteful spending. The next strategy for obtaining funds was to maintain a tax system that raised higher revenues due to economic growth. Between 1945 and 1973, government revenue increased rapidly as a result of economic growth rather than legislated tax increases. Finally, state-builders were forced to accept temporary deficits, which was difficult in a nation that continued to revere balanced budgets.[8] While scholars have considered budgetary deficits as a type of conscious economic policy promoted by Keynesians or supply-siders, it must be recognized that deficits offered the only viable solution for political actors who wanted to build a state with limited federal revenue. What is most notable about the conservative revolution of the 1980s is not just that conservatives mobilized support around tax resistance, but that the fiscal infrastructure did not disintegrate amidst this onslaught. The durability of the fiscal system that state-builders put into place, in response to popular resistance to taxation, continued the pattern in American political history in which federal politicians created a state that did not necessarily resemble European models but was nonetheless effective and powerful on its own terms.[9]

My interpretation makes four historiographical claims. First, the challenge of raising revenue must be put at the forefront of the new political history. While fiscal restraint has been one of the most powerful forces in national politics, historians have downplayed its importance among the pressures facing politicians. Second, my interpretation suggests that the history of taxation offers insights into the areas in which public policy, institutional development, and political culture intersected. Third, I raise questions about prevailing interpretations of American political history. My interpretation is critical of historians who have usually linked democratic politics to state-building while minimizing the persistent tensions that just as often existed between them. It simultaneously challenges New Left and race-centered scholars who exclusively blame corporate interests or conservative southern congressmen for subverting state-building while ignoring the role of a mass electorate that detested taxes. Finally, I argue that historians must pay closer attention to what has been achieved in American political history rather than alternatives that were rejected. Too often, political history has focused on the failures of state-building rather than on what was actually accomplished (consider, for example, the extensive literature on our lack of national health insurance, compared with the rather limited work on Medicare and Medicaid). The operating assumption has been that politicians stifled democratic pressure from the left, rather than that they faced equivalent, if not greater, pressure from the right.[10] When scholars take into account the formidable obstacles that state-builders faced, the importance of understanding American state-building on its own terms rather than only comparing it with European systems becomes evident.

Historians, Democracy, and the State

U.S. historians have generally postulated a harmonious relationship between democracy and state-building in the twentieth century. During the 1950s and 1960s, the leading interpretation of political history was termed the liberal synthesis. The scholars who developed this synthesis, including Arthur Schlesinger Jr. and William Leuchtenburg, argued that the expansion of the state corresponded with growing democratic demands.[11] Adopting a progressive teleology that pitted "selfish" economic interests against the virtuous "people," they described a series of liberal presidents (including Republican Dwight Eisenhower) who built federal programs as a countervailing force against big business. The New Deal, in this analysis, reflected the triumph of democratic politics. As Leuchtenburg wrote, "Roosevelt and his aides fashioned a government which consciously sought to make the industrial system more humane and to protect workers and their families from exploitation."[12]

In the 1960s, the liberal scholars were challenged by the "corporate liberal" synthesis.[13] Born of the domestic conflicts of the era, this synthesis claimed that the federal government had been expanded to protect the modern corporation, not to tame it. Corporate liberal scholars did not deny that most citizens wanted an expansive domestic state but instead argued that the institutions that emerged served the interests of big business. The state, in this view, aimed to quell destructive competition and social unrest. Taking populists and progressive labor unions as representatives of the democratic impulse, historian Gabriel Kolko wrote that business leaders concluded "the best way to thwart change was to channelize it."[14] These historians implied that popular state-building alternatives were rejected to fulfill the interests of corporate capitalism. Even social historians in the 1980s, whose outlook differed from that of this earlier generation of scholars, were primarily interested in tracing social support of the New Deal rather than the factors behind persistent citizen opposition.[15] Their focus reflected a professional lack of interest in the history of conservatism, which became a source of serious intellectual concern only in the 1990s.[16]

There was a less conspiratorial variant of the corporate liberal interpretation, called the "organizational synthesis," whose practitioners focused on the interdependence of corporations, the federal government, and the new professional class that emerged with the industrial economy. The organizational synthesis posited that at the turn of the century large-scale national institutions eclipsed the nineteenth-century society of "island communities."[17] This school abandoned the progressive teleology of liberal historians, examining instead how the nation's political and economic systems achieved equilibrium.[18] In depicting the inevitable growth of large-scale institutions, organizational historians paid minimal attention to the resistance that state-builders encountered, such as fiscal constraint or popular anxiety with large-scale institutions.[19] When these historians looked at failure, they focused on institutional weaknesses or conflicting visions of state-building that had hampered policy.

The most recent incarnation of political history has been developed by historical social scientists. These scholars have been extremely interested in why the development of the American state lagged behind those of Europe.[20] Everyone and everything has been suspect for limiting state growth, except for the majoritarian interests of voters themselves. In many versions of this scholarship, the power of southern Democrats has been featured as the major obstacle to expansive government, as they fought against state intervention to protect regional racist institutions.[21] Others working in this vein have blamed perceptions that politicians held about gender roles in economic life.[22] America's underdeveloped bureaucracy and federalism have also been prominent culprits. Still others have highlighted "political discourses" that restricted the scope of policy.[23] The common assumption is that without these obstacles, a sizable majority of citizens would have supported a larger state. Those who have acknowledged voter resistance to the federal government, particularly that of blue-collar workers who at one time championed the New Deal, have tended to present this opposition as centering on racial concerns rather than a broader distrust of government.[24] While all of this work points to important sources of resistance to government expansion, the work tends to downplay questions of taxation and broad-based anti-statism that have continually shaped American's political culture.[25]

Nonetheless, there are alternative schools that have moved historians closer to the problem of anti-statism. This essay builds on the work of a handful of scholars who have identified anti-statism as a central problem in American state-building.[26] One group of scholars has focused on political culture.[27] Emanating from the field of intellectual history, this approach has tended to focus on the abstract realm of Lockean individualism. These scholars argue that shared national values caused Americans to oppose centralized political power. However, this work has been vulnerable to attack; other scholars have pointed to shared national values that actually supported government. By not grappling with resistance to taxation—the most concrete manifestation of anti-statism—many of the scholars who have focused on anti-statism have often omitted the most striking evidence that supports their claims. Nonetheless, their works have played a pivotal role in channeling research into a new direction.[28] Another important body of research has come from neoconservatives who have approached the state more skeptically by highlighting grassroots resistance to government expansion.[29] From a different perspective, liberal scholars have shown how white voters were often extremely hostile to federal government programs as a result of racial tension.[30] Their research has raised important questions by placing anti-statism at the center, rather than periphery, of its analysis.

Recently, there has been renewed interest in the history of taxation. While most political historians have treated taxation as a technical matter that is not central to national politics, over the past few years a number of scholars have recognized the importance of taxation to political history.[31] In doing so, they have discovered the intense struggle that was required to construct the nation's existing, albeit limited, income tax system and to contain the proliferation of tax loopholes.[32]

Finally, some political scientists and economists have contributed pertinent research by examining business, professional, and investor opposition to the state.[33] Among most business leaders, David Vogel wrote, "a sense of suspicion toward the state has managed to survive the most impressive and decisive political triumphs."[34] Although these scholars have modified their argument to account for corporate liberalism, their work has explored how most capitalist leaders fought to keep taxes low. These scholars have discussed how businessmen limited taxation, partially because they encountered little public opposition in their efforts to do so. Even businessmen who supported a role for the federal government tended to champion Keynesian tax reductions.[35]

This historiographic analysis reveals that until recently political historians have tended to downplay the strong strain of anti-tax sentiment that has been an important component of the nation's political culture, and they have downplayed as well the problem of fiscal restraint. Most interpretations have posited that democracy and state-building have usually worked in tandem while overlooking public opposition to taxes that was given a strong voice through the democratic process. To undermine this premise would raise troubling questions for the teleology of these narratives. This essay does not claim democracy is *always* at odds with state expansion. Indeed, many federal programs in the twentieth century had strong grassroots support, without which they most likely would never have been enacted.[36]

Yet democratic pressure has also imposed a brake on government expansion. The most powerful evidence of this strand of democratic pressure has been the fact that most federal politicians have feared supporting direct and visible tax increases. State-builders have rarely identified a single source of tax opposition; the sentiment was blamed on business, the middle class, blue-collar workers, homeowners, wealthy families, and others. While different politicians targeted different coalitions, no social group escaped blame. This made it difficult to mobilize countercoalitions in favor of tax hikes.

Therefore, federal politicians of all parties, regions, and ideologies have been forced to grapple with the question, Where is the money coming from? But what has been obvious to politicians remains obscure in the historical literature. As a result, one of the largest obstacles that politicians have faced is a ghost in many scholarly accounts of state-building. Since the 1950s, historians have pointed to many forces working against the growth of government, from racism to weak institutions. But they have not looked at democratic pressure from voters to maintain low rates of taxation.

State-Building with Empty Pockets

Since the 1930s, state-builders have had to grapple with the problem of fiscal constraint. The American electorate has never moved toward an agenda of high taxes and high spending. During the biggest economic crisis in the nation's history, the Great Depression, resentment toward federal taxation remained strong. At the local level, intense opposition to rising property taxation produced organized tax revolts in parts of the country. In those revolts, voters passed measures that limited local and state taxes as over one thousand taxpayer organizations were formed by 1932.[37] Even in moderate states, constituents continued to elect state government officials who were unsympathetic to many New Deal programs and progressive government in general, including higher income taxes.[38]

At an institutional level, the nation did not have a federal mass income tax in the 1930s. Less than 5 percent of the population encountered income tax returns in those years.[39] The Roosevelt administration never pushed to broaden the tax base to the size needed to fund the New Deal. Instead, the government relied on hidden regressive taxes (including alcohol and tobacco taxes, the Social Security tax, and the agricultural-processing tax) and one increase, albeit watered down, on corporations. But even the famous tax on corporation profits, the centerpiece of Roosevelt's notorious shift to the left, was "more bluff than bludgeon" that affected only a small number of elite capitalists.[40] Except for programs with earmarked taxes, Roosevelt relied heavily on state and local spending while rejecting proposals that required significant increases in the federal income tax. Even with a strong liberal majority in Congress, Roosevelt's 1936 budget rejected a general tax increase and did not include permanent spending for public assistance.[41] The most significant new tax was the Social Security tax in 1935, which remained small until 1950. This earmarked tax was promoted by the Social Security Board as a "premium."[42]

The New Deal tax agenda left the federal government with a limited and inflexible revenue source. Deficits of the 1930s were largely a result of the increased need for public spending, combined with limited revenue sources. While Roosevelt used Keynesian rhetoric to justify a deficit in 1938, this was not the driving force behind his policies. Rather, the deficit resulted from having to enact programs without sufficient revenue.[43] This was problematic for liberals since Roosevelt and congressional leaders remained committed to fiscal conservatism, which severely restricted how much federal officials were able to spend.[44] Although he did not balance a budget, Roosevelt continued to strive for that objective, promoting expenditure reduction as soon as the economy improved. Progressive ideology, moreover, sometimes worked against the imposition of federal taxation. During the 1930s, influential congressional liberals and the Roosevelt administration would actively oppose popular congressional proposals for a national sales tax on the grounds that it would be regressive (and that implementation would be impossible).[45]

It was not until World War II that the American state adopted a mass federal income tax. Policymakers mobilized during the war to expand the fiscal infrastructure of the state. Strikingly, even during the war, federal officials felt the need to market this idea to the wage-earning public. The government launched a public relations campaign to sell the idea of taxpaying to average citizens. The

Department of Treasury used all sorts of messages that told Americans it was patriotic to pay their taxes. To promote the tax, the Office of War Information placed ads in magazines such as *Ladies' Home Journal*, *House Beautiful*, and *True Detective*. The Treasury broadcast radio jingles by Danny Kaye and Irving Berlin and released Disney animations in which Donald Duck taught citizens why they should pay taxes.[46] The campaign worked, as the government successfully expanded the income tax base to include over 40 million wage earners and implemented withholding at the source.

The wartime experience revealed how new politics could reconfigure politics.[47] By the time the war ended, there was no strong pressure to eliminate the mass income tax altogether. Most conservatives accepted a permanent mass income tax, just as liberals had accepted the regressive system of the New Deal era as a permanent feature in American politics. A majority of citizens and politicians had developed new conceptions of what types of government intervention were legitimate and essential. The tax system would never return to its prewar condition. Tax reductions after the Korean War meant lowering rates within the existing, progressive income tax system rather than retrenching the entire code. This was a significant change in a nation where most citizens had not been subject to this federal income tax until World War II. Once the mass tax was in place and the Cold War required high revenue permanently, the assumption about what constituted minimum taxation changed.

Just as World War II tax policies reconfigured notions about what was legitimate for the federal government to ask of its citizens, social policy in this era expanded popular conceptions of entitlement. A larger number of citizens came to expect certain types of programs ranging from Social Security retirement payments to farm subsidies. The most famous of these interest groups was the American Farm Bureau Federation, which made it virtually impossible for politicians to cut farm subsidies without facing severe political risks, as the Eisenhower administration learned when it attempted to take on this challenge. When the influence of the Farm Bureau waned, it was replaced by organizations representing particular commodities.[48] Interest groups were also willing to protect any particular tax mechanisms that were attached to their program. The elderly, for instance, would mobilize through the American Association of Retired Persons (AARP) several decades after Congress had created Social Security. This organization was founded in 1958 as a small vehicle for insurance and turned into an interest group by the 1980s and 1990s that aggressively lobbied legislators in support of Social Security. Interest groups such as the AARP represented the voices of different segments of the population, as Herbert Hoover had discerned back in 1928, and they helped protect federal programs such as contributory social insurance from retrenchment. When politicians attempted to reform Social Security, they encountered fierce electoral resistance from working- and middle-class constituents.

Despite the rising number of interest groups that formed to protect federal programs, after World War II public opposition to current federal tax rates rose as well. Whereas only 15 percent of those polled by Gallup in February 1943 said federal income taxes were unfair, that figure jumped to 38 percent by February 1946 and kept rising steadily.[49] Congress moved to reduce income taxes within the new institutional framework. In 1948, Congress passed a sizable tax reduction. When President Truman vetoed the bill, claiming that it would lead to inflation and be fiscally irresponsible, Congress succeeded in overriding him. Although the mass tax system was needed to pay for the Korean War in the early 1950s, Congress continued its incremental expansion of loopholes for all income brackets to help ease the tax burden. The tax recodification of 1954, which legitimated the progressive rate structure in effect during the Korean War, provided a wide array of loopholes for all classes of citizens. After the recodification, an extremely large number of citizens had a vested interest in the loophole system of the federal tax code. As Aaron Wildavsky and Carolyn Webber concluded, "The truth is out: As Pogo might have put it, we—the broad middle and lower classes—have met the special interests, and 'they is us.'"[50] It was clear to most politicians by the 1950s that large federal tax increases, other than those involving earmarked taxes, were off the table. Indeed, the horrors of German fascism, discoveries about the brutalities of the Soviet Union, and the domestic politics of the Cold War all heightened anti-statist sentiment within the public, thereby placing federal programs and proposals at risk of being tagged as Communist.[51] This reality governed policy decisions.

Throughout the 1950s, public opinion data continued to show support for lower taxes. When polled, a majority of Americans said consistently that they felt their taxes were too high (even when the question was worded in different ways) and that they supported proposals for tax reductions. In 1947, Gallup polls found that 54 percent of those polled thought taxes were too high; that number peaked in 1952 when 71 percent of those polled felt that their taxes were too high. While this number would drop by 1961, it steadily climbed back up to 69 percent by 1969. Between 1943 and 1997, the proportion of Americans who said they were satisfied with federal income tax rates was never more than 3 percent.[52] Although there were obvious discrepancies between these opinion polls and the reality that most citizens accepted a sizable overall tax burden (local, state, federal) in practice, opinion polls sent clear signals that raising non-earmarked federal taxes could have high electoral costs. Importantly, polls did not identify any single component of society as being the source of this opposition.

Nevertheless, few Americans actually paid the statutory income tax rates. Congress institutionalized tax reduction through a generous system of loopholes. Through this system, called "tax expenditures" by some experts, tax reductions were automatically granted even if Congress did not take action. The tax code subsidized the growth of private welfare benefits that employers at private companies offered their workers. Through indirect spending, legislators found a short-term solution to American's chronic fiscal dilemma. By international standards, the United States distributed generous tax loopholes, exemptions, and deductions. Although top tax rates reached 94 percent by the late 1950s, the system never yielded more than 10.6 percent of the GNP.[53] A variety of loopholes were available to citizens and organizations during much of the twentieth century. Technical errors in the tax code and vague statutory language, for instance, enabled lawyers to hide their clients' income. Furthermore, Congress enacted specific provisions with the intent of providing tax relief to certain industries; the most famous of these was the depletion allowance through which the oil industry avoided its tax obligations. Additionally, credits, exemptions, and exceptions were designed to encourage categories of citizens and industries to invest money in special ways, ranging from providing health-care coverage for workers, to home ownership, to investment in new industrial machinery. Political scientist John Witte concluded: "Unless faced with a dire alternative, people favor lower rather than higher taxes, and politicians have accommodated them. Although favoring base-broadening tax reform in theory, when details are presented they strongly support existing tax reduction provisions and seem eager to expand the tax expenditure system to include new and increased benefits."[54]

Since most policymakers never abandoned the precepts of fiscal conservatism, believing that deficits were economically harmful and a sign of political corruption and instability,[55] there was a constant tension between limited federal revenue and increased demand for government services. The impact of a limited tax base was relevant not just to domestic welfare policies in the 1950s but also to the Cold War. If there was any area of policy that commanded widespread popular support, it was the fight against international communism. But even here, revenue concerns loomed large. When the Truman administration attempted to expand the national security state, the president had to settle for a more modest plan than he had initially hoped for, due to fiscal constraint.[56] Military planners unsuccessfully proposed that the military budget be increased by 100, to 300 percent. Aaron Friedberg found that if military planners had achieved their objectives, the United States would have dedicated 15 percent of its national output to defense in the 1960s rather than 10 percent.[57] When Congress established a civil defense program to protect citizens in case of a nuclear attack, the program relied heavily on state and local government as well as voluntarism, so that Congress had to allocate only limited funds for the program, almost 50 percent less than President Eisenhower requested between 1954 and 1958.[58] Fiscal restraint worked both ways. Eisenhower, for example, opposed tax cut proposals during his second term, realizing that the combination of the entrenched federal state with the existing tax structure curtailed policymakers' budget flexibility.[59] He sensed that if taxes were cut too much, it would be extremely difficult to raise them in the future. Given that international and domestic commitments were not likely to disappear, excessive tax cuts seemed imprudent since inadequate taxes would lead to higher deficits, which would hamper investment and growth.

In addition to wartime crises, state-builders relied on accounting devices and earmarked taxes in the 1950s. Americans proved willing to pay specific types of taxes if they were distinguished by trust funds or packaged as earmarked contributions. As a result, politicians linked taxes with specific benefits that the contributor would receive in the future and created the appearance that such funds were to be protected from irresponsible spending. After fifteen years of uncertainty, Congress decided in 1950 that contributory old age insurance, financed through the earmarked payroll tax, would be the centerpiece of social provision for the elderly rather than means-tested public assistance, which was funded through general revenue.[60] The strategy proved to be successful. Unlike corporate and income taxes, which steadily declined during the postwar period, Social Security taxes would continue to rise. In 1950, the combined Social Security tax rate was 3.0 percent; by 1990, the combined rate reached 15.3 percent.[61] During this same period, federal income taxes were cut more than twelve times. At the creation of Social Security, policymakers equated the promised benefits with private insurance. Under this rhetoric, the Social Security "tax" was really a "contribution" or "premium" which entitled taxpayers to receive a benefit during their retirement years. Even after politicians downplayed the insurance rhetoric, the Social Security tax proved durable as citizens continued to believe their money was paying for a contributory, non-welfare program.

The extensive use of earmarked taxes and trust funds in American budgeting has been a testament to the fact that policymakers have felt pressure to deal with fiscal restraint while crafting durable policy commitments. The fact that Social Security and Medicare—the nation's two largest domestic programs—have been financed through these devices reveals the persistence of both tax resistance and policymakers' success in devising strategies around that problem. Earmarked taxes provided policymakers the latitude to build viable programs. By the 1990s, almost 40 percent of federal revenues were committed to trust funds, mainly for the Social Security and Medicare programs, but also for domestic programs such as highway construction, airport development, nature conservation, and the environmental Superfund.[62] In the end, the programs that relied on dedicated revenue sources have proved to be much more resistant against political retrenchment than those that relied on general revenue.

Another strategy through which state-builders were able to raise taxes in peacetime was automatic revenue. The income tax system was not indexed for inflation. As a result, an important method of tax collection by the 1950s and 1960s was the automatic increase in revenue generated by economic growth, not federal tax hikes. In the first two decades after World War II, economic growth pushed taxpayers into higher income brackets so that the federal government received increased levels of revenue. Because low inflation sustained the value of their dollars as incomes rose, citizens seemed tolerant of moving up to higher brackets. This phenomenon also benefited Social Security, as Congress found itself with extra revenue to distribute as cash benefits without raising taxes. Economic growth, together with earmarked taxes, made revenue-raising possible despite an electorate that fiercely protected its money.

The burst of state-building in the 1960s, like those of the New Deal and World War II, also took place in a context of limited fiscal capacity. In economic policy, liberals embraced tax reduction as an effective means of helping wage-earners and stimulating the economy, a stark alternative to increasing defense and welfare spending.[63] Congress never discussed increasing taxes dramatically when the new programs were being planned. From the start of the decade, President Kennedy and then Johnson set the tone of the policy agenda in 1963 and 1964 with the campaign for and passage of a $10 billion, across-the-board tax cut. The reduction was sold on the grounds that it would stimulate the economy and minimize "fiscal drag." Johnson explained that through the tax cut "the federal government will not have to do for the economy what the economy should do for itself."[64] According to the president's close advisor on domestic issues, Joseph Califano, "Johnson's extravagant rhetoric announcing new programs belied the modest funds he requested to begin them. Conservative members of Congress distrusted him because they believed that he was hiding his real intentions just to get a foot in the door. The Great Society's liberal advocates were frustrated because he wasn't asking for enough to smash the door open. And Congress was providing even less."[65] The guiding assumption of the period was that increased revenue would be produced automatically from economic growth. As a result of tax cuts and incentives passed in the 1960s, corporate taxes declined as well. After Congress passed a major investment credit to stimulate corporate investment in 1962, the top corporate tax rate declined from 70 percent in 1964 to 36 percent in 1986.[66] Tax breaks continued to erode the nation's tax base. By 1967, for example, the federal government spent almost $2.3 million in tax breaks for the elderly through provisions that included tax exemption, a tax credit for retirement income, and the exclusion of Social Security benefits from income taxation. Congress reported that in 1967 federal tax breaks cost $37 billion (21 percent of federal expenditures).[67]

The commitment to low taxes constrained state-building efforts in the 1960s, both in defense and domestic programs. Fiscal pressure remained evident in the 1960s when President Kennedy abandoned his goal of building a national network of underground bomb shelters because of insufficient revenue, and he angered defense advisors when he cut spending requests for the armed forces by $13 billion.[68] From the start, the War on Poverty received meager appropriations. President Johnson balanced his desire to help the poor with his perception that the federal budget needed to remain below $100 billion and that taxes could not be raised.[69] "The War on Poverty," Michael Brown explained, was "mortgaged to the tax cut." Johnson advisors Charles Schultze and Walter Heller embraced a targeted poverty program, abandoning proposals for liberalized cash transfers, job training, and social services, largely because of budgetary constraints.[70] The results of this budgetary decision were clear. The War on Poverty received $500 million, while Medicare received $6.5 million upon its creation. The largest social program, Medicare, was primarily paid for with increased Social Security taxes, not revenue derived from income taxes. Unlike other national healthcare programs that had previously been proposed in the United States, Medicare passed by substantial margins in 1965 in large part because proponents sold the program within the Social Security system and tied benefits to an earmarked payroll tax.[71] Based on polls, Medicare proponents believed from the start of their campaign that, unlike income taxes, citizens would be willing to accept higher Social Security taxes to pay for healthcare for the elderly.[72] But in other areas, those in charge of creating the War on Poverty never had the type of financial resources that they felt were necessary to succeed. Johnson embraced a course that reallocated existing federal funds rather than seeking new revenue. He explained his outlook when he warned his administration: "The Great Society will require substantial investment. This means: that as a nation we cannot afford to waste a single dollar of our resources on outmoded programs . . . [and] that as a government we must get the most out of every dollar of scarce budget resources, reforming old programs and using the savings for the new programs of the Great Society."[73] Johnson repeatedly frustrated his closest advisors by rejecting requests for more spending.

When the Vietnam War consumed federal funding, the War on Poverty suffered. Between 1966 and 1968, Johnson and his congressional allies fought for a $10 billion tax surcharge to finance the war in Vietnam while maintaining the War on Poverty. His administration also justified the measure as anti-inflationary. But, sticking to the policy agenda of the early 1960s, Congress forced the administration to accept steep spending cuts of more than $6 billion.[74] The president was told by the tax-writing committees that he could have either guns *or* butter, but he could not have both. When Johnson sacrificed the War on Poverty on the altar of Vietnam, he learned quickly about the impact of fiscal restraint on the possibilities of state-building. "That bitch of a war," Johnson lamented, "killed the lady I really loved—the Great Society."[75] Even though social welfare spending continued to rise in the next decade, the enthusiasm for expanding social programs had been quelled. "What was left," concludes the historian Robert Collins, "was not the powerful reform surge of mid-decade but only its inertia."[76]

By the 1960s, blue-collar workers—an integral part of the New Deal coalition—were becoming less tolerant of existing income tax rates as well. Beginning in World War II the union movement, policymakers looking for alternatives to direct government intervention, and welfare capitalists had constructed generous systems of private benefits within their institutions, ranging from health insurance to workers' pensions (all of which were subsidized by federal tax breaks). These benefits constituted an integral and sizable supplement to America's public welfare state. As Jacob Hacker has explained: "The United States, we have seen, ranks last according to the traditional measure of social welfare effort. But once we adjust for relative tax burdens, tax expenditures, and publicly subsidized private benefits . . . the United States rises to the middle of the pack." In none of the eleven nations that were the subject of an Organization for Economic Co-operation and Development report on this issue that used the most sophisticated measures, "does private social welfare spending comprise even half as large a share of total social spending as it does in the United States."[77] Combined with Social Security taxation, workers had less reason to support income taxation, since general welfare programs did not seem to benefit them. Many workers felt as if paying union dues and higher income taxes amounted to a "double tax." The private welfare state weaned blue-collar support away from the welfare state, thereby transforming this key constituency in the New Deal coalition into a prime opponent of taxation.[78] Republican presidents from Richard Nixon to Ronald Reagan capitalized on the resentment of the new middle class as they attempted to create a conservative majority.

Many successful state-building initiatives starting in the 1970s took place in the form of federal regulations that did not require direct tax increases. This became yet another way through which state-builders worked around the problem of fiscal restraint. "Governments short on money but desiring to have an impact," one scholar noted, "are likely to be drawn to regulatory mechanisms."[79] Indeed, many important policy breakthroughs in this decade emerged through the courts and bureaucracies rather than the legislative branch. The most dramatic extensions of government came through regulations to protect minorities, consumers, the environment, and individuals in the workplace.[80] One of the biggest domestic policy breakthroughs of the decade was deregulation, which of course consisted of the government diminishing its responsibilities.[81]

While anti-tax sentiment constrained state-builders since the 1930s, it bolstered the conservative movement that overtook domestic politics in the 1970s and 1980s. With the notable exception of the Cold War, nothing unified conservatives as much as resistance to taxation. In the 1970s, the animosity toward taxes did not emanate just from corporate quarters. It was particularly acute with wage-earners, who felt squeezed as inflation pushed them into higher tax brackets while weakening the value of their dollars. This dynamic was called "bracket creep." Conservative politicians played to this anger. At the grassroots level, conservatives mobilized around referendums to reduce property taxes.[82] The property tax revolt in California brought national attention to the problem of taxation. Some observers argued that rising anti-tax sentiment was a disguise for racial tensions.[83] While the argument had validity, it downplayed the deep-rooted resistance to taxation in the United States that extended beyond race and centered on a basic antipathy in funding the federal government.

The California tax revolt that resulted in the passage of Proposition 13 in 1978, which greatly reduced property taxes—and the debate that ensued in the media about all types of taxation—did not create broad opposition to taxation, as it is commonly portrayed in the scholarly and popular literature. The political drive to lower federal taxes was not a backlash against a "liberal" era when citizens had accepted high taxation. No such era ever existed: the New Deal did not endorse a mass tax, while Presidents Kennedy and Johnson launched the Great Society after cutting taxes. This is why policymakers in those times felt the need to rely on all sorts of complex mechanisms to raise revenue while building the government. As this essay attempts to show, state-builders constantly fretted about strong anti-tax sentiment. Raising money to pay for federal programs was always a problem. The conservative movement that coalesced at the national level in the 1970s was the first to articulate many antigovernment themes, but hostility toward high taxation was an age-old tradition.

While the conservative movement failed to retrench the nation's biggest federal policies, such as Social Security, it was able to weaken the federal tax system. President Ronald Reagan's administration passed the largest tax cut in history through Congress, the Economic Recovery Tax Act of 1981, and indexed the tax code to eliminate "bracket creep." Some of the 1981 tax cut was reversed in the coming years when fiscal conservatives raised taxes to lower the deficit. However, fiscal conservatives were unable to offset the 1981 reduction.[84] Indexation of the tax code deprived the American state of automatic revenue. It was costing the government approximately $180 billion a year by 1990. The top tenth of income-earners received the greatest benefit, since by that time the primary tax burden of wage-earners in the lower income brackets was Social Security and energy taxes.[85]

Changes in the budget process made things even more difficult for policymakers. In 1990, the Budget Enforcement Act created stringent rules. Discretionary spending would be subject to annual budget caps. Any legislated expenditure increases in entitlement programs had to be offset by reductions in other parts of the program, in another program, or by raising taxes. Until economic growth generated higher revenues, Congress had the choice of raising taxes or cutting spending to compensate for revenue shortfalls. Moreover, when Congress passed a sweeping tax-loophole-closing measure in 1986, it also agreed to a trade-off of steep rate cuts.[86] Income taxes as a share of all federal taxes fell to 57 percent in 1990 after reaching 63 percent in 1980.[87] By the 1990s, moreover, many of the loophole-closing tax reforms were reversed by the emergence of new breaks for industry and the middle class. So popular was opposition to taxation that the Earned Income Tax Credit, a tax benefit for the working poor, proved to be enormously strong in the 1980s, unlike other forms of welfare.[88] Federal tax breaks had increased to 35 percent of federal spending by 1984. In 1995, the federal tax breaks for social welfare alone cost $400 million.[89]

The most important outcome of the conservative era was that tax increases became more difficult politically because the system no longer generated sufficient revenue automatically. Increasing spending commitments combined with a stagnant revenue base. By 1986, Paul Pierson concluded, "the easiest roads to higher taxes are effectively blocked."[90] The impact of conservative tax cuts, combined with the success of postwar policymakers in using earmarked taxes and trust funds, became evident in the last decade of the century. By the 1990s, skyrocketing deficits and precommitted spending, particularly for entitlements for senior citizens, resulted in reduced levels of discretionary funds. A precommitted federal budget, large deficits and debt, and diminished income tax revenue left the government in what one fiscal expert called a "fiscal straitjacket."[91] As a result, domestic politics became "fiscalized" as debates were subsumed under the rubric of deficit reduction.[92] Lack of revenue constrained the types of policies that were even proposed. Upon taking office in 1993, President Clinton hoped to offer a welfare reform package that would end the existing welfare system but provide necessary services to help the poor find jobs. This involved a substantial expenditure, as became apparent in state-based initiatives such as those in Wisconsin. The administration realized that Congress would not redirect funds from another program toward this objective. Nor did the administration want to propose higher taxes for this purpose even when Democrats controlled both chambers of Congress. Liberal Democrats opposed proposals to reduce spending in other entitlement programs to pay for reform. Therefore, according to the leading account of welfare reform, insufficient money was the "biggest hurdle" that stifled the administration's initial welfare proposal.[93] As a result, the issue was left to the Republican majority elected in 1994. The final result was more stringent than Clinton's original plan, providing virtually no assistance to former welfare beneficiaries.

Even when budget surpluses returned in the late 1990s, politicians discovered that the projected long-term costs of Social Security and Medicare were so large that there was little room to discuss the creation of new initiatives. Rather, excess funds were geared to the protection of the long-term stability of entitlement programs. The first significant change in this pattern came as a result of the war against terrorism, launched after the devastating attacks on the United States on September 11, 2001. Despite starting his administration with a massive tax cut and promising to curtail spending, President George W. Bush's administration found, as had many presidents before him, that it is nearly impossible to hold down spending in times of war.[94] The result was a quick return to deficit government. Yet much of the deficit spending has shored up preexisting programs, including farm supports, and the amount of slack that is available to create fundamentally new initiatives remains limited.

While fiscal restraints did rein in government expansion, it is just as crucial that in the so-called conservative era politicians did not overturn the existing federal tax structure. Social insurance taxes continued to rise in the 1980s and 1990s. By 2001, 80 percent of working Americans were paying more in payroll taxes than in income taxes.[95] Meanwhile, conservatives cut the overall income tax burden only slightly from 1981 levels. Deficit reduction actually forced significant income tax *increases* in 1990, a decision that cost President George H.W. Bush substantial Republican support. President Clinton did the same in 1993, helping fuel the Republican takeover of government in 1994. The fact that the tax system remained intact meant that more automatic revenue would be generated once economic growth returned in the 1990s. Once again, conservative success at mobilizing tax opposition confronted the institutional inheritance of those who had built the federal tax system.

The Uneasy Relationship

Anti-tax sentiment has required that state-builders operate with limited fiscal capacity. Throughout the era of most intense state-building, limited revenue has simply been a fact of life as politicians feared the electoral impact of raising taxes on wage earners or business. The reality of strong anti-tax sentiment raises normative questions about state-building. At a fundamental level, state-building has often been at odds with crucial aspects of public opinion and the popular will as they were conveyed through the democratic process. While opinions of government vary depending on what policies are being discussed, public pressure has been relatively steadfast in its opposition to federal taxation. Ultimately, this reality has been the clearest manifestation of anti-statism.

The dissonance between democratic impulses and state-building challenges the teleology of several generations of historical narratives. Acknowledging fiscal restraint sheds new light on the process of American state-building. Most important, it helps us appreciate those politicians who succeeded in building an American state despite limited resources and constituent hostility. This story of tax resistance should not be surprising, since it is a basic fact of life in domestic politics. Indeed, it is a dilemma that politicians have faced since the emergence of the modern state.[96] However, historians have not integrated tax resistance and fiscal constraint into their narratives of recent political history. Taking this step will challenge the analytic frameworks that have been used to examine the history of twentieth-century state-building.

Coming to terms with anti-statism in modern America, as expressed through resistance to taxation and in other incarnations, is an important challenge facing the new generation of political historians. The project will take scholars into the heart of American democracy, where citizens and politicians retained old cultural fears even while accepting the need for new political institutions. The result of this dilemma was not always pristine. New institutions were constructed around all sorts of restraints, lack of revenue being one of the most powerful. In the end, American state-builders were able to construct an impressive government infrastructure given the opposition they faced. The story of how state-builders overcame their own constituencies must be a defining question for historians who now seek to reshape narratives of our political past.

SEVEN

The Forgotten Legacy of the New Deal: Fiscal Conservatism and the Roosevelt Administration, 1933–1938

When President William Clinton elevated deficit reduction to the top of his domestic agenda in 1993, he tapped into a long-standing Democratic tradition that was rooted in the 1930s.* Liberalism and fiscal conservatism have been interwoven since the construction of the New Deal state. Liberal Democratic presidents never felt that they could or should exclude fiscal conservatism from their agenda. Harry Truman, for example, fought with the military establishment to balance the budget, while John Kennedy and Lyndon Johnson adhered to modest levels of spending and only hesitantly accepted temporary deficits. Jimmy Carter emphasized deficit reduction more than a decade before Clinton championed the issue. In fact, liberal administrations have usually encountered great pressure to demonstrate a commitment to fiscal responsibility to refute conservative warnings that their policies would result in economic instability and limitless government expansion. Indeed, the histories of liberalism and fiscal conservatism have been intimately related. The key to some of the most durable state-building efforts in U.S. history has been a pragmatic alliance between liberals and moderate fiscal conservatives, who accepted an active role for government subject to budgetary constraints. This alliance produced bold federal initiatives in a nation historically resistant to centralized government.

Most accounts of the New Deal coalition downplay the influence of orthodox conservative ideas within the Roosevelt administration. The importance of fiscal conservatism to the New Deal has been acknowledged but rarely analyzed. Serious treatment of this tradition, like the rest of modern conservatism, has been relegated to the periphery of contemporary historical scholarship (Brinkley, 1994). Instead, historians have written Whiggish accounts of Keynesianism (Brinkley, 1995; Collins, 1987; May, 1981; Barber, 1985; Snowiss, 1971; Stein, 1969). They have paid little attention to the influence of fiscal conservatism—

* This essay originally appeared in *Presidential Studies Quarterly*, 30 (2000): 331–58.

defined as an agenda of balanced budgets, private capital investment, minimal government debt, stable currency, low inflation, and high savings—which remained normative for most of the New Deal period.

When New Deal historians mention fiscal conservatism in these years, moreover, they treat it as monolithic, static, and irrational. Liberal historians understood that Roosevelt was a fiscal conservative (Leuchtenburg, 1963; Schlesinger, 1959; Friedel, 1990). Yet, since they were interested in the expansion of liberalism, they never knew what to make of that fact. The ideology thus remains at the periphery of their analysis, a curious relic from earlier political times. More recently, social scientists have treated fiscal conservatism as a barrier to state-building. Mark Leff's landmark book on New Deal taxation lacks a detailed examination of the fiscal conservative ideology, and variations of that ideology, even though he admits that it influenced national politics during this period (Leff, 1984). At most points in his book, fiscal conservatives appear simply as sinister advisors who want to pay for the New Deal on the backs of the poor. But the ideology of fiscal conservatism was much richer and more nuanced than he suggests. Brown, another scholar to deal with this issue, also presents a limited understanding of Roosevelt's acceptance of fiscal conservatism (Brown, 1999). For Brown, fiscal conservatism was the key obstacle to state-building since low revenue constrained the growth of the federal government. He downplays the fact that Roosevelt succeeded in state-building, in part because he took fiscal concerns seriously. While Brown defines fiscal conservatism as the agenda of investors, Roosevelt felt that voters of all classes disliked taxes and wanted balanced budgets. Indeed, this was the principal reason the United States did not create a mass income tax until World War II. Given the broad cross-class aversion to taxes and deficits, portions of Brown's argument become less persuasive.

Building on the work of Savage and Kennedy, this article claims that fiscal conservatism constituted a key component of the New Deal (Savage, 1988; Kennedy, 1999). Roosevelt knew that fiscal conservatism was supported by investors and the business community, mainstream academic economists, think tanks, and the majority of the voting public. Conservative southern Democrats, who favored balanced budgets and were opposed to increased taxes, occupied almost all the key committee chairmanships. Roosevelt understood that large deficits would only exacerbate their hostility toward his agenda (Collins, 1987, pp. 39–52; Patterson, 1967; Leff, 1984, pp. 110–11; Smith, 1991, pp. 103–4; Snowiss, 1971). Even progressive Democrats in the 1930s regarded balanced budgets as essential to economic stability in the long run, although they were flexible in accepting short-term deficits (Jacobs, 2004, pp. 95–178). Moreover, opinion polls in the 1930s consistently documented public opposition to deficits and debt (Brinkley, 1994, p. 304). Throughout his time in office, Roosevelt recruited fiscal conservatives to serve in his administration. Ideologically, the president embraced their values. Politically, he shared the belief that fiscal conservatism enjoyed support from the electorate, Democrats, and business. In this context, fiscal conservatism evolved and the ideology influenced key policy decisions.

Although Roosevelt understood the importance of fiscal conservatism, the pressure to spend was enormous. During his presidency, Roosevelt could be convinced to change course at nearly any time since he rarely committed to a single ideological position. As historians have discovered, Roosevelt experimented with different strategies of government intervention rather than pursuing one course of action. In the process, he played advisors off each other and followed those who made the most compelling political argument at a given time. Like all policymakers in his administration, fiscal conservatives faced a formidable challenge if they were to influence policy outcomes amid the contradictory demands Roosevelt faced.

Given the prevailing concern with liberalism, social scientists have not probed into the advisors who struggled to keep Roosevelt faithful to fiscal conservatism. As a result, the process through which those ideals remained influential at the height of the Great Depression is not well understood. The task of maintaining pressure on Roosevelt to balance budgets largely fell to two members of the administration: Lewis Douglas, who served as Director of Budget from 1933 to 1934, and Henry Morgenthau Jr., Secretary of the Treasury from 1934 to 1945. Douglas and Morgenthau worked in the Department of the Treasury, an institution that nurtured policymakers known for their devotion to fiscal austerity. Both men understood that fiscal conservatism faced a challenge with the growth of budgets to unprecedented size. Douglas and Morgenthau worried about the detrimental impact of deficits on consumer prices, national savings, and the international stability of the dollar. They defined policy in terms of budgetary costs and tax burdens rather than needs, rights, or obligations. For Douglas and Morgenthau, fiscal conservatism was broader than a technical understanding of economics, a guise for protecting wealthy investors, or a catchy slogan. Rather, fiscal conservatism offered a means of restoring healthy economic conditions, constraining the state, limited interest groups, and retaining the faith of citizens in a disciplined government. Both saw fiscal conservatism as the moral obligation of current politicians to future generations of citizens as well as beneficial to investment and business leaders. Fiscally conservative policies would enable Roosevelt to build a sizable federal government *and* maintain relatively low tax rates in a nation hostile to taxation. Yet, Douglas and Morgenthau adopted different styles as advisors. While Douglas's rigid approach ultimately undermined his influence since he failed to transform his beliefs into a politically and economically viable agenda, Morgenthau's flexible entrepreneurship resulted in significant influence over policy and introduced a moderate vision of fiscal conservatism that could coexist with the modern state.

The Marginalization of Fiscal Extremism: Lewis Douglas, 1932–1934

Douglas insisted that fiscal conservatism was incompatible with an expansive centralized state. Several themes dominated Douglas's arguments against New

Deal liberalism: the centrality of the gold standard, the danger of inadequate savings, and the weakness of government spending. His ideas were grounded in a basic distrust of politicians, believing that without rigid institutional controls they would not refrain from destructive behavior. In his personal and public interaction with President Roosevelt, Douglas believed that a total commitment to minimal government spending and debt, regardless of changing economic and political conditions, was the only way to combat the pressure to spend. Because of his unyielding outlook, Douglas gradually lost clout within the administration. In the end, he resigned in frustration.

Douglas could not be criticized for inconsistency. He adamantly defended the principles of fiscal conservatism throughout his time in politics (Browder and Smith, 1986). Grounded in a distrust of the modern state, fiscal conservatism was a guiding ideology from which the government should never depart. Anti-statism framed Douglas's entire outlook. In light of developments in Russia and Germany, he believed that the state inevitably destroyed the right of the individual to initiate new industrial enterprise or to exercise "economic independence" (Douglas, 1935d, pp. 32, 135–36). Nor did he think that the state could possess the technical capacity to manage a national economy (1935d, pp. 28–29, 44). He distinguished good government "acting as an umpire of a game played by others under a certain simple set of rules" from bad government "participating itself as a player in the game" (pp. 104–6). His intense distrust of the state complemented an optimistic view of capitalism. Rejecting the "mature economy" thesis, Douglas argued that history demonstrated the inevitability of economic revival as long as there was no government interference (Rosenof, 1975, p. 27).

Born on July 2, 1984, Douglas was raised by a wealthy family that had accumulated its fortune through copper mining in Bisbee, Arizona. After graduating from Amherst College, he served as an officer in World War I. He won a seat in the Arizona state legislature in 1923 and three years later, voters elected him to the House of Representatives where he championed sound currency, free trade, limited spending, and efficiency in government. Douglas urged the Democratic Party to emphasize anti-inflationary monetary policy and fiscal austerity in the presidential campaign of 1932. His Democratic allies included Speaker of the House John Nance Garner, Senator James Byrnes, Governor William Murray of Oklahoma, former Secretary of War Newton Baker, and former Secretary of the Treasury William McAdoo. Before the election, Douglas participated in a bipartisan committee to investigate strategies for cutting federal spending and reorganizing government bureaus. The committee received high marks from conservative groups such as the National Organization to Reduce Public Expenditures and the National Economic League.[1]

Representative Douglas was extremely pleased when Democratic nominee Franklin Roosevelt devoted much of his campaign to attacking the "reckless" spending of Hoover. On the campaign trail, Roosevelt promised to balance the budget by reducing federal expenditures by 25 percent. Although Hoover clearly opposed chronic unbalanced budgets, he had learned to accept deficits during this administration to respond to the economic crisis. Roosevelt targeted Hoover's deficits even though the president had tried to balance the budget in 1931 by raising taxes. From the start of his presidential bid, he thus understood the appeal of these values.

Following the election, Roosevelt remained receptive to fiscal conservatism. The president understood that the business and investment communities were insistent on sound finance and low taxation (Collins, 1987, pp. 23–52). During his first term in office, Roosevelt courted these economic leaders. But it was not just investors with whom he was concerned. The president also believed that a large portion of the electorate still saw balanced budgets as a symbol of stable government. Moreover, the majority of citizens clearly shared the traditional American aversion to taxation, evidence by grassroots citizen revolts against local tax burdens in the early 1930s (Beito, 1989). The public believed that fiscally conservative policies guaranteed low taxes. Democratic leaders, ranging from progressive congressman Robert Wagner to businessman Bernard Baruch, all insisted on balancing the budget (Savage, 1988, pp. 169–70). Targeting federal deficits as a major source of the Depression, President of the American Federation of Labor William Green and President of the U.S. Chamber of Commerce Henry Harriman wrote a joint letter to President Roosevelt in 1933 that called for steep spending reductions to expand credit, stimulate investment, and encourage entrepreneurs.[2]

Since it made sense politically for Roosevelt to present his administration as fiscally conservative, Douglas was a logical choice to serve as a key advisor. Roosevelt invited Douglas to serve as Director of the Bureau of Budget (then located in the Treasury). The *New York Times*, like many other newspapers, interpreted the appointment as a signal that the administration was committed to expenditure control (February 25, 1933). Inside the White House, Douglas quickly became an important figure. During his first year, Douglas worked closely with the president on all areas of economic policy, serving as part of the elite "Bedside Cabinet." Unlike previous budget directors, he was invited to attend cabinet meetings. The evidence suggests that the president was pleased with his work. Roosevelt privately boasted to a close advisor that Douglas was the "greatest find" of the administration (Romasco, 1983, p. 67). Many in Roosevelt's administration were well aware of how the charismatic, educated, and intellectually persuasive Arizonian was usually able to raise serious doubts in the president's mind about new spending proposals (Perkins, 1946, p. 197).

In the first years of Roosevelt's administration, Douglas had reason to believe that fiscal conservatism would be a guiding ideal. Building on this campaign promise, one of Roosevelt's first legislative proposals centered on expenditure reduction. On March 10, 1933, the president told Congress that the federal government had been on the "road toward bankruptcy" for three years under Herbert Hoover. Deficits, he insisted, had contributed to the stagnation of the economy and the increase in unemployment. Roosevelt concluded,

> Our Government's house is not in order and for many reasons no effective action has been taken to restore it to order . . . Too often in recent history liberal governments have been wrecked on the rocks of loose fiscal policy. We must avoid this danger. (1939, pp. 49–50)

Secretary of Labor Frances Perkins, one of the most liberal members of the administration, later wrote,

> There is no doubt in my mind that Roosevelt did give him (Douglas) grounds to believe that he wanted a balanced budget and that he was at least doubtful of the wisdom of a public works program if it could not be achieved without throwing the budget out of balance. This was one of the conflicts in Roosevelt's nature and in his thinking. He wanted a balanced budget, but he also wanted to do the right thing by his unemployed citizens. If anyone could have shown him a way to get them back to work in normal, private industrial activities, he would have preferred it to a public works or relief program. (Perkins, 1946, p. 270)

Perkins herself admitted that "a great deal of what Douglas said had a sound economic basis" and that "one could not but share in his concern that heavy expenditures would create a great deficit in the budget and impair the credit of money." Perkins explained,

> He feared to spend money that could not be raised by taxation in a period of declining income. The national income, the taxing power of the Federal Government, and the balanced budget all hung together in Douglas's mind. He was persuasive. (1946, p. 273)

On March 20, Congress passed the Economy Act of 1933, Douglas's most notable contribution to policy. Titled "the Act to Maintain the Credit of the United States Government," the bill was written largely by Douglas (Moley, 1939, p. 153). The act reduced federal expenditures by $500 million by granting the president broad powers to reduce veterans' payments and the salaries for federal officers and employees. The act also strengthened the president's ability to enact administrative cuts through executive orders and sent a message about the importance of fiscal conservatism to the New Deal (Sargent, 1980). According to historian Frank Friedel, "The economy program was not a minor aberration of the spring of 1933, or a hypocritical concession to delighted conservatives. Rather it was an integral part of Roosevelt's overall New Deal" (Friedel, 1990, p. 96; see also Brinkley 1998, pp. 19–21; Kennedy, 1999, pp. 146–47; Leuchtenburg, 1963, p. 45). Roosevelt received enthusiastic support from citizen mail, the *New York Times*, and the American Legion (Baez, 1999). Whatever policies lay ahead, the Economy Act lent credence to Roosevelt's early promises that he would uphold strict budgetary limits.

Douglas knew that the president would encounter intense pressure to increase spending from interest groups, ranging from farmers to the military.

In response, he envisioned his role as a one-man lobby for fiscal responsibility. Likewise, Roosevelt saw the institutional function of the budget director in these terms. During a press conference on December 13, 1933, Roosevelt (1972) explained that

> Douglas' job is to prevent the Government from spending just as hard as he possibly can. That is his job. Somewhere between his efforts to spend nothing . . . and the point of view of the people who want to spend ten billion additional on public works, we will get somewhere.

Between 1933 and the summer of 1934, Douglas was able to cut government spending through executive authority by reducing the defense budget by $125 million, $75 million from the Post Office, $12 million from the Commerce, $75 million from government salaries, and $100 million from staff reorganization (Browder and Smith, 1986, pp. 96–97).

Nonetheless, the demands for spending were strong and the income tax system did not generate enough revenue to pay for the programs. While the president continued to aim for a balanced budget, he accepted that in time of crisis that goal would not be realized. In fact, the president undermined the Economy Act by using the savings in New Deal programs and making concessions to veterans. Deficits soon seemed inevitable. Roosevelt did not have the support to create a mass income tax to finance spending. Throughout the 1930s, not more than 3 percent of the population ever paid income taxes. During the New Deal, the administration relied on regressive excise and payroll taxes and income taxes on the wealthiest Americans. Even with steep rates, the latter only generated a limited amount of funds (Leff, 1984). Without sufficient revenue, Roosevelt had no other option but to rely on deficits if he intended to meet urgent needs.

Douglas soon felt that Roosevelt had relinquished any plans to balance the budget in the near future, signaled by the adoption of a "double budget" that separated "normal" from "emergency" expenditures to show that the former was balanced despite an overall deficit. In frustration, Douglas called this account method a "fiction of romantic minds" (Douglas, 1935d, p. 93). While some in the administration believed that conditions required temporary departures from basic principles even if those principles remained intact for the long term, Douglas found this to be intolerable. Postmaster General James Farley later complained that Douglas

> Was against spending because it put the budget out of balance and tended to raise taxes but he never, as far as I could discover, had anything definite to offer on how to feed the millions of people who were suffering from loss of jobs, loss of income, and loss of savings. (Farley, 1938, p. 218)

Given Douglas's understanding of the problems facing the economy, only annual balanced budgets or the clear intention to balance the budget in the immediate future could create an atmosphere conducive to investment, which would create economic conditions that would take care of those Farley saw suffering (Douglas, 1935a, pp. 19–20). In Douglas's view, balanced budgets strengthened the dollar by bolstering investor confidence and enabled the government to decrease its borrowing and pay off debt. Balanced budgets, he added, minimized the "destructive psychological effects of making mendicants of self-respecting American citizens" (Douglas, 1935e, p. 69; 1936, pp. 44–45). Like constitutional law, balanced budgets to Douglas established nonnegotiable boundaries on federal government expansion. Although balanced budgets did not eliminate government spending, they limited it. While Douglas admitted that the budget could not be balanced in 1935, he believed that it could be brought into an "approximate balance" by 1936 and into full balance by 1937. For Douglas, the balanced budget was the most important signal government leaders could send to investors about the future. Since Roosevelt no longer seemed committed to balanced budgets as the framework within which all other policies would be considered, Douglas began to feel that if the president did not change course, he would have to leave the administration.

Douglas adamantly objected to Roosevelt's inflationary monetary policies. For Douglas, the gold standard controlled the government by limiting individual discretion for inflationary policy. As with deficits, he refused to accept any flexibility in his position. A stable financial system, he argued, had to be preserved even in the most severe economic crisis:

> Rules for playing the game [must] be established and that those rules be rigidly and uncompromisingly followed—not changed, as in the past, when they began to be painful, for it is only by incurring slight and temporary pain that the violent fluctuations with their accompanying intense misery can be avoided! (Douglas, 135d, p. 130)

Douglas grew enraged when the administration decided to abandon the gold standard in March 1933; the bulwark against currency inflation was gone. Neither could Douglas tolerate the administration's willingness to purchase moderate amounts of silver and to print paper money. He warned hysterically that such monetary experimentation meant the "end of Western Civilization" (Moley, 1939, p. 160).

Roosevelt's decision led another key member of the administration, Raymond Moley, to leave. Moley had been an integral part of the Brain Trust and also served as assistant secretary of state. Moley, a professor of government at Barnard College, believed firmly in government-business cooperation and ridiculed notions of returning to a small entrepreneurial economy. But after influencing policy during the first 100 days, Moley became disillusioned with the administration. Enraged with Roosevelt's decision to abandon the gold standard, which he interpreted as a personal defeat and a move to the Left, Moley was forced to resign from the administration. As a journalist, he allied with the conservative wing of the Republican Party.

All of Roosevelt's actions, in the minds of staunch fiscal conservatives, threatened the credit of government. Douglas said to Roosevelt that a stringent budget had been "the heart of your recovery program."[3] In a letter, Douglas targeted the Public Works Administration (PWA) as a prime example of the flawed nature of New Deal policies. Douglas complained that the PWA was ineffective because it produced few jobs. Moreover, government investment in the heavy durable goods industry paled in comparison to what would be privately invested under proper conditions. The projects only exacerbated deficits that discouraged capital investment. Public works also involved contractual obligations that lasted for years and created vested interests that would block future cuts. Although Douglas understood the appeal of the program, he insisted that politicians had to be disciplined:

> We cannot always have what we want; we must deny ourselves in the interest of the general public welfare; and so, desirable as some of these things may appear to be to you, if the consequences of undertaking them means setting in motion the destructive forces of paper inflation, then, in the public interest, they should not be undertaken.[4]

Douglas warned that government spending offered a weak alternative to higher rates of productive savings, meaning private investment, claiming that government spending was merely a palliative to the depression since it produced expensive *temporary* employment. When the cost of these programs rose beyond acceptable limits, Douglas warned, they would inevitably fall under the budgetary knife. Workers would soon find themselves unemployed in an economy in the same dire condition as before the programs were enacted. While Roosevelt focused on alleviating immediate suffering through relief, Douglas wanted to repair the economy permanently through higher rates of private employment. He lamented that under Roosevelt "we are running on a treadmill under a constantly increasing burden of debt. We are paying billions, piling up Government debt, and getting nowhere" (Douglas, 1935b, pp. 410–11; 1935f, pp. 678–79). Furthermore, Douglas was unconvinced by promises that spending would subside once the depression ended since programs created vested interests. Congress had rarely displayed the self-control needed to stop subsidies in light of constituent pressure.

Choosing to act as a roadblock instead of an entrepreneur, Douglas failed to influence policy except for a short period. By his second year as budget director, Douglas was dismayed by the administration's move away from private capital investments as the key to saving the economy. Only private capital investment, he had told Roosevelt, could revitalize the heavy durable goods industry. Douglas supported a restoration of investor confidence through balanced budgets, curtailment of excessive banking regulations, presidential proclamations that the government would not interfere with the profit system, restrictions on the National Recovery Administration, and tariff reduction. Douglas also called for an executive order to centralize independent agencies under the Bureau of the

Budget to limit their freedom to spend. Although Roosevelt initially supported the order, PWA administrator Harold Ickes objected to the measure as a direct attack on his agency.[5] Despite a commitment to Douglas, the president canceled the order. This episode was characteristic of Roosevelt, who constantly played advisors off one another to promote his leadership. Douglas turned out to be ill-suited to President Roosevelt's fluctuating style of leadership.

Betrayed by these and other incidents, Douglas felt increasingly isolated within the administration. Amid the grave economic crisis, Roosevelt simply could not adhere to Douglas's rigid agenda. Douglas stayed in office as long as Roosevelt seemed committed to expenditure control. But in the summer of 1934, he no longer felt this to be true (Sargent, 1974, pp. 33–43). As a result, Douglas resigned on August 30, 1934. Roosevelt pleaded with Douglas to remain in the administration past the upcoming congressional elections. Despite the president's forceful appeal to him on "a patriotic basis and then as a Democrat," Douglas stood firm.[6] Although the president downplayed the resignation, newspapers such as the *New York Times* commented sympathetically on Douglas's values (September 2 and 4, 1934).

In Douglas's mind, staying in the administration had become impossible since Roosevelt's deficits were threatening the nation's future. By destroying confidence in the future value of currencies and government credit, Douglas argued, deficits were diminishing the incentives for individuals to invest. Ultimately, chronic deficits would decimate the core of a stable polity, the middle class, through inflation. For Douglas, inflation was more than a concern only to investors. By enticing government to print money or to use credit to finance its expenditures, deficit-induced inflation decreased the value of middle-class savings:

> It strikes with wicked, cruel violence the middle class, the laborer and all on fixed incomes, even the war disabled veteran. The speculator has a remote chance of surviving, and the wealthy may be able to protect themselves, at least in part. But it is the other group in society who carry the crushing burden on their back. (Douglas, 1935a, p. 18)

Even amid deflation, the threat of inflation seemed to him quite rational. Looking internationally, Douglas pointed to how inflation had opened the door to German fascism in the 1920s. Domestically, the Silver Purchase Act of 1934 signaled the strength of an influential congressional block of progressive Democrats and Republicans who promoted inflationary policies. The congressional coalition, led by Senator Elmer Thomas of Oklahoma, Senator Burton Wheeler of Colorado, Senator Key Pittman of Nevada, Representative Wright Patman of Texas, and Speaker of the House Henry Rainey of Illinois, fought to boost farmers' income (and the income of silver miners, although this was not explicitly discussed) by infusing silver into the monetary system and printing dollars to raise prices artificially.

Douglas argued that the most damaging effect of Roosevelt's chronic deficits was psychological. Americans were becoming accustomed to deficits as numbers became meaningless. Regarding deficits that approached billions of dollars, he wrote:

> There was a time not so long ago when even a million dollars seemed a rather stupendous figure. But now the word "billion" is bandied about freely. The nonchalant, careless, jovial sloshing of a billion dollars here and a billion dollars there has become so commonplace a part of the daily news that there is danger that we may not appreciate the real significance of the word . . . A billion dollars should never be thought of as merely a sum of money. It should be thought of as representing many years of labor by many thousands of people . . . Only then can we understand the extent to which we have mortgaged our future. (Douglas, 1935c, pp. 561–62)

Facing the challenge of chronic deficits, the federal government would eventually resort to printing paper money, expanding credit from private banks, or increasing taxes. Douglas warned that deficit spenders always justified their policies on the basis of "emergency" situations, promising that in the future, fiscal policy would return to normal: "It is one thing to rationalize a deficit. It is another thing to liquidate it" (Douglas, 1935c, pp. 561–62).

After his resignation, Douglas was even more extreme in his views as he became a leading public advocate for fiscal conservatism. Freed from any ties to Roosevelt, Douglas intensified his rhetoric in periodical and newspaper publications, two widely publicized books, and media coverage of his speeches at universities. Roosevelt angrily compared his attacks to wartime treason since Douglas's former position led the public to believe his claims.[7] After leaving the administration, he was still hesitant to oppose Roosevelt personally. He refused to join the American Liberty League in 1934 since it attacked the president personally and failed to renounce monopoly and high tariffs (Browder and Smith, 1986). But by 1936, Douglas pledged to vote for Republican Alfred Landon. In 1937, he helped mobilize the conservative coalition in Congress, and three years later he led a group of Democrats who supported Republican candidate Wendell Wilkie.

Douglas's experience reveals the tensions that emerged by 1934 between doctrinaire fiscal conservatives and the rest of Roosevelt's administration. In 1932, Douglas believed that Roosevelt was devoted to the goals outlined in his presidential campaign. The Economy Act of 1933 and subsequent budget cuts gave him confidence. By the fall of 1934, he sensed that fiscal conservatism as he understood it no longer had a role in the New Deal. Douglas's influence waned as he refused to adjust to new economic and political conditions. Although Roosevelt remained committed to controlling expenditures, limiting taxation, avoiding excessive inflation, protecting the dollar, and balancing the budget when it became possible, Douglas feared that Roosevelt had veered too far from his original principles.

The Virtues of Moderation: Henry Morgenthau Jr., 1934–1937

For others in the administration, however, fiscal conservatism still had an important role in the New Deal coalition. Henry Morgenthau Jr., a fiscal conservative, proved to be a much shrewder policy entrepreneur than Douglas. Although often dismissed as the least innovative or intelligent member of Roosevelt's cabinet, Morgenthau promoted a vision of moderate fiscal conservatism that influenced Roosevelt for three critical years in the period of the most intense state-building. He succeeded by continually redefining fiscal conservatism so that it would be politically viable. Decoupling the ideology from Douglas's antistatism, Morgenthau struggled to inscribe budgetary restraint within the New Deal. Although he suffered some major losses, Morgenthau also shaped the design of several key policies such as Social Security, veterans' pensions, and income taxation. By being flexible about when fiscal conservatism was politically obtainable or economically desirable, and by packaging fiscal conservatism as an ongoing objective rather than a fixed requirement, Morgenthau gained legitimacy for himself and his beliefs. In doing so, he left a stronger imprint on New Deal policies than Douglas and articulated an ideology that influenced presidential politics for the remainder of the century.

For Morgenthau, fiscal conservatism and New Deal liberalism were interdependent. Morgenthau shared almost all of the same values as Douglas: he championed the need for balanced budgets, stable currency, debt reduction, and private investment. Without controls on spending, Morgenthau claimed, there were no limits on government expansion. Morgenthau saw these values as long-term objectives. He accepted that under certain economic and political conditions, greater government activity and less fiscal restraint were necessary. Rather than using the budget to undercut the state, Morgenthau wanted to ensure budgetary restraint while creating domestic programs. His moderation enabled him to influence the administration even though he too was often frustrated with Roosevelt.

Like Douglas, Morgenthau was born into a wealthy family. His parents, Henry and Josephine Sykes Morgenthau, were German-Jewish immigrants who had become prominent members of the New York Democratic Party. In school, Morgenthau had encountered problems. He left Phillips Exeter after two years and dropped out of Cornell University after three unsuccessful semesters. As a youth, Morgenthau was influenced by the Progressive Era budget reform movement, which presented the budget as a tool to ensure efficient and accountable governance (May 1981, 29–31). In 1911, Morgenthau moved to Texas at twenty-one years of age to be cured from typhoid fever. Upon returning to New York, he pursued a career in farming and edited the *American Agriculturist*, a trade journal for state farmers. Morgenthau grew close to Roosevelt through their work in the Democratic Party. When voters elected Roosevelt as governor in 1928, he named Morgenthau as chair of the New York State Agricultural Advisory Commission and later appointed him to be the state conservation commissioner. Morgenthau wanted to be secretary of agriculture under President Roosevelt, but he settled for the Federal Farm Board. On November 13, 1933, after the resignation of Secretary of the Treasury William Wooden, Roosevelt asked Morgenthau to temporarily take over Treasury. Although pundits ridiculed the "farmer" as incapable of the job, he retained this important position until the end of World War II.

From the time he took office, Morgenthau embraced the basic tenets of New Deal liberalism. Within the administration, he championed programs to provide welfare, public jobs, pensions, labor regulations, and agricultural assistance. Despite his desire to curtail spending, he did not harbor the animosity toward the state that consumed Douglas. For example, he once told Treasury economists that it was "perfectly asinine to talk about immediate balance of the budget. Everybody knew that it could not be balanced now with any decent attention to human needs."[8] "Douglas' policy involved too great a gamble with human lives," Morgenthau later wrote when comparing himself and President Roosevelt with Douglas, "we differed from Lewis Douglas, not over whether a balanced budget was our ultimate goal, but over what sacrifices of relief and reform we were prepared to make in order to get it right away" (Blum, 1959, p. 230).

There was one important difference between Morgenthau and Douglas, which signaled an important shift in fiscal conservatism. Unlike his predecessor, Morgenthau was willing to experiment with the gold standard: "This country has had enough of that sort of worship of a monetary fetish."[9] In time of economic crisis, he believed that the administration could engage in modest monetary experimentation without losing control of inflation. Like Douglas, Morgenthau stressed that it was essential for the administration to protect the stability of currency, warning that monetary officials had to exercise extreme caution when purchasing and distributing silver (Everest, 1973). But after 1933, moderate fiscal conservatives such as Morgenthau no longer made the gold standard the defining principle of their agenda.

During his first two years as secretary, Morgenthau believed that the administration needed to show the public that it was at least moving toward a balanced budget. This did not mean always balancing the budget but showing that it remained a long-term goal. In America, he argued, the balanced budget carried weight as evidence of government restraint and healthy economic activity. With a balanced budget, private investors would be more willing to risk their capital since they had less fear about inflation and future taxation. Morgenthau told Roosevelt that being able to decrease spending would show that "we have broken the back of the depression."[10] Without that commitment, he said about federal spending, "Just where it will all end, heaven only knows."[11] In contrast to Douglas, Morgenthau accepted the double budget as legitimate evidence that even in crisis the administration was exercising budgetary prudence.[12] He distinguished between different economic conditions, agreeing that certain types of government action were needed in depressed times that would be unwise amid healthy economic conditions.

Morgenthau succeeded in his battle against a proposed veterans' bonus increase in 1935. Fiscal responsibility, according to Morgenthau, could limit the influence of interest groups. While accepting the need for substantial government spending, Morgenthau deplored special interests that seemed to receive a disproportionate share of limited federal funds. By trimming those particular allocations, Morgenthau felt that the government could continue to fund essential programs while maintaining a reasonable budget. This was a consistent theme in his tenure. For Morgenthau, the veterans' lobby was a prime example of budgeting that was driven by interest group pressure rather than economic need. Led by Representative Wright Patman (D-TX), Congress had pushed for veterans' bonuses of $4.8 billion to be financed by printing paper money. Morgenthau argued that accelerated veterans' payments would create inflation and undermine the value of government securities.[13] At first, Roosevelt promised a veto.[14] Before the Senate, Morgenthau said that adherence to the president's budget made it impossible to pass the legislation. Abandoning the balanced budget would result in a "grave injustice" to purchasers of government securities and "slow up" the recovery program.[15] During the days preceding the final vote, Morgenthau lobbied intensely against the bill. Calling prominent newspaper publishers, he criticized their blind support of the veterans and failure to inform the public about the budgetary cost of the benefits.[16] Morgenthau did not understand why scarce resources should be devoted to veterans rather than needier groups, something the media seemed to ignore.[17] What most concerned him was that the public and business leaders did not perceive the inflationary dangers at hand. At the last minute, Roosevelt shocked Morgenthau by telling him he was going to compromise. In his diaries, Morgenthau recounted the meeting:

> I had a sort of sinking feeling and found myself sort of gradually crumpling up and I said, if you want me to go on please do not talk that way to me because I am building a bonfire of support for you in your veto message. He said rather quickly with a smile, let's agree that I will not talk to you about any compromise if you will not talk to me about any bonfire. He said, in other words, never let your left hand know what your right is doing. I said, which hand am I Mr. President, and he said, my right hand. He said, but I keep my left hand under the table. This is the most frank expression of the real F.D.R. that I ever listened to and that is the real way that he works—but thank God I understand him.[18]

Nonetheless, Morgenthau was victorious. Heeding Morgenthau's warnings, Roosevelt vetoed the legislation.

Loophole-closing tax reform was central to Morgenthau's fiscal conservatism. Since such a small portion of the workforce paid income taxes, closing loopholes offered a way to increase revenue without taxing more citizens.

For years, Treasury experts had told Morgenthau that the tax system would be adequate under normal conditions.[19] Morgenthau justified tax reform as a revenue-raising measure rather than as a punitive measure against the rich. Hearing these arguments, Roosevelt joked that "we have Lew Douglas with us again."[20] Morgenthau led campaigns for reform between 1935 and 1937. He was also instrumental in the passage of the Undistributed Profits Tax, which raised levies on corporations (Brownlee, 1996, p. 79). Although these measures were far from revolutionary, they did close significant avenues of escape for the wealthy and brought in new sources of revenue to Treasury. Fiscal conservatives would continue to champion loophole-closing tax reform through the 1980s as a means of raising revenue without increasing taxes (Steuerle, 1992).

On numerous occasions, Roosevelt frustrated Morgenthau when political necessity trumped budgetary caution. For example, the Department of Agriculture's Rexford Tugwell told Budget Director Daniel Bell in January 1935 to release $67 million that had been earmarked for him but held back by the president. Morgenthau warned that should Tugwell receive the money, Secretaries Ickes and Hopkins, who were in a similar situation, would be enraged. Agreeing, the president told Morgenthau to temporarily hold up Tugwell's money. This decision, Morgenthau noted, was typical of the president.

> Instead of doing the straight forward thing and canceling Tugwell's authorization which could not have yet reached him, he doubled crosses Tugwell by telling me to tell Bell that Tugwell cannot have one cent until the budget passes on it. This makes a complete circle and everybody will be sore and nobody will be satisfied.[21]

Morgenthau also disliked Roosevelt's frequent manipulation of data to show declining deficits.

By the summer of 1935, Morgenthau expressed many of the frustrations that had been voiced by Douglas. Roosevelt had yet to balance a budget (Morgan, 1995, p. 3; Kimmel, 1959, p. 143). Morgenthau feared that chronic deficits would produce inflationary policies and he would take the blame. Morgenthau, moreover, doubted that many programs were making a dent in unemployment. Increasingly, the administration seemed concerned with spending for its own sake but not with rehabilitating private markets.[22] But in contrast to his predecessor, Morgenthau did not resign because of these frustrations. Rather, he continued to fight for mechanisms of restraint within new programs.

Secretary Morgenthau secured his greatest victory with the design of Social Security: the self-financed system would force savings by individuals and government. The Committee on Economic Security (CES), which drafted the legislation, originally called for the use of general revenue to fund a portion of old-age insurance. But at the last minute Morgenthau changed the plan to exclude general revenue. Morgenthau insisted that the program should be completely supported by payroll tax revenue and the interest from the reserve fund. The program would thus not rely on funds produced by income taxation; benefits would be limited to the money Congress obtained through the earmarked system. It was crucial to Morgenthau and the president that Social Security be fiscally conservative for political and moral reasons. Morgenthau intended the deflationary tax system to commit future officials to a particular policy design (Patashnik, 1997, p. 439). Along with Roosevelt, he believed that the self-financing tax system would guarantee the program's long-term solvency and help define payments as "earned benefits" that the elderly were entitled to receive (Leff, 1983). In the long term, the tax system would also protect the federal budget from the cost of this program. As Roosevelt told Frances Perkins,

> It is almost dishonest to build up an accumulated deficit for the Congress of the United States to meet in 1980. We can't do that. We can't sell the United States short in 1980 any more than in 1935. (Schlesinger, 1959, pp. 309–10)

Although recent histories of the New Deal have stressed the role of conservative southern Democrats in excluding farm workers and domestic servants from Social Security for racial purposes, it was Morgenthau who was also responsible for this fragmented structure (for good examples of the race-based analysis, see Lieberman, 1995; Quadagno, 1994). Financial, in addition to racial, concerns guided this crucial decision. Morgenthau was insistent on reducing the tax burden needed to finance insurance benefits. American policymakers were well aware that Britain's unemployment insurance program had gone bankrupt in the 1920s because of unsustainable liberalizations in coverage to include workers outside the industrial workforce (Davies and Derthick, 1997). Morgenthau also feared that it would be administratively impossible to collect taxes from those transient, nonindustrial workers (Kennedy, 1999, pp. 268–70). Members of the CES were surprised by Morgenthau's move away from universal coverage, but they were also worried about the deflationary effects of the Social Security tax, the long-term cost of benefits, and the "desirability" of such a large federal program. As a result, the CES, including Frances Perkins, agreed to temporarily limit coverage to a limited number of workers (Perkins, 1946, pp. 297–98).

In a different battle, Morgenthau tried to obtain administrative reform to impose tighter budgetary control. Like Douglas, Morgenthau proposed that independent agencies be centralized under the Bureau of the Budget. When Harold Ickes complained that these changes could harm the PWA, Morgenthau warned of inflation. Through this outburst, Morgenthau felt that he prevented the president from repeating the incident where he double-crossed Douglas. "I am going about it in a roundabout way and am sugar-coating it so that I hope they will not recognize it."[23] The administration adopted a compromise version of reorganization in 1936.

In 1935, Morgenthau sensed he was having an effect on Roosevelt. He received encouragement when the president said that he wanted to keep expenditures within the previous year's figures.[24] During the summer, the president promised Morgenthau to push states to reduce the number of public aid recipients. Following the conversation, Morgenthau noted,

> I have made a real start towards changing the whole picture of expenditure of the government . . . If I can accomplish this I will have made it possible to have avoided a deficit inflation and the printing of greenbacks and put this country back on a sound financial basis.[25]

In December, the president ordered a half-billion-dollar budget cut and made it clear that he wanted "to impress on the country the fact that the budget is balanced except for relief."[26]

Understanding the president's mentality, Morgenthau reminded the president that standing for sound finance would have electoral benefits in 1936. He warned that Roosevelt remained "extremely vulnerable to attack on his spending program" since the Republicans would focus on the administration's spending in the same fashion that he had attacked Hoover.[27] With the exception of the first six months of the New Deal, Morgenthau said,

> All of the publicity that came out of the White House was "spending" and "more spending" and not a single word about economizing; that it was still time to talk and practice economy and that if he waited very much longer they would simply accuse him of doing it for political effect.

The deficit for fiscal year 1936 was the administration's highest, and economic recovery had stimulated an "inflationary psychology."[28] Morgenthau stressed that polls showed higher taxes were unpopular and that

> if the President will really go through with this program and begin to talk and *practice* economy it may be the turning point in his whole hold on the people because there is no question that many many people are really worried about this spending program because they can see no end to it.[29]

In the months preceding the election, Morgenthau argued that the government could save up to $500 million by cutting unnecessary costs and unused funds in agencies such as the PWA. The president agreed with Morgenthau's advice and announced that agencies were to identify nonessential funds that could be reduced.[30]

While 1935 and 1936 are often remembered for Roosevelt's shift to the Left, his administration continued to rely on regressive tax schemes in these climactic years. Fearing a loss of business confidence and citizen revolts, Roosevelt was determined not to increase federal taxes by an excessive amount. The administration promoted a welfare state that relied heavily on state and local spending while constraining the federal tax burden. At the height of the New Deal, as progressive support for Roosevelt was increasing in Congress and the conservative coalition found itself weaker than ever before, the president still rejected proposals that would have significantly increased federal income taxes (Brown, 1999, p. 32).

By the spring of 1936, the challenge to fiscal austerity increased. Morgenthau faced another serious threat to a balanced budget. Congress passed a $2.2 billion veterans' bonus increase and this time overrode the presidential veto. The combination of the veterans' payments and the Supreme Court decision to invalidate the agricultural processing tax left the federal government in need of an additional $620 million. Morgenthau suggested the excess profits tax as one response to this dilemma, as well as a way to calm inflationary pressures.[31] Furthermore, Morgenthau complained that the president had authorized Secretary Ickes to receive $250 million from the Reconstruction Finance Corporation (RFC), thereby throwing the budget out of balance. When Roosevelt promised that Ickes would not spend the money, Morgenthau responded that the newspapers would still interpret the budget as being out of balance. He was frustrated with the president, who did not seem "manly enough to admit to me and I do not think to himself that through this deal he has definitely thrown his budget out of balance by 250 million dollars."[32]

Improving economic conditions eased the budget crunch in the summer of 1936 by generating increased tax revenue. Together with the passage of the Undistributed Profits Tax and loophole-closing reform, revenue seemed sufficient to cover expenditures.[33] Meanwhile, Morgenthau maintained pressure on agencies to set aside 5 percent "as a kitty" to bring expenditures below the previous year's level.[34] Roosevelt said that there would be debt reduction as soon as income rose to normal levels. At that time, he said, the problem

> will not be how we shall obtain funds to promote recovery, but how fast we shall reduce the public debt, how fast and which taxes we shall reduce, and how much revenue we shall continue to employ in discharge of the new responsibilities for the social welfare which have been accepted by the Federal Government under the present Administration.[35]

But the president refused to make definite statements about when the budget might be balanced.[36]

In December, Morgenthau learned that Marriner Eccles, chair of the Federal Reserve, was promoting deficit spending. When the president said he wanted to use portions of an Eccles memorandum in a speech, Morgenthau noted,

> This is one of the most important challenges to your intellectual ability because the President has absorbed Eccles' philosophy and you have the job of dynamiting Eccles stuff out of the President's brain and if you fail you will find that Eccles will become the President's fiscal adviser.[37]

At this time, because of victories on issues such as tax reform and Social Security, Morgenthau still felt secure that he was having a significant impact on the president's decisions. Eccles's threat stemmed from what he might convince Roosevelt to do in the future, not from anything he had already done.

Most of 1937 turned out to be a triumphant year for Morgenthau as the policy agenda shifted decisively toward expenditure reduction. The economy seemed to be on its way to recovery. National income rose, unemployment declined, and prices increased. In response to these improvements, Morgenthau pushed the administration to undertake a program of expenditure reduction to avoid inflation. He believed that the budget could be balanced in 1938 with existing revenues, as long as new expenditures were not added. If necessary, Morgenthau supported new taxes since it would "be better to injure few people by unfair taxes than to ruin the country by uncontrolled inflation."[38] In what became an infamous statement, Morgenthau said that it was time "to strip off the bandages, throw away the crutches and see if American enterprise could stand on its own feet" (Morgenthau, 1947a, p. 82).

During the spring of 1937, Roosevelt decided to balance the budget. Although Roosevelt had never balanced a budget as president, he still believed that it was a desirable objective and had gone to great efforts to maintain deficits that were as low as possible (Friedel, 1990, pp. 96–97; Stein, 1994, pp. 35–36). The Budget and Relief Message of 1937 called for a balanced budget in light of the success of the New Deal, marking a high point for Morgenthau. The president accepted a relief figure so low that it left Morgenthau "absolutely breathless" (Morgan, 1995, p. 34). In the end, Morgenthau noted,

> the President gave me in his Message everything I asked for and I told him that I was entirely satisfied . . . he must have come to the conclusion that if he wants this Administration to go forward with his reform program he must have a sound financial foundation or his whole program will completely fail.[39]

In Morgenthau's opinion, everyone in the administration seemed determined to balance the budget. Even Harold Ickes told him in several private conversations that he was "anxious to balance the budget, and he says he's sick and tired of being the whipping boy. I almost fainted. He said, as far as he's concerned, he isn't going to encourage any more spending."[40] Continuing to make the type of distinctions that Douglas rejected, Morgenthau argued that cuts should affect regular government operations rather than emergency programs. He praised Harry Hopkins (head of the Works Progress Administration, or WPA) as one of the new leaders to cut expenditures.[41] His leniency toward Hopkins reflected Morgenthau's desire to distinguish between different types of expenditures, given the fact that the WPA was one of the most generous public works programs in the democratic and industrialized world (Amenta, 1998).

Morgenthau understood that the Treasury had to demonstrate to the public "that the President *really* meant what he said in his Budget Message."[42] Rather than arguing for a reduction in all spending, he distinguished between agencies that were being frugal and those that were wasting programs. Throughout the year, he focused on the Department of Agriculture. Morgenthau felt that the farm program represented the dangerous pressure imposed by interest groups and their government allies on the budget, much in the way the veterans' lobby had in 1935. Agriculture was one of the largest drains on the budget, greater than public works or public relief. Secretary of Agriculture Henry Wallace epitomized the administrators who refused to go along with the national need to reduce deficits because of the demands they faced for their constituencies. Morgenthau told his staff that Wallace was "getting away with murder."[43] Frustrated with Wallace's influence and positive media coverage, Morgenthau said that Wallace was obtaining more government money than "he's entitled to" and Wallace was beholden to the American Farm Bureau.[44] Wallace, he pointed out, received one out of every six dollars that the administration spent. In Morgenthau's view, Wallace needed to accept retrenchment so that cuts did not just come "out of the hide of the unemployed."[45] Morgenthau summarized the difference between himself and supporters of unrestrained government spending by telling a colleague, "What you want is for the Government to keep spending in order to keep business going . . . I want business to do the spending in place of the Government."[46]

Morgenthau feared that neither the public nor the media had faith in promises for fiscal responsibility. He compared this to the skepticism that emerged during World War I, when the government kept promising that soldiers would return in the next month.[47] Even Budget Director Daniel Bell felt that the president would go along on expenditure reduction up to a certain point to make the public "feel good" and "then he will back out and back down on balancing the budget."[48] As the voice of fiscal responsibility, the Treasury needed to show that these promises were real. Morgenthau urged the president to veto a small appropriation of about $1 million to "vie a good stiff message." Whatever the president decided, Morgenthau insisted that he do something "to make these people believe" in promises to balance the budget.[49] Bold statements from the president were crucial to this effort:

> I don't know anything which would be more popular than if you began to talk about how you are going to balance the Budget . . . you will reach a group that pretty well overlaps the same group who are down on you for what you have done and said about the Courts . . . beat the drums and boast about it . . . you will have the country in back of you to balance the Budget and keep Congress from passing a lot of appropriations over and above your estimates.[50]

Bell had reported that congressional Democrats were being swamped by constituent mail, even from citizens who received federal benefits, urging them to cooperate with Republicans on the drive for economy.[51] Morgenthau insisted that as the economy seemed to be recovering, expenditure reduction, rather than tax increases, should accomplish this goal. Higher taxes, he insisted, would hamper investment at this crucial moment. Taxes also remained unpopular with business and the electorate. Following the court packing battles, Roosevelt no longer had the strong political support that he commanded in

1935. Neither could Roosevelt afford to repeat Hoover's politically disastrous tax increase of 1932.[52]

Morgenthau met with Roosevelt every week to sustain his support for expenditure reduction. He was especially nervous since inaccurate estimates had created a projected revenue shortfall. Yet, Morgenthau believed the revenue shortfall could serve as a restraint on spending.[53] He proposed that the targeted figure of 10 percent savings in each agency could be met partially by refraining from filling vacancies, canceling promotions, and eliminated unnecessary expenses.[54] Roosevelt sent a letter to each agency head calling for these types of savings. On October 11, the president also acknowledged that federal money was being spent for activities that should now be funded by state and local government.[55]

Finding himself in a similar role to that of Douglas, Morgenthau served as a voice for fiscal restraint. As he later explained, "The policy of the budget is not my job, but I do think it is my job to lay down limits."[56] Throughout the fall and winter of 1937, Morgenthau and his experts devised ways to reduce expenditures. They went through every facet of the budget to see where monies could be saved. Treasury held firm to the rule that agencies seeking money for new programs needed to either take funding away from an existing program or raise additional revenue. Morgenthau also grappled with guaranteed budgetary commitments that were making it increasingly difficult to balance the budget in the long term.[57]

Morgenthau shared Douglas's concern that Americans were becoming less knowledgeable about the overall fiscal condition of the government. He insisted that Treasury needed to provide sound information about the possibility of balancing the budget. Through his speeches, he wanted to stimulate a public "backing to really balance this budget in an intelligent manner and, if you wish, so that the people, when they do write to their Congressman, will know what they are writing about." Lack of accurate budgetary information, he believed, was one of the greatest obstacles to faith in government: "People don't believe when the President gives a statement, because he's been wrong too often . . . they keep saying, 'Well, he's going to balance the budget—ha ha ha!' and they just don't believe it."[58] Even the concept of the balanced budget had lost its meaning:

> I want to talk to the people as man to man, and say—I'm so sick and tired of hearing people talk about balancing the budget as a slogan, like "Eat more Campbell's soup" . . . Or "Smoke Luckies Because you're Satisfied." I mean they've gotten so they think it's a kind of slogan. But what do they mean when they say that? Now, let's just take the can-opener and take a look at the thing.[59]

Morgenthau encountered skepticism during a speech he made to the National Academy of Political Science, a group of prominent business and financial leaders. As Morgenthau prepared the speech in the fall of 1937, a severe recession began. In response, Morgenthau emphasized that the balanced budget was a tool for recovery (May 1981, 103). After spending several intense weeks writing the speech, Morgenthau did not apologize for earlier deficits, arguing that they were needed to fight a "war" against the economic crisis. Moreover, he said that the policy of deliberate deficits had worked. But the recovery in 1936 had created new demands for private capital funds that would otherwise be available for private investment. The purpose of budget policy was to

> promote a high level of healthy character of business activity, a maximum volume of employment at good wages in private industry, a reasonable return to capital and enterprise, fair treatment for agricultural population, and adequate revenues to meet the services now demanded of the Federal government.

He promised that the administration would not "allow anyone to starve nor will it abandon its broad purpose to protect the weak, to give human security and to seek a wider distribution of our national income."[60] This statement was inserted at Roosevelt's request.[61] The distrustful audience literally laughed out loud as Morgenthau said the president was dedicated to balancing the budget. In the end the administration did not balance the budget because of a revenue shortfall. Even though Morgenthau failed to achieve his ultimate goal, he was pleased that the direction of budget policy seemed to have shifted toward a balanced budget. Significant budget cuts had been made and the deficit reduced. The media portrayed Morgenthau as a person who led this campaign with the administration. The *Wall Street Journal* reported that "he stands today as probably the strongest advocate within the administration of an honest-to-goodness balanced budget not later than the next fiscal years" (November 20, 1937). In the first week of January 1938, Roosevelt's budget to Congress contained a message of economy in government and more than one-half billion dollars in expenditure cuts, lowering the federal deficit significantly.

Revisiting the "Keynesian Turn"

Morgenthau's worst defeat came in 1938 when Roosevelt accepted a deficit to stimulate the economy. As the severity of the recession became clear in November 1937, Morgenthau's campaign halted temporarily. Morgenthau admitted to the president that the nation might be headed into another depression.[62] He blamed the recession on inadequate investment confidence, skepticism about the deficit reduction, instabilities in Europe, and the tight money policies of the Federal Reserve. However, Morgenthau still wanted to continue a policy of budgetary austerity. He agreed with Lewis Douglas, who made the argument that the recession was a "corrective," a result of President Roosevelt's attack on the Supreme Court, sit-down strikes, trade restrictions, monopolistic price-fixing, and so many years of deficits.

But the increasingly influential consumptionist policymakers blamed the recession on fiscal restraint. While John Keynes is often credited for introducing the notion of compensatory fiscal policy to correct underconsumption, the idea had been promoted for several decades by economists such as Waddill Catchings and Stuart Chase (Brinkley, 1995). Consumptionists argued that spending, not investment, was the key to a healthy economy. Rejecting the traditional belief that production created its own demand, they insisted that underconsumption had caused the depression. To solve this problem, the government should compensate for inadequate private spending through increased public spending. These experts claimed that federal deficits placed extra money into the economy. Workers would spend the extra dollars, which business could then respend. As that money circulated, the rate of spending doubled (the Multiplier Effect). Consumptionists insisted that the American economy had reached a stage of maturity and could no longer grow at the levels seen in the industrial age. As a result, the government needed to implement a program of sustained fiscal intervention to boost consumption. The recession of 1937 and 1938, which took place immediately after the administration's spending cuts, offered them a window of opportunity to inject their ideas into fiscal policy. Within Roosevelt's administration, Marriner Eccles, Leon Henderson (economic advisor to the secretary of commerce), Harry Hopkins, and Lauchlin Currie (special assistant to the chair of the Federal Reserve) all lobbied for this position.

At a cabinet meeting in November, Roosevelt admitted that he did not regard balancing the budget as "the most important question before the country."[63] In April 1938, the tide turned against fiscal conservatives. Leon Henderson, Aubrey Williams, and Beardsley Ruml convinced the president to accept deliberate deficits; Morgenthau was vacationing in Georgia at the time and did not know about the meeting. After returning to Washington, Morgenthau learned that the White House was prepared to increase spending. On April 14, the president called for almost $3 billion in emergency spending and loans. Morgenthau complained that the president had worked out this program without consulting a single person at the Treasury and that "he wants to shoot the whole works as far as spending is concerned."[64]

From outside the administration, Douglas railed against the consumptionist outlook. He argued that a shortage of investment in capital goods industries, which he called productive savings, posed the most urgent economic problem. While savings had risen during the 1930s, most of that money went toward "unproductive" government securities that did not increase private employment. Douglas complained that the administration taxed profits and discouraged productive savings by fostering an atmosphere of hostility toward private enterprise, tension between employees and employers, and uncertainty about the financial future. He argued that the heavy durable goods industry was in much worse condition than the consumer goods industries. Thus, spending was not the answer. Grounded in neoclassic economics, Douglas insisted that savings were a dynamic component of the economy since business depended on them for investments. Given the centrality of savings, he saw attacks on thrift as dangerous.

> We are confronted on all sides by slogans, such as "Spend and Put Men Back to Work." "Buy Now and Lick the Depression." The man who lives well within his income has come to be regarded as unpatriotic and as a slacker in the fight against the depression.

In his view, consumptionists encouraged citizens to avoid the very actions needed for recovery. "Thrift" Douglas (1935g) insisted, "is still a virtue" (pp. 267–72). But amid the most severe conditions since the start of Roosevelt's administration, his arguments had little political appeal. Nor could Morgenthau, who used less inflammatory rhetoric, seem to gain the president's ear. By 1938, the U.S. government was spending a greater portion of its gross national product (GNP) on certain types of social provision than comparable nations in Western Europe (Amenta, 1998).

Roosevelt's temporary embrace of deficits almost caused Morgenthau to resign. But Roosevelt wanted this prominent fiscal conservative to remain in a top position within the administration. Roosevelt said that resignation would lead to the destruction of the Democratic Party, the creation of a third party, and the loss of his program in Congress. "All the time he was telling me this I could not help but remember that he used almost word for word the same arguments with Lew Douglas. [*sic*]" Morgenthau told the president that he was asking him to carry out a program when he had nothing to do with the planning. Despite feeling excluded from Roosevelt's inner circle, Morgenthau stayed. He later explained that although they were in disagreement about this component of administration policy, they were in "total agreement on all other broad questions," especially the conviction that "the first concern of government should be the masses of the people." He did not want to jeopardize "common objectives" because of his opposition to "one phase" of the program (Morgenthau, 1947b, p. 49). In this decision, Morgenthau's political instincts differed from those of Douglas.

However, Morgenthau never came into the Keynesian fold. Decades later, Morgenthau continued to insist that Roosevelt should have balanced the budget, although he never went as far as Douglas, who said Keynes "had done more harm to the world than any author in the course of the last 150 years."[65] While admitting that unbalanced budgets were not "automatic" disasters and could ensure extraordinary levels of production and employment, Morgenthau (1947b) insisted that it was crucial for the economic system to "run on its own power" (p. 49). Gradually, Morgenthau turned to mass income tax increases instead of expenditure reduction. He felt that the administration had little choice if it intended to curtail deficits.[66] He also rejected the Keynesian argument that expenditure cuts had been the source behind the 1937 recession, an argument later used as ammunition against fiscal conservatism. Morgenthau said that government spending had not dropped significantly. Rather, revenue had increased as a result of a stronger economy. Future economists would lend support to this argument (Stein, 1969, pp. 98–99). Furthermore, the deficit had started to decline almost a month before there were any signs of a recession.

Morgenthau believed that the acceptance of compensatory fiscal policy was "one of the tragedies of this Administration." But Morgenthau sensed that facts were useless since "they've got the Eccles speech [linking spending cuts to the recession and deficits to economic improvement] there and they're using that as a Bible."[67] Following the battle over the budget in 1938, Morgenthau continued to play an important role in the administration. His wartime policies, such as the creation of a mass tax and war bonds, fostering private savings, successfully curtailed inflation and expanded the capacity of the state to raise revenue. Morgenthau suffered another defeat in 1939 when Congress, in response to Keynesians and orthodox fiscal conservatives, abandoned the accumulation of large reserves in Social Security. The fiscal design of Social Security remained uncertain until the landmark 1950 amendments (Zelizer, 1997). Although Morgenthau worked with Truman following Roosevelt's death, he resigned in July 1945.

Despite Morgenthau's own sense of defeat, many scholars have exaggerated the significance of Keynesianism by presenting the 1938 deficit as a dramatic embrace of consumptionist economics and an abandonment of fiscal conservatism. But this account is misleading. Foremost, the decision did not come until the very end of the New Deal after most of the key New Deal initiatives had passed. Moreover, within a year, the president faced a conservative congressional coalition of southern Democrats and Republicans who regained power in 1938. The coalition applied considerable pressure on the president until the war for low levels of spending and deficits. Furthermore, the actual size of the 1938 deficit was modest. Far short of a Keynesian revolution, the $3 billion deficit was relatively small, given the $100 billion economy. It was smaller than the unintended deficit of 1936 (Kennedy, 1999, pp. 358–59). Finally, there is little evidence that the president himself had consciously undertaken a new fiscal path that rejected the goal of balanced budgets and debt reduction (Brownlee, 1996, pp. 87). Roosevelt's long-term position was unclear as the rest of his years in office were consumed by the exigencies of war. At best, as the historian Alan Brinkley (1995) argued, the 1938 deficit "was a small and tentative step—an augury of the timid, halfhearted way in which Americans would embrace Keynesianism for most of the next forty years" (p. 104).

Fiscal Conservatism and the New Deal

By 1938, Henry Morgenthau Jr. had guided fiscal conservatism through an important transformation. For Lewis Douglas, New Deal liberalism and fiscal conservatism were irreconcilable. He defined fiscal conservatism as a vision of the political economy that enabled the private market to survive, a vision of sound currency, balanced budgets, and low interest rates. Excessive government, he believed, created artificial rigidities in the market and led to inflation. This vision did not find a permanent place within Roosevelt's administration. But a more moderate strand of fiscal conservatism survived. Morgenthau decoupled fiscal conservatism from anti-statism and proved to be extremely flexible. He believed that fiscal conservatism bestowed legitimacy to New Deal liberalism. Like Douglas, he feared the dangers of inflation, high interest rates, and growing debt. But Morgenthau believed in the need for government to create domestic stability. As secretary of the Treasury, he attempted to demonstrate that fiscal conservatism legitimized the American state by ensuring discipline, accountability, and restraint; fiscal conservatism also protected private markets from excessive intervention and from inflation. Given the distrust of government in the national political culture, adherence to fiscal conservatism, Morgenthau believed, broadened support for the New Deal. Fiscal conservatism seemed to be a way to constrain New Deal liberalism so that it could survive. At the same time, embracing New Deal liberalism provided fiscal conservatives with political appeal and legitimacy. This accommodation was a political outlook that Lewis Douglas could not understand or tolerate.

Notwithstanding moments of intense conflict, Roosevelt never felt as if he could or should exclude fiscal conservatives from his governing coalition. Douglas and Morgenthau were joined by other fiscal conservatives such as George L. Harrison, governor of the Federal Reserve Bank of New York, Jesse Jones, head of the RFC, and Raymond Moley, presidential advisor. From its inception, New Deal liberalism included fiscal conservatism in its agenda. Even when New Deal liberalism veered toward deficits, moreover, it remained in a constant dialogue with fiscal conservatism. But it took the active efforts of policy entrepreneurs such as Morgenthau to make sure this overriding principle actually affected policy. Although Douglas failed to wield such influence because of his ideological rigidity, Morgenthau reconfigured his agenda so that it became politically and economically viable. His influence became clearly evident through key victories during battles over Social Security, taxation, and spending.

Throughout the 1930s, fiscal conservatives created a countervailing force within the New Deal coalition against unrestrained government expansion. Given their clout within the fiscal institutions of the state, including Treasury and the tax-writing committees, they checked Roosevelt's inclinations to spend. The president needed to compromise with fiscal conservatives as he brokered legislative deals. Roosevelt's deficits before 1940 never exceed $4.4 billion, nor did expenditures eve rise beyond $10 billion (Morgan, 1995, p. 150; Savage, 1988, p. 169). Like economic planning and business-government associationalism, fiscal conservatism was yet another component in the eclectic mix of economic ideas that characterized the New Deal.

Democratic fiscal conservatives from presidents Truman to Carter have continued to believe that they could realistically champion fiscal responsibility and accept the modern state. Even their Keynesian advisors would turn to automatic stabilizers and stimulative tax cuts, rather than public spending, to stimulate the economy while continuing to endorse balanced budgets under strong economic conditions (Collins, 1987; Stein, 1969). The presidents worked closely with leaders of the congressional tax-writing committees who shared similar concerns (Zelizer, 1998). By reexamining the role of fiscal conservatism in the New Deal, it becomes clear that when Clinton insisted fiscal restraint and the modern state were interdependent, rather than mutually exclusive, he embraced one of the most important, yet least appreciated, legacies of the New Deal.

References

Amenta, Edwin. 1998. *Bold Relief: Institutional Politics and the Origins of Modern American Social Policy*. Princeton, NJ: Princeton University Press.

Baez, Joseph A. 1999. The New Deal and veterans' benefits, 1933–1936. This unpublished manuscript is in the possession of the author.

Barber, William J. 1985. *From New Era to New Deal: Herbert Hoover, the Economists, and American Economic Policy*. Cambridge: Cambridge University Press.

Beito, David. 1989. *Taxpayers in Revolt: Tax Resistance during the Great Depression*. Chapel Hill: University of North Carolina Press.

Blum, John M. 1959. *From the Diaries: Years of Crisis, 1928–1938*. Boston: Houghton Mifflin

Brinkley, Alan. 1994. The problem of American conservatism. *American Historical Review* 99 (April): 409–29.

———. 1995. *The End of Reform: New Deal Liberalism in Recession and War*. New York: Knopf.

———. 1998. *Liberalism and Its Discontents*. Cambridge, MA: Harvard University Press.

Browder, Robert, and Thomas G. Smith. 1986. *Independent: A Biography of Lewis W. Douglas*. New York: Knopf.

Brown, Michael K. 1999. *Race, Money, and the American Welfare State*. Ithaca, NY: Cornell University Press.

Brownlee, W. Elliot. 1996. *Federal Taxation in America: A Short History*. Cambridge: Cambridge University Press.

Collins, Robert M. 1987. *The Business Response to Keynes, 1929–1964*. New York: Columbia University Press.

Davies, Gareth, and Martha Derthick. 1997. Race and social welfare policy: The Social Security Act of 1935. *Political Science Quarterly* 112 (Summer): 217–35.

Douglas, Lewis. 1935a. Address of Hon. Lewis W. Douglas. *The Consensus* 19 (January): 8–24.

———. 1935b. Can government spending cure unemployment? *Atlantic Monthly* 156 (October): 408–12.

———. 1935c. The danger of mounting deficits. *Atlantic Monthly* 156 (November): 561–67.

———. 1935d. *The Liberal Tradition: A Free People and a Free Economy*. New York: Van Nostrand.

———. 1935e. Recovery by balanced budget. *Reviews of Reviews* 91 (January): 25–26, 69.

———. 1935f. Sound recovery through a balance budget. *Atlantic Monthly* 156 (December): 676–80.

———. 1935g. There is one way out. *Atlantic Monthly* 156 (September): 267–72.

———. 1936. Blowing the bubble! *Atlantic Monthly* 157 (January): 40–45.

Everest, Allan S. 1973. *The New Deal and Silver: A Story of Pressure Politics*. New York: De Capo.

Farley, James A. 1938. *Behind the Ballots: The Personal History of a Politician*. New York: Harcourt, Brace.

Friedel, Frank. 1990. *Franklin D. Roosevelt: A Rendezvous with Destiny*. Boston: Back Bay Books.

Jacobs, Meg. 2004. *Pocketbook Politics: Economic Citizenship in Twentieth Century America*. Princeton, NJ: Princeton University Press.

Kennedy, David M. 1999. *Freedom from Fear: The American People in Depression and War, 1929–1945*. New York: Oxford University Press.

Kimmel, Lewis. 1959. *Federal Budget and Fiscal Policy, 1789–1958*. Washington, DC: Brookings.

Leff, Mark. 1983. Taxing the "forgotten man": The politics of Social Security finance in the New Deal. *Journal of American History* 70 (September): 359–81.

———. 1984. *The Limits of Symbolic Reform: The New Deal and Taxation, 1933–1939*. Cambridge: Cambridge University Press.

Leuchtenburg, William E. 1963. *Franklin D. Roosevelt and the New Deal, 1932–1940*. New York: Harper Torchbooks.

Lieberman, Robert. 1995. Race and the organization of welfare policy. In *Classifying by Race*, ed. Paul Peterson, 156–87. Princeton, NJ: Princeton University Press.

May, Dean L. 1981. *From New Deal to New Economics: The Liberal Response to the Recession*. New York: Garland.

Moley, Raymond. 1939. *After Seven Years*. New York: Harper.

Morgan, Iwan W. 1995. *Deficit Government: Taxing and Spending in Modern America*. Chicago: Ivan Dee.

Morgenthau, Henry, Jr. 1947a. The Morgenthau diaries: The fight to balance the budget. *Colliers* 27 (September): 11–13, 80–82.

———. 1947b. The Morgenthau diaries II: The struggle for a program. *Colliers* 7 (October): 20–45; 48–49.

Patashnik, Eric M. 1997. Unfolding promises: Trust funds and the politics of precommitment. *Political Science Quarterly* 112 (Fall): 431–52.

Patterson, James T. 1967. *Congressional Conservatism and the New Deal: The Growth of the Conservative Coalition in Congress, 1933–1939*. Lexington: University of Kentucky Press.

Perkins, Frances. 1946. *The Roosevelt I Knew*. New York: Viking.

Quadagno, Jill. 1994. *The Color of Welfare: How Racism Undermined the War on Poverty*. New York: Oxford University Press.

Romasco, Albert U. 1983. *The Politics of Recovery: Roosevelt's New Deal*. New York: Oxford University Press.

Roosevelt, Franklin. 1939. *The Public Papers and Addresses of Franklin D. Roosevelt: Volume Two*. New York: Russell and Russell.

———. 1972. *Complete Presidential Press Conferences of Franklin D. Roosevelt*. New York: De Capo.

Rosenof, Theodore. 1975. *Dogma, Depression, and the New Deal.* Port Washington, NY: Kennikat.

Sargent, James E. 1974. FDR and Lewis W. Douglas: Budget balancing and the early New Deal. *Prologue* 6 (Spring): 33–43.

———. 1980. Roosevelt's Economy Act: Fiscal conservatism and the early New Deal. *Congressional Studies* 7 (Winter): 33–51.

Savage, James D. 1988. *Balanced Budgets and American Politics.* Ithaca, NY: Cornell University Press.

Schlesinger, Arthur, Jr. 1959. *The Age of Roosevelt: The Coming of the New Deal.* Boston: Houghton Mifflin.

Smith, James A. 1991. *The Idea Brokers: Think Tanks and the Rise of the New Policy Elite.* New York: Free Press.

Snowiss, Sylvia. 1971. Presidential leadership of Congress: An analysis of Roosevelt's first hundred days. *Publius* 1: 59–66.

Stein, Herbert. 1969. *The Fiscal Revolution in America.* Chicago: University of Chicago Press.

———. 1994. *Presidential Economics: The Making of Economic Policy from Roosevelt to Clinton.* 3rd rev. Washington, DC: American Enterprise.

Steuerle, C. Eugene. 1992. *The Tax Decade: How Taxes Came to Dominate the Public Agenda.* Washington, DC: Urban Institute.

Zelizer, Julian E. 1997. "Where is the money coming from?" The reconstruction of Social Security finance, 1939–1950. *Journal of Policy History* 9 (Fall): 399–424.

———. 1998. *Taxing America: Wilbur D. Mills, Congress, and the State, 1945–1975.* Cambridge: Cambridge University Press.

EIGHT

"Where Is the Money Coming From?"[1]

The Reconstruction of Social Security Finance

Social Security has achieved a privileged status in American politics.[*] As a result of the Social Security tax, supporters claim, recipients have not received unearned benefits, nor has Congress felt as if it were building a massive welfare state. Indeed, the Social Security tax system has legitimated the program in the minds of policy experts, politicians, and recipients. Through Social Security, the American state has forged a strong alliance with the elderly and their descendants, both with retirees who received cash payments and with working families who did not have to finance their parents' retirement years.

Today, however, the future of Social Security seems uncertain. The enormous cost of the "baby boomer" retirement between 2010 and 2040 and the tax increases needed to finance their pensions threaten to undermine long-term support for the program. By 2030, according to one bipartisan congressional study, projected spending for Medicare, Social Security, and federal employee retirement programs will consume almost all the tax revenue collected by the federal government unless policy changes are made in the interim.[2] As policymakers and citizens debate this looming "Social Security Crisis," they would profit from understanding the influence of the earmarked tax system on the development of the Social Security program since 1935.

Most historical studies of the American state downplay the centrality of taxation to their analysis.[3] The revenue-raising functions of the state have been treated purely as a technical, administrative endeavor at the periphery of policy life. This essay, however, emphasizes the centrality of the earmarked tax system to the politics of Social Security. Without this system, social insurance would not have been as attractive, as generous, or as desired; the benefits, moreover, would not have been distributed without a means test. After all, the main reason citizens and politicians have privileged social insurance was the perception that it was an earned benefit. This definition of the policy was not inherent to

* This essay originally appeared in the *Journal of Policy History* 9 (1997): 339–424.

the benefit, but had to be constructed through a complex tax system, with its symbols and its rhetoric. By focusing on taxation, this article begins to reconstruct the discourse that was used during the internal debates over Social Security, thereby providing a richer sense of the logic that drove these important policy decisions. My findings suggest that issues other than race and gender, which most historical studies have focused on, were also crucial to the development of Social Security.[4] In particular, fiscal policymakers sought to create an expansive social insurance program—grounded in a distinct system of contributory finance—that could withstand politically the anti-statist culture of the United States.[5] Most important, policymakers and legislators were eager to find a common ground between fiscal conservatives and the welfare system.

The following pages focus on one crucial period in the history of Social Security finance. Between 1939 and 1950, the Social Security tax system came under fire when the program's financial principles were under attack. By 1943, Congress had undermined the two fiscal mechanisms that distinguished Old-Age Insurance from other forms of welfare. Foremost, Congress had abolished the mandate for a large reserve. Moreover, they authorized the use of general revenue to pay for benefits when payroll taxes became insufficient. By threatening the tax that justified the exclusion of a means test, these actions blurred the thin line that separated social insurance from public welfare.

The essay examines how program supporters reconstructed Social Security finance to meet this challenge, resulting in the Social Security Amendments of 1950. I begin by describing the earmarked tax system that Congress created in 1935. I then turn to the debate between 1939 and 1948 about the survival of the Social Security tax system and whether Social Security would be financed through the same monies as all other programs. Finally, I focus on how a cadre of policymakers, including Wilbur Mills, Democrat on the House Ways and Means Committee and future chairman of the committee, and Robert Myers, Chief Actuary of the Social Security Administration, redesigned the earmarked tax system into the structure that defined the program until 1972. The tax system constituted a seminal compromise between fiscal conservatism and the American state.

The Social Security Tax System

The New Deal had introduced into the American state a new concept in federal taxation. Through the Social Security Act of 1935, federal officials began to use earmarked taxes to distinguish entire categories of government benefits.[6] By earmarking taxes, the federal government designated a particular revenue source to a particular type of expenditure. This practice stood in contrast to general revenue financing, through which particular expenditures were financed by consolidated government monies.[7] When Congress enacted Social Security, it divided the program into two tracks, each characterized by the type of tax that paid for its benefits.

The "public assistance" track included Old-Age Assistance and Aid to Dependent Children. Even though federal funding for welfare represented a significant innovation, public assistance relied on a traditional system of finance. Congress paid for benefits through general government revenue raised primarily by personal and corporate income taxes. Like other general revenue programs, policymakers feared that benefits might become too generous over time; they frequently invoked Civil War pensions as an example of how noncontributory programs tended to become mired in corruption and partisan politics.[8] After all, Congress did not have to raise a specific tax each time it raised a noncontributory benefit, nor did recipients contribute anything directly to the program. To combat these problems, Congress imposed strict controls on OAA and ADC, including means-testing and low benefits. Although welfare experts spent the next fifty years debating over the expansion of benefits, few of them challenged its method of finance.[9]

In contrast, the "social insurance" track (Old-Age Insurance and Unemployment Compensation) stimulated a continual debate about the program's tax source.[10] Since the inception of Old-Age Insurance in 1935, Congress had imposed a monthly tax on the gross income of employees to pay for monthly benefits; both workers and their employers shared this tax burden. By paying the Social Security tax, participants would "earn" the right to their benefits; general revenue, moreover, could not be used to pay for the program.[11] Administrators claimed that Congress would use the payroll tax revenue in future years to pay for personal retirement benefits. Wage-related benefits were said to guarantee the connection between the individual's contributions and the benefits they received.[12] Unlike OAA, these benefits were federally administered. During the early years of the program, Social Security administrators directed intense public relations efforts to promote the concept of social insurance among the citizenry.[13]

The payroll tax constituted the heart and soul of Old-Age Insurance. According to the Social Security Act, the payroll "contribution" was a direct tax on the wage income of workers in covered occupations. While the tax applied to *all* income earned, no matter how small or large, the act imposed a maximum limit on the amount of wages on which taxes could be collected (this was called the earnings or wage base). By having contributed this payroll tax during their productive years, according to President Roosevelt, retirees would feel as if they had earned their benefits. The earmarked tax also justified the exclusion of a means test from the program.[14]

Under the terms of the Social Security Act, the Bureau of Internal Revenue would begin collecting payroll taxes in 1937. The Treasury was to place the taxes into the general revenue fund like all other tax revenue, where the monies could be used for anything from building battleships to constructing roads.[15] Nonetheless, the law required that Congress make an annual appropriation into the old-age reserve account that was sufficient to preserve a self-supporting system. In 1935, "self-supporting" meant a reserve large enough so that if the program ceased operating, all benefits earned at that time could be paid from the reserve.[16] The program would never need to depend on general revenue.

The founders of Old-Age Insurance claimed that scheduled taxes would exceed the cost of benefits over the long term. Contemplating that the cost of benefits would reach approximately $3.5 billion by 1980, the founders established a tax schedule that could finance 60 percent of these expenditures at a combined tax rate of 6 percent for the employer and employee. The excess of tax revenue collected during the early years of the program would create a reserve of $47 billion by 1980, which was sufficient to finance the remaining cost of benefits; Congress would invest the revenue in U.S. interest-bearing bonds. Under this byzantine system, in which the government invested its own monies in itself, workers could theoretically receive benefits that were equivalent to their tax contributions, with interest; the Social Security Administration claimed that U.S. bonds were the "safest investment in the world."[17]

The Perils of Uncertainty, 1939–1948

Within two years, however, strong opposition had mounted against collecting a surplus of revenue. First, Keynesian economists warned that the surpluses and the taxes themselves would drain consumer purchasing power. Reserves, they added, were unnecessary since the government always had the power to tax and since "policy-holders" could not withdraw their contributions. Second, the popular Townsendite movement promoted flat pensions that offered generous benefits and that were funded through general revenue. Third, fiscally conservative legislators and business leaders feared that Congress would use the surplus for extravagant public expenditures; instead, they preferred lowering the corporate tax burden. Finally, many financial analysts cautioned that large reserves meant higher costs to those who paid the income tax that financed the interest on federal bonds.[18]

In response to these challenges, Congress abandoned the principle of accumulating large reserves through the Social Security Amendments of 1939. Among the financial stipulations, the amendments legally earmarked payroll taxes by creating the Federal Old-Age and Survivors' Insurance Trust Fund; payroll tax revenue was to be placed directly into the fund and used for nothing else.[19] The amendments also established a Board of Trustees to report whenever the reserve exceeded three times the program's cost.[20] Although it was not specifically stated in the law, this implied that the system would be run on a "pay-as-you-go" basis with a little money to be deposited in a contingency reserve fund. To reduce the program's surplus by almost one-half, the tax-writing committees increased benefits, expanded coverage to the widows and children of participants who died before reaching the retirement age, and froze the tax rate at 2 percent.[21] After expanding coverage to widows and children, Congress changed the name of Old-Age Insurance to Old Age and Survivors' Insurance (OASI).

Politically, Congress was eager to reduce the actuarial surplus since this meant increasing benefits without raising taxes. By boosting cash benefits and by expanding coverage to those constituents who were not yet in the program, representatives could strengthen support within their district. The extension of coverage was particularly appealing during a period when many representatives did not yet have constituents who received Social Security. Of course, there were limits to this electoral payoff. Constituents perceived the benefits as an earned right—not as a government benefit—and politicians had defined their own role as brokers between the contributions and benefits of citizens in this insurance system. Nonetheless, representatives were aware that any type of monies that arrived to citizens via the federal government increased political satisfaction among the electorate. Congress thus agreed to abandon the plan for accumulating large reserves in the trust fund.

Without the original concept of a "full" reserve, Congress could now only rely on the symbolic value of the payroll tax, or the absence of general revenue funding, to distinguish social insurance finance from public assistance to justify the exclusion of a means test. Although social insurance was to be financed in the same fashion as all other public expenditures, with one group of citizens paying for the benefits of another group, most government officials explained the payroll tax as a special type of tax that *entitled* the contributor to receive a specific type of benefit in future years without a means test. According to the Social Security Board, the tax offered the "psychological basis" for OASI: unless every benefit recipient "makes a contribution, no matter how small, the whole system of Social Security, with relatively fixed benefits payable as a matter of right, would be jeopardized."[22] Or as Marion Folsom, an executive of the Eastman Kodak Company, explained:

> The contributions which an individual makes give him the feeling that he has earned the benefits as a right. This avoids and eliminates the need for a means test and the fear of being an object of charity . . . Sharing in the cost of the benefits should give the individual a better understanding of their value and of the workings of our economic system. It also helps to offset a tendency on the part of the individual to look toward the government for support. He realizes, too, that any increase in benefits may involve an increase in contributions.[23]

While general revenues meant welfare, payroll taxes meant earned benefits. Nonetheless, the 1939 amendments left open the possibility of using general revenue to pay for social insurance.[24] Even Secretary of Treasury Henry Morgenthau, who had been the strongest advocate for a full reserve in 1935, now suggested that "general tax revenues may be substituted—without substantial inequity—for a considerable proportion of the expected interest earnings from the large reserve contemplated by the present law."[25] Without the full reserve, future committees would have to pay for the benefits of current retirees either by raising payroll tax rates on working citizens or by using general revenue monies.[26] The

1939 amendments neither authorized nor excluded either option. By failing to resolve this issue, Congress left Social Security in a state of grave uncertainty.[27]

The tax-writing committees aggravated this situation by maintaining a tax freeze through the 1940s. Congress justified its position on the basis of the small number of elderly persons receiving social insurance benefits, the remaining surplus from 1939, and the rising wartime payrolls that resulted in larger Social Security tax collections.[28] The tax freeze according to Robert Myers, chief actuary of the Social Security Administration, found "unanimous" support from "Government, labor, and business representatives."[29] Some Social Security actuaries, moreover, sensed intense pressure from their bureaucratic leaders to avoid raising the issue of long-term cost. Myers complained: "There is the very serious limitation that the general philosophy of planners is to utterly disregard costs, if this might prove a deterrent. The planners also are not willing to face the problems and difficulties which an analytical actuarial mind will usually bring forth. Rather, the attitude is that any word of adverse criticism denotes a reactionary attitude or, in other words, you must all be in favor of it or all against it with no midway positions."[30]

Worse still, the tax-writing committees adopted the Vandenberg-Murray amendment (1944), which authorized general revenue appropriations into the Social Security trust fund when the cost of benefits exceeded the amount of payroll tax revenue.[31] The subsidy would begin in about fifteen years, when the government finished paying off the cost of the war and reconversion; the percentage of general revenue would increase gradually until it represented at least one-third of total annual expenditures.[32] When the House of Representatives voted to repeal the amendment in 1946, they were overruled by the Senate. The following year, Treasury officials accepted a temporary continuation of the tax freeze and assumed an eventual general revenue contribution to the program.[33]

The Advisory Council on Social Security, headed by Robert Ball, issued a series of reports in 1947 and 1948 about the program. The council argued that the best way to reduce dependency on welfare was to expand OASI into a universal program.

Besides raising benefits and expanding coverage, the Advisory Council recommended an immediate increase in the tax rate to one and a half percent for employers and employees. Congress, according to the council, should increase the tax rate to two and a half percent when the cost of benefits exceeded taxes. Thereafter, the "pay-as-you-go" system would be maintained through a general revenue contribution whenever benefits exceeded taxes. The council added that the federal contribution should never exceed one-third of the benefit disbursements.[34] Such a contribution could be legitimated on the grounds that the social insurance system was gradually taking over from public assistance a major part of the "burden" for caring for the aged, widows, and dependent children.[35]

Together, the Vandenberg-Murray amendment and the tax freeze had thus jeopardized one of the main distinctions of social insurance. Congress had not only eliminated the accumulation of reserve but also had authorized the use of general revenue to pay for insurance benefits. Although no one suggested that social insurance be means-tested, Congress had threatened the tax system that rationalized the distribution of benefits without regard to need. During the next two years, the Ways and Means Committee and the Social Security Administration teamed up to reestablish the stability of the payroll tax. Their efforts to prevent general revenue from "contaminating" social insurance began in the winter of 1949, when Ways and Means conducted hearings about a new series of proposals to broaden coverage in Old-Age and Survivors' Insurance.

Financing the Expansion, 1949–1950

As America entered the 1950s, federal officials initiated a campaign to expand social insurance and to eliminate most noncontributory public assistance. There were many factors behind this campaign. Some were microeconomic and ideological: collective bargaining for private pensions led corporate employers to support public pensions to minimize their own costs; a higher cost-of-living fueled a demand for higher benefits; and government officials were more willing to expand contributory social insurance for retirees who had "earned their benefits," as opposed to poor citizens in need of government handouts. Other factors were macroeconomic: rising incomes had generated enough revenue so that officials could raise benefits without a major increase in the tax rate. Meanwhile, there was a substantial revenue surplus since more people were paying for benefits than were receiving them.[36] These developments coincided with congressional elections, which provided an incentive for representatives from both parties to provide constituents with more cash.[37]

But the prospects for this expansion were uncertain. During the 1940s, welfare was expanding at a faster rate than social insurance.[38] Since OASI covered a limited segment of the population, rural agricultural laborers, domestic workers, state and local government employees, and the self-employed still relied on public assistance.[39] In 1949, the federal government spent almost three times as much on welfare as it did on insurance; the average OAA payment, for example, was 70 percent more than the average insurance benefit.[40] Given these statistics, advocates of social insurance feared that their program would be swamped by the continued growth of public welfare. As one administration staffer acknowledged, "Because of our failure to develop a much stronger social insurance system than we now have, it is nip and tuck as to whether . . . advocates of a general pension system may win out in the race between insurance and pensions."[41]

To avoid this outcome, the Social Security administration proposed a massive expansion of coverage that would, once and for all, establish the primacy of Old-Age and Survivors' Insurance over Old-Age Assistance. In response to the election of 1948, which kept Harry Truman in the presidency and enabled the Democrats to retake both chambers of Congress, the Democratic Party supported a massive expansion of Social Security. Wilbur Cohen, who was a top advisor to the Social Security Board, led the lobbying campaign to expand benefits and coverage.[42]

Between February and April 1949, Robert Doughton's Ways and Means Committee conducted public hearings. Doughton, a Democrat from North Carolina and chairman of the Ways and Means Committee, teamed up with Arthur Altmeyer, the commissioner of Social Security, to argue that an expansion of social insurance was crucial to eliminating the need for public assistance.[43] Most hearing participants agreed. Mills, for example, warned that "the longer Congress delays coverage under title II [Old-Age and Survivors' Insurance], the greater grows the momentum for increased assistance under title I [Old-Age Assistance]."[44] By extending social insurance benefits to domestic servants, farm workers, and the self-employed, he argued, Congress could reduce the demand for government handouts to the elderly.[45]

The convergence of the proposed expansion with the tax freeze and the Vandenberg-Murray amendment forced Congress finally to confront the issue of general revenue. Until Congress clearly defined the tax source behind OASI, its proponents would have difficulty selling social insurance as an alternative to welfare. As Mills lamented, "The present program is not sound, and the present rate of taxation provided to maintain that program is not sound."[46] Indeed, Myers now estimated that the general-revenue subsidy might be more than $6.5 billion by the year 2000.[47]

Policymakers came down on both sides of the general-revenue debate. Some experts supported the use of non-earmarked monies. Foremost, the Council of Economic Advisers argued that an eventual Treasury contribution offered an "economically sound and desirable course." Among themselves, they concluded that "in an economy whose vigor depends upon a high relative level of consumption, a social insurance scheme which depends entirely upon payroll taxes which bear on consumption is an anachronism which can defeat the most fundamental purpose of social security."[48] Likewise, Robert Ball concluded that "the Government's obligation to eventually make up the deficit of contribution of older workers and those who in the early years contribute at less than the actuarial rate should be explicitly stated in the legislation."[49] "For social insurance just as for private annuities," Ball wrote, "it is much easier for both workers and employers to pay a more or less level rate over a working lifetime." He continued to recommend a constant low tax rate combined with a general-revenue subsidy.[50]

But most Ways and Means members shied away from the general-revenue approach. The thought of placing non-earmarked tax money into the system seemed to undermine the basic premises of social insurance. Before expanding OASI, they insisted on restoring the connection between the payroll tax and the insurance benefit. Robert Kean (D-NJ), for example, warned that if the committee wanted "to pay to the individual as a matter of right, and then if we start to take out of the general tax revenues money which he has not earned through his insurance premiums, which would go to rich and poor alike, there ought to be a needs requirement which is entirely contrary to the idea of this whole system."[51] Similarly, Noah Mason (R-IL) argued that he was fooling his constituents "if I am promising them certain benefits which they will only partially pay for and the rest comes out of the air—as most of them think, when it comes out of the general Treasury."[52]

Wilbur Mills caught the eyes of Washington pundits by helping to resolve this historic debate. Mills was a Democratic representative from Arkansas who had entered Congress in 1938. In October 1942, Speaker of the House Sam Rayburn had placed Mills on the Ways and Means Committee.[53] In 1949, Mills confessed his "guilt" for accepting what "now appears to be a very ill-advised thing over the years, not permitting the original tax rate provided in the 1935 and 1939 acts to go into effect, but continuing to agree with the Senate that it should be frozen at 1 percent of payroll each on employer and employee."[54] Mills perceived the political payoff for legislation that protected the actuarial soundness of Social Security, even when that meant raising payroll taxes. After all, workers paid their "contribution" with the expectation that the program would remain sound through their own retirement. Members of Congress could thus gain electoral support not only by distributing immediate benefits to recipients, but by protecting the actuarial soundness of the earmarked tax system that was said to guarantee the future benefits of current contributors. This differed from the income tax system since citizens did not perceive a direct, concrete benefit that would result for themselves from an income tax hike.

Behind the scenes, Mills worked closely with Robert Myers to reestablish a close actuarial balance for the "pay-as-you-go" program. Myers had taken over as chief actuary of the Social Security Administration when his predecessor, W. R. Williams, quit following a public conflict with administrators over the use of insurance rhetoric to promote the program. At Chairman Doughton's request, Myers worked full-time as an actuary for Ways and Means in 1949 and 1950. Mills and Myers produced a formidable team. On the one hand, Mills pushed Myers toward publishing politically feasible data. On the other hand, Myers provided Mills with a respected "technician" whose vast knowledge intimidated his opponents; in 1949, these opponents even included top administration officials who privately acknowledge that "the tendencies toward weakening the contributory principle are not necessarily bad and . . . there is a certain amount of political appeal in not pressing the issue."[55]

While designing the proposed expansion in 1950, this dynamic tax duo took several steps toward strengthening the payroll system. Most important, they wanted to force Congress to pay for Old-Age and Survivors' Insurance entirely through the payroll tax with monthly contributions paying for monthly benefits. Unlike previous estimates, their new data assumed that there would not be any federal subsidy from general revenue.

When determining who should be covered by the program, they always began with the question of cost, after which they considered the issue of "rights" or "need."[56] For example, Myers criticized the recommendation made by the Advisory Council in 1948 that a level tax rate should be supplemented by a general revenue subsidy on "equitable grounds." Myers warned that, since actuarial cost estimates were never "precisely determinable," the amount of federal monies needed to pay for social insurance could climb much higher than Ball and the council had predicted.[57]

Mills and Myers used conservative estimates to guarantee the actuarial soundness of their proposals. One of their favorite devices, for example, was the "level earnings assumption," whereby they did not anticipate any increase in wage levels, even though the long-range trend of wages had been upward since 1890. Should wages continue to rise, as most economists agreed they would, the "unanticipated surplus" could provide Congress with enough revenue to liberalize benefits or expand coverage *without* raising taxes.[58] Under the level-wage assumption, Myers also estimated that Congress would not increase payroll tax rates or the wage base; if Congress did, representatives would once again find themselves with an "unanticipated surplus." According to Mills and Myers, however, this assumption postponed increases until economic conditions created the necessary revenue. Finally, they relied on a graduated contribution rate that would meet all benefit payments and produce a moderate amount of excess income for seventy-five years. By dealing with seventy-five-year periods, the two men hoped to avoid the short-term focus that had produced the tax freeze of the 1940s.[59]

Based on the actuarial work of Mills, Myers, and Cohen, Ways and Means reported out a bill to the House in August 1949. The opening paragraphs of their report began with the difficult choice facing Congress: "There are indications that if their insurance program is not strengthened and expanded, the old-age assistance program may develop into a very costly and ill-advised system of noncontributory pensions, payable not only to the needy but to all individuals at or above retirement age who are no longer employed." The time had come, the committee proclaimed, to "reaffirm the basic principle that a contributory system of social insurance in which workers share directly in meeting the cost of the protection afforded is the most satisfactory way of preventing dependency."[60] The bill expanded coverage to more than eleven million people and raised benefits for present and future retirees. The amendments promised benefits for retirees who were newly eligible to the program as the result of its expansion but who had never contributed taxes into the system because of their initial exclusion. Like the 1939 amendments, this liberalization further reduced the projected surplus by several billion dollars.[61]

To finance these changes, the legislation ended the tax freeze and eliminated the Vandenberg-Murray amendment.[62] The decision to exclude officially general revenue from the program, according to Wilbur Cohen, cut across ideological lines: "They all—the liberals and the conservatives—went for a completely self-supporting system. 'Let's not get into a Government subsidy.'"[63] The committee recommended "a tax schedule which . . . will make the system self-supporting . . . as nearly as can be foreseen under present circumstances." Recognizing that future experiences might differ from the estimates made at the time, Ways and Means stipulated that Congress would adjust the tax schedule when needed. Through this system, Myers explained, "no appropriated monies other than contributions from workers and employers will, over the long-run, be needed to pay the benefits (and also the administrative expenses)."[64] Additionally, the committee raised the wage base to $3,600, far below the amount sought by the administration.[65]

During the debate on the House floor, Ways and Means members conveyed the sense of crisis that had gripped Social Security policymakers. Representative Kean, for example, warned that "we are at the crossroads. The old-age assistance program has grown by leaps and bounds. More than twice as many of our older citizens are receiving old-age assistance as are receiving payments under OASI."[66] This proposal would protect social insurance by restoring the integrity of the payroll tax, the political glue that held the contributory system together. The hope of Ways and Means, Kean concluded, was that the "old-age assistance program will gradually taper off as more and more people become qualified under OASI."[67]

But it was Mills who captured the political imagination of the House. In his presentation, he explained that social insurance offered federal assistance without creating a welfare state:

> We have heard an awful lot in recent months about the development of the welfare state. It is significant that we hear that charge every time any legislation is presented to the Congress which has to do with the welfare of an individual. I challenge the statement that the creation of machinery providing security against need in old age constitutes a welfare state or is in the direction of a welfare state. If we should adopt some of these grandiose schemes which have been submitted to the House in the form of a bill providing for the payment of pensions to individuals who have reached the age of 65, whether they need those benefits or not, as some of our colleagues have signed a discharge petition to do so, we might be proceeding in the direction of a welfare state [here Mills was referring to a variant of the Townsend Plan]. But when we call upon the individual during his productive years to lay aside, in the form of a contribution, out of his wages and earnings an amount of money which will enable an agency of the Government to provide him with benefits after he becomes 65 years of age, how can it be said that we are doing something for that individual for nothing?[68]

When John Byrnes (R-WI) charged that OASI did not operate like private insurance, Mills responded that the taxpayer was at least "entitled to say" that he was "buying and paying for that security" against need in his old age, not that he had actually done so.[69]

Such arguments were effective. On October 5, the House passed the bill by a vote of 333 to 14 through a "splendid demonstration of teamwork" by committee Democrats.[70] The Senate postponed action until the following year. After five months of study, Senate Finance reported out a bill in May 1950, which the Senate passed by a vote of 81 to 2 following a well-orchestrated campaign by Wilbur Cohen.[71] Soon after, the conference report passed both chambers on August 28, 1950.

The Social Security Amendments of 1950 extended coverage to approximately ten million workers, including portions of the nonprofessional self-employed, agricultural workers, employees of nonprofit institutions, and domestic servants. The benefit amounts were roughly doubled, a reflection of the changes in wage levels and cost of living since the 1939 amendments; the retirement test (the amount of earnings permitted beneficiaries if they were to receive benefits) was notably liberalized.[72] This expansion helped to cement an alliance between the American state and the elderly through a social provision that appeared self-supporting and distinct from welfare; it also showed members of Congress that these types of benefits could be raised significantly without any apparent cost.

Ironically, despite all the rhetoric about a race to defeat welfare, the amendments increased the scope of public assistance: until the government had expanded social insurance to a sufficient level, most representatives agreed on the continued need for noncontributory welfare. In 1950, Congress created grants-in-aid, called "vendor payments," which partially financed medical providers for needy citizens;[73] they created a new category of federal grants-in-aid for needy individuals who were "permanently and totally" disabled; and, as a result of Mills's effort, they increased the rate of federal participation in OAA.[74]

Most important, the amendments transformed the "financial philosophy" of the Old-Age and Survivors' Insurance by resolving the uncertainty that had existed over the role of general revenue.[75] In short, Myers explained, Congress now intended that "the system should be completely self-supporting from the tax income provided. Accordingly, the provision for potential Government contribution to the system, which had been incorporated in 1943, is eliminated."[76] The Social Security Amendments of 1950 affirmed a "pay-as-you-go" approach by eliminating the Vandenberg-Murray amendment, by raising the wage base, and by establishing a graduated tax schedule that would meet the cost of the program for the next seventy-five years.[77] The small excess of tax contributions over benefits in the early years would be deposited in the trust fund. The money would be invested in government bonds and would equal the amount needed to help pay benefits in months when unexpected increases in benefits or decreases in tax revenues, or both, resulted in expenditures greater than revenues; the contingency reserve would most likely be used in the case of a severe economic recession.[78]

Based on the Ways and Means report, the conference committee recognized that long-range cost estimates could not be precise and that adjustments in the tax schedule might be necessary in the future.[79] The committee recommended that the system be financed by an increasing tax schedule that of necessity would ultimately rise higher than the level tax rate that Robert Ball had endorsed.[80] Finally, the committee did not suggest that earmarking taxes should be in all areas of fiscal policy; as one official explained: "A guiding principle of fiscal policy should be that the Government expends its funds where they are needed most, regardless of the source of the funds."[81] But earmarking taxes, according to the committee, could be used when there was a clear correlation between the benefit and the tax.[82]

Indeed, the amendments secured an exclusive link between the payroll tax and the insurance benefit, thereby virtually eliminating the possibility of financing OASI through general revenue. Congress would redistribute money across generations, from the paychecks of young wage-earners to the pockets of retirees. For government officials, this decision appeared to strengthen social insurance since they perceived the payroll tax as a superior type of tax that distinguished the programs it financed; the payroll tax, they contended, entitled the contributor to receive a certain type and amount of benefit in future years; it also disciplined representatives since they had to raise the tax each time they raised a benefit. Since the payroll taxpayer was "entitled" to future benefits, moreover, Congress would find it difficult to reduce the tax rate as they could with income taxes without decreasing future OASI benefits or destroying the actuarial balance of the system. According to the rules of the program, any additional revenue was to be kept in the trust fund in case of an emergency if the program lost unexpected revenue or an immediate benefit increase became essential.

Policymakers often acknowledged that these distinctions were primarily symbolic. After all, many of the economic arrangements were a fiction. Mills, for example, admitted to the House that "the net effect upon the individual who pays a tax is the same whether it is a social-security tax or an income tax: His income is decreased by the amount of the tax and so is his purchasing power. That is simple mathematics."[83] Regardless, they continued to encourage the belief that the earmarked tax system was the key feature that separated OASI from other forms of welfare: in their rhetoric, policymakers did not even call the payroll tax a "tax," but referred to it as a "contribution."[84] Once they established this distinction, they began an intensive campaign to expand social insurance and to eliminate federal participation in public assistance.

There were other factors besides symbolic distinctions that created the strong congressional support for the amendments. Throughout the summer of 1950, for example, Truman had been pushing Congress to raise income taxes in order to prevent inflation and to pay for the Korean War.[85] But Congress resisted such an unpopular action, especially during the election year. In fact, some representatives called for a reduction of the tax load through lower excise taxes and expanded loopholes. More fiscally conscientious representatives, however, designed subtle mechanisms for raising revenue; Mills, for example, proposed a speedup in the collection of corporate tax payments.[86] Within this context, the Social Security Amendments offered an alluring anti-inflationary weapon that provided tax increases that were rhetorically disguised as higher "contributions" for benefits.[87]

Nonetheless, most fiscal policymakers appear to have based their decisions on their deliberations on the need to reestablish the primacy of social insurance and to retain its distinction from the welfare payments, which were associated with the stigmatized members of American society. Within months, their plan appeared to be a success. By February 1951, the numbers of elderly citizens on insurance surpassed those on assistance. The number of persons on the old-age assistance rolls had decreased approximately 65,000 as of June 1951 from the high of September 1950; between 1950 and 1951, state agencies discontinued assistance for 44,000 recipients of old-age assistance and almost 6,900 families receiving aid to dependent children.[88]

Dwight Eisenhower's presidential election in 1952 brought in a Republican Congress for only the second time since 1933. Nevertheless, Congress continued its expansion of Social Security with strong bipartisan support. In 1952 and 1954, Congress extended coverage to more than ten million workers, including farm operators and more of the professional self-employed (except doctors, lawyers, and dentists); they provided coverage to employees of state and local government; they liberalized retirement tests; and they increased real benefits by an additional 12.5 percent. In addition, the 1954 amendments raised the contribution schedule to meet the increased cost of the benefit changes and to correct an "actuarial insufficiency" that had been discovered in the relationship between benefit distribution and tax intake.[89] Like Truman, Eisenhower perceived the political advantages that could be reaped from the continued expansion of this social program for the elderly.

There were still attacks on the "self-supporting" system. Representative Carl Curtis's Subcommittee on Social Security, for example, issued a report that attacked the claims that Social Security was modeled after private insurance. According to the report: "contractual rights" were non-existent and benefit claims had occasionally been eliminated by the SSA. The subcommittee insisted that Social Security was a "conditional" right, always subject to legislative change. Curtis submitted a legislative proposal that threatened to overturn the entire system.[90] These fierce attacks, however, caused a backlash against Curtis's position from supporters of Social Security, including Mills, Wilbur Cohen, and even President Eisenhower.[91] Although Curtis was correct in his critique of the program, he failed to grasp the importance, both to the providers and to the recipients of social insurance, of the language that symbolically distinguished their benefits from welfare.

By 1954, OASI had become a centerpiece of U.S. domestic policy. Meanwhile, public assistance programs were further marginalized, stigmatized, and relegated to state and local governments. The average monthly number of elderly receiving OAA declined at a steady rate; the average monthly number of families on ADC dropped significantly until 1955.[92] The Social Security Amendments of 1950 had allowed this to take place by reestablishing the connection between the payroll tax and social insurance, guaranteeing that the system would exclude general revenue from its system of finance.[93] Once this marriage had been consummated, policymakers could package OASI as an effective, fiscally conservative alternative to socialism or the welfare state.

The Social Security Amendments of 1950 set social insurance on a path of long-term incremental growth. When Wilbur Mills took over the chairmanship of Ways and Means in 1958 (a position he retained until his fall from power in 1974), a consensus had already formed around Old-Age and Survivors' Insurance: bureaucrats, think tanks, congressional representatives, interest groups, experts, and both political parties now fought to liberalize "self-supporting" social insurance and to eliminate public assistance. As Chairman Doughton once explained, OASI "dignifies the worker, upon his retirement, or his survivors, in the event of his untimely death, since it is a protection which the worker helps provide for himself."[94]

These amendments would continue to shape the politics of Social Security for the next three decades. Building on the earmarked tax system, Congress expanded social insurance to unprecedented levels. In 1965, for example, Congress brought health care into Social Security, through Medicare, without threatening the symbolic distinctions that separated social insurance from public assistance. Wilbur Cohen, Robert Ball, Robert Myers, and Mills would continue to be influenced by the Social Security Amendments of 1950, since the amendments had helped to distinguish them as the leading experts on Social Security finance and since the amendments had determined that payroll taxes would be the sole source of revenue for OASI benefits. By doing so, they distinguished OASI from welfare even as they transformed the program into one of the largest and most popular components of the state.

The earmarked tax system left the imprint of fiscal conservatism on Social Security by imposing certain long-term restrictions on the program. First, the tax system limited the type of benefit that Congress could distribute. Wage-related cash benefits were the only ones that justified the earmarked tax system and were the only type of benefit that maintained the insurance myth. Second, the tax system imposed a ceiling on the amount of benefits that the government could provide. Policymakers and legislators would insist on a balanced budget principle for Social Security, meaning that the federal government should only distribute, or plan to distribute, as much in benefits each month as it raised in taxes each month, leaving aside a small amount for a contingency reserve. Conservative actuarial assumptions, moreover, would protect the long-term fiscal soundness of the program.

Social Security finance would be reconstructed once again between 1969 and 1972, when Congress and the Social Security Administration implemented automatic cost-of-living adjustments for Social Security, when they abandoned the conservative actuarial practices that had ensured an excess of revenue, and when they enacted a dramatic liberalization in the amount of cash benefits.[95] These changes weakened significantly the compromise that had been created between fiscal conservatives and the American state. Today, as Social Security faces one of the most difficult fiscal crises in the program's history, policymakers should reexamine the tax system that Mills, Myers, Ball, and Cohen had constructed in 1950.

NINE

Paying for Medicare: Benefits, Budgets, and Wilbur Mills's Policy Legacy

Written with Eric Patashnik

During the past few years, dramatic proposals have been introduced for restructuring Medicare's financing.* The current financial structure of Medicare features two distinct federal government trust funds and three major revenue sources. Medicare Part A, which covers hospital stays, is financed by the Hospital Insurance (HI) Trust Fund, which in turn obtains its revenue primarily from a 2.90 percent payroll tax. Medicare Part B, which covers doctor visits and outpatient care, is financed by the Supplementary Medical Insurance (SMI) Trust Fund, three-quarters of which is now funded from general revenues and one-quarter from beneficiary premiums.[1] At the time of Medicare's enactment in 1965, separate financing of hospital and physician coverage was consistent with private-sector insurance models. Over time, however, healthcare financing and delivery have become integrated, both driven by the shift toward managed care and technological innovations that have blurred the lines between hospital stays and outpatient care. In 1999, a majority of the National Bipartisan Commission on the Future of Medicare proposed that the two Medicare trust funds be unified, while the Clinton administration urged that general revenues be used to meet a growing share of spending under Part A. In the 2000 presidential election campaign, George W. Bush basically endorsed the former approach and Al Gore embraced the latter. In this essay, we argue that although Medicare's inherited financing structure requires modification given changes in the healthcare system, policymakers should not abandon lightly the policy objectives that motivated the creation of this design in the first place.

Building on our recent books on trust fund financing and the political leadership of former Ways and Means Committee chair Wilbur D. Mills (D-AR), this essay explores the origins and consequences of Medicare's peculiar bifur-

* This essay originally appeared in *Journal of Health Policy, Politics, and Law* 26 (2001): 7–36.

cated structure. Our analysis speaks both to welfare state scholars unfamiliar with the details of Medicare finance as well as to health policy reformers who lack a deep understanding of Medicare's historical development. A central theme is that a commitment to fiscal discipline and spending restraint has been integral to Medicare throughout its thirty-five-year history, from its adoption in the expansionary years of the Great Society to the more recent era of large budget deficits. To be sure, the specific *reasons* for the salience of fiscal concerns in Medicare politics have varied over time. Originally, institutional budget guardians, most prominently Mills, feared that the adoption of Medicare would threaten the actuarial soundness of the Social Security system. More recently, Medicare's own financial sustainability and overall budgetary impact have been the overriding concerns. The crucial point, however, is that fiscal conservatism has been no less central to Medicare than the commitment to social insurance principles. How to maintain the delicate balance between fiscal discipline and the protection of benefit promises has been the major challenge of policymaking for Medicare. It remains so even in an era of large unified budget surpluses. By taking a long historical view, our discussion provides the background for understanding the politics of Medicare financing—past, present, and future.

Medicare Finance and Welfare State Scholarship

This is not the place for a review of the extensive literature on Medicare and the U.S. welfare state, but it is pertinent to situate our discussion in the context of several lines of analysis. The first is historical scholarship on American policy history. Our examination of Medicare contributes to a renewed interest among historians in the important role of *conservatism* in U.S. state-building. The substantive contributions of conservatism to public social provision have received little attention until recently. This neglect is rooted in three historiographical trends. The first is the failure of mainstream political historians to take conservatism seriously as a source of domestic policy innovation (on the reasons for historians' lack of attention to conservatism, see Brinkley, 1994). When the role of conservatives is discussed, historians typically focus on ideological extremists who rejected almost every type of federal intervention at the expense of moderates who have been more influential in policymaking. Inattention to the complex relationship between conservatism and U.S. state-building also stems from the executive-centered orientation of most political history, as exemplified by work on the "imperial presidency" (Burns, 1965; Schlesinger Jr., 1974). While political scientists will find this stunning, the contribution that members of Congress have made to the design of the modern American welfare state has received only limited attention from historians (Zelizer, 2000b).

There is a tendency in much of the literature to treat the president as the prime mover to the exclusion of a detailed examination of the independent role of Congress.[2] In this respect, historians are still locked into the traditional presidency-centered model of lawmaking that underwent substantial revision among political scientists in the 1990s (Peterson, 1990; Jones, 1994). When lawmakers—especially Southern Democrats—appear in recent narratives of postwar U.S. social policymaking, they are usually portrayed as roadblocks to the enactment of the initiatives of liberal presidential administrations (see, for example, Patterson, 1967; Quadagno, 1988; Gordon, 1994; and Lieberman, 1998; Howard, 1997). Finally, historians have not given sustained attention to tax policy (Brownlee, 1996, pp. 3–36), thus neglecting the very realm where moderate conservatives exerted their most important influence. In Julian Zelizer's recent book *Taxing America* (1998), he reintegrated the role of moderate congressional conservatives in the evolution of U.S. fiscal and social policy. These lawmakers, exemplified by the influential Mills, accepted an activist state, provided that the provision of social benefits was subject to meaningful fiscal constraints.

The part of our analysis on Medicare's legislative origins is much closer to two seminal political science works: Theodore R. Marmor's 1973 book *The Politics of Medicare*, and Martha Derthick's 1979 study *Policymaking for Social Security*. Both of these classic works give due attention to the leadership of Mills, whose influence over the final shape of the Medicare bill rivaled or surpassed that of any executive branch actor with the exception of Lyndon Johnson. Both studies recognize, for example, that Medicare's byzantine financial arrangements are inexplicable without attention to Mills's preoccupation with conservative financing of the Social Security system. Their work provides the foundation for Zelizer's book chapter on the origins of Medicare, which situates Mills's fiscal concerns in larger debates over social policy. Our primary contributions here will be to deepen the analysis of Mills's fiscal concerns about Medicare's adoption, and to extend the time frame of the narrative by tracing out the post-1965 consequences of Medicare's legislative design, including the system's recurrent financial crisis.

Our conclusions differ from two important recent studies of Medicare politics: Jonathan Oberlander's (1995) comprehensive dissertation on Medicare and the American state, and Marmor's new writing in his greatly expanded second edition of *The Politics of Medicare* (2000). While we cover some of the same historical ground, we offer a different interpretation of many of the key Medicare developments. A major theme in both Oberlander's and Marmor's analyses is that Medicare's evolution has been marked by a fundamental *irony*. According to Oberlander, Medicare's fiscal design has produced perverse effects. Although the Social Security Trust Fund for many decades produced actuarial surpluses that program builders could use to pay for benefit expansions, the HI Trust Fund has repeatedly been on the brink of insolvency, making the costs of Medicare spending more visible and providing ammunition to the program's sharpest critics (Oberlander, 1995). The "perversity thesis" is elaborated upon in Marmor's new chapters. Characterizing the HI Trust Fund as an "artifact" of social insurance financing, Marmor (2000, 94, p. 137) suggests that the program's recent financial troubles have produced effects "quite inimical" to the "expansionist intentions' of Medicare's original sponsors." He continues: "The social insurance philosophy that ensured its original appeal as a proposal used the trust fund terminology for Part A to suggest a sense of financial pre-commitment and thus political stability to Medicare. But over time, forecasts of the trust fund accounting—and projections of 'insolvency'—have partly undermined the very sense of security the trust fund was supposed to engender" (ibid., p. 171).

Like both Oberlander and Marmor, we recognize that liberal reformers during the 1960s viewed the adoption of hospitalization coverage as but the first step in an incremental march toward comprehensive national health insurance. We also acknowledge that many important developments in the context of Medicare policymaking—including the rate of medical inflation—have been largely unexpected. But more so than Oberlander and Marmor (in his new edition, at least), we view Mills as a crucial member of Medicare's enacting coalition and regard the program's trust funds and dedicated tax systems as more than mere accounting conventions. As a substantive matter, we argue that institutional features of Medicare's inherited design have served a valuable social purpose by periodically forcing policymakers to engage in a healthy examination of one of the nation's largest and most expensive social programs.

Historically, one of the prime motivations for the creation of federal government trust funds has in fact been a desire to protect the fisc and discipline expenditure demands (Patashnik, 1997, 2000). The Highway Trust Fund, for example, was adopted in 1956, in part, to ensure that Dwight Eisenhower's interstate system would be financed on a pay-as-we-build basis. In a similar vein, the Aviation Trust Fund drew support from key budget guardians (including Mills) in 1970 because it provided a vehicle for levying increased charges on aviation users. And of course Franklin Roosevelt himself viewed "sound financing" as both a political and moral imperative. Indeed, at the birth of New Deal liberalism, Roosevelt constantly attempted to balance the imperatives of fiscal conservatism and the modern welfare state (Zelizer, 2000a; Kennedy, 1999; Brown, 1999; Leff, 1983). To be sure, public trust funds differ substantially from their private-sector counterparts. They cannot really go bankrupt, for example, because Congress can always choose to inject unlimited general revenues into the programs. Nonetheless, the trust fund strategy has often appealed to fiscal conservatives precisely because it offers a mechanism for constraining long-term spending commitments, particularly when the trust funds draw their income in whole or in part from specific earmarked taxes or user fees, which cannot be increased without the passage of new legislation (Patashnik, 2000). It is therefore misleading to claim, as Oberlander and Marmor do, that the triggering of "bankruptcy crises" when trust fund balances are inadequate signifies that Medicare's design has produced perverse effects, since Medicare's trust fund system was designed in no small part to impose fiscal discipline to begin with. In short, we see more continuity, and less irony, in the salience of fiscal concerns in Medicare policymaking than do our colleagues.

The Logic of Mills's Financing Design

The story of Medicare's political development has been told elsewhere (see, for example, David, 1985; Jacobs, 1993). While most accounts have focused on the opposition of the American Medical Association as a central component of the story, here we focus on the emergence of the program's complex financing arrangements. We explain three aspects of Medicare's legislative design: (1) the financing scheme chosen for Hospital Insurance; (2) the financing scheme chosen for Supplementary Medical Insurance; and (3) why Medicare's financing came to be divided in the first place. Mills's decision along all three dimensions can be understood only if one appreciates his intense desire to control Medicare costs while protecting both Social Security and the general treasury in the process (Zelizer, 1998; see also Schlesinger, Blumenthal, and Drumheller, 1988).

THE PART A FINANCING DESIGN

Easiest to explain is the design of Part A. From the very beginning of the Medicare debate, liberal proponents had assumed that hospitalization coverage should be based on Social Security financing. Mills too approved of this approach to financing social insurance programs. "I want to make it clear that I have always thought there was great appeal in the argument that wage earners during their working lifetime should make payments into a fund to guard against the risk of financial disaster due to heavy medical costs," he said in a 1964 speech in his home state of Arkansas (*Congressional Quarterly Almanac* 1964, p. 232). But whereas liberals emphasized that reliance on earmarked payroll taxes was expansionary, Mills viewed this approach as inherently constraining. According to Mills,

> Whenever you have a program financed by a specific tax, the willingness of people to pay that tax, that specific tax, limits the benefits of that specific program . . . if you put a program, then, into the general fund of the Treasury, there is less likelihood that you control the package of benefits initially enacted than there is if you put it in a trust fund. . . . I can't help but reach the conclusion that a specific fund, supported by a payroll tax, is a more conservative method of financing something than to do it out of the general fund of the Treasury. (U.S. Congress, 1965a, pp. 803–4)

"The tax," Mills added, "serves to limit the benefit (804). After years of experience, he had concluded that "a payroll tax will tend to limit the growth of the benefit and will tend to do so to a greater extent than will be the case if that benefit cost is placed in the general fund of Treasury" (*Congressional Record*, 7 April 1965: 7223). Social Security Administration (SSA) officials agreed that linking a specific tax to a specific benefit encouraged "fiscal responsibility."[3]

Yet if Mills strongly approved of the use of earmarked taxes as a control mechanism, he nonetheless feared that Medicare's enactment would endanger the actuarial soundness of Social Security—a program with which he had developed a proprietary relationship (Derthick, 1979; Zelizer, 1998). From a historical perspective, one must recall that Social Security and its pay-as-you-go tax system had only been solidified in 1950 after years of tremendous legislative uncertainty (Zelizer, 1997; Leff, 1988). Because of his concern about Social Security's long-term viability, as well as the opposition of the American Medical Association, Mills remained a steadfast opponent of Medicare during the early 1960s. Nor was there enough support in the House to pass Medicare legislation.

Since taking over as chair of Ways and Means in 1958, Mills refused to let any bill out of committee that did not have an exceptional chance of passage (Manley, 1970). After the Democratic landslide election of 1964 transformed the ideological complexion of Congress, creating what Marmor (1973, p. 59) has aptly termed "the politics of legislative certainty," Mills recognized he could no longer prevent Medicare's adoption. Still, Mills remained the key gatekeeper, and he used his formidable institutional resources to limit the financial risks to the Social Security Trust Fund.

Since it was first proposed, Mills believed that Medicare posed two specific dangers to the basic pension program (see Derthick, 1979; Zelizer, 1998). First, he feared that the Social Security tax could not withstand the high cost of healthcare. Skyrocketing prices combined with constituent pressure for liberalized benefits—once voters learned that Medicare did not include the cost of physicians—could force Congress to raise Social Security taxes beyond tolerable levels. "I have always maintained that at some point there is a limit to the amount of a worker's wages, or the earnings of a self-employed person, that can reasonably be expected to finance the Social Security system," said Mills (*Congressional Quarterly Almanac* 1964, p. 231). Mills, ranking Ways and Means Republican John Byrnes (of Wisconsin), and most members of the SSA feared that constituents had been led to believe by the name Medicare (which newspaper reporters coined because it fit easily into a headline) that benefits would cover the cost of physicians. Mills feared that when constituents discovered this was not the case, it would be difficult to prevent the inclusion of those benefits under Social Security. Faced with skyrocketing costs, Congress would have to use general revenue to finance Social Security, a development that he saw as anathema to the program. Related to this, Mills was concerned that Medicare's costs would make future Social Security benefit expansions harder to enact by forcing Congress to devote the proceeds from increases in the wage base of the payroll tax to hospitalization costs rather than to higher cash benefits. In the past, raising the wage base had been a principal method through which Congress provided more generous pension benefits without having to increase payroll tax rates.

Mills's second major concern, which he shared with Byrnes, was that Medicare undermined the relationship between earmarked taxes and benefits by using wage-related revenue to pay for non-wage-related service benefits. Conservatives had perceived the wage-related benefit system in Social Security as an effective control against limitless benefits, since pension payments were scaled to what a person's wages had been.

But that relationship did not exist with hospitalization benefits. "That at the heart is the thing that constantly worried us," Byrnes (1967, pp. 39–40) explained, "this intermixture of non-wage related benefits with wage-related benefits; the putting on a payroll tax a benefit that had no relationship to wages; bringing everybody under it whether you presently had a system that took care of you." A sound contributory social insurance system, moreover, required accurate long-range forecasts of spending levels, but the future costs of service benefits were extremely uncertain. "The central fact which must be faced on a proposal to provide a form of service benefit—as contrasted to a cash benefit—is that it is very difficult to accurately estimate the cost," Mills said. "These difficult-to-predict future costs, when such a program is part of the Social Security program, could well have highly dangerous ramifications on the cash benefits proportion of the Social Security system" (*Congressional Quarterly Almanac* 1964, p. 232). During committee hearings, Mills pointed out to SSA officials that if Congress had passed previous Medicare proposals, their tax packages would have been inadequate because of actuarial miscalculations and incorrect assumptions. In 1963, for example, Mills explained that 1958 and 1960 proposals would have been one-third underfinanced (U.S. Congress 1963, pp. 140–41).

There were other technical ramifications to Medicare that made Mills uneasy. One concern had to do with the assumptions employed in actuarial forecasting. In their long-term projections for Social Security during the 1950s and 1960s, program actuaries had traditionally assumed that wages would remain static. The effect of this "level-wage" convention was to generate technically unanticipated trust fund surpluses when wages inevitably grew. Congress then used these surpluses to finance major benefit expansions (Derthick, 1979). While this technique was not incompatible with Social Security expansion, Mills and others (including the cautious Social Security chief actuary, Robert Myers) strongly believed it was a more fiscally responsible approach than assuming continued economic growth, something that many liberals at the time advocated. In this way, liberals at least were prevented from spending economic windfalls before they materialized (Zelizer, 1998, pp. 72–73). What particularly concerned Mills was that the level-wage assumption would not work for Medicare, because the cost of hospital insurance coverage was independent of the earnings of individual participants. "This same [level-earnings] assumption, which is conservative and safe for cash benefits, has just the opposite effect when applied to non-cash benefit such as hospitalization, which will become more costly rather than less costly when earnings rise," Mills worried (*Congressional Quarterly Almanac* 1964, p. 232).

After his landslide election victory in 1964, President Lyndon Johnson (1964a) instructed his Social Security advisors, including Wilbur Cohen and

Robert Myers, to work closely with Mills to "get him something" that "he can call a Mills bill." Legislative liaison Lawrence O'Brien told President Johnson that "this actuarial soundness thing is likely crucial to solving Mills" (Berkowitz, 1995, p. 213). Under Mills's guidance, Myers made numerous technical changes to the bill (Zelizer, 1998). To provide a greater margin of safety, Myers assumed that hospital utilization rates would be 20 percent higher than in the original proposal and that hospital prices would increase more rapidly. In addition, Mills required Myers to make his long-term actuarial forecasts of hospital spending on a twenty-five-year basis, rather than on the seventy-five-year basis that had traditionally been used for Social Security. This was done both to distinguish Medicare from Social Security as well as to take account of the greater difficulty of projecting the costs of a service benefit.[4]

Most important, Mills insisted that the payroll tax rate for Medicare be set much higher than in the administration's original plan. Mills explained: "I do not have any hesitancy [about increasing the tax]. Do not misunderstand me. In all the questions I have ever asked on this committee, I have never had any hesitancy at all in fixing the tax so as to take care of the cost. I just want to be certain that we do it. That is all I have ever wanted to do" (U.S. Congress 1965a, p. 85). Mills believed a sense of fiscal responsibility to future Congresses dictated these steps, even as he recognized that his successors would have the opportunity to make financing decisions of their own. Said Mills, "I do not like to get us in the position of making it necessary by our own action that Congress do something in the future. Let us do it now. If Congress wants to change it, let them do it, if Congress wants to repeal what we do, let them do it, but let us not enact it today with the specific knowledge that affirmative action must be taken by Congress at one specific time in the future" (ibid.). Under the final Medicare proposal, Mills assured colleagues, future payroll taxes would cover the cost of hospitalization so that increases in the wage base could still be used for higher cash benefits; Myers affirmed that "if the earnings base is increased, the gain to the system from raising the earnings base would stay in the OASDI trust funds." Mills called this a "fundamental difference" from the earlier proposals (ibid., pp. 80–81). In a 1968 interview with the Columbia University Social Security Project, Myers acknowledged that Mills's incessant concern about Medicare's future costs played an important role in his efforts to redesign Medicare's actuarial basis and design structure (Myers 1968).

The final version of the Medicare bill also constructed symbolic distinctions between Medicare and Social Security. Not only would there be a separate HI Trust Fund, but tax withholdings for Social Security and Medicare were required to be displayed by the Internal Revenue Service on separate lines on workers' W-2 forms. In view of scholarly arguments that Medicare's financing design has been less successful than Social Security's (Oberlander, 1995), it bears underlining that these symbolic steps were *not* intended to make Medicare a more perfect copy of Social Security. Rather, they were meant to protect the Social Security Trust Funds' future viability.

THE CREATION AND SEPARATE FINANCING OF PART B

Also requiring scrutiny are Mills's unexpected decision to add separate coverage of doctors' fees to the Medicare bill (which became Part B) and the specific financing approach chosen for this program. John Byrnes, an opponent of Medicare, introduced a voluntary plan known as Bettercare that was modeled after the federal government's employee health benefits program. In addition to hospitalization costs, the plan covered doctors' services and certain other medical expenses. It obtained its financing from a combination of general revenues and beneficiary premiums. Beneficiaries would thus have to pay for part of their benefits. Byrnes (1967, pp. 40–41) hoped that this would help limit cost by forcing beneficiaries to contribute to the system and that it would act as a disincentive for those who didn't need government benefits because they were already covered by private insurance.

The Byrnes and administration plans were presented as mutually exclusive alternatives (Marmor, 1973). But in closed hearings, Mills astonished his colleagues on the Ways and Means Committee by combining the two into a single package. This stunning combination was obviously not the result of years of careful planning. In that sense, it was an accident of history. Yet Mills must be seen as a *purposive* actor here, taking full advantage of the political opportunities that his position as a committee chair in the pre-reform House afforded him. In fact, at several times in 1964, Mills had discussed with Byrnes and administration officials the possibility of stitching together several different healthcare bills, although the particular combination he eventually offered took nearly everyone by surprise (Zelizer, 1998). In the end, Mills combined the two bills not merely because it allowed him to broker a compromise and respond to the pressure he faced, but also because it enabled him to protect Social Security and promote fiscal restraint in the process.

Foremost, the design restricted the immediate burden on the payroll tax. Since the reimbursement of doctors' fees was only to be offered under the voluntary and public assistance portions of the legislation, those unpredictable expenses would remain outside the compulsory social insurance system. With the final plan, Mills (1971) said, constituents would not demand that Congress use Social Security taxes to pay for physicians' costs (Manley, 1965). While SSA officials had worked to correct the misimpression that doctors would be covered under Medicare, Mills simply put the cost of physicians under a different part of the program. Besides taking the bite from AMA warnings of socialized medicine, this financial structure enabled Mills to build a "fence" around the Medicare program (Marmor, 1973, p. 69; see also Derthick, 1979, p. 332; Zelizer, 1998, pp. 241–43). Moreover, the legislation created Medicaid, which ensured that the cost of the poor remained outside Social Security. Based on Myers's assurances, Mills felt reasonably comfortable promising that the tax schedule would cover rising costs so that he could

> Assure colleagues who have had reservations in the past, as I have had reservations in the past about doing anything in any way that might jeopardize the cash benefit program that has developed over the past 30 years and that has become such an important part of every elderly person's life, without any hesitation, without any equivocation, that there is not one single, solitary thing in this bill which would permit or allow for $1 of the money which is set aside to go into the old-age and survivors disability insurance trust funds to ever get into the hospital insurance trust fund. (*Congressional Record,* 7 April 1965, p. 7213)

In addition to safeguarding Social Security, Mills's combined package was also meant to protect the general fisc. Cohen and Myers had warned several times that Byrnes's plan would cost more than Johnson's hospitalization proposal because it covered a wider array of services, and that this would have a very damaging impact on the operating budget. If all eligible-aged persons joined the plan, it would cost the federal government at the outset $2.4 billion annually (Cohen, 1965). After interrogating Myers and Byrnes about the cost of Byrnes's plan under high levels of participation, Mills concluded that the price tag was just too much (Manley, 1965). On the House floor, Mills attacked the Byrnes plan as fiscally irresponsible, arguing that it would exacerbate federal budget deficits. Under the final package, which placed hospital care under payroll taxation and physician's costs under general revenue, it seemed that neither revenue source would be detrimentally affected. Since hospital care was the biggest element in the program, Mills said the impact on Treasury would be limited (*Congressional Record,* 7 April 1965, p. 7214).

Part B's internal financing design was also meant to promote fiscal responsibility. To be sure, the design did force Mills to accept some use of general revenues in Medicare. In contrast to his position on Social Security, however, Mills was willing to accept this inconsistency since medical benefits were not directly wage-related. Moreover, the use of general revenue was all but politically unavoidable. Without a general fund subsidy, premium rates would have been prohibitive for seniors of age eighty if premium rates varied by age; but if premium rates were based on the average cost of all the elderly, the younger and healthier elderly persons would have found the program unattractive (Ball, 1995).

Still, Mills maneuvered to contain the inroads on general revenues. Byrnes had suggested that premiums be scaled to the level of Social Security benefits, but Mills insisted on a flat $3 premium to ensure that the amount raised from beneficiaries would cover half of the program's projected costs (Marmor, 1973, p. 65). Republican proponents of the Byrnes plan consistently argued that premiums would make "for a sounder program. This cost sharing will have a tendency to reduce excessive usage of the benefits" (U.S. Congress, 1965b, p. 255). Another closely related motivation was to decrease the share of Part B spending paid from general tax revenues. During floor debate, Representative Thomas

Curtis (R-MO) pointed out that the existence of a beneficiary premium "reduces the cost which is passed on to taxpayers under age 65" (*Congressional Record*, 7 April 1965, p. 7233). Although Mills did not comment on this specific point, it is reasonable to assume he accepted it since all policymakers at the time, without exception, understood fiscal rectitude to be a central function of the premium. This was not an issue subject to extensive debate; it was conventional wisdom. Indeed, just minutes before Mills proposed the "three-layer-cake" to his Ways and Means colleagues, the committee had been discussing the functional similarities between premiums and payroll taxation as ways to contain leakages of the general fisc (Manley, 1965).

In summary, Mills sought to strike a balance between safeguarding Social Security and protecting the general operating budget. "I have said consistently that I did not think that all of the medical costs incurred by those over 65 could be financed only through a payroll tax, because conceivably the payroll tax would be so high finally as to interfere with our capacity to compete in the world, with the payroll tax being charged as a cost of doing business," Mills said. "I have said repeatedly that we cannot run the risk of bankrupting the Federal Treasury once and for all by putting this entire cost upon the general fund of the Treasury. I think that the program has to be dealt with in a combination approach of two things: use of payroll tax and use of general revenue funds" (*Congressional Record*, 7 April 1965, p. 7213).

Medicare's Financing Since 1965

A comprehensive discussion of Medicare's evolution since 1965 is beyond the scope of this essay. Instead, we focus on financing developments. Our central claim is that the complex financing design adopted in 1965 has experienced a fair degree of success in perpetuating Mills's original vision of fiscal restraint. If the design has not achieved all that Mills hoped, neither has it been an abject failure. More specifically, the Part A financing scheme, by creating the possibility of distinct solvency crises, has forced policymakers repeatedly to examine the program's fiscal impact and take difficult actions they might otherwise have wished to avoid. As Mills intended, the Part B financing scheme has helped to protect Social Security's claim on payroll tax revenues. It has been less effective, however, in limiting general fund spending on Part B itself (Patashnik, 2000).

PART A FINANCING DYNAMICS SINCE 1965

The evolution of Medicare Part A has been shaped by the imperative of keeping the HI Trust Fund solvent. As it has in Social Security, Congress has traditionally adhered to a policy of self-support. This has obviously not meant that Congress has charged recipients actuarially fair rates for their hospital insurance coverage. Nor has it meant that Medicare has been kept in long-term actuarial

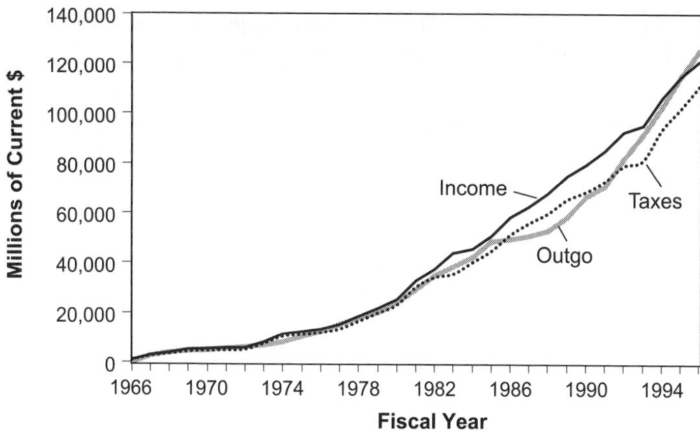

Figure 9.1. Financial History of HI Trust Fund, FY 1966–1996. Source: Annual Reports of the Medicare Board of Trustees, various years. Income includes taxes, interest earnings, and other revenues.

balance (for a critique of long-term Medicare cost estimates, see White, 1998). Medicare has large unfunded liabilities. But the commitment to self-support has nonetheless disciplined Part A spending in two ways. First, Congress has kept current revenues high enough to meet current expenditures—no mean accomplishment given the program's rapid growth (figure 9.1).

Self-support has also entailed a closely related commitment to maintaining the trust fund's solvency over the medium term. More than a dozen times between 1970 and 1997, the trustees reported that the HI Trust Fund would be depleted in ten or fewer years (table 9.1). Each time Congress took steps to keep the trust fund solvent, usually reducing payment schedules for providers, occasionally raising taxes, sometimes doing both (Rubin, 1995).

A major reason Congress was encouraged to act is because trust fund depletion can be analogized to "bankruptcy." From an economic perspective, of course, the analogy is quite misleading. The federal government is not a private business; there is no true danger of it going broke. Nonetheless, the image of trust fund bankruptcy resonates politically. U.S. lawmaking typically embodies popular conceptions of instrumental rationality. Members frame their actions in ways that can be easily explained to voters back home (Mayhew, 1986). "Saving" a trust fund from bankruptcy is a case in point. Part A solvency "crises" have come to serve as key "focusing events" that structure the Medicare policy agenda (Kingdon, 1984; Oberlander, 1995).

As Oberlander (1995) correctly stresses, trust fund solvency crises may create a strategic opening for hard-core opponents of social insurance to pursue broader retrenchment projects, generating public fears about Medicare's sustainability. Yet it must be stressed that the commitment to maintaining Part

Table 1. Number of Years From Medicare Hospital Insurance Part A: Trustees' Projection Until Insolvency, 1965–1999

Year of trustees' report	Years until insolvency Under intermediate forecast
1970	2
1971	2
1972	4
1973	None indicated
1974	None indicated
1975	About 20
1976	About 15
1977	About 10
1978	12
1979	13
1980	14
1981	10
1982	5
1983	7
1984	7
1985	13
1986	10
1987	15
1988	17
1989	None indicated
1990	13
1991	14
1992	10
1993	6
1994	7
1995	7
1996	5
1997	4
1998	10
1999	16

Source: Intermediate projections of various HI trustees' reports, 1970-1999.

A solvency has been a largely bipartisan affair. Even liberal Democrats have accepted the imperative to "save" Medicare. From a historical perspective, this acceptance has served to carry forward Mills's original goal of fiscal restraint within a contributory insurance framework, forcing lawmakers to confront policy trade-offs that they might well prefer to avoid in view of the power of the senior and medical lobbies. This is not to say that every Medicare development since 1965 would have been acceptable to Mills, or is the best that could have been accomplished, only that the consequences of an inherently conservative fiscal design have not been wholly *perverse.*

Certainly it would be gravely misleading to conclude that Mills had *crafted* the HI Trust Fund as a Trojan horse, with the secret hope that Medicare's future instabilities would destroy the social insurance project. Mills was a fiscal conservative, but he was no antigovernment libertarian. As noted above, Mills had worried endlessly about the program's fiscal stability in 1965 and had demanded that program actuaries design appropriate institutional safeguards. Despite these precautions, however, Part A forecasts during the 1960s and 1970s regularly proved much too optimistic. In part, the explosive growth in Medicare spending was due to exogenous factors. Prices climbed throughout the American economy during this period, particularly in the healthcare sector. But the increase in Medicare spending was also the product of factors endogenous to Medicare itself. Medicare's early administrators sought to accommodate providers to ensure the program's acceptance. Moreover, Medicare's legislative design had a built-in inflationary impetus. The 1965 act failed to provide precise definitions of key legislative terms, such as "reasonable costs," creating little incentive for providers to exercise self-restraint when seeking payments from the government (Marmor 2000).

Already by 1969, Mills knew Congress had not been cautious enough (Cohen, 1968b, 1968c, 1968d, and 1968e). While questioning Myers during a committee hearing on Medicare's mounting costs, Mills asked:

> Do you remember the interrogation that occurred when we were considering this matter in 1965 [Medicare], when former Secretary Celebrezze sat there and he was surrounded by some of the finest looking, most intelligent men I had seen up to that time—you, and Mr. Ball, and Mr. Cohen, and a few others—when I was interrogating you about the costs of this hospital program and whether or not there was a possibility that for 5 or 6 years of hospital costs might rise at a rate of about twice the increase of the earnings level? Do you remember all that . . . Without trying to make myself the one with the white hat and somebody else with the black hat, who turned out to be more nearly correct? Have hospital costs gone up over a 5-year period at about twice the rate of the rise in earnings levels? (U.S. Congress, 1969, p. 187)

Myers responded: "That, unfortunately, is correct," The chair found this situation "alarming" since there was no prospect of the rising cost leveling. Between

1970 and 1977 alone, Part A outlays tripled from $4.9 billion to $15.2 billion (OMB, 1995). Congress responded in part by increasing payroll tax rates from 1.6 percent in 1965 to 2.9 percent in 1977 (Myers, 1993).

But the HI Trust Fund's status progressively worsened over the early 1980s. The number of years until the trust fund's projected depletion fell from fourteen in 1980 to five in 1982 (Table 9.1). In 1982, Congress agreed to impose limits on hospital reimbursement for the next three years (Schick, 1987; Palmer and Torrey, 1982). In addition, it ordered the Health Care Financing Administration (HCFA) to develop a detailed plan for controlling hospital insurance spending. The result was a dramatic reform of hospital reimbursement under Medicare Part A. Previously, the government had reimbursed hospitals for the costs of treatment after Medicare services had been rendered. Under the new system, based on a schedule of "diagnosis-related groups" (DRGs), the government began paying hospitals *prospectively* for specific diagnoses. The reform helped to raise the real growth rate of Part A spending from 5.4 percent annually between 1980 and 1985 to just 1 percent annually between 1985 and 1990 (CBO, 1992, p. 58). This breathed about fourteen more years of life into the trust fund. In sum, Medicare Part A has faced "sustained budgetary pressure" despite the program's entitlement status and middle-class constituency (Pierson, 1994, p. 137).

PART B FINANCING DEVELOPMENTS SINCE 1965

As Mills intended, the creation of a separate Part B trust fund, which depends on general funds and beneficiary contributions for its income, has helped limit Medicare's claim on payroll taxes, thereby protecting Social Security's revenue base. To be sure, the HI tax rate has climbed higher than planned. Under the tax schedule contained in the original 1965 act, the combined employer-employee tax rate for Part A was to be 1.6 percent in 1986. In fact, it climbed to 2.9 percent. Yet the Medicare tax rate has not increased since 1986. At 2.9 percent, the payroll tax share of Medicare remains a small part of the FICA (Federal Insurance Contributions Act) total of 15.3 percent (Moon, 1993, p. 234).[5]

However, the Supplementary Medical Insurance Trust Fund (SMI) has historically been much less successful in limiting the share of Part B spending borne by general taxpayers—75 percent under current law. As the fiscally conservative Concord Coalition (1999, 1) notes, indeed laments, program solvency has not really been an issue with Part B because the SMI Trust Fund "has an open pipeline to the Treasury which automatically closes any gap between beneficiary premiums and expenditures." To be sure, Congress has restrained physician reimbursement levels to control costs and help lower the overall budget deficit. But while the 1965 Medicare Act called for beneficiaries to cover 50 percent of Part B spending, this cost-sharing framework did not prove durable. Congress did allow the premium to rise from $3 per month in 1966 to $5.80 six years later, an increase of 93 percent. In 1972, however, a Democratic Congress responded to the unpopularity of rapidly increasing premium rates by enacting a provision that limited future premium increases to the percentage increase in Social Security cash benefits (which would themselves be indexed for inflation beginning in 1975 [Myers, 1993; Weaver, 1988]).[6]

The decision to cap Part B premium increases actually represented a compromise between the more extreme positions of congressional liberals on the one hand and the Nixon administration on the other. Senator Frank Church's Special Commission on Aging sought to eliminate the Part B premium altogether. The argument was that high premiums undermined the income protection provided by Social Security. "I think it would be a sham for this Congress to act on increases in cash retirement benefits under social security on one hand, while allowing the government to take back part of these increases in the form of higher monthly premium payments on the other," said one lawmaker (*Congressional Record*, 5 April 1972, p. 11536). The Nixon administration, which was then proposing the creation of a single Medicare Trust Fund, agreed with the need to do away with the Part B premium. In sharp contrast to liberal Democrats, however, the administration plan would have had the $1.5 billion then represented by Part B premiums funded through the existing payroll tax.

By this time, Mills's authority as committee chair was under strong attack from liberals. Moreover, his struggle with alcoholism diminished his ability to lead (Strahan, 1990). Still, Mills remained active on the issue, arguing that the administration's financing plan would endanger the basic pension program. Mills remained ever the pragmatist on Medicare, seeking to help beneficiaries while simultaneously protecting Social Security and the government fisc. In a floor statement, Mills supported the indexing of the Part B premium as a way to reduce the financial burden on vulnerable seniors. But he was at pains to emphasize that the overall measure also included mechanisms to "provide incentives to limit program costs," including an increase in the Part B deductible from $50 to $60 and changes in certain coinsurance provisions (*Congressional Record*, 21 June 1971, p. 21093).

As matters turned out, however, medical inflation increased much faster than general inflation over the 1970s. Consequently, the share of Part B income accounted for by beneficiary premiums fell from 50 percent to approximately 25 percent during the mid-1980s (figure 9.2).[7] Meanwhile, Part B outlays soared, in a number of years exceeding the rate of the growth in Part A. The general fund subsidy climbed from $18 billion in 1986 to $62 billion in 1996.

In theory, Congress might have taken steps to prevent this. But without an explicit solvency crisis in the SMI Trust Fund, there was no triggering event for legislative action (Patashnik, 2000). "Part B deserves more attention than it gets," said Richard S. Foster, the chief HCFA actuary. "Under present law, it can't go broke . . . but it's not good to have outlays growing faster than your financing base" (quoted in Adams 1999). Ironically, the introduction of the DRG system for hospital insurance in 1983 may well have increased Part B spending in the mid- to late 1980s by creating an incentive for providers to accelerate the shift of procedures from inpatient hospital care to outpatient services, where reim-

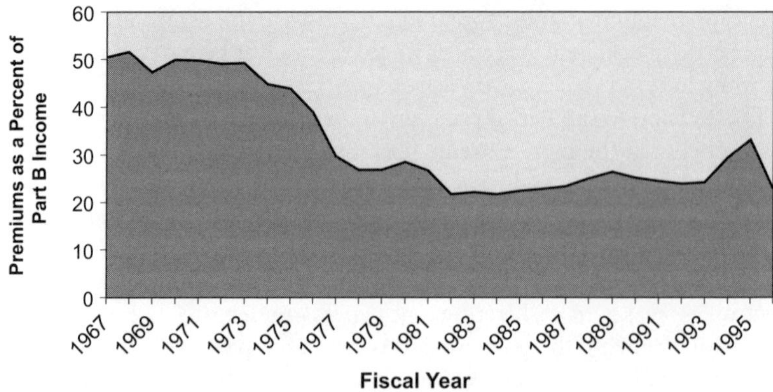

Figure 9.2. Premiums as a percentage of Part B Income. FY 1967–1996. Source: Annual Reports of the Medicare Board of Trustees, various years.

bursement schedules were than more generous (Moon and Mulvey, 1996). The Balanced Budget Act of 1997 permanently set the premium equal to 25 percent of Part B costs.

CONTESTING THE LINE BETWEEN PARTS A AND B

To summarize the discussion above, Medicare's legislative structure has mattered in the sense that it has caused the two parts of Medicare to experience distinctive political and financial dynamics (Aaron and Reischauer, 1995). This is not to suggest, however, that maintaining the program's historical bifurcation has been *unproblematic*. In 1965, the division of Medicare followed the distinction that private employers made between hospital (Blue Cross) insurance and medical services (Blue Shield) insurance. But healthcare financing and delivery has since become integrated. Physicians on an outpatient basis increasingly handle complex medical procedures that once could only be performed in a hospital setting. The traditional distinction between hospitalization and major medical insurance has disappeared in the private sector due to the merger of Blue Cross and Blue Shield and the shift to managed care. Yet Medicare's financing has remained fragmented, creating confusion among beneficiaries about payment rules for different services (Adams, 1999). Over the years, there have been repeated attempts—none yet successful—to completely dismantle Mills's policy legacy. To examine these past attempts provides perspective on proposals to restructure Medicare's financing for the future.

Within only a few years of Medicare's adoption, liberals were proposing that Medicare's two trust funds be folded into a single unified program. They viewed Medicare's bifurcated design as cumbersome and believed that the program's financing sources were insufficiently redistributive and incompatible with benefit expansion. The 1971 Advisory Council on Social Security proposed combining the two Medicare trust funds, adding some new medical benefits, and paying for the entire program two-thirds from payroll taxes and one-third from general revenues. A liberal majority on the 1975 Advisory Council would have gone even further, calling for general tax funds eventually to finance all of Medicare spending. In addition to making Medicare financing less regressive, by relying more heavily on progressive income taxes, this shift would have freed up more payroll tax revenues for Social Security, whose own trust fund was facing depletion.

But these liberal proposals for restructuring Medicare financing sparked resistance from fiscal conservatives. President Richard Nixon's secretary of health, education and welfare, Casper Weinberger, claimed that it was "inappropriate" for a program "whose strength" depended on working people to be financed from general revenues. Weinberger argued that general fund financing would destroy the "earned rights" principle of the HI Trust Fund and make Medicare more like welfare (U.S. Congress, 1975). President Gerald Ford took a similar position (Myers, 1975). Four conservative members of the 1975 council argued that general fund financing of Part A would hide the program's costs and "weaken even further the control over it." Finally, these members opposed efforts to solve Social Security's problems by shifting payroll taxes from the HI Trust Fund to Social Security and financing Part A out of general revenues, emphasizing that "the Treasury is not an inexhaustible source of funds" (Advisory Council on Social Security, 1975, p. 7).

Turf wars among congressional committees have also helped maintain the traditional boundary between Medicare's two programs. The revenue committees in Congress (the House Ways and Means and the Senate Finance) control the payroll tax–financed HI Trust Fund, but the commerce committees have jurisdiction over the SMI Trust Fund. Merging the two trust funds could force some committee leaders to give up power, which they have been reluctant to do (Gardner, 1998; on congressional jurisdictional disputes generally, see King, 1997).

While past attempts to create a unified Medicare financing system have failed, some movement of services between the program's divisions has nonetheless occurred in recent years as a result of political gamesmanship (see Moon, 1997). In 1997, President Bill Clinton proposed shifting a significant portion of the costs of home health services to Part B from Part A. By itself, this transfer would not reduce overall Medicare spending. The transparent motivation behind the proposal was to extend the solvency of the HI Trust fund without imposing large costs on constituents. Indeed, Clinton even proposed to exempt the home health costs from the calculation of the Part B premium. Congressional Republicans initially denounced the proposal as an accounting gimmick pure and simple. However, they ultimately went along with the transfer in the Balanced Budget Agreement (BBA), after modifying it to require that home health costs be phased into the calculation of the premium over seven years.

As a result of this change, and other provisions of the BBA, the share of total Medicare spending paid through beneficiary contributions, which declined from 13 percent in 1970 to 9 percent in 1980, is expected to again reach 13 percent by 2020 (Concord Coalition, 1999). In this respect, Medicare financing will have come full circle. However, since Part B spending is 75 percent funded through general revenues, and expected to grow more rapidly than Part A spending (in part because of the home healthcare shift), general revenues will constitute a larger share of total Medicare spending over time under current law. Based on 1998 estimates, which assume no use of unified budget surpluses for Part A, the general fund share of overall Medicare expenditures will rise from 2.45 percent of GDP in 1998 to 5.09 percent of GDP in 2030 (National Academy of Social Insurance, 1998).

Recent Medicare Reform Proposals: Competing Financing Approaches

While implementation of the BBA has extended Part A's solvency, there remains substantial interest in long-term Medicare financing reform. The BBA itself provided encouragement for a fresh look at the issue by establishing the Bipartisan Commission on the Future of Medicare, headed by Senator John Breaux (D-LA) and Representative Bill Thomas (R-CA).[8] Ironically, perhaps, the Medicare reform plan that contemplates the sharpest departure from Mills's vision of fiscal responsibility—Clinton's February 1999 proposal for allocating expected budget surpluses—would preserve, at least on paper, the system's traditional divided financing structure. In contrast, the reform plan that is in some ways closest in spirit to Mills's financing approach—the Breaux-Thomas proposal—would combine Part A and Part B into a single Medicare Trust Fund (for an excellent discussion on these financing proposals, see Posner 2000). It should be emphasized that these plans also call for sweeping *programmatic* reforms in Medicare. A detailed analysis of these reforms is beyond the scope of this essay. (For a useful analysis, see McClellan, 2000.) The discussion below focuses only on those features of the plans directly relevant to an understanding of Medicare financing.

Under Clinton's budget proposal, $334 billion of the projected non–Social Security surplus would be transferred to the HI Trust Fund to extend Part A's solvency for ten years.[9] Significantly, Clinton's plan, which is also Al Gore's plan, would give Part A guaranteed claim on future general revenues *even if large budget surpluses failed to materialize*. The underlying rationale for the transfer is that Medicare should receive a share of the economic benefits from the lower interest costs the federal government will face as publicly held debt is retired.

The Breaux-Thomas proposal would take a much different financing approach, folding the two parts of Medicare into a single Medicare Trust Fund.[10] While not explicitly stated, the proposal implies that the combined trust fund would be financed through a combination of payroll taxes, premiums, and general revenues. There are two rationales for unifying Medicare's financing under the Breaux-Thomas proposal. First, a combined program structure fits with the plan's major substantive reform of the Medicare benefit—the introduction of a variant of managed competition known as "premium-support." Under this approach, recipients would select from a range of benefit packages, which the government would subsidize up to the level of the average price charged by all competing plans. Those joining more expensive plans would have to pay additional amounts. By encouraging competition for Medicare dollars among health plans and giving recipients an incentive to be cost conscious, the approach naturally lends itself to eliminating the long-standing division between Parts A and B.[11]

The second rationale for combing Medicare's financing under Breaux-Thomas is to prevent the kind of budgetary legerdemain that occurred with the recent transfer of home healthcare. Under the plan, the Medicare Board of Trustees would be required to report each year on the proportion of the total program's funding supported by general revenue. To limit the general fund's exposure under a unified structure, general revenue contributions in excess of 40 percent of total Medicare spending would not be automatically transferred to the program. Once the 40 percent threshold is breached, which is expected to occur within a decade under current law, Medicare would be declared "programmatically insolvent." Congress would then be required to approve additional general fund infusions (Moon, 2000).

Given the declining ratio of workers to retirees, the use of general revenues as a permanent part of Medicare's financing structure is probably inevitable. Still, Clinton's proposal to subsidize Part A through future unified budget surpluses would constitute a major change in Medicare's financing design. The shift to general revenue financing has been masked by the political focus on putting emerging Part A surpluses, which would be smaller if home healthcare costs had not been shifted to Part B, into a new Medicare "lockbox." General fund infusions would effectively remove the possibility of a distinct solvency crisis in Part A, thereby eliminating any mechanism to signal the need for policy adjustments when spending exceeds a fixed revenue base. Moreover, by precommitting general tax revenues for Medicare, the Clinton plan would reduce the discretion of future Congresses to reallocate resources as spending needs change (Posner, 2000). In both of these respects, Clinton's proposals would arguably undermine the delicate balance that Mills tried to strike between protecting retirees and keeping society's options open.

The Breaux-Thomas financing plan, in contrast, seeks to maintain this balance. In this respect, at least, it seems more consistent with Mills's fiscal goals, even as the proposal's competitive, premium-support approach diverges from traditional fee-for-service Medicare. It is not clear, however, that the new concept of programmatic solvency will achieve its intended objectives. If the past is any guide, increases in general fund spending on Medicare alone will not create the sense of legislative urgency required to force policymakers to confront painful budgetary trade-offs. A stronger trigger for action than the Breaux-Thomas scheme might be required. One possibility would be an automatic reduction in provider reimbursement rates whenever the general fund contribution to Medicare exceeds some predetermined threshold.[12]

Conclusions

Examination of the evolution of Medicare financing sheds light on the trajectory of the U.S. welfare state as well as on very current social policy debates. We have argued that the politics of Medicare cannot be understood without focusing on the role of fiscal conservatives as key institutional designers. To be sure, the substantive importance of actors like Mills has been recognized in the political science literature on Medicare's enactment. Yet too often the concern with controlling Medicare expenditures, as symbolized by recent efforts to "save Medicare from bankruptcy," is treated as a sharp departure from the past, rather than as an effort to work out Medicare's original political understanding in a vastly changed fiscal and demographic environment. This original understanding, to repeat, was pragmatic, not ideologically pure. It accepted the principles of universalism and earned rights but insisted that spending on Medicare benefits be subject to fiscal restraints.

As we have noted, Chairman Mills was initially most worried about the potential for Medicare's adoption to damage Social Security. In actuality, Medicare's impact on the basic pension program has been mixed. Despite Mills's fears, there was not a revolt in the early 1970s, when payroll taxes first crossed the "unbreakable" 10 percent threshold directly to individuals. Yet if events have not unfolded exactly as Mills predicted, his fears about bringing Medicare into the welfare state were hardly unfounded. Even after the 1997 Balanced Budget Act, Medicare spending is projected to double as a share of GDP over the next forty years. Yet there is strong bipartisan sentiment against raising payroll tax rates any higher (McClellan, 2000). If emerging operating budget surpluses create pressure for large general tax cuts, the share of the total budget devoted to programs other than pensions and healthcare for the elderly will continue to decline in the years and decades ahead, especially if Congress establishes a major new Medicare prescription drug benefit.

Our purpose here has not been to provide a detailed analysis of every policy option but to place the current debate over Medicare financing reform in a larger historical perspective. In our view, the critical institutional design task is to update Medicare's financial structure without sacrificing the goals of either policy durability or fiscal rectitude. Only within such a structure, our analysis suggests, is it possible to manage the operations of long-term governmental commitments in a way that both recognizes the need of program beneficiaries for continuity and allows each generation to make important taxing and spending choices of its own.

References

Aaron, H., and Reischauer, R. 1995. The Medicare reform debate: what is the next step? *Health Affairs* 17 (4): 8–30.

Adams, R. 1999. Lawmakers envision a Medicare system greater than the sum of its parts. *Congressional Quarterly Weekly Report*, 27 April, 891.

Advisory Council on Social Security. 1975. *Reports of the Advisory Council on Social Security*. Washington, DC: Government Printing Office.

Ball, R. 1995. What Medicare's architects had in mind. *Health Affairs* 14(4): 62–72.

Berkowitz, E. 1995. *Mr. Social Security: The Life of Wilbur J. Cohen*. Lawrence: University of Kansas Press.

Board of Trustees of the Federal Hospital Insurance and Supplementary Medical Insurance Trust Funds. 1999. *1999 Annual Report of the Board of Trustees of the Federal Hospital Insurance and Supplementary Medical Insurance Trust Funds*. Washington, DC: Government Printing Office.

Brinkley, A. 1994. The problem of American conservatism. *American Historical Review* 99(2): 409–29.

Brown, M. 1999. *Race, Money, and the American Welfare State*. Ithaca, NY: Cornell University Press.

Brownlee, W., ed. 1996. *Funding the Modern American State, 1941–1995: The Rise and Fall of the Era of Easy Finance*. Cambridge: Cambridge University Press.

Burns, J. 1965. *Presidential Government: The Crucible of Leadership*. New York: Houghton Mifflin.

Byrnes, J. 1967. Interview with Peter Corning, Columbia University Oral History Project. Social Security Project. 23 February.

Cohen, W. J. 1965. Memorandum for President Johnson. Wilbur Cohen Papers. Wisconsin Historical Society. Madison, WI. Box 82, File 9. 29 January.

———. 1968a. Interview with David McComb. Lyndon Johnson Library. Oral History Interview with David McComb. Tapes 1 and 2. 8 December.

———. 1968b. Cohen, W., to W. Mills. Cohen Papers. Madison, WI. Box 97. File Unmarked. 13 June.

———. 1968c. Gorham, W., to W. Cohen. Cohen Papers. Box 109. File 4. 29 February.

———1968d. Rice, D., to W. Cohen. Cohen Papers. Box 109. File 4. 22 April.

———1968e. Cohen, W., to L. Johnson. Cohen Papers. Box 98. File Unmarked. 17 December.

Coleman, J. 1996. *Party Decline in America: Policy, Politics, and the Fiscal State*. Princeton, NJ: Princeton University Press.

Committee on Ways and Means. 1998. *1998 Green Book*. Washington, DC: Government Printing Office, 116–17.

Concord Coalition. 1999. *Issue Brief: The 1999 Report of the Social Security and Medicare Trust Funds*. Washington, DC: Concord Coalition.

Congressional Budget Office (CBO). 1992. *The Economic and Budget Outlook: Fiscal Years 1993–1997*. Washington, DC: Congressional Budget Office.

Congressional Quarterly Almanac. 1964. Medicare Program Dies in Conference. Washington, DC: *Congressional Quarterly*, 231–32.

David, S. 1985. *With Dignity: The Search for Medicare and Medicaid*. Westport, CT: Greenwood.

Derthick, M. 1979. *Policymaking for Social Security.* Washington, DC: Brookings Institution.

Gardner, J. 1998. A + B = Solution? Merging Two Medicare Parts Might Help Medicare Solvency. *Modern Healthcare*, 29 June, 134.

Gordon, L. 1994. *Pitied but Not Entitled: Single Mothers and the History of Welfare, 1890–1935.* New York: Free Press.

Howard, C. 1997. *The Hidden Welfare State: Tax Expenditures and Social Policy in the United States.* Princeton, NJ: Princeton University Press.

Jacobs, L. 1993. *The Health of Nations.* Ithaca, NY: Cornell University Press.

Johnson, L. B. 1964a. Telephone Conversation. Recording Tape WH6403.15.2612. Lyndon B. Johnson Presidential Library. 21 March.

———1964b. Telephone Conversations Recording. Tape WH6406.06.3868. Lyndon B. Johnson Presidential Library. 9 June.

Jones, C. 1994. *The Presidency in a Separated System.* Washington, DC: Brookings Institution.

Kennedy, D. 1999. *Freedom from Fear: The United States, 1929–1945.* New York: Oxford University Press.

King, D. 1997. *Turf Wars: How Congressional Committees Claim Jurisdiction.* Chicago: University of Chicago Press.

Kingdon, J. 1984. *Agendas, Alternatives, and Public Policies.* Boston: Little, Brown.

Leff, M. 1983. Taxing the "Forgotten Man": the politics of Social Security finance in the New Deal. *Journal of American History* 70: 359–81.

———. 1988. Speculating in Social Security futures: the perils of payroll tax financing, 1939–1950. In *Social Security: The First Half Century*, eds. G. Nash, N. Pugach, and R. Tomasson. Albuquerque: University of New Mexico Press.

Lieberman, R. 1998. *Shifting the Color Line: Race and the American Welfare State.* Cambridge, MA: Harvard University Press.

Manley, J. 1965. Handwritten Notes about Executive Medicare Sessions. John Manley Files. Box 5. Lyndon B. Johnson Presidential Library. 15 March.

———. 1970. *The Politics of Finance: The House Committee on Ways and Means.* Boston: Little, Brown.

Marmor, T. 1973. *The Politics of Medicare.* New York: Aldine.

———. 2000. *The Politics of Medicare*, 2d ed. New York: Aldine.

Mayhew, D. 1986. Legislation. In *Law and the Social Sciences*, ed. L. Lipson and S. Wheeler. New York: Russell Sage.

McClellan, M. 2000. Medicare reform: fundamental problems, incremental steps. *Journal of Economic Perspectives* 14(2): 21–44.

Mills, W. D. 1971. Oral history interview with Joe B. Franz. Lyndon B. Johnson Presidential Library. 2 November.

Moon, M. 1993. *Medicare Now and in the Future.* Washington, DC: Urban Institute.

———. 1997. No Medicare "Gimmick." *Washington Post*, 10 February, 19.

———, ed. 2000. *Competition with Constraints: Challenges Facing Medicare Reform.* Washington, DC: Urban Institute.

Moon, M., and J. Mulvey. 1996. *Entitlements and the Elderly.* Washington, DC: Urban Institute.

Myers, R. 1968. Interview with Peter Corning. Columbia Oral History Project. 10 October.

———. 1975. *Social Security*. Bryn Mawr, PA: Irwin.

———. 1993. *Social Security*, 4th ed. Philadelphia: University of Pennsylvania Press.

National Academy of Social Insurance. 1998. *The Financing Needs of a Restructured Medicare Program*. Washington, DC: National Academy of Social Insurance.

Oberlander, J. 1995. Medicare and the American State: The Politics of Federal Health Insurance, 1965–1995. PhD diss., Yale University.

Office of Management and Budget (OMB). 1995. *Budget for Fiscal Year 1995–Historical Tables*. Washington, DC: Office of Management and Budget, Table 13.1, 224–26.

Palmer, J., and B. Torrey. 1982. Health Care Financing and Pension Programs. In *Federal Budget Policy in the 1980s*, eds. G. Mills and J. Palmer. Washington, DC: Urban Institute.

Patashnik, E. 1997. Unfolding promises: trust funds and the politics of precommitment. *Political Science Quarterly* 112: 431–52.

———. 2000. *Putting Trust in the U.S. Budget: Federal Trust Funds and the Politics of Commitment*. Cambridge: Cambridge University Press.

Patterson, J. 1967. *Congressional Conservatism and the New Deal: The Growth of the Conservative Coalition in Congress, 1933–1939*. Lexington: University of Kentucky Press.

Peterson, M. 1990. *Legislating Together: The White House and Capitol Hill from Eisenhower to Reagan*. Cambridge, MA: Harvard University Press.

Pierson, P. 1994. *Dismantling the Welfare State?* New York: Cambridge University Press.

Posner, P. 2000. Testimony on Medicare Reform: Issues Associated with General Revenue Financing, before the Senate Committee on Aging, U.S. Congress, 27 March.

Quadagno, J. 1988. *The Transformation of Old Age Security: Class and Politics in the American Welfare State*. Chicago: University of Chicago Press.

Rubin, A. 1995. Medicare's woes, while nothing new, are politically charged this year. *Congressional Quarterly Weekly Report*, 6 May, 1228–29.

Schick, A. 1987. Controlling the "uncontrollable": budgeting for health care in an age of megadeficits. In *Charting the Future of Health Care*, eds. J. Palmer and M. Lewin. Washington, DC: American Enterprise.

Schlesinger Jr., A. M. 1974. *The Imperial Presidency*. New York: Popular Library.

Schlesinger, M., D. Blumenthal, and P. B. Drumheller, eds. 1988. *Renewing the Promise: Medicare and Its Reforms*. New York: Oxford University Press.

Strahan, R. 1990. *New Ways and Means: Reform and Change in a Congressional Committee*. Chapel Hill: University of North Carolina Press.

U.S. Congress, House Committee on Ways and Means. 1963. *Medical Care for the Aged: Executive Hearings*, 88th Cong., 1st sess.

———. 1965a. *Medical Care for the Aged: Executive Hearings*, 91st Cong., 1st sess.

———. 1965b. *Report of the Committee on Ways and Means of H.R. 6675*, 89th Cong., 1st sess.

———. 1969. *Social Security and Welfare Proposals: Hearings*, 91st Cong. 1st sess.

U.S. Congress, House. 1975. *Hearings before the Subcommittee on Social Security of the Committee on Ways and Means*, 94th Cong., 1st sess.

Weaver, K. 1988. *Automatic Government*. Washington, DC: Brookings Institution.

White, J. 1998. Saving Medicare—From What? Paper presented at the Annual Meeting of the American Political Science Association, Boston, Massachusetts, 3–6 September.

Zelizer, J. 1997. "Where Is the Money Coming From?" The reconstruction of Social Security finance, 1939–1950. *Journal of Policy History* 9: 399–424.
———. 1998. *Taxing America: Wilbur D. Mills, Congress, and the State, 1945–1975*. Cambridge: Cambridge University Press.
———. 2000a. The forgotten legacy of the New Deal: fiscal conservatism and the Roosevelt administration. *Presidential Studies Quarterly* 30(2): 331–58.
———. 2000b. Introduction. *Social Science History* 24(2): 307–16.

PART III

The Rules of the Game: The Politics of Process

The political process matters. Since the establishment of the country, political parties and political movements have become deeply invested in "changing the rules of the game," meaning the political procedures and processes through which policymakers, interest groups, social movements, and voters attempt to influence policy decisions and electoral outcomes.

The political process has opened up opportunities for certain kinds of policies and closed the door to others. In "Seeds of Cynicism" and "Bridging State and Society," I focus on how the political process became deeply enmeshed in broader political struggles over civil rights and other types of domestic reform that were taking place during the 1960s and 1970s.

Significant changes in the political process, as I argue in "Without Restraint," can have huge consequences for the nation's political culture and the way in which politics is conducted. With regard to Congress, I have found that the best way to conceptualize different political eras revolves around how the legislative process worked in specific moments in time. In my book, *On Capitol Hill*, I compared the legislative branch to an automobile. While drivers of various skills can take the automobile in different directions and along various types of roads, the internal machinery of the vehicle plays a crucial role in determining how smooth the drive will be as well as how far the driver can go, and this can be seen in all of the essays in this section.

The outcome of these battles over political process can profoundly impact the balance of power in Washington. In "Seizing Power" and "How Conservatives Learned to Stop Worrying and Love Presidential Power," I analyze how the conservative movement took advantage of reforms that had been put into place by liberals. Conservatives were able to master the political process that came out of the 1970s and used that process as a cudgel against Democrats and New Deal liberalism. The use of congressional procedures, such as ethics rules, budget reconciliation, and televised proceedings, turned into an effective mechanism for conservative Republicans to win control of Congress and to ensure that passage of their priority items.

Together, these process-oriented essays provide a much richer understanding of the connection between the mechanics and the substance of politics. The two cannot be disentangled. My essays, which bring together these two realms of political history—which have been too often separated by political historians in recent years—are heavily influenced by work in political science that has paid great attention to the importance of procedure and institutional design, and that offers hugely useful analytic tools for political historians.

TEN

Seeds of Cynicism: The Struggle over Campaign Finance, 1956–1974

"It is a cesspool, it is a source of infection for the body politic," Senator Hubert Humphrey (D-MN) warned his fellow senators in 1973 about the private financing of elections.* "[I]f it doesn't stop, there are going to be good men in this hall right here today who are going down the drain, not that you are guilty, not that you have done anything wrong, but that the public is disenchanted with all of us, and they are going to want somebody new and say I want a fresh one here."[1] From 1971 through President Nixon's resignation in 1974, Congress enacted the boldest campaign finance reforms in American history, including strong disclosure laws, public financing for presidential elections, contribution and spending limits, and an independent enforcement commission. Despite these reforms, after only a decade under the new laws, citizens still felt that campaign finance was corrupt.

Campaign finance is one of the most vexing problems in American democracy. To achieve reform, proponents must convince incumbent politicians to change a system in which they have succeeded. To make matters more difficult, campaign finance reform has never been driven by strong electoral pressure. The laws that passed in the early 1970s provide policy historians an opportunity to contribute to current debates about reforming the ties between money and politics.

In studying the 1970s reforms, the first puzzle historians must solve is how campaign finance reform passed despite enormous political opposition and lukewarm public support.[2] Although most accounts stress Watergate, this study suggests that a more complex intersection of events culminated in reform. By placing less explanatory weight on the Watergate scandal to evaluate the 1974 legislation, this essay stresses how antecedent political events created a window of opportunity for reformers at the same time that prior decisions limited the long-term impact of their accomplishments.[3]

* This essay originally appeared in "Seeds of Cynicism: The Struggle over Campaign Finance, 1956–1974," *Journal of Policy History* 14 (2002): 73–111.

In the 1960s, campaign finance reform did not emerge because of intense electoral pressure but, rather, emanated from a reform coalition that was neither a grassroots movement nor a group of elites at the center of political power. These were political actors operating at the margins of power who believed that representative government could be improved. The coalition, composed of legislators, experts, philanthropists, foundations, and public interest groups, was at the heart of the struggle over campaign finance. Members of this coalition claimed that substantive institutional reform was essential to restore public trust in democratic politics. Refusing to believe that politicians would independently monitor or cleanse their own institutions, the coalition supported a number of reforms in the political process ranging from the codification of ethics to the creation of an independent prosecutor. Campaign finance always maintained the most tenuous position of all the reforms (compared to filibuster reform, for example) since it touched on every interest in the political system, including legislators who were supportive of process reform. Still, the coalition was able to place campaign finance reform on the national agenda even without widespread public interest or support.[4]

But the efforts of this coalition were not sufficient for reform to pass.[5] Even without strong public pressure, politicians in the 1960s developed a self-interest in campaign finance reform as a result of escalating television costs and the evolving financial condition of the parties. A new adversarial media, moreover, created the perception that opposing campaign finance reform could be politically dangerous. These forces produced the political interest needed to make reform viable. Politicians then restructured the coalition's proposals to satisfy their own needs. Watergate created political support for reforms as legislators feared an angry constituency prepared to remove them from office. But scandal did not automatically produce reform. When Watergate occurred, the coalition was in place to take advantage of the favorable climate and additional conditions had created an interest for politicians.

The second puzzle historians must resolve is why reform failed to end public distrust of campaigns. Most accounts have focused on events after the passage of the 1974 legislation that undermined the reforms, ranging from the law of unintended consequences, to Supreme Court decisions, to the permanent power of special interest groups. While these factors are certainly important, this essay emphasizes critical choices and problems that reformers made before 1974. During the incubation period between 1956 and 1970, the coalition struggled to define how the debate would be framed.[6] The choices made during these years limited the ultimate impact of the reforms. Most important, the coalition left intact most of the underlying pressures on campaign finance. For example, they did not tackle the declining importance of political parties, leaving high-cost television as the principal medium of political communication. Although parties regained some importance in the 1990s, they served primarily as another source of campaign contributions for individual candidates rather than dominant forces of political communication, a function they had once served. Moreover, even with the substantial legislation that passed, the coalition made debilitating compromises, such as accepting political action committees (PACs) and limiting public financing of campaigns.

The most striking failure of the coalition was its inability to build sustained grassroots support for this issue. The major parties supported campaign finance reforms only where there was extreme internal financial pressure to do so. With limited electoral support, both parties immediately turned away from reform once it no longer served their interest. As a result of this weak electoral support, opponents were able to water down proposals or undermine laws after they passed. Key opponents of reform were rarely voted out of office because of their opposition to campaign finance. The leading opponent, Wayne Hays (D-OH), lost his power because of a notorious sex scandal, not because of his determined efforts to gut campaign finance laws. The coalition never obtained the popular support for the kinds of expansive government intervention, such as full government subsidies for all federal campaigns and free advertising, that was necessary to tame permanently the candidate-centered election.

The Pressures on Campaign Finance

Federal campaign finance laws originated in the Progressive Era. In 1907, Congress passed legislation that prohibited corporations and national banks from contributing to candidates in federal elections. This prohibition grew out of the belief that large contributions inherently corrupted politics. Reformers also believed it to be undemocratic for large organizations to use compulsory funds without the consent of contributors.[7] At this time, however, Congress rejected a proposal to finance presidential campaigns publicly. Instead, Congress required interstate party committees and congressional campaign committees to disclose campaign receipts only *after* the election, thereby diluting the effect of this reform. Nor did the laws apply to committees operating within a single state (designated "singe-state committees"). In 1911, Congress strengthened the disclosure requirements for the House and Senate and imposed spending limits. Congress again endorsed these provisions in 1925 by mandating federal regulation in all elections except in state primaries in accordance with a 1921 Supreme Court decision that ruled the federal government could not regulate state primaries.

The Progressive Era reforms had a negligible effect. Candidates easily found loopholes to evade unenforced regulations. Given the Supreme Court decision to limit federal regulation in the states, primary spending increased, obliterating the effects of reform in southern states. In addition, single-state committees were unregulated. Union contributions were also the source of great controversy. The Congress of Industrial Organizations (CIO) created the first political action committee in 1943 to support Democratic candidates.[8] Although the CIO first used general treasury funds, the union soon turned to voluntary $1 contributions from members. In 1947, following widely publicized congressional investigations into the CIO's influence in the 1944 and 1946 elections, Congress made permanent wartime prohibitions on union usage of general funds for campaigns. The right of unions to collect voluntary donations for campaign contributions remained contentious. Meanwhile, state-level initiatives foundered. Politicians underreported contributions, they withheld information from the public, and corruption survived even in state systems with public financing (Puerto Rico). With minimal reform, campaign finance changed very little.

During the post–World War II period, the Progressive Era laws failed to eliminate the four underlying factors that generated the strong incentives for candidates to seek private money. One was the declining organizational strength of parties. Unlike the nineteenth century, parties were no longer the primary vehicle for communicating issues or mobilizing voters during presidential and congressional campaigns. The organizational basis of parties weakened significantly throughout the century due to several factors, including Progressive Era reforms. Candidates began to communicate to voters through the media and professional campaign specialists rather than through the parties. The television "spot" became a main vehicle for candidates to communicate to the public, along with television news programs and newspapers, in the same fashion as the nineteenth-century party parade, picnic, and newspaper. Parties, which previously had been dominant, became the instrument of candidates. The second factor was the increase in campaign costs. As politicians used the radio and then television to communicate with voters, campaign costs rose dramatically for individual candidates. Third, there was little public pressure to reform campaign finance. Even though voters complained to pollsters that money corrupted politics, there was no substantive electoral pressure to change the system or to punish those who opposed reform legislation. Finally, the constitutional protection of free speech made it difficult to impose substantive restrictions on campaign spending.[9] Although it was unclear until 1976 how the Supreme Court would view legislation enforcing campaign spending limits, they gave indications in the 1950s and 1960s that they would deem them illegitimate.[10]

These four factors—weak parties, rising campaign costs, limited public pressure for reform, and the constitutional protection of free speech—shaped campaign finance for most of the period that followed the New Deal. But between 1956 and 1973, the convergence of several interdependent forces elevated the problems of this campaign system to the forefront of the political agenda as a reform coalition formed. As a result, tensions over campaign finance reached a boiling point when President Nixon began his second term in office.

The Reemergence of Reform, 1956–1964

Between 1956 and 1963, a small group of legislators realized that the Progressive Era campaign reforms were ineffective. Although each reformer had a different objective, most supported improved disclosure regulations in addition to tax incentives to encourage small contributions. Liberal Democrats such as Senators Albert Gore (D-TN) and Thomas Hennings (D-MO) hoped to constrain large contributors, limit corruption, and end the secrecy surrounding elections. Conservatives John McClellan (D-AR) and Barry Goldwater (R-AZ) used reform to attack organized labor. Although neither faction was able to pass legislation, their efforts caused two key factions to solidify their position. Organized labor emerged as the lead opponent of regulating PACs. Campaign finance experts became the external voice promoting reform.

In 1956, a congressional scandal involving campaign finance received national attention. On February 3, Senator Francis Case (R-SD) admitted that he had been offered cash by an oil company in exchange for supporting legislation. Although Case rejected the payment, the admission led President Dwight Eisenhower to veto the bill in question to avoid any appearance of corruption. The scandal increased congressional interest in the issue of campaign finance. Gore, for example, headed an investigation through the Privileges and Election Subcommittee of the Senate Rules Committee. The senator hired University of North Carolina Professor Alexander Heard, the leading expert on campaign finance and author of the landmark publication *The Cost of Democracy*, to serve as a consultant to the staff. Heard recruited Herbert Alexander, a newly minted political scientist from Yale. The committee produced an extensive analysis of campaign contributions. Soon after, John McClellan's Special Committee to Investigate Political Activities, Lobbying, and Campaign Contributions focused on labor's political activities. However, no legislation passed.

While legislation did not pass, these investigations put labor on the defensive. Organized labor felt that its political standing, only recently secured during the New Deal and World War II, was under attack from big business and conservatives in government. During the late 1950s, the government investigated union corruption. The National Association of Manufacturers was conducting a national anti-union campaign. In this context, union leaders perceived campaign finance reform as a tool for conservatives to emasculate their political power. Labor contributions were generally funneled through political action committees. When the American Federation of Labor (AFL) and CIO merged in 1955, leaders created the Committee on Political Education (COPE) to influence elections.[11] To avoid legal violations, COPE used voluntary member contributions deposited in a segregated account for cash contributions to candidates. Drawing on general AFL-CIO funds in addition to the voluntary contributions, COPE used these dollars for "political education." Unions could use compulsory dues for indirect expenditures such as providing campaign volunteers and publications about candidates. By 1956, there were 17 national union and 155 state and local affiliate political action committees.[12] Some unions also illegally directed union funds toward campaigns.

For these reasons, union leaders opposed PAC regulations. At this time, wealthy contributors known as "fat cats" were the main contributors to parties and candidates. They did not use formal PACs. Thus, PACs offered unions a counterweight to these contributors. By pooling contributions, unions created a lobbying presence and obtained access to politicians in a way that workers could never achieve individually. Since corporations were barred from making direct donations to candidates, corporate officials and their families contributed as individuals. Sometimes corporations illicitly concealed the source of donations through law firms. Unknown to the public, many corporations also maintained PAC-like operations without public knowledge: Gulf Oil, Union Carbide, McDonnell Douglas, Ford Motors, and General Electric had solicited executives and distributed the money to candidates since the 1950s.[13] Corporations often gave executives bonuses or inflated salaries with the implicit agreement that the money would be returned for campaign contributions.[14] Because the Justice Department ignored the Progressive Era laws, these activities went unpunished.

Unions argued that conservatives such as Senator Goldwater were using reform to combat labor's political power without doing anything about these corporate contributions.[15] Conservatives regularly proposed amendments that specifically targeted labor's committees. Regarding 1959 legislation, AFL-CIO Vice President Walter Reuther wrote President George Meany: "What little meaning the Bill has is aimed at labor and other liberal groups; if turned loose on the Senate floor in the present atmosphere, we would be faced with the strong probability that anti-labor forces in both parties would make an all out effort to amend the Bill so as to block and if possible prohibit all political activity by labor."[16] Labor continued through the 1970s to lobby against those who supported regulations on its committees.

Besides labor, another group that responded to campaign finance reform between 1956 and 1964 was composed of campaign finance experts. In an age when this issue generated little public interest and there was no major scandal to keep it at the forefront of public attention, these experts created a permanent constituency for reform and monitored campaigns in lieu of government enforcement. They would remain at the center of the reform coalition. Their efforts originated with William Vanderbilt, former governor of Rhode Island, who established the Committee on Campaign Contributions and Expenditures in January 1958. The committee included economist Seymour Harris, Eleanor Roosevelt, businessman Paul Hoffman, Harvard University Professor of Law Milton Katz, and President of Columbia University Grayson Kirk.[17] Even George Meany joined since it was good from the "standpoint of public relations."[18] The committee endorsed disclosure, centralized campaign committees, contribution limits, tax deductions for small contributors, and extending reforms to primaries.

Disclosure was the committee's most desired goal. At this time, there were virtually no data available on who contributed to campaigns or how campaign financing even worked. Information about the existing campaign finance system, in the minds of these experts and philanthropists, was the most important reform, as it could enable voters to make informed decisions. They assumed that voters would punish those who abused the laws. As the committee argued: "Full publicity is a key factor for there may well be no better test of propriety of a contribution or expenditure than the willingness to expose it to general public knowledge. It would also enable our citizens to know what the facts really are and to base plans for improvement on these facts, rather than guess and rumor."[19] Vanderbilt appointed Herbert Alexander, from Gore's investigations, to direct a research division that would analyze existing data and disseminate that data to the public through the media. The committee was renamed the Citizen's Research Foundation.

Information was difficult to obtain. Armed only with limited funds and a small staff, Alexander rummaged through the files of the Clerk of the House and Secretary of the Senate. The data were notoriously unreliable. To avoid interstate committee reporting requirements, candidates maintained campaign committees in one state. Single-state committees were immune from investigation. Even information from interstate committees often went unreported. To make matters worse, Alexander could not bring typewriters or adding machines into the Clerk's office, nor could he make photocopies.[20] In spite of these difficulties, Alexander found information by gathering what he could and drawing on information compiled by the Washington-based publication, *Congressional Quarterly*. Based on his research, the Citizen's Research Foundation released several studies of campaigns. One of its first major publications provided an unprecedented look into how the Democrats financed the 1960 presidential campaign.[21]

As president, Kennedy brought these campaign finance experts into the executive branch when he invited Alexander Heard to lead a Commission on Campaign Costs. Heard then hired Herbert Alexander to direct the staff. The White House insisted that its goal was to curtail big contributors, not to replace privately financed campaigns with public finance.[22] The 1962 commission report stressed the need to reduce the role of large donors through tax incentives for small contributors. At the same time, the commission said it was essential to minimize campaign costs and establish an independent commission to publicize data. Finally, they dismissed spending limits as ineffective and instead supported full disclosure.[23] Based on Heard's recommendations, Kennedy retained Alexander to lobby for a tax incentive.[24] But Congress rejected the measure; fiscal conservatives and tax reformers complained it cost too much, while liberals attacked it as regressive.

When Lyndon Johnson became president in 1963, he closed Alexander's operation and canceled a White House conference on the issue. Besides Johnson's lack of interest in reform, the Department of Justice challenged Kennedy's commission as being divorced from political reality. One official warned that if the government "scientifically" identified techniques to reduce costs, as the commission suggested, managers would spend the savings elsewhere.[25] Clearly not welcomed by Johnson, Alexander left the administration and returned to the Citizen's Research Foundation, where he received grants from the Ford and

Carnegie Foundations to write case studies on campaigns. His work continued to receive media attention.

As a result of the Case bribery scandal and the events it triggered, two vital interests in this battle had emerged. On the one hand, labor developed a hostile stand toward regulation of political action committees. On the other hand, campaign finance experts supported by philanthropists and foundations devoted themselves to the production of knowledge on campaign costs. If the government would not provide reliable information on elections, the experts would privately supply research and the media would publicize their findings. Failing to produce legislation, these experts built momentum for future efforts and helped define a policy agenda.

Television, Parties, and Scandal, 1964–1969

This cadre of experts and legislators in the reform coalition were not enough to sustain support for reform. Although Johnson dismissed campaign reform during his first years in office, external forces drove the issue to national attention. Skyrocketing television costs placed extraordinary pressure on politicians to secure funds. The evolving financial structure of the parties triggered Republican and Democratic interest in reform. Finally, a series of scandals before Watergate led reporters and politicians to focus on this issue.

Television drove up campaign costs to unprecedented levels. As the traditional role of parties continued to decline, candidates relied increasingly on television "spots" to sell themselves in elections. Television did not have a discernable financial impact in the 1950s when campaign costs rose only at the rate of inflation.[26] The effects of television on campaigns were striking and became a subject of constant discussion. More campaigning took place through advertising rather than parties. The Citizens' Research Foundation reported that election spending in 1968 was 25 percent higher than 1964.[27] In 1956, each vote cast cost 19 cents, while by 1968 that figure had risen to 56 cents.[28] Politicians faced significant pressure to obtain enough funds.

The parties responded with different financial strategies. Republicans supplemented their traditional large donors by broadening their contributor base to conservative groups and individual citizens. Conservative campaign specialist Richard Viguerie mastered the use of direct mail. He went to the files of the Clerk of the House to see who had donated more than $50 to conservative candidates. Using computers, he then sent out personalized mail to those supporters requesting small donations. In 1964, as a result of these mailings, individual citizens and single-issue groups funded much of Goldwater's presidential campaign. The senator had received 380,000 responses to direct mail with contributions of $100 each.[29] Given their broad support base and reliance on informal corporate contributions, Republicans endorsed incentives for small contributors and allied with southern Democrats to support the regulation of PACs.

Since they controlled the presidency and Congress, Democrats felt less pressure to innovate in the 1960s, even though the party had accumulated astronomical debt. Democrats also stayed with their old tactics by leaning more on large contributors. Non-southern congressional incumbents continued their reliance on labor and liberal organizations. In 1961, Democrats launched the President's Club, where members made donations in exchange for invitations to monthly events with prominent officials, including the president. There were more than 4,400 President's Club members by 1965.[30] The Democrats raised money through corporate advertising books for conventions. Without supporting candidates, corporations purchased tax-deductible ads. In 1964, the party produced a $15,000-a-page advertising book. Republicans copied this method, although not as effectively, since they were in the minority. While Democrats expanded their small contributor drive in 1966, these efforts were ancillary.[31] With Democrats in the White House and labor controlling PACs, this plan worked. But after Richard Nixon's victory in 1968, large contributors turned away from the party. Republicans also started to benefit from the PACs formed by the American Medical Association in 1961 and NAM in 1963. This change would lead more mainstream Democrats to support public financing and campaign regulations.

This third major development involved an increasingly aggressive news media that uncovered a series of 1960s scandals involving campaign finance. One involved Senator Thomas Dodd, a prominent senior Democrat from Connecticut. In their nationally syndicated column, Drew Pearson and Jack Anderson revealed the senator's illicit activities such as Dodd's use of campaign money for personal purposes. The Senate censured Dodd on June 23, 1967. In reporting the story, the papers detailed how Dodd raised money from wealthy individuals at "testimonial dinners" where politicians spoke to crowds paying $100 a plate. The dramatic scandal, which unfolded on the front pages of newspapers and magazines, produced extensive coverage into unregulated campaign practices.[32]

Democratic fund-raising tactics were the center of attention in 1965 and 1966. Republicans revealed how Democrats solicited funds from corporate executives with large military contracts. The charges were based on information from the Citizens' Research Foundation and *Congressional Quarterly*. In response to this scandal, Senator John Williams (R-DE) successfully added an amendment to 1966 tax legislation which eliminated the deduction businesses received for the contributions. In addition to this disincentive, many companies stopped donating because they were being "badgered by reporters" about why they had contributed to Democrats and "what they were promised in return."[33] Notwithstanding the scandals, Democrats still courted large contributors. For example, the Democrats held a $500-a-plate dinner with organizers and simply refrained from using the term "President's Club."[34]

Public opinion polls reflected contradictory attitudes toward campaign reform in the late 1960s. On the one hand, a majority of those polled favored limits on the total amount of money that candidates for federal office could spend. Yet Americans rarely demonstrated strong support for alternative forms of campaign finance. In 1956, only 31 percent of Americans said they would donate $5 to the party of their choice; 50 percent said they would not. Twelve years later, not more than 49 percent responded that they would make a donation to the party of their choice, while opposition still hovered at 50 percent.[35] Nor was government the answer. A 1964 poll found 71 percent of those surveyed were opposed to publicly financed presidential campaigns.[36] In this period, Americans never rated campaign reform as a key problem.

With Republicans attacking Democratic fund-raising tactics, President Johnson called on Congress in May 1966 to extend disclosure laws into primary and general elections and to create a tax deduction for contributions up to $100. However, the president refrained from supporting an independent commission. He told Congress that it was time for a change since "we have tolerated the growth of seeds in cynicism from the underbrush surrounding our present methods of financing political campaigns."[37] Senator Joseph Clark (D-PA) attempted unsuccessfully to move Johnson's proposals forward. He encountered hostility on almost every measure and received weak support from the administration. The Senate Rules and Administration Committee passed a watered-down version of the bill written by Senator Cannon's (D-NV) Privileges and Elections Subcommittee. In the House, Robert Ashmore (D-SC), chair of the Subcommittee on Elections in the House Administration Committee, and Republican Charles Goodell (R-NY) introduced a stronger measure (drafted by Herbert Alexander) that expanded disclosure, established an independent commission, ended spending limits, and prevented unions and corporations from using voluntary contributions for political expenditures. Although the subcommittee reported a bill on October 3, Chairman Omar Burleson's (D-TX) House Administration Committee killed the legislation.

In 1966, Congress passed a direct subsidy for presidential elections as an alternative to Johnson's proposal. Senator Russell Long (D-LA) proposed an amendment in June, along with Senators Nelson, Metcalf, and Douglas, to establish a Presidential Campaign Fund. The measure for the first time introduced public finance into presidential elections without imposing any contribution or spending restrictions. Wilbur Mills (D-AR), chair of the House Ways and Means Committee, surprised colleagues by accepting a provision he previously opposed as too costly. Long favored a subsidy over tax incentives as more progressive, but a direct appropriation was unacceptable politically.[38] Therefore, Long proposed a tax checkoff where individuals could allocate a dollar of taxes. Money would go to the major parties; minor parties qualified by obtaining four million votes. This subsidy soon came under fire. Senator Williams attacked it as too expensive, while Gore warned that third parties would be crippled. Without barring spending limits, he added, the subsidy was just a boon to the parties. Despite this criticism, Congress passed the legislation and for the first time subsidized elections. Johnson signed the legislation into law.

Behind closed doors, as Congress passed the direct subsidy, President Johnson formed a task force in September 1966 under the direction of Harvard

University's Richard Neustadt. Neustadt worked with Heard, then the chancellor of Vanderbilt University, and Malcolm Moos of the Ford Foundation, a former political scientist at Johns Hopkins University and former assistant to President Eisenhower. At first, the group was charged with reexamining old proposals. But the passage of Long's campaign fund changed the task force's agenda to protecting public subsidies from being attacked as a "grab-bag" for incumbents. The task force discovered that many politicians and experts opposed public subsidies for elections, instead favoring incentives for small contributions.[39] Heard, for example, warned that there were "great dangers" in the federal subsidy relating to the "voluntary character" of political activities in America. He also worried about the effect of "bureaucratic rigidities" on parties. Another member warned that "creating a beast which won't work will add to the already great cynicism over political financing."[40] Senator Robert Kennedy (D-NY) acknowledged that direct subsidies promoted the centralization of political power and raised constitutional problems by curtailing freedom of speech by requiring contribution and spending limits. Public subsidies, he said, were antithetical to the tradition of individual participation.[41] Politically, Mills told the task force that Congress would never vote for the extension of subsidies to the legislative branch since that would "finance the opponents of Congressional incumbents."[42] Hostility toward public finance became clear when Congress rendered Long's program ineffective in May 1967. After a bitter struggle, Gore was able to delay the implementation of the direct subsidy until technical guidelines were determined. This indefinite delay made the fund inoperative.

The month Congress short-circuited Long's campaign fund, Johnson proposed an Election Reform Act that included direct appropriations from presidential elections, regulations on primaries, and disclosure laws for all political committees spending more than $1,000. The administration believed that it had the legislative support to obtain a compromise on these issues based on a head count that Treasury made of the Senate Finance Committee. Johnson made a speech in which he said that there was more "loophole than law" in campaign finance. Key members of the administration were skeptical about free airtime from the networks since it might not be in the interest of the Democratic Party. The networks would only finance public service appearances or debates, but would not finance the crucial type of "spot announcements" that Johnson and Goldwater had used in 1964. Moreover, presidential aide Joseph Barr was concerned that free airtime would benefit third-party candidates such as George Wallace.[43] Clark Clifford, who did not believe any legislation would pass in the end because of the free speech problems raised by contribution limitations, suggested that the president promote his legislation from a "public relations" standpoint even though it would fail.[44] At the June Senate hearings and behind closed doors, there was considerable support for the reforms.[45] Senator Scott proposed an independent commission which Republicans considered essential so that the disclosed information, now controlled by the Democratic Congress, would not be used against them. After a bill was reported from committee, the

Senate rejected two amendments: one by Clark to require congressional members and candidates to disclose outside income and another from Williams to ban all corporate and union spending of funds on political activities. Senators Ted Kennedy (D-MA) and Walter Mondale (D-MN) defeated the amendment. The Senate bill limited individual contributions, expanded disclosure, and eliminated spending ceilings.

Within the House, Representatives Ashmore and Goodell promoted the ideas that had been rejected the year before. Their Subcommittee on Elections reported a bill in June that expanded reporting requirements to primary elections and to all political committees, created a bipartisan commission, strengthened regulations on political action committees, and eliminated spending ceilings. The AFL-CIO warned that the definition of "committee" was so broad it would include spending on political education. AFL-CIO lobbyist Andrew Biemiller felt that the union needed to obtain language that would "pull the teeth of the bad provisions" and at the same time "look like we're just being boy scouts."[46] The legislation encountered resistance in the full committee from southerners, liberal Democrats, and Republicans. Liberal Democrat Frank Thompson (D-NJ) fought against provisions on PACs, southerners opposed primary regulations, and Republicans wanted stronger PAC limits. The deadlock ended when the committee abandoned the provisions against labor, which enabled liberal Democrats to support the legislation. Although the House Administration passed the measure, the Rules Committee prevented it from reaching the floor. Thus, despite passage of the Senate bill, the House never voted on any legislation.

Advocates of reform doubted that campaign spending limits would survive constitutional challenge. While the Supreme Court did not review any cases directly and sent mixed messages on this issue, several rulings in the 1950s and 1960s indicated a bias toward protecting speech in elections.[47] In the 1964 decision *New York Times Co. v. Sullivan*, for example, the Court ruled that the public had to be exposed to a full range of information about public concerns.[48] In *Mills v. Alabama* (1966), the court overturned an Alabama action where a newspaper publisher was convicted for publishing an editorial in favor of a candidate on the day of an election. The publication had violated an Alabama statute prohibiting vote solicitation on the day of an election. The Court ruled that Alabama had violated the First Amendment and warned against any restrictions on speech during campaigns.[49] In law review articles, Dr. Alexander Meiklejohn spent much of the decade writing about how there should be no restrictions on information reaching voters in times of elections, a key to effective democratic governance.[50]

By the late 1960s, policymakers were considering campaign reform with increased frequency as a result of the publications by campaign finance experts, the cost of campaigns, the evolving financial practices of the major political parties, and a series of scandals. These debates revolved around reforming, not replacing, the candidate-centered election system. The biggest development came with the passage of public finance for presidential elections, although this was quickly dismantled. The reform coalition did not yet have the political support needed to pass and maintain substantive change.

1969–1963: Reform without Scandal

The political support emerged between 1969 and 1973. Congress passed legislation in 1971 that improved disclosure and limited costs. Just as important, the reform coalition actively monitored the laws after Congress failed to create any independent enforcement mechanisms. The coalition's reports resulted in unprecedented publicity about money in politics, thereby increasing the political incentives for reform. Much of the information released during this period became central to the Watergate investigations. Without the legislation or the reform coalition, the Watergate scandal of 1974 might not have been nearly as severe.

By 1970, before Watergate, citizens were becoming distrustful of political institutions as a result of Vietnam. Political scientist Gary Orren has shown that public trust in the American government began to decline in 1964 and continued to deteriorate ever since then.[51] This political culture made institutional reform seem appealing.

The debate over reform in 1969 began around issues of cost rather than scandal. In 1970, policymakers voiced concerns about increased election costs. A prominent task force study sponsored by the Twentieth Century Fund found that incumbents enjoyed a significant advantage since challengers could not raise the funds needed to manage a successful campaign.[52] Democrats were particularly aware of this cost pressure since the party faced a large deficit. Following their widely publicized study on television costs, the National Committee for an Effective Congress (a political action committee composed of liberals) drafted legislation to enable congressional candidates to purchase airtime at a reduced rate. They also proposed ending the equal-time provision of the Communications Act of 1934. The provision discouraged presidential debates by requiring networks to provide every candidate with an opportunity to participate. Although Congress suspended the requirement in 1960, no debates were held in the election of 1968 and the issue subsided. Network executives supported a suspension.[53] The proposal reemerged in 1969 as part of the general effort to broaden candidate access to television.

Congress took up legislation in 1969 and 1970, beginning with a bill that included free spots for candidates and additional time at reduced rates. Senators Philip Hart (D-MI), James Pearson (R-KS), and Representative Torbert MacDonald (D-MA) introduced a bill based on the recommendations of the National Committee for an Effective Congress.[54] In response, network executives promised to discount rates voluntarily while adamantly opposing free airtime. The Commerce Committee reported a bill that suspended the equal-time provision and limited the rates broadcasters could charge candidates. On

April 14, the Senate passed the legislation 58-27 with eight Republicans in favor. Democrats were very aware of how this legislation could change their electoral fortunes. One representative wrote the Speaker that the failure of reform would "hand a big advantage to well financed Republican candidates" in his state and similar harm to Democrats in "marginal districts."[55] The House bill also guaranteed reduced advertising rates and stronger disclosure regulations.

The conference committee eliminated the most controversial provision: an independent commission. Most Democrats opposed the creation of a commission since it would increase enforcement of the laws. Republicans feared that without a commission Democrats would use information for partisan purposes. Under the existing system, candidates submitted their campaign data to the Clerk of the House and Secretary of Senate, both of whom reported to Democratic leaders. Responding to the powerful network executives, the committee also settled on watered-down cost control through reduced rates. Using these concerns as an excuse for his general opposition to any reform, President Nixon vetoed the legislation on October 12. He claimed that the bill opened more loopholes than it closed and that it fell short of solving all the problems of campaign finance. It also discriminated unfairly against the broadcast media and benefited incumbents.[56] Democrats charged Nixon with sacrificing reform on the altar of partisan interests; reformers equated Nixon's reasoning with "a man who decided not to undergo a much needed appendectomy because the doctor was not prepared to deal with his liver and back problems at the same time."[57]

As Nixon's veto and the Democratic response made clear, partisan interests and divided government added heat to the campaign finance debate. Since his inauguration, Nixon and the Democrats had been locked in a fierce battle. One advisor warned Nixon that this was the first administration in 120 years to "begin with a hostile Congress" and that aggressive liberals were defining the party leadership instead of moderates.[58] Just as Democrats attacked Nixon by focusing on the excessive power of the executive branch, Nixon went after liberal Democrats by highlighting the chronic failures of Congress. The volatile atmosphere led to an "arms war" of institutional criticism with each side escalating its attack of the other.

Traditionally, campaign finance reform had been promoted by a small coalition of experts, reform legislators, and reporters. Many organizations sympathetic to other process reforms, such as the AFL-CIO, had been much less interested in the issue of campaign finance. But starting in 1970, the coalition gained its own interest group. Johnson's former Secretary of Health, Education, and Welfare John Gardner founded Common Cause, an organization devoted to good government reforms to curtail the power of interest groups and to end corruption. The Common Cause founders believed that interest-group liberalism, which had promised that the struggle between organized interests would balance each other out for the public good, had not worked as planned. It had disempowered individuals who were not connected to interest groups, which were largely unrepresentative even of those they served.[59] For Gardner, campaign finance was needed before any other change was possible. Common Cause brought organizational muscle to the reform coalition. Common Cause claimed more than one hundred thousand members and $1.75 million in contributions by 1971. The members tended to be educated, middle-class professionals, most of whom did little more than contribute money.[60]

Ironically, Common Cause adopted the techniques of sophisticated specialized lobbyists to promote the needs of the "public" and fight interest-group politics: placing advertisements and op-eds in newspapers, bombarding legislators with position papers, and orchestrating "mass" letter writing campaigns. The organization thus used all the weapons of a traditional interest group, including donations, in the name of reforming government. Democrats had to strike a delicate balance between Common Cause, which insisted on the broadest reforms, and organized labor, which opposed many reforms (such as PAC limitations) since they did not want to risk losing their hard-earned political influence. Another addition was Philip Stern, liberal heir of the Sears Roebuck fortune, who devoted his life to advocacy of institutional reform and founded the Center for the Public Financing of Elections. Director Susan King developed strong ties with other reform groups to lobby Congress.[61] By 1974, there would be eighteen of these groups working on the lobby for campaign reform.[62]

Public interest groups such as Common Cause shared the Progressive Era fear that corruption was undermining democratic politics.[63] These public interest reformers were deeply suspicious of political parties and attacked the organizational mechanisms of parties that had traditionally served as intermediaries between voters and elected officials (urban machines, for example).[64] Gardner said that parties were "virtually useless as instruments of the popular will."[65] The National Committee for an Effective Congress believed that it was urgent to "break the southern and city-machine stranglehold on the power structure of the party."[66] Common Cause and allied organizations also chose to influence policy through Washington-based activities rather than building locally based coalitions to support campaign finance reform. Accepting the permanence of the existing framework for electoral politics, the leaders of Common Cause reasoned that if reformers did not employ the tactics of interest groups their campaign would fail.

Common Cause introduced a new tactic in the struggle for campaign reform: the class action lawsuit. On January 11, 1971, it filed a lawsuit in a U.S. District Court against the Democratic and Republican National Committees and the Conservative Party of New York to enjoin them from violating the campaign laws. Common Cause claimed that both parties regularly flouted the 1925 laws. According to this suit, these political parties were creating multiple committees for candidates and spending more on single candidates than the laws allowed. Gardner issued a statement, lamenting: "I find it less easy to excuse the parties, which had they chosen to do so—could long since have joined forces to put an end to the fraud and humbug. They have paid a healthy price for not doing so. A recent Newsweek-Gallup poll of student opinion found political parties rated lowest on a list of American institutions."[67] Common Cause was joined in its class action suit by the Americans for Democratic Action, the Twentieth Century Fund, and the National Committee for an Effective Congress. Ruling for the interest group, the district court formalized the "right of private enforcement" of campaign finance laws since no strong public commission existed. As a result, groups such as Common Cause gained the right to bring class action suits against the parties on behalf of voters.[68]

As reformers turned to the courts between 1969 and 1973, the news media extensively reported on corruption. The stories surrounding campaign finance were written by a new generation of professionally trained journalists and editors who had adopted a critical role toward politicians since the mid-1960s. The conflict over civil rights and Vietnam inspired many reporters and editors to challenge politicians. This adversarial relationship meshed with the needs of the print and television media in their fierce competition for dramatic stories.[69] Reporters in both mediums could now draw on a wealth of data from experts in the reform coalition, housed in the Citizen's Research Foundation, Common Cause, and the Center for Public Financing, who produced studies of how parties and candidates received money from vested interests. In turn, the media produced a record number of articles and editorials endorsing reform.[70] Sidney Scheuer, the chairman of the National Committee for an Effective Congress, pointed out to Congress that in 1970 alone, "countless newspapers and magazines" had appeared with such "glaring" headlines as "Unseen Fund Raisers Financing Lobbyists," "Bank PAC Funds Data Surfaced After Vote," and "Five Political Funds Don't Report Aid." Regardless of whether each story pointed to a clear violation of laws, Scheuer argued, "each instance stokes the fires of public cynicism and the common suspicion of widespread wrong-doing. As a result, the reputation of politics and all politicians suffers."[71]

In addition to reformers and an aggressive media, partisan interests also energized the drive for campaign finance reform. As political scientist Robert Mutch argued, "principle and partisanship" were "inextricably entangled in all of these regulations."[72] By 1971, the Democratic Party was aggressively supporting reform.[73] This support had as much to do with raw economic self-interest, if not more so, than ideological motivation. Large donors had shifted their resources toward the Republican Party after Nixon took over the presidency and the Democrats fell into disarray. At the same time, Republicans continued to expand their small contributor base by sending personalized letters to targeted individuals requesting small solicitations. Democrats needed to catch up. This is one of the reasons that the Senate housed the strongest proponents of congressional campaign reform. Since senators faced more competitive elections than representatives and needed to finance more media expenditures to cover entire states, they were more concerned about the pressures of campaign finance. There were internal Democratic efforts to revamp private fund-raising. Under the new leadership of Robert Strauss, the Democratic National Committee focused on fund-raising to avoid becoming fiscally irrelevant. In 1972,

Strauss inaugurated a telethon that raised $4 million.[74] The party also increased its small contributor base from 16,000 to 45,000.[75] But this was not enough to match the overflowing Republican coffers. Democrats needed new revenue. In blunt language, AFL-CIO lobbyist Andrew Biemiller warned that without publicly financed elections, "the Democratic Party will be in desperate shape" in 1972.[76] Just as partisan interests led Democrats to support public finance, Republicans now sensed that it no longer served their interest to appear as the party of obstruction in the light of increased media attention on the subject. In March, Republican National Committee Chairman Robert Dole told reporters that the president would not repeat his veto of a bill imposing a ceiling on costs.[77] Working with Democrats, moderate Republican Senators Hugh Scott and Charles Mathias proposed legislation to establish a limit for overall costs, media spending ceilings, and improved disclosure.

The Senate passed the regulations by a vote of 88-2 on August 5, removing limitations on private contributions, creating a six-person independent commission, requiring television and radio stations to charge the lowest price possible to candidates, and strengthening disclosure laws. Common Cause had worked behind the scenes successfully to obtain Senator Pearson's amendment for an independent commission (a measure based on language they had drafted).[78] For Common Cause's John Gardner, Congress's decision to eliminate the commission would create the "appearance of reform without the reality."[79] To gain bipartisan support, Common Cause accepted a commission with six members with three from each party.[80] Labor also supported this structure.[81] Controversy formed around Senator Dominick's amendment to prohibit organizations from using dues to support candidates, but labor-backed Democrats defeated the amendment.

When the Senate legislation reached the House, both the Interstate and Foreign Commerce and Administration Committees had jurisdiction over the measure. While the former was sympathetic to moderate reform, the House Administration Committee was chaired by Wayne Hays (D-OH), an avid opponent. Hays was powerful because his committee controlled the allowances for the office expenses of members and chaired another committee that distributed campaign funds. The acerbic Hays displayed little respect for Common Cause or John Gardner. But Hays was not alone in opposing the bill. Another committee member, Bill Frenzel (R-MN), said spending limits would help incumbents who had free exposure. Without being able to spend enough money, challengers would not match such visibility.[82] There were strong supporters of reform on the committee, including John Anderson (R-IL) and Morris Udall (D-AZ). Anderson believed that if the committee did not pass reform before the next election cycle began, partisanship would undermine the effort.[83]

The AFL-CIO feared for the future of its PACs. The Supreme Court was considering a case of union leaders convicted of violating the prohibition of using general fund money for contributions to federal elections. Evidence revealed that the St. Louis Pipefitters Local Union No. 562 maintained a fund between 1949 and 1962 to which union members were required to contribute. In 1963, they converted it to an independent fund and contributions were made voluntary. The jury found the union guilty, since union officers administered the funds. Those officers were paid by the general funds. When the case reached the Supreme Court, the Justice Department raised the stakes by claiming that it was not legal for unions to engage in any political activities, even with voluntary funds.[84] This argument threatened all union political committees.[85]

In January 1972, Congress passed a bill that limited media spending, forced broadcasters to sell reduced-cost advertising, reasserted the right of Congress to regulate primaries (which the Supreme Court had overturned in 1921), strengthened reporting requirements for all campaign committees, legitimated PACs, and deemed contribution limits to be illegitimate. The legislation authorized labor to seek contributions for political funds as long as they were voluntarily donated without any type of physical intimidation or employment threat. To gain administration support, Democrats inserted a sixty-day delay so that it took effect only on April 7, after the New Hampshire, Florida, Illinois, and Wisconsin primaries. Nixon signed the legislation on February 7, realizing that he no longer had support for a veto. In addition, Senate Democrats unexpectedly attached language providing for public financing of presidential elections to tax legislation. Nixon threatened a veto, saying the bill was too costly.[86] Ways and Means Chairman Wilbur Mills felt the tax legislation was too important to risk, so he engineered a compromise: taxpayers could allocate money in 1972, but Congress could not distribute funds until 1976. For reformers, this compromise resembled Senate action in 1967, which effectively killed the legislation through postponement.

One immediate effect was to stimulate intense fund-raising before the laws went into effect. Nixon's team led the way as Maurice Stans went on a whirlwind tour to solicit contributors. The press intercepted an administration letter urging donors to make anonymous donations before the disclosure laws went into effect.[87] While a few Democrats voluntarily disclosed information before April 7, responding to a challenge from Common Cause, presidential candidates Wilbur Mills, Henry Jackson, and Nixon refused. The flurry of fund-raising during these weeks would become a central issue in the Watergate investigation.

Since Congress had not created an independent commission to enforce the laws, the reform coalition took this responsibility upon themselves. The courts were a key avenue for enforcement. As soon as Nixon signed the legislation in 1972, Ralph Nader's Public Citizen, the Federation of Homemakers, and the D.C. Consumer's Association filed a lawsuit claiming that the president accepted money from the milk co-ops in exchange for reversing a decision by the Department of Agriculture that had lowered milk prices.[88] In a separate action, Public Citizen filed a suit against the Department of Justice, claiming that the department had not enforced campaign finance legislation. Public Citizen and the National Committee for an Effective Congress filed a petition in March 1972 requesting that the Securities and Exchange Commission force corporations with "voluntary" committees to disclose fully their transactions. Finally, Common Cause filed a suit on September 6 charging that the Committee to Reelect the President had violated the 1925 election disclosure laws. The suit was partially settled on November 1, 1972, with Nixon revealing the sources of $5 million in donations. On July 24, 1973, the court ruled that Nixon had to disclose the remaining donations. The information that emerged from these suits was soon on the front pages of many newspapers.

Besides the courts, the reform coalition called on its members to enforce the laws. Starting on March 30, Common Cause launched a national monitoring project of the 1972 election. The project aimed to determine how much was being spent and who was contributing. Common Cause trained more than one thousand volunteers throughout the states to analyze reports. The volunteers established networks in state capitals and near the offices of the major congressmen who would be the focus of the study.[89] Common Cause leader Fred Wertheimer said that this was the only way to keep the issue of campaign reform alive without administrative enforcement.[90] He also believed that Common Cause could establish itself as the major player on this issue.[91] Based on initial findings, Common Cause filed complaints against 128 Democrats and 98 Republicans. In 1973, the group released the data through carefully planned encounters with reporters.[92] When Wayne Hays attempted to subvert the regulations, Common Cause responded. For instance, Common Cause reported that TRW, a large company with major government contracts, maintained an illegal campaign fund solicited from employees. Common Cause filed a suit against TRW, which led the company to end the practice.[93] Without public hearings, Hays's committee repealed the law that allowed this suit by exempting corporate and union contractors from Section 611, the provision that barred voluntary campaign gifts from persons involved with government contracts.[94] Senators, under intense pressure from Common Cause, killed the measure.[95]

Unions rested a little easier following the Supreme Court decision in June 1972, *Pipefitters v. United States*, which protected the right of unions to establish PACs as long as donations were voluntary and maintained in a separate account. The basis of the prohibition against unions and corporations, the Court explained, was that large organization money corrupted politics. But if the money was voluntarily contributed by individuals, the rationale did not apply. Based on the 1972 legislation and precedents since the 1940s, the Court did not deny unions this right. Union officers, moreover, could administer the funds as long as they were maintained in a separate account. The case legitimated political action committees. In his ominous dissent, Justice Powell warned that this opinion provided a "blueprint" for corporations and unions to flood the political system with contributions without regulation.[96]

Even with this decision, unions were still wary of reform. While the AFL-CIO supported federal subsidies for presidential elections, they wanted a mixed system that included some private contributions because, as one senior counsel wrote, "the opportunity to make contributions to our friends is one which repays us during the course of the legislative and executive processes." Since labor spent most of its money on congressional candidates, they were less concerned with presidential elections.[97] The AFL-CIO was skeptical of contribution limits because unions, which aggregated the funds of many individuals with modest incomes, might be inequitably treated in the same fashion as those from single wealthy contributors.[98]

Watergate, the scandal that was riveting national attention by 1973, revolved around rampant campaign corruption. The story broke around the bugging of Democratic national headquarters to obtain information on campaign strategies. Gradually the story expanded to include other campaign abuses, including illicit contributions in 1972. The news emanated from the *Washington Post* within the context of a preexisting reform coalition that was seeking to enforce new laws. It also took place in an explosive partisan environment pitting the Democratic Congress against a Republican president, each fighting to curtail the power of the other.

Congress, the courts, and the media furthered this effort to make the existing campaign laws effective through the Watergate investigations. The Select Committee on Presidential Campaign Activities, charged by Senator Sam Ervin (D-NC), conducted highly rated televised hearings on the 1972 presidential campaign. The hearings focused both on the break-in at the Watergate and the subversion of campaign laws.[99] The hearings, which introduced many Americans to the corrupt campaign practices of the administration, were filled with dramatic stories such as an administration official, G. Gordon Liddy, obtaining a briefcase containing $83,000 and the president reversing policies because the milk industry made donations. During the second half of December 1973, the committee examined in great detail the activities of the milk producers during the 1972 campaign.[100] Ervin's panel also looked into the campaigns of Mills, McGovern, Muskie, and Humphrey, and found evidence of illicit corporate contributions to their campaigns.[101] Attorney General John Mitchell and Secretary of Commerce Maurice Stans were indicted on campaign charges. The prosecution presented evidence that these officials had secretly accepted union contributions in exchange for stopping Justice Department investigations.

More Republicans began to call for reform. Watergate turned campaign finance into a political liability for Republicans as many Democrats were preparing to use it as a campaign issue. As one Democrat told colleagues: "It is very possible you will find that if you are against public financing you might be accused of being in favor of what has just happened in Watergate; in other words, it may be the most popular thing right now for everybody to be in favor of public financing rather than to think that you are being accused of wanting a slush fund."[102] To separate themselves from the scandal, Republicans stressed that Watergate was the product of a corrupt system, not a corrupt individual or party. William Brock (R-TN), chairman of the Republican Senatorial Campaign Committee, called for stronger disclosure laws, contribution limits, and stronger restraints on campaign costs. He also wanted to require candidates to designate a single financial institution to hold their funds. The bank would publish the names and Social Security numbers of contributors.[103] Nixon even called for a nonpartisan commission.[104] Few took him seriously. Charles Colson, former special assistant to the president, published a piece in the *New York Times* which argued that public financing and complete financial disclosure were essential for the nation to move beyond Watergate.[105] However, most Republicans still opposed public finance on the grounds that it was unconstitutional and costly and that it protected incumbents. Even with Watergate, Republicans had less need for public money and did not want Democrats to benefit from the new public funds.

By 1973, most congressional Democrats agreed on the need for public subsidies, contribution and spending limits, and an independent commission. Yet there were still important divisions within the party. One disagreement revolved around the relationship between Watergate and reform. Some Democrats, such as Senator Joseph Biden (D-DE), wanted to target Nixon, while others, such as Senator John Pastore (D-RI), stressed the need to keep the issue bipartisan. A second division was over whether to call for public financing in congressional or just presidential elections. Pastore and others warned of the need to limit reforms in terms of cost and coverage, or risk losing support. Likewise, Long believed that public financing for congressional elections, based on his experience in 1966, would be seen as a subsidy for incumbents while public finance for presidential elections could pass: "You ought to start right out with the Presidency where the people can understand it. That is where we have already acted and where we have already managed to put something on the statute books and the public has come to accept it."[106] A few Democrats such as Representative James O'Hara (D-MI) argued that campaign finance had to be completely subsidized by the federal government. Even a matching funds system, he said, left open the door for corruption.[107]

In July 1973, the Senate Rules and Administration Committee reported legislation limiting campaign spending, restricting contributions, repealing the equal-time provision, and creating an independent commission to regulate elections. Support for a commission had become much stronger as the abuses of the Department of Justice under Nixon became clear. Watergate had made it much more difficult to contend that members of the administration could uphold the laws. The complete ineffectiveness of federal controls on campaign costs, Director of the General Accounting Office Philip Hughes claimed, showed that stronger machinery was needed.[108] While the Senate rejected public subsidies for presidential elections, it did so by an extremely narrow vote. In the House, Anderson and Udall received more support for public finance than ever before but were unsuccessful getting it through committee. When a bipartisan coalition of senators attached a rider for publicly financed elections to legislation, they were forced to drop the measure as a result of Senator James Allen's (D-AL) filibuster.

The years between 1969 and 1973 witnessed an increase in the momentum for reforming the candidate-centered system even before Watergate exploded.

Congress passed legislation in 1971, which the reform coalition used to expose election corruption. There was now a sense that reform could work. Senator Claiborne Pell (D-RI) told fellow Democratic senators that the 1971 bill "is a pretty darn good law, because a lot of things exposed in the Watergate would not have come up if it hadn't been for the present law."[109] More than forty states adopted reforms before the federal legislation of 1974.[110] None of the reforms resulted automatically from scandal, but from a reform coalition actively pursuing change and responding to policy windows as they emerged.

1974: Watergate

Watergate offered a "focusing event" for the coalition to push their proposals that had incubated over many years. When the press publicized Nixon's misdeeds, there was a reform coalition inside and outside Congress that was prepared to move forward with legislation. As Senator Joseph Biden explained in 1973: "Watergate isn't the question. Watergate is merely a vehicle through which we can get through what we originally could not get through because the fellows on the other team are in a very compromising position as a consequence of it."[111] Without the reform coalition, the Watergate scandal might have produced less legislation and the scandal itself might not have been as dramatic. But without a scandal as shocking as Watergate, the coalition might not have been able to secure legislative support for reform.

Conservative organizations continued to oppose federal subsidies for elections. While supporting some reforms, the Chamber of Commerce warned that public subsidies would control "political freedom" by requiring spending limits. Calling for the government to limit private contributions and to distribute public contributions to all candidates equally, they said, was the "height of arrogance."[112] The American Enterprise Institute, a conservative think tank, published a report that claimed private money appropriately weeded out unpopular candidates. Since most citizens did not have the energy for other types of political activity, moreover, private contributions were an integral method of political participation. It seemed hypocritical, the report added, for Common Cause to contribute funds yet deny that same right to others.[113] Amid public outrage at the activities of President Nixon and his staff, an IRS study found that only 4 percent of taxpayers had used the opportunity in 1972 to earmark a dollar for elections, and the number rose to 14 percent in 1973.[114]

Even the Democratic Party, which was now aggressive in the pursuit for reform, still needed money. Under the direction of Lloyd Bentsen (D-TX), the Democratic Senatorial Campaign Committee promoted its new private fund-raising techniques. The committee organized a $500-a-plate dinner that raised $1 million for senatorial candidates. The committee also sent experts to teach candidates effective fund-raising techniques. Bentsen encouraged colleagues to lean harder on interest groups, who were reluctant to contribute in light of the negative press coverage of campaign finance in the Watergate scandal. The committee also tried to broaden its small contributor base through direct mail, targeting those who had written senators about Nixon's impeachment and resignation.[115]

Notwithstanding these fund-raising activities, most Democratic leaders perceived campaign finance as a defining issue in 1974.[116] Public opinion polls confirmed that Watergate had heightened public interest in taking action against campaign corruption. Americans now ranked government corruption as one of the most important problems. Of those polled, 65 percent said that they favored the use of public funding in presidential and congressional elections. Support was high regardless of educational backgrounds or party affiliation. That figure had risen from 58 percent between June and October 1973. Seventy-four percent of those polled said that they would like the 1971 federal disclosure laws applied to their state.[117]

The Senate passed a bill that mandated public funds for all federal elections and created an independent commission. Nixon could no longer afford to oppose these legislators as Congress deliberated his impeachment. Several weeks after Nixon's key fund-raiser pleaded guilty to managing illegal contributions, the president called for an independent commission, stronger disclosure laws, rules against "dirty tricks," and strict reporting requirements for PACs.[118] Critics were angry that he refused to endorse publicly financed elections.[119] Senate Minority Leader Hugh Scott had reversed his position because of Watergate by supporting publicly financed presidential elections. Ardent campaign finance opponent Senator James Allen mounted another filibuster hoping to stop the bill or at least to water it down. Common Cause, along with Senators Ted Kennedy and Scott, lobbied for cloture. The Senate ended the filibuster and passed legislation on April 11 by 53-32. The bill included public financing for congressional and presidential elections, an independent commission, contribution and spending limits, and a repeal of the equal-time provision.

The Senate legislation reached the House, where Wayne Hays, sensing that federal subsidies for presidential elections were inevitable, focused on preventing public subsidies in congressional elections.[120] Consequently, Hays's committee reported legislation that included public financing for presidential, but not congressional, elections. John Brademas (D-IN), who supported the provision for congressional elections, brokered that compromise. Anderson and Udall vowed to fight for an amendment to extend public finance to congressional campaigns. Frenzel, along with other Republicans, attacked public financing and the lack of a commission in the bill. While the committee was deliberating, the Senate Watergate Committee released its final 2,217-page report. Although Sam Ervin's committee opposed public financing on the grounds that it was a serious threat to constitutional rights, most of the publicity surrounding this report centered on its lurid evidence of campaign corruption. Other developments surrounding this investigation generated momentum for reform. Former Secretary of Treasury John Connally was indicted for accepting a bribe from the milk industry. Criminal information filed against the Associated Milk Producers, Inc., revealed its donations to Democratic presidential candidates Mills, Humphrey, and Muskie.

The legislation passed by the House created two regulatory systems: public financing would attempt to constrain private contributions in presidential elections, while strict contribution limitations would achieve the same goal in Congress. After rejecting an amendment for publicly financed congressional elections and accepting one for an independent commission, the House passed the legislation on August 8, by a vote of 355-48, hours before President Nixon resigned from office. The bill included contribution and spending limits, publicly financed presidential elections, and a part-time independent commission.

As late as August 21, key advisors to President Gerald Ford believed there was a possibility that Hays would block the legislation in conference committee, where the House and Senate had to settle their differences.[121] Hays still wanted to stop the bill, which he felt he had been forced to pass, but he needed someone else to take the blame.[122] The bills went to conference with public finance for congressional elections (which was in the Senate but not the House bill) and the strength of the independent commission (stronger in the Senate than the House bill) being the two unresolved issues. Enough Democrats were willing to abandon public financing for congressional elections to obtain the other reforms. John Gardner predicted support for further reform once citizens saw how the program operated in presidential elections. Others in Congress were interested in reforming the presidency but not themselves. In conference, the House accepted a stronger commission in exchange for dropping the Senate's publicly financed congressional elections. Spending limits were set low so that incumbents felt they would help defeat challengers.[123] The Senate passed the bill 60-16 and the House by 365-24.

The final legislation established contribution and spending limits, public financing for presidential elections, and an independent election commission. The legislation did not impose any serious restriction on PACs and even permitted corporations with government contracts to establish these committees.[124] Candidates could not spend more than $50,000 from their personal funds. Independent expenditures, those made on behalf of a candidate but not in any way solicited or connected to his or her campaign committee, were limited to $1,000 a year. The FEC was given the power to conduct investigations, initiate civil actions, and refer criminal violations to the Attorney General. The House, Senate, and President would each nominate commissioners. Congress retained the power to veto regulations.

Although the legislation did not provide public financing for congressional elections, reformers claimed victory. John Gardner told reporters that while this was only a "half loaf," it was a "great half loaf." He explained that this legislation bought Congress two years before they would be forced, because of the inconsistency in the two election systems, to reform themselves. Frenzel called the bill a "hoax." Low spending caps and contribution limits, he said, would turn this bill into a boon for incumbents without doing anything about campaign abuses.[125] Common Cause acknowledged that House election challengers had difficulty raising funds. But the reformers were convinced that incumbents raised more money from interest groups than challengers, so public financing would make elections more competitive.[126] President Ford opposed the legislation but realized that he had little choice but to sign it. A veto was now politically dangerous and Congress might override it.[127] On October 15, Ford hesitantly signed the bill.[128]

The following month, Democrats swept the congressional elections in one of the worst showings for Republicans since the New Deal. The victories were a partial vindication for reformers. Although Democrats generally refrained from using Watergate directly, many candidates discussed the "integrity" issue in their campaigns.[129] Some elections were linked directly to Watergate. In the eighth district of Michigan, Republican Jim Sparling lost because Nixon had strongly supported him during an earlier election. Sparling acknowledged that the "taint" of Watergate had defeated him. Five Republican members of the House Judiciary Committee who supported Nixon were defeated. Senator Robert Dole, who had chaired the Republican National Committee, survived an unexpectedly close race with sharp reduction in the number of votes he received. Dole said that the "wreckage of Watergate" and Ford's pardon made it difficult for Republicans that year. He thought he would lose.[130]

The election dampened enthusiasm among congressional Democrats, who relied more on interest groups than party funds, for public subsidies in congressional elections. Given the importance of economic issues, organized labor spent record amounts on this election, obtaining great success.[131] In a dramatic turn of fortune, Democrats raised more overall money than the Republicans.[132] Some reformers were still optimistic. The previous vote on public financing for congressional elections had been supported by 187 representatives. In November, a Common Cause survey of House candidates found 242 supporting a mixed system of public finance for congressional elections, including 59 Republicans.[133] But reformers soon found themselves protecting what Congress had passed rather than expanding measures into new arenas.

By 1982, Common Cause would launch another campaign for campaign reform, this time focusing on PACs. Between 1974 and 1982, the new regulatory system experienced setbacks. In 1976, the Supreme Court had voided spending limitations and regulations on independent contributions. The FEC had become an enfeebled commission that had little support from either party. As reformers failed to extend public financing to congressional elections, interest groups focused on making donations to candidates through PACs. Equally important, as this essay makes clear, were critical choices made by the reform coalition during the incubation period, such as the failure to place PAC regulation at the top of their agenda.

The reforms did not achieve all their objectives. Campaign costs continued to rise, while wealthy citizens and congressional candidates could spend as much as they wanted on campaigns. The growth of PACs indicated to many reformers that private interests continued to dominate politics through contributions. Candidates were as desperately in need of private money as ever before, and PACs are a bountiful source. By forcing politicians to seek smaller contributions from a broader base of supporters, moreover, fund-raising became even more important than in previous decades. Even contribution limits were undermined by the unregulated donations to parties. Institutional reform was not the magic bullet that reformers had promised. While the many reasons behind distrust in national politics are beyond the scope of this essay, the new campaign system could only offer limited results. Changing the election process could not stop many Americans from hating politics.[134]

Nonetheless, the accomplishments of the reform coalition should not be discounted. There was a revolution in the disclosure of political information. Until the 1960s, there was little public knowledge about contributions. By 1974, that system had ended. The United States imposed some of the most stringent disclosure regulations in the world.[135] After 1974, moreover, politicians were forced to seek smaller contributions from a broad base of donors. No single entity wielded the singular influence once held by the Rockefeller or Dupont families.

Until 1988, the role of private donations diminished in presidential elections. In the end, the reforms created a more transparent and porous process where single contributors could no longer dominate the system without public knowledge.

ELEVEN

Bridging State and Society: The Origins of 1970s Congressional Reform

Congressional scholars have a unique opportunity to reconnect the histories of American state and society, a task central to the new generation of political historians.* As Mark Leff (1995, 852) recently argued, social and political historians have come to realize that they "ignored the other at their peril" and that "interaction was the only way to interrogate power—how it was structured and changed, where it was contested, how it was exerted, what its impact was, and what assumptions shaped the discourse that framed it" (see also Gillon, 1997). To accomplish the challenge of integrating social and political history, congressional historians will have to examine how the institution's development related to external forces. Much of what has been written about Congress thus far remains insular.

A handful of books published in the past two decades suggest how integration can be accomplished. In *Sectionalism and American Political Development 1880–1980*, Richard Bensel (1984) situates the internal development of Congress within the larger context of sectional tensions between the "industrial northern core" and the "underdeveloped southern and western periphery." He pays close attention to key policy decisions and the ongoing struggle between decentralized committee and centralized partisan power to show the influence of sectionalism. Similarly, Bruce Schulman (1991) situates southern congressmen and their politics within the broader relationship that developed between the South and the federal government following the New Deal. Jonathan Bean's (1996) *Beyond the Broker State*, on government-business relations, traces the key role played by a group of congressional entrepreneurs in the evolution of small business policy between the New Deal and the 1960s. Far from being passive observers of the executive branch, Bean argues, Emanuel Celler (D-NY), Robert Taft (R-OH), Wright Patman (D-TX), and James Murray (D-

* This essay originally appeared in *Social Science History*, Volume 24 (2000): 379–93.

MT) were crucial to the creation of programs aimed to protect small business in the era of the national corporation. But Bean simultaneously contextualizes these congressmen within a larger history of other political institutions and the relations between business and government. In a different policy domain, Edward Berkowitz (1995, 1996) thoroughly integrates the role of congressional representatives, such as Wilbur Mills and Russell Long, into his analysis of a broader network inside Washington that drove the expansion of the social welfare system, especially Social Security, between 1950 and 1972. Dealing with similar policies, my book (Zelizer, 1998) examined Ways and Means Chairman Wilbur D. Mills's (D-AR) close relationship with a policy community. Finally, an excellent example of this new approach to congressional history was written by Paul Milazzo (2006). His research demonstrates convincingly how congressional entrepreneurs actively shaped the environmental policy agenda during the postwar period. Although these works are useful models, much historical work remains to be done.

Nowhere has the insulation of congressional history, as written by political scientists, been clearer than in the voluminous literature on congressional reform (Adler, 1996; Sinclair, 1989, 1997; Rhode, 1991; Strahan, 1990; Riselbach, 1986). At numerous points in the twentieth century, there were movements to topple the entrenched congressional leadership and to alter the legislative process. One of the most sweeping efforts took place during the 1970s, when reformers diminished the power of committee chairmen, increased the influence of partisan leaders, created a stronger regulatory structure for campaign finance, codified ethics, and opened much of the congressional process to public scrutiny. In major policy areas such as the budget and military, moreover, Congress as a whole increased its strength in relation to the executive branch. While scholars have noted that many reforms were not as bold as originally intended or that they produced unanticipated results, most agree that there was a significant change in Congress and the legislative process as a result of these political battles.

In explaining the origins of 1970s reform, most of these outstanding accounts present congressional reform as the product of increasingly powerful liberal Democrats within Congress who were dissatisfied with the committee system. While these accounts often mention larger forces, such as the Vietnam War and the civil rights movement, they usually do so in passing and without rigorous analysis. Steven Smith and Christopher Deering (1990, 45–46) in their path-breaking book on congressional committees, captured the spirit of much of this scholarship: "These demands were especially strong among junior members and some long-standing liberal Democrats, who found their efforts to shape public policy stymied by their more conservative senior colleagues. These members, and the outsiders whose causes they supported, were concerned about issues that were not receiving active committee consideration and did not fall easily into existing committee jurisdictions." In numerous respects, this struggle over institutional reform in the 1970s offers historians an excellent opportunity to reconceptualize the way in which we study Congress.

In this essay, I focus on a few findings from my research on the origins of congressional reform in the 1970s (Zelizer, 1999). While scholars have acknowledged that a reform coalition within Congress emerged before the 1970s, they have provided a limited analysis of why reform took place with such vigor, why it took the form it did, and how it evolved. To understand the origins of congressional reform, it is necessary to look at some of the several forces outside Congress in the 1960s that established a strong foundation for congressional reform in the 1970s: the Supreme Court and voters, the news media, and the political discourse about institutional reform.

The Supreme Court and Voters

The first force involved the courts and voters. Inter-institutional challenges from the Supreme Court transformed the electoral landscape. Weakening the electoral base of southern Democrats made the reforms of the 1970s possible. While scholars have not yet systematically linked the redistricting decisions to the institutional reforms that took place in Congress during the 1970s, the relationship was extremely important. Under Chief Justice Earl Warren, the Supreme Court took a highly interventionist stance toward legislative institutions. Their decisions resulted in major changes in the electoral system, changes that gradually diminished the stability of the entrenched congressional leadership of primarily southern Democrats. Between 1962 and 1965, the electoral system had had privileged their white, rural voting based come under fire. This system had been in place since Reconstruction and had fostered high rates of incumbency among conservative southern Democrats.

Following the departure of Justice Felix Frankfurter, a strong advocate of judicial restraint, the Warren Court adopted an aggressive approach toward judicial intervention in legislative affairs. In a series of historic decisions—*Baker v. Carr* (1962), *Wesberry v. Sanders* (1964), *Reynolds v. Sims* (1964)—the court deemed that it had a right to intervene in congressional districting to ensure fair representation.[1] They rejected the traditional argument that these were "political" questions that were "not justiciable." Instead, the majority ordered the implementation of the one-man, one-vote principle for congressional districts. *Wesberry v. Sanders* stated that the size of the population in each congressional district must be roughly equal so that the vote of each citizen carried the same weight. Existing apportionment statutes, the majority argued, unfairly reduced the value of urban votes as they increased the value of rural votes. The electoral imbalance between rural and urban voting power had intensified noticeably in the years after World War II as large portions of the population moved to the cities. By the end of the decade, the justices had undercut the electoral foundation of southern Democrats. Ironically, Republicans benefited most by capturing the expanding suburban vote in the South. While redistricting did not mean a victory for liberalism, it helped reformers by weakening the senior congressional establishment who were vested in the institutional status quo.

The court decisions were issued at the same time that civil rights activists focused on voting. In 1964 and 1965, the movement struggled to increase African American voting registration and to obtain legislation to end racial voting barriers in the South. The campaign resulted in bitter clashes between protesters and local police. Soon after the tragic events of Bloody Sunday on March 7, 1965, when demonstrators were brutally attacked by Alabama police and state troopers, Congress enacted the 1965 Voting Rights Act. The legislation outlawed remaining practices that prevented African Americans from voting and empowered the federal government to combat racial discrimination.

The legislation gave muscle to the new electoral system by increasing the power of African American voters (Alt 1994). African Americans had been migrating to the North in search of economic opportunity, thereby expanding the voting base of northern liberal Democrats (Polsby 1990). The congressional elections of 1958 and 1964 brought into Congress large numbers of liberal Democrats from outside the South. The 1964 election, for example, produced a Democratic majority of 295 to 140 Republicans in the House and 68 Democrats to 32 Republicans in the Senate. These results foreshadowed the elections of 1972, 1974, and 1976, all of which showed strong Democratic gains. The Democrats elected in 1958 and 1964 were devoted to a more activist agenda. They helped launch the reform effort during the 1960s in response to fierce resistance to their proposals, particularly from southern Democrats, on healthcare and civil rights. Meanwhile, suburbanization in the postwar southern economy produced a new generation of moderate politicians who focused largely on economic development. When reformers mounted their attack in the 1970s, they found conservative southern Democrats weaker electorally than at any time since the conservative coalition's victories in 1938 (Patterson, 1967).

The News Media and Scandal

The second major development that led to congressional reform involved the media and its coverage of congressional scandals in the 1960s. These incidents involved prominent politicians and legislative staff such as Representative Adam Clayton Powell (D-NY), chairman of the House Labor and Education Committee, and Senator Thomas Dodd (D-CT), senior member of the Senate. Through the scandals, the media revealed the unrestrained power of senior congressmen and created an image of leaders operating without accountability to any rules or majority. Within the House and Senate, the scandals resulted in the creation of ethics committees.

The stories focused the mainstream news media on the issue of scandal in congressional politics. Until very recently, historians have not paid close attention to the media as a serious political institution, capable of stimulating and driving—not just reflecting—political change (Sparrow, 1999; Cook, 1998). Despite the work of communications scholars, recent research by political historians has still tended to focus on how politicians have manipulated the media to enhance their own political position (Allen, 1993; Bernhard, 1999). Scholars have paid less attention to how the media shaped politics.

The history of congressional reform indicates clearly how the media influenced politics. The congressional scandals of the 1960s regularly commanded front-page headlines in major newspapers and magazines such as the *New York Times*, the *Wall Street Journal*, the *Washington Post*, *Time*, and *U.S. News and World Report*. Although Nixon's election team had not yet broken into the Watergate and Wilbur Mills had not yet been caught with an Argentinean stripper in the Tidal Basin, editors in the 1960s were already devoting more front-page and editorial space to the abuse of power by senior congressional leaders. In many respects, the scandals provided the press with a personalized way to examine larger structural issues. It was more accessible for reporters to talk about the problems of "seniority" by focusing on a particular congressman who seemed both incompetent and powerful simply as a result of his years in office. As political scientist Bartholomew Sparrow (1999, 125) argues, "reporters and their editors use *persons* as the vehicles through which to tell stories about national politics. Even the complex and the abstract are explained in terms of, or reduced to, something more finite and more comprehensible: an individual person." Scandal offered reporters and editors dramatic stories full of intrigue. Through these sordid tales, the media provided unprecedented daily coverage of how Congress *really* operated behind the scenes.

Coverage of congressional scandal in the 1960s grew out of changes in the news media. The ethos of "Watchdog Journalism" influenced a new generation of middle-class journalists who were trained in professional schools and who distanced themselves from the older press with its ties to parochial local interests. Watershed events such as the Vietnam War undercut the deferential relationship that previously existed among many journalists toward politicians (Sabato, 1991). At the same time, the print media saw a practical value in sensational stories as they faced greater competition from television.

Before the nation had ever heard of Woodward and Bernstein, reporters were already investigating political scandal on a regular basis and were prepared to take on powerful politicians implicated in the stories. Most of the major newspapers and magazines brought to Americans the story of Powell, who the House eventually excluded for his misuse of congressional funds, inappropriate relations with staff, and failure to attend to the duties of his office. The New York congressman's boisterous personality made perfect fodder for the press. Reporters and editorials constantly pointed to Powell as an example of how the seniority system elevated to leadership positions representatives who were not competent and who abused their power. Even when critics accused the media of unfairly focusing on Powell, while ignoring white committee chairmen who were guilty of worse abuses, this criticism produced detailed coverage on how the institution operated.

During the 1960s, the media did not just report on scandals passively but played an active role in uncovering the stories. Take the case of Senator Thomas Dodd (D-CT), whom the Senate censured in 1967. The stories about Senator Dodd emerged through Jack Anderson and Drew Pearson's syndicated column, "The Washington Merry-Go-Round." In more than thirty installments, Anderson and Pearson shared the content of secret documents that Dodd's staff copied for them directly from the senator's files (Pearson and Anderson, 1966a, 1966b, 1966c, 1966d). Sounding more like a James Bond movie than congressional history, the documents described in lurid detail favors Dodd had performed for a wealthy lobbyist and registered agent for the West German government. The case quickly led to demands in the press for stronger disclosure laws, ethics codes, and campaign finance reform. Several members of Congress privately told reporters that they were concerned about public confidence in government and wanted the ethics investigation to tackle the larger issues; failure to do so, they said, would raise questions about the integrity of congressional self-regulation on ethics. While Dodd offered a dramatic example of the media's role in shaping the politics of scandal, there were other smaller cases. *Life*, for example, published several stories of congressional corruption. One article focused on Representative Cornelius Gallager (D-NJ), who the magazine claimed had intimate ties to the mafia.

Political Discourse on Institutional Reform

Finally, during the 1960s, a discourse about institutional reform helped unite a broad coalition aiming to change Congress. Discourse, one intellectual historian has argued, develops "over time, centering around certain problems, setting the terms of discussion for those who enter into it, and at the same time responding to the different intentions of participants" (Ross, 1991, xviii–xix). The central assumption of the 1960s reform discourse was that if institutions were fixed, liberalism would flourish: the institutional structure and norms of Congress discouraged policy innovation, shielded leadership, and protected the status quo. Believers in this discourse particularly resented the seniority system that automatically provided older southern Democrats control over powerful, insulated committees, leaving northern liberals unable to challenge their decisions. The institution protected these Democrats from public and partisan scrutiny. Others spoke of the filibuster, which allowed southern conservative senators to block popular legislation.

Institutional structures, those who used this discourse warned, also weakened Congress in relation to the executive branch. Until Congress reformed itself, the legislature would never be as strong and vigorous as it had been in the nineteenth century. As a result, the "Imperial Presidency" would continue to dominate policymaking and media coverage. One cartoonist captured this logic when he depicted three elderly men sitting in wheelchairs—marked

Congress—rolling down a hill with their arms in the air toward the White House, yelling "Charge!" (*Washington Post,* 1973).

There were two groups who used this discourse. First, Great Society liberals argued that the legislative process and norms supported an entrenched regime opposed to reform. Most of these liberal representatives and senators entered office between 1958 and 1964. Congressional resistance to civil rights, the collapse of the War on Poverty, and the persistence of the war in Vietnam proved that a powerful minority in the House and Senate maintained control over the agenda. Invigorated by the elections of 1958 and 1964, this discourse shaped numerous legislative changes in the 1960s, including the reform of the House Rules Committee in 1961, hearings on congressional reform in 1965, repeated challenges to the Senate filibuster, and the reinvigoration of the Democratic Caucus. Many of the campaigns for reform were led by the Democratic Study Group (DSG), a group of liberal congressional Democrats who believed firmly in the need for substantive institutional reform. The group's publications focused on attacking problems such as seniority and secrecy. Secrecy in the congressional process, DSG claimed, fostered "arbitrary" and "undemocratic" procedures that nourished illegitimate leadership, undermined public confidence in legislative institutions, and allowed the conservatives to wield massive influence without public knowledge (Democratic Study Group Papers 1970). Along with other reformers, DSG members were clearly motivated as much by self-interest—the desire to obtain the positions of power—as ideology. But they drew on this discourse to articulate their objectives.

Public interest reformers were the second group who relied on the reform discourse. Emerging in the late 1960s, public interest reformers supported expanding government into new areas of importance to the professional middle class, such as the environment and consumer protection. To enact broad-based programs in the face of the opposition from particularistic interest groups and to restore the public's faith in the legitimacy of politics, public interest reformers called for institutional renewal through the democratization and cleansing of the political process.

One prominent organization that promoted public interest reform was Common Cause, a group that formed in 1970 around the issue of congressional reform. During its first five years, the organization focused exclusively on what they called "structure and process issues" (Common Cause Papers, 1975). Common Cause founder John Gardner wrote his members, "Of all the things that can and must be done to improve the workings of the American political system, none is more important than Congressional reform. And the crucial first item is abolition of the seniority system" (Common Cause Papers, 1970). To promote this campaign, Common Cause placed advertisements in major newspapers and produced radio shows that attempted to popularize these complex issues in the broader public. The organization sensed the need to "throw light" on the issues in which voters had little interest. Most Americans, the founders noted, did not realize how these procedural questions affected them in the same fashion as "bread-and-butter" issues (Common Cause Papers, 1972). The organization also appropriated all the tools of the modern interest group, thereby enabling them to apply full pressure on legislators for reform.

Academics also played an important role in the development of this discourse. In particular, political scientists produced a stream of scholarship that focused on congressional reform. Their publications, based on extensive interviews with members and their staffs, focused on how committees dominated internal procedures and diminished the power of Congress. In 1964, the American Political Science Association (APSA) inaugurated the Study of Congress under the direction of Ralph Huitt. They received $230,000 from the Carnegie Foundation, and the project kicked off with a small conference at the Airlie Conference Center in Warrenton, Virginia. The goal was to produce data for any future joint committees of Congress or citizen's commissions (Mike Monroney Papers, 1964a, 1964b).

Political scientists usually favored congressional reorganization (Grazia, 1966). As one book noted: "'The failure of Congress' is a hoary theme that for years has been propounded by academics in textbooks and from lecture platforms. The congressional rogues' gallery—seniority, the House Rules Committee, filibusters, inefficient procedures, and so on—no doubt affirms the general impression among academics that 'something ought to be done about Congress"' (Davidson et al., 1966, 39). Scholars who focused on the House of Representatives generally concluded that committees were "virtually autonomous," "instruments of personal influence and prestige," "symbolic of American's growth and of many of the interests of society," "unrepresentative of the parent chamber," and "convenient graveyards for inept proposals.[2] These scholars were developing relationships with congressmen and their staff. Many who produced this work participated directly in reform efforts of the 1960s and 1970s, either as staff or through testifying at hearings (Davidson and Oleszek, 1979).

The reform discourse gained power when many citizens were increasingly distrustful of political institutions, as evidenced by public opinion polls, popular culture, and protest movements. The discourse helped foster a broad coalition inside and outside Congress that sought substantive institutional reform in the 1970s. Other reformers used this same discourse during controversial campaigns to transform the party system and administrative law (Milkis, 1998; Shafer, 1983).

Conclusion

Together, these three developments in the 1960s—electoral reform, changing media coverage on congressional scandal, and the emergence of a discourse about institutional reform—established a strong foundation for reform in the next decade. All combined to focus new attention on how Congress operated, who ran Congress, and how Congress fit within the larger needs of the nation's political system. By the 1970s, an activist group of Democrats and Republicans—

including Richard Bolling (D-MO), Phillip Burton (D-CA), Thomas Foley (D-WA), John Brademas (D-IN), Henry Waxman (D-CA), Edward Kennedy (D-MA), Hubert Humphrey (D-MN), Barber Conable (R-NY), and William Frenzel (R-MN)—led the movement within Congress. This movement was centered in organizations such as the Democratic Study Group and the Democratic Caucus. Other parts of the reform movement were located outside of Congress. African American voters in newly drawn districts curtailed the electoral base of older southern white Democrats, while campaign workers in northern and Midwestern states rallied voters to support reform candidates. Public interest groups and nonprofit organizations (including Common Cause, the National Committee for an Effective Congress, Congress Watch, and the Citizens' Research Foundation) mobilized resources for reform, while individuals such as Brian Lamb and Ralph Nader directed particular efforts. The movement contained numerous factions, some weakly related and others in conflict. But all were determined to change the institutional basis of legislative policymaking. They sometimes found support from Republicans who also believed (with different policy objectives) that the current institutions supported an entrenched leadership, which was corrupt and incompetent and which promoted an excessively liberal political agenda.

The history of this reform movement, and its consequences, reminds historians that Congress cannot be studied in isolation. Congressional reform shows that historians must connect legislative history with other parts of society such as the media, courts, and voters, as well as with other parts of American culture such as larger discourses that shaped national debates over politics. The roots of 1970s reform show that a variety of forces ultimately combined to create a vigorous movement that aimed to improve, and even transform, Congress.

As political historians reconceive how to study Congress, social and cultural historians must also accept the centrality of legislative institutions to their research. Indeed, the legislative process became a central issue for many of the mass movements that shaped this era as efforts to change the political process moved to the forefront of national debate. In expanding their interests, social and cultural historians will have to shed some of the intellectual hostility toward what Joel Silbey (1999) called "ordinary politics," which has defined the profession since the 1960s. If both parties in our intellectual community acknowledge the insights of the other, the result can be an exciting revitalization of congressional history and its integration into larger narratives about the American past.

References

Adler, Scott E. 1996. Changing the rules of the game: Distributive, informational, and partisan approaches to congressional reform. PhD diss., Columbia University.

Allen, Craig. 1993. *Eisenhower and the Mass Media: Peace, Prosperity, and Prime-Time TV*. Chapel Hill: University of North Carolina Press.

Alt, James E. 1994. The impact of the Voting Rights Act on black and white voter registration in the South. In *Quiet Revolution in the South: The Impact of the Voting Rights Act, 1965–1990*, eds. Chandler Davidson and Bernard Goffman. Princeton, NJ: Princeton University Press, 351–77.

Bean, Jonathan J. 1996. *Beyond the Broker State: Federal Policies toward Small Business, 1936–1961*. Chapel Hill: University of North Carolina Press.

Bensel, Richard. 1984. *Sectionalism and American Political Development, 1880–1980*. Madison: University of Wisconsin Press.

Berkowitz, Edward E. 1995. Social Security and the financing of the American state. In *Funding the Modern American State, 1941–1995: The Rise and Fall of the Era of Easy Finance*, ed. W. Elliot Brownlee. Cambridge: Cambridge University Press; Washington, DC: Woodrow Wilson Center Press, 148–93.

———. 1996. *Mr. Social Security: The Life of Wilbur J. Cohen*. Lawrence: University Press of Kansas.

Bernhard, Nancy E. 1999. *U.S. Television News and Cold War Propaganda, 1947–1960*. Cambridge: Cambridge University Press.

Common Cause Papers, Princeton University. 1970. Gardner, John, to Members. Box 10. File: Early CC Misc. Memos September–December 1970.

———. 1972. Congressional Reform. Box 30. File: September 1970–January 1972.

———. 1975. Governing board minutes January 23–24, 1975. Box 32. File: 24 January–April 1975.

Cook, Timothy E. 1998. *Governing with the News: The News Media as a Political Institution*. Chicago: University of Chicago Press.

Davidson, Roger H., and Walter Oleszek. 1979. *Congress against Itself*. Bloomington: Indiana University Press.

Davidson, Roger H., David M. Kovenock, and Michael K. O'Leary. 1966. *Congress in Crisis: Politics and Congressional Reform*. Belmont, CA: Wadsworth.

Democratic Study Group Papers, Library of Congress. 1970. Secrecy in the House of Representatives. Box 34. Unfiled.

Gillon, Steven M. 1997. The future of political history. *Journal of Policy History* 9: 240–55.

Grazia, Alfred de, ed. 1966. *Congress: The First Branch of Government*. Garden City, NY: Anchor.

Leff, Mark H. 1995. Revisioning U.S. political history. *American Historical Review* 100: 848–53.

Mike Monroney Papers, Carl Albert Center, University of Oklahoma. 1964a. Progress Report to the Advisory Committee. Box 1. Folder 2.

———. 1946b. Huitt, Ralph to Monroney, Mike. Box 1. Folder 2.

Milazzo, Paul C. 2006. *Unlikely Environmentalists: Congress and Clean Water, 1945–1972*. Lawrence: University Press of Kansas.

Milkis, Sidney M. 1998. Remaking government institutions in the 1970s: Participatory democracy and the triumph of administrative politics. *Journal of Policy History* 10: 51–74.

Patterson, James T. 1967. *Congressional Conservatism and the New Deal: The Growth of the Conservative Coalition in Congress, 1933–1939*. Lexington: University of Kentucky Press.

Pearson, Drew, and Jack Anderson. 1966a. Dodd aid to foreign agent cited. *Washington Post*, 29 January.

———. 1966b. Klein wrote letters for Dodd. *Washington Post*, 18 February.

———. 1966c. Spanel pushed by Dodd as envoy. *Washington Post*, 1 March.

———. 1966d. Dodd started campaign in '61. *Washington Post*, 25 March.

Polsby, Nelson W. 1990. Political change and the character of the contemporary Congress. In *The American Political System*, ed. Anthony King. Washington, DC: American Enterprise Institute, 29–46.

Rhode, David W. 1991. *Parties and Leaders in the Postreform House*. Chicago: University of Chicago Press.

Riselbach, Leroy. 1986. *Congressional Reform*. Washington, DC: Congressional Quarterly Press.

Ross, Dorothy. 1991. *The Origins of American Social Science*. Cambridge: Cambridge University Press.

Sabato, Larry J. 1991. *Feeding Frenzy: How Attack Journalism Has Transformed American Politics*. New York: Free Press.

Schulman, Bruce J. 1991. *From Cotton Belt to Sunbelt: Federal Policy, Economic Development, and the Transformation of the South, 1938–1980*. New York: Oxford University Press.

Shafer, Byron. 1983. *The Quiet Revolution: The Struggle for the Democratic Party and the Shaping of Post-Reform Politics*. New York: Russell Sage.

Silbey, Joel. 1999. The state and practice of American political history at the millennium: The nineteenth century as a test case. *Journal of Policy History* 11: 10–30.

Sinclair, Barbara. 1989. *The Transformation of the U.S. Senate*. Baltimore, MD: Johns Hopkins University Press.

———. 1997. *Unorthodox Lawmaking: New Legislative Processes in the U.S. Congress*. Washington, DC: Congressional Quarterly Press.

Smith, Steven S., and Christopher J. Deering. 1990. *Committees in Congress*, 2nd ed. Washington, DC: Congressional Quarterly Press.

Sparrow, Bartholomew H. 1999. *Uncertain Guardians: The News Media as a Political Institution*. Baltimore, MD: Johns Hopkins University Press.

Strahan, Randall. 1990. *New Ways and Means: Reform and Change in Congressional Committee*. Chapel Hill: University of North Carolina Press.

Washington Post. 1973. Charge! (cartoon) 4 February.

Zelizer, Julian E. 1998. *Taxing America: Wilbur D. Mills, Congress, and the State, 1945–1975*. Cambridge: Cambridge University Press.

———. 1999. The constructive generation: Thinking about Congress in the 1960s. *Mid-America: A Historical Review* 81: 265–98.

TWELVE

Without Restraint: Scandal and Politics in America

"What began 25 years ago with Watergate as a solemn and necessary process to force a president to adhere to the rule of law, has grown beyond our control so that now we are routinely using criminal accusations and scandal to win the political battles and ideological differences we cannot settle at the ballot box. It has been used with reckless abandon by both parties."* So lamented Representative Charles Schumer (D-NY) during the debate over impeaching President William Clinton in 1998. By then, scandal had become a driving force in politics. Many of Schumer's colleagues resembled weary soldiers surveying a bloody battlefield, shocked by what their conflict had wrought. While scandals had been part of American politics since the Revolution, never had they been so pervasive as in the last three decades of the twentieth century. No longer occasional or ancillary events, they had become integral to partisan strategy, political reform, and the public perception of government. While many citizens once viewed Watergate as the climax of scandal politics, it is now clear that President Richard Nixon's downfall in 1974 was only the opening chapter of a much larger story.

During the second half of the twentieth century, scandals became crucial to America's political style. The nation witnessed an unprecedented number of major ones: in Republican and Democratic administrations, in the legislative and executive branches, and in weak and strong economies. The impact was breathtaking. Two presidents were consumed by scandal, with one forced to resign and another impeached. Two more sitting presidents have been subject to intense investigation. Several influential congressmen have been forced out of office because of scandal, including three speakers of the House, two chairmen of the House Ways and Means Committee, and many powerful senators. A nominee for the Supreme Court was rejected because of drug use, while sev-

*This essay originally appeared in *The Columbia History of Post-World War II America*, ed. Mark C. Carnes (New York: Columbia University Press, 2007), 226–54. Copyright © 2007 Columbia University Press. Reprinted with permission of the publisher.

eral cabinet members and a vice president have resigned because of conflict-of-interest violations. In 1970, the federal government indicted forty-five state, federal, and local politicians and government employees on allegations of corruption. By 1995, that number had reached 824.[1] The types of issues capable of damaging an established politician, moreover, expanded dramatically. A plethora of congressional committees, independent commissions, prosecutors, and ethics codes had been created to fight corruption. Unlike earlier periods, when scandal politics was linked to a particular issue such as communist espionage, scandal had become a usual weapon with which politicians fought their battles.

Of course, scandal politics was not unique to post–World War II America. Democracies have always faced the potential to be consumed by scandal. In state-centered countries, such as China or the Soviet Union, the threat has been insignificant. There was scant opportunity for the revelation of corruptions, since in them a unified political elite controlled mass communication, political participation, and the legal system. In democracies, the press tended to be granted significant autonomy, and fewer controls existed on political opposition. Democratic governments usually created internal mechanisms that could be used to expose and punish corruption. Until the 1970s, politicians in the United States relied on "auxiliary precautions" created by the founding fathers that were meant to protect American democracy from excessive power and corrupt politicians, which included the separation of power, freedom of the press, and impeachment.

American history has been replete with scandal. During the Gilded Age, which lasted from roughly 1877 to 1900, for example, upper-class reformers called Mugwumps, Republican supporters of Democratic presidential candidate Grover Cleveland, revealed how big business influenced the decisions of machine politicians. In those years, the Crédit Mobilier scandal exposed government officials who had accepted stock in exchange for political favors. At the turn of the twentieth century, Progressive-Era reforms were motivated by, and helped to instigate, national revelations of extensive corruption in city and state governments. During Warren Harding's administration in the early 1920s, investigators brought to light evidence of politicians who leased property to oil executives and received payment in return—the Teapot Dome scandal.

Like economic corruption, sex scandals also have a long tradition in the United States. Simultaneously reflecting and contradicting the nation's Puritan cultural heritage, politicians have often been willing to wield the weapon of sexual impropriety. In the presidential campaigns of 1824 and 1828, for instance, opponents accused Andrew Jackson of adultery, while in 1884, Republicans lambasted Grover Cleveland for his illegitimate child.

The relationship between politics and scandal thus has deep roots in American history dating back to the Revolution. What changed during the post-1960s period was a gradual erosion of institutional and cultural forces that had temporarily prevented scandal from becoming the dominant partner in that relationship since the end of the Progressive Era. In contrast to the nineteenth century, moreover, politicians engaged in scandal warfare during a period when Americans retained minimal connection to their civic institutions, thereby creating a situation where there was little to counteract the disenchantment that scandal generated toward government. The centrality of scandal politics cannot be attributed to any single source. Instead, it must be understood as an outgrowth of the 1970s political turmoil that mounted fundamental challenges to American politics, culture, and economics. The transformation of America's political style began with an alliance between liberal northern Democrats and middle-class good-government reform in the 1960s and 1970s. While young liberal Democrats and Republicans were primarily interested in ending the power of southern conservatives—as opposed to good-government reformers whose interest began with preventing corruption—nobody in the coalition believed that politicians would expose or penalize corrupt behavior, nor did they think that the electorate was capable of handling that responsibility. Unlike their predecessors in the Progressive Era, the reform coalition created a permanent base for themselves in journalism, public interest organizations, and Congress. The conflicts over Vietnam, civil rights, and Watergate generated widespread public support for their outlook. The institutional infrastructure created by reformers became destabilizing in a new mass media and cultural environment. When politicians turned to scandal after 1980, they encountered few obstacles to prevent them from using it as a partisan weapon. The result was explosive.

The Early Postwar Era, 1945–1964

Right from the end of World War II, scandal played a prominent role in national politics. Numerous charges were brought against President Harry Truman's administration. Televised congressional hearings disclosed intimate connections between local gangsters and the Kansas City Democratic political machine from which Truman had received his initial political support. Several federal agencies were implicated as well. Investigators in 1951, for instance, discovered that hundreds of low-level tax collectors for the Internal Revenue Service (IRS) had accepted bribes from taxpayers.

While these charges of corruption had aided Dwight Eisenhower's presidential bid against Adlai Stevenson in 1952, he was not immune from scandal. During his campaign, the *New York Post* attacked his vice presidential candidate, Richard Nixon, for maintaining a secret slush fund financed by California millionaires. In a televised speech in which he famously insisted that his wife "doesn't have a mink coat, but she does have a respectable Republican cloth coat," while admitting that he had accepted a little cocker spaniel that his six-year-old daughter Tricia had named Checkers, Nixon defended himself as a decent man under attack from overzealous opponents. By speaking directly to the voters, and overcoming the demands that he resign from the ticket, Nixon's so-called Checkers speech indicated the important role of television in scandal warfare. Six years later, Eisenhower forced senior advisor Sherman Adams to resign when it became public that he had helped a businessman receive special treatment from the Federal Trade Commission and the Securities and Exchange Commission. Of course, the most dramatic scandals revolved around anticommunism. Between 1948 and 1954, several prominent members of the national security establishment were brought down by charges of espionage, even if those charges turned out to be false and often of malicious intent. Senator Joseph McCarthy (R-WI) led the charge, showing how scandal could enable a politician to move up the ranks rapidly—but also how it could lead to downfall.

Still, during the 1950s and 1960s, scandal politics was limited in scale and scope. In terms of quantity, the number of prominent officials involved in, and seriously harmed by, these incidents remained small. The IRS scandal, for example, did not touch the higher echelons of the agency. The most intense period of the anticommunist crusade that lasted throughout the 1950s was perhaps more noteworthy for its sloppiness than its excesses. Recent information from Soviet archives has proven that espionage in the United States was more extensive than most suspected. Furthermore, the most intense periods of scandal were usually defined by specific issues such as espionage, rather than a usual means of transacting politics. Except in a few cases, scandal failed to dominate news coverage.

Countervailing forces curtailed the importance of scandal within the political system. One force was the power of the senior politicians. Within Congress, for example, senior senators and representatives maintained control over legislative proceedings. Norms of reciprocity, deference to seniority, and institutional patriotism tended to discourage personal attacks on colleagues. Although a few mavericks such as McCarthy were able to elude control, they were outliers. Within the House, those who attempted to outflank senior Democrats were punished by being given inferior committee assignments. "If you want to get along," Speaker Sam Rayburn (D-TX) always advised new members, "go along." Such norms promoted professional civility between congressmen even across party lines.

A different type of senior establishment existed in other areas of politics. In presidential elections, urban and southern party leaders retained strong influence over the campaign process. Notwithstanding the introduction of primaries earlier in the century, party operatives selected most delegates to the Democratic and Republican conventions. The media had limited influence in the selection of candidates, and this further inhibited communication with voters.

Scandal was also muted because much of the policymaking process remained hidden from public view. Most legislative deliberations, for instance, were closed to the public. Despite a democratic electoral system, laws requiring disclosure of election contributions were ineffective, and no independent commission tracked campaign data. The national security establishment, which was constructed between 1947 and 1950 as part of the Cold War, entrenched an institutional network that conducted foreign policy in a highly secretive and tightly controlled environment.

Nor did American culture foster a great demand for scandal politics. Amid unprecedented economic prosperity, Americans trusted their political institutions. By the early 1960s, one poll indicated, 75 percent of Americans trusted government to make the right decision. World War II, in which the government defeated fascism, seemed to prove that politicians could be effective. Cold War nationalism intensified loyalty to political leaders by creating a mood favoring politicians rather than discrediting them.

This trust extended to other parts of American society. In 1959, Americans were shocked by news that television executives tampered with a popular quiz show, *Twenty One*, to secure high ratings. They provided answers to contestants, including the handsome young academic Charles Van Doren, whose appearances drew huge ratings. The revelation triggered congressional hearings, while the networks expanded news programming to regain legitimacy. Besides trust, privacy was a cherished cultural value. Americans became more conscious of this right as modern technology and a more intrusive federal government posed a greater threat. Within this early postwar culture, there were strong boundaries to what the public would tolerate. Even with some liberalization in film and television (the men's magazine *Playboy*, for example, first appeared in 1953), open discussion of sexual matters outside a medical context was rare.

The mainstream news media also exhibited restraint. To be sure, some journalists, such as Drew Pearson and I. F. Stone, continued the muckraking tradition by exposing the wrongdoing of public officials. But they were not the norm. Until the mid-1960s, the press was generally respectful of the political establishment. The norm of objectivity, or at least the appearance of objectivity, remained a desired goal. This in itself limited how far reporters would go in attacking politicians. Reporters tried to remove themselves and their opinions from stories by presenting facts without much analysis, along with considerable paraphrasing of the politicians' positions. On television, the image of the reporter did not appear as much as the elected officials they were covering: the average "sound bite" of politicians on television was forty-two seconds in 1968, where it would shrink to ten seconds by 1988.[2] (By several estimates, it was six seconds as of 2006.) Joseph McCarthy, for one, knew that reporters would publish what he said without critical commentary. In his case, the passivity of the press, not its investigatory efforts, facilitated scandal warfare.

Many prominent members of the media, moreover, had close ties to government. Like the public, most editors refused to publish on most aspects of a politician's private life. Despite the widespread knowledge of President John F. Kennedy's sexual escapades and Senator Russell Long's alcoholism, reporters refused to write about these stories. As political reporter Jack Germond wrote, "a politician who was a notorious drunk would be described as somebody with a reputation for excessive conviviality. A politician who chased women was known as someone who appreciated a well-turned ankle. And this was the way we went at this. Everyone knew except the reader."[3] Within the media there were boundaries between "news" and "entertainment" shows. The producers of news shows strove to maintain a degree of decorum that would distinguish them from "cruder" entertainment.

The final force inhibiting scandal politics during the early postwar decades was the salience of other issues: the continued growth of the federal government, the Cold War, the civil rights movement, and the war in Vietnam. During the 1950s and 1960s, civil rights dominated public debates. Other controversial policies, ranging from healthcare to crime, provided ample material for politicians to battle without resorting to scandal. When scandal emerged in these years, it had to compete for attention with the robust issue agenda of the period.

Institutionalizing the Public Interest, 1958–1973

Democracy and scandal have gone hand in hand, but before 1965, there were countervailing forces working to constrain scandal. Between 1958 and 1973, those countervailing forces started to disintegrate. The change started with liberal Democrats who railed against a political process that, they felt, benefited southern conservatives in the 1950s. Middle-class activists who focused on government corruption joined them in the 1960s. The baby boom generation, as well as older Democrats who were frustrated with their colleagues, lost faith in politicians because of Vietnam, compromises on civil rights, and violent official responses to student protest. As large segments of the population became suspicious of, if not downright hostile toward, government institutions amidst the political turmoil of the mid-1960s, the time was ripe for those who wanted to reform the political process permanently.

A small group of liberal Democrats attacked the political process that empowered conservative southern Democrats. The 1958 and 1964 elections produced an influx of these liberals in the House and Senate. They argued that legislative conventions such as seniority and the filibuster favored southerners who were stifling the party's agenda by resisting civil rights and prolonging segregation. Younger Democrats such as Senator Joseph Clark of Pennsylvania flagrantly ignored institutional norms in their fight for a new system.

Mainstream journalists became more adversarial in their coverage of politicians in the 1960s. Driven by the same concerns that absorbed students in the universities, many middle-class, well-educated reporters came to regard journalism as political activism. Professionally, scandal provided the media with identifiable characters and dramatic stories full of intrigue. It was a way for them to write in compelling fashion about the problems facing the nation's political institutions. In an age when competition from television news was becoming more pronounced, the print media required stories that would attract readers. Likewise, television newscasters sought dramatic visual images to build their audience. This new journalism was connected to a broader political movement. Its heroes were the reporters who exposed government lies about the war in Vietnam. Colleagues, for example, praised Harrison Salisbury of the *New York Times* for his shocking stories that revealed false claims that President Johnson was issuing about the nature and progress of the Vietnam War. Objectivity was no longer a virtue. Younger journalists regarded themselves as guardians, as key players in politics.

Toward the end of the 1960s, reporters applied this investigative method to the private behavior of politicians. While reporters had refused to write about the sexual escapades of John F. Kennedy in 1961, his brother Senator Edward Kennedy (D-MA) faced a new breed of journalists at the end of the decade. In the early morning of July 18, 1969, after attending a party on Chappaquiddick Island, Massachusetts, Senator Kennedy drove his car off a bridge. His companion, a young staffer named Mary Joe Kopechne, drowned. Kennedy escaped but did not tell the police about the incident until the next morning. Although Kennedy claimed that he immediately went to find help, the print media, which covered the story on front pages, discovered that this was untrue. Reporters openly speculated that Kennedy was afraid the scandal would destroy his career. Kennedy, who was married, insisted that he was not sexually involved with Kopechne. Pulling a page from the Nixon "Checkers" speech, Kennedy went on television to defend himself, claiming that his disorientation after the crash explained his delay in reporting the accident. Although Massachusetts voters repeatedly returned Kennedy to the Senate, the scandal cost him any future presidential aspirations. In May 2006, Kennedy's son Patrick, a congressman, would explain an automobile crash at the Capitol by claiming disorientation as well, but the resulting scandal was short-lived.

Middle-class reformers who operated through interest-group politics became closely allied with the new journalists. The reformers focused on the idea that institutional renewal was needed to protect the democratic process and preserve faith in government. Before sound policymaking could prevail, corruption had to be eliminated. Common Cause became the main proponent of political reform. The organization was founded in 1970 by John Gardner, former secretary of the Department of Health, Education, and Welfare under Lyndon Johnson. Common Cause emphasized the mass media, both print and television, and aspired to create a broad membership base.

Although most Common Cause members did little more than contribute a few dollars, the leadership emerged as a formidable presence in politics by 1971. Its leaders were frequent guests on television talk shows, while its studies, advertisements, and press releases regularly made it into the pages of the nation's leading newspapers. Common Cause spawned imitators, and by 1974 there were eighteen public interest organizations conducting similar activities. After the elections of 1974 and 1976, such groups obtained strong legislative support from the influx of liberal congressional Democrats representing middle-class, suburban areas who shared their concerns. Focusing primarily on what he called "structure and process issues," Gardner encouraged public interest organizations to repair institutions to prevent corrupt individuals from gaining power.

The reformers scored several important early victories. In 1971, Democrats instituted a series of party reforms that weakened the power of the political machines in selecting presidential nominees. New party rules opened up the delegate selection process to suburbanites, women, and members of various ethnic and racial minorities whom old party leaders had ignored. This enhanced the power of political activists, who tended to represent the extremes of the spectrum. At the same time, primaries became the principal means for selecting nominees as the party convention became irrelevant and ceremonial. The new rules marked a decisive blow to the traditional party machines, while elevating the role of the television news media to new levels. The results were evident in 1976 when Jimmy Carter became the Democratic nominee, despite having a weak relationship with the party's national leadership. Public interest organizations were also instrumental in the passage of the campaign finance amendments of 1972 and 1974, which created stringent disclosure requirements and limited campaign contributions.

Working in concert with liberal Democrats, public interest organizations helped put corruption on the national agenda. Their concerns made sense to the baby boomers, who had participated in an anti-war movement that questioned the legitimacy of government elites. Middle-class reformers distrusted politicians and championed laws that would make leaders more accountable to the public. They articulated the concerns that were driving an entire generation of younger Americans who had lost faith in their leaders as a result of Vietnam and the failure of ending racism across the nation. Although it drew on the ideas that motivated progressive reformers, this generation was able to establish a stronger organizational presence in national politics through the media, interest groups, and legislation.

Reform Politics: 1972–1978

The politics of reform dominated the years between 1972 and 1978, when a series of scandals shook Washington, culminating in extensive reform of the political process and the downfall of powerful politicians. In this period, scandal was the product of liberal Democrats and public interest reformers who were struggling to open up the democratic process by unseating an entrenched, and, in their minds, corrupt political establishment. The biggest scandal of the era started with a burglary at the Democratic National Committee headquarters, housed in Washington's Watergate Complex, in June 1972. Five men were arrested and charged. Two local reporters for the *Washington Post*, Bob Woodward and Carl Bernstein, discovered that the burglars had links to President Nixon's Committee to Re-Elect the President (CREEP), as well as to the anti-Castro Cuban exile community and to the Central Intelligence Agency (CIA).

Federal District Judge John Sirica, who handled the trial of the burglars, concluded that the crime somehow related to the presidential campaign. Woodward and Bernstein revealed that high-level officials in the Nixon White House had orchestrated the break-in. One of the burglars, James McCord, chief of security for CREEP, implicated higher-level officials. Under intense pressure, Attorney General Elliot Richardson appointed Archibald Cox to be special prosecutor and investigate the crime. *CBS News* anchor Walter Cronkite hosted a special that wove together all the threads into a broader picture.

The different investigations uncovered broad patterns of executive abuse of power. Whether the president was personally responsible remained in doubt. Then, in July 1973, Alexander Butterfield revealed that Nixon had tape-recorded all Oval Office conversations. The various investigators, along with the media, clamored for release of the tapes. Nixon refused, claiming that a president had the right to withhold documents from the public under certain circumstances. When special prosecutor Cox persisted in demanding the tapes, Nixon fired him in October 1973 in what critics called the "Saturday Night Massacre." This provoked a fierce backlash from critics and from the media. In July 1974, the Supreme Court ruled that executive privilege did not apply in a criminal matter and that Nixon would have to release the tapes.

Those recordings, which included some suspicious erasures—one of them, famously, eighteen and a half minutes long—revealed that the president had attempted to obstruct the investigation of the burglary. Other charges soon emerged: that Nixon had made policy decisions in exchange for campaign contributions; that he had used federal agencies to intimidate political opponents; and that his operatives had broken into the office of Daniel Ellsberg's psychologist. Ellsberg, a former national security staffer working for the Rand Corporation, had leaked the "Pentagon Papers," secret documents detailing the government's conduct of the Vietnam War, to the *New York Times*. Nixon's travails captivated the public. When the Senate conducted televised hearings in 1973, high numbers of viewers tuned in to watch Congress investigate the scandal. Polls revealed public approval of what they saw. Senator Sam Ervin (D-NC), a white-haired, folksy eminence once known for his opposition to civil rights, became an overnight celebrity. The investigations confirmed that televised hearings offered one of the few opportunities for legislators to gain media coverage that would propel them to national attention. After the House Judiciary Committee voted to impeach Nixon, the president resigned in August 1974 before the whole membership could vote.

Watergate was a turning point in the politics of scandal. Nixon embodied the corruption that reformers had attacked since the late 1960s, and Watergate was symptomatic of the abuses of those in power. The story marked a major success for the new forces seeking to make politicians accountable to a higher ethical standard. Nixon's activities also provided ample evidence for stronger laws to enforce ethical behavior among public officials. The "auxiliary precautions" that the nation's founders had created in the Constitution were insufficient. Two months after Nixon resigned, Congress enacted campaign finance legislation that created an independent commission to enforce disclosure regulations and imposed new limits on campaign contributions. Congress also passed spending limits, but the Supreme Court overturned them in 1976. The 1978 Ethics in Government Law created the Special Prosecutor's Office to investigate allegations of wrongdoing by high-ranking officials in the executive branch. The law made it extremely difficult for the attorney general to remove the prosecutor. Ethics legislation also strengthened restrictions on lobbying activities and financial disclosure requirements, including the creation of an Office of Government Ethics, to oversee executive branch conflict-of-interest rules. Congress also imposed stringent conflict-of-interest laws on the personal financial transactions of its own members. The power of the new laws became immediately apparent during the administration of President Jimmy Carter, who had campaigned on a platform of integrity. When top members of his staff were accused of activities that ranged from cocaine use to financial improprieties, a special prosecutor was appointed to investigate the charges.

During the 1970s, the executive branch as a whole lost much of its insulation. Congress expanded its oversight power to review the work of federal agencies and bureaus. In 1975, Congress authorized money to support citizen groups such as Common Cause to participate in administrative politics. As more external forces were able to monitor their activities, federal agencies became more porous. The national security establishment also came under fire after Vietnam. Senator Frank Church (D-ID) chaired committee hearings in the mid-1970s that revealed the types of activities that the CIA had supported, including attempts to assassinate foreign politicians and covert spying on individuals living in the United States. In response to the hearings, Congress imposed numerous regulations and openness requirements on the CIA and other military bodies.

Thanks to the era's reforms, the nation would no longer have to wait until an election to punish government officials, nor would it have to depend on politicians to decide when an investigation was needed. Liberal Democrats and middle-class reformers had institutionalized a concern with corruption so that after the memory of Watergate had faded, the investigatory infrastructure would remain.[4] Those who focused on corruption, including journalists, public interest organizations, and congressional committees, were given powerful weapons with which to pursue their objectives.

Just as Watergate confirmed distrust of politicians, it elevated journalists who had fought against corruption. Although Woodward and Bernstein were not the first to practice this new style of journalism, they embodied the new adversarial style. Their role in uncovering the scandal legitimated the new outlook. Their popularity soared after they became the subject of a film starring Robert Redford and Dustin Hoffman. They were even credited with causing a marked increase in applications to journalism schools across the country.

The Watergate crisis hit as the nation underwent a serious economic decline. High rates of inflation, high unemployment, and an oil crisis crippled the national economy. Whereas unprecedented rates of economic growth in the postwar years had buttressed public trust in government, rapid economic decline in the 1970s fueled general disillusionment. The government appeared incapable of sustaining a strong economy forever, and the era of endless growth came to a dramatic halt. The stagnant economy intensified the impact of Watergate as Americans searched for villains in government to explain the decline.

Although Watergate received more attention than any other political scandal of the time, Congress had its own problems in the 1970s. Partly this was the work of liberal Democrats and public interest reformers who sought to weaken the committee chairmen who ruled Congress, most of whom were southern Democrats, and to eliminate the secrecy that surrounded the legislative process. Until 1974, the established leadership was able to protect committee leaders from being deposed.

Then, in the early hours of October 7, 1974, the Washington Park Police stopped House Ways and Means Committee Chairman Wilbur Mills's (D-AR) speeding car near the Tidal Basin. One of his fellow passengers, Annabel Battistella, a stripper who performed locally as "Fanne Fox, the Argentine Firecracker," jumped out of the car and into the Tidal Basin. A cameraman captured the arrest on film. The media, now attuned to scandal, reported that Battistella was having an affair with Mills and that Mills had been an alcoholic and was also addicted to prescription drugs. Although Mills won reelection in November 1974, he could not control his drinking. In December, before shocked members of the media, Mills staggered onto the stage during Battistella's first public appearance in a Boston strip club. As chairman of the powerful Ways and Means Committee, a stronghold of congressional power, Mills had been able to subvert many reforms in the House. But the day after Mills's Boston debacle, House Democrats divested Ways and Means of its power to assign members to committees and ended rules that helped them control the legislative process. The Democratic leadership forced Mills to step down from the chairmanship.

Emboldened by Mills's downfall and by the success of liberal Democrats in the November election, freshmen moved against other powerful senior chairmen. In 1975, seventy-five freshmen Democrats took over the Democratic Caucus by removing three older congressional leaders from committee chairmanships, including Wright Patman (D-TX), chairman of the Banking, Currency and Housing Committee; W. R. Poage (D-TX), chairman of the Agriculture Committee; and F. Edward Hébert (D-LA), chairman of the Armed Services Committee. In 1975 and 1976, further reforms decreased the power of committees and opened deliberations to the public. Representatives began to challenge norms of deference by frequently proposing floor amendments, an indication that the tenor of Congress had changed. Scandal brought down other prominent legislators, such as Ohio Democrat Wayne Hays, who was chairman of the House Administration Committee and of the Democratic Congressional Campaign Committee (DCCC), which distributed campaign funds to Democratic candidates.

The concern about the personal behavior of congressmen was fueled in part by the feminist movement of the 1970s. Growing out of the argument that the "personal was political," public officials were expected to uphold certain standards of conduct. Feminists argued that men exercised power through all of their personal relationships, from those in the home to those in the workplace. To empower women, feminists argued, it was essential to eliminate the type of abusive personal behavior by men that denied women equal standing—and this included males who treated female employees and co-workers as sexual objects. Charges were leveled with more frequency than ever before. The charges emerged as these types of issues became prevalent in workplaces across America. The rapid influx of women into journalism during the 1970s heightened awareness of these concerns within the profession. While the interest in private behavior of politicians was rooted in liberalism, the emerging grassroots conservative movement also made private behavior a major issue calling for "morally virtuous" behavior by politicians. While the impetus for policing private behavior emerged from the left, the right joined in as well.

These post-Watergate reforms of the mid-1970s made Congress far more volatile. As the infrastructure upon which senior leaders was eroded, young renegade legislators were freer to pursue their own agendas. Moreover, "sunshine laws" opened many congressional hearings to the public. Without norms discouraging younger members from speaking to the media, the Sunday morning talk shows provided ambitious legislators with another national forum.

The conservative movement that flourished in the 1970s thrived in this atmosphere, and the Republican legislators associated with the movement used scandal effectively to advance their political objectives. Given that the central message of conservatism revolved around distrust in the federal government, persistent attacks on politicians as personally and politically corrupt meshed with their broader message. Nowhere was this clearer than with Newt Gingrich (R-GA). A young Gingrich, elected in 1978, used the new cable station C-SPAN to gain the attention of voters through special order speeches. Gingrich's combative style, well suited to television, featured the explicit use of scandal as a partisan weapon. While rising to power, Gingrich showed no respect for congressional hierarchies. Speaker Tip O'Neill complained that party discipline had gone "out the window," adding, "New members once were seen and not heard, but now it seemed that even the lowliest freshman could be a power in the House."[5] Conditions became more volatile as centrists disappeared from Congress over the next two decades. Both Democrats and Republicans elected officials who were at the far side of the political spectrum, while moderates retired or were defeated. Government leaders moved farther to the extremes of the political spectrum, while voters remained squarely in the middle.[6] Over the next two decades, moreover, a larger number of elected officials would come from the baby boom generation, which grew up in an era of low trust in government institutions. As a result, they tended to display less reverence for the institutions than their predecessors.

In Scandal We Trust, 1978–1992

The 1970s witnessed a sea change in political style that gradually encouraged the latent tendency of democratic politics to veer into scandal. A system that was more porous, more partisan, and subject to more intense oversight combined with a political culture that, by the 1980s, had become obsessed with corruption. There were many reasons that politicians, as they had in the past, turned to scandal warfare in the era of Ronald Reagan. One was that skyrocketing deficits and sacrosanct entitlements, such as Social Security, resulted in reduced levels of discretionary funds.[7] This, combined with a conservative movement that made it difficult to contemplate starting any programs, meant that the federal government could not really undertake new initiatives. Without as many policy issues on the agenda, especially as the Cold War came to a conclusion, politicians turned to scandal to distinguish themselves.

Another reason behind the renewed interest in scandal was the revitalization of partisanship in the 1980s and 1990s that resulted from two internally homogeneous parties that were eager to tear their opponents apart through these sorts of attacks. As southern conservatives fled the Democratic Party and northeastern liberals abandoned the GOP, both parties moved toward the extremes of the political spectrum and left behind a polarized Washington. There was little room left for anyone seeking a middle ground. Republicans attacked Democrats as the party of bloated bureaucracies, government handouts, cultural hedonism, high taxes, and spineless pacifism. Democrats accused Republicans of favoring tax cuts for the wealthy, privileging puritanical moralism, and recklessly using military power at the expense of international support. Without either party able to maintain complete, long-term control of the federal government, scandal warfare was instrumental in their efforts to gain political ground.

When the politicians made the decision to pursue scandal warfare, there was little to restrain them. Most Americans had grown distrustful of government. According to one Gallup poll, in 1964, 80 percent of the American people trusted Washington officials to "do what is right all or most of the time." By 1994, less than 20 percent felt the same. Whereas in the 1970s reformers accepted the need for government but distrusted those elected to lead it, conservatives in the 1980s trusted neither the politicians nor the government. Bureaucrats became the equivalent of the nineteenth-century robber baron.

Even norms of privacy were under strain as more Americans were subjected to monitoring within their own workplace. In the 1980s, for example, more than two million private-sector employees or job applicants were asked to take lie-detector tests or were made subject to drug testing, a consequence of the Reagan administration's vaunted "just say no" policies. In 1989, the Supreme Court legalized drug testing for a large percentage of federal employees. By the 1990s, employer monitoring reached new levels through the surveillance of email correspondence and Internet usage.[8] New regulations subjected personal activities between male and female employees to official sanction. As citizens came under greater scrutiny, they became more willing to pry into lives of political figures as well.

Not only had the pressures against scandal diminished, but reformers of the 1970s had actually created institutions to pursue corruption. The clearest example was the independent prosecutor. Each administration after Jimmy Carter's came under nearly constant legal scrutiny. Despite concerted efforts by Republicans to allow the independent prosecutor law to expire, Democrats kept extending the law. The largest investigation directed by Independent Prosecutor Lawrence Walsh took place during the second term of President Ronald Reagan. Walsh launched a multimillion-dollar investigation of the National Security Council, learning that senior Reagan administration staffer Lt. Col. Oliver North and National Security Advisor John Poindexter had secretly traded weapons to Iran for hostages and cash. The money was then given to fund anticommunist opponents of Nicaragua's Sandinista government, despite a congressional ban on such activities. Although investigators failed to turn up firm proof that Reagan had knowledge of the most damaging violations, congressional hearings were held on what came to be known as the Iran-Contra affair. The hearings, broadcast on cable television, generated mixed reactions. While some citizens became disenchanted with the Republican administration for these secret activities, other sympathized with the accused or perceived the independent prosecutor as overzealous.

The independent prosecutor was not the only unelected official directing investigations into official corruption. The Federal Bureau of Investigation (FBI) turned away from fighting communism and civil dissent and launched highly publicized investigations of bribery among congressmen. In 1980, the FBI rented a house in Washington, DC, where FBI officers disguised themselves as Arab employees of a Middle Eastern oil sheik. Six congressmen were convicted of accepting bribes in the so-called Abscam affair.

Politicians were increasingly brought down for actions that once eluded scrutiny. Conflict-of-interest rules adopted in the 1970s criminalized many once-routine activities. House Ways and Means Chairman Dan Rostenkowski (D-IL) was the first to face criminal indictment for violating House rules. He was charged with employing family friends and misusing House mailing privileges. One congressman explained that Rostenkowski, who came to the House in the 1950s, foolishly continued to use the same rules in the 1990s: "The standards changed and he didn't change with them."[9]

Supreme Court nominations also became part of the landscape of scandal warfare. Senate Democrats derailed President Reagan's 1987 nomination of Judge Robert Bork through an intense interest-group campaign that focused on Bork's ideological biases and character rather than on his record as a jurist. Opponents painted Bork as an unlikable character who was unsympathetic to African Americans, other ethnic minorities, and women. They went so far as to leak to the press records of Bork's video rentals. The Senate voted 42-58 against his confirmation, and the saga gave rise to a new term, "to be Borked," meaning to be subject to a confirmation process that fails as a result of character assassination. Reagan's next nominee, Judge Douglas Ginsberg, fell to defeat in November 1987 following revelations that he had occasionally smoked marijuana in the 1960s and 1970s. "Unfortunately," Ginsberg said, "all the attention has been focused on our personal lives, and much of that on events of many years ago. My views on the law and on what kind of Supreme Court justice I would make have been drowned out in the clamor." Democratic presidential contenders Senator Albert Gore Jr. of Tennessee and Arizona governor Bruce Babbitt immediately felt the need to acknowledge that they, too, had smoked marijuana. "I'd much rather be here talking about arms control or the stock market crash," Gore quipped.[10]

Higher standards of sexual behavior undid other politicians. Senator Robert Packwood (R-OR), chairman of the Senate Finance Committee, was forced to resign on allegations of sexual harassment, and Senator John Tower (R-TX) failed to be confirmed as secretary of defense because of charges of alcoholism and womanizing. In 1991, the military experienced its own scandal. That year, eighty-three women reported being assaulted and harassed at the thirty-fifth annual convention of the Tailhook Association, a private group whose members and activities were associated with the U.S. Navy. More than a hundred officers were implicated, with almost half fined or disciplined. Secretary of the Navy Lawrence H. Garrett III resigned.

It was clear to those whose careers were damaged that scandal politics had been thoroughly institutionalized. When politicians turned to scandal in the 1980s, they discovered an environment highly conducive to these tactics. In fact, the environment often drove politicians into scandal politics rather than vice versa.

Televising Scandal: 1980–1996

Another powerful force in this new environment was a communications industry that exploited scandal for its own institutional interests. Television had gradually become the primary medium through which Americans obtained their news. But in the 1980s, television itself changed with cable, where each channel targeted narrow segments of the population. By 1987, more than two-thirds of the population had access to cable television. The advent and widespread distribution of remote controls, which allowed viewers to easily switch channels from their seats, facilitated this proliferation of channels.

From the start, cable television and politics were linked. In 1980, entrepreneur Ted Turner launched the Cable News Network (CNN). CNN broadcast news twenty-four hours a day. By 1985, CNN claimed 2.5 million viewing households. CNN's constant news cycle obliged reporters to search for new material incessantly. Satellite technology enabled networks to broadcast a story immediately from anywhere in the world. The turning point for CNN came in 1991 with its coverage of the Gulf War. Slickly packaged as a show, not just news, the coverage led the cable channels to envision unprecedented strategies for presenting news events as entertainment. With the rapid speed with which stories made it onto the air, network editors and producers had difficulty controlling the release of information, and journalists and politicians alike were often caught off guard by events as they were unfolding.

Cable also brought fierce programming competition between the major firms in the news industry (even as economic competition diminished through corporate consolidation). In the two decades that followed the creation of CNN, news channels and shows proliferated at a brisk pace. NBC, for example, launched two twenty-four-hour cable news stations, CNBC and MSNBC. Specialized channels such as the Christian Broadcast Network devoted time to political news as well. The traditional networks increased the number of news shows in their programming. Nighttime programs such as *Nightline* and *Dateline*, as well as live broadcasts of breaking events, allowed the networks to compete with cable. While the original news shows of the 1960s centered on hosts reading dry descriptions of daily events, cable-era news revolved around celebrity hosts openly challenging their guests. NBC pundit Tim Russert warned, "With satellites, everyone now has access to the same pictures and sound bites, and news becomes old with amazing speed, things have changed; networks are feeling the competition. We've become more aggressive . . . 10 or 15 years ago, the networks acted as if there was a tacit agreement to be 'highbrow' in their definition of news. Now we've got *Geraldo*, *Inside Edition*, *Current Affair*, and *Entertainment Tonight*. Will their presence drive us, consciously or unconsciously, to gravitate toward more sex and scandal coverage?"[11]

The line between "highbrow" news and "popular" entertainment shows began to blur. In 1992, Democratic presidential candidate Bill Clinton went on a late-night show to play saxophone while joking with young viewers of the cable music station MTV about his underwear. Independent Ross Perot circumvented the traditional political media by speaking directly to voters through Larry King's CNN talk show.

Computer technology had a similar effect. The spread of the Internet in the 1990s expanded the number of outlets producing news around the clock. Networks, magazines, individuals, and political organizations established Websites through which they published news the moment it happened. By the 1990s, the Internet allowed information to be conveyed directly to computer users without the intermediary institutions of news organizations. The resources required to maintain Websites were minimal compared to traditional forms of communication. There was almost no control, moreover, over who could establish a site. As the price of personal computers plummeted, more Americans obtained access to the information the Internet provided. In this atmosphere, the speed at which information was disseminated accelerated exponentially, as did the media's desperate search to find original material that could attract viewers.

Newspapers struggled to compete. Many city papers closed down, while family-owned publications were bought out by large multimedia conglomerates. The slow production speed of print news constituted a serious structural problem. By the time newspapers hit the stands, their news was often stale. In response, newspapers emulated the style of television. With its premier in 1983, *USA Today*, using color pictures and two-paragraph articles, published sensational stories previously reserved for tabloids or entertainment magazines. Many newspapers followed suit to attract readers. They also upgraded their Web-based operations.

In this hypercompetitive environment, political scandal offered all parties a subject that would attract viewers. Scandals blurred the lines between news and entertainment. Like television drama, scandals were easily understood and dramatic enough to capture viewer attention. Scandals offered heroes and villains in easily understood stories that unfolded in dramatic fashion.

The appeal of scandal was not limited to politics. The 1980s and 1990s were an era where scandal saturated all aspects of American culture. Televangelist Jim Bakker lost his multimillion-dollar empire in 1987 because of his sexual relationship with a young woman. The media seemingly could not get enough of real estate mogul Donald Trump's sexual trysts or the illicit financial schemes of Wall Street financier Michael Milken. Ordinary citizens were caught up in the action as well. Americans became familiar with Lorena Bobbitt, who cut off her husband's penis after he physically abused her. Another citizen celebrity was Mary Jo Buttafuoco, shot in 1992 by a seventeen-year-old with whom her husband had been having an affair. Nothing earned better ratings, of course, than celebrity scandal. Whereas Americans were uncomfortable watching even a modicum of sexuality in 1950s cinema, in 1995 millions tuned to a late-night talk show when the popular British actor Hugh Grant discussed his arrest for soliciting a prostitute. The entire country was mesmerized by the daily coverage of former professional football player O. J. Simpson's 1995 trial for the murder of his ex-wife and a friend of hers. Each scandal pushed the boundaries of what stories were legitimate "news."

Throughout television, film, radio, and print, sex was presented more frequently and more explicitly. While reporting on Lorena Bobbitt, for example, newscasters started to use the word "penis." The news was, at times, equally salacious. One lurid scandal was launched on June 30, 1982, when *CBS Evening News* broadcast a story featuring a young page who claimed that he had organized a homosexual prostitution ring for congressmen and himself had had sex with a prominent member; the other said that he had been sexually harassed. As other news outlets flocked to the story, the charges escalated to include widespread cocaine use among congressmen. Although a House Ethics Committee revealed that most of the charges were untrue, it also discovered that two congressmen, Gerry Studds (D-MA) and Daniel Crane (R-IL), had had sexual relationships with pages. The House censured both.

Sexual behavior was featured during the Supreme Court confirmation of Clarence Thomas in 1991. Anita Hill confidentially told the Senate Judiciary

Committee that Thomas had sexually harassed her when she worked for him. Although he never threatened her for spurning his advances, Hill claimed that Thomas's sexual innuendo had created a hostile work environment. One week before the Senate committee was to vote on Thomas's confirmation, Nina Totenberg of National Public Radio and Timothy Phelps of *Newsday* revealed Hill's accusation to the public. Feminist organizations called on the Senate to reject Thomas. Conservatives claimed that Thomas was being persecuted for his conservative beliefs. Hill and Thomas testified during the final hearings, which were broadcast live, and featured frank discussions of Thomas's pornographic tastes and details of his alleged comments to Hill. The Senate confirmed Thomas, but by a narrow vote.

The impact of television was evident in elections. Candidates now communicated directly to voters through television. As they did, the interests of the news media played more of a role in structuring campaigns. This was important, since reporters focused on the competition itself rather than the policies, ideas, or issues in question. By covering campaigns as horse races, reporters were especially drawn to the revelatory scandal that would decide the election. The correlation was simple: because television had a bigger role in campaigns, and scandal was important to television, scandals became more influential in campaigns. Some prominent candidates were destroyed by them. During the 1987 Democratic primaries for president, for example, the *Miami Herald* alleged that Gary Hart, a former senator from Colorado, was having an affair with a young model. Hart challenged the media to prove their allegations. Soon after, the *National Inquirer* obtained pictures of a young model named Donna Rice sitting on Hart's lap on a yacht named *Monkey Business*. Once the pictures were published, Hart dropped out of the race, even though no connection between his private actions and his professional conduct had been demonstrated.

Not all scandals, through, were about sex. Walter Mondale's vice presidential nominee, Geraldine Ferraro, was subject to a ferocious media attack in the 1984 campaign. Reporters accused her husband of unethical business transactions that included Mafia connections. Senator Joseph Biden's (D-DE) campaign for the Democratic nomination in 1988 failed in part because of evidence that he plagiarized speeches from Neil Kinnock, the leader of Britain's Labour party.

Yet the media often refrained from covering scandals that lacked simplicity or drama. The most notable "missed" scandal involved the savings and loan industry. After Congress deregulated the industry in the early 1980s, savings and loan officials made highly risky investments in order to gain quick profits. Several congressmen had received campaign contributions from industry officials who had profited from deregulation, but who continued to be protected by federal subsidies for investment losses. The financial crisis, which cost the government (and taxpayers) as much as $150 billion, involved top law firms, elected politicians, and two government agencies. Yet it took years for the story to make the news.

The news industry had thus undergone a dramatic transformation between 1980, when Ted Turner founded CNN, and 1996, when NBC launched MSNBC. The reconstructed industry was sympathetic to scandal politics and offered unlimited airtime to broadcast these stories. While ideological changes in journalism had pushed reporters toward an investigative outlook in the 1970s, it was the structural reconfiguration of the news industry that cemented a decisive shift toward scandal politics. The advent of Fox News, and the end of the Fairness Doctrine, also opened the media to openly partisan reporting.

The Impeachment of Bill Clinton, 1997–1999

The era of scandal politics culminated with the impeachment of President William Jefferson Clinton in 1999. Since he first ran for the presidency, Clinton had been under investigation. During his 1992 campaign, allegations of an affair with Gennifer Flowers broke right before the crucial New Hampshire primary. Clinton effectively responded by appearing with his wife Hillary on CBS's *60 Minutes*. But during his first term, the investigations continued. The Justice Department appointed independent prosecutors to investigate a questionable real estate transaction that took place while he was governor of Arkansas and to look into the controversial firing of the White House travel office staff. The suicide of Deputy White House Counsel Vincent Foster, a friend of the Clintons, prompted speculation about corruption in high office. When Republicans took over both the House and Senate in 1994, the president's situation deteriorated.

Between 1995 and 1998, the Republican Congress conducted thirty-seven investigations into the White House. Nonetheless, Clinton and his cabinet survived each investigation, partly because of the failure of prosecutors to uncover sufficient evidence and partly because of his staff's skillful use of the media. One notable challenge took place in his 1996 reelection campaign when the tabloids revealed, on the final day of the Democratic convention, that advisor Dick Morris frequently employed the services of a prostitute. The tabloids printed photographs to prove it. Mainstream news organizations picked up the story immediately. But even this incident did not harm the media-savvy president.

Yet Clinton's fortune took a dramatic turn for the worse in 1997. On May 6, 1994, former Arkansas state employee Paula Jones had sued Clinton for sexual harassment. She claimed that three years earlier, Clinton, then governor of the state, had made sexual advances on her in a hotel room. On May 27, 1997, in a landmark decision, the Supreme Court allowed the suit to proceed against the sitting president. Jones's lawyers sought to prove the accusations by showing a pattern of such behavior. When prosecutors added the name of former White House intern Monica Lewinsky to the witness list in December, Clinton became concerned. Judge Susan Webber Wright then ruled that prosecutors could investigate other alleged affairs of the president. On December 17, Clinton suggested to Lewinsky that she could avoid being deposed by filing an affidavit affirming that she had not been sexually involved with the president. Vernon Jordan, a confidant of Clinton's who had met with Lewinsky earlier, helped her secure a job at the Revlon Corporation the day after she signed the affidavit. On January 17, during his deposition, the interrogators surprised the president by asking him a series of pointed questions about his relationship with Lewinsky, the former intern. Clinton emphatically denied having any type of sexual relations with her.

An independent prosecutor was simultaneously investigating the Lewinsky affair. Kenneth Starr, a respected solicitor general and federal appellate court judge, had been appointed in 1994 to investigate the Clintons' allegedly questionable real estate dealings in Arkansas, which became known as the Whitewater affair. Early in January, Linda Tripp, a Pentagon employee and a friend of Lewinsky, provided Star with audiotapes of phone conversations in which Lewinsky revealed intimate details of her sexual encounters with the president. Tripp also told Starr that Lewinsky had been offered a job in New York in exchange for her silence. FBI prosecutors and staff from Starr's office confronted Lewinsky in a room at the Ritz-Carlton hotel with evidence that Lewinsky's deposition was untruthful.

On January 21, 1998, the *Washington Post* published the first story on Clinton's affair with Lewinsky. The news media swarmed over the story, which was now driven chiefly by cable television and Internet newscasters such as Matt Drudge and Internet magazines such as *Salon*. Lewinsky found herself at the center of a media hurricane. Journalist Jeffrey Toobin noted that she had become "the object of the most intense media surveillance since O. J. Simpson's dash across Southern California."[12]

Clinton, too, was in trouble. Dick Morris advised Clinton that his polls showed that the public would want him out of office if the affair was true. Taking this advice, the president lied. During a television appearance, Clinton wagged his finger at the camera and denied having sexual interactions with Lewinsky. Clinton also told cabinet officials that the story was not true. Meanwhile, Starr continued his investigation. His staff and the courts gradually whittled away the privileges of the president by forcing secret service agents and White House counsel to testify before the grand jury. No longer did anyone in politics seem beyond the reach of investigation.

The scandal evoked fierce reactions. Republican leaders, determined to make sure the president was punished, recalled that many of their colleagues had been destroyed by similar charges. The Republicans also claimed that perjury and obstruction of justice were serious crimes. In response, Clinton and his staff bombarded the media with claims that the investigation was being driven by a cabal of right-wing leaders. From the start, congressional Democrats decided to focus on charging that Republicans were mounting a partisan investigation, rather than challenging the charges themselves. On January 27, the day of the State of the Union address, Hillary Clinton appeared on NBC's *Today* show and blamed her husband's problems on a "vast right-wing conspiracy." While Nixon had attempted to end Archibald Cox's bothersome investigation by firing him, Clinton and his allies undermined Starr's credibility through the media.

In the process of the investigation, Republicans sacrificed one of their own, forcing Speaker Newt Gingrich to resign because of his affair with an aide. On the day of the impeachment vote, his successor, Speaker Robert Livingston (R-LA), announced on the House floor that he too would resign and called on Clinton to do likewise. It soon emerged that men's magazine publisher Larry Flynt, who had offered a reward for evidence of sexual dalliances by Republicans, was about to reveal Livingston's infidelity.

Scandal politics were creating strange bedfellows. Political organizations did the opposite of what was expected. For two decades, feminists had insisted that male politicians be held accountable for their behavior toward women: but now organizations such as the National Organization of Women headed the lobby against Clinton's impeachment. Conservatives, who had attacked the notion of an independent prosecutor as an extra-constitutional institution, stood behind Starr.

On July 28, 1998, Lewinsky agreed to cooperate with the independent prosecutor and admitted that she had an affair with the president. She produced as evidence an unwashed dress stained with what she claimed was Clinton's semen. DNA tests were conducted. On August 17, 1998, Clinton testified on closed-circuit television to Starr's grand jury and admitted to having an "improper relationship" with Lewinsky, but insisted that he had not had sexual relations with her as he defined the term. Soon afterward, Starr's office revealed that DNA tests confirmed that the stain was from the president.

On September 9, 1998, Starr sent a report to Congress, which concluded that the president had twice committed perjury and had obstructed justice by coaching witnesses. In the post-sunshine Congress, most of the evidence from the case was made directly available to the public. On September 21, Congress broadcast the president's grand jury testimony on television. Americans saw crucial evidence before Congress deliberated. Congress also posted on the Internet the Starr report, a lurid document filled with sexual details. On October 8, the House Judiciary Committee, chaired by Henry Hyde (R-IL), began its investigation. They were interrupted in November by the midterm elections, in which Republicans suffered unexpected losses, indicating to many observers that the public did not favor impeachment. At the end of November, Judiciary Committee Republicans sent Clinton a list of questions. The president responded defiantly, insisting that he had told the truth to the Jones lawyers and grand jurors. In a fiercely partisan atmosphere, committee members from each party were not talking to each other, let alone negotiating a compromise. On strict party lines, the Judiciary Committee approved four articles of impeachment against Clinton for perjury and obstruction of justice.

Throughout the saga, the worlds of entertainment and politics morphed. Earlier in 1997, director Barry Levinson had released the movie *Wag the Dog*, starring Robert DeNiro and Dustin Hoffman. That fictional movie, filmed before the Lewinsky affair had become public, portrayed a secret team of presidential advisors seeking to cover up a president's sexual encounter with a young girl in the White House. In the film, the presidential staff works with a Hollywood producer to deflect media attention by orchestrating a fake war with Albania. Reflecting the realities of the 1990s, DeNiro's and Hoffman's characters calculate every move based on what television broadcasts. At key moments during the impeachment, Clinton initiated two military conflicts. Cabinet members were forced to deny allegations that Clinton had adopted a *Wag the Dog* strategy.

On December 19, 1998, House Republicans voted to impeach the president. The Senate began its trial on January 7, 1999, and broadcast videotaped witness testimony on February 6, 1999. All deliberations, except the final Senate debate, were televised. Enough Republicans defected from the party line so that the president was not convicted.

The impeachment was a product of the developments that had transformed politics since Vietnam. The investigation was driven by the independent prosecutor, framed by the new sexual norms of the 1970s, and judged within a partisan and televised congressional process. Legislators associated with the conservative movement headed the attack, once again claiming that the leaders of the nation's government were corrupt. Cable and Internet organizations dominated the news coverage of the scandal. In the 1950s, McCarthy had furthered his campaign by taking advantage of press that reported uncritically the charges he made. But in the 1990s, Democrats and Republicans desperately tried to keep up with the media. The saga also uncovered an uneasiness many Americans had with scandal politics. Many thought that Clinton's actions warranted severe punishment, but simultaneously believed that impeachment was excessive. Yet the volatile political world of the 1990s lacked any mechanism or senior establishment that could achieve compromise. The handful of centrists who agreed with public opinion were no longer influential. Information leaked out of Washington at a rapid pace. While the implications of Clinton's crisis remained unclear, Democrats and Republicans agreed on one issue. The independent prosecutor law was allowed to expire quietly. Almost no one called for its renewal.

The 2000 presidential election offered a fitting end to the post–World War II period. Candidates Al Gore Jr. and George W. Bush squared off in a fierce campaign that revealed a country deeply divided ideologically. The election ended in scandal. After an extremely narrow victory, Democrats questioned whether the voting had been fairly conducted in Florida, a state with a decisive twenty-five electoral votes. Democrats and Republicans squared off in the courts—making the electoral process itself fair game in the scandal wars taking place between the parties—while challenging the vote and fighting over recounts. Democrats charged that Republicans were suppressing votes and disenfranchising citizens, while Republicans argued that Democrats were trying to fabricate votes and discounting votes from groups such as the military. On December 12, the Supreme Court (in a split ruling of 5-4) stopped further recounts in Florida. George W. Bush emerged as president. Allegations of election fraud followed his victory in the 2004 race as well.

A New Century?

Although some commentators hoped that the elimination of the independent prosecutor would offer a cure, that seems unlikely. Even the trauma of the terrorist attacks of September 11, 2001, did not prevent the parties from engaging in scandal warfare over all sorts of issues ranging from the conduct of war to ethics and campaign finance. Indeed, by 2006, the Republican majority faced a serious political crisis as a result of scandals revolving around lobbying and corruption. The GOP entered into a political freefall going into the final weeks of the election as a result of a sex scandal centered on a legislator who had exchanged inappropriate emails and text messages with underaged pages.

This should not be a surprise. Scandal politics has become deeply embedded in the structure and culture of our polity. It was the product of a fundamental reorientation in national politics. The first stage involved a shift in what was to be expected from politicians. A reform movement located in Congress, the media, and public interest organizations raised the standards of behavior for politicians. To remove decisions from untrustworthy politicians or voters, the movement institutionalized investigation. The reform orientation became appealing within a national culture that distrusted government and in a political era that lacked many issues to debate. Members of the conservative movement jumped on scandal as a way to legitimate their claims about the nature of government. When politicians turned to scandal in the 1980s, they found none of the countervailing forces that had prevented them from taking this path earlier. Combined with these reforms was an important transformation in the news industry resulting from the advent of cable television and Internet-based media. As a result of these large-scale changes, scandal became the principal weapon with which political battles were fought.

The impact of a partisan political system where scandal plays such a prominent role is harmful to the body politic. Partisan-based scandal warfare was important in the nineteenth century, but there was a big difference between the two eras. During the 1800s, parties truly connected enfranchised citizens to their government. The parties remained central to social life as well as politics; partisan affiliation crucially defined the identities of American citizens. Party organizations maintained close ties to those Americans who had the right to vote, seducing them during campaigns with parades, picnics, and other events that made politics a form of public entertainment. Parties also used heavy-handed tactics: supplying voters with liquor, intimidating them, even offering outright bribes. The hurly-burly of nineteenth-century democracy led to high voter turnout (among those eligible to vote) and strong party loyalties. Americans identified with the party to which their families belonged and maintained a strong sense of allegiance to these groups. In a nation of joiners, partisan ties overlapped with other associations—church memberships, fraternal organizations, veterans groups, social clubs, ethic networks, labor unions, and reform societies.

By the end of the twentieth century, however, those affiliations had thinned. Campaigns centered on individual candidates; parties often functioned as fundraising mechanisms rather than sources of political mobilization. Low rates of voter turnout signaled just how many Americans remained alienated from their government and the political process. Party affiliation mattered only on Election Day, if even then. Democracy, according to one expert, had become more like a "kind of consumer good and spectator sport" than an exercise in civic participation.[13]

Today parties are quite strong in influencing politicians and organized interest groups, but they no longer involve Americans in government on a regular basis. The result is a rancorous political system where it is difficult to find compromise and where there is little room for constructive negotiation. Parties devastate each other through scandal warfare, while disaffected citizens watch the ugliest aspects of their system with disgust. Worse yet, the system does not have the beneficial nineteenth-century effect of integrating average people into the political process. We now have intense partisan polarization without durable grassroots connections to political parties; a deeply divided nation watches polarized politicians with whom they feel little identification or trust. In this respect, the dynamics of scandal are very different today from those in previous eras.

The future of scandal politics remains unclear. Some citizens are content with a system that holds politicians accountable and ensures constant surveillance for corruption. Others fear that the prominence of scandal has poisoned relations among political elites to the point that policymaking is impossible. Some of the nation's finest citizens, critics add, refuse to enter into the fray. All of this has become particularly troubling as the nation was thrust into a new dangerous era of warfare after the terrorist attacks against it. What Clinton's impeachment revealed, however, is that eliminating the centrality of scandal would require the nation to reconstruct the processes and culture that have defined national politics since the mid-1960s. Diminishing the role of scandal would likely require bringing back aspects of postwar American politics, such as greater secrecy in the policymaking process and an absence of formal rules governing the behavior of politicians, that were once (and probably remain) unpalatable to a large portion of the American public. Whether citizens have the desire to put the genie back in the bottle will become clear as the new century unfolds.

Bibliographic Note

Despite its importance, few historians have examined the political history of scandal. A handful of political scientists, journalists, and historians have attempted to explain why scandal became so important. The first argument has been that corruption actually increased over time: see Larry L. Berg, Harlan Hahn, and John R. Schidhauser, *Corruption in the American Political System* (1976), and Elizabeth Drew, *The Corruption of American Politics* (1999). Another thesis posits a cyclical process in American history that alternates between periods of corruption and reform; see Abraham S. Eisenstadt, "Political Corruption in American History: Some Further Thoughts," in *Before Watergate*, eds. Abraham S. Eisenstadt, Ari Hoogenboom, and Hans L. Trefousse (1978), 537–56. A third explanation is that politicians were largely responsible because they turned to scandal as an alternative to electoral politics; see Benjamin Ginsberg and Martin Shefter, *Politics by Other Means* (1990). Others claim that specific laws such as the Office of the Independent Prosecutor created a destructive "culture" of distrust; see Suzanne Garment, *Scandal* (1991). One work locates the source of scandal in presidential morality: Charles W. Dunn, *The Scarlet Thread of Scandal* (2000). Finally, John Summers, in an article focusing on why sexual scandal vanished as an issue after the nineteenth century, suggests that the fragmentation of journalism and diminished trust in government produced a return of scandal in politics after its long absence: John H. Summers, "What Happened to Sexual Scandals? Politics and Peccadilloes, Jefferson to Kennedy," *Journal of American History* (2000): 825–54.

None of these arguments is entirely satisfactory. There is scant evidence, for example, that the amount of corruption actually increased over time. A cyclical model fails to explain why scandal has been consistently prevalent over the last twenty-five years. While politicians have turned to scandal warfare as an alternative to electoral competition, this argument does not explain why similar strategies were less effective earlier in the postwar period or were eventually stifled. Finally, scandal intensified before the creation of the independent prosecutor. In fact, the law was reflective of a political culture distrustful of politics, rather than the instigator of change.

Like any synthetic work, this essay relies on a large body of research conducted by historians, political scientists, and journalists to piece together my story. It also grows out of archival research that I undertook for a book about the transformation of Congress after World War II. A sizable volume of scholarship has documented declining trust in American political institutions since the 1960s: see Hugh Heclo, "The Sixties' False Dawn: Awakenings, Movements, and Postmodern Policy-making," *Journal of Policy History* (1996): 34–63. *Why People Don't Trust Government*, eds. Joseph S. Nye, Jr., Philip D. Zelikow, and David C. King (1997); and E. J. Dionne Jr., *Why Americans Hate Politics* (1991). Work on scandals during the Truman period tend to be more descriptive than analytical; see Irwin F. Gellman, *The Contender* (1999), 372–90, and Andrew Dunar, *The Truman Scandals and the Politics of Morality* (1984). The best treatment of scandal in this period links anticommunism to partisan politics; see Robert Griffith, *The Politics of Fear: Joseph R. McCarthy and the Senate*, 2nd ed. (1970). There has also been work explaining how ethics laws were institutionalized, particularly the independent prosecutor; see Robert N. Roberts, *White House Ethics* (1988); Terry Eastland, *Ethics, Politics, and the Independent Counsel* (1989); Katy J. Harriger, *Independent Justice* (1992); and Martin and Susan J. Tolchin, *Glass Houses* (2001). James T. Patterson, *Grand Expectations* (1996), and Michael A. Berstein and David E. Adler, *Understanding American Economic Decline* (1994), have analyzed the relationship between economic conditions and public attitudes toward government.

Political scientists, sociologists, and journalists have provided excellent accounts of how media practices changed since the advent of television. They have tended to focus on how the commercial structure of the media impacted the type of news presented as well as the emergence of aggressive, watchdog journalism in the 1970s. Moreover, these observers have traced how investigative journalism eventually transformed into news presented as quasi-entertainment. See Larry J. Sabato, *Feeding Frenzy* (1991); Austin Ranney, "Broadcasting, Narrowcasting, and Politics, in *The New American Political System*, ed. Anthony King (1990), 175–201; Michael Schudson, *Discovering the News* (1978); Stephen Hess, *Live From Capitol Hill!* (1991); Martin Mayer, *Making News* (1987); Timothy E. Cook, *Governing with the News* (1998); Thomas E. Patterson, *Out of Order* (1993); Howard Kurtz, *Media Circus* (1993) and *Spin Cycle* (1998); Bartholomew H. Sparrow, *Uncertain Guardians* (1999); Nancy E. Bernhard, *U.S. Television News and Cold War Propaganda, 1947–1960* (1999); and John B. Thompson, *Political Scandal* (2000).

Political scientists spent a considerable amount of energy examining the reforms of the 1970s, with particular interest in the breakdown of an older system dominated by economic interest groups and machine-based political parties: Jeffrey M. Berry, *Lobbying for the People* (1977); Andrew S. McFarland, *Common Cause* (1984); Nelson W. Polsby, *Consequences of Party Reform* (1976); Byron E. Shafer, *Quiet Revolution* (1983); Sidney M. Milkis, *Political Parties and Constitutional Government* (1999). Furthermore, political scientists have examined the disintegration of the committee-based congressional system. Among the books that deal with this are Steve Smith, *Call to Order* (1989); Randall Strahan, *New Ways and Means* (1990); Roger H. Davidson and Walter J. Oleszek, *Congress Against Itself* (1979); Leroy N. Rieselbach, *Congressional Reform: The Changing Modern Congress* (1994); and Julian E. Zelizer, *On Capitol Hill: The Struggle to Reform Congress and its Consequences, 1948–2000* (2004).

The best place to start any examination of scandal during the postwar period would be the two presidential scandals that have received the greatest attention, namely, those surrounding Richard Nixon and Bill Clinton. The books on Nixon debate how much of the scandal was the product of Nixon himself versus the institution of the presidency. The work on Clinton, given its recentness, has tended to be descriptive, although it has tried to situate the drama within the political context of the 1990s. My account relies on Stanley I. Kutler, *The Wars of Watergate* (1990); Fred Emery, *Watergate* (1995); Michael Schudson, *Watergate in American Memory* (1992); Richard Posner, *An Affair of State* (1999); and Peter Baker, *The Breach* (2000).

THIRTEEN

Seizing Power: Conservatives and Congress Since the 1970s

The scene seemed as if someone writing a parody about the American Congress scripted it.* In the summer of 2003, the House Ways and Means Committee was debating legislation dealing with pensions and retirement savings. The committee started by reading the language of the bill. Suddenly, committee chairman Bill Thomas (R-CA) introduced a ninety-page substitute measure that had only been released around midnight the previous evening. When New York Democrat Charles Rangel protested that the minority had not been given any opportunity to review the language of the substitute, Thomas ignored him. Condemning what they saw as another attempt by the GOP to use the power of the majority to force legislation down the throats of their opposition, Democrats stormed out of the committee room and into an adjacent library to map out a strategy. Before leaving, Democrats required a full reading of the bill to delay action. A furious Chairman Thomas instructed his staff and the U.S. Capitol Police to round up the Democrats so that the committee could complete its work; Rangel refused to return. Back in the committee room, Thomas dispensed with reading the bill, leading the lone remaining Democrat, Pete Stark (CA), to protest in vitriolic rhetoric. When Republican Scott McInnis (R-CO) yelled at Stark to shut his mouth, the Californian responded by challenging McInnis to force him to be quiet. In the heat of the moment, Stark called his Republican counterpart a "fruitcake." After the story broke in the media, Republicans said that Democrats were blowing the incident out of proportion and exaggerating events for political effect. "Only one [police officer] walked in, and then walked out, on each of three occasions. For that, [Democrats] want to call us Nazis," complained a Republican aide (Cohen, 2003).

* This essay originally appeared in *The Transformation of American Politics: Activist Government and the Rise of Conservatism*, eds. Theda Skocpol and Paul Pierson (Princeton, NJ: Princeton University Press, 2007), 105–34.

While those Americans who noticed this incident were deeply troubled by these events, it was especially disappointing to older liberal Democrats who had struggled in the 1960s and 1970s to bring an end to the committee-era Congress. Although they intended to create an institution that was more progressive, their reforms backfired. The pension confrontation was just one among many stories that revealed how legislators associated with the conservative movement thrived in a congressional process that liberals had helped to create. This essay examines what went wrong.

During the 1970s, Congress underwent sweeping institutional reforms that closed down an era in legislative history when the chairmen of autonomous committees in the House and Senate dictated the pace of events while operating behind closed doors (for examples of the extensive political science literature on congressional reform in the 1970s, see Shepsle, 1989; Polsby, 2004; and Sinclair, 1989). In addition to electoral changes that resulted in more homogeneous party caucuses, the 1970s congressional reforms had been driven by a liberal coalition of interest groups, legislators, and activists who believed that institutional reform was essential if they wanted to expand the American state into new policy domains and to defend recent gains from retrenchment (Zelizer, 2004). While political scientists have focused on the transformation of the committee system, equally important were changes in the media coverage of Congress, campaign finance, and ethics rules. The congressional reforms, broadly defined, of the 1970s fostered decentralization and centralization simultaneously with the hope of creating an institution where strong parties thrived but where it was difficult for legislative leaders to gain the autonomy that committee chairs enjoyed in the previous era.

To the disappointment of liberals, the institutional reforms that were intended to protect the American state created opportunity structures for politicians with a very different policy agenda. During the 1980s, legislators associated with the conservative movement proved adept at working within the new institutional structures of national politics (for discussions of the conservative movement, see McGirr, 2001; Perlstein, 2001; Schoenwald, 2001; Hodgson, 1996; Dionne, 1991; Nash, 1976). Like southern Democrats in the earlier part of the twentieth century, conservative Republicans were highly cognizant that institutions mattered. Conservative Republicans devoted considerable effort to learning how to master the decentralizing processes created by the reforms when they were still a minority (in the 1970s and 1980s) and the centralizing processes when they were a majority (after 1994). Focusing on the House of Representatives, the history presented in this essay also reveals how congressional conservatives experienced more limited success at curtailing the American state. The tension between the political success of conservatives and their policy failures, namely, the endurance of the state in an era when national politics moved to the right, has defined congressional history since the 1960s.

How Congress Was Reformed in the 1970s

The American Congress was a very different place after the 1970s than it was between the 1920s and 1960s. As a result of a reform coalition, electoral transformations in the South and West, as well as changes in institutions external to Congress, the House and Senate moved out of the committee era and into the contemporary era. These institutional changes were extremely important because they changed the fundamental character of legislative politics.

THE COMMITTEE ERA, 1920S–1960S

During the committee era, the chairmen of standing committees held enormous power in both chambers, and party caucuses were weak. Committee chairs were shielded from significant pressure because they were selected through seniority, which meant that legislators gained positions of power by remaining in office long enough to reach the highest point in the queue rather than by displaying loyalty to any set of policies or individuals (Hinckley, 1971; Polsby, Gallaher, and Rundquist, 1969, pp. 787–807; Patterson, 1967). Professional norms discouraged mavericks or freshmen from taking action, and there were rarely floor challenges to committee legislation (S. Smith, 1989). Even in the Senate, where each individual had the right to filibuster, committee chairs were dominant (Sinclair, 1989, pp. 25–28; Matthews, 1960). Most deliberations took place behind closed doors. The Board of Education was one of the most famous landmarks of the period, a daily meeting where Speaker Sam Rayburn (D-TX) met, drank, and deliberated with top members of his party to determine how Democrats should act on major issues. The committee system existed in a particular institutional environment, one where the composition of districts favored rural constituents, campaigns revolved around a secretive process that favored concentrated, large contributions, and the print media generally refrained from aggressive investigative reporting.

Politically, southern Democrats were very powerful in the committee era. Southerners enjoyed a large portion of the major chairmanships and relied on a voting alliance with Republicans when legislation that they opposed made it to the floor. Known as "the conservative coalition," southern Democrats and Republicans presented a formidable challenge to liberal presidents and legislators between the 1940s and 1960s on such issues as civil rights legislation and the extension of federal protection for organized labor (Katznelson, Geiger, and Kryder, 1993, pp. 283–302; Plotke, 1996, pp. 226–61, 350–51; Key, 1949, pp. 314–82). Southern conservatives used the pillars of the committee process, such as the House Rules Committee and the House on Un-American Activities Committee, as an institutional base from which to protect themselves from legislative proposals and policy innovation that they opposed (Schickler, 2001, pp. 163–74).

THE REFORM COALITION, 1958–1974

The committee-era Congress ended in the 1970s as a result of several factors. One was the influence of an interinstitutional reform coalition of legislators and interest groups that worked for decades committed to extending New Deal liberalism in areas such as civil rights. Reformers included politicians such as Richard Bolling (Missouri), Hubert Humphrey and Donald Fraser (Minnesota), and Phil Burton (California), as well as organizations like the Americans for Democratic Action, the AFL-CIO, and the NAACP. They morphed into a "reform coalition" in the 1960s by absorbing organizations and individuals (such as Common Cause) who were devoted to broad institutional reform as an end in itself rather than primarily a means to a specific policy objective. The coalition dismantled the procedural foundations of the committee era by obtaining incremental reforms and by taking advantage of focusing events such as scandals and watershed elections.[1]

The coalition believed that institutional reform was essential to expanding the American state. Following three long decades where southern Democrats had used the design of Congress to block important measures, postwar liberals were convinced that if they wanted to create programs that appealed to suburban voters, such as environmental regulations, and to defend hard-fought gains, including civil rights, they needed to transform congressional norms and processes. Much of the policy success of liberalism in the 1960s, according to reformers, had depended on the unusually large Democratic majorities that emerged after the 1964 elections, as well as congressional reforms passed in the early 1960s, such as the expansion of the House Rules committee.

The coalition obtained many important reforms in the first half of the 1970s. The reforms purposely strengthened decentralization and centralization in both chambers with the intention of creating a system that fostered strong partisanship while forcing party leaders to be responsive to the membership. As a result of the reforms adopted between 1970 and 1978, party caucuses gained power over committees in the House and Senate. They did so as a result of formal mechanisms, such as the adoption of procedures granting caucuses the ability to easily vote on each chairman, the enhancement of party fund-raising mechanisms that allowed leaders to lean on their members, the centralized budget process that protected certain legislation from a filibuster, and more. New informal norms were likewise important, such as the diminished deference exhibited toward committee chairs. At the same time, reformers strengthened the forces of decentralization—thereby curtailing the autonomy of party leaders and allowing individual legislators to influence debate—through a variety of changes. The reformers opened more congressional deliberations to the public and media, created specialized caucuses, allowed television cameras to cover floor proceedings (although the Senate held off on this change until 1984), codified ethics rules that affected all legislators (including party leaders), strengthened regulations on campaign finance practices, and lowered the number of senators needed to end a filibuster. The Subcommittee Bill of Rights (1973) granted House subcommittee chairs the power to hire staff and ensured them the right to review legislation.

There was some early evidence that the reforms would fulfill the political objectives of liberals. Democrats who entered Congress in the 1970s used the process effectively. California Representative Henry Waxman, for instance, was one of the "Watergate Babies" elected in 1974. Waxman capitalized on the Subcommittee Bill of Rights to use his subcommittee chairmanship to push several important polities—often opposed by senior Democrats—such as national regulations to curb smoking, requirements that automobile manufacturers use tougher safety measures, and new environmental initiatives.

EXTERNAL INSTITUTIONS AND ELECTORAL CHANGE

There were likewise important changes in the institutions external to Congress that weakened the hold of committee chairmen while offering new opportunities for party leaders to enhance their influence, as well as for individual legislators who were outside the leadership. Foremost, the national news media was transformed with the success of adversarial journalism and the advent of cable television technology. By the 1980s, legislators faced a twenty-four-hour, adversarial media where it was difficult to control or respond to the flow of information. The media environment offered party leaders a way to promote their agenda, as well as a means for mavericks to attack those in power. The Supreme Court, moreover, issued its one-man, one-vote rulings in the early 1960s, which eroded the rural-based legislative districts upon which southern Democratic power had depended. Meanwhile, the proliferation and segmentation of professionally managed interest groups and trade associations made it more difficult for legislators to sustain coalitions. The presidency remained strong, despite the hopes of reformers in the 1970s that they would tame the institution.

In addition to the reforms and institutional changes, electoral transformations greatly impacted Congress. The most important was the success of the Republican Party in breaking the Democratic monopoly in the South. Dixiecrats lost their place in the Democratic Caucus. Republicans won conservative votes in the region. Migration into the South from northern states, facilitated by the advent of air conditioning and suburbanization, created a competitive partisan atmosphere in a region once dominated by Democrats (Polsby, 2004). As Republicans gained a stronger foothold in the southern states, conservatives lost their centrality within the Democratic Party (Black and Black, 2002). The result was that congressional Democrats moved further to the left. More dramatically, though, the GOP moved sharply to the right as the party absorbed southern conservatives and abandoned northeastern liberals. The persistence of partisan gerrymandering resulted in a diminishing number of competitive seats. As primaries became the central contest for legislators in every region of the country, they played to the extreme elements of their constituency who tended to turn out to vote in primaries. With moderates dwindling in both parties, the electoral incentives in the 1990s were for legislators to vote exclusively along party lines (Rohde, 1991; Binder, 1996, pp. 36–39).

THE CONTEMPORARY CONGRESS

The contemporary Congress is quite different from the committee-era Congress. Since the 1960s, party caucuses have been the dominant force in the institution. Party leaders have a large number of institutional weapons at their disposal. This is true in the Senate, where the filibuster still offers individuals a tool to block legislative progress. Senate party leaders have used the post–1974 budget process to avoid filibusters and campaign funds to maintain party cohesion. Even the filibuster has turned into a tool of party warfare since the 1970s, as opposed to one primarily used by bipartisan factions or individual legislators. Scandal warfare has also become normalized in both chambers, as politicians have been willing to engage in the politics of personal destruction to achieve improved political standing (Ginsberg and Shefter, 2002). Strong partisanship and scandal warfare—facilitated by the rules of the game and electoral incentives—have made it extremely difficult to devise durable compromises. Finally, both chambers are more open to public scrutiny as a result of sunshine reforms and the twenty-four-hour media environment.

While parties are strong in the contemporary Congress, party leaders continually encounter many threats and challenges. The legislative process crafted in the 1970s offered considerable political space for mavericks, specialized caucuses, the chamber minority, disaffected legislators, and others to challenge leaders through ethics rules, scandal warfare, and the media. Congress is much more open to public scrutiny in the current era, and that meant that it was far more difficult for leaders to shield themselves and control political outcomes. All legislators, including party leaders, are forced to maneuver within an endless and instant news cycle, and partisan media, that could be perilous to politicians caught in a frenzy.

The Conservative Movement

The new legislative process turned out to be central to the fortunes of the conservative movement. The conservative movement that emerged in the 1970s constituted several networks, individual leaders, and organizations that had formed in response to liberalism. Conservatives defined themselves in opposition to Great Society liberalism. The continued growth of the American state in the 1970s belied the notion that Richard Nixon's election as president in 1968 had marked the defeat of American liberalism. "Looking back on the budget, economic and social policies of the Republican years," lamented Nixon's conservative speechwriter Pat Buchanan in 1976, "it would not be unfair to conclude that the political verdict of 1968 had brought reaffirmation, rather than repudiation, of Great Society liberalism" (Hayward, 2001, p. 286). In domestic policy, the federal government was expanding in size and substance. In foreign policy, conservatives felt that politicians were hamstrung by the legacy of Vietnam. Nixon's presidency had been especially disappointing to conservative activists. The onetime darling of anticommunist conservatives had campaigned in 1968 by promising to represent the concerns of the right, yet he ended up presiding over a massive expansion of the federal government before resigning from office in 1974. He also introduced the policy of détente, whereby the United States negotiated with the Soviet Union and China over arms limitations and trade. Making matters worse, the Watergate scandal threatened to destroy the party vehicle through which conservatives hoped to reclaim control of government. The "New Right," as they were often called, hoped to reverse these trends by tapping into the conservative traditions of America and giving them organizational muscle: "The conservatism was always there," wrote direct-mail guru Richard Viguerie. "It took the new right to give it leadership, organization, and direction" (Viguerie, 1981, p. 6).

THE MEANINGS OF MODERN CONSERVATISM

Within the broad context of opposing the growth of domestic programs and attacks on post-Vietnam foreign policy, the conservative movement included several factions. Neoconservatives were former New Deal Democrats who had grown disaffected with the Democratic Party as its members turned leftward on foreign policy and social issues in the 1960s. The religious right, consisting of individuals who had become frustrated with dominant social and cultural norms of the country, was rooted in the South and Southwest. Members who identified with the religious right were concerned with a series of Supreme Court decisions in the 1960s and 1970s that outlawed school prayer, limited the power of the government to regulate obscenity, allowed for the sale of sexual contraception and the medical practice of abortion, and protected the rights of criminals. Furthermore, the movement included business and financial leaders whose main policy concerns were deregulation and lowering federal taxes.

Although there were many areas of disagreement within the conservative movement, the various factions did share certain common beliefs: these included the need for a strong military stand against communism and other international threats, the centrality of tax reductions to overcome stagflation and revive the economy, and the belief that the 1960s was a decade when American society moved in the wrong direction. The conservative movement defined itself through a distinct set of organizations that represented these concerns before members of Congress. Terry Dolan headed the National Conservative Political Action Committee, which was devoted to promoting the New Right. Campaign specialist Richard Viguerie taught conservatives to use direct mail to solicit small contributions from a broad base of citizens. Paul Weyrich organized the Committee for the Survival of a Free Congress, which assisted allied legislators in their rise to power through fund-raising, propaganda, and grassroots organizing. Conservatives relied on certain think tanks, both new and old, such as the American Enterprise Institute and the Cato Institute, to promote ideas that could be used against liberal programs. One of the most influential of these think tanks was the Heritage Foundation, formed in 1973 by Joseph Coors, Paul Weyrich, Richard Scaife, and Edward Noble. Heritage abandoned the restrained approach of the Brookings Institution by packaging and promoting ideas aggressively and with the intention of providing political advocacy information. They also relied on talk radio, and later cable television, to sell their message.

The conservative movement was thoroughly partisan since its inception. To a greater extent than most twentieth-century social movements, conservatism not only linked itself to a political party (Republican) but also committed a large amount of resources to improving the party's electoral standing. Although the movement reached out to the remaining southern conservative Democrats, most of the individuals and organizations associated with the movement staked their fortunes on the GOP. As Hodgson (2004, p. 38) wrote, "the conservative movement came of age. In the 1970s it captured the Republican Party."

Congressional Conservatives and the Power of Decentralization, 1978–1993

Because conservatives felt that they had been excluded from power for three decades, movement activists were keenly sensitive to the way in which institutions mattered. Although voters determined whether someone entered office, conservative Republicans believed that institutional politics held a key to success once a person was elected. The institutional reforms of liberals in the early 1970s, they were quick to see, offered opportunity structures for conducting attacks against the state, rather than just expanding it. Congress was a primary arena where conservatives felt as if they needed to thrive. The challenge was not simply to become a majority in both chambers, but to learn to use the institution more effectively even when they were in a minority. There was a cohort of young Republicans who entered Congress between 1972 and 1982 who were closely linked to the conservative movement. Many were southern, southwestern, or western conservatives who came into Congress with a strong ideological mission, yet they were simultaneously committed to playing hardball politics so that they were not relegated to the margins. In the early years, they capitalized on the decentralizing reforms of the 1970s to cause enormous problems for Democrats. At first, the senior leaders of the party looked at them with suspicion and feared that their renegade attitude would subvert the effectiveness of the GOP at influencing legislation and isolate Republicans from the mainstream electorate.

THE YOUNG TURKS, 1972–1982

The most prominent conservative Republicans came from the South and the West and were on a crusade to transform the GOP. They came from all walks of life. There were intellectuals in this group. One of them was Newt Gingrich, a brash and idealistic army brat who spent much of his youth traveling through the United States and Europe. Born in 1943 in Pennsylvania, his biological father was an alcoholic with a nasty temper who left the family when Newt was three years old. His mother remarried to Bob Gingrich, a tough disciplinarian. Gingrich earned his PhD in history at Tulane University in 1971. He taught for several years at West Georgia College. It took Gingrich several attempts to win a seat in the House to represent the sixth congressional district of Georgia (which stretched from the Atlanta suburbs to rural west Georgia). After losing in 1974 and 1976, Gingrich won the seat when John Flynt, a southern conservative Democrat, vacated it in 1978. In his first two campaigns, Gingrich had run as a southern moderate. In the last campaign, he ran as a conservative. In contrast, Flynt had become alienated from the voters in his district as a result of suburbanization and redistricting (Fenno, 2000). Gingrich was known for having a brilliant intellect. He could comprehend broad political trends in deep historical context. Critics, and allies, knew that he suffered from a massive ego as well, as indicated in the tendency to overplay his hand. Furthermore, his emphasis on big ideas sometimes caused him to overlook practical strategy. "If I have any criticisms of your style at all," Republican Dick Armey wrote Gingrich in October 1993, "it would be that you sometimes allow the forest to obscure the trees" (Garrett, 2005, p. 281).

Other movement Republicans entered Congress through the traditional path of law. Trent Lott of Mississippi was born in 1941 and raised in Pascagoula, Mississippi. His father was a shipyard worker and a teacher. After graduating from the University of Mississippi law school, he practiced law at a private firm and worked for the notorious conservative southern Democrat, William Colmer (D-MS), Howard Smith's (D-VA) chief ally on the House Rules Committee. Symbolizing the regional shift that was taking place during this period, Lott replaced Colmer in 1972, who endorsed his protégé. As the youngest member of the House Judiciary Committee, Lott stood as one of Nixon's most ardent defenders during Watergate. Lott moved up the ranks of the party quickly, becoming whip in 1980. While he earned a public reputation for conservatism, he consistently showed his inclination to negotiate and make deals.

A few members of the movement were journalists. John Vincent Weber (known as Vin Weber) grew up in Minnesota and studied political science at the state university. Weber spent a few years co-publishing his family's newspaper, the *Murray County Herald*, and managed the U.S. Senate campaign of Rudy Boschwitz in 1978. Constituents in the sixth district of Minnesota elected Weber to represent them in the House in 1980. He was skilled at using computers for fund-raising and using television in politics.

Finally, there were many career politicians who, ironically, came to embody a movement that bashed politicians. The most famous example was Richard Cheney of Wyoming. Before entering Congress, Cheney had gained considerable experience in the executive branch, such as serving as chief of staff for President Gerald Ford in 1975 and 1976. Cheney had been greatly disappointed when Ford courted Republican moderates on issues such as détente, at the expense of pleasing the right wing, who almost helped Ronald Reagan win the party nomination in 1976. When the representative of Wyoming, Democrat Teno Roncalio, retired in 1977, Cheney ran for the seat. Despite suffering a heart attack during the campaign, he won at thirty-seven years of age. Cheney avoided the spotlight, preferring to work behind the scenes. He was a conservative on both domestic and foreign policy.

Gingrich, Lott, Cheney, Weber, and other young Republicans kept close contact with conservative activists about the progress of "the coalition" in weakening Democratic power.[2] As a minority, they wanted to bring the Democrats to their knees and were determined to turn the GOP into a congressional majority. When Republicans took control of the Senate in 1980, their enthusiasm only grew in anticipation of a united government.

Not surprisingly, the young Republicans adopted similar legislative tactics as the Democratic Watergate Babies. Both cohorts had entered right as the committee-era Congress came to an end. Members of this legislative generation, both Republicans and Democrats, were comfortable with post-committee legislative politics because this was the process they experienced from the start. They were familiar with partisan decision-making, using scandal warfare as a normal tactic of battle, maneuvering through the decentralized opportunity structures offered by subcommittees and specialized caucuses, and surviving in the news cycle of television. Regarding the importance of television, for instance, Gingrich explained that "television is the dominant medium of our society . . . the guys and gals in Congress who don't master it get killed" (Lamb, 1998, p. 117).

Just like the Watergate Babies, young conservative Republicans made their voices heard immediately upon entering office. Elected in 1978, Daniel Lungren (R-CA), explained:

> We didn't come here accepting that things take time and compromise. We wanted to challenge the institution and raise issues that ought to be raised . . . we have to be willing to shake up the system in the House in ways that may make us uncomfortable . . . because there is a natural tendency to want to be liked. No one, for example, wants to read in the newspapers that the Speaker called us ruthless, as he did, or wants to call for votes that inconvenience other Members. (Cohen, 1984, pp. 413–17)

In 1979 and 1980, the new House Republicans held more than forty meetings to discuss pending legislation. Gingrich organized an informal strategy group to coordinate legislative and political action (Cohen, 1980). While reaching out to the Republican leadership, the younger Republicans were simultaneously critical of House Minority Leader Robert Michel, a plainspoken Illinois representative whose proclivity was to work with Democrats when possible. Michel disapproved of Gingrich's tactics. Rejecting Michel's accommodationist approach, Gingrich explained in 1982 that "the best Republican strategy is to recognize that the Democrats run the House and will do all they can to butcher the budget. . . . We should point out their obstruction from now until November and emphasize the opportunities of the Reagan budget. Bob Michel should relax, concentrate on the impotence of Tip O'Neill and refuse to take up the burden of being Speaker himself" (Cohen, 1982; see also Cohen, 1981). Gingrich saw guerrilla warfare as a defensive tactic: "Liberal Democrats intend to act bipartisan before the news media while acting ruthlessly partisan in changing the rules of the House, stacking committees, apportioning staff and questioning the administration."[3]

Most young conservatives were devout followers of President Ronald Reagan, whose election in 1980 symbolized to them a watershed moment akin to the election of Franklin Roosevelt for liberals. They believed that Reagan could bring together the diverse coalition that constituted the conservative movement and articulate their ideas in a fashion that would attract broad-based support from the population. They perceived the historic tax cut that the Reagan administration moved through Congress in 1981 as a turning point in American politics. While the Republican Party had always tended to balance the demands of tax and deficit reductions, Gingrich's cohort was much more interested in tax cuts. A large number of the younger members, including Gingrich, had run on this issue in the 1978 congressional elections (Hayward, 2001, pp. 529–30). New York Representative, and former professional football player, Jack Kemp became an intellectual guru for the group by promoting a theory of economics whereby tax cuts for the wealthy would trickle down to help everyone and eliminate deficits by bringing money to the federal government through economic growth. Gingrich was even willing to freeze defense spending to save tax cuts (White and Wildavsky, 1989, p. 259). He was not alone. In the 1980s, Grover Norquist, president of a conservative advocacy group called Americans for Tax Reform, convinced more than 90 percent of House Republicans to sign a pledge stating that they would never vote to raise taxes under any circumstances (Gourevitch, 2004).

Yet within a few years of Reagan's election, many movement conservatives were frustrated because so many of his policy promises seemed unfulfilled. For instance, the administration compromised by agreeing to sizable tax increases to reduce the federal deficit. The failure to restrain the federal tax system emerged as one of the central fault lines that divided these young conservatives from older members of the Republican Party. Responding to the 1983 tax increase, Gingrich (1983, pp. 30–32) wrote: "From January to August of 1981, it [the nation] lived through a truly revolutionary period in the tradition of the early New Deal. We conservatives began to change the direction of federal spending, we changed the direction of national defense, we changed the pattern of regulatory bureaucracy, and we changed the pattern of taxation. But from that point on to the present, we have essentially been muddling." Gingrich feared that the administration had been captured by moderates, who he defined as "people who articulate conservative goals and beliefs but who try to govern inside Washington. They believe that, in the end, you have to compromise inside Washington and that you have to govern within the values of that city, which is by definition impossible."

THE CONSERVATIVE OPPORTUNITY SOCIETY, 1983–1989

Exercising control in the House, Gingrich and his colleagues concluded, was essential if Republicans wanted to fulfill the Reagan revolution. After all, the House constituted a liberal bastion in a federal government now dominated by a Republican president and Senate. Like the persistence of a big federal government, the continued power of House Democrats—who used the centralizing procedures obtained in the 1970s to manhandle the GOP and isolate conservatives within their own ranks—greatly frustrated conservative Republicans. The young maverick Republicans formed the Conservative Opportunity Society (in 1983) as a vehicle to promote their message and to design legislative strategy. They defined the term in opposition to the liberal welfare state, which they hoped that they could replace through their bold policies (Broder, 1983).

COS was created following a weekend conference in Baltimore, chaired by Newt Gingrich and freshman Connie Mack (Florida), where Republicans spent most of their time trading war stories about how Democrats used the procedural power of the majority to stifle their participation (Cohen, 1984). During the Baltimore meeting, they divided themselves up with different tasks. Gingrich would be in charge of formulating policy and tactics. Vin Weber was named the coordinator because he was well liked by his colleagues. Robert Walker, another member of the group who represented Pennsylvania, was made floor leader because of his knowledge about parliamentary tactics and reputation for being willing to be aggressive when needed. "Oh, yeah, they think I'm a pain," Walker said in one interview. "But see, you don't win a lot of friends in my job" (Reid, 1984). Following the conference, COS began meeting every Wednesday morning in the office of Vin Weber. COS realized that the procedures and norms of the post-committee House offered numerous methods for challenging the majority. Cheney, who had clout with senior GOP members as a result of his work in the Ford administration, served as a liaison between COS and the leadership. "I was the grease between the grinding gears to some extent," he said (Remini, 2006, p. 463).

Just as the Democratic Study Group had offered young liberals assistance in the 1960s, COS worked with Republicans elected in 1984 who were seeking a different kind of conservative politics. Gingrich and his allies, for instance, were quick to embrace Tom DeLay, who was elected in 1984 to represent the suburbs of Houston and symbolized the rising power of affluent suburban conservative Republicans. This Texan was just the kind of legislator COS was looking for, one with a strong commitment to the ideological principles of modern conservatism and a brazen individual who was willing to use the toughest tactics to combat Democrats and moderate Republicans. DeLay was born in Laredo, Texas, to a family that was in the oil business. He graduated from the University of Houston in 1970. While he was the owner of a pest control company, DeLay developed an intense dislike for federal agencies (particularly the Environmental Protection Agency). He served for six years in the state House of Texas before winning election to the U.S. House in 1984. A devout Baptist, DeLay's twenty-second district was a model of the new suburban South, filled with upscale residential developments as well as churches and civic associations. While Anglo-Americans constituted the largest part of his solidly Republican district, there was a sizable percentage of Hispanics and Asians. If the 1960s counter-culture had redefined American culture, most of his constituents had missed the news.

COS conceived of numerous plans to achieve their objectives. Gingrich, for example, devised an elaborate media strategy for Republicans. He urged GOP legislators to coordinate their responses for national interviews on the evening news shows and on the Sunday morning talk shows in order to offer a consistent message. Gingrich implored Republicans to act as partisans in front of reporters by pinning blame on Democrats and claiming credit for themselves.[4] Although Michel and other senior leaders initially dismissed Gingrich's media ideas, they gradually embraced them as their own after they began to realize that COS was succeeding at influencing the agenda and building a following. For example, the GOP leadership adopted a central tactic of Gingrich's group when they launched a well-coordinated national media campaign depicting Democrats as corrupt.[5]

COS used the post-committee legislative process effectively. "It is my tactic to confront them so hard they have to respond," Gingrich said (Rogers, 1984). As a minority, for example, the Republicans understood that the televised Congress (the House authorized televised floor proceedings in 1978, and C-SPAN was founded in 1979) could be used as an effective weapon for individuals and the minority to challenge the party in power. Although C-SPAN was a small station compared to the networks, Gingrich concluded that the viewership still ranged between a quarter of a million to a half million people each day. "My test was very simple," Gingrich explained, "How far would you go to speak to five thousand people. The average politician would go around the planet" (Clift and Brazaitis, 1996, p. 228). In 1984, COS coordinated televised one-minute and special-order speeches on C-SPAN where they attacked Democrats for various policy issues. The practice became the center of controversy in May 1984, when COS members criticized the foreign policy positions of Democrats. After each speech, Republicans would ask Democrats to respond to the charges of their being weak on fighting communism. Viewers were unaware that the chamber was empty, so it appeared as if Democrats had nothing to say. David Obey (D-WI) compared this to the anticommunist scares of the 1950s: "He may look prettier than Joe McCarthy, but 'it still looks like a duck to me.'"[6] Speaker O'Neill was livid when COS attacked his close friend Eddie Boland (D-MA). "What really infuriated me about these guys," O'Neill later recalled, "is that they had no real interest in legislation. As far as they were concerned, the House was no more than a pulpit, a sound stage from which to reach the people at home. If the TV cameras were facing the city dump, that's where they'd be speaking" (O'Neill and Novak, 1987, pp. 353–54). To retaliate for the attacks, the Speaker ordered the cameraman to pan the chamber in order to show that it was empty (thereby violating the rules of the House). Although at first "CAMSCAM" seemed to reveal the tricks that COS employed, COS turned the incident against O'Neill by launching television ads that depicted the Speaker as a corrupt boss who violated and manipulated the rules. Jack Kemp wrote Republicans: "Since he has become Speaker in 1977, he has manipulated and maneuvered the system to insure his ironfisted control." With CAMSCAM, Kemp argued: "O'Neill alone altered procedure and tried to use the televising of the House to embarrass the Republicans."[7] All of the three major networks covered the events, so Gingrich's name gained national attention.

The incident established COS as a serious player in the Republican Party. Understanding the irony of how events unfolded, O'Neill said to Gingrich that "when I came out on the floor and attacked you, you were nothing but backbench-rabble rousers. I made you" (Farrell, 2001, p. 636). In January 1984, the Conservative Opportunity Society drafted its own budget, which included curtailing the growth of Medicare and across-the-board freezes on domestic programs. Gingrich publicly criticized Reagan for "feeding the liberal welfare state instead of changing it" (Birnbaum, 1984). In the summer of 1984, the young Republicans shunted moderates such as Robert Dole (Kansas) and Howard Baker (Tennessee) and rewrote the Republican platform. Describing himself as a "visionary conservative," Gingrich wanted Reagan to launch a "dynamic, audacious first 100 days reminiscent of [Franklin] Roosevelt's first term" (Thomas, 1984, pp. 34–35). Some moderate Republicans were angry. Jim Leach of Iowa, head of the Republican Mainstream Committee, said of the revised platform: "I do not identify with the Republican platform and view it as an embarrassment. I will run on my record" (*U.S. News and World Report*, 1984, p. 23). But these kinds of activities gave the impression that House Republicans were now the source of ideas in the GOP. Former Indiana representative Dan Quayle, elected to the Senate in 1980, said of Gingrich and his allies: "They are conducting the intellectual work of the Republican Party" (Shribman and Rogers, 1985).

In addition to televised proceedings, conservative Republicans also relied on the congressional ethics code that had been enacted in 1977 and 1978. The most infamous example involved the downfall of Speaker James Wright (D-TX). Wright had been elected as Speaker in 1987. Although he started his career as a centrist southern Democrat, Wright moved with the congressional base of the party to the left by the mid-1980s. By the time that Democrats elected him as Speaker, Wright understood that he had to push for the national agenda of the party or he would face retribution from the caucus. Therefore, Wright ruthlessly used the rules that the majority had gained in the 1970s. For instance, he worked closely with the House Rules Committee to make sure that party-based legislation received favorable treatment. As a result, in the 1970s reforms, the Rules Committee had become an instrument of the caucus rather than an independent fiefdom, as it had been in the committee era (S. Smith, 1998). Following the 1984 election, the Democratic majority voted to seat a Democratic legislator over a Republican, who had been certified by the Indiana state authorities to represent the eighth district, following a series of controversial and partisan recounts. Not only were young Republicans unhappy with the Democratic leadership but with senior Republicans as well for their apparent indifference (Evans and Novak, 1985). Gingrich proposed civil disobedience. Richard Cheney complained, 'What choice does a self-respecting Republican have . . . except confrontation? If you play by the rules, the Democrats change the rules so they win" (Balz, 1985). In 1987, moreover, the Speaker held open a vote on tax increase legislation beyond the allotted time just so that Democrats could find someone to switch his vote and thereby gain a victory. "Can we lock the damn door?" asked Trent Lott in protest. Republicans who had cheered when Wright initially declared that time had expired and the vote stood at 206-205 against the measure, started to boo and yell at him. "They had to cheat to win it," complained Minnesota Representative Bill Frenzel, who added that "it was a bad day for the speaker and for the country." The House approved the $12.3 billion tax increase by a narrow one-vote margin (Birnbaum and Langley, 1987).

Gingrich perceived an opening to attack the Speaker through the ethics rules. Common Cause, an organization that had formed in 1970 to fight for government reform, accused Speaker Wright of ethics violations. Gingrich realized that Wright offered a perfect target: it seemed that he had really abused the laws, and he had so many enemies in both parties (many Democrats personally disliked Wright because of his gruff style). Gingrich called for a House Ethics Committee investigation with a professional staff that was granted subpoena powers.[8] Common Cause and Gingrich made several accusations. They charged the Speaker with having violated the rules regarding outside income by forcing trade associations to purchase copies of his book—a collection of floor speeches—when he made an appearance. William Carlos Moore, a friend of Wright from Texas whose business had received more than $600,000 in consulting fees from the Speaker's reelection committee, published the book. Another accusation involved the claim that Wright once intervened with the Egyptian president to help a business friend obtain oil rights in the country and that he had approached the head of a savings and loan in Texas for special assistance. When Gingrich called this situation a crisis for the House,[9] Wright responded that he had "violated no rule and certainly violated no commonly accepted ethical standard" (Carlson, 1988, p. 21). Importantly, most of the aforementioned activities would have been tolerated during the committee era (W. Schneider, 1989). To spearhead his defense, the Speaker released a twenty-three-page pamphlet refuting each of the charges. He called this an inquiry being driven by partisanship and targeted the seventy-two Republicans mounting the attack, while ignoring the role of Common Cause (*Time*, 1988, p. 31; Borger, 1988, p. 20). Bill Alexander (D-AR), one of Wright's closest allies, took a different tack. He raised questions about Gingrich's ethics, claiming that he had engaged in inappropriate financial deals. Alexander also said that "Gingrich is clearly an extension of the Republican 'Southern Strategy' based on confrontational, demagogical politics that began with Richard Nixon and Harry Dent of South Carolina and is now being continued by Lee Atwater, Roger Ailes, and Ed Rollins. This strategy has established a political base for Republicans in the south."[10] Gingrich himself did not care about public perceptions that he was mean: "If voters see a race as a nice-guy Republican against a nice-guy Democrat, we lose" (Dionne, 1991, 296).

The House Ethics Committee began an investigation into Wright on June 9, 1988. The Republicans pressured the Ethics Committee into conducting a thorough investigation. They also appeared regularly on the media to keep these charges at the forefront of attention. Republicans elected Gingrich as minority whip in 1989, and then the partisan warfare accelerated into high gear. Gingrich told PBS's *MacNeil/Lehrer News-Hour*: "It is my honest belief as a citizen that you now have Tammany Hall on Capitol Hill . . . that is a sick institution, and that it has no legitimate authority, has enormous power, and that it has no legitimate authority; it does not represent the constitutional government. It is, in fact, a subversion of the process of free elections" (*National Journal*, 2001). In April 1989, the Ethics Committee released a full report stating that Wright had violated the ethics rules on multiple occasions.[11] Sensing that he would be removed, Wright decided to resign on May 31, 1989. Before he stepped down, the Speaker warned his colleagues that they needed to stop the "mindless cannibalism" that was sweeping through the chamber as both parties eviscerated each other through scandal warfare.[12] As with CAMSCAM, the deposition of Wright revealed that COS was a force to be reckoned with. Not only had these mavericks gained a secure foothold in the GOP, but they had also toppled the most powerful legislator in the House.

A few years later, conservative Republicans would strike once again with their campaign to depict Democrats as a corrupt majority.[13] In 1991, the GOP pressured Democrats to launch an investigation following a report from the General Accounting Office in 1991 that showed 269 sitting representatives had bounced checks at the House Bank without having been required to pay a penalty. The scandal was complicated, because the House Bank was not actually a bank. Rather, it was a depositing service offered to legislators that covered bad checks. Republicans kept the issue in the spotlight, however, despite attempts by Democrats to quiet them down. Once the investigation began, Republicans pushed for an even broader inquiry. Representative James Nussle (R-IA), part of the notorious "Gang of Seven" who favored confrontational styles, wore a bag over his head before the C-SPAN cameras to indicate disgust with his colleagues.

In the spring of 1992, the House Ethics Committee released the names of the worst offenders, which included 252 sitting lawmakers. The Justice Department hired a special counsel to investigate the worst cases. The revelations seemed to have an effect, earning the House some of the worst press that the institution had faced in years. During the 1992 elections, voters produced the largest House turnover in forty years with 110 new members. Of the 269 sitting members implicated in the scandal, 77 retired or were defeated. The scandal also caused a significant number of retirements and primary defeats. While many accused survived, there were enough losses to vindicate the Republican campaign.

THE FRUSTRATION WITH PRESIDENT GEORGE H. W. BUSH, 1990–1992

When it came to public policy, however, the young Republicans were not as successful. Indeed, one of the factors that motivated congressional conservatives to maintain such high levels of discipline and energy was that, despite their increased political success, they were unable to curb the growth of the American state. Their disappointment was evident with the presidency of George H. W. Bush, who signaled to conservatives that Republicans were regressing. During Bush's presidency, a series of historic expansions in the scope of government occurred, including the Civil Rights Act of 1989 and the Americans with Disabilities Act of 1990. The defining moment for congressional conservatives occurred in 1990 when, faced with pressure from Republican and Democratic budget hawks, Bush agreed to raise taxes in exchange for spending cuts. Upon hearing of the president's decision to renege on his famous promise in 1988 not to raise taxes, Gingrich lambasted it as "the fiscal equivalent of Yalta" (Critchlow, 2004, p. 719).

Gingrich and his allies would not tolerate the tax hikes, as they had with Reagan, because they already did not trust Bush and believed he was an old-guard compromiser (Gould, 2003, p. 448). Bush was so angry with Gingrich for defying him that he refused to shake his hand during a White House ceremony. Gingrich said that "there was a sense in the White House that the admiral of the fleet had made the decision and I was but a disloyal ship captain . . . I think that is a total misunderstanding of politics. For me to have voted for that compromise would have destroyed my effectiveness" (Clift and Brazaitis, 1996, p. 245). Many conservatives never forgave Bush for raising taxes. His opponent in the 1992 Republican primaries, Patrick Buchanan, said to fellow conservatives: "George Bush, if you'll pardon the expression . . . has come out of the closet as an Eastern Establishment liberal" (Hodgson, 1996, p. 250).

Frustration with Bush further energized congressional Republicans to stifle President Clinton (although they were certainly prepared to attack, regardless of the experience with Bush). During the 103rd Congress, despite Democrats controlling both chambers of Congress, Republicans maintained tremendous discipline and made it difficult for Democrats to pass major legislative accomplishments. Congressional Republicans were even able to block Clinton's healthcare reform proposal in 1993, turning what was meant to be a centerpiece of his presidency into an electoral liability that would cost Democrats control of Congress in 1994 (Jones, 1999, pp. 82–87). Congressional Republicans worked together in the months running up to the midterm elections of 1994, relying on congressional investigations in the House and the Senate filibuster to block Clinton's agenda. Clinton was able to pass an economic stimulus package in 1993 that included a tax increase and other deficit-reduction measures, but he did so without Republican support.

Congressional Conservatives and the Power of Centralizaton, 1994–2004

The election of 1994 had been a watershed year in congressional history. Republicans took control of both chambers of Congress for the first time since 1954. Senate Republicans increased their number to 52 by gaining eight seats; two Democrats then switched parties. House Republicans took over the chamber with 230 seats. Importantly, the biggest Republican gains were in the South, Midwest, and West. Most politicians and pundits credited Minority Whip Newt Gingrich for having orchestrated a national campaign based on the conservative ideas (including a balanced budget, term limits for legislators, capital-gains tax cuts, a policy to prevent U.S. troops from being placed under the authority of the United Nations, and requirements promoting personal responsibility and self-sufficiency for citizens on welfare) that were outlined in the "Contract with America." This was a slick document, published in *TV Guide*, that Republicans promoted through a sophisticated public relations campaign. As a result of the election, the individuals who came from COS were now in control of Congress and of the party. The Republicans showed themselves to be children of the 1970s reforms and had little interest in turning back the clock to the committee era. Most of the reforms that they passed in 1995 cemented, and accelerated, the trends of the 1970s.

THE REPUBLICAN REFORMS IN 1995

After years of using the decentralizing aspects of the legislative process to their advantage, conservative Republicans switched course. Speaker Gingrich continued to strengthen parties through a variety of methods. He created task forces that reported directly to the Speaker to craft legislative proposals and committee agendas. Gingrich organized the Speaker's Advisory Group (SAG) to meet every week and design policy (Dodd and Oppenheimer, 1997, p. 43; Wolfensberger, 2000, pp. 175–91). The Speaker and others in House leadership also stacked the key committees with individuals and chairmen who were loyal to the new Republican agenda, while imposing six-year term limits for committee chairs in the House and Senate. House Republicans created a twenty-six-person Steering Committee that obtained the responsibility of naming committee chairs. The Speaker chaired the committee and had more votes than the other members (S. Smith and Lawrence, 1997, p. 174). Republicans did reverse some of the 1970s changes by eroding the balance between centralization and decentralization that reformers had hoped to achieve. For example, the Republican leadership under Gingrich weakened the Subcommittee Bill of Rights by granting committee chairs the power to name subcommittee chairs and to hire staff (Schickler, 2001, p. 272). Republicans also limited the number of subcommittees that most committees could have to five. "In the Commerce Committee," lamented Henry Waxman, "the subcommittees are practically irrelevant" (S. Smith and Lawrence 1997, p. 179).

Yet Gingrich understood that the decentralizing tools of the 1970s reforms were still in place and that he needed to remain responsive to his membership. In this respect, the post-committee reforms worked by creating opportunities for strong party caucuses while leaving party leaders susceptible to attack. The forces of decentralization, though not as strong after 1994, were still very relevant. Gingrich depended on the seventy-three freshmen as a solid voting block, and he was always aware of the trouble they could cause him. This was a big challenge because the freshmen were a volatile bunch. While sharing the ideological outlook of the founders of COS, they were more extreme than their predecessors in their refusal to learn how to work in the political system or to build any kind of coalitions. Most of this class never intended to stay in politics. Only twenty-six of the freshmen had any previous legislative experience, and almost none of them envisioned themselves as career politicians. As a result, most were willing to put everything on the line.

The freshmen included South Carolina's Lindsey Graham, a single Baptist who was born in 1955 and raised in Pickens County by a family that owned a bar. He studied at the University of South Carolina following the early death of his parents, and he was the first person in his family to earn a college degree. Graham went on to earn a law degree at the University of South Carolina. He worked as an attorney for the Air Force. After practicing law in Seneca and serving in the Gulf War, he worked for two years in state government before being elected to the House in 1994. In his campaign, he ran against state senator Jim Bryan on a platform that emphasized increased military spending, term limits, and cultural conservatism. Another freshman was Mark Foley, who represented the sixteenth district of Florida that included beachfront resort communities, affluent suburban areas, and farmers. A Massachusetts native, Foley's family had moved to Florida when he was three. Unlike Graham, Foley did not do as well in school. He never completed his work at Palm Beach Community College and instead opened a restaurant. Before his election in 1994, Foley served in state politics for only four years. From the time he arrived in Washington, Foley became known for his independence and willingness to challenge any authority, including the Republican leadership. Then there was Mark Neumann, a self-made millionaire who had worked his way through undergraduate and graduate school at the University of Wisconsin by taking jobs in restaurants and coaching sports teams. Neumann had earned his millions through a real estate company; he financed much of his own campaigns. Despite his self-accumulated wealth, Neumann did not embrace the lifestyle of a millionaire. This workaholic maintained a cluttered and messy office on Capitol Hill, and he rejected most of the perks that came with working in Washington. Neumann developed a passion—bordering on an obsession—with the size of federal deficits. He entered office with a determination to cut the cost of federal spending, even when that meant that he would have to do battle with Republican leaders (Browning 1995).

Freshmen such as Graham, Foley, and Neumann made their voices heard. When Robert Livingston (R-LA) tried to remove Neumann from the defense appropriations subcommittee for voting against a piece of legislation, the freshmen intimidated Gingrich into placing Neumann on the Budget Committee instead. During one of the budget battles between President Clinton and the Republican Congress in 1995, Neumann added an amendment to an appropriations bill that would have blocked the $600,000 that was earmarked for the African Elephant Conservation Act and $200,000 that was to go to a fund to help developing nations protect certain animals that were headed toward extinction. Gingrich was angry because he supported the appropriations, especially the first measure that would have sent money to the Atlanta Zoo. Gingrich also felt that Neumann was practicing a kind of budget-balancing extremism that had little effect on the overall budget but earned GOP scorn among constituents. In response to criticism that $800,000 was a trivial amount of money, Neumann said: "Some people here in Washington would have us believe that $800,000 is not worth worrying about. Let me respond . . . I understand it takes $1 per day to keep a starving child alive in some of these countries. That means we could use these same tax dollars to keep 2,100 starving children alive (for a year), rather than spend the money to preserve tigers, elephants and rhinos." Neumann moved forward with his amendment despite Gingrich's fervent opposition. Although the House rejected Neumann's measure, it was a bold sign of defiance. Neumann was not the only young Republican willing to take on the leadership. At a retreat that followed the 1994 elections, some Republicans asked why the party shouldn't impose term limits on the Speaker as it had with committee chairs. The idea "caught on like wildfire," recalled Lindsey Graham, and the freshmen imposed an eight-year term limit. "Ain't nothing was off-limits, buddy. You could feed us, wash us, and comb us, but we'd still bite," Graham said (Baumann, 2004).

Additionally, these conservative legislators used advocacy think tanks to gain ground in the battle over ideas (Ricci, 1993; J. Smith, 1991). Republicans likewise depended on the new campaign finance system to gain political advantage, capitalizing on their broader base of support to mobilize small contributions and political action committees. After years of exile, Republicans became prominent in the mainstream media. Besides gaining attention in the network news shows, they relied on talk radio shows, C-SPAN, Internet Websites, and cable television.

THE TRAVAILS OF CONSERVATISM, 1995–1999

In the coming years, Gingrich realized that lower-ranking Republicans could cause him enormous problems. As Speaker, Gingrich had to confront the tension between the strength of the conservative movement of which he was a part and the persistence, as well as entrenchment, of the American state. When Republicans squared off against President Clinton in 1995 over the federal budget for fiscal year 1996, attempting to obtain deep cuts in spending and complete Reagan's revolution, they found themselves in a bind. Republicans proposed over $1 trillion in spending cuts over a seven-year period, as well as $353 billion in tax cuts and increases in defense spending. They packaged most of their proposals within the budget process since the rules created in 1974 offered a means of avoiding the filibuster in the Senate (Sinclair, 1997, p. 216). They also relied on a number of highly restrictive rules to limit debate. For instance, upon introducing the budget resolution in the House, Republican leaders required that any substitute could show it would balance the budget in seven years. Until then, only narrow amendments had been barred from consideration when dealing with budget resolutions (Sinclair, 1997, p. 185). Clinton responded by calling for $1.1 trillion in spending cuts over ten years and a much smaller tax cut that would only benefit the middle class. "The White House," Gingrich told his colleagues early on in the battle, "has crossed the line. We want them to understand that if they want a long-term stand-off, we are prepared to stay the course for as long as it takes" (Thurber, 1997, p. 337).

During the budget battles, Republicans learned that it was extremely difficult to dismantle the American state. President Clinton was able to link the proposed Republican Medicare cuts to their proposed tax cuts, presenting this budget as an attempt by the GOP to transfer money from the poor to the rich. Clinton also honed in on specific cuts in the budget that affected programs that had public support, such as food stamps, school lunches, and healthcare (Witcover, 2003, p. 676). Gingrich, however, had little room to maneuver since the freshmen remained adamant regardless of the political costs. As Clinton's top advisor said, "the freshman had become Newt's Frankenstein monster—and my new best friend" (Stephanopoulos, 1999, p. 406). When the intransigence of both sides caused a series of government shutdowns in December 1995 and January 1996, the media turned on the Republicans by presenting them as unwilling to compromise and as prepared to abandon popular government services ranging from the National Zoo, to federal monuments, to travel visas. Republicans had not perceived that most voters would blame the Congress, rather than Clinton, for a government shutdown—particularly after they spent so much time wielding this as a threat in public. The tension between Republicans and the White House became so severe that at one point during a shutdown, as House GOP leaders complained to the president about an insulting picture the White House had provided to *Time* magazine, Gingrich picked up the phone and cursed at Clinton, accusing him of being a "goddamn lying son of a bitch!" (Garrett, 2005, p. 125).

In the end, Republicans agreed to a federal budget that did not significantly cut into the strength of the federal government. Kansas Senator Robert Dole was instrumental at reaching a compromise, in part because he was concerned about how the budget shutdown would affect his presidential campaign. Politically, Clinton emerged from the battles with renewed strength as congressional Republicans had lost some of the luster they gained following the 1994 elections. Gingrich personally suffered as the national media developed an unfavorable caricature of the Speaker as immature, mean-spirited, and out of control.

Nonetheless, congressional Republicans would score some important victories. In January 1996, Clinton sent a message to Congress with a plan to balance the budget by 2002, thereby adopting a central platform of the Republicans in the budget battles. Moreover, in 1996, Clinton agreed to sign legislation that ended the federal welfare program, Aid to Families with Dependent Children. Clinton also made the famous proclamation that the "era of big government is over," which seemed to confirm the ideological message of the conservative movement. In 1997, Clinton agreed to a budget that constrained discretionary spending below the predicted rate of inflation, opened the door for Medicare reform, and reduced income taxes. In exchange, Clinton ameliorated certain parts of the welfare reform and obtained a new healthcare program to cover low-income children. Republicans would also prevent programs from being updated to meet current conditions, an effective way to retrench programs without eliminating them (Hacker, 2004). Despite the Republicans' accomplishments in the second term, however, most parts of the American state remained intact throughout the 1990s, and spending did not decline in dramatic fashion.

Once again, the persistence of the American state inspired Republicans to remain aggressive in employing the tools of the majority to achieve their goals. Their political victories were not translating into the kind of policy victories that they desired, so many in the GOP did not feel as successful as they thought they should. The leadership continued to use House rules to curtail dissent within their caucus and to limit Democratic opposition. Republican investigations into the White House were a central tactic that they used to combat Clinton, culminating with the investigation of Clinton's affair with a White House intern named Monica Lewinsky. As the House of Representatives considered whether to impeach President Clinton in 1998, Majority Whip Tom DeLay prevented Democrats and moderate Republicans from offering a censure resolution that would likely have attracted the support of many legislators (Baker, 2000, pp. 217–37).

EXERCISING MAJORITARIAN POWER IN AN ERA OF UNITED GOVERNMENT, 2000–2004

Once the era of divided government ended with the election of President George W. Bush in 2000, House Republicans accelerated their efforts to use the centralizing aspects of the 1970s reforms. With Gingrich out of office (he was forced by Republicans to resign during the Clinton impeachment), Tom DeLay stepped into the power vacuum. As whip and then majority leader, DeLay used House rules without restraint. One Republican colleague called DeLay's office "a cross between the concierge at the Plaza and the mafia. They can get you anything you want, but it will cost you" (*National Journal*, 2003). The role of committees continued to decline, as was evident from the diminished number of committee meetings and hearings (*National Journal*, 2001).[14] Between 2000 and 2004, Republicans also blocked Democratic participation in committee deliberations, refused to give Democrats access to the language of legislative proposals until hours before a vote, and made it hard for them to gain attention in the media. Even the tragedy of 9/11 did not stop House Republicans from employing their procedural power. Initially, Speaker Hastert tried to work across partisan lines. According to one report, shortly after 9/11, Congress was working on legislation to stimulate economic recovery. Senator Tom Daschle's (D-SD) and Richard Gephardt's (D-MO) staff convened with Hastert's staff in a conference room to work on an airline bailout package in the late hours of evening. After hearing about this, DeLay personally dashed into the conference room without announcement. In a fury, DeLay screamed at the Democratic staffers: "Who elected you to Congress?" He ordered the Republican staffers to leave immediately. Thereafter, he dismantled the work completed in the discussions. The Republican leadership removed all of the Democratic provisions the following day before the House voted on the legislation (Crowley, 2003).

But with a Republican in the White House and fewer GOP centrists to stop them, the skill of conservatives at institutional politics started to reap big dividends. In 2001, the Republican Congress passed a massive tax reduction, the largest in postwar history, which made deep inroads into the fiscal capacity of the state. In 2003, in the midst of a war against terrorism, Congress passed a smaller tax reduction that nonetheless broke the historic tradition in the United States of increasing federal tax contributions when American troops were fighting abroad. The $350 billion tax cut of 2003 included lower rates for dividends and long-term capital gains, various benefits to individual taxpayers, and business tax benefits such as improved depreciation rates. The rules were important to a smooth passage. House Democrats, for example, were only granted one hour to debate their less costly and more progressive $150 billion alternative; Democrats were not even allowed to vote on their plan. Republicans were so successful at stifling Democratic proposals through restrictive rules that the media reported as if Democrats had agreed to the Republican plan rather than being shut out of debate (Crowley, 2003).

House Republican leaders employed many tactics throughout other battles in Bush's first term. Republicans only allowed 15 percent of the bills in 2004 to be open for amendment (Milligan, 2004). In numerous committee meetings, Republicans prohibited Democratic amendments. During a vote on a prescription drug benefit in 2002, Democrats were not allowed to vote on their plan. Republicans also have delayed omnibus spending legislation until the very last minute so that Democrats had to scramble to influence legislation without having much time to devise strategy. Frequently, Republicans prevented Democrats from obtaining access to critical information. Democrats had been denied meeting space on some occasions or have been locked out of conference committees. The House Rules Committee barely gave notification about meetings on important rules decisions, while the markup of most legislation was handled by party leaders, administration staff, and lobbyists without the consultation of members of the conference committees (Mann and Ornstein, 2006, pp. 172–73).

With control of the White House and Congress secured, congressional Republicans also strengthened the K Street Project. Begun in 1994, this was an effort by conservative legislators to master the campaign finance and lobbying systems that had emerged in the 1970s. Conservatives understood that, in order to thrive, they needed command over the relationship between private contributions, interest-group lobbying, and governance. Congressional Republicans felt that so many decades of Democratic rule had biased the entire Washington community against them. The connections between Congress and lobbyists had become all that much more important after the 1960s as the number of trade associations exploded in Washington and the costs of campaigns skyrocketed. Through the K Street Project, Republicans attempted to make certain that top interest groups hired Republicans who had worked in Congress or the White House, thereby ensuring GOP dominance over money in politics. After 2001, Senator Rick Santorum of Pennsylvania met every Tuesday on Capitol Hill with carefully selected lobbyists. They discussed new job openings and the best candidates for the positions.

The lobbyists in the K Street Project were usually devoted Republicans, who had been working with activists in the conservative movement for more than a decade. Jack Abramoff, for example, had become involved in politics while he was an undergraduate at Brandeis University. In the 1980 election, he helped organize, along with Grover Norquist (who was then a graduate student at the Harvard Business School), Massachusetts college students who supported Ronald Reagan for president. After the election, Abramoff and Norquist moved to Washington where they worked with the activist Ralph Reed to transform college Republicans into a national force. Following his experience with the college Republicans, Abramoff directed a small grassroots operation (Citizens for America) that lobbied for U.S. assistance to the anticommunist Nicaraguan Contras. The Republican takeover of Congress in 1994 convinced Abramoff to turn his energy toward lobbying. Abramoff met Tom DeLay's fund-raiser in 1995, and the two men would quickly form a strong alliance (Schmidt and Grimaldi, 2005).

The Abramoff and DeLay relationship was not unique. Following the election in 1994, Tom DeLay had sent a strong message when he put together a list of four hundred of the biggest political action committees along with the amount of money that they had contributed to candidates. Having asked the lobbyists to come to his office, DeLay revealed whether they were in the "friendly or unfriendly" column on his list. "If you want to play in our revolution," he told them, "you have to live by our rules" (Confessore, 2003). According to Grover Norquist, "Ninety percent of the new top hires are going to Republicans; it should be 100 percent . . . it would be suicidal of them to go to a Democrat" (Chaddock, 2003). The K Street Project was a well-orchestrated effort to solidify a machine with its own spoils system, namely jobs in the private sector, which was comparable to the urban Democratic machines from the Gilded Age that relied on public patronage (Confessore, 2003; Drew, 2005).

After the 2004 election, emboldened Republicans moved to further weaken the constraints on party leaders. When the new Congress convened, Republicans pushed through a rule change stipulating that the House would be required to dismiss an ethics complaint if the House Ethics Committee found itself in a deadlock. Previously, as a result of a 1997 modification, an investigation was automatically triggered if the ethics committee (which was split evenly between parties) did not act on a complaint within forty-five days. The change adopted in January 2005 diminished the chances for new ethics investigations. To be sure, Republicans decided against moving forward with other changes—including when the caucus decided to reinstate a party rule whereby an indicted member could not serve in the leadership (which they had just overturned a few weeks earlier to protect DeLay). The GOP reversed the decision, however, only after DeLay told them in closed-door session that he was confident he would not be charged and that the leadership feared the political costs of the recent decision. This change, which prevented an investigation if the ethics committee was deadlocked, was significant. As Zach Wamp, a Republican from Tennessee, said, the change removed "a ball and chain around our foot" (Allen, 2005).

Yet even in an era of homogeneous parties, united government, and skilled legislative leadership, the American state did not disappear. In fact it grew. During President Bush's first three years as president, federal spending increased from 18 percent of the economy in 1999 to 20 percent in 2003. Discretionary spending, which rose at a rate of 2.4 percent a year during the 1990s, grew by more than 27 percent in 2002 and 2003 (*Albany Times Union*, 2003).

Much of this money went toward nonmilitary items such as transportation, education, and farm subsidies. Despite the emphasis of the 1994 class on balanced budgets, the government was drowning in a sea of red ink by its ten-year anniversary. "If Bill Clinton had tolerated this," noted the *Wall Street Journal*, "Republicans would be shouting from the rooftops" (*Wall Street Journal*, 2003; see also Rosenbaum, 2003). When House Republicans gathered in Arizona in January 2004 to reminisce ten years after the Republican revolution, most of the talk was about what had gone wrong and why so many "revolutionaries" had compromised their principles. "After three years or so," said Michael Franc, vice president of the Heritage Foundation, "they went from revolutionaries to members of a committee or a state's delegation . . . They shifted their senses of identity, and it became a lot easier for them to say, 'Well we have to get this project.' They lost their way with respect to the size and scope of government." The new Republicans in 2005 promised that things would be different. "They came back to their senses," said Thomas Fitton, president of Judicial Watch, "We returned to our moorings, to our foundations . . . Those of us who remain are more committed to the reform agenda that brought us here" (Klein, 2005).

Republicans, moreover, have been struggling with the dangers that the legislative process poses to leaders of any party. During the period of reform in the 1970s, liberal Democrats had created numerous mechanisms that could be used to bring down congressional leaders in order to make certain that the legislative system did not facilitate the type of long-term, unchecked power that had existed in the committee era. Young conservative Republicans had depended on these mechanisms to attack Democrats when they were in the majority of the House and Senate and to weaken GOP leaders who had played to the center in the 1980s. Over a decade since the Republican takeover, conservative Republicans were finding themselves struggling on Capitol Hill. Majority Leader Tom DeLay was forced to resign in April 2006 after being indicted for campaign finance violations and implicated in a massive lobbying scandal. Senate Majority Leader Bill Frist of Tennessee has been under investigation for ethics violations involving his personal finances. A congressional sex scandal involving Mark Foley's interaction with underage pages—and evidence that the Republican leadership had failed to act on earlier warnings of this—wrought havoc on the GOP one month before the 2006 midterm elections. Key figures from the notorious K Street Group—including the lobbyists Jack Abramoff and Michael Scanlon and the legislators who they had worked with—came under scrutiny. Abramoff, the kingpin of the operation, pled guilty to criminal felony counts. Meanwhile, maverick Republicans and Democrats started to flex their muscle and cause serious problems for the GOP leadership.

As a result, one of the big questions remains whether conservative Republicans can survive the immense challenges that have emerged ever since the Bush administration stumbled in its response to Hurricane Katrina, faced its own ethics scandal with the indictment of Lewis "Scooter" Libby, and confronted questions about how it handled intelligence before starting the war in Iraq. "Conservatives are in power but out of sorts," complained the commentator David Brooks

(2005). "Fifty years after the founding of the modern right, conservatives hold just about every important government job, yet the conservative agenda has stalled." Republicans lost control of Congress in 2006. Democrats regained control of the White House in 2008, and kept the Senate after the brutal 2010 midterms.

Conclusion

America's Congress underwent significant reform in the 1970s at the hands of liberals who hoped to make the institution more progressive and accountable. But reformers learned that it is impossible to control these kinds of changes, as conservative Republicans proved to be extremely adept at operating in the new institutions to achieve political power. A new generation of Republicans who entered Congress in the 1970s and maintained close ties to the conservative movement, mastered the post-committee legislative process—both the decentralizing features that benefited the minority or mavericks, as well as the centralizing features that favored the majority leadership—and used the process to achieve influence in national politics.

But the political success of conservatism in Congress did not slay the dragon of the American state. Republicans watched as the state proved to be extremely durable in the conservative era—even as the GOP was able to chip away at its edges. Although there were some instances when retrenchment occurred, such as with welfare reform in 1996 and the federal tax intake after 2001, overall, the government remained substantial through 2009. Whether congressional conservatives can finally translate their political success into policy remains one of the most vexing puzzles of the twenty-first century. Republicans must also find out if they can succeed in the volatile nature of the political process upon which they have depended as they climbed to the top.

References

Albany Times Union. 2003. Big spenders. 24 November.

Allen, Mike. 2005. GOP shifts gears on ethics rules. *Washington Post*, 5 January.

Baker, Peter. 2000. *The Breach: Inside the Impeachment and Trial of William Jefferson Clinton*. New York: Scribner.

Balz, Dan. 1985. Frustrations embitter House GOP. *Washington Post*, 29 April.

Baumann, David. 2004. Grading the Class of '94. *National Journal*, 1 May.

Binder, Sarah. 1996. The disappearing political center. *Brookings Review* 14 (Fall): 36–39.

Birnbaum, Jeffrey H. 1984. GOP Conservatives join to assail Reagan on budget strategy. *Wall Street Journal*, 24 January.

Birnbaum, Jeffrey H., and Langley, Monica. 1987. House passes bill to increase taxes by $12.3 billion. *Wall Street Journal*, 30 October.

Black, Earl, and Merle Black. 2002. *The Rise of Southern Republicans*. Cambridge, MA: Belknap Press, Harvard University Press.

Borger, Gloria. 1988. The GOP's sleaze pinup: For Jim Wright and his Party, what goes around comes around. *U.S. News and World Report*, 20 June.

Broder, David. 1983. Opening GOP minds. *Washington Post*, 23 October.

Brooks, David. 2005. Running out of steam. *New York Times*, 8 December.

Carlson, Margaret. 1988. The foul stench of money; in Congress the scandal is not what's illegal—it's what's legal. *Time*, 4 July, 21.

Chaddock, Gail Russell. 2003. Republicans take over K Street. *Christian Science Monitor*, 29 August.

Clift, Eleanor, and Tom Brazaitis. 1996. *War without Bloodshed: The Art of Politics*. New York: Simon & Schuster.

Cohen, Richard. 1980. House GOP conflicts may surface if Party gains in fall elections. *National Journal*, 12 July.

———. 1981. The "Revolution" on Capitol Hill: Is it just a temporary coup? *National Journal*, 29 August.

———. 1982. His troops restless over the budget, GOP leader Michel is on the spot. *National Journal*, 20 February.

———. 1984. Frustrated House Republicans seek more aggressive strategy for 1984 and beyond. *National Journal*, 3 March.

———. 2003. In the House, a fleeting cease fire. *National Journal*, 26 July.

Confessore, Nicholas. 2003. Welcome to the machine. *Washington Monthly* 35, nos. 7–8 (July–August): 30–37.

Critchlow, Donald. 2004. When Republicans become revolutionaries. In *The American Congress: The Building of Democracy*, ed. Julian E. Zelizer, 703–31. Boston: Houghton Mifflin.

Crowley, Michael. 2003. Oppressed minority. *New Republic*, 23 June.

Dionne, E. J., Jr. 1991. *Why Americans Hate Politics*. New York: Touchstone.

Dodd, Lawrence C., and Bruce I. Oppenheimer. 1997. Revolution in the House: testing the limits of Party government. In *Congress Reconsidered*, eds. Lawrence C. Dodd and Bruce I. Oppenheimer, 29–60. 6th ed. Washington, DC: Congressional Quarterly Press.

Drew, Elizabeth. 2005. Selling Washington. *New York Review of Books*, 23 June.

Evans, Rowland, and Novak, Robert. 1985. The Michel/Gingrich split. *Washington Post*, 11 March.

Farrell, John Aloysius. 2001. *Tip O'Neill and the Democratic Century*. Boston: Little Brown.

Fenno, Richard F. 2000. *Congress at the Grassroots: Representational Change in the South, 1970–1998*. Chapel Hill: University of North Carolina Press.

Garrett, Major. 2005. *The Enduring Revolution: How the Contract with America Continues to Shape the Nation*. New York: Crown Forum.

Gingrich, Newt. 1983. Battle plan for business in politics: stand firm. *Nation's Business*, April, 30–32.

Ginsberg, Benjamin, and Martin Shefter. 2002. *Politics by Other Means: Politicians, Prosecutors, and the Press from Watergate to Whitewater*. 3rd ed. New York: W. W. Norton.

Gould, Lewis. 2003. *Grand Old Party: A History of the Republicans*. New York: Random House.

Gourevitch, Philip. 2004. The fight on the right. *New Yorker*, 12 April.

Hacker, Jacob S. 2004. Privatizing risk without privatizing the welfare state: The hidden politics of social policy retrenchment in the United States." *American Political Science Review* 98 (2): 243–60.

Hayward, Steven F. 2001. *The Age of Reagan: The Fall of the Old Liberal Order, 1964–1980*. Roseville, CA: Forum.

Hinckley, Barbara. 1971. *The Seniority System in Congress*. Bloomington: Indiana University Press.

Hodgson, Godfrey. 1996. *The World Turned Right Side Up: A History of the Conservative Ascendancy in America*. Boston: Houghton Mifflin.

———. 2004. *More Equal Than Others: America from Nixon to the New Century*. Princeton, NJ: Princeton University Press.

Jones, Charles O. 1999. *Clinton and Congress, 1993–1996: Risk, Restoration, and Reelection*. Norman: University of Oklahoma Press.

Katznelson, Ira, Kim Geiger, and Daniel Kryder. 1993. Limiting liberalism: The Southern veto in Congress, 1933–1950. *Political Science Quarterly* 108 (June): 283–302.

Key, V. O., Jr. 1949. *Southern Politics in State and Nation*. New York: Knopf.

Klein, Rick. 2005. House GOP seen straying from pledges in "contract.' *Boston Globe*, 10 January.

Lamb, Brian. 1998. *C-SPAN: America's Town Hall*. Washington, DC: Acropolis Books.

Mann, Thomas E., and Norman J. Ornstein. 2006. *The Broken Branch: How Congress Is Failing America and How to Get It Back on Track*. New York: Oxford University Press.

Matthews, Donald R. 1960. *U.S. Senators and Their World*. Chapel Hill: University of North Carolina Press.

McGirr, Lisa. 2001. *Suburban Warriors: The Origins of the New American Right*. Princeton, NJ: Princeton University Press.

Milligan, Susan. 2004. Back-room dealing a capitol trend. *Boston Globe*, 3 October.

Nash, George H. 1976. *The Conservative Intellectual Movement in America since 1945*. New York: Basic Books.

National Journal. 2001. The mean season at Ways and Means. 20 October.

———. 2003. Representative Tom Delay. 14 July.

O'Neill, Thomas P., and Novak, William. 1987. *Man of the House: The Life and Political Memoirs of Speaker Tip O'Neill*. New York: Random House.

Patterson, James. 1967. *Congressional Conservatism and the New Deal: The Growth of the Conservative Coalition in Congress, 1933–1939*. Lexington: University of Kentucky Press.

Perlstein, Rick. 2001. *Before the Storm: Barry Goldwater and the Unmaking of the American Consensus*. New York: Hill & Wang.

Plotke, David. 1996. *Building a Democratic Political Order: Reshaping America Liberalism in the 1930s and 1940s*. New York: Cambridge University Press.

Polsby, Nelson W. 2004. *How Congress Evolves: Social Basis of Institutional Change*. New York: Oxford University Press.

Polsby, Nelson W., Miriam Gallaher, and Barry Spencer Rundquist. 1969. The growth of the seniority system in the U.S. House of Representatives. *American Political Science Review* 63 (September): 787–807.

Reid, T. R. 1984. "Minority Objector" conscientiously flays foes with House rules. *Washington Post*, 21 March.

Remini, Robert V. 2006. *The House: The History of the House of Representatives.* New York: Smithsonian.

Ricci, David M. 1993. *The Transformation of American Politics: The New Washington and the Rise of Think Tanks.* New Haven, CT: Yale University Press.

Rogers, David. 1984. Assault from the Right. *Wall Street Journal,* 23 May.

Rohde, David W. 1991. *Parties and Leaders in the Postreform House.* Chicago: University of Chicago Press.

Rosenbaum, David E. 2003. Spending discipline proves unfashionable this year. *New York Times,* 25 November.

Schickler, Eric. 2001. *Disjointed Pluralism: Institutional Innovation in the U.S. Congress.* Princeton, NJ: Princeton University Press.

Schmidt, Susan, and James V. Grimaldi. 2005. Abramoff probe spells trouble for Congress. *Washington Post,* 29 December.

Schneider, William. 1989. New rules for the game of politics. *National Journal,* 1 April.

Schoenwald, Jonathan. 2001. *A Time for Choosing: The Rise of Modern Conservatism.* New York: Oxford University Press.

Shepsle, Kenneth A. 1989. The changing textbook Congress. In *Can the Government Govern?* eds. John E. Chubb and Paul E. Peterson, 228–66. Washington, DC: Brookings.

Shribman, David, and David Rogers. 1985. Relationship is tense between Republicans in House and Senate." *Wall Street Journal,* 1 May.

Sinclair, Barbara. 1989. *The Transformation of the U.S. Senate.* Baltimore: Johns Hopkins University Press.

———. 1997. *Unorthodox Lawmaking: New Legislative Processes in the U.S. Congress.* Washington, DC: Congressional Quarterly Press.

Smith, James A. 1991. *The Idea Brokers: Think Tanks and the Rise of the New Policy Elite.* New York: Free Press.

Smith, Steven S. 1989. *Call to Order: Floor Politics in the House and Senate.* Washington, DC: Brookings.

———.1998. *Managing Uncertainty in the House of Representatives: Adaptation and Innovation in Special Rules.* Washington, DC: Brookings.

Smith, Steven S., and Lawrence Eric. 1997. Party control of Committees. In *Congress Reconsidered,* eds. Lawrence C. Dodd and Bruce I. Oppenheimer, 163–92. 6th ed. Washington, DC: Congressional Quarterly Press.

Stephanopoulos, George. 1999. *All Too Human: A Political Education.* Boston: Little, Brown.

Thomas, Evan. 1984. Struggling for a Party's Soul: G.O.P. Factions Jockey for 1988, and Beyond. *Time,* 3 September, 34–37.

Thurber, James A. 1997. Centralization, devolution, and turf protection in the congressional budget process. In *Congress Reconsidered,* eds. Lawrence C. Dodd and Bruce I. Oppenheimer, 325–46. 6th ed. Washington, DC: Congressional Quarterly Press.

Time. 1988. The Speaker on the spot. 20 June, 31.

U.S. News and World Report. 1984."Choosing up sides for control of the GOP. 3 September, 23.

Viguerie, Richard A. 1981. *The New Right—We're Ready to Lead.* Falls Church, VA: Viguerie Company.

Wall Street Journal. 2003. The GOP'S spending spree. 25 November.
White, Joseph, and Aaron Wildavsky. 1989. *The Deficit and the Public Interest: The Search for Responsible Budgeting in the 1980s*. Berkeley: University of California Press; New York: Russell Sage Foundation.
Witcover, Jules. 2003. *Party of the People: A History of the Democrats*. New York: Random House.
Wolfensberger, Donald R. 2000. *Congress and the People: Deliberative Democracy on Trial*. Baltimore: Johns Hopkins University Press.
Zelizer, Julian E. 2004. *On Capitol Hill: The Struggle to Reform Congress and Its Consequences, 1948–2000*. New York: Cambridge University Press.

FOURTEEN

How Conservatives Learned to Stop Worrying and Love Presidential Power

The vast expansion of presidential power under President George W. Bush was as troubling for many on the right as it was for those on the left.* The conservative columnist George Will lamented that "conservatives' wholesome wariness of presidential power has been a casualty of conservative presidents winning seven of the past 10 elections."[1]

There is certainly a grain of truth to the claims of conservatives who didn't want to link themselves to a strong presidency, and in this respect they legitimately disassociated themselves from Bush. Twentieth-century liberals, until the 1970s, were the people who most actively promoted the importance of a powerful president. Following the presidency of Theodore Roosevelt, contemporary liberals came to believe that executive power was integral to achieving domestic reform, designing internationalist foreign policies, and overcoming the obstacles from the legislative and judicial branches. Franklin Roosevelt's presidency during the Great Depression and World War II became a model for liberal governance. Even liberal internationalists in Congress, such as Senator William Fulbright, who promoted diplomacy and warned of the need to avoid overextending the military, accepted the superiority of the presidency as an institution relative to the legislature.[2] One need only look at Arthur Schlesinger Jr.'s magisterial three-volume history of the New Deal published in 1957, 1958, and 1960, to gain a sense of just how much capacity liberals saw in the office of the president. In Schlesinger's narrative, Roosevelt heroically saved the nation from the depths of its economic crisis while preventing equally dangerous threats from the left and the right. Liberals continued to champion this vision until frustration among the New Left with President Lyndon Johnson's policies toward race and war, as well as the scandals of President Richard Nixon, created overwhelming fears of an "imperial presidency." These anxieties shattered liberal confidence in the executive branch.

* This essay appeared in *The Presidency of George W. Bush: A First Historical Assessment* (Princeton, NJ: Princeton University Press, 2010), ed. Julian E. Zelizer, 15–38.

Before the 1970s, moreover, there were some conservative activists skeptical of, if not downright hostile toward, presidential power. Contemporary conservatives had cut their teeth railing against the presidency in the 1930s. Senator Frederick Steiwer of Oregon said in 1933, "Italy is under a dictatorship; Russia is under a dictatorship; Germany is under a dictatorship, and those who are here pressing this legislation [the Economy Act and banking legislation] are seeking to put the United States of America under a dictatorship!"[3] Formed in 1934, the American Liberty League made such attacks central to their agenda. Roosevelt's court-packing plan and executive reorganization subsequently become symbols of how the president aimed to create the same kind of dictatorial government that existed in Japan and Germany. These kinds of arguments informed the writing of conservatives who feared the future of constitutional government. The warnings gained more power after the midterm elections of 1938, when conservative Democrats and Republicans were elected to Congress in large numbers. The bipartisan coalition of southern Democrats and Republicans used the committee system to block civil rights and union legislation that threatened their mutual interests. The conservative intellectual James Burnham published a book in 1959 in which he claimed that the founding fathers privileged the legislature: "Legislative supremacy was thus not a novelty for the Fathers, but a starting assumption . . . [T]he primacy of the legislature in the intent of the Constitution is plain on the face of that document [the Constitution]."[4]

Nonetheless, recent conservative criticism of the Bush presidency ignores how deeply ingrained presidential power has become to the conservative movement. Starting early in the Cold War, and vastly accelerating during the succeeding three and a half decades, a growing number of conservatives have learned to love the presidency. While conservatives have justified their position through arguments that the presidency is often the best way to achieve smaller and more accountable government, they have also counted on an aggressive and centralized presidency to pursue the aims of the conservative movement. Bush's presidency thus falls on a larger historical trajectory, even as he has clearly pushed this tradition far beyond its previous limits.

A key turning point was the 1970s, a decade that has come to be seen as more important in recent years.[5] For many conservatives, the congressional reforms that were passed in the aftermath of Watergate dangerously weakened the power of the executive branch and were a symbol of what went wrong as a result of the 1960s. The gradual delegation of authority to independent agencies, in this line of thought, had resulted in decisions being made by bureaucrats who were beyond the control of elected officials.[6]

The Nixon Years

Some conservatives, such as William Buckley, had come to accept during the early Cold War years that broader executive power would be essential in the fight against communism. Under President Dwight Eisenhower, some conservatives joined the president in warding off efforts by Republicans such as Senator John Bricker to curtail executive power. Buckley wrote that conservatives had to "accept Big Government for the duration—for neither an offensive nor a defensive war can be waged . . . except through the instrument of a totalitarian bureaucracy within our shores." He explained that Republicans "will have to support large armies and air forces, atomic energy, central intelligence, war production boards, and the attendant centralization of power in Washington—even with Truman at the reins of it all."[7]

But the conservative embrace of presidential power really began to take shape with the presidency of Richard Nixon between 1969 and 1974. Merging conservatism and presidential power was one of Nixon's most lasting achievements. Nixon identified as a conservative Republican who came of age during the anticommunist crusades of the early Cold War era. From the beginning of his presidency, Nixon demonstrated how presidential power could be an effective tool against liberalism. He entered office convinced that liberalism was powerful because the ideology had proponents that were entrenched in Congress, the media, the bureaucracy, and academia.

The fact that he took office in a time of divided government reified this perception. Despite his victory in 1968, Democrats had retained control of the House, 243 to 192, and the Senate, 57 to 43. Not only did Democrats control Congress, liberals had been gaining more power in the House and Senate as elections and reforms weakened the power of older southern Democrats and their conservative coalition. The president believed he faced a more difficult political atmosphere than had the last Republican president, Dwight Eisenhower. Nixon and his advisors felt that congressional Democrats were being driven by the party's most partisan figures and that the administration should use this in its public relations campaigns.[8] Nixon was infuriated when Senate liberals blocked two nominations for the Supreme Court in 1969. Top advisors lamented that "not since Zachary Taylor has a new President had to try to form a new Administration with a hostile Congress second-guessing every move."[9] In October 1969, Nixon told congressional Republicans that he wanted a "systematic program of putting the blame on Congress for frustrating the legislative program." Nixon targeted the "super-partisans" in the Democratic leadership, and he presented Congress as inefficient and incapable of governing.[10] Nixon perceived that liberals would work through the bureaucracy and regulatory bodies to defend their programs.[11] Therefore, presidential power was essential, Nixon believed, to undercut liberal power.

Nixon used several tools to curtail the influence of the Democratic Congress. For instance, the president relied on the impoundment of funds to prevent the use of money Congress had appropriated for specific domestic programs. He also attempted to expand domestic programs in ways that would be politically detrimental to Congress. When a debate emerged between 1969 and 1972 over the need to liberalize Social Security benefits to meet the rate of inflation, Nixon supported indexing rather than relying on the traditional route of discretionary increases by Congress. Legislators immediately realized this would deny them the credit—and the power—they had enjoyed since 1950, when Congress made benefit increases a normal part of the congressional calendar. In the end, Congress passed indexation and discretionary increases to satisfy both sides. In foreign policy, Nixon conducted national security operations in Southeast Asia without congressional knowledge. The liberal historian Arthur Schlesinger Jr. noted in his diaries that "Nixon has gone further, I guess, than any President in ignoring even the forms of congressional consultation. I fear that those uncritical theories of the strong presidency that historians and political scientists, myself among them, were propagating with such enthusiasm in the fifties have come home to roost."[12]

Most famously, Nixon depended on presidential power in his struggles against congressional investigation. He attempted to block the *New York Times* from publishing the *Pentagon Papers* (documents that held the real history of the Vietnam War) in 1971 by claiming executive privilege. He was stopped only when the Supreme Court deemed his actions unconstitutional. During the Watergate process, Nixon tried to withhold the famous White House tapes until the courts once again ruled he had to relinquish them. He also came under intense fire for authorizing covert programs through the White House to intimidate domestic protesters. Nixon claimed executive privilege on six different occasions.[13]

In response to Nixon, Congress passed reforms such as the War Powers Act (1973) and the Budget Reform Act (1974), which attempted to strengthen the role of Congress in key areas of the policymaking process. Although those reforms turned out to be less effective than their creators had hoped, at the time they were perceived as significant efforts to restore the balance between the branches of government.[14]

While Nixon demonstrated to conservatives how effective presidential power could be when turned against liberalism, his own relationship with the conservative movement became tenuous toward the end of his term. As president, Nixon attempted to build a broad coalition that could insure his reelection. He took positions on domestic and foreign policy that angered many on the right. The passage of landmark environmental policies and the indexing of Social Security defied any claims that this Republican was truly committed to reducing the size of the welfare state. Nixon's foreign policy of détente, moreover, opened diplomatic ties with Communist China and led to arms agreements with the Soviet Union. These dramatic steps by the administration angered right-wing Republicans like Ronald Reagan, who defined themselves in large part through their staunch anticommunism.

Notwithstanding Nixon's tensions with conservatives, as well as the embarrassment that Watergate caused the GOP, his use of presidential power against liberal objectives offered a model for the Right as the conservative movement took form in the 1970s. Many up-and-coming conservative policymakers would come out of the Nixon and Ford White House, including Richard Cheney and Donald Rumsfeld. They were deeply influenced by his strategy even as they distanced themselves from his tarnished legacy. In the November 1974 issue of the *National Review*, Jeffrey Hart called on conservatives to reexamine their long-standing opposition to a strong presidency, given that the executive was needed to tame the bureaucracy and liberal media.[15]

Congress Reforms the National Security State

Whereas Nixon demonstrated the strategy for conservatives to use presidential power, heightened congressional activism between 1974 and 1978 helped liberals see that a strong Congress was in their interest. The feeling of betrayal by Lyndon Johnson over Vietnam caused many Democrats to rethink their glorification of the White House as an instrument of progress. Those frustrations greatly intensified when a Republican was in the White House. One of Senator Fulbright's first major legislative moves in the Nixon era occurred on June 25, 1969, when the Senate, by a resounding vote of 70-16, passed the National Commitments Resolution stating that the Senate needed to repair the balance among the three branches of government when dealing with foreign policy.

The sense of optimism among liberals in the legislature increased further as a result of turnover in the membership, and institutional reforms that weakened the power of senior southern conservatives who had benefited from the committee system. This movement culminated in the election of the "Watergate Babies" in 1974, mostly Democratic legislators who promised to reform government and give Congress a greater role in policymaking and oversight. Senator Barry Goldwater called them the "most dangerous Congress" the country had seen, while CIA director William Colby noted that the new members were "exultant in the muscle that they had used to bring a President down, willing and able to challenge the Executive as well as its own Congressional hierarchy, intense over morality in government, [and] extremely sensitive to press and public pressures."[16]

During the presidencies of Gerald Ford and Jimmy Carter, congressional reforms to constrain the powers and common abuses of presidents angered many conservatives. Given the dynamics of the era, reform of the executive branch came to be seen as a liberal objective. Ford vetoed sixty-six bills in the span of his short tenure. He also created various policy commissions to enhance his influence. For instance, Ford created the Economic Policy Board (EPB) by executive order on September 30, 1974. The EPB was a joint cabinet-staff agency, headed by the secretary of the treasury and including a number of cabinet secretaries, the director of the Office of Management and Budget (OMB), the chairman of the CEA, and sometimes the chairman of the Federal Reserve. The president also created an Energy Resources Council and an Intelligence Oversight Board.[17] When Cambodia captured an American ship and its crew of thirty-nine in May 1975, the president sent in the Marines. The operation was a success, although forty-one Americans were killed. The president took these military steps in Cambodia without congressional authorization, despite the recently passed War Powers Resolution.

Notwithstanding this exercise of presidential power, many top members of the administration felt they were constantly on the defense. Congress was aggressive and, just as important, Ford's exercise of executive power was limited. Ford had to be cautious, given the turmoil that had unfolded surrounding Nixon's use of the presidency against his adversaries. As the historian Douglas Brinkley wrote in 2007, "throughout his 896 days in the White House, it seemed that Ford, the veteran Congressman from Michigan's Fiftieth District, didn't fully comprehend the massive executive power at his disposal."[18] Conservatives who were working in these administrations in the 1970s watched as Congress, sometimes with the hesitant endorsement of the president, rapidly expanded social regulations, including federal intervention in environmental issues, consumer protection, workplace safety, transportation, and more.[19]

The tensions over executive power were central to the CIA crisis that unfolded after an internal report in 1975 revealed the agency had sponsored assassination plots against foreign leaders. In the legislative branch, Idaho senator Frank Church chaired hearings that received substantial coverage in the press. The committee staff numbered ninety-two people at a cost of $2 million a year. Church's committee issued a report making a number of recommendations for reform, including restrictions on wiretapping, the harassment of domestic protest groups, assassination plots, and other forms of surveillance. "In the absence of war," Church argued, "no Government agency can be given license to murder. The President is not a glorified Godfather."[20] As the Senate deliberated, Church released portions of the findings on his own. Church also published articles in *Playboy* and *Penthouse*, to the chagrin of some of his advisors, who were thinking about his 1976 presidential run and conservative voters in Idaho. The Senate soon published a six-volume report and expanded oversight of the CIA. Representative Otis Pike organized similar hearings in the House, and information was leaked to papers such as the *Village Voice*. National Security Advisor Henry Kissinger called these leaks a "new version of McCarthyism."[21]

Ford, feeling pressure to disprove charges that he had attempted to whitewash the revelations about the CIA, issued an executive order on February 18, 1976, that granted the National Security Council greater power over intelligence gathering, established a Committee on Foreign Intelligence and Operations Advisor Group to monitor the CIA, as well as an Intelligence Oversight Board, imposed restrictions on surveillance, and banned assassinations of foreign leaders. Ford told Congress his reforms would "help to restore public confidence in these agencies and encourage our citizens to appreciate the valuable contribution they make to our national security."[22] In response to the Senate revelations, the FBI crafted a set of strict guidelines that curtailed the authority of officials in investigations.

Congress drafted legislation that mandated warrants for domestic surveillance. Despite the opposition of Ford, Cheney, and Rumsfeld, this would eventually pass as the Foreign Intelligence Surveillance Act (FISA) of 1978. President Carter, who had accepted the creation of the Senate and House Intelligence Committees in 1976 and 1977, agreed to this reform. He had made this promise in the campaign, in response to the Church committees. The bills were handled through the Intelligence and Judicial Committees, so Church did not play a central role in this final stage as much as Senator Birch Bayh (D-IN) and Edward Kennedy (D-MA) did. In the House, Eddie Boland (D-MA), who was the first House Intelligence Committee chairman, handled the bill. The House and Senate passed it over the objections of conservatives, who claimed that many of the prohibitions on intelligence gathering would hamper executive power, while at the same time many felt the creation of an independent court to monitor intelligence would remove this authority from a democratically elected president and give it to an unaccountable body of judges. Senator Bayh, who took over this issue in this final phase of the process as Church turned his attention to other issues, such as managing the SALT II agreements on the Senate floor, promised the bill would remove intelligence activities from the total control of the executive branch.

The boldest move was to give the courts authority over this matter, not just Congress. The conference committee made compromises, including the addition of a provision that exempted the National Security Agency from many of these regulations as long as the attorney general certified that a surveillance program met certain guidelines, a decision Kennedy said would place a high burden on the attorney general to ensure the guidelines were not violated. Boland insisted the exemption was needed to pass the measure in the House. Conservatives complained that the legislation would prevent the executive branch from conducting the kind of operations needed for national security. The four Republicans on the House Intelligence Committee—Ashbrook (OH), Robert McClory (IL), Bob Wilson (CA), and Kenneth Robinson (VA)—offered this as their dissenting view.

Building on a 1972 Supreme Court decision that deemed electronic domestic surveillance to be unconstitutional, the legislation created strict, judicially enforced procedures that had to be followed when any agency conducted foreign intelligence surveillance. The legislation thus established a legal infrastructure that criminalized particular national security activities by the executive branch. The new standard, according to Chairman Bayh, aimed to create "safeguards, against unjustified wiretaps of Americans on the basis of political activities."[23]

Although the final reforms were much milder than many critics had hoped for, and Congress did not dismantle executive power in the area of national security (Seymour Hersh lamented that the investigations "generated a lot of new information, but ultimately they didn't come up with much"),[24] conservatives did perceive the hearings and ensuing legislation as far-reaching, and the congressional decisions profoundly shaped right-wing perceptions about why the legislature was the most dangerous branch of government.

In addition, the 1978 Ethics in Government Act created the Office of the Independent Counsel (Title VI). The legislation was a response to Watergate and an effort to prevent future presidents from taking the kind of steps Nixon had taken with the Saturday Night Massacre (when he fired the special prosecutor investigating the scandal). Under the law, the attorney general would request the appointment of a prosecutor if there was evidence of wrongdoing in the executive branch. The attorney general was instructed to seek a prosecutor upon receiving "specific information" about violations of the law. Following the request, a three-person panel drawn from the U.S. Court of Appeals for the District of Columbia would appoint a special prosecutor to conduct an investigation. The prosecutor would have few budgetary or political restraints. The legislation constituted a substantial blow to presidential power by creating an unelected mechanism outside the full control of the executive branch to pursue charges of corruption.

Conservatives criticized the law as an unconstitutional and dangerous delegation of power. One congressional Republican warned that "if an attorney general cannot be trusted to enforce the law against the executive, the remedy is impeachment and not the cloning of an additional attorney general to do the job of the first."[25] Former President Ford lamented to the American Enterprise Institute that Congress was making an "imperial presidency . . . an imperiled presidency."[26]

The Conservatives' President

Ronald Reagan strengthened the marriage between conservatism and presidential power that had begun under Richard Nixon. Like Nixon, Reagan believed in the centrality of the presidency. His political role model was Franklin Roosevelt. However, Reagan quickly learned that Congress presented a major obstacle to conservatives, even when Republicans controlled the Senate between 1981 and 1987. When the president attempted to cut Social Security spending in 1981, he suffered a major defeat. A bipartisan coalition of legislators, under intense pressure from voters and interest groups, forced the administration to abandon its plans. Following the 1982 midterm elections, the number of liberal northern Democrats in the House increased. Congress took a number of steps that angered the White House, including a decision to increase taxes in order to cut deficits. House Democrats also passed amendments restricting assistance in Central America. Reagan believed in peace through strength. He thought the United States needed to demonstrate its willingness to use force in areas such as Central America if it wanted to create viable conditions for negotiating with the Soviet Union and its communist allies.[27] In the president's mind, congressional Democrats did not understand that by failing to support a strong defense, they undermined the possibility for peace.

In response, Reagan and his cabinet aggressively relied on executive power to achieve conservative objectives that otherwise would have been defeated. Through executive orders, for instance, Reagan attacked environmental policies that Congress defended. Under Reagan, the Executive Office of the President supported regulations that allowed the federal government to intervene in state authority over environmental programs. The White House enhanced the power of the OMB to exert more control over agencies and how they spent funds.[28]

Conservatives attempted to reconcile their acceptance of muscular presidential power with the antigovernment arguments. They claimed that stronger presidents were needed since twentieth-century liberals had abandoned the nondelegation doctrine (Article I, Section 1, of the Constitution, which granted all legislative power to the legislative branch) in favor of agencies that could make regulatory decisions. Centralizing control in the White House, they said, was thus needed to curtail other forms of government. At the same time, enhancing presidential authority could diminish the influence of institutions such as Congress or bureaucracies that were more prone to creating intrusive federal initiatives.

According to their writing, there were three reasons to support expansive presidential power on organizational grounds. The first was that centralized power produced a more efficient administration of policy. The second was that the president had greater capacity than Congress to coordinate decision-making and achieve the best results. The final argument was that a centralized presidency was more democratically accountable than other power-sharing arrangements.

Besides an acceptance of more expansive executive power to achieve conservative ends, there was a cohort of young attorneys in the Department of Justice that promoted the theory of the unitary executive. The ideas flowed out of a growing body of conservative legal scholarship in the mid-1980s that opposed the Office of the Independent Counsel on the grounds that it violated the president's total control over the executive branch (given that the courts appointed the prosecutor).[29] Proponents of these arguments insisted that all executive power should be vested in the president rather than disbursed among independent agencies.

Attorney General Edwin Meese's Justice Department became a nursery for conservative legal arguments that promoted an expansive vision of presidential authority. Lawyers associated with the Federalist Society helped to craft a new understanding of the separation of powers that enhanced the freedom of executive branch officials. Justice officials in the Reagan administration expanded the theory of the unitary executive so far as to claim that the Constitution created a total separation of powers so that no branch could infringe on the power of any other.[30]

Throughout the 1980s, the Department of Justice led the opposition to the Office of the Independent Counsel. Their constitutional concerns were probably compounded by the fact that Meese himself came under investigation from an independent prosecutor for being complicit in a scandal involving the Wedtech Corporation. The company had received generous no-bid defense contracts from the Department of Defense when Meese was their lobbyist (Meese resigned from the Justice Department in 1988).

Republicans in Congress defended executive power. Between 1968 and 1986, according to one study, conservatives in Congress voted for the pro-presidential-authority positions more often than other legislators. Presidents Nixon, Ford, and Reagan received far more votes from Republicans than from Democrats when seeking legislation concerning the power of the presidency.[31]

One of the most important moments for congressional Republicans took place during the Iran-Contra arms scandal of 1986. The scandal involved revelations that National Security Council officials had sold arms to Iran and used the money to provide assistance to the Nicaraguan Contras, assistance that Congress had prohibited. Congressional Republicans were not apologetic about what had happened, dismissing Democratic criticism as partisan and supporting the principles behind the administration's policies. The minority report, signed by eight Republicans on the Iran-Contra Committee, rested on the claim that the nation needed to vest tremendous power and accountability directly in the president.[32]

When all the major players implicated had escaped significant political or legal damage by the end of Reagan's presidency, conservatives became more willing to defend strong presidential power. The courts reversed the convictions of Oliver North and Admiral Poindexter. When President George H. W. Bush pardoned former secretary of defense Casper Weinberger, former national security advisor Robert McFarlane, and former assistant secretary of state Elliot Abrams shortly before the 1992 election, he did not apologize for their actions.

Conservatives were also furious with Independent Counsel Lawrence Walsh, who conducted a multimillion-dollar investigation of the administration on this matter (he was appointed in 1987). Congress extended the Independent Counsel Reorganization Act in 1987. Reagan signed the bill, though he thought it was unconstitutional. Upon signing the legislation, the president reiterated his concern that the policy allowed the judiciary to appoint prosecutors for the executive branch, thus violating the separation of powers. He expressed his disappointment with the fact that the legislature "has not heeded these concerns, apparently convinced that it is empowered to divest the president of his fundamental constitutional authority to enforce our nation's laws." The following year, the U.S. Court of Appeals for the District of Columbia struck down the law as a violation of the appointments clause of Article II of the Constitution and an infringement of the separation of powers.

But the Supreme Court in *Morrison v. Olson* ruled that the law was constitutional. Chief Justice William Rehnquist joined six other justices to argue that the independent counsel was an "inferior officer" and could be appointed by a panel of judges. The office was not independent because it remained subordinate to the attorney general. Justice Anton Scalia dissented, arguing that the law clearly aimed to undermine executive power: "That is what this suit is about. Power. The allocation of power among Congress, the President, and the courts in such fashion as to preserve the equilibrium the Constitution sought to establish . . . frequently an issue of this sort will come before the Court clad, so to speak, in sheep's clothing: the potential of the asserted principle to effect important change in the equilibrium of power is not immediately evident, and must be discerned by a careful and perspective analysis. But this wolf comes as a wolf."[33]

George H. W. Bush continued to champion executive power. In July 1989, William Barr, head of the Office of Legal Council, sent a memo to the counsels of each executive agency defending the concept of the unitary executive.[34] Throughout December 1990, Bush and his top advisors, including Secretary of Defense Cheney, insisted that congressional authorization to send troops to defend Kuwait against Iraq was unnecessary. The administration obtained a congressional resolution of support from Congress, but it never sought a declaration of war. In case there was any confusion on Capitol Hill, Bush stated that "my signing this resolution does not constitute any change in the long-standing positions of the executive branch on either the president's constitutional authority to use the armed forces to defend vital U.S. interests or the constitutionality of the War Powers Resolution."[35] Republicans in Congress were still in agreement about the presidency. In 1992, they blocked the renewal of the independent counsel law as they were furious about Walsh's multimillion-dollar investigation, which concluded shortly before the presidential election, producing a report that suggested Bush played a larger role in the scandal than he had previously indicated. Senate Republican leader Robert Dole called Walsh and his assistants "assassins," while the *Wall Street Journal* wrote that he had attempted to "criminalize policy differences."[36] Senator Carl Levin of Michigan complained that Republicans were "killing the most important single Watergate reform on the books."[37] Republican William Cohen, one of the architects of the original law, agreed, saying that if Clinton won the election, Republicans "might rue the day they presided over the final rites of this legislation."[38]

Bust most congressional Republicans agreed with Dole. In response to Levin, they pointed out that many Democrats were happy to let the law expire as they dealt with a series of scandals that rocked the House. Clinton and Attorney General Janet Reno persuaded Congress to restore the law in 1994. More Republicans supported the law, as Clinton was facing charges about his and his wife's role in an Arkansas land deal connected to the Whitewater Development Company (although many, like Iowa's James Leach, said that the attorney general was fully capable of making sure that a prosecutor remained independent).[39] Dole now said that "if there was ever a need, it is when one party controls everything."[40]

Facing Another Democratic White House

During most of the Clinton years, Republicans held control of Congress (with the 1994 elections) as Democrats secured their hold on the White House. Clinton continued the aggressive use of executive power. As partisan polarization and the frequent use of the Senate filibuster had made legislative deal-making more difficult on Capitol Hill, presidents from both parties saw incentives to working around Congress rather than through the institution. For example, Clinton withheld materials from Hillary Clinton's healthcare task force. He also created programs by using executive orders, such as prohibiting the construction of roads throughout national forests, providing Medicare coverage to patients who were participating in clinical trials, improving water quality standards, and more.[41] One of Clinton's most controversial actions was to rely on the 1906 Antiquities Act, which enabled the president to place sites under federal protection, to create numerous national monuments. The act did not allow subsequent presidents to reverse the decision through proclamations but only through legislation. Clinton protected more than two million acres of land in his final months as president.[42]

Republicans responded, but not consistently. Although conservatives had become much more comfortable with presidential power, they still harbored older fears about the executive branch and exhibited a sort of institutional schizophrenia. One factor behind their push against the presidency had to do with ideology. There were many Republicans who, like Newt Gingrich, believed in a strong role for the legislature in the nation's polity. Equally important, they had pragmatic reasons to resist presidential power now that their party no longer controlled the White House. Congressional Republicans tried to pass legislation and amendments that would limit presidential discretion in sending troops under UN command and for specific "nation-building" efforts. Most of these proposals failed. The most dramatic example of congressional attacks on the executive branch occurred later in the decade, when Republicans slowly whittled away at executive privilege during various fights over investigations and Clinton's impeachment.

Despite these efforts, the 1990s did not witness a complete philosophical reversal among conservatives against the presidency. Indeed, the Republicans' 1994 Contract with America, widely promoted by Newt Gingrich, included proposals for a line-item veto for the president. Speaker Gingrich and the 1994 Republicans attempted to repeal the War Powers Act. Unlike in the 1970s, when Democrats railed against the presidency once a Republican was in office and tried to pass reforms to constrain executive power, numerous prominent conservatives in the 1990s remained comfortable with a strong presidency despite having a Democrat in the White House. When the independent counsel law, one of the greatest symbols of congressional resurgence from the 1970s, expired on June 30, 1999, after the failed effort to remove Clinton from office, there were few members of either party excited about extending the measure. The Republican Congress happily allowed this measure to expire.

There were also a number of prominent conservatives who defended President Clinton when he bombed Kosovo without the authorization of Congress in 1999, and continued the operation even after the House of Representatives failed to authorize it. Berkeley law professor John Yoo, a young star in the world of conservative legal thought, argued that the Constitution supported Clinton's actions.[43]

Many of the conservative legal scholars who worked in Reagan's Department of Justice spent most of the 1990s working in the court system or teaching at law schools, where they refined arguments about the unitary executive theory and presidential power. These conservative legal minds would influence younger scholars and lawyers who found themselves on the front line of political debate in the next decade.[44]

The War on Terrorism

When George W. Bush was elected president in 2001, he continued to build on the conservative pro-presidential-authority tradition. Working with a cooperative and disciplined Republican majority, he pushed that tradition far beyond anything that had preceded it. Starting with Richard Cheney as vice president, he staffed the White House with conservative veterans of the 1970s and 1980s who believed that the executive branch remained the most effective base from which to assert themselves without having to compromise, as in Congress. Expanding presidential power was a central objective.[45]

The arguments that Republicans made in defense of the White House during the Iran-Contra arms scandal served as an intellectual foundation for how they felt domestic and national security issues should be handled in the twenty-first century.[46] Bush targeted the executive orders Clinton had used to circumvent Congress—by using executive orders. For instance, he issued orders that stopped the provision of assistance to international family planning groups and reversed Clinton's regulations on arsenic levels in drinking water.[47] Vice President Cheney crafted the administration's energy program in secrecy by coordinating with private industry officials. When Congress attempted to force the White House to release the records from these meetings, Cheney relied on an expanded claim of executive privilege—one that covered the vice president—to withhold the documents.

Indeed, Vice President Cheney was the driving force within the administration pushing for this understanding of executive power. Cheney, who had cut his political teeth in the interbranch battles of the 1970s while serving as chief of staff for President Ford, believed that congressional reforms had dangerously undercut executive power and that no president, including Reagan, had been able to reestablish a sound balance. Cheney, as he had explained in the Iran-Contra hearings, did not believe that Congress was an efficient institution and he felt that sometimes extraordinary measures were needed to make sure the nation was safe.[48]

Influenced by Cheney, the president focused his efforts on expanding what might be called the hard power of the presidency. It is useful to think about the distinction that diplomatic scholars have made between "soft" and "hard" power to describe how the United States influences nations overseas. In foreign policy, hard power involves the use of military force and economic sanctions to coerce opponents into accepting American demands. In contrast, soft power refers to a reliance on exporting cultural and ideological values—using the power of argument and the power of persuasion—to expand America's influence in a much more subtle fashion.

Bush's White House focused on expanding hard presidential power in terms of strengthening the institutional muscle of the office and using brute force to achieve its objectives. President Clinton had made these kinds of arguments as well, but he had followed the post–World War II route of justifying such actions on technical interpretations of the law while accepting certain congressional limitations on his authority. In contrast, the Bush administration made dramatic constitutional arguments about unbounded presidential power and was defiant, if not downright hostile, about any kind of congressional restrictions whatsoever.[49]

When responding to the 9/11 attacks, Alberto Gonzales (White House counsel), John Yoo (Department of Justice), and David Addington and Lewis Libby (both Office of the Vice President) claimed that executive power was essential to fighting the war. Convinced that congressional restraints on executive power had been responsible for the failure of the government to stop al Qaeda, the president's advisors sought authority to overcome the barriers imposed by FISA, which they said had hampered domestic intelligence operations. Gonzales argued there was a strong precedent to grant the commander in chief virtually unlimited power in war and that the president could not be bound by congressional law or international treaties. A high level of executive authority was needed, they added, in the current crisis, given that speed was essential to stopping irrational enemies of the United States who were stateless and capable of lethal attacks.

Gonzales designed a plan to liberate the executive branch and military officials from most international and domestic constraints when dealing with the detainment and prosecution of prisoners. The Office of the Vice President was the driving force, pushing Justice Department officials beyond their comfort zone, in obtaining an expansive view of how much torture was tolerable.[50] Based on the memos of Yoo and Addington, Gonzales insisted that the United States needed to abandon the "cops and robbers" model that had previously been used to deal with captured terrorists, a model that relied on normal judicial channels and due process protections, and instead shift toward a war powers model. By strengthening the hand of the president, Gonzales claimed, the government could achieve faster, speedier, and more efficient results. On November 13, President Bush signed a directive that called for the use of military tribunals to prosecute alleged terrorists. The Department of Justice would also produce a series of memos justifying the use of torture, including waterboarding.

Notably, the administration had the consent and cooperation of Congress. With Congress under Republican control from 2000 to 2006 (except for a brief period when the Senate was split in 2001), Republicans used the procedural rules to push through Bush's proposals. Congressional Republican leaders and the White House converged on an executive-centered approach to governance, from domestic to national security policies.

By 2004 and 2005, the media, third parties, and some members of both parties were criticizing Bush's understanding of presidential power. In April, for instance, the media reported that Bush had relied on presidential signing statements as a means of circumventing the legislature.[51] In *Hamdan v. Rumsfeld*, the Supreme Court ruled on June 29 that the military tribunals at Guantánamo violated the Geneva Conventions as well as the Uniform Code of Military Justice.

But the backlash against Bush's executive power had limited effect. After taking over Congress in the 2006 midterm elections, Democrats were unable to roll back the institutional changes implemented since 2001. Legislative efforts to curtail programs such as the national surveillance program have failed. Many conservatives, particularly with the issue of national security, remain firmly committed to a strong presidency and have no intention of reverting back to the nineteenth or even the early twentieth century. In January 2007, the Democratic Congress seemed flummoxed when Bush signed a directive that empowered the president to shape rules and policy statements related to public health, safety, the environment, and civil rights. The directive stipulated that all agencies would establish regulatory offices, run by political appointees, to oversee material that had an impact on industry.[52] Even with his presidential ratings reaching historical lows and conservatives in the presidential primaries openly nervous about the possible demise of the Reagan coalition, President Bush did not flinch from his defense of executive power. In March 2008, the president vetoed legislation that would have prohibited the CIA from using various types of interrogation techniques such as waterboarding.

As Bush's time in office came to an end, no apologies were made. Vice President Cheney told one reporter that "If you think about what Abraham Lincoln did during the Civil War, what F.D.R. did during World War II. They went far beyond anything we've done in a global war on terror. But we have exercised, I think, the legitimate authority of the president under Article II of the Constitution as commander in chief in order to put in place policies and programs that have successfully defended the nation."[53]

One of the great ironies of this presidency is that George W. Bush's administration, which worked harder than almost any other in recent memory to expand presidential power, ended with Americans thinking so poorly of the institution. According to a Gallup poll released in September 2008, public satisfaction with the executive branch reached its lowest level seen since Watergate. Only 42 percent of Americans said they had a "great deal" or a "fair amount" of trust in the executive branch, compared with 40 percent in April 1974.

The chances for restoring a better balance of power remain unclear. There was a notable silence in the 2008 campaign about this issue from either candidate. Since the election, the prospects for change remain murky. While congressional Democrats and President Obama have been extremely critical of Bush's muscular approach to the executive branch, with Obama having promised to reverse a number of executive decisions made by his predecessor, it is hard to tell how far he is willing to go. In the first few months of his administration, Obama made a few important moves to distinguish himself from Bush. He signed an executive order announcing that the Guantánamo interrogation facility would be closed, and he released top-secret documents from the Bush administration that revealed how certain forms of torture had been authorized. Yet there is still minimal evidence that Obama will substantially roll back the gains in presidential power. Indeed, it has been extremely rare for presidents in the postwar period to voluntarily relinquish power. Democrats in Congress might not be willing to do to Obama what they did to Richard Nixon or even to Jimmy Carter in the 1970s. After decades of Republican rule, Democrats now believe they have an opportunity to build a new majority, and in a time of true crisis there will be less incentive to challenge the institutional prerogatives of their president. When Obama threatened to use executive power if Congress attempted to gain the release of interrogation photographs, some Democrats complained, but ultimately agreed to let the issue go. The Department of Justice has protected secret spying programs established as part of the war on terror, and the administration has continued to take similar positions in court as Bush did with regard to the treatment of detainees. Since Obama's first year as president was a time of economic crisis and continued international danger, Democrats govern under the exact conditions that have traditionally been used since World War II to justify granting presidents expanded power.

Conclusion

Recent events have confirmed how conservatism and presidential power have become intertwined since the 1970s. The Right cannot legitimately divorce itself from strong presidential power. The war on terrorism has highlighted the reality that presidential power is integral, rather than aberrational, to modern conservatism. The relationship is more than simply a product of political pragmatism under conditions of divided government. Since the 1960s, the Right, rather than the Left, has been a much more vociferous champion of an all-powerful White House.

This historical account of conservatism and presidential power contributes to an expanding historical literature that is attempting to revise our knowledge about conservatism by demonstrating how conservatives have had a more complex and less adversarial relationship with the modern state than we previously assumed.[54] But even with their arguments about how centralized presidential power is necessary as a tool to restrain other forms of government intervention, conservatives must acknowledge that their movement, too, has helped build big government in America. Regardless of the reasons behind its expansion, centralized presidential authority is a significant form of government power, and the impact has been clear during the war on terrorism. Conservatives must reassess their own antigovernment rhetoric and reexamine the impact of the enormous expansion in executive power they have promoted over the decades.

PART IV

Politics and Policy: The Case of National Security

One of my biggest efforts has been to root the history of national security—a policy that has usually been described as separate and distinct from other issues—squarely within the domestic political realm. In "Détente and Domestic Politics" and "Conservatives, Carter, and the Politics of National Security," I show how debates over foreign policy can only be understood by taking into account domestic political forces. American policymakers rarely enjoy any kind of strong insulation from the campaign trail and they have almost always been forced to contend with the electoral pressures that emerge every two years.

My essays differ from the two prevailing approaches toward understanding this relationship. One of these is the literature on the growth of the "military-industrial complex." Scholars in several disciplines had looked at how World War II and the Cold War produced an iron triangle of defense contractors, congressional committee chairs, and Pentagon officials who coordinated to push for a bigger defense budget and who refused to allow for substantive reforms in the ways that the federal government spent defense appropriations. A second contingent of historians who were influenced by William Appleman Williams wrote about how economic interests determined what areas would be of concern to policymakers. Others looked at how national cultural ideals, such as imperialism or American Exceptionalism, to explain why a once isolationist country ended up in the business of state-building.

All of this work is important and provides useful arguments about American politics. The problem is that the analysis is so broad and generalized that it often doesn't help analyze the specific political battles that took place in Washington over time. This work is good at explaining the parameters of policymaking (although there are many specific cases that challenge each of these claims) but less helpful when dealing with the many important choices that are made, as well as the bitter and meaningful struggles that occur, within any consensus.

These works also tended to miss how certain essential dynamics in our democratic political system, such as the election cycle and partisan strategy, deeply impacted how elected officials thought about problems. The following essays stress how partisan interests, partisan ideologies, and inter-branch struggles for power were extremely central to the story. I challenge the conventional wisdom that national security did not matter to domestic politics because polls often show that voters rank this issue lower than other domestic problems. These polls, I have argued, confuse more than clarify. Most important, voters often form their opinions about how parties are doing in terms of leadership and performance after being exposed constantly to news coverage of politicians' handling of national security crises. Even if voters say that they are primarily concerned about the economy, their understanding of political performance is certainly influenced, consciously and subconsciously, by how they see officials deal with national security.

More important, politicians focus on national security so much because they don't want it to become a number one issue. They understand that when national security becomes more important than bread-and-butter concerns such as unemployment and jobs, it can be devastating and decisive politically. The stakes of avoiding political mistakes on national security questions are thus sometimes higher than with domestic issues—even if polls register that domestic concerns are more common. In addition to intra-partisan and inter-partisan battles, Congress and the president have, as I examine in "Congress and the Politics of Troop Withdrawal, 1966–1973," engaged in tough institutional turf battles to gain control over this issue.

In my effort to connect policy and politics through the history of national security, I have returned to an issue that concerned an older generation of political historians but which was relegated to the sidelines in recent decades, namely that elections matter. Debates over national security policymaking have been profoundly shaped by the electoral timetable. Ironically, too much recent work on political history, whether focusing on social movements or institutions, has downplayed this basic element of our political system. Washington time runs according to the political clock that is imposed by our constant election cycle requiring that every two years, a large number of politicians are forced to come up for reelection. Presidents and legislators never forget this and rarely do they find the space to govern on domestic or foreign policy problems outside of the electoral timetable. Even if a certain politician is not up for reelection, the coalition on which they depend usually is often at risk in the ballot box. In this final section, through national security, I attempt to unpack the connections between institutions, policy, and electoral politics that have shaped the nation's political development.

FIFTEEN

Congress and the Politics of Troop Withdrawal, 1966–1973

According to most politicians, pundits, and voters, the executive is the dominant branch of the U.S. federal government.* Despite a brief period in the 1970s when Congress reined in presidential power, the Imperial Presidency remains alive and well. National security has been the issue area where presidents have enjoyed the greatest increase in their strength. Presidents have become accustomed to sending troops overseas without obtaining from Congress a formal declaration of war and have sanctioned a vast expansion of the national security apparatus within the executive branch.

President George W. Bush is the most recent White House occupant to have expanded the power of the executive branch, continuing the steady emasculation of Congress that has been taking place since the Progressive Era. Confronting the greatest national security crisis since Pearl Harbor with 9/11, the administration insisted that it had to overcome perceived legislative excess by reinvigorating the executive branch.

Yet concern about legislative encroachment on executive prerogatives has been neither partisan in origin nor unique to the Bush administration. Republican and Democratic presidents dating back to Harry Truman have all been frustrated by the power of Congress on matters involving national security. Consider, for example, congressional activism following Truman's recall of General Douglas MacArthur from Korea, or Ronald Reagan's efforts to evade Congress in pursuing anti-Communist policies in Central America, or George H.W. Bush's concerns about congressional support prior to and during the 1991 Gulf War, or especially Bill Clinton's troubles with Congress over allowing homosexuals to serve in the military or the conduct of peace-keeping missions in Somalia, Bosnia, and elsewhere. But the most conspicuous example of efforts to reassert congressional control over U.S. foreign policy came during the Vietnam

* This essay originally appeared in *Diplomatic History* 34 (2010): 529–41. Copyright © 2010. With permission of John Wiley and Sons.

War. The politics of a U.S. troop withdrawal from Vietnam during the 1960s and 1970s offers a window into the multitude of strategies Congress employed to check an imperial executive and to regain its constitutional prerogatives.

When the war in Vietnam escalated in 1964 and 1965, most policymakers, including Lyndon Johnson, were very sensitive to the role Congress might play in its evolution. As has been well documented, the Vietnam-era Congress had many failings. Lawmakers too often deferred to presidential decisions that they knew to be flawed. They hesitated to challenge presidents directly. Democrats and Republicans took action after the fact and agreed to watered-down compromises. Most importantly, Congress never forced an immediate end to the war. To the contrary, in 1964, Congress granted the president broad authority to use force, and in the late 1960s and early 1970s it continued to fund military operations after the war had turned into a quagmire.[1]

But the Congress also left behind a significant record of challenging presidential decisions and helping to create the political pressure that led to a drawdown in U.S. troops fighting war. Historians have devoted a great deal of attention to the antiwar movement that rocked college campuses and produced huge marches on the streets of our cities. They have paid much less attention to the legislators on Capitol Hill who popularized antiwar arguments among middle-class Americans and the media, threatened and cajoled the president, and gradually circumscribed the political options that were available to Richard Nixon as he started his first term.[2]

Criticism about the war in the mainstream press gained momentum as a result of congressional hearings. Before grassroots antiwar protesters had started to impact American society, one prominent liberal internationalist, Senator J. William Fulbright, brought the problems with the war to the forefront of public debate. Fulbright (D-AR) was the chair of the Senate Foreign Relations Committee, which conducted hearings in February 1966, parts of which were broadcast on national television. In an effort to distract the public, the administration convened a summit with the South Vietnamese in Hawaii the night before the hearings began. But the strategy did not work. The hearings captivated public attention. The nation watched as Fulbright and his colleagues grilled administration officials and former policymakers such as Secretary of State Dean Rusk, George F. Kennan, and Former Ambassador to South Vietnam Maxwell D. Taylor. Fulbright directly challenged the claims of Rusk and others, rejecting the notion that South Vietnam was essential to American interests and that the United States, therefore, had no choice but further escalation of the war. The significance of the hearings, according to Fulbright biographer Randall Bennett Woods, was that they "opened a psychological door for the great American middle class . . . if the administration intended to wage the war in Vietnam from the political center in America, the 1966 hearings were indeed a blow to that effort."[3]

Fulbright's activism extended beyond Capitol Hill. Delivering the Christian Herter lectures that May at the Johns Hopkins University School of Advanced

International Studies, Fulbright argued that the United States had misused its military power. In one of the most provocative portions of his speech, Fulbright said that "both literally and figuratively, Saigon has become an American brothel." He then published his thoughts in *The Arrogance of Power*, a book that quickly moved to the top of the *New York Times* bestseller list and sold over a million copies. According to the historian Ronald Steel, whose review appeared in the *Washington Post*, the book "mark[ed] the passage of Senator Fulbright from a relatively orthodox supporter of the liberal line on foreign policy to a spokesman for the post-cold-war generation."

Fulbright focused his remarks on other issues as well, including reports of covert activities by the CIA. He turned against executive power as he came to believe that presidents had been pursuing imperialist aims, abusing the authority granted to them. In the coming year, Congress would hold hearings on other war-related issues, such as the draft, employing the power of investigation to cause immense problems for the president. While many factors, including the antiwar movement, stoked opposition to Johnson's policies, congressional hearings and criticism by legislators such as Fulbright were crucial elements in the expansion of such opposition beyond the college campuses and the New Left. The Fulbright hearings played a role in that development, as Johnson's advisors recognized. As presidential assistant Joseph Califano put it, "the Fulbright hearings particularly are doing a tremendous amount to confuse the American people."[4] Likewise, Senator Barry Goldwater (R-AZ) accused Fulbright of having given "aid and comfort to the enemy" through his words.[5] In their many encounters through the end of his presidency, Johnson was constantly frustrated by his inability to win over Fulbright, whom he derided as "Senator Halfbright," with his famous "treatment."

But congressional pressure on Lyndon Johnson came from the political Right as well as the Left, especially as the looming 1966 midterm elections helped push Johnson deeper into war. In our efforts to find when Congress has or has not caused presidents to curb military operations, historians have often overlooked how Congress has created pressure on the executive branch to intensify its use of force. Conservatives had never been thrilled about the war in Vietnam, believing it to be a distraction from the need for a military buildup to match Soviet power as well as from their ongoing concern about China. Once war started, conservatives supported the operation—Senate Republicans, such as Everett Dirksen, were the president's strongest allies—but they called for a strategy that focused on intense bombing, limited ground troops, and a quick exit. As the war dragged on, Republicans became increasingly critical and cited Johnson's failure to adopt their strategy as an example of how Democrats were mishandling the Cold War. Former Vice President Richard Nixon led the charge, traveling around the country and criticizing the administration's policies as he stumped for Republican candidates.

Johnson was very sensitive to these kinds of political attacks. After all, politics had been crucial to the president's decision to escalate America's involve-

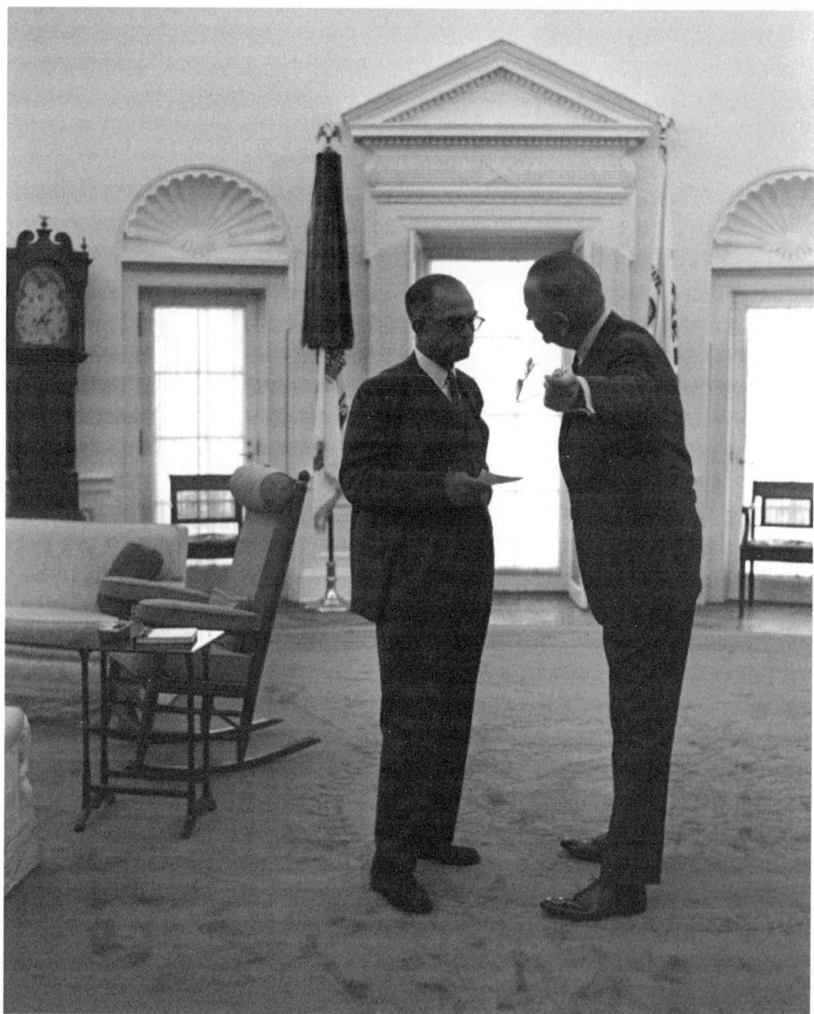

Figure 15.1. Senator J. William Fulbright speaking with President Lyndon Baines Johnson. LBJ Library, Austin, Texas. Photo by Yoichi Okamoto, C9834-21A, May 1, 1968.

ment and to sustain the country's presence in the region even as the conflict became troublesome. Johnson remained extremely sensitive to congressional Republicans who were criticizing the president's timidity at using air power and demanding an intensification of the bombing campaign. He had served as Senate Minority and Majority Leader in the 1950s, when the Grand Old Party (GOP) effectively used attacks about "Who Lost China?" to undermine his party's national security advantage that FDR had achieved with World War II. While Johnson shared Republican concerns and said so privately, he publicly dismissed critics of the war, largely because he feared that Democrats could lose control of the House. "If we lose the Congress, as we could very well," Johnson told Secretary of Defense Robert S. McNamara on May 7, "then the next two years, as we go into election, they'll tear the Democratic Party wide open and it will be in much worse shape than it was when [Illinois governor Adlai E.] Stevenson took it in '52 for the '68 election . . . liberals are not prudent folks, and they don't evaluate carefully and they don't see that."[6]

Although the 1966 midterm election outcome was not as bad as Johnson had feared, Republicans increased their numbers in the House by forty-seven seats and by three seats in the Senate. They also gained seven hundred state legislative seats (thus reversing losses from 1964) and eight governorships. The conservative coalition was thus reinvigorated after the devastating defeats of 1964. Polls indicated that concern over the war was central to Republican success, as voters were seeking a way to bring the conflict to an end.

Congressional moderates from the southern wing of the Democratic Party also forced Johnson to deal with the budgetary consequences of the war, further alienating mainstream liberals from the mission. While Johnson believed that he could fund both domestic and wartime spending, some members of Congress, including conservative Democrats, forced him to make difficult choices. In January 1967, Johnson agreed to a tax surcharge to quell the inflationary impact of the war and to continue to fund the War on Poverty. But objections came from Wilbur Mills (D-AR), the chairman of the powerful House Ways and Means Committee, which controlled taxation. Mills was a southern fiscal conservative, and he argued that if the administration wanted to increase taxes, it would have to reduce domestic spending. He feared that tax reductions would be undercut by the costs of Vietnam and the Great Society. Mills insisted that Johnson would have to decide between guns and butter.[7]

While the administration agreed to spending cuts, it did not want to go as far as Mills. The confrontation escalated in 1968 when an international financial crisis put intense pressure on the United States to lower the budget deficit. Johnson used the crisis to try to influence Mills. During one conversation, Johnson promised him that he would not try to go around him through the Senate: "I'm not going to screw you. I'm going to put this on you . . . I think we're in the most dangerous thing I ever saw in my life and I think it is going to blow right in our face and ruin all of us, and all of us go down together." Johnson told Mills that he was boxed in and did not have more room to compromise on spending cuts. Southern Democrats did not like him to begin with and the Republicans would not support the president, so all he had left were "regular" Democrats who did not want spending cuts. Therefore, the decision came down to Mills. But the administration blinked anyway, as Johnson agreed to accept $6 billion in budget cuts so that Congress would pass the tax surcharge.[8]

While conservatives were not happy with the tax hike, they were eager to curb the deficit and strike a blow against the Great Society. Budget cuts put a damper on the movement by liberals toward further programmatic expansion at the domestic level. At the same time, the tax surcharge revealed clearly to liberals the costs of the war and the kind of trade-offs they needed to make. Liberal support for the war further deteriorated as these costs became increasingly clear.[9] And with Democrats losing House seats in 1966, the conservative coalition in both the House and Senate increased its strength.

By the time that Richard Nixon was elected president in November 1968, the antiwar coalition had expanded in Congress to include former Democratic hawks, such as Democratic senator Stuart Symington of Missouri, and northeastern liberal Republicans like New York senator Jacob Javits. With party discipline being weak and the committee system allowing legislators to work across party lines, bipartisan alliances were common in this period.

Nixon's presidency quickly changed the political dynamics of the war with the creation of divided government. A few months into the Nixon administration, Senator Fulbright visited the president. Pointing to polls, which showed that a majority of the nation opposed the war, Fulbright warned Nixon that his honeymoon would not last long and that the conflict would soon be known as "Nixon's War." Similarly, Senate Majority Leader Mike Mansfield wrote the president a letter, urging him to announce a unilateral cease-fire and immediate withdrawal. Nixon, Mansfield argued, could claim that he had no choice but to end the war because of the pressure from liberals. Nixon refused to take the bait, yet he did understand that he needed a strategy in between immediate, complete withdrawal and the continuation of the status quo.[10]

His chosen path, Vietnamization, pleased many in the antiwar coalition since it constituted a gradual withdrawal of American troops. The United States, according to this policy, would take its troops out of the region slowly while allowing the South to fight the ground war on its own. Nixon's decision was extremely political. After having observed the turmoil that engulfed his predecessor, Nixon was convinced that ending the Vietnam War was essential if he wanted to break the back of the Democratic Congress and the liberal media.

Initially, many antiwar Democrats, such as Senator Frank Church of Idaho, were enthused that they had won the debate and that this was the beginning of the end. Church said that "Too much blood has been lost, too much patience gone unrewarded, while the war continues to poison our society. If the Executive Branch will not take the initiative, then the Congress and the people must."[11] Indeed, National Security Adviser Henry Kissinger was extremely concerned about Vietnamization; he feared it would lead to a total withdrawal in the near future and thus undermine America's standing abroad. Kissinger said the American public would become addicted to withdrawal like "salted peanuts . . . the more U.S. troops come home, the more will be demanded."[12] Nixon subsequently agreed that the withdrawals would not wind down until *after* the 1972 election in order to protect himself from the right wing of his party.

But using Vietnamization to break the back of Congress entailed working with it, and it was here that personal networks between Congress and the White House allowed for legislative influence on the withdrawal process. Former representative Melvin Laird (R-WI), who served as Nixon's secretary of defense, was the liaison to legislators who opposed the war. Laird was the administration's prime mover behind both Vietnamization and the shift to a professional army, which took place in 1973 when the government ended the draft. Like his former Wisconsin constituents, Laird was profoundly uneasy with Vietnam. As defense secretary, he worked with legislators who assisted him in building support for the withdrawal plans, just as Congress was able to promote antiwar sentiment within the administration through the Pentagon's leadership. "I knew that time was running out for us," Laird later acknowledged, "because the public wasn't going to support the war any longer."[13]

Notwithstanding the huge political shift that occurred with Vietnamization, congressional Democrats continued to place immense pressure on the administration. There were strong demands from Congress to cut defense spending. Nixon and Kissinger perceived this as the political reality of the era. Senator Ted Kennedy said that "We should not repeat the mistakes of the fifties and sixties, when we overreacted to cold war fears and helped to stimulate the spiraling arms race . . . Since the federal budget is being sharply cut in so many areas, no aspect of military expenditures should be free from scrutiny."[14] In addition, the schedule of gradual withdrawal, combined with Nixon's covert program of bombing, resulted in distrust on Capitol Hill and a growing sense that the war would never really come to an end. On June 25, 1969, the Senate, by a vote of 70-16, passed a "national commitments" resolution stating that Congress needed to reclaim its power. Later that summer, after the administration acknowledged a secret plan to help fight any insurgency that might erupt in Thailand, Congress pressured Nixon to announce a reduction of the U.S. military presence there. And following a two-week trip to Southeast Asia, Mansfield demanded that Nixon start reducing the size of U.S. military forces in the region. Some Republicans joined in. New York GOP representative Charles Goodell proposed a bill that would establish a deadline of December 1970 to pull troops out of Vietnam. Fulbright also announced that he would hold new hearings on the war. And Senator Fred Harris, chairman of the Democratic National Committee, said he would "take the gloves off" with the president.[15]

On December 6, 1969, Congress finally used the power of the purse. In a closed-floor session, Senators Church and John Sherman Cooper (R-KY) offered an amendment to a defense spending bill to prevent the further use of money in Laos or Thailand. The amendment received the support of seventy-three senators. Church called the amendment a "reassertion of congressional prerogatives" on foreign policy. It survived the House-Senate conference committee and Nixon signed the legislation.

But in the spring of 1970, Church and Cooper became concerned that Nixon was planning to use military force to support General Lon Nol, who had recently taken over Cambodia in a coup. Following Nixon's televised speech on April 30, in which he revealed that he had authorized a combined bombing and ground attack on North Vietnamese forces in Cambodia, Church and Cooper offered a new amendment that extended the 1969 prohibition to include Cambodia.

The administration mounted an intense lobbying effort to keep legislators from supporting the amendment. The American Legion sent letters to senators warning of such action. White House Chief of Staff H. R. Haldeman authorized the use of "inflammatory types [such as Senators Robert Dole and Barry Goldwater] to attack Senate doves—for knife in back disloyalty—lack of patriotism." Nixon told his advisors to "hit 'em in the gut."[16]

Following an intense seven weeks of floor debate over the constitutional balance of power, the Senate voted on June 30, 1970, to pass the Church-Cooper amendment with fifty-eight votes. The amendment stipulated that the administration could not spend funds for soldiers, combat assistants, advisors, or bombing operations in Cambodia. To broaden support for the measure, the sponsors agreed to alter the language for the amendment to work "in concert" with the administration's policies. They also declared that the amendment did not deny any constitutional powers to the president. In his memoirs, Henry Kissinger recalled that "Senate opponents of the war would introduce one amendment after another, forcing the Administration into unending rearguard actions to preserve a minimum of flexibility for negotiations." He added that "Hanoi could only be encouraged to stall, waiting to harvest the results of our domestic dissent."[17]

Fulbright played a diminished role at this stage in the debate, in large part because he found himself allying with Henry Kissinger in promoting détente—the easing of tension between the Soviet Union and the United States. Fulbright respected Kissinger's objectives, and the two men got along extremely well. Fulbright also thought that the best way to restrain the president was to build public opposition to the executive branch rather than by relying on legislation.[18]

In contrast to the seven-week debate in the Senate, it took the House less than an hour to table a motion instructing conferees to agree to the Church-Cooper amendment. In response, Church and Cooper compromised on several matters, such as a provision to limit the amendment to a supplemental aid bill that passed both the House and the Senate. While the authors understood that Nixon was already taking troops out of Cambodia and that the measure would have limited effect, it was nonetheless another political blow to the president and a warning of how far he could go. Congress sent the measure to the president in late December. While some antiwar critics preferred the Senate amendment proposed by South Dakota Democrat George McGovern and Oregon Republican Mark Hatfield, which would have required a withdrawal of forces from Vietnam by the end of the following year, the passage of the Church-Cooper amendment marked the first successful use of congressional budgetary authority to limit the war.

The legislative pressures behind the amendment convinced Nixon that he would have to restrict ground operations in Cambodia and elsewhere. State Department William Bundy recalled that "the Cooper-Church Amendment, and the sentiment it represented, continued to hang over the White House." Nixon National Security Council staffer John Lehman later said that "the impact on executive policies actually ran much deeper. It . . . narrowed the parameters of future options to be considered. Everyone was aware that ground had been yielded and public tolerance eroded." Opinion polls revealed that by the winter of 1970, 84 percent of the public supported the withdrawal of U.S. troops. A mere 7 percent stated that they supported an escalation of the fighting.[19] The proposals to restrict funds and to pursue withdrawal produced intense pressure on Nixon to bring an end to the war on his own terms before his legislative opponents gained too much ground. During Nixon's first term, Congress had conducted eighty roll call votes on the war; there had been only fourteen between 1966 and 1968. Congress also repealed the Gulf of Tonkin Resolution. In 1971, Mansfield attached an amendment to three pieces of legislation that required the withdrawal of U.S. forces nine months after their passage. The White House warned that the president would not abide by this declaration. Congress agreed to pass the amendment, but only after deleting the withdrawal date and declaring it to be a sense-of-Congress resolution rather than a policy declaration.

While the Senate watered down the amendment, the expanding number of supportive votes made the administration well aware of active opposition in Congress. In 1972, Church and Republican senator Clifford Case of New Jersey obtained support for an amendment to foreign aid legislation that ended funding for all operations in Southeast Asia, except for withdrawal (subject to the release of prisoners of war). When the Senate passed the bill, with an amendment attached, it marked the first time either chamber had adopted a provision that cut off funds for the war. Though House and Senate conferees failed to reach agreement on the measure, the administration interpreted its general support as another sign that antiwar forces were gaining strength. Earlier poll results had shown that public support for the McGovern-Hatfield amendment stood at 73 percent.

During the final negotiations with the Vietnamese over ending the war, culminating with the 1972 Christmas Bombings and the Paris Peace Accords in January 1973, the president knew he had limited time before Congress used the power of the purse to bring the war to an end altogether. Indeed, to make certain that the president could not reverse course, Congress, in June 1973, passed legislation that included an amendment sponsored by Church and Case to prohibit the use of more funds in Southeast Asia after August 15. Sixty-four senators voted in favor. When the House assented, its vote marked the first time that chamber had also agreed to cut off funds.

More importantly, Congress passed the War Powers Act in 1973 over Nixon's veto, imposing restrictions on the executive branch to ensure that the president would have to consult with the House and Senate before deploying troops for longer periods of time. The final blow to executive latitude came in April 1975, when Congress denied President Gerald R. Ford's budgetary requests for additional funding for Vietnam. By the end of the month, the enfeebled leadership of South Vietnam would surrender to the advancing Communists, a moment that Ford described as "the saddest hour of my time in the White House."[20]

Many policymakers were seriously concerned about the assertive stance of Congress. Serving as chief of the U.S. Liaison Office in the People's Republic of China in February 1975, George H. W. Bush noted that State Department and Chinese officials were apprehensive over the implications of such newfound power. "The State Department worries about whether they will be able to keep commitments. I am wondering what other governments will say if they see us make commitments and then have the Congress undo them. There has got to be close cooperation or something to guarantee that we can keep our commitments. The mood was gloomy at State over Vietnam and Cambodia and there seems to be no will by the Congress to fulfill commitments already made."[21]

Indeed, the battles over troop withdrawal became a precedent for Congress to take other sorts of actions. Legislators, for instance, have used their power over the purse to limit presidential options on the size and structure of the defense budget. Substantive reforms to the composition of the defense budget have been virtually impossible since the early Cold War. Legislators who depend on government funds for defense contractors in their states and districts, as well as military bases, have been steadfast in their opposition to executive efforts to cut or redirect spending. In addition, when presidents have attempted to initiate base closings, they often ran directly into congressional roadblocks. In 1977, Congress created a process that made base closing so difficult that none were shut between 1977 and 1991. The process required that the secretary of defense provide a formal request for closing a base with the annual appropriations proposal, as well as the likely economic, environmental, fiscal, and strategic effects of the closing. This left considerable room for legislators to block the request.[22]

In the aftermath of Vietnam and congressional hearings about the secret activities of the Central Intelligence Agency (CIA), Congress enacted the Foreign Intelligence Surveillance Act (FISA) in 1978. The FISA legislation created strict, judicially enforced procedures for conducting foreign intelligence surveillance.[23] The legislation created a legal infrastructure that criminalized particular national security activities by the executive branch. Senator Birch Bayh of Indiana boasted that the legislation "is a triumph for our constitutional system of checks and balances. It establishes that the authority to conduct foreign intelligence surveillance in this country will be shared by all three branches of the government. It will no longer be the exclusive domain of the executive branch."[24] As Jack Goldsmith has argued, the infrastructure was a powerful force in shaping how the Bush administration responded to 9/11.[25]

Congress would continue to exert its influence in the coming decades. During the 1980s, legislative restrictions pushed the executive branch toward covert and, some say, illegal methods for sending funds to the Nicaraguan Contras, a development that led to the Iran-Contra scandal in 1986. Congressional pressure has also influenced presidential decisions to launch military operations. Opposition to Panamanian strongman Manuel Noriega came from liberal Democrats, such as Massachusetts senators John Kerry and Edward Kennedy, who called for tougher sanctions on Noriega because of his human rights abuses, and from conservative Republicans, like Senators Jesse Helms (NC) and Alfonse D'Amato (NY), who believed that Noriega made a mockery of the "War on Drugs" that the GOP had been promoting. The subsequent invasion of Panama, with its congressional origins, became a template for the use of force after Vietnam.

In 1991, President George H. W. Bush sent troops to Kuwait to fight the invading Iraqi forces. Bush sought a resolution from Congress, though many of his advisors, including Secretary of Defense Richard Cheney, did not think he needed it. But Bush, remembering Vietnam, decided that congressional support would be politically valuable. Though many Democrats opposed the resolution, the vote was helpful as Bush built his coalition. Realizing that his congressional backing was thin, though, Bush felt extremely reluctant to broaden the mission beyond Kuwait and, in the end, rejected proposals to march on Baghdad. Many factors influenced this decision, but fears about triggering congressional opposition—grounded in memories of the 1970s—were crucial considerations.

Following a disastrous humanitarian effort in Somalia in 1993, Congress passed legislation stating that the United States had to be taken out of the UN operation by March 31, 1994. Congress imposed further restrictions on President Clinton in the late 1990s, limiting the president's military options. Following the 9/11 attacks, the Bush administration shaped specific proposals during the debates over the creation of the Department of Homeland Security and military tribunals based upon what they anticipated Congress would desire. Indeed, the proposal for a Department of Homeland Security emanated from Congress, not the executive branch.[26]

In the most recent battle over Iraq, the Republican Party made a deliberate decision in 2002, with Democratic support, to authorize the use of force to remove Saddam Hussein's regime. Republicans were motivated by strategic imperatives stemming from the neoconservative and nationalist Republican belief that Iraq constituted a central threat in the Persian Gulf region. They were also moved by their desire to solidify their electoral advantage on national security issues that was amplified after the attacks of 9/11. Similarly, the outcome of debates over changing course in Iraq resulted directly from a cohesive and disciplined Republican minority effectively using its power to defend the status quo.

As the 2008 election came to a close, the influence of Congress was once again evident in debates over foreign policy. The Democratic takeover of Congress in 2006 changed the terms of public debate over Iraq, shifting discussion toward the need for an exit strategy. While Bush resisted legislative pressure to begin an immediate withdrawal, he did undertake a surge of troops and reorientation of military strategy that focused on winning the support of local Iraqis rather than defeating insurgents. Though most Democrats perceived that Bush was ignoring public opinion, in fact the surge reflected the president's understanding that the status quo was no longer tolerable.[27] By 2008, Bush had agreed to a schedule for ending American involvement in the war. Americans elected a president, Senator Barack Obama (D-IL)—part of the coalition in the Senate pushing for an end to the war—who promised to fulfill the hopes of his colleagues. By late November 2008, the Iraqi parliament itself had ratified a plan to terminate the U.S. troop presence. As soon as President Obama ordered an escalation of U.S. troops in Afghanistan in December 2009, the tensions between the branches were immediately evident when senators grilled administration officials about what they hoped to do.

While we have seen a vast expansion of presidential power throughout this period, legislators have found a number of ways to influence policy, debate, and presidential options. Short of declaring or refusing to declare war—which of course has been a huge delegation of power—members of the House and Senate have proven to be more entrepreneurial through private persuasion and legislation. Unfortunately, we know remarkably little about this back-and-forth interaction. Studying the politics of troop withdrawal is a perfect place to begin. And a closer look at these interbranch struggles can open up a richer history of the polity.

SIXTEEN

Détente and Domestic Politics

During the first half of the 1970s, Presidents Richard Nixon and Gerald Ford responded to the aftermath of Vietnam by avoiding the extremes of the era: massive military retrenchment (left) and massive military escalation (right).* The presidents had different reasons for seeking a centrist national security agenda. The Republican presidents were willing to accept and actively pursue arms and trade agreements with the Soviet Union and China. Nixon concluded that appealing to moderates was essential in order to protect a muscular national security state from retrenchment in the aftermath of the 1960s and to ensure his own electoral success. His successor, Gerald Ford, believed that détente with the Soviets could rebuild public confidence in the post-Watergate GOP.

But the foreign policy of détente drowned in the turbulent waters of domestic politics in the 1970s. Nixon's and Ford's national security centrism failed to create a stable political majority within the Republican Party. The political weakness of each president as well as contradictions in their policies exposed them to domestic attack. At the same time, Soviet aggression undermined their ability to deliver on the promise of détente. Politicians allied with the conservative movement took advantage of presidential vulnerability to move national security politics toward the right. Each president ran head first into two factions in the burgeoning conservative movement, both of which rejected moderation: neoconservatives, who were Democrats disaffected with the leftward drift of their party as a result of the 1960s; and hawkish Republicans, who were rooted in the anticommunist politics of the early Cold War.

In addition to the historiography on détente and the conservative movement, the struggles of the 1970s offer us a powerful example of how domestic politics shaped foreign policy, a complex relationship that until recently has been downplayed by historians and social scientists.[1]

* This essay originally appeared in *Diplomatic History* 4 (2009): 653–70.

Figure 16.1. Spiro Agnew, Bob Hope, Richard Nixon, and Ronald Reagan and their wives (1971). (National Archives)

Defining the National Security Center

Richard Nixon believed that the strength of America's national security state had been severely jeopardized by the political unrest of the 1960s. Nixon decided that opening relations with China and pursuing détente with the Soviets could reaffirm American power abroad and restore domestic support for an aggressive national security agenda.

Because he had a strong conservative base, Nixon was confident that he could risk an apparent move toward the center without suffering political disaster. Through détente, the administration would accept the permanence of the Cold War and attempt to create a favorable set of rules for the superpowers that would benefit the United States.[2] The aim was to capitalize on divisions between the Soviets and China and simultaneously demonstrate to voters that Republicans could avoid international weakness while keeping the nation out of war.[3]

The individual who most eloquently articulated the concepts behind détente was Henry Kissinger, Nixon's national security advisor (and secretary of state after 1973). In his scholarship on European history, Kissinger had come to admire the balance of power achieved at the Congress of Vienna in 1815 and hoped to replicate such a system of international governance.[4] Kissinger did not invent the policy of "détente," which had been discussed by American policymakers throughout the 1960s.

Figure 16.2. Richard Nixon and Mao (1972). (National Archives)

Under Nixon, the strategy had three components. The first was negotiation with China and the Soviet Union over weapons and territorial conflicts. The second was economic trade with the two communist superpowers. The third was building America's defense capacity and undertaking targeted military operations in order to demonstrate the nation's willingness to use force. Nixon would authorize bombing, expand operations in Cambodia, and only gradually withdraw forces (taking over four years to leave) to also ensure that he had political protection from right-wing attacks about the Vietnam withdrawal and détente.

The first component of his strategy began in 1970 and 1971 when Nixon and Kissinger conducted a series of high-level negotiations with China and the Soviets. The talks culminated with the president traveling to China in February 1972, an act of historic proportion. Nixon feared angering the Republican right, which continued to promote a moralistic vision of national security and argued that the United States was engaged in a struggle against fundamentally evil regimes with the Soviet Union and China. They did not think that communists could be trusted in negotiations. Nixon was attempting to appeal to a broader base than conservatives while using politicians such as Ronald Reagan and Barry Goldwater to keep the right wing of the GOP within his electoral coalition since he needed their votes.[5] Conservative Republicans who had cut their teeth on the Cold War battles over "Who Lost China?" were very unhappy with the president. Yet because of his personal background and outreach effort, Nixon was able to keep most of them by his side.

By playing off the competitive rivalry between the two communist superpowers, Nixon hoped to create the incentives for agreements with the Soviets. By courting the Soviets with the possibility of agreements, he and Kissinger hoped to compel them to place pressure on the North Vietnamese to bring an end to the war. Soviet Premier Leonid Brezhnev hoped that détente would curtail the growing threat of China and limit the amount of expenditures that the Soviets would have to allocate for defense.[6] Initially, Soviet actions suggested that Nixon's strategy was working as planned. In 1972, the Soviets agreed to the Strategic Arms Limitation Talks (SALT I). This landmark agreement imposed restrictions on the future construction of weapon systems, including land- and sea-based intercontinental warheads as well as antiballistic systems.[7]

The second component of Nixon's strategy was to improve economic trade with the enemy and link economic trade with diplomatic relations. The United States would attempt to create incentives for favorable Soviet foreign policy actions. The Soviets, saddled with a stagnant economy, needed access to modern technology and economic trade with the West in order to boost productivity.[8] Nixon lobbied Congress to ease trade restrictions by granting the Soviet Union most-favored nation trade status, which would have the effect of normalizing trade with the country.

Finally, Nixon's strategy required American policymakers to support the use of military force. Diplomacy would only work, Nixon told fellow Republicans, if the Soviets and China believed that U.S. threats were credible. The United States would therefore need to maintain large defense budgets and embark on targeted military actions.

Nixon's three-party strategy was rooted in the realist tradition, which stressed that the United States should not concern itself with the internal composition of other nations or ideological concerns. Instead, realists claimed that foreign policy should focus on strategic self-interest within a world of states that were constantly competing.

Opening relations with China and practicing détente with the Soviets were also pragmatic responses to domestic political pressure. The president believed that Congress was intent on curtailing the national security state. Détente, in Nixon's mind, could freeze the amount that the Soviets would spend on weapons systems and thereby diminish the immediate pressure that he faced when seeking higher appropriations.[9] By improving Nixon's chances for reelection in 1972, détente would also help Nixon obtain the electoral environment he needed to fight Democrats for higher defense appropriations down the road.[10]

The Neoconservative Critique

In addition to the Republican right, the other opponents of Nixon's strategy were an elite group of Democratic politicians, staffers, and intellectuals who were convinced that their party had moved too far to the left in the 1960s.[11]

These Democrats—later called neoconservatives—were concerned that the turmoil over Vietnam had caused many of their allies to lose sight of the need for aggressive policies to combat communism and to embrace moral relativism when dealing with foreign policy. The Committee to Maintain a Prudent Defense Policy, a Washington-based group founded by Paul Nitze in 1950 to champion the policies in National Security Council Report 68 (NSC-68) which was revived in the 1960s, promoted these ideas on Capitol Hill and in the media.

The most prominent neoconservative was Washington Senator Henry "Scoop" Jackson. Although liberal on most domestic issues, Jackson was a conservative on national security. While Nixon contemplated moves to attract moderates, Senator Jackson emerged as the champion of Democrats who wanted to maintain an aggressive position on national security. Jackson capitalized on his institutional base as the chair of the Permanent Investigations Subcommittee of Government Operations and as a senior member of the Armed Services Committee.[12]

Jackson and his allies demanded that the Soviet Union liberalize its policies toward Jews. This became a centerpiece of their attack on détente. In 1972 and 1973, Senator Jackson opposed Nixon's proposals to grant the Soviet Union most-favored national status unless Brezhnev allowed more Jewish citizens to leave the country. In August, the Soviets implemented a new "exit tax" on emigrants from their country, many of whom were Jews. Jackson called these policies a gross violation of human rights and a sign that the Soviets could not be trusted.

With regard to his opponents in Congress, Nixon felt that Jackson—who ran for president in 1972 and was planning to run again in 1976—would never compromise and was solely motivated by the national attention these controversies brought. Nixon and Kissinger rejected the argument that foreign policy should attempt to sway the internal behavior of the Soviets. In fact, the administration argued that Jackson was making things worse for Soviet Jews. "They [the Soviets] feel they're being deliberately humiliated," Kissinger warned one colleague, "and that every time they yield on something, immediately another demand is made."[13] Nixon told Jewish organizations that the "politically favorable course of action" that Jackson pursued would only make the Soviets feel more isolated and thus cause them to completely lock their doors to the Jews.[14]

Despite the attacks on détente, Nixon was able to benefit from his centrist national security agenda. His impeccable credentials as a conservative offered the president considerable protection from attacks from the right. Nixon's uncanny political ability helped him use dramatic events to sell the abstract concepts behind his strategy. Privately, Nixon made concessions to Jackson at the time of the 1972 election, giving clear signals he would start supporting a harder line in arms negotiations. Jackson, who one newspaper said was the person who "upped the price of détente," used the resurgent feeling in Congress toward executive power to constrain President Nixon's foreign policy options.[15]

Many pundits credited his landslide victory in 1972 to his national security policies. In an administration beset by scandal, détente stood as one of Nixon's most glorious achievements. When the North and South Vietnamese signed a Peace Accord in 1973, Nixon pointed to this as proof that détente worked. Tired of the war, many Americans agreed. Détente was a policy, from the perspective of 1974, which his successor could confidently inherit.

Détente and Gerald Ford

President Ford continued to promote détente. "It would be very unwise for a President—me or anyone else—to abandon détente," Ford explained. "I think détente is in the best interest of the country. It is in the best interest of world stability, world peace."[16] He reappointed Henry Kissinger to serve in the dual roles of national security advisor and secretary of state. Ford and Kissinger argued that détente promoted a sound diplomatic strategy and diminished the appeal of liberalism by showing voters that Republicans could maintain peaceful relations across the globe.[17]

But Watergate had tarnished everything associated with Nixon's administration, including détente, more than was apparent at the time. The atmosphere surrounding Watergate also allowed Dale Bumpers to upset Senator Fulbright in the Arkansas primary. This was costly to the GOP, since Senator Fulbright was one of the strongest proponents of détente and a close ally of Henry Kissinger. The Watergate scandal weakened the senior Fulbright as it did most legislators who were seen as part of the political "establishment." Fulbright was also attacked for his positions about Israel. As a capstone of his career, Fulbright was planning to hold high-profile hearings about détente in the summer of 1974. As a result of the Watergate scandal the hearings were postponed until the end of the summer, and the key participant—Kissinger—pulled out to help at the White House. Fulbright conducted the hearings but they barely received any media attention as a result of Watergate.[18] Without this influential Democratic supporter of détente in the Senate, the base of legislative support for the policies became even thinner than it already was. In addition to the detrimental effect of Watergate, President Ford was the wrong man to protect détente from the national security challenges that his administration confronted. Ford lacked the foreign policy experience that was required, and he did not possess the same talent as Nixon in this area.

In September 1974, Ford saw how shaky détente's political base was. Senator Jackson intensified his demands that the Soviets allow a minimum number of citizens to emigrate each year. Jackson wanted to attach this requirement to pending trade legislation in 1974, thus making normal trade status for the Soviets contingent on agreement on a specified number of emigrants. Senators Jacob Javits of New York (R) and Abraham Ribicoff of Connecticut (D), as well as Ohio Representative Charles Vanik (D), worked with him. Each time that Ford obtained a verbal commitment from the Soviets, Jackson publicly insisted on a higher number and a written agreement.

The pressure from Jackson came at a difficult time for the administration. On September 8, Ford had ensured that voters would not forget Watergate when he pardoned Nixon for crimes that he might have committed. Democrats turned the controversial pardon into a campaign issue, and Watergate became a central media story. Ford's popularity plummeted as a result of the pardon.

As the president struggled with the fallout from the pardon, on September 20, 1974, Ford, Jackson, and the Soviets privately agreed to a compromise. Under the agreement, Congress would pass an amendment to trade legislation stating that the United States could not offer most-favored nation status to countries that had poor human rights records. Under the deal, the Soviets would be granted a temporary eighteen-month waiver during which they would need to release a certain number of emigrants. The waiver was subject to congressional review after eighteen months, which Jackson had timed to occur in the middle of the next electoral cycle.[19]

But at a White House meeting on October 14 to complete the agreement, Jackson publicly boasted that the Soviets had caved to U.S. pressure and specified that 60,000 Jews would be allowed to leave. The Soviets were livid, since they had never approved that figure and had clearly objected to the release of official documents involving this matter. Although Ford opposed the Jackson-Vanik amendment, he concluded that he had no choice and signed it into law with the Trade Reform Act of 1974.

The Jackson-Vanik amendment constituted a political setback to détente since it legitimated the notions that human rights should be relevant to diplomacy. Imposing human rights requirements that the Communist leadership was not likely to accept made economic trade with the Soviets—a key component of détente—difficult. The amendment undermined the president's credibility to offer economic benefits in exchange for certain types of Soviet foreign policy decisions.

Just as southern Democrats had joined Republicans in the 1940s and 1950s to form a coalition against liberal domestic policies, neoconservative Democrats in Congress allied with hawkish Republicans in the 1970s to subvert presidential initiatives on détente. The alliance was fragile given that the two factions in this coalition disagreed on as many issues as those that brought them together (not unlike the situation with the conservative coalition of the 1940s and 1950s). Indeed, the opposition to détente was that much more potent because it served as the unifying theme for this alliance.

By 1974, a conservative movement had taken form, which claimed a network of intellectuals (William Buckley), politicians (Jesse Helms), issue organizations (the National Rifle Association), think tanks (Heritage Foundation, American Enterprise Institute), fund-raising operations (Committee for the Survival of a Free Congress, the National Conservative Political Action Committee), and evangelical leaders (Jerry Falwell), as well as activists and campaign professionals (Phyllis Schlafly, Richard Viguerie, Terry Dolan, Paul Weyrich).[20] Since the 1950s and 1960s, these activists had been as concerned with moderates within the Republican Party as they were with Democrats who had power in the White House and Congress.[21] Many of these activists, such as Joseph Coors and Richard Viguerie, had gone so far as to form the Committee on Conservative Alternatives to consider creating a third party.[22]

Trouble in 1975

The crucial year in the battle over détente took place in 1975. A series of crises allowed a more ardent form of conservatism—more attuned to the conservative internationalism that had been promoted by the right since the 1940s than the ideological mutt that Presidents Nixon and Ford championed to win support from the center—to gain the upper hand. As Ford attempted to keep détente alive, the Soviet Union became involved (although often to a lesser extent than American policymakers believed) in a number of conflicts that created the perception of bolder ambitions among the Communist leadership.

The fall of South Vietnam to communism in 1975 was a huge blow to the administration's standing among conservatives, even though Ford tried to blame Congress for having refused his requests for military assistance. On April 30, the enfeebled leadership of South Vietnam surrendered to the Communists. The Provisional Revolutionary Government turned Saigon into Ho Chi Minh City. "It was the saddest hour of my time in the White House," Ford said.[23]

Ford's tension with conservatives became worse in July when the Soviet dissident Aleksander Solzhenitsyn visited the United States, five months after he had been expelled from the USSR. Solzhenitsyn objected to détente. He argued that Soviet leaders were simply using the term and policy to mask their expansionist desires and brutal dictatorship. Conservative Republicans greeted Solzhenitsyn as a hero when he arrived on a visit to the United States in the summer of 1975. When the AFL-CIO asked the president to attend a dinner honoring Solzhenitsyn, Ford turned down the request. The president also declined an invitation from Republican Senators Strom Thurmond and Jesse Helms to organize a dinner with Solzhenitsyn on July 4. Kissinger and his staff advised Ford that a meeting with Solzhenitsyn would offend the Soviets with less than a month remaining before the president was scheduled to travel to a summit with the Soviets in Helsinki.[24] "I decided to subordinate political gains," Ford later wrote, "to foreign policy considerations."[25]

Ford's decision angered hawkish Republicans and disaffected Democrats.[26] Deputy Chief of Staff Richard Cheney warned Secretary of Defense Donald Rumsfeld that insulting Solzhenitsyn would harm "the President's capability to deal with the right wing in America."[27] The neoconservative Democratic congressional staffers who had lobbied against détente were furious with Ford. One Ford staffer concluded that "our refusal to see Solzhenitsyn will come to symbolize a Munich-like deafness in this period."[28] When the president privately sent an invitation to Solzhenitsyn to meet with him in secret (a compromise that was worked out by Kissinger) after he returned from the Soviet summit, the insulted dissident refused.

Even when Ford took actions that should have placated critics of détente, he faltered. This was evident when the United States signed onto a set of agreements with the Soviet Union on August 1 at a thirty-five country summit in Helsinki. The agreements had two components. The first outlined a bold set of human rights principles (such as the right of families to reunify across borders and the freedom to travel). Ford thus obtained the first formal statement from the Soviet Union that human rights were a legitimate diplomatic concern.

Tough rhetoric did not suffice, however. The human rights aspect of the Helsinki agreements was overshadowed by the second component, in which the participating countries recognized the territorial claims of the Soviet Union over Eastern Europe. Conservatives were furious about this proclamation. Underestimating the political impact the statement would have in the United States, Ford believed that this part of the agreement merely acknowledged what had been a political reality since World War II. Upon signing the agreements, Ford proclaimed that "the era of confrontation that has divided Europe since the end of the Second World War may now be ending."[29] According to one Ford speechwriter, conservatives in America saw the agreement as "a 'new Yalta'"[30]

The final blow to Ford's relationship with conservatives came in the fall of 1975 as a result of civil conflict in Angola. Following the announcement by the new government of Portugal in 1974 that they would withdraw from their former colonies, three factions attempted to take control of Angola and its oil: the Popular Movement for the Liberation of Angola (MPLA) which was supported by Cuba, Mozambique, and the Soviet Union; the National Front for the Liberation of Angola (FNLA), which received support from China and Zaire and covert assistance from the Central Intelligence Agency (CIA); and the National Union for Total Independence of Angola (UNITA), which received support from South Africa and the United States (the CIA supported two factions). The administration provided covert assistance in this civil war in order to display that the U.S. government was still willing to take action even after Vietnam.[31] Ford said that Soviet involvement in Angola was damaging the prospects for détente.[32]

At first, most legislators paid little attention to reports about Angola. There was minimal knowledge on the Hill about Africa in general. But attitudes changed by December 1975, when Ford made a request for money to fund the operation. South Africa's recent intervention in the war had angered many liberals. Many congressional Democrats said they were outraged to learn about the CIA activities and called for cutting off the funds. Besides the fact that aid was distributed in secrecy, many Democrats felt this was a lost cause. The Senate passed an amendment, sponsored by John Tunney (D-CA), to military spending legislation in December 1975 that killed the program, which Dick Clark (D-IA) extended with his own amendment to a foreign aid bill that same month. Ford called the action irresponsible. The House confirmed this decision through legislation passed in January. Both chambers rejected presidential requests for direct assistance.

When MPLA took control of the country, Ford blamed the Democratic Congress. But conservatives blamed the president for allowing a communist victory. The joint effort by the Soviets (which only hesitantly provided its support) and Cuba seemed to be a turnaround from the late 1960s when relations between those two countries had reached an all-time low.[33]

The assertion of congressional power by liberal Democrats had the unintended effect of fueling conservative demands for tougher anticommunist policies.[34] Conservatives pointed to Angola as another example of how détente encouraged communists to expand their reach and how the Ford administration's timid responses to military crises were inadequate to stopping the communist threat.[35]

Behind closed doors, the president was worried. In November, campaign advisor Robert Teeter warned that "détente is a particularly unpopular idea with most Republican primary voters and the word is worse. We ought to stop using the word whenever possible."[36] By the winter, the president had shelved any further discussions of arms limitation with the Soviets. The move was primarily political. "I never backed away from détente as a means for achieving a more stable relationship with our Communist adversaries," Ford explained, "but the situation that developed in connection with the presidential primaries and the fight at the convention made it necessary to deemphasize détente."[37]

The Republican Primaries

The final blow to détente within the GOP took place during the 1976 Republican primaries. Ford nearly lost to Ronald Reagan, the candidate who had come to embody the conservative movement in the post-Vietnam era. Going into the campaign season, most Republicans underestimated the seriousness of the threat that he faced from conservative Republicans in the primaries.[38] In September 1975, Nixon told Ford advisor Jerry Jones that Reagan was a lightweight.[39] Moreover, Ford was still committed to détente as a viable strategy. "My feeling is SALT II is in the best interest of the United States and the world," he told Kissinger.[40] Yet the Republican primaries would force him to change course.

More than any other politician in the 1970s, Ronald Reagan tapped into the energies of the conservative movement. The Young America's Foundation, for instance, conducted an extensive fund-raising campaign for Reagan and collected the names of potential supporters. The conservative magazine *Human Events* sponsored Reagan's radio addresses.[41] But in late 1975, conservative Republican activists had not yet proven that they could be commanding electoral force. Most Republicans remembered the failed campaign of Goldwater in 1964. When Reagan announced his candidacy, Ford released a statement saying that "the simple political fact is that he cannot defeat any candidate the

Democrats put up. Reagan's constituency is much too narrow, even within the Republican Party."[42]

Reagan began his campaign by focusing on domestic issues. The early results were poor. Reagan lost New Hampshire by a narrow margin, followed by defeats in Florida, Illinois, Massachusetts, and Vermont. Pundits speculated that he would have to drop out of the race. By March, most of his staff was working without pay, while others were let go.[43]

Facing the possibility of defeat in March, Reagan turned almost all of his attention to the issue of national security. Early in the month, the issue excited his followers in Florida when he proclaimed that, "Under Messrs. Kissinger and Ford this nation has become number two in military power in a world where it is dangerous—if not fatal—to be second best."[44] On NBC television's *Meet the Press*, Reagan lashed out against détente by saying, "it has been a one-way street. We are making the concessions, we are giving them [the Soviet Union] the things they want; we ask nothing in return. In fact, we give them things before we ask for the return."[45]

Sensing trouble, Ford took a more proactive approach. On March 1, the president stopped saying "détente."[46] On March 11, presidential advisor David Gergen warned that the president needed to "posture himself as sufficiently hard-line that no major candidate can run to the right of him on defense and foreign policy."[47] Defending Kissinger and his foreign policy, Ford started to raise doubts about whether a SALT agreement could be reached.[48] But Ford had trouble stopping Reagan's momentum. On March 22, Reagan exploited the language of a news story written by Robert Evans and Robert Novak about a memo from State Department official Helmut Sonnenfeldt regarding the "organic union" that existed between the Soviet Union and Eastern Europe. Reagan also warned voters that Ford was secretly conducting high-level talks with the Panamanian government to give back the Panama Canal. Reagan turned this into a major issue and litmus test for the strength of national security policy. Kissinger became a central target for Reagan since the secretary of state offered a way to criticize the administration without directly attacking the president, who was, after all, a fellow Republican.

In North Carolina, Reagan received support from the state's first twentieth-century Republican senator. Jesse Helms had close ties to the grassroots conservative movement. Elected in 1972, Helms's National Congressional Club, located in Raleigh, quickly became a hub for the activists who were building the "New Right." Helms commanded significant power. He had provided financial and manpower assistance to young Republicans in southern states. While his close ties to Nixon kept him silent in the early 1970s, Helms, like many conservative Republicans, felt no personal or political loyalty toward Ford. In March, Helms traveled across North Carolina to promote Reagan. The National Congressional Club ran a cutting-edge get-out-the vote effort that targeted disaffected Democrats. The Young Americans for Freedom, the American Conservative Union, and other allied organizations mobilized North Carolinian voters.[49]

Reagan shocked most observers when he won the North Carolina primary on March 23 with 52 percent of the vote. On March 31, Reagan purchased airtime on NBC. "There's one problem that must be solved, or everything else is meaningless. I'm speaking of the problem of our national security. Our nation is in danger," Reagan said. Mocking Ford for merely replacing the term détente with "peace through strength" while sticking with the same policy, Reagan told the audience that "I believe in the peace of which Mr. Ford spoke—as much as any man. But peace does not come from weakness or from retreat. It comes from restoration of American military superiority."[50]

Reagan followed his triumph in North Carolina with a string of victories in Texas, Alabama, Georgia, Nebraska, California, and Indiana. Texas was a watershed that caused serious introspection within the Ford administration about the newfound electoral power of the Republican right. As the reporter Jules Witcover noted, "Where Ford went and conducted Q&A sessions, Reagan's issues—the Panama Canal, détente, U.S. Military strength—always seemed to come up. Reagan just got tougher, saying he'd go to war if necessary to protect and keep the canal."[51]

Reagan's victories caused Ford to move to the right on national security. Only five days after he lost North Carolina, Ford lashed out against House Democrats for proposing a $7 billion defense cut. The statement was part of a larger strategy in which the administration tried to appeal to the right by fighting for an increased defense budget. In March, Rumsfeld published a report that warned of a massive shift of power as Soviet weapons technology improved.[52] Ford continued to shelve discussions of SALT II. Regaining some momentum, Ford defeated Reagan in June with crucial victories in Ohio and New Jersey.

The race was neck and neck. When the primaries ended, neither of the candidates had a majority of delegates. Almost 140 delegates remained uncommitted going into the convention. Between the primaries and the convention, Reagan had hurt himself by announcing that his running mate would be Richard Schweiker, a liberal Republican who embodied the type of moderate political views that Reagan supporters detested. This was a last-minute attempt by Reagan campaign official John Sears to win over the very moderates from whom Reagan had distanced himself in order to save the nomination. The plan backfired.

During the Republican convention in Kansas City, Reagan tried one last time to influence the party's agenda. His supporters proposed a plank for the platform entitled "Morality in Foreign Policy." The plank called for a new vision in foreign policy and was critical of Nixon's and Ford's records.[53] After reading the text of the plank, Ford was furious because it amounted to "nothing less than a slick denunciation of Administration foreign policy."[54] Yet Ford decided that by not attacking the language he would avoid being provoked into a confrontation with conservatives, which was Reagan's hope. Instead, Ford told his delegates to vote for the language that discussed morality in foreign policy with the goal of making it appear like the president's idea, not Reagan's.[55]

The final results could not be seen as any mandate. Ford secured the nomination, but by a narrow margin of 1,187 to 1,070. Even though Ford had won, Reagan had both defined the terms of the contest and profoundly influenced the agenda of the GOP. "Reagan was the dominating presence of the 1976 campaign," concluded William Buckley Jr., "even though Ford was the formal victor."[56]

Democrats selected Georgia Governor Jimmy Carter. Throughout his campaign, Carter had presented himself as an "outsider" who could restore trust in government. In contrast to the other Democratic candidates, his southern upbringing offered the possibility of appealing to core Democratic voters. Carter conducted an effective primary campaign that played into this perception while he retained the trust of enough core Democratic voters to win the nomination. Regarding national security, Carter was hard to pin down. He endorsed most of the policies of détente, although he criticized the secrecy through which the policies had been conducted under Kissinger.[57] When asked, Carter was hesitant about allying directly with Democrats such as Scoop Jackson.[58] Yet he ran a campaign that appealed to their critique of foreign policy as he sought to distance himself from how mainstream Democrats were handling international relations. Carter also promised to promote human rights. As his speechwriter explained, human rights policy was "seen politically as a no-lose issue. Liberals liked human rights because it involved political freedom and getting liberals out of jail in dictatorships, and conservatives liked it because it involved criticisms of Russia."[59]

The general campaign was difficult for Ford. The memories of Nixon and Watergate haunted his campaign. The one-two punch of economic stagnation and high inflation left citizens disillusioned with economic expectations that had been widespread since World War II.[60] Ford's economic policies had failed to curb the rapid decline of the U.S. economy in the 1970s. The comedic depiction of Ford as a klutz did not help. Ford also made mistakes that reinforced the poor impressions many Americans had about him. The criticism about détente continued to plague him. For instance, during the second debate with Carter, Ford said that Eastern Europe was not under the control of the Soviet Union. When advisors implored him to apologize, Ford refused.[61] Finally, Ford's shift to the right in the primaries had forced him into positions that alienated him from the mainstream—exactly the type of voters who he had hoped to court throughout his entire career.[62]

Despite these problems, Ford remained strong in the polls until the end. Carter won by one of the narrowest margins in U.S. history, receiving 50.1 percent of the popular vote and 297 electoral votes to Ford's 48 percent of the popular vote and 240 electoral votes (Reagan received 1 vote). Democrats retained control of Congress. Although Carter won the general election, one of the most important developments in the campaign with far-reaching national consequences was the shift within the GOP in 1976. When Ford ended his presidency, so too did the centrist foreign policy agenda that Republican presidents had pursued since 1968. Looking back at the primary and the general election,

Ford would later lament that "If I'd been elected in '76, the party wouldn't be as far right as it is at the present time."[63]

Following the election, conservatives were reenergized by reports from an independent study about CIA intelligence. During the 1976 primaries, because he was feeling so much pressure from Ronald Reagan, Ford decided to allow for an independent review in June 1976.[64] Official CIA intelligence estimates had come under increasing criticism from Lieutenant General Daniel Graham of the Arms Control and Disarmament Agency and General George Keegan, who worked for the intelligence operations of the U.S. Army. The critics said that the CIA had underestimated the strength of the Soviet Union. Team B, as the commission was called, concluded that the CIA's National Intelligence Estimate on Soviet Strategic Objectives (NIE) had underestimated the strength of the Soviet military. Just as conservatives had been warning, the commission found that the world's strategic balance of power was threatened as a result of Soviet advances in the development of intercontinental missiles and other weapons. The Soviets, they said, had abandoned the concept of parity, which was the bedrock of Mutual Assured Destruction, in pursuit of military superiority.[65] Although scholars later found that Team B had made a series of errors about Soviet advances, at the time the finds were dramatic. The study supported the arguments of military officials who had been complaining in 1976 that declining military expenditures were crippling the armed forces.[66]

Inspired by this report and related arguments, a group of policymakers sympathetic to the arguments from Team B formed the Committee on the Present Danger. The committee, which included such prominent figures as Paul Nitze, Eugene Rostow, Richard Perle, and Georgetown Professor Jeane Kirkpatrick, aimed to produce an intellectual counterweight to détente.

Laying the Groundwork for the Election of 1980

As Ford's presidency came to an unhappy conclusion, the possibility of a centrist agenda on national security with the GOP had almost vanished. The defeat of détente in the 1970s quickly became a defining moment for conservatives. Although Reagan lost the 1976 primary, his candidacy helped push the GOP toward the right. His success would culminate with the 1980 election. With Reagan's election as president, the challenge to conservatives would change dramatically. After a tough three-decade struggle against liberal internationalism, right-wing isolationism, and moderates in both parties, hawkish conservative Republicans would finally triumph politically and ideologically by capturing the White House, Senate, and the GOP in 1980. Although between 1985 and 1987, President Reagan reached back to some of the arguments made by proponents of détente, leaders of the Republican Party would generally shy away from the rhetoric of the 1970s and instead adopted a more militaristic outlook toward international affairs.

SEVENTEEN

Conservatives, Carter, and the Politics of National Security

The new year of 1980 was not a happy one for President Jimmy Carter.* On December 27, the Soviet Union invaded Afghanistan. When Carter heard the reports, he blurted out, "there goes SALT II." The invasion seemed to confirm everything that conservatives had been saying about the president, his national security policies, and the weakness of the Democratic Party. The president's wife, Rosalynn, had never seen him more upset. "We will help to make sure that Afghanistan will be their Vietnam," the shaken Carter vowed to his spouse.[1] In the coming weeks, the president imposed a grain embargo against the Soviet Union, endorsed substantial increases in defense spending, and announced the United States' boycott of the Moscow Summer Olympics.

The invasion of Afghanistan and its political aftermath ended a decade-long quest among Democrats and moderate Republicans for a centrist national security agency. During the 1970s, all three American presidents had responded to the aftermath of Vietnam by promoting national security agendas that avoided extreme positions toward the Soviet Union. Earlier in the decade, the Republican version of centrism, *détente*, had revolved around arms and trade agreements with the Soviet Union and China. Although President Richard Nixon enjoyed significant success with this policy, he came under attack from two factions in the burgeoning conservative movement: "neoconservative" Democrats, who had become disaffected with the leftward drift of their party, and hawkish Republicans. President Gerald Ford continued the policy of détente since he believed it to be one of the more successful inheritances from his predecessor. Ford, though, discovered that Watergate had tarnished everything associated with Nixon, détente included. And Ford did not possess the skills needed to

* "Conservatives, Carter, and the Politics of National Security," reprinted by permission of the publisher from *Rightward Bound: Making America Conservative in the 1970s*, eds. Bruce J. Schulman and Julian E. Zelizer, pp. 265-287, Cambridge, MA: Harvard University Press.

fend off the pressure from the Right to adopt a more hawkish posture. In 1976, with the support of the conservative movement, Ronald Reagan nearly defeated Ford in the primaries and signaled the future of the GOP.

This essay examines how the conservative movement capitalized on President Jimmy Carter's struggles to redefine and champion centrism. When Carter struggled politically and the Soviet Union undertook actions that undermined the promise of détente, conservatives took advantage of the situation. Following the national security problems encountered by Nixon and Ford, Carter both added a human rights component to détente and moderated the military aspects of foreign policy to form a Democratic Party vision of centrism. He, unsurprisingly, courted moderates. The conventional wisdom in the 1970s stipulated that presidents should try to please voters who occupied the political center. The forces that would soon push politics toward the extremes, such as a reformed primary system that privileged party activists, had not yet fully taken hold. The memory of Barry Goldwater's defeat in 1964 compounded by George McGovern's loss in 1972 loomed large as proof that voters preferred candidates who eschewed extremist rhetoric. In the 1970s, congressional moderates in both parties continued to enjoy powerful positions. The electoral forces that had tended to push politicians toward the center, such as southern Democratic voters, were still fulfilling their traditional role.

During the 1976 primaries, Democrats selected Georgia governor Jimmy Carter as their candidate. Throughout this campaign, Carter presented himself as an outsider who could restore trust in government. In contrast to the other Democratic candidates, his southern upbringing offered the possibility of appealing to core Democratic voters. Carter conducted an effective primary campaign that played into this perception while retaining the trust of enough core Democratic voters to win the nomination. Regarding national security, Carter was hard to pin down. He endorsed most of the policies of détente, although he criticized the secrecy through which the policies had been conducted under Kissinger. When asked, Carter was hesitant about allying directly with such Democrats as Senator Henry "Scoop" Jackson. Yet he ran a campaign that appealed to their critique of foreign policy as he sought to distance himself from the way mainstream Democrats were handling international relations. Carter also promised to promote human rights policy. As his speechwriter explained, a human rights policy was "seen politically as a no-lose issue. Liberals liked human rights because it involved political freedom and getting liberals out of jail in dictatorships, and conservatives liked it because it involved criticisms of Russia."[2]

The memories of Richard Nixon and Watergate haunted Gerald Ford's campaign. The one-two punch of economic stagnation and high inflation left citizens disillusioned with economic expectations that had been widespread since World War II. Ford's economic policies had failed to curb the rapid decline of the U.S. economy in the 1970s. Comedic depictions of Ford as a klutz did not help. Ford also made mistakes that reinforced the poor impressions many Americans had about him. The criticism about détente from the Right continued to plague him. For instance, during his second debate with Carter, Ford said that Eastern Europe was not under the control of the Soviet Union. When advisors implored him to apologize, Ford refused.

Carter defeated Ford by one of the narrowest margins in U.S. history, receiving 50.1 percent of the popular vote and 297 electoral votes to Ford's 48 percent of the popular vote and 240 electoral votes (Ronald Reagan received 1 vote). Democrats retained control of the Congress. Although Carter won the general election, one of the most important developments in the campaign with far-reaching national consequences was the shift within the GOP in 1976. When Ford ended his presidency, so too ended the centrist foreign policy agenda that Republican presidents had pursued since 1968.

Despite Carter's victory, conservatives were re-energized soon after the election by an independent study that was commissioned by the CIA of its own intelligence. Official CIA data had come under criticism from the Right for underestimating the military strength of the Soviet Union. The study's staff included Lieutenant General Daniel Graham; Harvard historian Richard Pipes; former deputy secretary of defense Paul Nitze, who had been a main author of NSC-68, a secret 1950 State Department report that called for a huge increase in defense spending; and State Department official Paul Wolfowitz.

Team B, as the commission was called, concluded that the CIA's National Intelligence Estimate on Soviet Strategic Objectives had downplayed the strength of the Soviet military. Just as conservatives had been warning, the commission found that the world's strategic balance of power was threatened as a result of Soviet advances in the development of intercontinental missiles and other weapons. The Soviets, they said, had abandoned the concept of parity, which was the bedrock of Mutual Assured Destruction, in pursuit of military superiority.[3] Although scholars would later find that Team B had overstated Soviet advances, at the time the findings were dramatic. The commission's report constituted a watershed moment for many conservatives by confirming their worst fears about the effects of Vietnam and détente on the national security establishment, which in turn galvanized them.

Inspired by this report and related arguments, a group of policymakers sympathetic to the claims from Team B formed the Committee on the Present Danger. The committee, which included such prominent Democrats as Nitze, Eugene Rostow, Richard Perle, and Georgetown professor Jeane Kirkpatrick, aimed to produce an intellectual counterweight to détente. Expressing the committee's mission, Kirkpatrick complained that the "Vietnam syndrome" (which she defined as the fear among policymakers to authorize military operations as a result of Vietnam) had nurtured a "culture of appeasement, which finds reasons not only against the use of force, but denies its place in the world."[4]

But in contrast to the rightward drift of Team B, during his transition to the presidency Carter hoped to develop a different set of policies that transcended Left/Right divisions and achieved more than merely containing Communism.[5] While resisting pressure from the Right in early 1977, Carter refused to ally with the liberal wing of his party. There was still more than enough reason for him to believe that a national security center was politically attractive. After all, Carter had defeated Ford, and Democrats controlled Congress. Thus, Carter pursued all the hallmarks of détente, including arms negotiations, trade agreements, and territorial compromises. He dismissed the findings of Team B and promoted a more optimistic vision of what could be achieved in negotiations with the Soviets.

Unlike his Republican predecessors, as he started his presidency Carter elevated the issue of human rights to the center of his policies. Conservatives had used human rights to attack détente's efficacy. For Carter, supporting human rights and practicing détente could be compatible policies. He thought he could demand that the Soviets and their allies improve their human rights records while simultaneously negotiating arms agreements to reduce the possibility of nuclear war. In unstable regions such as Africa, he felt that the recognition of majority rule was essential to countering the appeal of the Soviets and Cubans.

Besides Carter's ideological commitment to the issue, the political logic behind his stance was simple. With human rights integral to his agenda, critics would not be able to charge the administration with downplaying the importance of democratic and civil liberties in pursuit to arms and trade agreements. Human rights offered political advantages in addition to ideological appeal. Most important, the administration thought the strategy had the potential to unite neoconservatives and liberals in the Democratic Party. Crafting a foreign policy that advanced human rights, Carter explained in 1977, required policymakers to overcome the "inordinate fear of communism, which once led us to embrace any dictator who joined us in that fear."[6]

During the first months of his administration, conservatives in both parties joined liberals and moderates in praising Carter's human rights efforts. Before the specific direction of his human rights initiatives became clear, there was enough reason for neoconservative Democrats, and even some Republicans, to believe that they might not be that far apart from the president on this particular issue. On May 14, the neoconservative Coalition for a Democratic Majority sent the president a letter congratulating him on his decision to make human rights a diplomatic issue, which they said had "reminded us what our foreign policy is supposed to be about: protecting our own interests, to be sure, but primary among these interests the defense and preservation of freedom in the world."[7] The appointment of Zbigniew Brzezinski—a Columbia professor who was seen as extremely sympathetic to the arguments of neoconservative Democrats—as national security advisor counteracted some of Carter's more dovish appointments, such as Cyrus Vance as secretary of state. Senator George McGovern became concerned that "the Carter [human rights] policy looks like a reincarnation of John Foster Dulles's attempt to bring Communism down by encouraging dissent and revolt in Eastern Europe."[8]

By embracing human rights, Carter built on a strong base of preexisting congressional and interest group support. In addition to support from the neoconservatives, Carter found allies among a liberal human rights lobby that included such legislators as Tom Harkin of Iowa.[9] Other supportive organizations included the Human Rights Working Group of the Coalition for a New Foreign and Military Policy, Amnesty International, and Freedom House. President Carter even went so far as to institutionalize his priority of human rights. For example, he established a Bureau of Human Rights and Humanitarian Affairs in the State Department.

But over time, the administration failed to achieve a consensus. The contradictions in the policy proved to be problematic. Despite early enthusiasm, conservatives quickly started to complain that most of Carter's human rights initiatives targeted right-wing governments in Latin America or Africa rather than governments allied with the Soviets. Neoconservative Democrats and conservative Republicans thought that the focus of human rights had to be the Soviet Union above any other authoritarian regime, on the grounds that the Soviets were the worst and most dangerous violators of these principles. Another dilemma that Carter encountered was the difficulty of avoiding the tensions that existed between simultaneously promoting human rights and practicing détente with the Soviets. When Carter explained to Soviet ambassador Anatoly Dobrynin that he did not intend to interfere with the internal affairs of the Soviets or to embarrass them for their human rights records, the Soviet ambassador angrily suggested that in return the Soviets might point out the human rights failures of the United States, such as with the nation's treatment of African Americans.[10]

The difficulty of combining human rights rhetoric with détente became apparent in the debate over Soviet dissidents in the summer of 1978. Just as Carter was negotiating the Strategic Arms Limitation Treaty (SALT) agreements, the Soviets initiated trials against dissidents such as Alexander Ginzburg and Anatoly Scharansky. Human rights official Jessica Tuchman feared that the trials were a "turning point" that could undermine the administration's initiatives in this area. "If we do not respond," Tuchman wrote, "the Soviets will feel free to crack down even harder, and it will not be difficult for U.S. press and public opinion to draw the obvious connection."[11] In July, Carter announced that the United States would limit the sale of oil and computer technology to the Soviets. After the trials of the dissidents, though, Carter shifted his attention away from the Soviets and focused his human rights efforts on other governments, a decision that opened him up to criticism.[12]

The situation in Congress made things even more difficult. Carter immediately had trouble working with the Democratic leadership on Capitol Hill given that Congress, as a result of 1970s reforms, had become highly unpredictable. The reforms weakened the authority of committee chairs, decentralized power, and opened more proceedings to the public and press.[13] The president began his term expecting harmonious relationships with the legislative branch and loyalty toward his administration. The reality was quite different.

As the president tried to complete the types of international agreements pursued by Nixon and Ford earlier in the 1970s, he found himself snarled in the same web as his predecessors. Soviet aggression did not make things easy for Carter. Like Nixon and Ford, Carter had to defend détente at the same time that the Soviets seemed to become more expansionist. In 1977 and 1978, a war between Somalia and Ethiopia offered evidence to conservatives that the Soviets, as well as the Cubans, were committed to expansion and could not be trusted to negotiate over an arms limitation agreement. The Soviets and the Cubans supported Ethiopia in this war. Carter admitted that Soviet policies in Somalia would weaken public confidence in détente. Most members of the administration perceived the Horn of Africa as a test of whether the Soviets were willing to take actions that they understood to be damaging to détente. Zbigniew Brzezinski feared that the Soviets were trying to secure control of the area around Saudi Arabia—and its oil.[14] "SALT lies buried in the sands of Ogaden," he later wrote.[15]

The most contentious issue in President Carter's relationship with conservatives turned out to be the Panama Canal. Carter decided that, given the anger that had developed in Panama about continued U.S. control of the canal, returning authority over the canal was essential to securing regional peace in Latin America. There had been sizable protests within Panama about America's continued presence. Panama, according to Carter, could serve as a symbol that the United States was prepared to take bold steps to ease tensions in regions turned "hot" by the Cold War and to back off from policies that had been criticized as imperialistic.

Carter understood the political risks of tackling this issue. When he proposed the treaties in August 1978, polls showed that 78 percent of Americans opposed returning the canal. One White House official noted that the challenger was to "mobilize middle-of-the-road public support for a SALT Treaty, while avoiding a left-wing vs. right-wing fight [over the Panama Canal] reminiscent of the Sixties. If we fail to act promptly, well-established peace organizations will take the lead, and the anti-disarmament forces will have an opportunity to label us as 'soft.'"[16] They were worried that peace organizations would claim this issue and make it appear that the treaties were a demand of America's left wing rather than a part of Carter's centrist agenda.

And the opposition was energized. According to White House advisor Hamilton Jordan, conservatives considered the fight over Panama to be a "dry run" for the upcoming debate over SALT II. Republicans, he said, were planning to "use the Treaty as a partisan issue" and to embarrass the Democratic president.[17] While there were some genuine fears about how a diminished U.S. role in Panama could pose a security threat in the region, the Panama Canal was an issue that could serve the "conservatives" larger political interest in building support for their organizations and attacking Democrats. "It's patriotism, and that's the issue we do the best with," explained Howard Phillips, head of the Conservative Caucus.[18]

As expected, conservatives attacked through a variety of lobbying groups including the American Conservative Union, the Conservative Caucus, the

Committee for the Survival of a Free Congress, the American Security Council, and the Young Americans for Freedom. The conservative lobby that formed against the treaties sent out a "truth squad" of prominent figures, including Ronald Reagan and Senator Paul Laxalt, to speak in major media markets.[19] They argued that the Soviets would use American withdrawal to gain a stronger foothold in Latin America by expanding Communist influence.

For conservative activists, a victory on the treaties was less important than using Panama to expand the movement's political and financial base and to publicize their movement, which they accomplished. Although Carter and allied liberal interest groups fought hard for the treaties, they were not as organized and they lacked a grassroots force. The most effective tactic that Carter employed was lobbying senators personally. Carter also turned to old-fashioned horse-trading and took advantage of divisions within the conservative movement to garner support for his Panama treaty.

These tactics were sufficient for the president to win the battle over the treaties. In March 1978, the Senate ratified the first Panama treaty by one vote (68 to 32, with two-thirds of the Senate needed for ratification) and ratified the second treaty in April 1978 with the same vote.

Carter saw the treaties as an important success. But conservatives emerged in 1978 with renewed vigor, organizational strength, and disciplined opposition. Carter had cashed in most of his political chips over the Panama Canal.[20] Public opinion about the treaties remained tepid. Carter's popularity plummeted.

Carter confronted conservatives for a second, charged time in 1978 when he initiated negotiations over SALT II. The president based his support for a new arms control agreement on a sunnier view of America's military position than the one held by neoconservatives. And he gave Soviet leaders the benefit of the doubt on their desire to reach an agreement.

Although polls indicated public support for an arms limitation agreement, the administration realized that the domestic path to SALT II would be rough. Many Americans who supported the goals of SALT II doubted that the Soviets could be trusted to keep their end of the bargain.[21] Based on Ford's experience, Carter's advisors concluded that the legislative support for SALT II was thin. These were serious problems for the president, who did not have the hawkish background of Nixon to assuage conservative anxieties.[22]

Throughout the debates in 1978, conservatives demonstrated that they were better prepared to challenge SALT II than the administration was ready to defend it. The anti-SALT forces had strong representation at all levels. In Congress, a well-prepared group that included reputable senators like Scoop Jackson made it difficult for Carter to depict his opponents as extremists. Unlike with the Panama treaty, Republicans were unified on SALT II.

No one in the Senate leadership strongly supported SALT II. Majority Leader Robert Byrd (D-WV) had little trust of the Soviets and greatly respected, and feared, the hawks in his party. Early on, Senate Minority Leader Howard Baker (R-TN) decided that he could not consent to another controversial Carter initiative. Moderates in both parties were skeptical about negotiations. While the administration remained cautious in making any statements for fear of jeopardizing negotiations, Senator Jackson and the right wing showed no hesitation in leveling accusations about the dangers of negotiating with the Soviets and thus received much more press attention than Carter.[23] The "anti-Soviet climate on the Hill," according to congressional liaison Frank Moore, was also making it difficult to achieve an agreement.[24] Conservatives were gradually broadening their support in the Senate thanks to the battles over the Panama treaties. Soviet actions did not help either. As with the Ethiopia-Somalia war, Soviets again added fuel to the fire with their decision to deploy on their borders intermediate range missiles, called SS-20s, that were capable of striking Western Europe. Although Carter considered SALT II to be his most important policy objective because he thought it would lessen the possibility of nuclear war, he could not garner enough senatorial support. Whereas Panama brought Carter an immediate policy victory with significant political costs, the fight for SALT II did not produce any benefit for the president.

The conflicts between Carter and the conservative movement were important to the congressional elections of 1978. Although Democrats retained control of both chambers (59-41 in the Senate and 277-158 in the House), Republicans increased their numbers in the House by fifteen seats and in the Senate by three seats. Five liberal Democrats on whom Carter was counting to vote for SALT II, including one influential member of the Senate Armed Services Committee, were defeated by conservatives whose electoral support included opponents of the Panama treaties. "There are as many interpretations of the mid-term congressional elections as there are interpreters," noted the *Economist*, "but as the dust settled one conclusion seemed even clearer: in the area of foreign policy, the United States Senate has moved significantly to the right."[25] Conservative Republicans from the South and Southwest—who won support from former Democrats—were the most notable victors.

The new Republican legislators, such as Representative Newt Gingrich of Georgia, were not interested in compromising with Democrats. They believed that the GOP needed to embrace the conservative movement as a way to take control of government. Strengthening America's military presence abroad and cutting taxes were their prime concerns. If Carter's policy battles with conservatives had not convinced the president that he faced a serious threat on the Right, the 1978 elections made this threat real and impossible to ignore.

What made matters even more trying for Carter was that he had never developed a strong working relationship with the Democratic leadership in Congress. Most congressional Democrats personally disliked Carter and his Georgia advisors. Speaker Tip O'Neill (D-MA) felt that "Carter rode into town like a knight on a white horse. But while the gentleman leading the charge was capable, too many of the troops he brought with him were amateurs. They didn't know much about Washington, but that didn't prevent them from being arrogant."[26] Legislators were also troubled by media reports about ongoing tensions between Brzezinski and Secretary of State Cyrus Vance. Whereas Brzezinski agreed with neoconservative positions, Vance tended to oppose military operations and focused more heavily on negotiations. The stories of strife created the impression that the president did not fully control his own White House.

Following the elections of 1978, Carter shifted his rhetoric and policies. After two years of holding the line on military budgets, the president called on NATO members to increase defense spending by 3 percent above the rate of inflation each year. On February 28, 1979, Brzezinski outlined a new national security framework centering on the Persian Gulf. The "return to militarism," as one historian called it, was under way.[27]

By the time the "crisis years" began for Carter, his administration was grappling with tremendous political challenges. Administration policies had come under intense fire from the conservative movement. "To the communists and those others who are hostile to our country," Ronald Reagan wrote, "Carter and his supporters in the Congress seem like Santa Claus."[28]

Carter had one reason to be optimistic in 1979 as he helped broker a historic peace agreement between Israel and Egypt. Despite a series of compromises made to reach agreement, the handshake between Anwar Sadat and Menachim Begin on March 26 received international acclaim. The agreement stipulated that Israel would remove troops from the Sinai. Egypt would recognize Israel and open diplomatic channels. The agreement left out the issue of settlements around the Palestinian territories as well as the status of the West Bank. All three American networks covered the event live. While in the cities of Jerusalem and Tel Aviv Israelis flooded the streets to dance to folk music and sing nationalistic songs, most Arab countries opposed the treaties. Many conservatives in the United States feared that the agreement signaled diminished support for Israel, but given the strong public enthusiasm for the accord, most of them remained quiet.

But political problems quickly pushed this peace agreement out of the limelight. Four events between the summer and winter of 1979 created the perception that America was in crisis and that the Cold War was heating up: a revolution in Nicaragua, the revelation of a Soviet brigade in Cuba, the Iran hostage crisis, and the Soviet invasion of Afghanistan.

The first crisis took place in Nicaragua, when the authoritarian regime of Anastasio Somoza collapsed in July. The regime was overthrown by a left-wing revolution under the leadership of the Sandinista National Liberation Front. Prior to the revolution, Carter had refused to support Somoza's Western-friendly regime because of its violation of human rights. Conservatives saw the revolution as proof that the administration was not interested in preventing the spread of Communism in this region.[29]

The second explosive incident involved the revelation of a Soviet brigade in Cuba. After Leonid Brezhnev and President Carter signed the SALT II agreement in Vienna in June 1979, the president sent the treaty to the Senate for ratification. At the signing ceremony, Carter infuriated conservatives by embracing Brezhnev in front of the cameras. Shortly after, Senator Richard Stone (D-FL) and Senator Frank Church (D-ID), chair of the Senate Foreign Relations committee and presidential aspirant, revealed that intelligence reports had uncovered a Soviet brigade of about 2,000 men station in Cuba. For Church, a famous Vietnam opponent who had supported the Panama Canal treaties, this revelation offered him an opportunity to appear tough on foreign policy and to appeal to the conservative electorate of his state. Church had run into trouble in the 1978 elections when conservative organizations purchased ads that superimposed his face next to Fidel Castro. The other senator who publicized the presence of the Soviet brigade, Richard Stone, had taken a tough stand against Cuba since entering the Senate. When the media picked up on the revelation in July, the neoconservative Senator Scoop Jackson immediately called for every Soviet aircraft in Cuba to be removed.[30]

Most military experts agreed that the brigade did not really threaten national security. On September 7, Carter told reporters that the United States had a right to ask that the brigade be removed but that the forces did not represent a danger to the country because they were primarily used to train proxy armies for Africa. "Politics and nuclear arsenals do not mix," the president said.[31] The speech did not change Republican minds or their agenda.[32] A group of bipartisan security experts agreed that regardless of its accuracy, the release of the information had placed SALT in jeopardy by spreading evidence that suggested that the Soviets could still not be trusted.[33]

Conservative legislators called the brigade further proof that the Soviets had not abandoned their expansionist aims. Many senators who were wavering on SALT II withdrew their support. The agreement remained ungratified.

A third crisis arose in early November when militant Iranian students took American diplomats hostage in Tehran. The troubled history of U.S.-Iranian relations dated back to 1953. The Eisenhower administration had authorized the CIA to mount a coup against the democratically elected government of Muhammad Mossadegh, which had moved to nationalize its oil supplies, and to install a regime that would be sympathetic to Western interests. The new regime ended up being that of Shah Pahlavi, with whom the United States had a strong relationship into the 1970s. Many Iranians despised the shah because of his efforts to modernize the country, his authoritarian regime, and his brutal secret police. The human rights lobby had been extremely critical of the shah. Despite his support of human rights and his concerns about the shah, Carter defended his economic support for Pahlavi.

In August and September 1978, revolutionaries in Tehran attacked the government. The revolution included secular intelligentsia and Islamic fundamentalists who were loyal to the Ayatollah Ruhollah Khomeini. Most members of the administration believed that this crisis was part of the Cold War.[34] Some were scared that Khomeini was supported by the Soviets, while others feared that any instability opened up opportunities for the Soviets to influence the region. Brzezinski warned of the "Arc of Crisis" that threatened the Persian Gulf—with the arc extending from Afghanistan to the Horn of Africa.

Carter struggled over his response when the shah requested permission in 1979 to enter the United States to receive medical treatment for cancer. Admitting the shah was a choice that worried the president, as the political fallout could be grave. These concerns were outweighed, however, by the fact that the shah had many influential American supporters. Carter finally decided to allow the shah to enter the United States for treatment in October.

Iranian rebels were furious upon receiving news of the decision. It seemed to many of them that the United States was protecting the shah. On November 4, 1979, students stormed the American embassy in Tehran with fears that the events of 1953 would happen all over again. The Iranians took fifty-two soldiers and diplomats hostage. In their view, the United States was protecting a tyrant by allowing him to avoid trial in his home country. Khomeini praised the "ten thousand martyrs" who had led the revolution. He demanded that "the Great Satan Carter" send the shah back to Iran so that he could stand trial and that the United States return the money that the shah had taken from the Iranian people.[35] Although Americans had seen a series of terrorist incidents in the 1970s, none hit so close to home and none demanded so much attention as the hostage crisis.[36]

Things got worse. In the month after the hostages were taken, the Soviets invaded Afghanistan. The Soviets had maintained close ties to the government of Afghanistan. But Muslim fundamentalists had formed alliances with various tribal leaders to fight against the divided Afghan Communist leadership. The conflicts in Afghanistan caused tremendous concern for the Soviets, who decided to invade and reestablish control in this troublesome country on its border. Brzezinski told the president that the Soviets were trying to achieve their "age-long dream" of direct access to the Indian Ocean. The United States was already involved even before this event. Following the 1979 assassination of the U.S. ambassador in Kabul, Carter had secretly sent support to Muslim guerrillas fighting the Afghan Communists.

Despite this history and the U.S. involvement, President Carter was genuinely shocked when on December 27 Soviet troops crossed the border, moving for the first time into a country that was not part of the Warsaw Pact. The invasion appeared to confirm the gravest warnings of conservatives: the Soviets were committed to reckless expansionism and did not care how the world interpreted their actions. The neoconservative Ben Wattenberg wrote supporters of his Coalition for a Democratic Majority that "people keep saying 'all those lies you've been telling us—are true!'"[37]

"This is the most serious international development that has occurred," Carter wrote in his diary on January 3, 1980, "since I have been President, and unless the Soviets recognize that it has been counterproductive for them, we will face additional problems with invasions or subversion in the future."[38] On January 3, the president requested that Senate Democrats delay further discussions of SALT II in the Senate. The administration concluded that it was not advisable to bring the treaty up for a vote at the time.

It did not take long for these international issues to bubble up and pervade domestic politics. Republicans dismissed the president's tone. They blamed Carter by saying that the Soviets had been emboldened to invade Afghanistan as a result of the administration's foreign policies. In early January, Republicans launched a political offensive against the president. Bill Brock, director of the Republican National Committee, put Democrats on notice. On *Good Morning America*, he stated that "the policy of patience" is the "policy of weakness."[39]

Yet these attacks did not deter the president. During his State of the Union address in 1980, he outlined his "Carter Doctrine" in which he announced a formal U.S. commitment to protect the Persian Gulf Region from Communism. He called for a large increase in defense spending (a 4.5 percent annual increase for five years) and an aggressive response to Soviet activities. "The Soviet attack on Afghanistan and the ruthless extermination of its government," Carter announced, "have highlighted in the starkest terms the darker side of their policies—going well beyond competition and the legitimate pursuit of national interest, and violating all norms of international law and practice."[40]

Throughout the year, and as the presidential election season heated up, Carter strove to demonstrate his toughness on defense. In July 1980, he signed a national security document (PD-59) that endorsed further increased defense spending and planning for targeted nuclear attacks against strategic Soviet sites. The president also convinced Congress to pass legislation that required all males when they reached the age of eighteen to register for a draft—should a system be reinstated. The previous year, Carter officials had resisted this move, despite pressure from the military. While it was good to separate politics from policy, one staffer had said, Democrats Jerry Brown or Massachusetts senator Ted Kennedy would capitalize on such a decision in the 1980 primaries to portray Carter as too much of a hawk.[41] Just in September 1979, after receiving reports on the dire state of the army, the House had killed a proposal for registration by a vote of 2 to 1.

After Afghanistan, however, Carter went so far as to consider reinstating the draft. He was dissuaded from doing so by Vice President Walter Mondale and domestic policy advisor Stuart Eizenstat on the grounds that it would be a political disaster. Nonetheless, with true fears of a full-scale crisis as America struggled on multiple fronts, the president insisted on a registration system owing to his concern that the all-volunteer forces were not up to the job. Since the termination of the draft in 1973, the all-volunteer forces had suffered. Enrollment levels remained low, while pay and bonuses were inadequate. Secretary of Defense Harold Brown had also convinced the president that registration would send a strong message to the Soviets. Even liberal senators who had opposed the draft and registration, such as Alan Cranston (D-CA), said they were willing to consider registration.[42] In the end, Carter concluded that a registration system would be necessary, sufficient, and the most he could realistically obtain. Reagan, who opposed the draft and was Carter's most outspoken foe, said that registration would do nothing for national security.

Carter's most important symbolic move was his announcement that the United States would boycott the Moscow Olympics, an action that conservatives had promoted since 1976. After the invasion of Afghanistan, Carter and his advisors agreed. "There is no single action we could take," said Marshall Brement of the National Security Council, "which could have a greater effect in the Soviet Union."[43] Carter believed that a boycott would punish the Russians and constitute a declaration of moral principle. Carter sent a letter to the president of the Olympic Committee asking for the Games to be moved to a different site if the Soviets did not withdraw within a month. Although critics warned that the boycott would not have a major economic impact on the Soviet Union, proponents believed that a boycott would damage the prestige of the Soviets.

Olympic officials were shocked that any nation would consider boycotting the Games, let alone calling for them to be transferred. The U.S. Olympic Committee claimed that the boycott would punish athletes unfairly. Nonetheless, Carter found public support for the boycott to be strong, including sportswriters and athletes (although there were many athletes who were upset that Carter was mixing politics and sports). One poll found that the public supported the boycott by more than two to one.[44] Strong congressional support existed for the boycott.[45] Democratic and Republican leaders together wrote the Olympic Committee that "we must not let the Olympics be prostituted by the Soviets."[46]

When the International Olympic Committee denied the request to change the venue, the U.S. Olympic Committee voted by a 2-1 margin to endorse the boycott. The majority of the committee did so reluctantly because they were under significant pressure from the president and Congress. After tense negotiations, sixty countries agreed to boycott the events, although many American allies, including Britain, France, and Italy, decided to participate. The Soviets warned the European nations, such as Germany, that the success of the Moscow Olympics was essential to the continuation of détente.

By this time, the forces of anti-Communism were growing around the globe. In Rome, Pope John Paul II mobilized the Catholic Church around the cause of anti-Communism, focusing on the anti-Soviet forces that had emerged in his original home of Poland. In 1979, Margaret Thatcher became the prime minister of England and drew on sharply conservative rhetoric, more akin to Reagan than to Ford, for her harsh words against Communism.

Carter's shift to the Right occurred as the 1980 presidential election was gathering momentum. Before the general election, Carter first had to fend off a primary challenge. Many Democrats thought the party should move left, not right. Throughout the 1970s, politicians such as George McGovern and Frank Church had supported budget cuts in defense spending along with the stern regulations on national security operations, both at home and abroad. Like proponents of détente, these Democrats endorsed negotiations which the nation's adversaries called for policymakers to distinguish between nationalist movements that experimented with socialism and those that were Communist, and endorse aggressive efforts to reach agreements on the reduction of the world's nuclear arsenal. Senator Kennedy, who supported many of these positions, announced his candidacy in 1979. During his campaign, Kennedy lashed out at the president for lacking focus on national security and for unleashing a dangerous, militaristic rhetoric.

The deteriorating crisis in Iran did not help Carter. By January 1980, CBS News anchor Walter Cronkite was ending each broadcast by reminding viewers how long the hostages had been in captivity. When Carter finally decided to use military force to attempt to free the hostages, it was a failure. Without telling Secretary of State Vance, Carter authorized a military rescue attempt on April 24. But the two helicopters crashed in a sandstorm, leaving eight American soldiers dead. With the hostages still captive, the incident turned into a grotesque embarrassment.

In the meantime, Republicans had nominated Ronald Reagan to run for president. From the start of his campaign, Reagan focused on and skewered Carter's national security record. The Iran hostage crisis and Afghanistan served as potent symbols of an administration that had lost control. Reagan also attacked the inefficiencies of such domestic programs as welfare, and he called for steep tax reductions. As the campaign took shape, according to pollster Patrick Caddell, the situation did not look good for the president. Caddell believed that the president was in "jeopardy of losing the center to Reagan." Independent candidate John Anderson (a former Republican from Illinois) was also eating away at Carter's "natural liberal base."[47]

Hawkish Republicans passionately supported Reagan. They saw him as embodying the type of politics that their wing of the GOP had promoted since the 1940s. Although many neoconservatives were torn about how to express their anger toward Carter, a large number would vote for Reagan and begin their break from the party.

The Carter campaign could not figure out a way to overcome Reagan's charisma. The former actor's campaign of renewal and hope contrasted starkly with the image of Carter as an inept president who could not respond to international crises or economic decline. "Our President's admission the other day that he at last believes that the Soviets are not to be trusted would be laughable," Reagan wrote, "if it were not so tragic. Even as he said it, he acknowledged that he would probably be willing to trust them in the near future when he will once again take up the SALT II treaty."[48] While Reagan gave speeches calling for Americans to believe in their country again, Carter delivered speeches about limits. Reagan offered shining optimism, Carter sobering realism.

In the end, Carter's efforts failed to create a stable political majority at home. When crises struck in 1979, centrism was already in political trouble. The president's weakness as a politician and contradictions in his policies had exposed him to domestic attack. Soviet aggression in Somalia, and then Afghanistan, undermined his ability to deliver on the promise of détente. Politicians allied with the conservative movement took advantage of Carter's vulnerability and moved national security politics toward the right.

The defeat of the center in national security politics during the 1970s was a defining moment in the history of modern conservatism. After the tough three-decade struggle against liberal internationalism, right-wing isolationism, and moderates in both parties, hawkish Republicans allied with the conservative movement captured the White House, Senate, and the GOP in 1980.

In one important respect, the 1970s marked the end rather than the beginning of an era for conservatism with regard to national security. The 1970s was the last moment when the movement was an oppositional force rather than one with formal power and responsibilities. Conservatives now needed to demonstrate that they could marshal the same type of political success while governing. Either in the White House or Congress, conservatives would hold positions of influence throughout the next two and a half decades. Along the road to power, conservatives had made crucial decisions that helped them to win on the campaign trail, such as the decision to promote an ambitious vision of what America's national security institutions could achieve. These choices would present major challenges when conservatives were in power.

After the 1970s, American politics would look very different: sustaining moderate positions in national politics would be extremely difficult. When politicians, including President Bill Clinton, adopted this strategy, they did so with thin legislative and party support. By 2000, President George W. Bush and his top strategist Karl Rove would decide to ignore moderate voters on the grounds that Republicans could achieve bigger gains by pleasing the right wing and increasing their voter participation on Election Day. Campaign consultant Matthew Dowd outlined this strategy in a memo that showed how only a minute fraction of the electorate consisted of swing voters.[49] The electorate, Rove and Bush concluded, had become so divided that there were only a limited number of voters who could be persuaded to change their voting patterns. As was evident in national security, the shift was not just a product of institutional or demographic changes, as social scientists argue, but also of a concerted effort by younger conservatives and liberals to defeat the bipartisan center, on national security and other issues, which they felt had stifled politics for too long.

Notes

Introduction

1. Carl N. Degler, "Remaking American History," *Journal of American History* 67 (June 1980): 8–10.

2. Fernand Braudel, *The Mediterranean World in the Age of Philip II*, volume I (Berkeley: University of California Press, 1996).

3. William Leuchtenburg, "The Pertinence of Political History: Reflections on the Significance of the State in America," *Journal of American History* 73 (December 1986): 586.

4. For a good discussion of this literature, see Peter Novick, *That Noble Dream: The 'Objectivity Question' and the American Historical Profession* (New York: Cambridge University Press, 1988), 415–629.

5. Leuchtenburg, "The Pertinence of Political History," 585.

6. Thomas Bender, "Wholes and Parts: The Need for Synthesis in American History," *Journal of American History* 67 (June 1980), 120–136.

7. Julian E. Zelizer, "Introduction to Roundtable," *Social Science History* 24 (2000): 307–16.

TWO: Clio's Lost Tribe

1. For another insightful history of policy history, see Hugh Davis Graham, "The Stunted Career of Policy History: A Critique and an Agenda," *Public Historian* 15 (1993): 15–37. My work focuses much more on the professional and intellectual history of what policy historians have written since the 1970s. I would like to thank Edward Berkowitz, Donald Critchlow, Michael Grossberg, Richard Hamm, Michael Katz, Morton Keller, Eric Patashnik, Beryl Radin, and Nora Zelizer for their suggestions. I would especially like to thank Ellis Hawley for sharing his valuable documents with me.

2. Paula Baker, "Remarks at a Roundtable Discussion on the State of Policy History and Its Future," 27 May 1999, paper presented at the 1999 History Conference, Clayton, Missouri.

3. Edward D. Berkowitz, "The Historian as Policy Analyst: The Challenge of HEW," *Public Historian* 1 (1979): 17–18.

4. For examples of articles that speak to the concerns of the historical profession, see Steven M. Gillon, "The Future of Political History," *Journal of Policy History* 9 (1997): 240–55; Joel H. Silbey, "The State of American Political History at the Millennium: The Nineteenth Century as a Test Case," *Journal of Policy History* 11 (1999): 1–30.

5. Arthur M. Schlesinger Jr., *The Age of Roosevelt: The Coming of the New Deal* (Boston, 1959); William M. Leuchtenburg, *Franklin Roosevelt and the New Deal* (New York, 1963); Richard Hofstadter, *The Age of Reform: From Bryan to F.D.R.* (New York, 1955).

6. Some of the landmark books that dealt with economic regulation in the Progressive and New Deal eras include Gabriel Kolko, *The Triumph of Conservatism* (Glencoe, 1963); James Weinstein, *The Corporate Ideal in the Liberal State* (Boston, 1966). To be sure, there were moderates who studied the relationship between business and economic policy. For one of the best works in this period, see Ellis Hawley, *The New Deal and the Problem of Monopoly* (Princeton, 1966).

7. See, for examples, Roy Lubove, *The Professional Altruist: The Emergence of Social Work as a Career, 1880–1930* (Cambridge, MA, 1965); Michael B. Katz, *The Irony of Early School Reform: Educational Innovation in Mid-Nineteenth-Century Massachusetts* (Cambridge, MA, 1968).

8. Mark H. Leff, "Revisioning U.S. Political History," *American Historical Review* 100 (1995): 829–53.

9. Samuel P. Hays, "The Social Analysis of American Political History," *Political Science Quarterly 80* (1865): 373–94; Paul Kleppner, *The Cross of Culture: A Social Analysis of Midwestern Politics* (New York, 1970); Joel H. Silbey, Allan G. Bogue, and William H. Flanigan, eds., *The History of American Electoral Behavior* (Princeton, 1978).

10. John Higham, *History: Professional Scholarship in America* (Baltimore, 1989), 68–86. See also Benjamin Franklin Cooling, "History Programs in the Department of Defense," *Public Historian* 12 (1990): 43–63; Roger R. Trask, "Small Federal History Offices in the Nation's Capital," *Public Historian* 13 (1991): 47–60.

11. Richard G. Hewlett, "The Practice of History in the Federal Government," *Public Historian* 1 (1978): 30–31.

12. Patricia Mooney-Melvin, "Professional Historians and 'Destiny's Gate,'" *Public Historian* 17 (1995): 21–24.

13. Robert Kelley, "Public History: Its Origins, Nature, and Prospects," *Public Historian* 1 (1978): 24–28.

14. Cited in Theodore S. Hamerow, *Reflections on History and Historians* (Madison, 1987), 8.

15. "Editor's Preface," *Public Historian* 1 (1978): 5.

16. Peter Novick, *That Noble Dream: The "Objectivity Question" and the American Historical Profession* (Cambridge, 1988), 512–21.

17. Both quotations cited in Novick, *That Noble Dream*, 516–17.

18. See, for example, David Rothman, *The Discovery of the Asylum: Social Order and Disorder in the Early Republic* (Boston, 1971); and Paul Boyer, *Urban Masses and Moral Order in America, 1820–1920* (Cambridge, 1978). Much of the scholarship on social control was influenced by Frances Fox Piven and Richard A. Cloward, *Regulating the Poor: The Functions of Public Welfare* (New York, 1971).

19. Louis Galambos, "The Emerging Organizational Synthesis in Modern American History," *Business History Review* 44 (1970): 279–90; Galambos, "Technology, Political Economy, and Professionalization," *Business History Review* 57 (1983): 471–93.

20. Correspondence from Morton Keller, 26 August 1999.

21. Ellis Hawley, "Remarks at a Roundtable Discussion on the State of Policy History and Its Future," 27 May 1999, paper presented at the 1999 Policy History Conference.

22. Morton Keller and Tom McGraw to Ellis Hawley, 13 July 1978, Hawley Papers.

23. Michael Grossberg, "A Report of the Conference on the History of American Public Policy," *Public Historian* 1 (1979): 24.

24. Ibid., 25.

25. Graham, "The Stunted Career of Policy History," 18.

26. James A. Smith, *The Idea Brokers: Think Tanks and the Rise of the New Policy Elite* (New York, 1991).

27. Home Page of the Association for Public Policy Analysis and Management, http://ww.appam.org.

28. Joseph Badaracco, "Report of the Conference on the History of American Public Policy," 2–3 November 1979; and Morton Keller and Thomas McGraw to Ellis Hawley, 23 June 1980.

29. See, for example, Stephen W. Grable, "Applying Urban History to City Planning: A Case Study in Atlanta," *Public Historian* 1 (1979): 45–59; Peter N. Stearns, "History and Policy Analysis: Toward Maturity," *Public Historian* 4 (1982): 5–29.

30. See, for example, W. Andrew Achenbaum, "American Medical History: Social History and Medical History," and Daniel Fox, "History and Health Policy," in *Journal of Social History* 18 (1985): 343–64; James Reed, "Public Policy on Human Reproduction and the Historian," *Journal of Social History* 18 (1985): 383–97.

31. David J. Rothman and Stanton Wheeler, eds., *Social History and Social Policy* (New York, 1981).

32. Herbert G. Gutman, "Mirrors of Hard, Distorted Glass: An Examination of Some Influential Historical Assumptions About the Afro-American Family and the Shaping of Public Policies, 1861–1965," in *Social History and Social Policy*, 239–73.

33. Morton Keller, *Affairs of State: Public Life in Late Nineteenth-Century America* (Cambridge, MA, 1977); Edward Berkowitz and Kim McQuaid, *Creating the Welfare State: The Political Economy of Twentieth-Century Reform* (New York, 1980); William Graebner, *A History of Retirement: The Meaning and Function of an American Institution, 1885–1978* (New Haven, 1980); James T. Patterson, *America's Struggle Against Poverty, 1900–1980* (Cambridge, MA, 1981); W. Andrew Achenbaum, *Shades of Gray: Old Age, American Values, and Federal Policing Since 1920* (Boston, 1983); Michael B. Katz, *In The Shadow of the Poorhouse: A Social History of Welfare in America* (New York, 1986).

34. Thomas K. McCraw, *Prophets of Regulation: Charles Francis Adams, Louis D. Brandeis, James M. Landis, and Alfred E. Kahn* (Cambridge, MA, 1984).

35. Ernest R. May, *Lessons of the Past: The Use and Misuse of History in American Policy* (New York, 1973).

36. Richard E. Neustadt and Ernest R. May, *Thinking in Time: The Uses of History for Decision Makers* (New York, 1986), 275–84.

37. Robert B. and Rosemary Stevens, *Welfare Medicine in America: A Case Study of Medicaid* (New York, 1974); Gilbert Steiner, *The Children's Cause* (Washington, DC, 1976), Henry Aaron, *Politics and the Professors: The Great Society in Perspective* (Washington, DC, 1978); and Martha Derthick, *Policymaking for Social Security* (Washington, DC, 1979); Derthick and Paul J. Quirk, *The Politics of Deregulation* (Washington, D.C., 1985).

38. Novick, *That Noble Dream*, 522–72.

39. Donald Critchlow to Ellis Hawley, 9 January 1984, and Donald Critchlow to Ellis Hawley, 1 February 1984, Hawley Papers.

40. Ibid.

41. Donald T. Critchlow and Ellis W. Hawley, eds., *Federal Social Policy: The Historical Dimension* (University Park, PA, 1988).

42. Ibid., 6.

43. Donald T. Critchlow and Ellis W. Hawley, eds., *Poverty and Public Policy in Modern America* (Chicago, 1989).

44. Andrew Abbot, *The System of Professions: An Essay on the Division of Expert Labor* (Chicago, 1988).

45. David B. Mock, "History in the Public Arena," in *Public History: An Introduction*, eds. Barbara J. Howe and Emory Kemp (Malabar, FL, 1986).

46. Edward Berkowitz, "History, Public Policy and Reality," *Journal of Social History* 18 (1984): 79–89.

47. Neustadt and May, *Thinking in Time*.

48. Ibid., xxii.

49. Hugh Graham later echoed this proposal by claiming that historians were able to understand the "institutions that drive the policy process—their personality and culture, their values and memory, the legacy of their leaders." Hugh Davis Graham, "The Stunted Career of Policy History: A Critique and Agenda," *Public Historian* 15 (1993): 35–36.

50. Margaret Jane Wyszomirski, "Book Review: Thinking in Time," *Journal of Politics* 49 (1987): 607.

51. W. Andrew Achenbaum, "Public History's Past, Present, and Prospects," *American Historical Review* 92 (1987): 1162.

52. Donald Critchlow to Ellis Hawley, 20 February 1987, Hawley Papers. Arnold stepped down in 1990 because of his responsibilities to the Department of Political Science, leaving Critchlow as the only editor. Critchlow moved to Saint Louis University in 1991.

53. Stephen Skowronek, *Building a New American State: The Expansion of National Administrative Capacities, 1877–1920* (Cambridge, 1982); Dietrich Rueschemeyer, Theda Skocpol, and Peter Evans, *Bringing the State Back In* (Cambridge, 1985).

54. Leff, "Revisioning U.S. Political History," 849.

55. One exemplary publication comes from Sarah Binder. Her recent publication draws on a wealth of historical data to argue that partisan interests in the nineteenth and twentieth centuries were the primary factors shaping parliamentary rules for minority rights in Congress. Her work demonstrates clearly how majorities must grapple with rules inherited from the past. Sarah Binder, *Minority Rights, Majority Rules: Partisanship and the Development of Congress* (Cambridge, 1997).

56. Ellis W. Hawley, "Remarks at a Roundtable Discussion," 27 May 1999, paper presented to the 1999 Policy History Conference, Clayton, Missouri.

57. There were exceptions to this trend, which are discussed in the next section of this essay.

58. Jeff Shartlet, "Why Diplomatic Historians May Be the Victims of American Triumphalism," *Chronicle of Higher Education*, 24 September 1999.

59. For a wonderful overview of the public history movement, see the special issue of their journal, *Public Historian* 21 (1999).

60. Otis L. Graham Jr., "The Organization of American Historians and Public History—A Progress," *Public Historian* 18 (1996): 7–10.

61. American Historical Association, *Perspectives* 37 (1999): 59.

62. Patricia Mooney-Melvin, "Professional Historians and 'Destiny's Gate.'"

63. Page Putnam Miller, "Reflections on the Public History Movement," *Public Historian* 14 (1992): 69.

64. Richard A. Posner, *An Affair of State: The Investigation, Impeachment, and Trial of President Clinton* (Cambridge, MA, 1999), 230–40.

65. Cited in Otis L. Graham, "Editor's Corner," *Public Historian* 15 (1993): 12. For the excellent book that emerged, see Otis L. Graham, *Losing Time: The Industrial Policy Debate* (Cambridge, MA, 1992).

66. One notable example is Michael B. Katz, *The "Underclass" Debate Views from History* (Princeton, 1993).

67. Hugh Davis Graham, "The Stunted Career of Policy History: A Critique and an Agenda," *Public Historian* 15 (1993): 16.

68. "JPH Editor's Note," *Journal of Policy History* 3 (1991): 350.

69. W. Andrew Achenbaum, "Politics, Power, and Problems: Perspectives on Writing Policy History," *Journal of Policy History* 1 (1989): 208.

70. Michael B. Katz, *The Undeserving Poor: From Poverty to the War on Welfare* (New York, 1989).

71. Sven Steinmo, *Taxation and Democracy: Swedish, British, and American Approaches to Financing the Modern State* (New Haven, 1993).

72. Linda Gordon, *Pitied But Not Entitled: Single Mothers and the History of Welfare* (New York, 1994), 306. See also Alice Kessler-Harris, "Designing Women and Old Fools: The Construction of the Social Security Amendments of 1939," in *U.S. History as Women's History: New Feminist Essays*, eds. Linda Kerber, Alice Kessler-Harris, and Kathryn Kish Sklar (Chapel Hill, 1995), 87–106; Eileen Boris, *Home to Work: Motherhood and the Politics of Industrial Homework in the United States* (Cambridge, 1994); Nancy Fraser and Linda Gordon, "'Dependency' Demystified: Inscriptions of Power in a Keyword of the Welfare State," *Social Politics* 1 (1994): 4–31; Robyn Muncy, "Gender and Professionalization in the Origins of the U.S. Welfare State: The Careers of Sophonisba Breckinridge and Edith Abbott, 1890–1935," *Journal of Policy History* 2 (1990); 290–315. For a nuanced and innovative analysis of this issue, see Suzanne Mettler, "The Stratification of Social Citizenship: Gender and Federalism in the Formation of Old Age Insurance and Aid to Dependent Children," *Journal of Policy History* 11 (1999): 31–58.

73. Robert C. Lieberman, *Shifting the Color Line: Race and the American Welfare State* (Cambridge, MA, 1998); Jill Quadagno, *The Color of Welfare: How Racism Undermined the War on Poverty* (New York, 1994). For a pointed critique of this type of policy analysis, see Gareth Davies and Martha Derthick, "Race and Social Welfare Policy: The Social Security Act of 1935," *Political Science Quarterly* 112 (1997): 217–35.

74. Theda Skocpol, *Protecting Soldiers and Mothers* (Cambridge, MA, 1992), 539. See also Molly Ladd-Taylor, *Mother Work: Women, Child Welfare, and the State 1890–1930* (Urbana, IL, 1994).

75. Amy Sue Bix, "Diseases Chasing Money and Power: Breast Cancer and AIDS Activism Challenging Authority," *Journal of Policy History* 9 (1997): 5–32. See also William B. Turner "Lesbian/Gay Rights and Immigration Policy: Lobbying to End the Medical Model," *Journal of Policy History* 7 (1995): 208–25.

76. Edward Berkowitz, *Mr. Social Security: The Life of Wilbur Cohen* (Lawrence, KS, 1995).

77. See, for example, Frederic S. Lee, "From Multi-Industry Planning to Keynesian Planning: Gardiner Means, the American Keynesians, and National Economic Planning at the National Resources Committee," *Journal of Policy History* 2 (1990):186–212; Peter Skerry, "The Ambivalent Minority: Mexican Americans and the Voting Rights Act," *Journal of Policy History* 6 (1994): 73–95; Julian E. Zelizer, "'Where Is the Money Coming From?' The Reconstruction of Social Security Finance, 1939–1950," *Journal of Policy History* 9 (1997): 399–424; Meg Jacobs, "The Politics of Purchasing Power: State-Building, Political Economy, and Consumption Politics, 1909–1959 (Ph.D. diss., University of Virginia, 1999); Alan Brinkley, *The End of Reform: New Deal Liberalism in Recession and War* (New York, 1995); Margaret Weir, *Politics and Jobs: The Boundaries of Employment Policy in the United States* (Princeton, 1992).

78. Hugh David Graham, "Race, History, and Policy: African Americans and Civil Rights Since 1964," *Journal of Policy History* 6 (1994): 12–39; Graham, *The Civil Rights Era: Origins and Development of National Policy, 1960–1972* (New York, 1990). Gareth Davies showed how Lyndon Johnson's initial campaign against poverty framed its programs within popular American ideals of individualism and self-sufficiency. The book traces why these efforts were abandoned by the 1970s, but also hints that those older programs offered a vision of federal assistance that might have been more successful politically. See Gareth Davies, *From Opportunity to Entitlement: The Transformation and Decline of Great Society Liberalism* (Lawrence, KS, 1996).

79. Hugh Davis Graham, "Legacies of the 1960s: The American 'Rights Revolution' in an Era of Divided Governance," *Journal of Policy History* 10 (1998): 284.

80. Martha Derthick, "Crossing Thresholds: Federalism in the 1960s," *Journal of Policy History* 8 (1996): 64–80.

81. Helene Silverberg, "State Building, Health Policy, and the Persistence of the American Abortion Debate," *Journal of Policy History* 9 (1997): 311–38. For another insightful example of international comparison to understand alternatives, see Gareth Davies, "Understanding the War on Poverty: The Advantages of Canadian Perspective," *Journal of Policy History* 9 (1997): 425–49.

82. Alfred E. Eckes, "Revisiting Smoot-Hawley," *Journal of Policy History* 7 (1995): 295–310.

83. Michael W. Flamm, "Price Controls, Politics, and the Perils of Policy by Analogy: Economic Demobilization After World War II," *Journal of Policy History* 8 (1996): 335–55.

84. Thomas J. Sugrue, *The Origins of the Urban Crisis: Race and Inequality in Postwar Detroit* (Princeton, 1996).

85. David T. Beito, "Mutual Aid, State Welfare, and Organized Charity: Fraternal Societies and the 'Deserving' and 'Undeserving' Poor, 1990–1930," *Journal of Policy History* 5 (1993): 419–34.

86. Christopher Howard, *The Hidden Welfare State: Tax Expenditures and Social Policy in the United States* (Princeton, 1997).

87. Edwin Amenta, *Bold Relief: Institutional Politics and the Origins of Modern American Social Policy* (Princeton, 1998).

88. Timothy J. Minchin, "Federal Policy and the Racial Integration of Southern Industry, 1961–1980," *Journal of Policy History* 11 (1999): 347–78.

89. Jo Freeman, "The Political Culture of the Democratic and Republican Parties," *Political Science Quarterly* 101 (1986): 327–28.

90. For examples, see the following articles: Gary Mucciaroni, "Political Learning and Economic Policy Innovation: The United States and Sweden in the Post–World War

II Era," *Journal of Policy History* 1 (1989): 391–418; William R. Childs, "Origins of the Texas Railroad Commission's Power and Control Production of Petroleum: Regulatory Strategies in the 1920s," *Journal of Policy History* 2 (1990): 353–87; Douglas Clark Kinder, "Shutting Out the Evil: Nativism and Narcotics Control in the United States," *Journal of Policy History* 3 (1991): 468–93; Carl Abbott, "Five Downtown Strategies: Policy Discourse and Downtown Planning," *Journal of Policy History* 5 (1993): 5–27; Marc Allen Eisner, "Discovering Patterns in Regulatory History: Continuity, Change, and Regulatory Regimes," *Journal of Policy History* 6 (1994): 157–87; Matthew Lasar, "The Triumph of the Visual: Stages and Cycles in the Pornography Controversy from the McCarthy Era to the Present," *Journal of Policy History* 7 (1995): 181–207; Daryl Michael Scott, "The Politics of Pathology: The Ideological Origins of the Moynihan Controversy," *Journal of Policy History* 8 (1996): 81–105.

91. Robert Kelley, *Battling the Inland Sea: Floods, Public Policy, and the Sacramento Valley*, 2d ed. (Berkeley and Los Angeles, 1998), 319–24. See also Kelley, "The Interplay of American Political Culture and Public Policy: The Sacramento River as a Case Study," *Journal of Policy History* 1 (1989): 19; Carolyn Webber and Aaron Wildavsky, *A History of Taxation and Expenditure in the Western World* (New York, 1986), and Frank Dobbin, *Forging Industrial Policy: The United States, Britain, and France in the Railway Age* (Cambridge, 1994). In my own book, I tried to show how political culture influenced Representative Wilbur Mills, chairman of the House Ways and Means Committee, and the tax policy community between the 1940s and 1970s. See Julian E. Zelizer, *Taxing America: Wilbur D. Mills, Congress, and the State, 1945–1975* (Cambridge, 1998).

92. Samuel P. Hays, *Beauty, Health, and Permanence: Environmental Politics in the United States, 1955–1985* (Cambridge, 1987).

93. Donald T. Critchlow, *Intended Consequences: Birth Control, Abortion, and the Federal Government in Modern America* (New York, 1999).

94. Marc Allen Eisner, "Institutional History and Policy Change: Exploring the Origins of the New Antitrust," *Journal of Policy History* 2 (1990): 261–289.

95. Keller, *Affairs of State*. In his more recent work, Keller continued to pursue these themes. See, for example, Keller, *Regulating a New Economy: Public Policy and Economic Change in America 1900–1933* (Cambridge, 1990).

96. Brian Balogh, *Chain Reaction: Expert Debate and Public Participation in American Commercial Nuclear Power, 1945–1975* (Cambridge, 1991), 326.

97. John Earl Haynes, "Applied History or Propaganda? The Influence of History on Farm Credit Legislation in Minnesota," *Public Historian* 10 (1988): 32–33.

THREE: History and Political Science

1. Charles Beard, *An Economic Interpretation of the Constitution of the United States* (New York, 1913).

2. Arthur M. Schlesinger Jr., *The Coming of the New Deal* (Boston, 1959); Ellis Hawley, *The New Deal and the Problem of Monopoly: A Study in Economic Ambivalence* (Princeton, 1966); Arthur E. Bentley, *The Process of Government: A Study of Social Pressures* (Chicago, 1908); Louis Hartz, *The Liberal Tradition in America: An Interpretation of American Political Thought Since the Revolution* (New York, 1955).

3. Richard Hofstadter, *The Age of Reform: From Bryan to F.D.R.* (New York, 1955).

4. Gabriel Kolko, *The Triumph of Conservatism: A Reinterpretation of American History, 1900–1916* (New York, 1963); James Weinstein, *The Corporate Ideal in the Liberal State, 1900-1918* (Boston, 1968).

5. Dorothy Ross, *The Origins of American Social Science* (Cambridge, 1991).

6. Martha Derthick, *Policymaking for Social Security* (Washington, DC, 1979); Hugh Heclo, *Government of Strangers: Executive Politics in Washington* (Washington, DC, 1971); James L. Sundquist, *Politics and Policy: The Eisenhower, Kennedy and Johnson Years* (Washington, DC, 1968); Michael P. Rogin, *The Intellectuals and McCarthy: The Radical Specter* (Cambridge, MA, 1967).

7. Clifford Geertz, *The Interpretation of Cultures: Selected Essays* (New York, 1973).

8. Joel H. Silbey, Allan G. Bogue, and William H. Flanigan, eds., *The History of American Electoral Behavior* (Princeton, 1978).

9. Louis Galambos, "The Emerging Organizational Synthesis in Modern American History," *Business History Review* 44 (1970): 279–90; Galambos, "Technology, Political Economy, and Professionalization," *Business History Review* 57 (1983): 471–93.

10. Julian E. Zelizer, "Clio's Lost Tribe: Public Policy History Since 1978," *Journal of Policy History* 12 (2000): 369–94.

11. Julian E. Zelizer, "Beyond the Presidential Synthesis: Reordering Political Time," in *A Companion to Post-1945 America*, eds. Jean-Christophe Agnew and Roy Rosenzweig (Oxford, 2002): 345–70.

12. Julian E. Zelizer, "Stephen Skowronek's *Building a New American State* and the Origins of American Political Development," *Social Science History* 27 (Fall 2003): 425–41.

13. Peter B. Evans, Dietrich Rueschemeyer, and Theda Skocpol, eds., *Bringing the State Back In* (Cambridge, 1985); Margaret Weir, Ann Shola Orloff, and Theda Skocpol, eds., *The Politics of Social Policy in the United States* (Princeton 1988); Richard Bensel, *Sectionalism and American Political Development, 1880–1980* (Madison, 1984); Stephen Skowronek, *Building a New American State: The Expansion of National Administrative Capacities, 1877–1920* (Cambridge, 1982); Elizabeth M. Sanders, *The Regulation of Natural Gas: Policy and Politics, 1938–1978* (Philadelphia, 1981); Ira Katznelson, *City Trenches: Urban Politics and the Patterning of Class in the United States* (New York, 1981).

14. Stephen Skowronek, *The Politics Presidents Make: Leadership from John Adams to George Bush* (Cambridge, MA, 1993).

15. Brian Balogh, *Chain Reaction: Expert Debate and Public Participation in American Commercial Nuclear Power, 1945–1975* (Cambridge, 1991).

16. Edward D. Berkowitz, *Disabled Policy: America's Program for the Handicapped* (Cambridge, 1978); Berkowitz, *America's Welfare State: From Roosevelt to Reagan* (Baltimore, 1991); Berkowitz, *Mr. Social Security: The Life of Wilbur J. Cohen* (Lawrence, KS, 1995).

17. Richard R. John, *Spreading the News: The American Postal System from Franklin to Morse* (Cambridge, MA, 1995).

18. Julian E. Zelizer, *Taxing America: Wilbur D. Mills, Congress, and the State, 1945–1975* (Cambridge, 1998).

19. Hugh Heclo, "Issue Networks and the Executive Establishment," in *The New American Political System*, ed. Anthony King (Washington, DC, 1978), 90–121; John W. Kingdon, *Agendas, Alternatives, and Public Policies* (Boston, 1984); Frank R. Baumgartner and Bryan D. Jones, *Agendas and Instabilities in American Politics* (Chicago, 1993).

20. Ira Katznelson and Helen V. Milner, eds., *Political Science: State of the Discipline* (New York, 2002).

21. See, for example, Robert D. Putnam, *Bowling Alone: The Collapse and Revival of American Community* (New York, 2000); Theda Skocpol and Morris P. Fiorina, eds., *Civic Engagement in American Democracy* (Washington, DC, and New York, 1999).

22. Kay Lehman Schlozman, "Citizen Participation in America: What Do We Know? Why Do We Care? In *Political Science*, 433–61.

23. Michael C. Dawson, *Black Visions: The Roots of Contemporary African American Political Ideologies* (Chicago, 2001); Dawson, *Behind the Mule: Race, Class, and African American Politics* (Princeton, 2000); and Cathy J. Cohen, *The Boundaries of Blackness: AIDS and the Breakdown of Black Politics* (Chicago, 1999).

24. See, for example, Eric Oliver, *Democracy in Suburbia* (Princeton, 2001).

25. Jennifer L. Hochschild, *Facing Up to the American Dream* (Princeton, 1995); Robert C. Lieberman, *Shifting the Color Line: Race and the American Welfare State* (Cambridge, MA, 1998); Rogers M. Smith, *Civic Ideals: Conflicting Visions of Citizenship in U.S. History* (New Haven, 1997); Martin Gilens, *Why Americans Hate Welfare: Race, Media, and the Politics of Antipoverty Policy* (Chicago, 1999).

26. Michael C. Dawson and Cathy Cohen, "Problems in the Study of the Politics of Race," in *Political Science*, 488–510.

27. Jeffry Frieden and Lisa L. Martin, "International Political Economy: Global and Domestic Interactions," in *Political Science*, 118–46.

28. Daniel T. Rodgers, *Atlantic Crossings: Social Politics in a Progressive Era* (Cambridge, 1998).

29. Paul Pierson, *Politics in Time* (Princeton, 2004).

30. Some notable exceptions by historians that look into their craft include Peter Novick, *That Noble Dream: The "Objectivity Question" and the American Historical Profession* (Cambridge, 1988); Joyce Appleby, Lynn Hunt, and Margaret Jacobs, *Telling the Truth About History* (New York, 1994); John Higham, *History: Professional Scholarship in America*, rev. ed. (Baltimore, 1983); J.G.A. Pocock, *Politics, Language, and Time: Essays on Political Thought and History* (Chicago, 1989); Marc Bloch, *Historians' Craft* (New York, 1953).

31. See, for examples, Pierson, *Politics in Time*; Richard Bensel, "Of Rules and Speakers: Toward a Theory of Institutional Change for the U.S. House of Representatives," *Social Science History* 24 (Summer 2000): 349–66; Elizabeth S. Clemens and James M. Cook, "Politics and Institutionalism: Explaining Durability and Change," *Annual Review of Sociology* 25 (1999): 441–66; Karen Orren and Stephen Skowronek, "Regimes and Regime Building in American Government: A Review of Literature on the 1940s," *Political Science Quarterly* 113 (1998–99): 689–702.

32. See, for example, Julian E. Zelizer, *On Capitol Hill: The Struggle to Reform Congress and Its Consequences, 1948–2000* (Cambridge, 2004).

33. David R. Mayhew, "Supermajority Rule in the U.S. Senate," *PS: Political Science & Politics* 26 (January 2003): 31–36.

34. Pierson, *Politics in Time.*

35. Novick, *That Noble Dream.*

FOUR: Rethinking the History of American Conservatism

1. I would like to thank Meg Jacobs, Kevin Kruse, Dan Rodgers, Bruce Schulman, and Thomas Slaughter for their comments.

2. Alan Brinkley, "The Problem of American Conservatism," and Leo Ribuffo, "Why Is There So Much Conservatism in the United States and Why Do So Few Historians Know Anything About It," *American Historical Review* 99 (April 1994): 409–49. Michael Kazin had written about similar concerns in Kazin, "The Grass-roots Right: New Histories of U.S. Conservatism in the Twentieth Century," *American Historical Review* 97 (February 1992): 429. The best early account of the history of conservatism was written by George H. Nash, *The Conservative Intellectual Movement in America Since 1945* (1976).

3. Meg Jacobs, William Novak, and Julian E. Zelizer, eds., *The Democratic Experiment: New Directions in American Political History* (2003).

4. Thomas Byrne Edsall and Mary D. Edsall, *Chain Reaction: The Impact of Race, Rights, and Taxes on American Politics* (1991); Susan Faludi, *Backlash: The Undeclared War Against Women* (1991); Steve Fraser and Gary Gerstle, eds., *The Rise and Fall of the New Deal Order* (1989).

5. Dan T. Carter, *From George Wallace to Newt Gingrich: Race in the Conservative Counterrevolution, 1963–1994* (1996).

6. Matthew D. Lassiter and Joseph Crespino, eds., *The Myth of Southern Exceptionalism* (2009).

7. Kevin M. Kruse, *White Flight: Atlanta and the Making of Modern Conservatism* (2005); Matthew D. Lassiter, *The Silent Majority: Suburban Politics in the Sunbelt South* (2005); and Joseph Crespino, *In Search of Another Country: Mississippi and the Conservative Counterrevolution* (2007).

8. Thomas J. Sugrue, *The Origins of the Urban Crisis: Race and Inequality in Postwar Detroit* (1996).

9. Cited in Patricia Cohen, "Interpreting Some Overlooked Stories from the South," *New York Times*, May 1, 2007.

10. Lisa McGirr, *Suburban Warriors: The Origins of the New American Right* (2001), 15.

11. Paul Boyer, "The Evangelical Resurgence in 1970s American Protestantism," in *Rightward Bound: Making American Conservative in the 1970s*, eds. Bruce J. Schulman and Julian E. Zelizer (2008), 29–51.

12. Bruce J. Schulman, *The Seventies: The Great Shift in American Culture, Society and Politics* (2001), 202; Joseph Crespino, "Civil Rights and the Religious Right," in Schulman and Zelizer, eds., *Rightward Bound*, 90–105.

13. Matthew D. Lassiter, "Inventing Family Values," in Schulman and Zelizer, eds., *Rightward Bound*, 13–28.

14. Shane Hamilton, *Trucking Country: The Road to America's Wal-Mart Economy* (2008).

15. Elizabeth Tandy Shermer, "Origins of the Conservative Ascendency: Barry Goldwater's Early Senate Career and the Delegitimization of Organized Labor," *Journal of American History* 95 (2008): 678–709.

16. James Morton Turner, "'The Specter of Environmentalism': Wilderness, Environmental Politics, and the Evolution of the New Right," *Journal of American History* 96 (June 2009): 123–48.

17. Steve M. Teles, *The Rise of the Conservative Legal Movement* (2008).

18. Rick Perlstein, *Before the Storm: Barry Goldwater and the Unmaking of the American Consensus* (2001).

19. Jonathan M. Schoenwald, *A Time for Choosing: The Rise of Modern American Conservatism* (2001), 260–61.

20. Alice O'Connor, "Financing the Counterrevolution," in Schulman and Zelizer, eds., *Rightward Bound*, 148–68; Kimberly Phillips-Fein, *Invisible Hands: The Making of the Conservative Movement from the New Deal to Reagan* (2009).

21. The concept of a movement culture comes from Lawrence Goodwyn, *The Populist Moment: A Short History of the Agrarian Revolt in America* (1978).

22. George Nash, *The Conservative Intellectual Movement in America Since 1945*. For a recent book that expands on Nash's arguments, see Patrick Allit, *The Conservatives: Ideas and Personalities Throughout American History* (2009).

23. E. J. Dionne Jr., *Why Americans Hate Politics* (1991), 161, 166, 231–32, 258.

24. Godfrey Hodgson, *The World Turned Right Side Up: A History of the Conservative Ascendancy in America* (1996), 244.

25. McGirr, *Suburban Warriors*, 260–61, 272.

26. Neil J. Young, "We Gather Together: Catholics, Mormons, Southern Baptists and the Question of Interfaith Politics, 1972–1984," PhD diss., Columbia University, 2008.

27. Benjamin Cooper Waterhouse, "A Lobby for Capital: Organized Business and the Pursuit of Pro-Market Politics, 1967–1986," Ph.D. diss., Harvard University, 2009.

28. Steven M. Gillon, *The Pact: Bill Clinton, Newt Gingrich, and the Rivalry that Defined a Generation* (2008), 191.

29. Ryan Sager, *The Elephant in the Room: Evangelicals, Libertarians, and the Battle to Control the Republican Party* (2006), 22.

30. Hugh Graham, *Collision Course: The Strange Convergence of Affirmative Action and Immigration Policy in America* (2002), 75; Paul Pierson, "The Rise and Reconfiguration of Activist Government," in *The Transformation of American Politics: Activist Government and the Rise of Conservatism*, eds. Paul Pierson and Theda Skocpol (2007), 24–26; Marc K. Landy and Martin Levin, eds., *The New Politics of Public Policy* (1995); David Vogel, *Kindred Strangers: The Uneasy Relationship Between Politics and Business in America* (1996), 141–94, 298–388; Vogel, "The 'New' Social Regulation," in *Regulation in Perspective: Historical Essays*, ed. Thomas McGraw (1981), 155–85.

31. Gareth Davies, "Towards Big-Government Conservatism: Conservatives and Federal Aid to Education in the 1970s," *Journal of Contemporary History* 43 (2008): 622.

32. Paul Pierson, *Dismantling the Welfare State? Reagan, Thatcher, and the Politics of Retrenchment* (1994), 69.

33. James T. Patterson, *Restless Giant: The United States from Watergate to Bush v. Gore* (2005), 165.

34. Gareth Davies, *See Government Grow: Education Politics from Johnson to Reagan* (2007), 4.

35. Jacob S. Hacker and Paul Pierson, *Off Center: The Republican Revolution and the Erosion of American Democracy* (2006), 52.

36. Ibid., 46. On gradual policy retrenchment, see Jacob S. Hacker, "Privatizing Risk Without Privatizing the Welfare State: The Hidden Politics of Social Policy Retrenchment in the United States," *American Political Science Review* 98 (May 2004): 243–60; Nolan McCarty, "The Policy Effects of Political Polarization," in Pierson and Skocpol, eds., *The Transformation of American Politics*, 223–55.

37. Martha Derthick and Paul J. Quirk, *The Politics of Deregulation* (1985); Eduardo Canedo, "The Rise of the Deregulation Movement in Modern America, 1957–1980," PhD Diss., Columbia University, 2008.

38. Paul Frymer, *Black and Blue: African Americans, the Labor Movement and the Decline of the Democratic Party* (2008).

39. Nelson Lichtenstein, *State of the Union: A Century of American Labor* (2002), 212–76.

40. Benjamin Edelman, "Red Light States: Who Buys Online Adult Entertainment?" *Journal of Economic Perspectives* 23 (Winter 2009): 209–20.

41. Jeffrey M. Berry, *The New Liberalism: The Rising Power of Citizen Groups* (1999), 1.

42. Samuel P. Hays, *Beauty, Health and Permanence: Environment Politics in the United States, 1955–1985* (1987), 513–20.

43. Everett Carll Ladd Jr. with Charles D. Hadley, *Transformations of the American Party System: Political Coalitions from the New Deal to the 1970s* (1975).

44. David W. Rhode, *Parties and Leaders in the Postreform House* (1991); Sean M. Theriault, *Party Polarization in Congress* (2008).

45. For the best critique of realignment theory, see David R. Mayhew, *Electoral Realignments: A Critique of an American Genre* (2002).

46. John B. Judis and Ray Teixeira, *The Emerging Democratic Majority* (2004).

47. Bruce Miroff, *The Liberals' Moment: The McGovern Insurgency and the Identity Crisis of the Democratic Party* (2007), 3.

48. Stephen Tuck, "'We Are Taking Up Where the Movement of the 1960s Left Off': The Proliferation and Power of African American Protest during the 1970s," *Journal of Contemporary History* 43 (2008): 637–54.

49. Thomas J. Sugrue, *Sweet Land of Liberty: The Forgotten Struggle for Civil Rights in the North* (2008), 501–5.

50. Joshua Zeitz, "Rejecting the Center: Radical Grassroots Politics in the 1970s: Second-wave Feminism as a Case Study," *Journal of Contemporary History* 43 (2008): 677.

51. Jeremy W. Peters, "Why There's No King or Steinem for the Gay Movement," *New York Times*, June 21, 2009.

52. Mary Bernstein, "Identities and Politics: Toward a Historical Understanding of the Lesbian and Gay Movement," *Social Science History* 26 (Fall 2002): 547, 564; Dudley Clendin and Adam Nagourney, *Out for Good: The Struggle to Build a Gay Rights Movement in America* (1999); David Eisenbach, *Gay Power: An American Revolution* (2006).

53. Guian McKee, "'I've Never Dealt with a Government Agency Before': Philadelphia's Somerset Knitting Mills Project, the Local State, and the Missed Opportunities of Urban Renewal," *Journal of Urban History* 35 (March 2009): 387–409.

54. Lawrence S. Wittner, *Toward Nuclear Abolition: A History of the World Nuclear Disarmament Movement, 1971 to the Present* (2003), 486.

55. Julian E. Zelizer, *Arsenal of Democracy: The Politics of National Security—From World War II to the War on Terrorism* (2010).

56. Martin Anderson and Annelise Anderson, *Reagan's Secret War: The Untold Story of His Fight to Save the World from Nuclear Disaster* (2009); James Mann, *The Rebellion of Ronald Reagan: A History of the End of the Cold War* (2009); Paul Lettow, *Ronald Reagan and His Quest to Abolish Nuclear Weapons* (2006). For one of the earlier interpretations of Reagan, see Frances Fitzgerald, *Way Out There in the Blue: Reagan, Star Wars and the End of the Cold War* (2000).

57. Two exceptions are Wittner, *Toward Nuclear Abolition*, and Sean Wilentz, *The Age of Reagan: A History, 1974–2008* (2008).

58. Nash's work on the intellectual history of conservatism was told from this perspective. Most of the recent literature was not, with the exception of Donald T. Critchlow, *Phyllis Schlafly and Grassroots Conservatism: A Woman's Crusade* (2005).

59. Maurice Isserman and Michael Kazin, *American Divided: The Civil War of the 1960s* (2000).

60. Jefferson Cowie and Nick Salvatore, "The Long Exception: Rethinking the Place of the New Deal in American History," *International Labor and Working-Class History* 74 (2008): 3–32; Steve Fraser, *Wall Street: A Cultural History* (2005).

61. Donald T. Critchlow, *The Conservative Ascendancy: How the Right Made Political History* (2007), 286.

62. Paul Pierson and Theda Skocpol, "American Politics in the Long Run," in Pierson and Skocpol, eds., *The Transformation of American Politics*, 4–5.

63. Bruce J. Schulman and Julian E. Zelizer, "Introduction," in Schulman and Zelizer, eds., *Rightward Bound*, 4.

64. Meg Jacobs and Julian E. Zelizer, *The Reagan Revolution* (2010). See also Zelizer, *Arsenal of Democracy*.

65. Daniel T. Rodgers, "In Search of Progressivism," *Reviews in American History* 10 (December 1982): 127.

SIX: The Uneasy Relationship

1. Thomas J. Sugrue, "All Politics Is Local: The Persistence of Localism in Twentieth Century America," *The Democratic Experiment: New Directions in American Political History* (Princeton, NJ: Princeton University Press, 2003), 301–26.

2. Steven R. Weisman, *The Great Tax Wars: Lincoln to Wilson—The Fierce Battles over Money and Power That Transformed the Nation* (New York: Simon & Schuster, 2002).

3. On the legal state of the nineteenth century, see Stephen Skowronek, *Building a New American State: The Expansion of National Administrative Capacities, 1877–1920* (Cambridge: Cambridge University Press, 1982), and William Novak, *The People's Welfare: Law and Regulation in Nineteenth-Century America* (Chapel Hill: University of North Carolina Press, 1996).

4. Paul Pierson, *Dismantling the Welfare State? Reagan, Thatcher, and the Politics of Retrenchment* (Cambridge: Cambridge University Press, 1994).

5. Brian Balogh, "'Mirrors of Desires': Interest Groups, Elections, and the Targeted Style in Twentieth Century Politics," in *The Democratic Experiment: New Directions in American Political History* (Princeton, NJ: Princeton University Press, 2003), 222–49.

6. Anthony J. Badger, "The Limits of Federal Power and Social Politics, 1910–1955, " in *Contesting Democracy: Substance and Structure in American Political History, 1775–2000*, eds. Byron E. Shafter and Anthony J. Badger (Lawrence: University Press of Kansas, 2001), 194–95; Lisa McGirr, *Suburban Warriors: The Origins of the New American Right* (Princeton, NJ: Princeton University Press, 2001); Patricia Nelson Limerick, *The Legacy of Conquest: The Unbroken Past of the American West* (New York: Norton, 1988).

7. Michael S. Sherry, *In the Shadow of War: The United States since the 1930s* (New Haven, CT: Yale University Press, 1995), 261–62.

8. James Savage, *Balanced Budgets and American Politics* (Ithaca, NY: Cornell University Press, 1988), 161–286.

9. Although focusing on an earlier era, Ira Katznelson has shrewdly urged scholars of American political history to avoid using European models of state-building to understand this country and to abandon the "weak state" versus "strong state" dichotomy. See

Katznelson, "Flexible Capacity: The Military and Early American Statebuilding," in *Shaped by War and Trade: International Influences on American Political Development*, eds., Ira Katznelson and Martin Shefter (Princeton, NJ: Princeton University Press, 2002), 82–86.

10. For alternative narratives that take the threat of the right more seriously, see David Plotke, *Building a Democratic Political Order: Reshaping American Liberalism in the 1930s and 1940s* (Cambridge: Cambridge University Press, 1996); Elizabeth Fones-Wolf, *Selling Free Enterprise: The Business Assault on Labor and Liberalism, 1945–1960* (Urbana: University of Illinois Press, 1994); Robert Griffith, "Forging America's Postwar Order: Domestic Politics and Political Economy in the Age of Truman," in *The Truman Presidency*, ed. Michael J. Lacey (Cambridge and Washington, DC: Cambridge University Press and Woodrow Wilson International Center for Scholars, 1989), 57–88.

11. Arthur Schlesinger Jr., *The Age of Roosevelt*, 3 vols. (Boston: Houghton Mifflin, 1957–1960); William E. Leuchtenburg, *Franklin D. Roosevelt and the New Deal, 1932–1940* (New York: Harper Torchbooks, 1963).

12. Leuchtenburg, *Franklin D. Roosevelt*, 332–33.

13. See, for example, Martin J. Sklar, *The Corporate Reconstruction of American Capitalism, 1890–1916: The Market, the Law, and Politics* (Cambridge: Cambridge University Press, 1988); David F. Noble, *America by Design: Science, Technology, and the Rise of Corporate Capitalism* (New York: Knopf, 1977); James Weinstein, *The Corporate Ideal and the Liberal State, 1900–1918* (Boston: Beacon Press, 1968); Gabriel Kolko, *Triumph of Conservatism* (New York: Free Press, 1963).

14. Kolko, *Triumph of Conservatism*, 58.

15. Lizabeth Cohen, *Making a New Deal* (Cambridge: Cambridge University Press, 1990).

16. "AHR Forum: The Problem of American Conservatism," *American Historical Review* 99 (April 1994): 409–52.

17. Louis Galambos, "The Emerging Organizational Synthesis in Modern American History," *Business History Review* 44 (August 1970): 279–90; Samuel P. Hays, *The Response to Industrialism, 1885–1914* (Chicago: University of Chicago Press, 1957); Robert Wiebe, *The Search for Order, 1877–1920* (New York: Hill & Wang, 1967).

18. Louis Galambos, "Parsonian Sociology and Post-Progressive History," *Social Science Quarterly* 50 (June 1969): 25–45.

19. For two insightful critiques of the organizational synthesis that stress inevitability and lack of attention to opposition, see Brian Balogh, "Reorganizing the Organizational Synthesis: Federal-Professional Relations in Modern America," *Studies in American Political Development* 5 (Spring 1991): 119–72, and Alan Brinkley, "Writing the History of Contemporary America: Dilemmas and Challenges," *Deadalus* 113 (Summer 1984): 121–41.

20. For an excellent review of this literature, see Theda Skocpol, *Protecting Soldiers and Mothers: The Political Origins of Social Policy in the United States* (Cambridge, MA: Belknap Press of Harvard University Press, 1992), 1–62.

21. Robert Lieberman, *Shifting the Color Line: Race and the American Welfare State* (Cambridge, MA: Harvard University Press, 1998); Jill Quadagno, *The Color of Welfare: How Racism Undermined the War on Poverty* (New York: Oxford University Press, 1994); Ira Katznelson, Kim Geiger, and Daniel Kryder, "Limiting Liberalism: The Southern Veto in Congress, 1935–1950," *Political Science Quarterly* 108 (1993): 283–302; Quadagno, *The Transformation of Old Age Security: Class and Politics in the American Welfare State* (Chicago: University of Chicago Press, 1988).

22. Linda Gordon, *Pitied but Not Entitled: Single Mothers and the History of Welfare, 1890–1935* (New York: Free Press, 1994); Eileen Boris, *Home to Work: Motherhood and the Politics of Industrial Homework in the United States* (Cambridge: Cambridge University Press, 1994).

23. Michael B. Katz, *The Undeserving Poor: From Poverty to the War on Welfare* (New York: Pantheon, 1989).

24. Thomas Byrne Edsall and Mary D. Edsall, *Chain Reaction: The Impact of Race, Rights, and Taxes on American Politics* (New York: W.W. Norton, 1991); Thomas J. Sugrue, *The Origins of the Urban Crisis* (Princeton, NJ: Princeton University Press, 1998). My point is not to deny that racial animosity fueled resistance to government expansion at key points in American history, since it clearly did. Rather, I argue that these claims are too narrow as explanatory models. I believe that anti-statism, and particularly anti-tax sentiment, was not always about race. It involved a broader distrust of federal government intervention and, more important, an unwillingness to pay money for its services.

25. Gareth Davies and Martha Derthick, "Race and Social Welfare Policy: The Social Security Act of 1935," *Political Science Quarterly* 112 (Summer 1997): 217–35.

26. James Morone, *The Democratic Wish: Popular Participation and the Limits of American Government*, rev. ed. (New Haven, CT: Yale University Press, 1998); Morton Keller, *Affairs of State: Public Life in Late-Nineteenth-Century America* (Cambridge, MA: Belknap Press of Harvard University Press, 1977); Ellis W. Hawley, "Social Policy and the Liberal State in Twentieth-Century America," in *Federal Social Policy: The Historical Dimension*, eds. Donald T. Critchlow and Ellis W. Hawley (University Park: Pennsylvania State University Press, 1988), 117–39; Ellis W. Hawley, *The New Deal and the Problem of Monopoly: A Study in Economic Ambivalence* (Princeton, NJ: Princeton University Press, 1966).

27. See, for example, Anthony King, "Ideas Institutions, and the Policies of Governments: A Comparative Analysis," part 3, *British Journal of Political Science* 3 (October 1973): 409–23; Charles Lockhart, *Gaining Ground: Tailoring Social Programs to American Values* (Berkeley: University of California Press, 1989); Alan Brinkley, *Voices of Protest: Huey Long, Father Coughlin, and the Great Depression* (New York: Vintage, 1982); John W. Kingdon, *America the Unusual* (New York: Worth, 1998).

28. Recently, political scientists have also started to develop a more nuanced understanding of anti-statism by showing how different groups of Americans opposed particular types of government rather than federal intervention altogether. See Elizabeth Sanders, *Roots of Reform: Farmers, Workers, and the American State, 1877–1917* (Chicago: University of Chicago Press, 1999).

29. Robert Higgs, *Crisis and Leviathan: Critical Episodes in the Growth of American Government* (New York: Oxford University Press, 1987); David Beito, *Taxpayers in Revolt: Tax Resistance during the Great Depression* (Chapel Hill: University of North Carolina Press, 1989); Mark Thornton and Chetley Weise, "The Great Depression Tax Revolts Revisited," *Journal of Libertarian Studies* 15 (Summer 2001): 95–105.

30. Sugrue, *Origins of the Urban Crisis.*

31. W. Elliot Brownlee, ed., *Funding the Modern American State, 1941–1995: The Rise and Fall of the Era of Easy Finance* (Cambridge and Washington, DC: Cambridge University Press and Woodrow Wilson Center Press, 1996); Julian E. Zelizer, *Taxing America: Wilbur D. Mills, Congress, and the State, 1945–1975* (Cambridge: Cambridge University Press, 1998); Christopher Howard, *The Hidden Welfare State* (Princeton, NJ: Princeton University Press, 1997).

32. Robin Einhorn has documented how slavery hindered the construction of a national tax system during the founding period. See Robin L. Einhorn, "Slavery and the Politics of Taxation in the Early United States," *Studies in American Political Development* 14 (Fall 2000): 156–83.

33. See, for example, Michael Brown, *Race, Money, and the American Welfare State* (Ithaca, NY: Cornell University Press, 1999); Cathie J. Martin, *Shifting the Burden: The Struggle over Growth and Corporate Taxation* (Chicago: University of Chicago Press, 1991); Ronald F. King, *Money, Time, and Politics: Investment Tax Subsidies and American Democracy* (New Haven, CT: Yale University Press, 1993); James R. O'Connor, *The Fiscal Crisis of the State* (New York: St. Martin's, 1973).

34. David Vogel, *Kindred Strangers: The Uneasy Relationship between Politics and Business in America* (Princeton, NJ: Princeton University Press, 1996), 30.

35. Robert M. Collins, *The Business Response to Keynes* (New York: Columbia University Press, 1981).

36. See, for example, Sanders, *Roots to Reform*.

37. Beito, *Taxpayers in Revolt*, 161.

38. James T. Patterson, *The New Deal and the States: Federalism in Transition* (Princeton, NJ: Princeton University Press, 1969), 168–93.

39. Mark Leff, *The Limits of Symbolic Reform: The New Deal and Taxation, 1933–1939* (Cambridge: Cambridge University Press, 1984), 287.

40. David M. Kennedy, *Freedom from Fear: The American People in Depression and War, 1929–1945* (New York: Oxford University Press, 1999), 284. Leff provides an excellent account of the "symbolic" nature of Roosevelt's taxes on the rich in *Limits of Symbolic Reform*.

41. Brown, *Race, Money, and the American Welfare State*, 32.

42. Jerry R. Cates, *Insuring Inequality: Administrative Leadership in Social Security, 1935–1954* (Ann Arbor: University of Michigan Press, 1983); Brian Balogh, "Securing Support: The Emergence of the Social Security Board as a Political Actor, 1935–1959," in *Federal Social Policy*, ed. Critchlow and Hawley, 55–78.

43. Herbert Stein, *The Fiscal Revolution in America: Policy in Pursuit of Reality*, 2nd ed. (Washington, DC: AEI Press, 1996), 122.

44. Julian E. Zelizer, "The Forgotten Legacy of the New Deal: Fiscal Conservatism and the Roosevelt Administration, 1933–1938," *Presidential Studies Quarterly* 30 (June 2000): 331–58.

45. W. Elliot Brownlee, *Federal Taxation in America: A Short History* (Cambridge and Washington, DC: Cambridge University Press and Woodrow Wilson Center Press, 1996), 67–72.

46. Carolyn C. Jones, "Mass-Based Income Taxation: Creating a Taxpaying Culture, 1940–1952," in *Funding the Modern American State*, ed. Brownlee, 121–25.

47. Theodore J. Lowi, "Four Systems of Policy, Politics, and Choice," *Public Administration Review* 32 (July/August 1972): 299.

48. John Mark Hansen, *Gaining Access: Congress and the Farm Lobby, 1919–1981* (Chicago: University of Chicago Press, 1991), 176–77.

49. Karlyn Bowman, "The History of Taxing Questions in America," *Roll Call*, March 26, 1998. To be sure, polls are an imperfect gauge of public opinion, yet they remain one of the best measures we have of how representative groups of citizens felt on issues in the past, and they have been considered crucial by policymakers (along with interest groups, the media, and elections) as a sign of the "public will."

50. Carolyn Webber and Aaron Wildavsky, *A History of Taxation and Expenditure in the Western World* (New York: Simon & Schuster, 1986), 531.

51. Jill Quadagno, "Culture as Politics in Action: How the 'Red Menace' Derailed National Health Insurance," paper presented at New York University, 2001; Aaron L. Friedberg, "American Antistatism and the Founding of the Cold War State," in *Shaped by War and Trade: International Influences on American Political Development*, eds. Ira Katznelson and Martin Shefter (Princeton, NJ: Princeton University Press, 2002), 246–47.

52. Bowman, "History of Taxing Questions."

53. Sven Steinmo, *Taxation and Democracy: Swedish, British, and American Approaches to Financing the Modern State* (New Haven, CT: Yale University Press, 1993), 39.

54. John F. Witte, *The Politics and Development of the Federal Income Tax* (Madison: University of Wisconsin Press, 1985), 364. For excellent data on polls, see pp. 339–63.

55. Savage, *Balanced Budgets and American Politics*, 1–8.

56. Michael J. Hogan, *A Cross of Iron: Harry S. Truman and the Origins of the National Security State* (Cambridge: Cambridge University Press, 1998).

57. Aaron L. Friedberg, *In the Shadow of the Garrison State: America's Antistatism and Its Cold War Grand Strategy* (Princeton, NJ: Princeton University Press, 2000), 82.

58. Laura McEnaney, *Civil Defense Begins at Home: Militarization Meets Everyday Life in the Fifties* (Princeton, NJ: Princeton University Press, 2000), 25–26.

59. Iwan W. Morgan, *Deficit Government: Taxing and Spending in Modern America* (Chicago: Ivan R. Dee, 1995), 83–84. See also Morgan, *Eisenhower versus "The Spenders": The Eisenhower Administration, the Democrats, and the Budget, 1953–1960* (New York: St. Martin's, 1990).

60. Julian E. Zelizer, "'Where Is the Money Coming From?' The Reconstruction of Social Security Finance, 1939–1950," *Journal of Policy History* 9 (Fall 1997): 339–424.

61. C. Eugene Steuerle, "Financing the American State at the Turn of the Century," in *Funding the Modern American State*, ed. Brownlee, 420.

62. Eric M. Patashnik, *Putting Trust in the US Budget: Federal Trust Funds and the Politics of Commitment* (Cambridge: Cambridge University Press, 2000), 2.

63. Robert M. Collins, *More: The Politics of Economic Growth in Postwar America* (New York: Oxford University Press, 2000).

64. Robert Dallek, *Flawed Giant: Lyndon Johnson and His Times, 1961–1973* (New York: Oxford University Press, 1998), 74.

65. Joseph A. Califano Jr., *The Triumph and Tragedy of Lyndon Johnson: The White House Years* (New York: Simon & Schuster, 1991), 148.

66. Martin, *Shifting the Burden*, 19.

67. Brownlee, "Tax Regimes, National Crisis, and State Building," in *Funding the Modern American State*, ed. Brownlee, 100.

68. Friedberg, *In the Shadow of the Garrison State*, 141–42.

69. Gareth Davies, *From Opportunity to Entitlement: The Transformation and Decline of Great Society Liberalism* (Lawrence: University Press of Kansas, 1996), 52–53.

70. Brown, *Race, Money, and the American Welfare State*, 227–30.

71. Julian E. Zelizer and Eric Patashnik, "Paying for Medicare: Benefits, Budgets, and Wilbur Mills's Policy Legacy," *Journal of Health Policy, Politics, and Law* 26 (February 2001): 7–36.

72. Lawrence Jacobs, *The Health of Nations* (Ithaca, NY: Cornell University Press, 1993), 140.

73. Cited in Brown, *Race, Money, and the American Welfare State*, 241.

74. Zelizer, *Taxing America*, 255–82.

75. Cited in Bruce J. Schulman, *Lyndon B. Johnson and American Liberalism: A Brief Biography with Documents* (Boston: Bedford Books, 1995), 101.

76. Robert M. Collins, "The Economic Crisis of 1968 and the Waning of the 'American Century,'" *American Historical Review* 101 (April 1996): 422.

77. Jacob S. Hacker, *The Divided Welfare State: The Battle over Public and Private Social Benefits in the United States* (Cambridge: Cambridge University Press, 2002), 13–16.

78. Nelson Lichtenstein, "Labor in the Truman Era: Origins of the 'Private Welfare State,'" in *The Truman Presidency*, ed. Lacey, 128–55; Sanford M. Jacoby, *Modern Manors: Welfare Capitalism since the New Deal* (Princeton, NJ: Princeton University Press, 1997); Michael B. Katz, *The Price of Citizenship: Redefining the American Welfare State* (New York: Metropolitan Books, 2001), 177.

79. Paul Pierson, "From Expansion to Austerity: The New Politics of Taxing and Spending," in *Seeking the Center: Politics and Policymaking at the New Century*, eds. Martin A. Levin, Marc K. Landy, and Martin Shapiro (Washington, DC: Georgetown University Press, 2001), 73.

80. Gareth Davies, "The Great Society after Johnson: The Case of Bilingual Education," *Journal of American History* 88 (March 2002): 1405–29; Sidney M. Milkis, *Political Parties and Constitutional Government: Remaking American Democracy* (Baltimore: Johns Hopkins University Press, 1999), 103–73; Hugh Davis Graham, "Since 1964: the Paradox of American Civil Rights Regulation," in *Taking Stock: American Government in the Twentieth Century*, eds. Morton Keller and R. Shep Melnick (Cambridge and Washington, DC: Cambridge University Press and Woodrow Wilson Center Press, 1999), 187–218; Marc K. Landy and Martin A. Levin, eds., *The New Politics of Public Policy* (Baltimore: Johns Hopkins University Press, 1995); Hugh Davis Graham, *The Civil Rights Era: Origins and Development of National Policy, 1960–1972* (New York: Oxford University Press, 1990); Samuel P. Hays, *Beauty, Health, and Permanence: Environmental Politics in the United States, 1955–1985* (Cambridge: Cambridge University Press, 1987).

81. Martha Derthick and Paul J. Quirk, *The Politics of Deregulation* (Washington, DC: Brookings, 1985).

82. Godfrey Hodgson, *The World Turned Right Side Up: A History of the Conservative Ascendancy in America* (Boston: Houghton Mifflin, 1996), 205.

83. Edsall and Edsall, *Chain Reaction*.

84. Pierson, *Dismantling the Welfare State?* 154–55.

85. Morgan, *Deficit Government*, 156.

86. Jeffrey H. Birnbaum and Alan S. Murray, *Showdown at Gucci Gulch: Lawmakers, Lobbyists, and the Unlikely Triumph of Tax Reform* (New York: Random House, 1987).

87. Brownlee, "Tax Regimes, National Crisis, and State Building," 101.

88. Christopher Howard, "Protean Lure for the Working Poor: Party Competition and the Earned Income Tax Credit," *Studies in American Political Development* 9 (Fall 1995): 404–36.

89. Howard, *Hidden Welfare State*, 25.

90. Pierson, *Dismantling the Welfare State?* 154.

91. Steuerle, "Financing the American State," 430.

92. Paul Pierson, "The Deficit and the Politics of Domestic Reform," in *The Social Divide: Political Parties and the Future of Activist Government*, ed. Margaret Weir (New York and Washington, DC: Russell Sage Foundation and Brookings, 1998), 127.

93. R. Kent Weaver, *Ending Welfare as We Know It* (Washington, DC: Brookings Institution Press, 2000), 240–41.

94. Editorial, "Guns and Butter," *Wall Street Journal*, May 17, 2002.

95. Glenn Kessler, "Payroll Tax: The Burden Untouched," *Washington Post*, February 6, 2001.

96. Margaret Levi, *Of Rule and Revenue* (Berkeley: University of California Press, 1988).

SEVEN: Forgotten Legacy of the New Deal

1. National Organization to Reduce Public Expenditures, "Can Government Cut Costs—A Program of National Economy," 1932, Franklin D. Roosevelt Library (FDRL), Hyde Park, NY, Democratic National Committee collection, Box 862, File: Budget.

2. Henry I. Harriman and William Green to Franklin Roosevelt, February 22, 1933, FDRL, President's Personal File 1483: Chamber of Commerce of the United States.

3. Lewis Douglas to Franklin Roosevelt, December 30, 1933, FDRL, President's Personal File, File: Lewis Douglas, 1914.

4. Ibid. See also Lewis Douglas to Franklin Roosevelt, April 13, 1934, FDRL, President's Official File, OF78, Box 1, File: 1933–1934.

5. Diary Entry, September 11, 1934, FDRL, Morgenthau Diaries, Roll 1.

6. Diary Entry, September 6, 1934, FDRL, Morgenthau Diaries, Roll I. See also Lewis Douglas to Franklin Roosevelt, August 30, 1934, FDRL, President's Personal File, File: Lewis Douglas, 1934; Lewis Douglas to Franklin Roosevelt, November 28, 1934, FDRL, President's Personal File, File: Lewis Douglas, 1914.

7. Diary Entry, March 1935, FDRL, Morgenthau Diaries, Roll 2.

8. Diary Entry, November 11, 1935, FDRL, Morgenthau Diaries, Roll 4. For the most comprehensive treatment of Morgenthau, see John Blum's masterful work: *The Morgenthau Diaries* (Boston: Houghton Mifflin, 1959). Since Blum and I both used the Morgenthau diaries, we often draw on similar quotations or events. Blum does not provide much of an analysis comparing Douglas and Morgenthau. For scholars who are interested in a much more comprehensive and detailed study of Morgenthau, within the context of his own personal and professional development rather than within the context of fiscal conservatism, see Blum's study.

9. Diary Entry, October 13, 1936, FDRL, Morgenthau Diaries, Roll 11.

10. Diary Entry, January 1, 1935, FDRL, Morgenthau Diaries, Roll 1.

11. Diary Entry, September 11, 1934, FDRL, Morgenthau Diaries, Roll 1.

12. Ibid.

13. Diary Entry, April 23, 1935, FDRL, Morgenthau Diaries, Roll 2.

14. Meeting Minutes, April 22, 1935, FDRL, Morgenthau Papers, Box 517, File: The President.

15. Diary Entry, April 23, 1935, FDRL, Morgenthau Diaries, Roll 2.

16. Telephone Transcript, May 20, 1935, FDRL, Morgenthau Diaries, Roll 2.

17. Telephone Transcript, May 21, 1935, FDRL, Morgenthau Diaries, Roll 2.

18. Diary Entry, May 23, 1935, FDRL, Morgenthau Diaries, Roll 2.

19. George Haas to Henry Morgenthau, September 4, 1935, FDRL, President's Official File, OF21/Department of Treasury, Box 2, File: 1935; Henry Morgenthau to Franklin Roosevelt, August 10, 1936, FDRL, Morgenthau Diaries, Roll 9.

20. Diary Entry, June 19, 1935, FDRL, Morgenthau Diaries, Roll 3.
21. Diary Entry, January 22, 1935, FDRL, Morgenthau Diaries, Roll 1.
22. Diary Entry, July 3, 1935, FDRL, Morgenthau Diaries, Roll 3.
23. Diary Entry, January 1, 1935, FDRL, Morgenthau Diaries, Roll 1. See also Diary Entry, September 11, 1934, FDRL, Morgenthau Diaries, Roll 1; Diary Entry, August 5, 1935, FDRL, Morgenthau Diaries, Roll 3.
24. Diary Entry, July 1, 1935, FDRL, Morgenthau Diaries, Roll 3.
25. Diary Entry, July 23, 1935, FDRL, Morgenthau Diaries, Roll 3.
26. Diary Entry, November 21, 1935, FDRL, Morgenthau Diaries, Roll 4.
27. Diary Entry, February 2, 1936, FDRL, Morgenthau Diaries, Roll 5.
28. George Haas to Henry Morgenthau, April 28, 1936, FDRL, Morgenthau Diaries, Roll 6.
29. Diary Entry, February 2, 1936, FDRL, Morgenthau Diaries, Roll 5.
30. Diary Entry, February 3, 1936, FDRL, Morgenthau Diaries, Roll 5; Diary Entry, February 11, 1936, FDRL, Morgenthau Diaries, Roll 5.
31. Diary Entry, May 11, 1936, FDRL, Morgenthau Diaries, Roll 7.
32. Diary Entry, May 27, 1936, FDRL, Morgenthau Diaries, Roll 7.
33. Henry Morgenthau Jr. to Franklin Roosevelt, August 10, 1936, FDRL, Morgenthau Diaries, Roll 9.
34. Diary Entry, August 18, 1936, FDRL, Morgenthau Diaries, Roll 9.
35. Diary Entry, August 23, 1936, FDRL, Morgenthau Diaries, Roll 9.
36. Diary Entry, October 1, 1936, FDRL, Morgenthau Diaries, Roll 10.
37. Diary Entry, December 28, 1936, FDRL, Morgenthau Diaries, Roll 13.
38. Roswell Magill to Henry Morgenthau, February 15, 1937, FDRL, Morgenthau Diaries, Roll 15.
39. Diary Entry, April 21, 1937, FDRL, Morgenthau Diaries, Roll 18.
40. Meeting Transcript, September 30, 1937, FDRL, Morgenthau Diaries, Roll 23.
41. Diary Entry, April 19, 1937, FDRL, Morgenthau Diaries, Roll 18.
42. Diary Entry, April 21, 1937, FDRL, Morgenthau Diaries, Roll 18.
43. Meeting Transcript, April 15, 1937, FDRL, Morgenthau Diaries, Roll 18.
44. Meeting Transcript, April 21, 1937, FDRL, Morgenthau Diaries, Roll 18.
45. Meeting Transcript, May 12, 1937, FDRL, Morgenthau Diaries, Roll 19.
46. Meeting Transcript, October 26, 1937, FDRL, Morgenthau Diaries, Roll 25.
47. Telephone Transcript, April 23, 1937, FDRL, Morgenthau Diaries, Roll 18.
48. Diary Entry, October 11, 1937, FDRL, Morgenthau Diaries, Roll 24.
49. Telephone Transcript, April 23, 1937, FDRL, Morgenthau Diaries, Roll 18.
50. Diary Entry, September 20, 1937, FDRL, Morgenthau Diaries, Roll 23.
51. Meeting Transcript, April 26, 1937, FDRL, Morgenthau Diaries, Roll 18.
52. Meeting Transcript, October 29, 1937 and November 8, 1937, FDRL, Morgenthau Diaries, Roll 25.
53. Diary Entry, May 10, 1937, FDRL, Morgenthau Diaries, Roll 19.
54. Diary Entry, July 8, 1937, FDRL, Morgenthau Diaries, Roll 21.
55. Diary Entry, October 11, 1937, FDRL, Morgenthau Diaries, Roll 24. See also Franklin Roosevelt to the Secretary of Agriculture, July 8, 1937, FDRL, Morgenthau Diaries, Roll 21.
56. Meeting Transcript, October 27, 1937, FDL, Morgenthau Diaries, Roll 25.
57. Meeting Transcript, April 21, 1937 and April 22, 1937, FDRL, Morgenthau Diaries, Roll 18.

58. Meeting Transcript, December 15, 1937, FDRL, Morgenthau Diaries, Roll 27.

59. Meeting Transcript, October 22, 1937, FDRL, Morgenthau Diaries, Roll 25.

60. Henry Morgenthau Jr., "Address of the Secretary of Treasury before the Academy of Political Science," November 10, 1937, FDRL, Morgenthau Diaries, Roll 25.

61. Meeting Transcript, November 12, 1937, FDRL, Morgenthau Diaries, Roll 26.

62. Henry Morgenthau Jr. to Franklin Roosevelt, November 4, 1937, FDRL, Morgenthau Diaries, Roll 23.

63. Meeting Transcript, November 12, 1937, FDRL, Morgenthau Diaries, Roll 26.

64. Diary Entry, April 11, 1938, FDRL, Morgenthau Presidential Diaries.

65. Lewis Douglas to Alexander Sachs, February 19, 1952, FDRL, Alexander Sachs Papers, Box 20, File: Lewis Douglas.

66. Meeting Transcript, December 9, 1938, FDRL, Diaries, Roll 42.

67. Meeting Transcript, December 30, 1938, FDRL, Diaries, Roll 42.

EIGHT: "Where Is the Money Coming From?"

1. This quotation comes from Representative Noah Mason (R-IL), who was describing the key issue behind any decision on social welfare. U.S. Congress, House Committee on Ways and Means, *Social Security Legislation: Hearings*, 85th Congress, 2d sess., 1958, 56. The following abbreviations are used in these endnotes: COHP, Columbia University Oral History Project (New York); NA, National Archives: Papers of Ways and Means and the Joint Committee on Internal Revenue Taxation (Washington, DC); NAS, National Archives: Records of the Social Security Administration (College Park, MD): NAT, National Archives: General Records of the Department of Treasury (College Park, MD); RMP, Robert J. Myers Papers, Wisconsin Historical Society (Madison); WCP, Wilbur J. Cohen Papers, Wisconsin Historical Society (Madison); WMPC, Wilbur D. Mills Paper Collection (Conway, AR); HTL, Harry S. Truman Library (Independence, MO); DEL, Dwight D. Eisenhower Presidential Library (Abilene, KS).

2. Bipartisan Commission on Entitlement and Tax Reform, *Final Report to the President*, Washington, DC, January 1995, 8.

3. W. Elliot Brownlee, "Reflections on the History of Taxation," in *Funding the Modern American State, 1941–1995: The Rise and Fall of the Era of Easy Finance*, ed. W. Elliot Brownlee (Cambridge, 1996), 3–36.

4. Much of the recent historiography about Social Security has focused on the racial and gendered exclusions that were embedded, according to their analyses, in the policies. See, for example, Gwendolyn Mink, *The Wages of Motherhood: Inequality in the Welfare State, 1917–1942* (Ithaca, 1995); Linda Gordon, *Pitied But Not Entitled: Single Mothers and the History of Welfare* (New York, 1994); Nancy Fraser and Linda Gordon, "'Dependency' Demystified: Inscriptions of Power in a Keyword of the Welfare State," *Social Politics* 1 (Spring 1994): 12–14; Jill Quadagno, *The Color of Welfare: How Racism Undermined the War on Poverty* (New York, 1994); Quadagno, *The Transformation of Old Age Security: Class and Politics in the American Welfare State* (Chicago, 1988); Rickie Solinger, *Wake Up Little Susie: Single Pregnancy and Race Before Roe v. Wade* (New York, 1992); Michael Katz, *The Undeserving Poor: From the War on Poverty to the War on Welfare* (New York, 1989); James T. Patterson, *America's Struggle Against Poverty, 1900–1985* (Cambridge, MA, 1981).

My work raises three issues regarding the aforementioned literature. First, my findings suggest that there were many other crucial issues on the minds of policy experts and politicians, other than excluding particular groups, that drove the dynamics of Social Security politics. Finance was among the most important. Second, some of the limits built into the program, such as the regressive tax system, were implemented on pragmatic grounds so that the program could withstand political attack. Finally, Social Security policymakers believed in a gradual, incremental expansion of the program and many of the exclusions were gradually eroded. Many African American farm workers, for example, who were initially excluded from the program, were brought into the program through the 1950 amendments. It is essential to understand this long-term strategy in order to understand some of the policy exclusions initially built into the law. In short, my work begins with the question: How did federal policymakers accomplish what they did, despite the nation's anti-statist political culture? as opposed to the question, Why were the accomplishments so limited?

5. For a discussion of the historical relationship between this anti-statist tradition and public policy, see the following: Morton Keller, *Affairs of State: Public Life in Late Nineteenth-Century America* (Cambridge, MA, 1977), and Ellis W. Hawley, "Social Policy and the Liberal State in Twentieth-Century America," in *Federal Social Policy: The Historical Dimension*, eds. Donald T. Critchlow and Ellis W. Hawley (University Park, PA, 1988), 117–41; Barry D. Karl, *The Uneasy State: The United States from 1915 to 1945* (Chicago, 1983).

6. There were many precedents for the use of earmarked taxes to pay for contributory programs. On the federal level, there were a series of smaller programs for selected government workers that used a "contributory system" of finance. These included programs for employees of the federal and District of Columbia governments (1920); officers of the Foreign Service (1924); workers on the Panama Canal (1931); employees of Federal Reserve Banks and the retirement system (1934); and railroad workers (1934). On the state and local level, the Wisconsin unemployment program required firms to pay taxes into their own reserve, which then funded benefits to workers when they were unemployed. Finally, in the private market, the insurance industry provided the clearest model for the use of earmarked contributions. Nonetheless, the Social Security Act marked a dramatic departure in scale and scope from anything that had existed in the past at the federal level. For the best work on the origins of earmarked taxes before the 1930s in the United States and abroad, see Richard Richards, *Closing the Door to Destitution: The Shaping of the Social Security Acts of the United States and New Zealand* (University Park, PA, 1994), chap. 2; Gordon, *Pitied but Not Entitled*, chap. 6; Theda Skocpol, *Protecting Soldiers and Mothers: The Political Origins of Social Policy in the United States* (Cambridge, MA, 1992), chap. 3; Peter Baldwin, *The Politics of Social Solidarity: Class Bases of the European Welfare State, 1875–1975* (Cambridge, 1990).

7. Ranjit S. Teja and Barry Bracewell-Milnes, *The Case for Earmarked Taxes: Government Spending and Public Choice* (London, 1991), 11.

8. Skocpol, *Protecting Soldiers and Mothers.*

9. The main exception involves the debates over a negative income tax between 1964 and 1971. See Daniel P. Moynihan, *The Politics of a Guaranteed Income: The Nixon Administration and the Family Assistance Plan* (New York, 1973); Quadagno, *The Color of Welfare*, 117–34.

10. See, for example, Felicity Skidmore, ed., *Social Security Financing* (Cambridge, MA, 1981); Colin D. Campbell, ed., *Financing Social Security: A Conference Sponsored by the American Enterprise Institute for Public Policy Research* (Washington, DC , 1979). In this article, I discuss only Old-Age Insurance. The Unemployment Compensation

program, which also included an earmarked tax system, offers another important area of study that followed a different trajectory than Old-Age Insurance or Public Assistance.

11. On the debates over the payroll tax during the New Deal, see Mark Leff, *The Limits of Symbolic Reform: The New Deal and Taxation, 1933–39* (Cambridge, 1984), chap. 1; Edward D. Berkowitz, *America's Welfare State: From Roosevelt to Reagan* (Baltimore, 1991), 13–65; Robert J. Myers, "Pay-As-You-Go Financing for Social Security Is the Only Way to Go," *Journal of the American Society of CLU & CHFC* (January 1991): 52–58; Ann Shola Orloff, *The Politics of Pensions: A Comparative Analysis of Britain, Canada, and the United States, 1880–1940* (Madison, WI, 1993); Richards, *Closing the Door to Destitution*, chaps. 2, 5, and 6; Robert M. Ball, *Social Security Today and Tomorrow* (New York, 1978); Otto Eckstein, "Financing the System of Social Insurance," and Joseph A. Pechman, "Discussion of the Paper by Otto Eckstein," in *The Princeton Symposium on the American System of Social Insurance: Its Philosophy, Impact, and Future Development* (New York, 1968), 47–73. For the best analysis of the corporate interests and influence behind this legislation, see Colin Gordon, *New Deals: Business, Labor, and Politics in America, 1920–1935* (Cambridge, 1994), chap. 7.

12. Jerry Cates, *Insuring Inequality: Administrative Leadership in Social Security, 1935–1954* (Ann Arbor, 1983); Martha Derthick, *Policymaking for Social Security* (Washington, DC, 1979), chaps.12, 13, and 17; W. Andrew Achenbaum, *Social Security: Visions and Revisions* (Cambridge, 1986).

13. Cheryl Zollars and Theda Skocpol, "Cultural Mythmaking as a Policy Tool: The Social Security Board and the Construction of a Social Citizenship of Self-Interest," in *Political Culture and Political Structure: Theoretical and Empirical Studies*, ed. Frederick D. Weil for *Research on Democracy and Society* 2 (1994): 381–408; Brian Balogh, "Securing Support: The Emergence of the Social Security Board as a Political Actor, 1935–1939," in *Federal Social Policy: The Historical Dimension*, eds. Donald T. Critchlow and Ellis Hawley (University Park, PA, 1988), 55–78.

14. G. John Ikenberry and Theda Skocpol, "Expanding Social Benefits: The Role of Social Security," *Political Science Quarterly* 102 (Fall 1987): 404–7; Robert J. Myers, "Estimates of the Reserves Under the Old-Age Insurance System in the United States," 18 September 1950, NAS, RG 47, Office of the Actuary, Box 37, File: 705, 1950.

15. Ralph T. Compton, *Social Security Payroll Taxes* (New York, 1940), 31.

16. Robert J. Myers, "Methodology Involved in Developing Long-Range Cost Estimates for the Old-Age, Survivors, and Disability Insurance System," May 1959, Actuarial Study No. 49, RMP, Unprocessed, 48–49; Myers, "Actuarial Aspects of Financing Old-Age and Survivors Insurance," *Social Security Bulletin* 16 (June 1953): 7; Myers to Wilbur Cohen, 11 January 1950, WCP, Box 33, Folder 3.

17. Social Security Administration, "Facts About the Trust Fund of the Federal Old-Age and Survivors Insurance System," January 1950, NAS, Office of the Actuary, Box 37, File: 705, 1950.

18. Carolyn L. Weaver, *The Crisis in Social Security: Economic and Political Origins* (Durham, NC, 1982), chap. 6; Berkowitz, "The First Advisory Council and the 1939 Amendments," in *Social Security After Fifty: Successes and Failures*, ed. Edward D. Berkowitz (New York, 1987), 55–78; Cates, *Insuring Inequality*.

19. Wilbur Cohen to Myer Jacobstein, 31 August 1948, WCP, Box 28, Folder 4. For the best institutional analysis of the Social Security trust fund, see Eric M. Patashnik, "Credible Commitments? The Politics of Federal Government Trust Funds" (Ph.D. diss., University of California, Berkeley, 1996).

20. Myers, "Actuarial Aspects of Financing Old-Age and Survivors Insurance"; Myers, "Old-Age, Survivors, and Disability Insurance Provisions: Summary of Legislation, 1935–1956," *Social Security Bulletin* 20 (July 1957): 3–8; James S. Parker, "Financial Policy in Old-Age and Survivors Insurance, 1935–1950," *Social Security Bulletin* 14 (June 1951): 3–10; Myers to Cohen, 11 January 1950, WCP, Box 33, Folder 3.

21. U.S. Congress, House Committee on Ways and Means, *Social Security Act Amendment of 1939*, 76th Congress, 1st sess., 1939; Weaver, *The Crisis in Social Security*, 118–19.

22. U.S. Department of Treasury, Division of Tax Research, "The Extension of Old-Age and Survivors Insurance to the Self-Employed," 5 December 1945, HTL, Papers of Fred Vinson, Roll 19. See also Wilbur Cohen to Professor Milton Handler, 12 October 1949, WCP, Box 29, Folder 4.

23. Marion Folsom, "Greater Security for Your Old Age," 21 December 1948, NAS, RG 47, Office of the Actuary, Box 26, File: Folsom.

24. Robert J. Myers, "Estimates of the Reserves Under the Old-Age Insurance System in the United States," 18 September 1950, NAS, RG 47, Office of the Actuary, Box 37, File 705, 1950.

25. Technical Staff of the Office of the Secretary of the Treasury, "Questions and Answers on Social Security," 11 March 1949, HTL, Papers of John W. Snyder, Box 85, Folder: Questions and Answers on Social Security.

26. Robert Myers to Wilbur Cohen, 11 January 1950, WCP, Box 33, Folder 3; Myers "The Financial Principle of Self-Support in the Old-Age and Survivors Insurance System," April 1955, Actuarial Study No. 40, RMP, Unprocessed.

27. Roy Blough to Secretary Vinson, 28 February 1946, HTL, Papers of Fred Vinson, Roll 19.

28. Mark H. Leff, "Speculating in Social Security Futures: The Perils of Payroll Tax Financing, 1939–1950," in *Social Security: The First Half-Century*, eds. Gerald D. Nash, Noel H. Pugach, and Richard E. Tomasson (Albuquerque, 1988), 243–78; The American Forum of the Air, "Should We Freeze the Social Security Tax?" 5 December 1944, NAT, RG 56, Office of Tax Policy, Box 40, File: Social Security Finance.

29. Robert Myers to Mr. Williamson, 24 October 1946, NAS, Office of the Actuary, Box 40, File: 750.

30. Robert Myers to G. W. Calvert, 10 July 1947, NAS, Office of the Actuary, Box 26, File: C.

31. U.S. Congress, House Committee on Ways and Means, *Social Security Amendments of 1949: Report Number 1300*, 81st Congress, 1st sess., 1949, 4. For a brief scholarly discussion of the Murray amendment, see E. J. Crowley, "Financing the Social Security Program—Then and Now," U.S. Congress, Joint Economic Committee, Subcommittee on Fiscal Policy, *Studies in Public Welfare: Paper No. 18*, 93d Congress, 2d sess., 1974, 29–32; Wilbur Cohen, "Financing" 1960, WCP, Box 72, Folder 6; Derthick, *Policymaking for Social Security*, 240–41; Leff, "Speculating in Social Security Futures," 243–79, and Leff, "Historical Perspectives on Old-Age Insurance: The State of the Art on the Art of the State," in *Social Security After Fifty*, 29–55.

32. Wilbur J. Cohen, "Cost Factors Under the Wagner-Murray and Dingell Bills," 26 July 1943, WCP, Box 40, Folder 2; Robert Myers to Robert Ball, 17 June 1949, NAS, RG 47, Office of the Actuary, Box 38, File: 710; Myers, "Estimates of the Reserves Under the Old-Age Insurance System in the United States," 18 September 1950, NAS, RG 47, Office of the Actuary, Box 37, File: 705, 1950.

33. Acting Secretary of the Treasury to James Webb, 1 August 1947, HTL, White House Bill File, Box 29, Folder: August 6, 1947 (H.R. 3813-H.R. 4079); Technical Staff of the Office of the Secretary of the Treasury, "Questions and Answers on Social Security," 11 March 1949, HTL, Papers of John W. Snyder, Box 85, Folder: Questions and Answers on Social Security. See also J. S. Parker to Daniel Gerig, 23 April 1946, NAS, RG 47, Office of the Actuary, Box 1, File: Ways and Means Committee (1946).

34. Robert Myers, "Estimates of the Reserves Under the Old-Age Insurance System in the United States," 18 September 1950, NAS, RG 47, Office of the Actuary, Box 37, File: 705, 1950.

35. Robert Myers, "Material for the Meeting of the Advisory Council on Social Security," 12–13 March 1948, NAS, RG 47, Office of the Actuary, Box 5; U.S. Department of Treasury, "Comments on Congressman Reed's Statement on the Old-Age Insurance System," 29 March 1939, NAT, RG 56, Office of Tax Policy, Box 36, File: Social Security and Relief.

36. In 1940, for example, there were only 222,000 people, less than 1 percent of the elderly population, receiving Social Security benefits. Weaver, *The Crisis in Social Security*, 126.

37. This paragraph is drawn from the following works: Nelson Lichtenstein, "From Corporation to Collective Bargaining: Organized Labor and Eclipse of Social Democracy in the Postwar Era," In *The Rise and Fall of the New Deal Order, 1930–1980*, eds. Steve Fraser and Gary Gerstle (Princeton, 1989), 140–45; Beth Stevens, "Blurring the Boundaries: How the Federal Government Has Influenced Welfare Benefits in the Private Sector, "In *Politics of Social Policy in the United States*, eds. Margaret Weir, Ann Shola Orloff, and Theda Skocpol (Princeton, 1988), 123–48; Quadagno, *The Color of Welfare*, 155–73; Gordon, *Pitied But Not Entitled*, 1–3, 287–306; Berkowitz, "Social Security and the Financing of the American State," in *Funding the Modern American State, 1941–1995: The Rise and Fall of the Era of Easy Finance*, ed. W. Elliot Brownlee (Chicago, 1996), 148–93; Weaver, *The Crisis in Social Security*; Derthick, *Policymaking for Social Security*; Cates, *Insuring Inequality*.

38. Derthick, *Policymaking for Social Security*, 273; Berkowitz, *America's Welfare State*, 55–65; Cates, *Insuring Inequality*, 104–53; Jules H. Berman, "State Public Assistance Legislation," *Social Security Bulletin* 12 (December 1949): 3–10.

39. Quadagno, *The Transformation of Old Age Security and the Color of Welfare*; Theodore Marmor, Jerry Mashaw, and Philip Harvey, *America's Misunderstood Welfare State: Persistent Myths, Enduring Realities* (New York, 1990).

40. Derthick, *Policymaking for Social Security*, 271–74; Wilbur Cohen to Herbert Seibert, WCP, Box 66, Folder 5.

41. Staff Comments, "Memorandum for Mr. Murphy: Expansion and Extension of Social Security System," 14 February 1949, WCP, Box 28, Folder 8. This document is also in HTL, Files of Charles S. Murphy, Box 27, Folder: Social Security [Folder 2]. See also W. Rulon Williamson to Robert Myers, 26 March 1949, RMP, Box M86-W3, Unprocessed.

42. Edward D. Berkowitz, *Mr. Social Security: The Life of Wilbur J. Cohen* (Lawrence, KS, 1995), 65–67.

43. U.S. Congress, House Committee on Ways and Means, *Social Security Act Amendments of 1949: Hearings*, 81st Congress, 1st sess., 1949, 1081–83; 1221. See also Arthur Altmeyer, "Old-Age Survivors, and Disability Insurance," *Social Security Bulletin* 12, no. 4 (April 1949): 3–15; Richard Neustadt to Gerhard Colm, 16 December 1949, HTL, Papers

of Richard Neustadt, Box 1, Folder: Chron. Files, 1947–56; Mr. Kirby to Mr. Lynch, 9 November 1948, HTL, Papers of L. Laszlo Ecker-Racz, Box 1, Bound Book.

44. U.S. Congress, House Committee on Ways and Means, *Social Security Act Amendments of 1949: Hearings*, 81st Congress, 1st sess., 1949, 1390.

45. Wilbur Cohen to Arthur Altmeyer, 15 April 1948, WCP, Box 28, Folder 2; Robert Myers to M. A. Linton, 22 April 1949, RMP, Box M86-43, Unprocessed. To improve the chances for passing this bill, Mills and the administration decided to avoid more controversial issues such as health insurance. See Charles Murphy to President Truman, 14 February 1949, and Murphy for the Files, 11 February 1949, HTL, Files of Charles S. Murphy, Box 27, Folder: Social Security [Folder 2].

46. U.S. Congress, House of Representatives, *Congressional Record*, 81st Congress, 1st sess., 5 October 1949, 13905.

47. Robert Myers to Wilbur Cohen, 25 February 1949, RMP, Box M83-106, Unprocessed; Myers to Carl Curtis, 5 May 1949, RMP, Box M86-43, Unprocessed; Myers, "Question Raised by Mr. Byrnes," 5 April 1949, RMP, Box M83-106, Unprocessed; Myers to Wilbur Cohen, 4 June 1947, RMP, Box M83-106, Unprocessed; Myers to Cohen, 24 June 1947, RMP, Box M83-106, Unprocessed. His views were seconded by an Advisory Council on Social Security, which recommended a substantial general-revenue contribution in future years. See Cohen and A. J. Altmeyer, 23 March 1948, WCP, Box 28, Folder 2; Myers, "Actuarial Cost Estimates for Proposals of Social Security Administration and Advisory Council," 14 January 1948, RMP, Box M83-106, Unprocessed.

48. Gerhard Colm and David Christian to Leon Keyserling, 25 January 1949, HTL, Papers of Leon Keyserling, Box 9, Folder: Social Security Program.

49. Robert M. Ball, "What Contribution Rate for Old-Age and Survivors Insurance?" *Social Security Bulletin* 12 (July 1949): 9. Likewise, the CIO and AFL proposed a provision allowing the balance of the cost to be paid through general revenues. See, for example, William Green to President Truman, 14 January 1949, HTL, Official Files 121-A, Box 665, Folder O.F. 121-A, Unemployment Insurance, Social Insurance (May 1949–February 1949).

50. Cited in Derthick, *Policymaking for Social Security*, 240.

51. U.S. Congress, House Committee on Ways and Means, *Social Security Act Amendments of 1949: Hearings*, 81st Congress, 1st sess., 1219.

52. Ibid., 1236.

53. Julian E. Zelizer, "Learning the Ways and Means: Wilbur Mills and a Fiscal Community, 1954–1964," in *Funding the Modern American State, 1941–1995*, 289–352; Zelizer, Taxing America: Wilbur Mills and the Culture of Fiscal Policy, 1949–1969" (PhD diss., Johns Hopkins University, 1996).

54. U.S. Congress, House of Representatives, *Congressional Record*, 81st Congress, 1st sess., 5 October 1949, 13905. Also cited in Leff, "Speculating in Social Security Futures," 266. See also Colin Stam to Wilbur Mills, 28 May 1949, WMPC, Box 38, File: HR 6000.

55. Richard Neustadt to Charles Murphy, 14 July 1950, and Murphy to Wilbur Mills, 14 July 1950, HTL, Papers of Richard Neustadt, Box 1, Folder: Chron. Files, 1947–56. See also David Christian to Leon Keyserling, 2 February 1949, HTL, Papers of Leon Keyserling, Box 9, Folder: Social Security Program. For examples of how Myers attacked critiques of the emerging proposals, see Myers to M. A. Linton, 7 April 1949; Myers to Gordon McKinney, 11 April 1949; Linton to Myers, 20 April 1949; Myers to Reinhard Hohaus, 21 April 1949; Myers to Mills, 27 April 1949; Myers to Linton, 3 May 1949. The

aforementioned documents are in RMP, Box M86-43, Unprocessed. See also Derthick, *Policymaking for Social Security*, 55–58.

56. For a glimpse into the discourse in which Mills, Myers, and Cohen engaged, see the following documents: U.S. Congress, House Committee on Ways and Means, *Actuarial Cost Estimates for the Old-Age and Survivors Insurance System as Modified by the Social Security Act Amendments of 1950*, 27 July 1950, H4488 (Committee–Print); Robert Myers to Wilbur Cohen, 25 January 1950, WCP, Box 29, Folder 6; Myers to Cohen, 25 February 1949; Myers, "Question Raised by Mr. Byrnes," 5 April 1949; Myers to Wilbur Cohen, 2 November 1949; Myers, "Actuarial Cost Estimates on H.R. 6000," 2 November 1949. All the aforementioned documents between Mills and Myers are located in RMP, Box M83-106, Unprocessed. See also Myers to Mills, 29 March 1949; Myers to Mills 15 April 1949; Myers to Mills, 26 April 1949; Myers to Mills, 27 April 1949; Myers to Mills, 5 May 1949; Myers to Mills, 9 May 1949; Myers to M. A. Linton, 22 April 1949; Myers to Reinhard Hohaus, 26 April 1949; Myers to Gordon McKinney, 11 April 1949; Linton to Myers, 20 April 1949, all in RMP, Box M86-43, Unprocessed; Myers to Mills, 23 April 1949, NAS, RG 47, Office of the Actuary, Box 1, File: H 2893.

57. Robert Myers to Ida Merriam, 15 July 1949, RG 47, Office of the Actuary, Box 38, File: 710.

58. Robert J. Myers, "Methodology Involved in Developing Long-Range Cost Estimates for Old-Age, Survivors, and Disability Insurance System," May 1959, Actuarial Study No. 49, RMP, Unprocessed; Myers, "Underlying Factors in Long-Range Actuarial Cost Estimates for OASDI System," 8 June 1962, RMP, Box M83-106, Unprocessed; Myers to Wilbur Cohen, 16 December 1948, WCP, Box 28, Folder 6; Myers to Cohen, 21 May 1948, WCP, Box 41, Folder 3; Myers, interviewed with Peter Corning, 8 March 1967, COHP Interview #1, 7–8; Myers to Jacob Perlman, 6 May 1949, and Perlman to Cohen, 21 April 1948, MAS, RG 47, Office of the Actuary, Box 17, File: 1950–1946.

59. Myers, "Methodology Involved in Developing Long-Range Cost Estimates for Old-Age, Survivors, and Disability Insurance System," May 1959, Actuarial Study No. 49, and Myers, "Long-Range Cost Estimates for the Old-Age and Survivors Insurance: 1954," Actuarial Study No. 39, RMP, Unprocessed; U.S. Congress, House Committee on Ways and Means, *Social Security Act Amendments of 1949: Report Number 1300*, 81st Congress, 1st sess., 1949, 32; Myers to Wilbur Cohen, 25 February 1949, RMP Box M83-106, Unprocessed; Myers to Wilbur Mills, 5 May 1949, RMP, Box M86-43, Unprocessed; Myers to Wilbur Cohen, 5 January 1949, WCP, Box 28, Folder 7; Robert Myers to Mr. Williamson, 14 October 1946, NAS, Office of the Actuary, Box 40, File: 750.

60. U.S. Congress, House Committee on Ways and Means, *Social Security Act Amendments of 1949: Report Number 1300*, 81st Congress, 1st sess., 1949, 2–3. See also The Advisor by Unemployment Benefit Advisors, Inc., 16 June 1949, WCP, Box 36, Folder 3; The Advisor by Unemployment Benefit Advisors, Inc., "Status of Deliberations in Ways and Means—Second Chapter," 5 July 1949, WCP, Box 36, Folder 3; Wilbur Cohen to Edwin Witte, 28 September 1949, WCP, Box 29, Folder 3.

61. Acting Assistant Director, Legislative Reference to William Hopkins, 24 August 1950, HTL, White House Bill File, Box 75, Folder: August 28, 1950 [H.R. 6000-Folder 1].

62. U.S. Congress, House Committee on Ways and Means, *Social Security Act Amendments of 1949: Report Number 1300*, 81st Congress, 1st sess., 1949.

63. Wilbur Cohen, "Bureau Directors' Meeting with Commissioner," August 15 1949, WCP, Box 36, Folder 3.

64. Robert J. Myers, "The Financial Principle of Self-Support in the Old-Age and Survivors Insurance System," RMP, Unprocessed.

65. Oscar Ewing to President Truman, 6 July 1949, HTL, Files of Charles S. Murphy, Box 27, Folder: Social Security.

66. U.S. Congress, House of Representatives, *Congressional Record*, 81st Congress, 1st sess., 4 October 1949, 13835.

67. Ibid., 13836–7.

68. U.S. Congress, House of Representatives, *Congressional Record*, 81st Congress, 1st sess., 5 October 1949, 13835.

69. Cited in Derthick, *Policymaking for Social Security*, 249.

70. Charles S. Murphy to President Truman, 6 October 1949, HTL, Files of Charles S. Murphy, Box 27, Folder: Social Security.

71. Richard Neustadt to Stephen Spingarn, 21 May 1950, HTL, Papers of Richard Neustadt, Box 1, Folder: Chron. Files, 1947–56.

72. Robert J. Myers, "Old-Age, Survivors, and Disability Insurance Provisions: Summary of Legislation, 1935–1958," *Social Security Bulletin* 22 (January 1959): 18; Wilbur J. Cohen, "The Social Security Act Amendments of 1950: Legislative History of the Coverage Provisions," n.d., WCP, Box 249, Folder 3.

73. Wilbur J. Cohen, "The Need for More Adequate Financing of Medical Assistance," n.d., WCP, Box 49, Folder 2; Ruth White, "Vendor Payments for Medical Assistance," *Social Security Bulletin* 13 (June 1950): 3–10; Robert B. Stevens and Rosemary Stevens, *Welfare Medicine in America: A Case Study of Medicaid* (New York, 1974).

74. Richard Neustadt to Charles Murphy, 14 July 1950, HTL, Papers of Richard Neustadt, Box 1, Folder: Chron. Files, 1947–56.

75. Robert J. Myers, "The Financial Principle of Self-Support in the Old-Age and Survivors Insurance System," April 1955, Actuarial Study No. 40, RMP, Unprocessed.

76. Robert J. Myers, "Estimates of the Reserve Under the Old-Age Insurance System in the United States," 18 September 1950, NAS, RG 47, Office of the Actuary, Box 37, File: 705, 1950.

77. U.S. Congress, House Committee on Ways and Means, *Actuarial Cost Estimates for the Old-Age and Survivors Insurance System as Modified by the Social Security Act Amendments of 1950*, 27 July 1950, H4488 (Committee—Print), 3–12; U.S. Department of Treasury, Tax Advisory Staff of the Secretary, "Financing Social Security," 18 January 1952, HTL, Papers of L. Laszlo Ecker-Racz, Box 6, Bound; Robert Myers to Wilbur Cohen, 10 November 1949, and Myers to Cohen, 2 November 1949, in NAS, RG 47, Office of the Actuary, Box 2, File: 1949.

78. Robert J. Myers, "Financing Policy," 1954, Papers of Oveta Culp Hobby, Box 60, Folder: Background Book for 1954 Hearings, OASI.

79. Robert Myers to Wilbur Cohen, 11 January 1950. See also Myers, "Actuarial Balance of OASI System," 25 May 1951; Myers to Cohen, 6 September 1951: Myers, "Actuarial Basis of the Old-Age and Survivors Insurance System as Contrasted with that of Private Life Insurance," 6 June 1952, WCP, Box 33, Folder 3.

80. Robert J. Myers, "Old-Age, Survivors, and Disability Insurance: Financing Basis and Policy Under the 1958 Amendments," *Social Security Bulletin* 21 (October 1958): 15–21.

81. Richard Neustadt to the Director, 14 December 1949, HTL, Papers of Richard Neustadt, Box 1, Folder: Chron. Files, 1947–56.

82. Wilbur D. Mills, "Remarks to the Pulaski County Bar Association," 30 October 1964, WMPC, Box 591, Folder: Mills, Speeches.

83. U.S. Congress, House of Representatives, *Congressional Record*, 83d Congress, 2d sess., 18 March 1954, 3525.

84. Technical Staff of the Office of the Secretary of the Treasury, "Questions and Answers on Social Security," 11 March 1949, HTL, Papers of John W. Snyder, Box 85, Folder: Questions and Answers on Social Security; U.S. Congress, House Committee on Ways and Means, *Social Security Act Amendments of 1949: Hearings*, 81st Congress, 1st sess. 1949, 1371.

85. President Truman to Senator Walter George, 25 July 1950, HTL, Official Files, Box 700, Folder: O.F. 137 (March–April 1951).

86. David E. Bell to Charles Murphy, 23 May 1950, HTL, President's Secretary's Files, Box 160, Folder: Treasury, Secy of (folder 2); Mr. Lynch to Secretary John Snyder, 21 June 1950, HTL, President's Secretary's Files, Box 160, Folder: Treasury, Secy of (folder2); Joseph Pechman to L. Laszlo Ecker-Racz, 7 March 1950, HTL, Papers of L. Laszlo Ecker-Racz, Box 2, Bound; L. Laszlo Ecker-Racz to Assistant Secretary Graham, 31 May 1950, HTL, Papers of L. Laszlo Ecker-Racz, Box 1, Bound; "Representative Mills Would Balance Budget by Speeding up Corporation Tax Collections," 17 May 1949, WMPC, Box 0701, File 1; Press Release, 17 May 1949, WMPC, Box 707, File 1 and Box 40, File 1.

87. Gerhard Colm and David Christian to Leon Keyserling, 25 January 1949, HTL, Papers of Leon Keyserling, Box 9, Folder: Social Security Program.

88. Wilbur J. Cohen, "Should Old-Age Assistance Again Outpace Old-Age Insurance?" WCP, Box 249, Folder 3; Robert J. Myers, "Long-Range Trends in Old-Age Assistance," *Social Security Bulletin* 16 (February 1953): 13–15; "Public Assistance: Effect on the Increase in Current Old-Age and Survivors Insurance Benefits," *Social Security Bulletin* 14 (September 1951): 3–6.

89. Robert J. Myers, "The Financial Principle of Self-Support in the Old-Age and Survivors Insurance System," April 1955, Actuarial Study No. 40, RMP, Unprocessed; Myers, "Long-Range Cost Estimates for Old-Age and Survivors Insurance: 1954," Actuarial Study No. 39, RMP, Unprocessed.

90. Berkowitz, *Mr. Social Security*, 71–94. Within the Treasury, there were also economists who continued to support alternatives to the payroll tax to finance a portion of social insurance. See U.S. Department of Treasury, Tax Advisory Staff of the Secretary, "Financing Social Security," 18 January 1952, HTL, Papers of L. Laszlo Ecker-Racz, Box 6, Bound.

91. See Wilbur J. Cohen, interview with Maclyn P. Burg, 31 March 1976, DEL, Oral History Interview Collection, 16–22; L. A. Minnich Jr., "Legislative Leadership Conference," 17–19 December 1953, DEL, Ann Whitman File, Legislative Meetings Series, Box 1, Folder: Legislative Meetings—1953(6) [August–December]; Dwight D. Eisenhower to J. Earl Schaefer (Boeing Airplane Company), 30 September 1954, DEL, Ann Whitman File, DDE Diary Series, Box 8, Folder: September 1954(1); Eisenhower to the Director of the Bureau of the Budget, 5 November 1953, DEL, Ann Whitman File, DDE Diary Series, Box 3, Folder: November 1953 (3); George Humphrey to Dwight Eisenhower, 5 November 1953, DEL, Ann Whitman File, Administration Series, Box 20, Folder: Humphrey, George M. 1953 (2); Arthur Burns to the Eisenhower Cabinet; 17 May 1954, DEL, Ann Whitman File, Cabinets Series, Box 3, Folder: Cabinet Meeting of April 2, 1954; Robert J. Myers, "Financing Policy," 1954, DEL, Papers of Oveta Culp Hobby, Box 60, Folder: Background Book for 1954 Hearings, OASI; "Extracts from Secretary of the Treasury Humphrey's Press Conference," 21 May 1953, DEL, White House Central Files, Official Files, Box 172, Folder: 9 May 1953; Berkowitz, "Social Security and the Financing of the American State."

92. Berkowitz, *America's Welfare State*, 92–93.

93. Robert J. Myers, "Financing Policy," 1954, and Myers, "The Interrelationship of the OASI Contribution Schedule and the Long-Range Cost Estimates," 22 October 1953, DEL, Papers of Oveta Culp Hobby, Box 60, Folder: Background Book for 1954 Hearings, OASI.

94. Robert Doughton to President Truman, 12 July 1952, HTL, Official Files 121-A, Box 656, Folder: O.F. 121-A, H.R. 7800, Social Security Amendments of 1952.

95. Julian E. Zelizer, *Taxing America: Wilbur D. Mills, Congress, and the State, 1945–1974* (Cambridge, 1998).

NINE: Paying for Medicare

1. Both trust funds also receive income from interest earnings on their holdings of Treasury securities. In addition to payroll taxes, the Hospital Insurance trust Fund derives income from taxation of Social Security benefits, railroad retirement account transfers, reimbursements for uninsured pensions, premiums from voluntary enrollees, and payments for military wage credits.

2. We owe this formulation to Martha Derthick.

3. As commissioner of Social Security, Robert Ball explained to members of the House Ways and Means Committee, "When a worker covered by social security gets a slip in his pay envelope showing how much has been deducted from his pay in social security taxes and how much in earnings has been credited toward benefits he cannot fail to be aware, very concretely, that he is paying toward the cost of his future benefits and that if he wants them to be higher he will have to pay more" (U.S. Congress 1965a: 824).

4. It would not be until the 1980s that seventy-five-year forecasts would be used for Medicare, promoted by concern about the demographic shifts caused by the looming retirement of the massive baby boom generation.

5. Medicare's claim on payroll tax revenues is actually larger than its share of the FICA tax rate implies because there is no cap on the wages subject to the Medicare portion of the tax. By contrast, under Social Security, workers do not pay taxes on wages above $76,200.

6. The 1972 amendments provided for a 20 percent increase in Social Security benefits and automatic adjustment of pension benefits for inflation. Mills himself sponsored the benefit hike. This was a point in Mills's career when he was running for president. He was also starting to experience his battle with alcoholism. In this fight, Mills abandoned his normal fiscal demands in response to his own political ambitions. He would later say that this was one of the biggest mistakes of his career.

7. During the 1980s, Congress regularly voted to set Part B premiums at 25 percent of program costs. In 1990, however, it set specific dollar figures rather than a percentage. These dollar figures reflected CBO's estimate of what 25 percent of program costs would be over the next few years. Program costs grew at a slower rate than expected, however, causing the premium level temporarily to reach 31.5 percent of program costs. See Committee on Ways and Means 1998.

8. The 1999 Breaux-Thomas Medicare Reform Proposal is available online at Thomas.loc.gov/medicare/bbmtt31599.html

9. Based on actuarial estimates made at the time, Clinton's plan was expected to extend Part A's solvency to 2025 from 2015 (the date of the HI Trust Fund's projected

exhaustion according to the 1999 Trustees' Report). As a result of continued economic growth and slower than expected Medicare spending, the 2000 Trustees Report extended the projection of Part A solvency to 2025. Given this updated forecast, Clinton's proposed general fund transfer would thus keep the HI Trust Fund solvent to approximately 2035.

10. The 1999 Breaux-Thomas Medicare reform plan fell one vote short of the supermajority required for the Bipartisan Commission's formal endorsement.

11. Although the right of recipients to healthcare benefits would be retained, the premium-support approach would constitute a significant change from traditional Medicare, which guarantees seniors an entitlement to receive services with unlimited choice of providers in a fee-for-service setting. By contrast, under Clinton's "competitive defined-benefit" proposal for Medicare reform, government support would be tied not to the cost of the average plan but to the cost of the traditional plan. This would offer more protection for seniors but at the expense of placing more financial risk on the government.

12. Robert Reischauer has suggested this idea.

TEN: Seeds of Cynicism

1. Minutes of the Senate Democratic Conference, 9 May 1973, MMP, Collection 65: Mansfield-Mike-U.S. Senate, Series XXXII: Leadership, Box 91, Folder 1.

2. I would like to thank Professor Alan Brinkley for suggesting that I use this puzzle to frame my analysis.

3. The best historical treatment of campaign finance reform, the only one, comes from political scientist Robert E. Mutch, *Campaigns, Congress, and the Courts: The Making of Federal Campaign Finance Law* (New York, 1988), 191. While his book provides the sole historical overview of this subject, it is unsatisfying for a historian since he organizes the book by topic. Besides its lack of a strong analytic argument, the structure obscures how the various components and factions of reform unfolded over time in relation to each other. By compartmentalizing each area of reform, the book fails to explain satisfactorily the chronology of how this issue unfolded—the major task of the historian. Mutch acknowledges the fact that many reforms were proposed before Watergate, and he presents snapshots of the debates in his scattered topical history, but he does not incorporate this fact into any type of systematic analytical framework for understanding the history of the period. Mutch stresses the centrality of scandal to producing reform legislation, while I emphasize the importance of a reform coalition. Another useful, albeit brief, historical article is Anthony Corrado, "Money and Politics: A History of Federal Campaign Finance Law," in *Campaign Finance Reform: A Sourcebook*, eds. Anthony Corrado, Thomas E. Mann, Daniel Ortiz, Trever Potter, and Frank J. Sorauf (Washington, DC, 1997), 27–35. Although I take issue with his thesis, the best historical account of campaign finance reform that relies on the unintended consequences argument is Steven M. Gillon's *"That's Not What We Meant To Do": Reform and Its Unintended Consequences in Twentieth-Century America* (New York, 2000), 200–234. The best nonhistorical overviews of campaign finance are Frank J. Sorauf's *Money in American Politics* (Glenview, IL, 1988) and Sorauf, *Inside Campaign Finance* (New Haven, 1992); Burton D. Sheppard, *Rethinking Congressional Reform: The Reform Roots of the Special Interest Congress* (Cambridge, MA, 1985); Larry J. Sabato, *PAC Power: Inside the World of Politi-*

cal Action Committees (New York, 1984); Elizabeth Drew, *Politics and Money: The New Road to Corruption* (New York, 1983).

4. This reform coalition, and its broader efforts to change Congress, is the focus of my book, *On Capitol Hill.*

5. By stressing the political self-interest in reform, I differ in some respects with the political science literature that stresses how ideas can overcome interest. See, for example, Martha Derthick and Paul J. Quirk, *The Politics of Deregulation* (Washington, DC, 1985), and Gary Mucciaroni, *Reversals of Fortune: Public Policy and Private Interests* (Washington, DC, 1995).

6. On policy incubation, see Nelson W. Polsby, *Political Innovation in America: The Politics of Policy Innovation* (New Haven, 1984), 153–54.

7. Albert Sacks, "Election Contributions and Expenditures: Present Federal Law and Proposals for Change," 15 January 1958, George Meany Archives (GMA), Department of Legislation, Box 7, File 21.

8. Steven Fraser, *Labor Will Rule: Sidney Hillman and the Rise of American Labor* (New York, 1991), 503–17.

9. These pressures are gleaned from a survey of the social science literature on campaign finance. See, for example, Sorauf, *Money in American Elections,* and *Party Politics in America,* 5th ed. (Boston, 1984); Larry Sabato, *The Rise of Political Consultants: The New Ways of Winning Elections* (New York, 1981); and Nelson W. Polsby, "Money in Presidential Campaigns," in *New Federalist Papers: Essays in Defense of the Constitution,* eds. Alan Brinkley, Nelson W. Polsby, and Kathleen M. Sullivan (New York, 1997), 51–58.

10. Martin H. Redish, "Campaign Spending Laws and the First Amendment," *New York University Law Review* 46 (1971): 900–934.

11. Alan Draper, *A Rope of Sand: The AFL-CIO Committee on Political Education* (New York, 1989).

12. Lawton Chiles, "PAC's: Congress on the Auction Block," in *Funding Federal Political Campaigns: PACs, Corporate Activities and Contributions, and Lobbying Laws* (Washington, DC, 1986), 275.

13. William H. Jones, "Political Muscle Desire Began Payoffs," *Washington Post,* 4 January 1976, Sunday, section B; Walter Pincus, "Silent Spenders in Politics—They Really Give at the Office," 1971, GMA, Department of Legislation, Box 7, Folder 20.

14. Edwin M. Epstein, *Corporations, Contributions, and Political Campaigns: Federal Regulation in Perspective* (Berkeley, 1968), 74.

15. George Riley to George Meany, 8 October 1956, GMA, Department of Legislation, Box 32, Folder 23; George Meany, "The Lobby Probe," *AFL-CIO American Federationist* 63 (April 1956): 16–17.

16. Walter Reuther to George Meany, 5 August 1959, GMA, Department of Legislation, Box 10, Folder 27.

17. William Vanderbilt to Members of the Committee on Campaign Expenditures, 12 June 1958, GMA, Department of Legislation, Box 7, File 21.

18. Jim McDevitt to George Meany, 8 May 1958, GMA, Department of Legislation, Box 7, Folder 21.

19. Committee on Campaign Contributions and Expenditures to Senators and Representatives in Congress, 4 November 1958, GMA, Department of Legislation, Box 7, File 21.

20. Herbert Alexander, interview with Julian Zelizer, Washington, DC, 4 March 1999.

21. Citizen's Research Foundation, *Financing the 1960 Election* (Princeton, 1961).

22. Office of the White House Press Secretary, Press Release, 4 October 1961, John F. Kennedy Library [JFKL], Presidential Office Files, Box 93.

23. President's Commission on Campaign Costs, *Financing Presidential Campaigns*, April 1962, JFKL, Presidential Office Files, Box 93.

24. Harold Reis, Memorandum, 3 July 1962, and Alexander Heard to Lee White, 13 July 1962, in JFKL, White House Central Files, Box 206.

25. Robert J. Rosthal to Fred Vinson, 26 July 1965, LBJL, Office Files of Matthew Nimetz, Box 3, File: Financing Political Campaigns.

26. Herbert E. Alexander, *Money in Politics* (Washington, DC, 1972), 33.

27. Terry Robards, "Election Funds May Set Record," *New York Times*, 31 March 1968.

28. "Campaign Spending Regulation: Failure of the First Step," *Harvard Journal of Legislation* 8 (1971): 642.

29. Godfrey Hodgson, *The World Turned Right Side Up: A History of the Conservative Ascendancy in America* (Boston, 1996).

30. Democratic National Committee, Financial Report, 25 March 1965, Lyndon B. Johnson Library [LBJL], Files of Marvin Watson, Box 19, File: DNC/Financial Reports.

31. Democratic National Committee, Financial Records, 1965 and 1966, LBJL, Files of Marvin Watson, Box 19, File: DC/Financial Reports.

32. Julian E. Zelizer, "The Constructive Generation: Thinking about Congress in the 1960s," *Mid-America* 81 (1999): 265–98, and Zelizer, "Bridging State and Society: The Origins of 1970s Congressional Reform," *Social Science History* 12 (2000): 379–90.

33. Arthur Krim to Marvin Watson, 2 November 1967, LBJL, Files of Marvin Watson, Box 19, File: DNC/Financial Reports.

34. Marvin Watson to President Johnson, 25 January 1967, LBJL, Files of Marvin Watson, Box 19, File: DNC/Financial Reports; John Criswell to William White, 16 November 1967, LBJL, Files of Marvin Watson, Box 19, File: DNC/Financial Reports.

35. George H. Gallup, *The Gallup Poll: Public Opinion 1935–1971: Volume Three* (New York, 1972), 2070: 2116–17; George H. Gallup, *The Gallup Pool: Public Opinion 1935–1971: Volume Two* (New York, 1972) 1391, 1445.

36. David Adamy and George Agree, "Election Campaign Financing: The 1974 Reforms," *Political Science Quarterly* 90, no. 2 (Summer 1975): 206.

37. John P. Pomfret, "Johnson Urges Strict New Law on Election Gifts," *New York Times*, 7 May 1966.

38. "Position of Various Senators on Political Campaign Problems," 1967, LBJL, Office Files of John E. Robson and Stanford G. Ross, Box 15, File: Political Process.

39. Richard Neustadt to the President, 20 December 1966, LBJL, Task Force Reports, Box 3, File: 1966 Task Force on Campaign Financing.

40. Record of Meeting, 22 October 1966, LBJL, Task Force Reports, Box 3, File: 1966 Task Force on Campaign Financing.

41. "Testimony of Senator Robert F. Kennedy On Campaign Financing," 6 June 1967, LBJL, Office Files of John Robson and Stanford Ross, Box 15, File: Political Process.

42. Memorandum of a Telephone Conversation, 2 December 1966, LBJL, Task Force Reports, Box 3, File: 1966 Task Force on Campaign Financing.

43. Joseph Califano to President Johnson, 1967, LBJL, White House Aide Files: Papers of Joseph Califano, Box 57, File: Political Process.

44. Joseph Califano to President Johnson, 23 May 1967, LBJL, White House Aide Files: Papers of Joseph Califano, Box 57, File: Political Process.

45. Joseph Barr to President Johnson, 10 June 1967, LBJL, White House Aide Files: Papers of Joseph Califano, Box 57, File: Political Process.

46. Andrew Biemiller to Tom Harris, 29 June 1967, GMA, Department of Legislation, Box 7, Folder 20.

47. Lucas A. Powe Jr., *The Warren Court and American Politics* (Cambridge, MA, 2000), 303–35.

48. *New York Times Co. v. Sullivan*, 376 U.S. 254 (1964).

49. *Mills v. Alabama*, 384 U.S. 214 (1966).

50. Martin H. Redish, "Campaign Spending Laws and the First Amendment," *New York University Law Review* 46 (1971): 900–934.

51. Gary Orren, "Fall from Grace: The Public's Loss of Faith in Government," in *Why People Don't Trust Government*, eds. Joseph S. Nye Jr., Philip D. Zelikow, and David C. King (Cambridge, MA, 1997), 80–81.

52. Twentieth Century Fund Task Force on Financing Congressional Campaigns, *Electing Congress: The Financial Dilemma* (New York, 1970).

53. Fred Vinson Jr. to Ramsey Clark, 14 February 1966, LBJL, Office Files of Matthew Nimetz, Box 3, File: Financing Political Campaigns.

54. National Committee for an Effective Congress, July 1969, and Philip Hart and James Pearson to Fred Harris, 5 August 1969, CAC, Fred Harris Papers, Box 279, File 12.

55. James Abourezk to Carl Albert, 22 September 1971, Carl Albert Collection (CAC), Carl Albert Legislative Files, Box 147, File 5.

56. U.S. Congress, Senate, Committee on Commerce, Subcommittee on Communications, *Hearings: Federal Election Campaign Act of 1971*, 92d Cong., 1st sess., 2–31 March and 1 April 1971, 146–48.

57. Common Cause, "Making Congress Work," November 1970, Common Cause Papers (CCP), Box 216, File: Open-Up-The System.

58. Bryce Harlow, Memorandum for the President, 6 October 1969, Richard Nixon Papers (RNP), White House Central Files, Subject Files FG 31-1: Bryce Harlow, Box 5, Folder 4; Richard Poff, "Diary of White House Leadership Meetings—91st Congress," 7 October 1969, Gerald Ford Library (GFL), Robert Hartmann Papers, Box 106, File: White House-Congressional Leadership Meeting 7 October 1969.

59. Report by Tom Mathews, 1971, and "Statement of John W. Gardner Re Common Cause Lawsuit," 11 January 1971, CCP, Box 27, File: Tom Mathews—1971.

60. For the best existing work on Common Cause, see Andrew S. McFarland, *Common Cause: Lobbying in the Public Interest* (Chatham, NJ, 1984), and Lawrence S. Rothenberg, *Linking Citizens to Government: Interest Group Politics at Common Cause* (Cambridge, MA, 1992).

61. Mutch, *Campaigns, Congress, and Courts*, 46.

62. Adamany and Agree, "Election Campaign Financing," 207.

63. McFarland, *Common Cause: Lobbying in the Public Interest*; Sorauf, *Money in American Politics*, 229.

64. Nelson Polsby, *Consequences of Party Reform* (New York, 1983), 131–56; Byron E. Shafer, *Quiet Revolution: The Struggle for the Democratic Party and the Shaping of Post-Reform Politics* (New York, 1983), 410–13.

65. Nick Thimmesch, "Gardner: Common Cause," *Newsday*, 6 May 1971.

66. Richard E. Cohen, *Rostenkowski: The Pursuit of Power and the End of the Old Politics* (Chicago, 1999), 68.

67. "Statement of John W. Gardner Re Common Cause Lawsuit," 11 January 1971, CCP, Box 27, File: Tom Mathews–1971.

68. Mutch, *Campaigns, Congress, and Courts*, 45.

69. Zelizer, "The Constructive Generation"; Larry J. Sabato, *Feeding Frenzy: How Attack Journalism Has Transformed American Politics* (New York, 1991), 25–26.

70. Numerous examples can be found in U.S. Congress, Senate, Committee on Commerce, Subcommittee on Communications, *Hearings: Federal Election Campaign Act of 1971*, 220–79.

71. U.S. Congress, Senate, Committee on Rules and Administration, Subcommittee on Privileges and Elections, *Hearings: Federal Election Campaign Act of 1971*, 92nd Cong., 1st sess., 24–25, May 1971, 92–93.

72. Ibid., 189.

73. Press Release, 23 June 1971, CAC, Box 147, File 91; Democratic Advisory Council, Democratic National Committee, "Report to the DNC Executive Committee," 19 July 1973, Democratic National Committee Papers (DNCP), Box 22, File: Democratic Advisory Council 1973.

74. Robert Strauss to Democratic Senators and Representatives, 13 May 1974, CAC, Tom Steed Collection, Box 62, File: Democratic Party 1 of 2.

75. Lawrence O'Brien to Members and Friends of the Democratic Party, 27 December 1970, CAC, Tom Steed Papers, Box 43, File: Democratic 2 of 3.

76. Andrew Biemiller to Edward Kennedy, 9 June 1971, GMA, Department of Legislation, Box 7, File 20.

77. Warren Weaver Jr., "Nixon Shift Seen on Campaign Bill," *New York Times*, 17 March 1971.

78. Lowell Beck to John Gardner, 21 June 1971, CCP, Box 28, File: Tom Mathews–1971 III.

79. John Gardner to Senator Frank Moss, 27 June 1971, CCP, Box 28, File: Tom Mathews–1971 III.

80. Robert E. Gallamore to John Gardner, 23 July 1971, CCP, Box 28, File: Tom Mathews–1971 III.

81. Larry Gold to Tom Harris, Ken Young, and Mary Zon, 1 June 1973, GMA, Department of Legislation, Box 7, File 20.

82. Bill Frenzel to John Gardner, 7 July 1971, CCP, Box 23, File: 1971.

83. U.S. Congress, House of Representatives, Committee on House Administration, Subcommittee on Elections, *Hearings: To Limit Campaign Expenditures*, 92nd Cong., 1st sess., 1971, 28.

84. Al Barkan to George Meany, 11 November 1971, GMA, Office of the President: George Meany Files, Box 95, File: Political Education, 1970–72.

85. "Proceedings of the Tenth Constitutional Convention of the AFL-CIO: Volume II," 18–23 October 1973, GMA, 236.

86. "Statement of Clark MacGregor," 29 November 1971, CAC, Carl Albert Legislative Files, Box 144, Folder 1.

87. Editorial, "Nixon's Responsibility . . ." *New York Times*, 30 March 1972.

88. Democratic Study Group, "The Most Corrupt Administration in History," 13 October 1972, Issue Report No. 13, Democratic Study Group Papers (DSGP), Box 22, File: Issue Report #13.

89. Common Cause, Press Release, "The Federal Election Campaign Act of 1971—Is It the Real Thing, or Only a Sham?" 24 February 1972, CCP, Box 136, File: January–March 1972; Minutes of the Executive Committee Meeting of the Policy Council, 22 October 1971, CCP, Box 30, File: September 1970–January 1972.

90. Minutes, Executive Committee Meeting of the Policy Council," January 1972, CCP, Box 30, File: 13 September 1972.

91. Minutes of the Meeting of the Governing Board of Common Cause, 15 February 1972, CCP, Box 30, File: February–July 1972.

92. Minutes, Governing Board of Common Cause, 28–29 September 1973, CCP, Box 31, Folder: 20 July–November 1973.

93. Jack Conway to Carl Albert, 20 September 1972, CAC, Box 134, File 19.

94. John Gardner, Memorandum, 3 October 1972, CCP, Box 23, Folder 1972.

95. John W. Gardner, "We, The People of the United States and Common Cause: Remarks Delivered to Common Cause Membership Meeting," 1 February 1973, CCP, Box 25, File: Speeches—March 1973.

96. *Pipefitters v. United States* 407 U.S. 385 (1972).

97. Alexander, *Money in Politics,* 171.

98. Larry Gold to Tom Harris, Ken Young, and Mary Zon, 1 June 1973, GMA, Department of Legislation, Box 7, File 20. See also "Alice in Wonderland of Campaign Reform," *Memo from COPE,* 14 June 1974, DSGP, Box 27, File: Unmarked.

99. U.S. Congress, Senate, Select Committee on Presidential Campaign Activities, *Hearings: Presidential Campaign Activities of 1972,* 93d Cong., 1st sess., 17–24 May 1973.

100. Ibid., 14–21 December 1973.

101. Ibid., 5–24 October, 12–19 November, 4 December 1973, and 28 January 1974.

102. "Minutes of the Senate Democratic Conference," 9 May 1973, MMP Collection 65: Mansfield-Mike-U.S. Senate, Series XXII: Leadership, Box 91, Folder 1.

103. Bill Brock to Carl Albert, 4 May 1973, CAC, Carl Albert Legislative Files, Box 160, Folder 1.

104. The White House, Press Release, 16 May 1973, GFL, Ford Vice Presidential Papers, Box 143, File: Election Reform.

105. Charles W. Colson, "Public Office, Public Funds," *New York Times,* 19 November 1973.

106. "Minutes of the Senate Democratic Conference," 9 May 1973, MMP, Collection 65: Mansfield-Mike-U.S. Senate, Series XXII: Leadership, Box 91, Folder 1.

107. James O'Hara, "Remarks at the St. Clair Rotary Club, St. Clair, Michigan," 13 August 1973, James O'Hara Papers (JOP), Box 33, File: Speeches January–August 1973.

108. U.S. Congress, Senate, Committee on Rules and Administration, Subcommittee on Privileges and Elections, *Hearings: Federal Election Reform, 1973,* 93d Cong., 1st sess., 11–12 April and 6–7 June 1973, 66–67.

109. "Minutes of the Senate Democratic Congress," 9 May 1973.

110. Michael J. Malbin and Thomas L. Gais, *The Day After Reform: Sobering Campaign Finance Lessons from the American States* (Albany, 1998), 13–14.

111. "Minutes of the Senate Democratic Conference," 9 May 1973.

112. Arch Booth to Members, 8 February 1974, GMA, Department of Legislation, Box 7, File 20.

113. Ralph K. Winter Jr., *Domestic Affairs Studies: Campaign Financing and Political Freedom* (Washington, DC, 1978).

114. "GAO Issues 'Q&Q' Explanation of $1 Income Tax Check-off," 14 March 1974, CAC, Carl Albert Legislative Files, Box 188, Folder 10.

115. "Minutes of the Senate Democratic Conference," 30 January 1974, MMP, Collection 65: Mansfield-Mike-U.S. Senate, Series XXII: Leadership, Box 91, Folder 1.

116. "Minutes of the Democratic Conference," 24 January 1974, MMP, Collection 65: Mansfield-Mike-U.S. Senate, Series XXII: Leadership, Box 91, Folder 1.

117. George Gallup, *The Gallup Poll: Public Opinion, 1972–1977 Volume I* (New York, 1978), 146–86.

118. President Richard Nixon to Speaker Carl Albert, 27 March 1974, RNP, White House Subject Files, FG 34, Box 15, File: 2 of 3.

119. Editorial, "Inadequate Reform," *New York Times*, 16 March 1974: "Pastore Criticizes Nixon Proposals for Vote Reforms," *New York Times*, 16 March 1974.

120. Christopher Lydon, "Hays Opposes Public Subsidies for House and Senate Campaigns in Election Reform Bill," *New York Times*, 28 February 1974.

121. Ken Cole to President Ford, 21 August 1974, GFL, White House Central Files, Box 77, File: PL2.

122. William Timmons, "Meeting with Rep. Hays," 12 September 1974, GFL, William Timmons Files, Box 5, File: Meeting with Representatives & Senators—Briefing Papers September 1974.

123. NBC Nightly News, 17 September 1974, GFL, Weekly News Summary Videos, Tape 1, File: F073.

124. Mutch, *Campaigns, Congress, and Courts*, 164–65.

125. CBS Nightly News, 13 September 1974, GFL, Weekly News Summary Videos, Tape F069B.

126. Minutes, Governing Board of Common Cause, 28–29 September 1973, CCP, Box 31, Folder: 20 July–10 November 1973.

127. William Timmons to President Ford, 9 October 1974, GFL, William Timmons Files, Box 2, File: Campaign Financing Reform Legislation. See also Ken Cole to President Ford, 26 August 1974, GFL, William Timmons Files, Box 2 File: Campaign Financing Reform Legislation.

128. White House, Press Release, 15 October 1974, GFL, Philip Buchen Files, Box 14, File: Federal Election Campaign Act Amendments—1974.

129. Congressional Quarterly, *The 1974 Election Report*, 12 October 1974, 2714.

130. ABC Nightly News, 5 November 1974, GFL, Weekly News Summary, Tape F134.

131. "Labor and A.M.A. Top List in '74 Spending on Politics," *New York Times*, 29 October 1974; David E. Rosenbaum, "Special Interests Donate $8.5 Million So Far in '74," *New York Times*, 1 November 1974; "The 1974 Elections: The New Potential," *AFL-CIO American Federationist* 81, no. 12 (December 1974): 1–5, "Proceedings of the Eleventh Constitutional Convention of the AFL-CIO: Volume II," 2–7 October 1975, GMA, 351–52.

132. David E. Rosenbaum, "Who Is Paying for the Election? People Who Want Something," *New York Times*, 3 November 1974, Sunday, section IV.

133. "Statement by John W. Gardner," 20 November 1974, CCP, Box 216, File: Open-Up-The-System.

134. For an alternative explanation of why Americans continued to hate politics, see E. J. Dionne Jr., *Why Americans Hate Politics* (New York, 1991).

135. Herbert E. Alexander, "Political Finance Regulation in International Perspective," in *Parties, Interest Groups, and Campaign Finance Laws*, ed. Michael J. Malbin (Washington, DC, 1980), 336.

ELEVEN: Bridging State and Society

1. *Baker v. Carr*, 369 U.S. 186 (1962); *Wesberry v. Sanders*, 376 U.S. 1 (1964); and *Reynolds v. Sims* 377 U.S. 533 (1964).

2. Terrence T. Finn to members of the Select Committee on Committees, House of Representatives, 1973, Personal Papers of Walter Oleszek (Congressional Research Service). Oleszek allowed me access to his papers, and a copy of this document is in my possession.

TWELVE: Without Restraint

1. Ronald Brownstein, "Life in the Time of Scandal," *U.S. News & World Report*, 27 April 1998, 15.

2. Thomas E. Patterson, "The United States: News in a Free-Market Society," in *Democracy and the Media: A Comparative Perspective*, eds. Richard Gunther and Anthony Mughan (New York: Cambridge University Press, 2000), 250–51.

3. Cited in Larry J. Sabato, *Feeding Frenzy: How Attack Journalism Has Transformed American Politics* (New York: Free Press, 1991), 31.

4. Michael Schudson, *Watergate in American Memory: How We Remember, Forget, and Reconstruct the Past* (New York: Basic Books, 1992), 88–90.

5. Tip O'Neill with William Novak, *Man of the House: The Life and Political Memoirs of Speaker Tip O'Neill* (New York: Random House, 1987), 282–84.

6. David C. King, "The Polarization of American Parties and Mistrust of Government," in *Why People Don't Trust Government,* eds. Joseph S. Nye Jr., Philip D. Zelikow, and David C. King (Cambridge, MA: Harvard University Press, 1997), 155–78; Sarah A. Binder, "The Disappearing Political Center: Congress and the Incredible Shrinking Middle," *Brookings Review* 14 (1996): 36–39.

7. C. Eugene Steuerle, "Financing the American State at the Turn of the Century," in *Funding the Modern American State, 1941–1995: The Rise and Fall of the Era of Easy Finance*, ed. W. Elliot Brownlee (New York: Cambridge University Press, 1996), 409–44.

8. Philippa Strum, *Privacy* (New York: Harcourt Brace, 1998), 1–21.

9. Cited in Richard E. Cohen, *Rostenkowski: The Pursuit of Power and the End of the Old Politics* (Chicago: Ivan R. Dee, 1999), 246.

10. Dennis Hevesi, "Drug Use Emerges as Campaign Issue," and "Judge Ginsburg's State," *New York Times*, 8 November 1987.

11. Cited in Suzanne Garment, *Scandal: The Culture of Mistrust in American Politics* (New York: Doubleday, 1991), 69–70.

12. Jeffrey Toobin, "The Secret War in Starr's Office," *New Yorker*, 15 November 1999, 72.

13. Todd S. Purdum, "The Year of Passion," *New York Times*, 31 October 2004.

THIRTEEN: Seizing Power

1. These arguments and issues are explored in much greater detail in my book *On Capitol Hill* (2004). For an outstanding history of the tensions conservatives faced between ideology and the needs of governing, see Donald Critchlow's essay in *The American Congress: The Building of Democracy* (2004).

2. Newt Gingrich to Paul Weyrich, 18 December 1980, Tip O'Neill Papers, Kirk O'Donnell Papers, box 1, file: Newt Gingrich, 1982–1985, Boston College, Boston, MA.

3. Newt Gingrich to Republican Colleagues, 8 February 1983, Tip O'Neill Papers, Kirk O'Donnell Papers, box 1, file: Newt Gingrich, 1982–1985.

4. Newt Gingrich to Fellow Republican, 18 March 1982, Tip O'Neill Papers, Kirk O'Donnell Papers, box 1, file: Newt Gingrich, 1982–1985.

5. "Republican Agenda for the Remainder of 1983," 17 October 1983, Robert Michel Papers, Press Series, box I, file: Memoranda 1981–1988(2), Dirksen Congressional Center, Pekin, IL.

6. David Obey to Tony Coelho, 3 May 1984, Tip O'Neill Papers, Kirk O'Donnell Papers, box 1, file: Newt Gingrich, 1980–1989.

7. Jack Kemp to Friends, 1984, Tip O'Neill Papers, Kirk O'Donnell Papers, box 1, file: Newt Gingrich, 1982–1985.

8. Newt Gingrich to Colleagues, 15 December 1987, Jim Wright Papers, RC box 18-4, The Capital, Suite H 324, Steering and Policy Committee, file: Newt Gingrich, Texas Christian University, Fort Worth.

9. Newt Gingrich to Colleagues, 17 February 1988, Jim Wright Papers, RC box 18-4, The Capital, Suite H 324, Steering and Policy Committee, file: New Gingrich.

10. Bill Alexander to Colleague, 7 April 1989, Jim Wright Papers, RC box 18-4, The Capital, Suite H 324, Steering and Policy Committee, file: Newt Gingrich.

11. U.S. Congress, House of Representatives, Committee on Standards of Official Conduct, *Statement of Alleged Violation in the Matter of Representative James C. Wright, Jr.*, 101st Congress, 1st session, 13 April 1989.

12. U.S. Congress, House of Representatives, *Congressional Record*, 101st Congress, 1st Session, 31 May 1989, p. 10400.

13. Jerry Solomon to House Republican Leadership, 6 December 1990, Robert Michel Papers, Staff Series, K. Bullard, box 132, file: Legislative Agenda for 102nd Congress.

14. In the House, for instance, there were 5,388 House committee hearings in the 100th Congress (1987–1988); 5,152 House committee hearings in the 102nd Congress (1991–1992); 3,786 House committee hearings in the 104th Congress (1995–1996); and 3,347 House committee hearings in the 106th Congress (1999–2000).

FOURTEEN: How Conservatives Learned to Stop Worrying and Love Presidential Power

1. George F. Will, "Why Didn't He Ask Congress?" *Washington Post*, December 20, 2005.

2. Randall B. Woods, *LBJ: Architect of American Ambition* (New York: Free Press, 2006).

3. Paul J. Kern, "The President as 'Dictator' in the Light of Our History," *New York Times*, March 26, 1933.

4. James Burnham, *Congress and the American Tradition* (Chicago: Regnery, 1959), 93–97.

5. Bruce Schulman and Julian E. Zelizer, eds., *Rightward Bound: Making America Conservative in the 1970s* (Cambridge, MA: Harvard University Press, 2008).

6. An abbreviated version of this essay can be found in Julian E. Zelizer, "The Conservative Embrace of Presidential Power," *Boston University Law Review*, 88 (2006), 100–105.

7. Ronald Lora, "Conservative Intellectuals: The Cold War and McCarthy," in *The Specter: Original Essays on the Cold War and the Origins of McCarthyism*, eds. Robert Griffith and Athan Theoharis (New York: New Viewpoints, 1974), 60.

8. "Diary of White House Leadership Meetings—91st Congress," October 7, 1969, RNP (Richard Nixon Papers, College Park, MD), box 106, file: White House-Congressional Leadership Meeting 10/7/69.

9. Bryce Harlow to President Nixon, October 6, 1969, RNP, White House Central Files, Subject Files FG 31-1, box 5, file 4.

10. "Diary of White House Leadership Meetings—91st Congress."

11. Gareth Davies, *See Government Grow: Education Politics from Johnson to Reagan* (Lawrence: University Press of Kansas, 2007).

12. Arthur M. Schlesinger Jr., *Journals: 1952–2000* (New York: Penguin, 2007), 352.

13. Congressional Research Service, *Presidential Claims of Executive Privilege: History, Law, Practice and Recent Development*, September 17, 2007, 37.

14. James L. Sundquist, *The Decline and Resurgence of Congress* (Washington, DC: Brookings, 1981).

15. Jeffrey Hart, "The Presidency: Shifting Conservative Perspectives?" *National Review*, November 1974.

16. Kathryn S. Olmsted, *Challenging the Secret Government: The Post-Watergate Investigations of the CIA and FBI* (Chapel Hill: University of North Carolina Press, 1996), 48.

17. John Robert Greene, *The Presidency of Gerald R. Ford* (Lawrence: University Press of Kansas, 1995), 69, 70, 106.

18. Douglas Brinkley, *Gerald R. Ford* (New York: Times Books, 2007), 147.

19. Hugh Graham, *Collision Course: The Strange Convergence of Affirmative Action and Immigration Policy in America* (New York: Oxford University Press, 2002), 75; Paul Pierson, "The Rise and Reconfiguration of Activist Government," in *The Transformation of American Politics: Activist Government and the Rise of Conservatism*, eds. Paul Pierson and Theda Skocpol (Princeton, NJ: Princeton University Press, 2007), 24–26; Marc K. Landy and Martin Levin, eds., *The New Politics of Public Policy* (Baltimore: Johns Hopkins University Press, 1995); David Vogel, *Kindred Strangers: The Uneasy Relationship Between Politics and Business in America* (Princeton, NJ: Princeton University Press, 1996), 141–94, 298–388; Vogel, "The 'New' Social Regulation," in *Regulation in Perspective: Historical Essays*, ed. Thomas McGraw (Cambridge, MA: Harvard University Press, 1981), 155–85.

20. "Church: 'Entering the 1984 Decade,'" *Time*, March 24, 1975, 26.

21. "Backlash over All Those Leaks," *Time*, February 23, 1976.

22. "Text of Ford Plan on Intelligence Units and Excerpts from His Executive Order," *New York Times*, February 19, 1976.

23. David Burnham, "Compromise Bill Is Drafted on Electronic Surveillance," *New York Times*, February 8, 1978.

24. Olmsted, *Challenging the Secret Government*, 3.

25. *Congressional Quarterly Almanac* (Washington, DC: CQ Press, 1978), 843.

26. David S. Broder, "Presidential Power Is Defended by Ford," *Washington Power*, December 14, 1978.

27. Melvyn P. Leffler, *For the Soul of Mankind: The United States, the Soviet Union, and the Cold War* (New York: Hill & Wang, 2007), 346.

28. Samuel P. Hays, *Beauty, Health, and Permanence: Environmental Politics in the United States, 1955–1988* (New York: Cambridge University Press, 1987), 535–36.

29. Terry Eastland, *Ethics, Politics and the Independent Counsel: Executive Power, Executive Vice, 1789–1989* (Washington, DC: National Legal Center for the Public Interest, 1989).

30. Frederick A. O. Schwarz Jr. and Aziz Z. Huq, *Unchecked and Unbalanced: Presidential Power in a Time of Terror* (New York: New Press, 2007), 156.

31. Richard Pious, "Why Do Presidents Fail," *Presidential Studies Quarterly* 32 (December 2002): 739–40; Richard Piper, "Situational Constitutionalism and Presidential Power," *Presidential Studies Quarterly* 24 (1994): 577–96.

32. Michael A. Fitts, "The Paradox of Power in the Modern State: Why a Unitary, Centralized Presidency May Not Exhibit Effective or Legitimate Leadership," *University of Pennsylvania Law Review* 144 (1996): 847–50.

33. *Morrison v. Olson*, 487 U.S. 654, 699 (1988).

34. Charlie Savage, *Takeover: The Return of the Imperial Presidency and the Subversion of American Democracy* (New York: Little, Brown, 2007), 57–58.

35. Louis Fisher, "War Power," in *The American Congress: The Building of Democracy*, ed. Julian E. Zelizer (Boston: Houghton Mifflin, 2004), 695–96.

36. Stuart Taylor Jr., "Keep the Special Counsel," *New York Times*, June 22, 1992.

37. *Congressional Quarterly Almanac*, 1992, 317.

38. Adam Clymer, "Republicans in About-Face on Special Prosecutor Law," *New York Times*, November 18, 1993.

39. *Congressional Quarterly Almanac*, 1994, 295.

40. Clymer, "Republicans in About-Face on Special Prosecutor Law."

41. Kenneth R. Mayer and Kevin Price, "Unilateral Presidential Powers: Significant Executive Orders, 1949–1999," *Presidential Studies Quarterly* 32 (June 2002): 369.

42. William G. Howell and Kenneth R. Mayer, "The Last One Hundred Days," *Presidential Studies Quarterly* 35 (September 2005): 546–47.

43. John Yoo, "Kosovo, War Powers, and the Multilateral Future," *Pennsylvania Law Review* 148 (2000): 1673–1731.

44. Steven M. Teles, *The Rise of the Conservative Legal Movement: The Battle for Control of the Law* (Princeton, NJ: Princeton University Press, 2008).

45. Savage, *Takeover*.

46. Jane Mayer, "The Hidden Power," *New Yorker*, July 3, 2006, 44.

47. Mayer and Price, "Unilateral Presidential Power," 369.

48. Barton Gellman, *Angler: The Cheney Vice Presidency* (New York: Penguin, 2008), 81–107.

49. David J. Barron and Martin S. Lederman, "The Commander in Chief at the Lowest Ebb: A Constitutional History," *Harvard Law Review* 121 (February 2008): 1087–97.

50. Barton Gellman and Jo Becker, "Pushing the Envelope on Presidential Power," *Washington Post*, June 25, 2007.

51. Charlie Savage, "Bush Challenges Hundreds of Laws," *Boston Globe*, April 30, 2006.

52. Robert Pear, "Bush Directive Increases Sway on Regulation," *New York Times*, January 30, 2007.

53. Rachel L. Swarns, "Cheney, Needling Biden, Defends Bush's Record on Executive Power," *New York Times*, December 22, 2008.

54. See, e.g., the contributions in Schulman and Zelizer, eds., *Rightward Bound*; Donald T. Critchlow, *The Conservative Ascendency: How the GOP Right Made Political History* (Cambridge, MA: Harvard University Press, 2007).

FIFTEEN: Congress and the Politics of Troop Withdrawal

1. A good example of this interpretation is Robert Mann, *A Grand Delusion: America's Descent Into Vietnam* (New York, 2001). For a broader history of the politics of national security policy, see Julian E. Zelizer, *Arsenal of Democracy: The Politics of National Security—From World War II to the War on Terrorism* (New York, 2010).

2. One interesting book that has begun to explore this subject is Gary Stone, *Elites for Peace: The Senate and the Vietnam War, 1965–1968* (Knoxville, TN, 2007).

3. Randall Bennett Woods, *Fulbright: A Biography* (New York, 1995), 411.

4. Ibid., 406.

5. David S. Broder, "Goldwater Says Johnson Plays Politics with War," *New York Times*, May 6, 1966.

6. Telephone Conversation, Audio Tape, Lyndon Johnson and Robert McNamara, Tape WH6605.01, Citation 10106, Lyndon B. Johnson Presidential Library and Museum, Austin, TX (hereafter LBJL).

7. Julian E. Zelizer, *Taxing America: Wilbur D. Mills, Congress and the State, 1945–1975* (New York, 1998), 255–82.

8. Telephone Conversation, Lyndon Johnson and Wilbur Mills, March 24, 1968, Tape WH6803.05, Citation 12848, LBJL.

9. Robert M. Collins, "The Economic Crisis of 1968 and the Waning of the 'American Century,'" *American Historical Review* 101 (1996): 396–422.

10. Conrad Black, *Richard M. Nixon: A Life in Full* (New York, 2007), 636–37.

11. Lewis L. Gould, *The Most Exclusive Club: A History of the Modern United States Senate* (New York, 2005), 258.

12. Robert Dallek, *Nixon and Kissinger: Partners in Power* (New York, 2007), 153–54.

13. Ibid., 130.

14. Henry Kissinger, *White House Years* (Boston, 1979), 214.

15. Max Frankel, "Now It Is 'Nixon's War,'" *New York Times*, September 18, 1969.

16. Robert David Johnson, *Congress and the Cold War* (New York, 2006), 165.

17. Kissinger, *White House Years*, 513.

18. William C. Brennan, *William Fulbright and the Vietnam War: The Dissent of a Political Realist* (Kent, OH, 1988), 179–80.

19. Dallek, *Nixon and Kissinger*, 183.

20. James Cannon, *Time and Chance: Gerald Ford's Appointment with History* (New York, 1994), 397.

21. Jeffrey A. Engel, ed., *The China Diary of George H. W. Bush: The Making of a Global President* (Princeton, NJ, 2008), 151.

22. David Lockwood and George Siehl, "Military Base Closures: A Historical Review from 1988 to 1995," *Congressional Research Service Report*, October 18, 1994.

23. The best history of FISA can be found in Kathy Olmsted, *Challenging the Secret Government: The Post-Watergate Investigations of the CIA and FBI* (Chapel Hill, NC, 1996).

24. George Lardner Jr., "Carter Signs Bill Limiting Foreign Intelligence Surveillance," *Washington Post*, October 26, 1978.

25. Jack Goldsmith, *The Terror Presidency: Law and Judgment Inside the Bush Administration* (New York, 2007), 66, 180–82.

26. William G. Howell and Jon Pevenhouse, "When Congress Stops Wars," *Foreign Affairs*, September/October 1997.

27. Thomas Ricks, *The Gamble: General David Petraeus and the American Military Adventure in Iraq 2006–2008* (New York, 2009); Zelizer, *Arsenal of Democracy*, 499.

SIXTEEN: Détente and Domestic Politics

1. Robert McMahon, "Diplomatic History and Policy History: Finding Common Ground," *Journal of Policy History* 1 (2005): 94. For another excellent critique of this historiographical trend, see Fredrik Logevall, "A Critique of Containment," *Diplomatic History* 28 (September 2004): 473–99. See also Julian E. Zelizer, *Arsenal of Democracy: The Politics of National Security from World War II to the War on Terrorism* (New York, 2010).

2. John Lewis Gaddis, *The Cold War: A New History* (New York, 2006), 198. The archives cited in this essay include: Richard Nixon Presidential Materials, College Park, MD (hereafter RNP); Gerald Ford Presidential Library, Ann Arbor, MI (GFPL); and the Vanderbilt Television News Archives, Nashville, TN (hereafter VTA).

3. Joan Hoff, *Nixon Reconsidered* (New York, 1994), 201.

4. Jeremi Suri, *Henry Kissinger and the American Century* (Cambridge, MA, 2007), 150–57.

5. NBC Evening News, Record 454847, November 17, 1971, VTA.

6. Odd Arne Westad, *The Global Cold War* (New York, 2005), 194–95.

7. Edward Berkowitz, *Something Happened: A Political and Cultural Overview of the Seventies* (New York, 2006), 45.

8. Henry Kissinger to Richard Nixon June 14, 1973, National Security Council Papers, Henry Kissinger Office Files, Box 75, File: Meetings with Brezhnev, RNP.

9. Congressional Democrats were voting to reduce defense spending.

10. H. R. Haldeman, *The Haldeman Diaries* (New York, 1994), 274.

11. Peter Steinfels, *The Neoconservatives: The Men Who Are Changing American Politics* (New York, 1978), 294.

12. William Bundy, *A Tangled Web: The Making of Foreign Policy in the Nixon Presidency* (New York, 1998), 344.

13. Telephone Transcript, 6:30 p.m., May 11, 1973, Henry Kissinger Telephone Conversation Transcripts, Box 20, File: 11–15 May 1973, RNP.

14. "Synopsis of Meeting with President Richard Nixon at the Waldorf Astoria Hotel," September 26, 1972, President's Office File, Box 90, File: September 26, 1972, RNP.

15. Bundy, *A Tangled Web*, 346–47; Robert David Johnson, *Congress and the Cold War* (New York, 2006), 199–200.

16. Raymond L. Garthoff, *Détente and Confrontation: American-Soviet Relations from Nixon to Reagan* (Washington, DC, 1985), 548.

17. Memorandum of Conversation, May 12, 1975, 9:15 a.m., National Security Agency, Memoranda of Conversations, Box 11, File: May 12, 1975, GFPL.

18. Roy Reed, "Fulbright and Bumpers," *New York Times*, May 26, 1974; William C. Berman, *William Fulbright and the Vietnam War: The Dissent of a Political Realist* (Kent, OH, 1988), 194.

19. John Robert Greene, *The Presidency of George Bush* (Lawrence, KS, 2000), 122–23.

20. Bruce J. Schulman, *The Seventies: The Great Shift in American Culture, Society, and Politics* (New York, 2001), 196–205.

21. Lisa McGirr, *Suburban Warriors: The Origins of the New American Right* (Princeton, NJ, 2001), 66–67.

22. Craig Shirley, *Reagan's Revolution: The Untold Story of the Campaign that Started It All* (Nashville, TN, 2005), 36–37.

23. James Cannon, *Time and Chance: Gerald Ford's Appointment with History* (New York, 1994), 397.

24. Russ Rourke to Jack Marsh, June 26, 1975, John Marsh Files, Box 30, File: Solzhenitsyn, GFPL.

25. Douglas Brinkley, *Gerald R. Ford* (New York, 2007), 108.

26. Max Friedersdorf to the President, July 12, 1975, John Marsh Files, Box 30, File: Solzhenitsyn, GFPL.

27. Dick Cheney to Donald Rumsfeld, July 8, 1975, Richard Cheney Files, Box 10, File: Solzhenitsyn, Aleksander, GFPL.

28. Stef Halper to Dave Gergen, April 20, 1976, Dave Gergen Files, Box 8, File: Alexsander Solzhenitsyn, GFPL.

29. "Ford: 'A Challenge, Not a Conclusion," *Washington Post*, August 2, 1975.

30. John J. Casserly, *The Ford White House: The Diary of a Speechwriter* (Boulder, CO, 1977), 131.

31. Piero Gleijeses, *Conflicting Missions: Havana, Washington, and Africa, 1959–1976* (Chapel Hill, NC, 2002), 331, 389.

32. ABC Evening News, Record 35410, December 20, 1975, VTA.

33. Central Intelligence Agency, *Bolsheviks and Heroes: The USSR and Cuba: Special Memorandum*, November 21, 1967, National Security Online Archive (NSOA).

34. Robert David Johnson, "The Unintended Consequences of Congressional Reform," *Diplomatic History* 27 (April 2003): 237–38.

35. William Safire, "Cold War II," *New York Times*, December 29, 1975.

36. Robert Teeter to Richard Cheney, November 12, 1975, Robert Teeter Papers, Box 63, File: Analysis of Early Research, GFPL. See also "Remarks and a Question-and-Answer Session at a Public Forum in Atlanta," April 23, 1976, in *Public Papers of the Presidents of the United States: Gerald R. Ford, 1976–1977*, Book II (Washington, DC, 1979), 1191; Jussi Hanhimaki, *The Flawed Architect: Henry Kissinger and American Foreign Policy* (New York, 2004), 445.

37. A. James Reichley, *Conservatives in an Age of Change: The Nixon and Ford Administrations* (Washington, DC, 1981), 353–54.

38. Gerald R. Ford, *A Time to Heal: The Autobiography of Gerald R. Ford* (New York, 1979), 294–95; Max Friedersdorf, interview with Stephen Knott and Russell L. Riley, 24–25 October 2002, Ronald Reagan Oral History Project, Miller Center of Public Affairs, University of Virginia, 35.

39. Jerry Jones to Dick Cheney, November 18, 1975, Richard Cheney Files, Box 18, File: President Ford Committee—Advisory Committee Meeting 11/17/75, GFPL; Jerry Jones

to Don Rumsfeld and Dick Cheney, September 26, 1975, Jerry Jones Files, Box 35, File: Ronald Reagan (1), GFPL.

40. Memorandum of Conversation, January 8, 1976, 9:23 a.m.—10:30 a.m., NSOA.

41. Lou Cannon, *President Reagan: The Role of a Lifetime* (New York, 2000), 54–55.

42. Shirley, *Reagan's Revolution*, 94.

43. Ibid., 159.

44. "Statement by Ronald Reagan, in Orlando, Florida," March 4, 1976, Robert Hartmann Files, Box 26, File: Ronald Reagan, GFPL.

45. Transcript, Meet the Press, March 7, 1976, Ron Nessen Papers, Box 71, File: Meet the Press, GFPL.

46. Murrey Marder, "Ford Stirs Flurry on Détente," *Washington Post*, March 3, 1976. For an outstanding account that examines some of these same historical moments through the lens of neoconservative staffers and intellectuals, see James Mann, *Rise of the Vulcans: The History of Bush's War Cabinet* (New York, 2004), 56–78.

47. Dave Gergen and Dick Cheney, March 11, 1976, Michael Raoul-Duval Papers, Box 16, File: David Gergen, GFPL.

48. NBC Evening News, Record 487411, March 12, 1976, VTA.

49. William A. Rusher, *The Rise of the Right* (New York, 1984), 278.

50. "Ronald Reagan Paid Political Broadcast," Record 834566, March 31, 1976, VTA.

51. See, for instance, "An Explanation of the Reagan Victories in Texas and the Caucus States," 1976, GFPL, Jerry Jones Files, Box 25, File: Ronald Reagan (2); Jules Witcover, *Marathon: The Pursuit of the Presidency 1972–1976* (New York, 1977), 420.

52. Donald H. Rumsfeld, "Implications of Recent Trends in the United States and Soviet Military Balance," March 24, 1976, James E. Connor Files, Box 1, File: Defense, Donald Rumsfeld, GFPL.

53. Republican Party Platform, 1976, Online Documents, GFPL.

54. Ford, *A Time to Heal*, 398.

55. Martin Anderson, interview with Stephen Knott and James Sterling Young, December 11–12, 2001, Ronald Reagan Oral History Project, Miller Center of Public Affairs, University of Virginia, 31.

56. William F. Buckley Jr., "The President Comes Alive with the Conservative Spirit," *Los Angeles Times*, August 26, 1976.

57. Gaddis Smith, *Morality, Reason and Power: American Diplomacy in the Carter Years* (New York, 1986), 30; William Stueck, "Placing Jimmy Carter's Foreign Policy." In *The Carter Presidency: Policy Choices in the Post-New Deal Era*, eds. Gary M. Fink and Hugh Davis Graham (Lawrence, KS, 1988), 244–45.

58. Dick Holbrooke and Stu Eizenstat to Governor Carter, September 1, 1976, 1976 Presidential Campaign, Box 25, File: Memos–Jimmy Carter 9/76–10/76, Jimmy Carter Presidential Library, Atlanta, Georgia.

59. Joshua Muravchik, "Our Worst Ex-President," *Commentary*, February 2007.

60. James Patterson, *Grand Expectations: The United States, 1945–1975* (New York, 1996).

61. Yanek Mieczkowski, *Gerald Ford and the Challenges of the 1970s* (Lexington, KY, 2005), 333.

62. Brinkley, *Gerald R. Ford*, 139.

63. Michael Beschloss, "Ford's Long Shadow," *Newsweek*, January 8, 2007.

64. Donald R. Baucom, *SDI: The Origins of SDI 1944–1983* (Lawrence, KS, 1992), 81.

65. Richard Pipes, "Team B: The Reality Behind the Myth," *Commentary*, October 1986, 25–40.

66. Dale R. Herspring, *The Pentagon and the Presidency: Civil-Military Relations from FDR to George W. Bush* (Lawrence, KS, 2005), 241.

SEVENTEEN: Conservatives, Carter, and the Politics of National Security

1. Rosalynn Carter, *First Lady from Plains* (New York: Fawcett Gold Metal, 1984), 298.
2. Joshua Muravchik, "Our Worst Ex-President," *Commentary* (February 2007).
3. James Mann, *Rise of the Vulcans: The History of Bush's War Cabinet* (New York: Viking, 2004), 73–75.
4. Jay Winik, *On the Brink: The Dramatic, Behind-the-Scenes Saga of the Reagan Era and the Men and Women Who Won the Cold War* (New York: Simon & Schuster, 1996), 111.
5. William Stueck, "Placing Jimmy Carter's Foreign Policy," in *The Carter Presidency: Policy Choices in the Post-New Deal Era*, eds. Gary M. Fink and Hugh Davis Graham (Lawrence: University Press of Kansas, 1998), 245–48.
6. Jimmy Carter, "University of Notre Dame: Address at Commencement Exercises," May 22, 1977, in *Public Papers of Presidents of the United States: Jimmy Carter, 1977*, vol. 1 (Washington, DC: U.S. Government Printing Office, 1977), 956.
7. Coalition for a Democratic Majority to President Carter, May 14, 1977, Lyndon Johnson Presidential Library (Austin, TX), Papers of Peter Rosenblatt, box 49, File: Open Letter to Carter.
8. Steven F. Hayward, *The Age of Reagan: The Fall of the Old Liberal Order 1964–1980* (Roseville, CA: Forum, 2001), 536–37.
9. Joshua Muravchik, *The Uncertain Crusade: Jimmy Carter and the Dilemmas of Human Rights Policy* (Lanham, MD: Hamilton Press, 1986), 161–95.
10. Memorandum of Conversation, February 1, 1977, Carter Library, NSA, Brzezinski Material, Subject File, box 34, File: Memocons, President 2/77.
11. Jessica Tuchman Matthews to Zbigniew Brzezinski, July 7, 1978, Carter Library, White House Central File, Subject File, Human Rights, box HU-1, File: 7/1/78–8/31/78.
12. Peter Beinart, *The Good Fight: Why Liberals—and Only Liberals—Can Win the War on Terror and Make America Great Again* (New York: HarperCollins, 2006), 58–59.
13. Julian E. Zelizer, *On Capitol Hill: The Struggle to Reform Congress and Its Consequence, 1948–2000* (New York: Cambridge University Press, 2004).
14. Rachel Bronson, *Thicker Than Oil: America's Uneasy Partnership with Saudi Arabia* (New York: Oxford University Press, 2006), 134.
15. Zbigniew Brzezinski, *Power and Principle: Memoirs of the National Security Adviser* (New York: Farrar, Straus, Giroux, 1983), 189.
16. Landon Butler to Hamilton Jordan, March 17, 1977, Carter Library, Office of Chief of Staff, box 37, File: SALT, 1977.
17. Hamilton Jordan to President Carter, June 28, 1977, Carter Library, Hamilton Jordan Papers, box 34, File: Foreign Policy/Domestic Politics Memo 6/77.
18. David Skidmore, *Reversing Course: Carter's Foreign Policy, Domestic Politics, and the Failure of Reform* (Nashville: Vanderbilt University Press, 1996), 117.
19. J. Michael Hogan, *The Panama Canal in American Politics: Domestic Advocacy and the Evolution of Policy* (Carbondale: Southern Illinois University Press, 1986), 114–31.
20. Richard A. Viguerie, *The New Right: We're Ready to Lead* (Falls Church, VA: Viguerie Company, 1981), 70–71.

21. Patrick Caddell, "A Memorandum on Current Public Attitudes on SALT," Carter Library, Office of Chief of Staff, box 37, File: SALT 1979.

22. Dan Tate to Frank Moore, November 18, 1977, Carter Library, Office of Chief of Staff, box 37, File: SALT, 1977.

23. Frank Moore and Hamilton Jordan to the President, 1979, Carter Library, Office of Congressional Liaison, box 230, File: SALT II Memo, 7/30/79—8/17/79.

24. Frank Moore to President Carter, July 7, 1978, Carter Library, Hamilton Jordan Papers, box 34, File: Comprehensive Test Ban Treaty, SALT, 1978.

25. "What Chance Now of Selling SALT to the Senate?" *The Economist*, November 18, 1978, 19.

26. Tip O'Neill with William Novak, *Man of the House: The Life and Political Memoirs of Speaker Tip O'Neill* (New York: Random House, 1987), 308.

27. Gaddis Smith, *Morality, Reason, and Power: American Diplomacy in the Carter Years* (New York: Hill & Wang, 1986), 9.

28. Ibid., 115.

29. Philip Jenkins, *Decade of Nightmares: The End of the Sixties and the Making of Eighties America* (New York: Oxford University Press, 2006), 156–57.

30. David D. Newsom, *The Soviet Brigade in Cuba: A Study in Political Diplomacy* (Bloomington: Indiana University Press, 1987), 16, 40.

31. Jimmy Carter, "Address to the Nation on Soviet Combat Troops in Cuba and the Strategic Arms Limitation Treaty," October 1, 1979, in *Public Papers of the Presidents of the United States: Jimmy Carter 1979*, vol. 2 (Washington, DC: U.S. Government Printing Office, 1980), 1806.

32. Albert R. Hunt, "Carter Apparently Didn't Boost Chances for Passage of SALT with Cuban Speech, *Wall Street Journal*, October 3, 1979.

33. Hedley Donovan to Zbigniew Brzezinski and Lloyd Cutler, September 27, 1979, Carter Library, NSA, Brzezinski Material, box 16, File: Cuba Soviet Brigade (Meetings) 9/79.

34. David Farber, *Taken Hostage: The Iran Hostage Crisis and America's Encounter with Radical Islam* (Princeton, NJ: Princeton University Press, 2005), 5, 187.

35. Robert D. Schulzinger, *U.S. Diplomacy since 1900*, 5th ed. (New York: Oxford University Press, 2002), 329.

36. For the best history of terrorism in the 1970s, see Timothy Naftali, *Blind Spot: The Secret History of American Counterterrorism* (New York: Basic Books, 2005), 1–115.

37. See Wattenberg letters from January 1980 in Johnson Library, Papers of Peter Rosenblatt, box 59, File: White House Meeting.

38. Jimmy Carter, *Keeping Faith: Memoirs of a President* (New York: Bantam Books, 1982), 473.

39. David S. Broder, "Bipartisan Support Wanes for Carter's Iran Policy," *Washington Post*, January 3, 1980.

40. Jimmy Carter, "Annual Message to Congress," January 21, 1980, in *Public Papers of the Presidents of the United States: Jimmy Carter, 1980–1981*, vol. 1 (Washington, DC: U.S. Government Printing Office, 1981), 164.

41. Les Francis to Frank Moore, June 11, 1979, Carter Library, Office of Congressional Liaison, box 228, File: Registration and the Draft.

42. ABC Evening News, Reference 62358, January 24, 1980, Vanderbilt Television Archives.

43. Marshall Brement to Zbigniew Brzezinski, January 10, 1980, Carter Library, Brzezinski Material, Subject File, box 48, File: Olympics 6/79–2/80.

44. William Dyess to the Deputy Secretary of State, March 21, 1980, Carter Library, Office of the Press Secretary, box 66, File: Olympic Boycott 1/80.

45. Lloyd Cutler, interview with Marie Allen, March 2, 1981, Carter Library, Exit Interview Collection, 7–8.

46. Tip O'Neill, John Brademas, Clement Zablocki, Jim Wright, John Rhodes, and William Broomfield to U.S. Olympic Committee, April 1, 1980, Carter Library, NSA, Brzezinski Material, Subject File, box 48, File: Olympics 6/79–2/80.

47. Patrick Caddell to Les Francis, May 26, 1980, Carter Library, Office of Chief of Staff, box 77, File: Campaign Strategy—Caddell.

48. Kiron S. Skinner, Annelise Anderson, and Martin Anderson, *Reagan: A Life in Letters* (New York: Free Press, 2003), 400.

49. Thomas B. Edsall, *Building Red America: The Conservative Coalition and the Drive for Permanent Power* (New York: Basic Books, 2006), 50–52.

Index

Note: Page numbers in italic type indicate photographs.

Aaron, Henry, 47
Abbot, Andrew, 48
Abramoff, Jack, 282–83, 284
Abrams, Elliot, 299
Abscam affair, 245
Achenbaum, Andrew, 47, 49, 53
Adams, Sherman, 235
Addington, David, 303
Advisory Council on Social Security, 185
Afghanistan, Soviet invasion of, 335, 343, 345–46, 348
AFL-CIO, 206, 211, 213–14, 262, 328
African Americans, 85, 224. *See also* race
agenda-setting, 23
Agnew, Spiro, 322
Aid to Dependent Children, 155
Aid to Families with Dependent Children, 280
Ailes, Roger, 274
Alexander, Herbert, 199, 201–2, 204
Allen, James, 215, 217
Allison, Graham, 45
Altmeyer, Arthur, 160
AMA. *See* American Medical Association
Ambrose, Stephen, 16, 20
Amenta, Edwin, 57
American Association of Retired Persons (AARP), 114
American conservatism: and anticommunism, 70, 73, 77–78, 94; beliefs of, 265; in Bush Jr. years, 281–85, 349; and Bush Sr., 275; and Carter, 335–48; causal factors in, 69–71; and centralization, 276–85; in Congress, 259–85; and decentralization, 266–76; and Ford, 328–30; and foreign policy, 321, 324–25, 335–48; fragmentation of, 72–75, 265, 277–81; frustrations and failures of, 77–79, 269–70, 275, 284; fusionist consensus behind, 72–73; future of scholarship on, 87–89; governance challenges for, 75–80, 275–76, 279–81, 349; history of, 68–89; and liberalism's persistence, 81–87; and Medicare, 169; modern, 265–66; new political history and, 93–95; and Nixon, 293, 322–23; organizations of, 265; post–congressional reform, 264–70; and presidential power, 290–306; prominent individuals in, 267–68, 277–78, 327–28; and race, 69–70, 94; and Reagan, 74, 78, 100, 121, 269–70, 272, 297–300, 330–34, 336, 348; and religion, 70, 77, 94, 265; southern Democrats and, 170, 261, 266; and state-building, 169; successes of, 79–80, 276, 280, 349; and Supreme Court, 265; tactics of, 71; and taxation, 79–80, 120–21, 269, 275, 281. *See also* neoconservatives

American Conservative Union, 331, 340
American Enterprise Institute, 216, 266, 327
American Farm Bureau Federation, 114, 143
American Federation of Labor (AFL), 199. *See also* AFL-CIO
American Historical Association, 44, 60
American Historical Review (journal), 27, 41, 68
American Legion, 316
American Liberty League, 134, 291
American Medical Association (AMA), 172, 173, 176, 203
American Political Development (APD), 3, 5, 6, 23, 61–64, 90, 92, 97–98
American Political Science Association, 22, 50, 60, 62, 228
American Security Council, 341
Americans for Democratic Action, 13, 210, 262
Americans for Tax Reform, 269
Americans with Disabilities Act (1990), 275
AmeriCorps, 83
Amnesty International, 339
Anderson, Jack, 203
Anderson, John, 211, 215, 217, 226, 348
Angola, 329–30
Annales school, 2, 65
anticommunism, 70, 73, 77–78, 94, 235, 322–23, 347
Antiquities Act (1906), 301
anti-statism: business role in, 112; and fiscal conservatism, 127; popular, 108, 115; race and, 365n24; scholarship on, 107, 111; taxation and, 111, 123
APD. *See* American Political Development
Armey, Dick, 267
Arnold, Peri, 49
Ashbrook, John, 296
Ashmore, Robert, 204, 206
Associated Milk Producers, 218
Association for Policy Analysis and Management, 46
Atwater, Lee, 274
automatic revenue, 117–18
Aviation Trust Fund, 171
Babbitt, Bruce, 246
Baker, Howard, 272, 341
Baker, Newton, 127
Baker, Paula, 28, 41
Baker v. Carr (1962), 223
Bakker, Jim, 248
balanced budget, 124–47. *See also* budget deficits; deficit reduction; fiscal conservatism
Balanced Budget Act (1997), 184
Balanced Budget Agreement, 185–86
balance of power, 322
Ball, Robert, 160, 164, 167
Balogh, Brian, 28, 49, 58, 62, 95–97, 108
Barber, J., 15
Barr, Joseph, 205
Barr, William, 300
Baruch, Bernard, 128
Battistella, Annabel, 242
Bayh, Birch, 296, 318
Bean, Jonathan, 221–22
Beard, Charles, 9–10, 60
Begin, Menachim, 343
Beito, David, 56
Bell, Daniel, 138, 143
Bensel, Richard, 23, 61, 221
Bentsen, Lloyd, 216
Berkowitz, Edward, 45, 48, 49, 55, 62, 222
Berlin, Irving, 114
Bernstein, Carl, 239–40, 241
Berry, Jeffrey, 81
Beschloss, Michael, 19, 58
Bettercare, 176
Biden, Joseph, 215, 216, 249
Biemiller, Andrew, 206, 211
big government. *See* government: size of
Binder, Sarah, 354n55
Bipartisan Commission on the Future of Medicare, 186
Bix, Amy Sue, 55
Blue Cross Blue Shield, 184
Blum, John, 369n8
Board of Education (congressional group), 261
Bobbitt, Lorena, 248
Boland, Eddie, 272, 296

Boland Amendments, 78
Bolling, Richard, 229, 262
Boris, E., 99
Bork, Robert, 245–46
Boschwitz, Rudy, 267
Bosnia, 74, 309
"bottom up" historiography, 2, 19, 42, 61, 91
Bowling Green University, 50
bracket creep, 120, 121
Brademas, John, 217, 229
Breaux, John, 186
Brement, Marshall, 347
Brezhnev, Leonid, 324, 325, 343
Bricker, John, 292
Brinkley, Alan, 68, 93, 148
Brinkley, Douglas, 295
Brock, William (Bill), 214, 346
Brookings Institution, 266
Brooks, David, 285
Brown, Harold, 346
Brown, Jerry, 346
Brown, Michael, 118, 125
Brownlee, W. Elliot, 30
Brzezinski, Zbigniew, 338, 340, 343–45
Buchanan, Pat, 265, 275
Buckley, William, Jr., 73, 291, 327, 333
Budget and Relief Message (1937), 142
budget deficits, 108–9, 113, 116, 121–22, 128, 130–31, 133–34, 147. *See also* balanced budget; deficit reduction
Budget Enforcement Act (1990), 121
Budget Reform Act (1974), 293
Bumpers, Dale, 326
Bundy, William, 316
Bureau of the Budget, 132–33, 139
Burleson, Omar, 204
Burnham, James, 14, 291
Burnham, Walter Dean, 21–22, 29–30
Burns, James MacGregor, 14, 16
Burton, Phillip, 229, 262
Bush, George H. W., 78, 82, 122, 275, 299, 300, 309, 318, 319
Bush, George W., 74–75, 77–80, 88, 122, 168, 253–54, 283, 290–91, 302–4, 309, 319, 349
business: and campaign finance, 200; government in relation to, 110, 112; and taxation, 112, 118
Business Roundtable, 73
Buttafuoco, Mary Jo, 248
Butterfield, Alexander, 240
Byrd, Robert, 341
Byrnes, James, 127
Byrnes, John, 173–74, 176, 177

Cable News Network (CNN), 246–47
cable television, 246–47, 263
Caddell, Patrick, 348
Califano, Joseph, 118, 311
Cambodia, 294–95, 315–16
campaign finance, 195–220; accomplishments concerning, 220; coalition for reforming, 196, 200, 208, 213, 216; conservative Republicans and, 282–83; disclosure of, 200–201, 204, 212–13, 220; and election costs, 207; experts on, 200–201; news coverage of, 210; obstacles to, 198; public financing and, 201, 203–5, 207, 209–12, 214–15, 217–18; public opinion on, 203–4, 217; puzzles concerning, 195–97; reform efforts (1956–1964) in, 198–202; reform efforts (1969–1973) in, 207–16; roots of reforms in, 197–98; scandals involving, 199, 203, 214–18; Watergate and, 214–18, 241
CAMSCAM, 272
Cannon, Howard, 204
Carnegie Foundation, 201–2, 228
Carnegie Mellon University, 46
Carpenter, D. P., 98
Carter, Jimmy, 18, 20, 124, 239, 241, 294, 296, 333, 335–48
Carter, Rosalynn, 335
Case, Clifford, 317
Case, Francis, 199
Castro, Fidel, 239, 344
Catchings, Waddill, 146
Catholic Church, 347
Cato Institute, 266
caucuses, party, 262, 264, 273

CBS Evening News (television show), 248
Celler, Emanuel, 221
Center for the Public Financing of Elections, 209, 210
Central America, 78, 297, 309
Central Intelligence Agency (CIA), 239, 241, 295, 304, 311, 318, 329, 334, 337, 344
centralization, congressional conservatives and, 276–85
centrism, 335–49
Chamber of Commerce, 216
Chandler, Alfred, 27
Chase, Stuart, 146
Cheney, Richard (Dick), 78, 268, 270, 273, 294, 296, 300, 302–4, 319, 328
China, 21, 265, 318, 322–24, 329, 335
Christian Broadcast Network, 247
Church, Frank, 183, 241, 295, 296, 314–17, 344, 347
Citizens for America, 283
Citizens' Research Foundation, 201, 202, 203, 210, 229
civic participation, 63
Civil Rights Act (1964), 55
Civil Rights Act (1989), 275
Clark, Dick, 329
Clark, Joseph, 204, 206, 237
class action lawsuits, 209–10
Clerk of the House, 201, 202, 208
Cleveland, Grover, 233
Clifford, Clark, 205
Clinton, Bill, 51, 59, 74, 81–83, 122, 124, 150, 168, 185–87, 232, 247, 250–53, 276, 278–81, 300–303, 309, 319, 349
Clinton, Hillary, 250–52, 300, 301
CNBC, 247
CNN. *See* Cable News Network
Coalition for a Democratic Majority, 338, 345
Cochran, Thomas, 11
Cohen, Cathy, 64
Cohen, Lizabeth, 92
Cohen, Wilbur, 55, 159, 162, 163, 166, 167, 174, 177
Cohen, William, 300
Colby, William, 294
Cold War, 15, 16, 18, 114, 116, 235–36, 244, 291–92, 311, 315, 322, 340, 343, 344
Collins, Robert, 31
Colmer, William, 267
Colson, Charles, 215
Commission on Campaign Costs, 201
Committee for the Survival of a Free Congress, 266, 327, 341
Committee on Campaign Contributions and Expenditures, 200–201
Committee on Economic Security (CES), 138–39
Committee on Foreign Intelligence and Operations Advisor Group, 295
Committee on Political Education (COPE), 199
Committee on the Present Danger, 334, 337
Committee to Maintain a Prudent Defense Policy, 325
Committee to Reelect the President (CREEP), 213, 239–40
Common Cause, 208–13, 216, 217, 219, 227, 229, 238, 241, 262, 273–74
Communications Act (1934), 207
Comparative Politics, 64
Conable, Barber, 229
Concord Coalition, 182
conflicts of interest, 233, 241, 245
Congress: and campaign finance, 197–98, 204–8, 210–19, 241; committee era (1920s–1960s) of, 261; conservatism in, 259–85; elections for, 223–24; ethical issues in, 272–75, 283, 284; historiography focused on, 5–6; institutional reform and, 226–28; and Medicare, 172–88; and military/national security matters, 16, 291–92, 300, 309–20, 329–30; news coverage of, 224–26; Nixon vs., 292–93; policy role of, 22; post-reform, 264–70; power of, 14, 17–18, 318; and presidential power, 13–15; reform of, in 1970s, 222–29, 242, 260, 262–63, 294; Republican reforms (1995) of, 276–78; scandals involving, 224–26, 235, 242–43,

245, 284; scholarship on, 30; seniority in, 222, 224–27, 235, 237, 242–43, 261; and Social Security, 154, 156–58, 160–67; Supreme Court and, 223–24; transparency of, 235, 243, 261; and troop withdrawal, 314–20; and Vietnam War, 309–18
Congressional Black Caucus, 85
Congressional Budget and Impoundment Act (1974), 17
Congressional Quarterly (journal), 201, 203
Congress of Industrial Organizations (CIO), 197–99. *See also* AFL-CIO
Congress of Vienna (1815), 322
Congress Watch, 229
Connally, John, 217
conservatism. *See* American conservatism
Conservative Caucus, 340
Conservative Opportunity Society (COS), 270–72, 274, 276, 277
consumptionism, 146–47
Contract with America, 276, 301
Contras. *See* Iran-Contra affair
Cook, Blanche Weisen, 16
Cooper, John Sherman, 315–16
Coors, Joseph, 266, 328
corporate liberal synthesis, 110
corporations. *See* business
corruption. *See under* scandals
Corwin, Edward, 14
COS. *See* Conservative Opportunity Society
Council of Economic Advisers, 160, 161
Cox, Archibald, 240, 252
Crane, Daniel, 248
Cranston, Alan, 346
Crédit Mobilier scandal, 233
Crespino, Joseph, 69, 94
Critchlow, Donald, 48, 49, 57, 88
Cronkite, Walter, 240, 348
C-SPAN, 243, 271, 275
Cuba, 329–30, 338, 340, 343–44
cultural historians and cultural history, 50, 229
Currie, Lauchlin, 146
Curtis, Carl, 166
Curtis, Thomas, 177–78
Dahl, Robert, 60
D'Amato, Alfonse, 319
Daschle, Tom, 281
Dateline (television show), 247
Davies, Gareth, 76, 100, 356n78
Davis, Michele, 79
Dawson, Michael, 64
D.C. Consumer's Association, 212
decentralization, congressional conservatives and, 266–76
Deering, Christopher, 222
deficit reduction, 122, 124, 128. *See also* balanced budget; budget deficits; fiscal conservatism
DeLay, Tom, 271, 281, 283, 284
democracy: and corruption, 233; state-building and, 108, 110, 112; and taxation, 107–23
Democratic Caucus, 82, 85, 227, 229, 242
Democratic Party: and campaign finance, 203, 207–8, 210–19; Carter and, 339, 342; and congressional reform, 224; liberalism's persistence and, 81–87; Nixon vs., 292–93; reforms of, 239; Republican conservatives vs., 263, 268–85. *See also* southern Democrats
Democratic Study Group (DSG), 227, 229
DeNiro, Robert, 253
Dent, Harry, 274
Department of Agriculture, 142–43, 212
Department of Defense, 298
Department of Education, 77
Department of Homeland Security, 319
Department of Justice, 200, 201, 212, 215, 250, 275, 298, 303, 305
Department of State, 339
deregulation, 80
Derthick, Martha, 22, 47, 56, 61, 170
détente, 265, 268, 293, 316, 321–36, 338–40, 347, 348
Diner, Steven, 46
Dionne, E. J., 72–73
direct mail, 202, 210, 266
Dirksen, Everett, 311
Divine, Robert, 16

Dobrynin, Anatoly, 339
Dobson, James, 70, 94
Dodd, Thomas, 203, 224, 226
Dolan, Terry, 265, 327
Dole, Robert, 211, 219, 272, 280, 300, 316
domestic politics, and foreign policy, 307–8, 311–13, 321–34
Dorsey Press, 48
Doughton, Robert, 159, 161, 167
Douglas, Lewis, 126–34, 136, 145–49
Dowd, Matthew, 349
draft, military, 346
Drudge, Matt, 251
Duke University, 46
Dulles, John Foster, 338

earmarked taxes, 117, 154–56, 164–65, 167, 172, 372n6
Eccles, Marriner, 141, 146, 148
economic history, 31
Economic Policy Board, 294
Economic Recovery Tax Act (1981), 79, 121
Economist (newspaper), 342
Economy Act (1933), 129–30
Edelman, Benjamin, 80
Edsall, Thomas, 69
Edwards, George, 25
Egypt, 343
Eisenach, Eldon, 50
Eisenhower, Dwight, 15–16, 20, 25, 114, 116, 166, 171, 199, 234–35, 292, 344
Eisner, Marc, 57
Eizenstat, Stuart, 346
Election Reform Act, 205
electoral politics, 6–7, 308. *See also* presidential primaries
Elementary and Secondary Education Act (1965), 76
Ellsberg, Daniel, 240
Energy Resources Council, 294
environmental regulations, 297–98
Equal Employment Opportunity Commission v. Sears, Roebuck & Company, 51
Ervin, Sam, 214, 217, 240
Ethics in Government Act (1978), 18, 241, 297
Ethiopia, 340
Evans, Robert, 331
executive branch. *See* presidency
executive orders, 129, 297, 301, 302

Faludi, Susan, 69
Falwell, Jerry, 70, 94, 327
Farley, James, 130–31
FEC. *See* Federal Election Commission
Federal Bureau of Investigation (FBI), 51, 245
Federal Election Commission (FEC), 218, 219
Federalist Society, 298
Federal Old-Age and Survivors' Insurance Trust Fund, 156
Federal Trade Commission, 46, 235
Federation of Homemakers, 212
feminism, 85, 243, 249, 252. *See also* gender
Fenno, Richard, 22
Ferraro, Geraldine, 249
filibusters, 226–28, 237, 261–64, 264
FISA. *See* Foreign Intelligence Surveillance Act (FISA, 1978)
fiscal concerns, and taxation in democracies, 107–23
fiscal conservatism: anti-statism and, 127; benefits of, 126; defined, 124–25; Douglas and, 126–34; liberalism and, 124–25; and Medicare, 169, 175, 185; Morgenthau and, 135–45; New Deal, 124–50, 171; post–New Deal, 108, 112–23; public opinion on, 128; and Social Security, 167; state-building and, 125; Vietnam War and, 313. *See also* balanced budget
Fitton, Thomas, 284
Flowers, Gennifer, 250
Flynt, John, 267
Flynt, Larry, 252
Foley, Mark, 277–78, 284
Foley, Thomas, 229
Folsom, Marion, 157
Foner, Eric, 91
Ford, Gerald, 76, 185, 218, 219, 268, 294–96, 317–18, 321, 326–37

Ford Foundation, 46, 201–2
Ford Motors, 200
Foreign Intelligence Surveillance Act (FISA, 1978), 296, 303, 318
foreign policy: domestic politics and, 307–8, 311–13, 321–34; electoral politics and, 308; Ford and, 326–34; Nixon and, 322–26; presidential power and, 15. *See also* national security
Foster, Richard S., 183
Foster, Vincent, 250
Franc, Michael, 284
Frankfurter, Felix, 223
Fraser, Donald, 262
Freedom House, 339
Frenzel, William (Bill), 211, 217, 229, 273
Friedberg, Aaron, 116
Friedel, Frank, 129
Friedman, Milton, 73
Frist, Bill, 284
Fulbright, William, 290, 294, 310–11, *312*, 314–16, 326

Galambos, Louis, 27, 45
Gallager, Cornelius, 226
Gardner, John, 208–9, 211, 218–19, 227, 238–39
Garner, Nance, 127
Garrett, Lawrence H., III, 246
gay rights, 85–86
Geertz, Clifford, 61
gender, 28, 54, 371n4. *See also* feminism
General Electric, 200
Geneva Conventions, 304
Gephardt, Richard, 281
Gergen, David, 331
Germond, Jack, 236–37
Gilens, Martin, 64
Gillon, Steve, 74
Gingrich, Newt, 74, 243, 252, 267–79, 301, 342
Ginsberg, Douglas, 246
Ginzburg, Alexander, 339
Goldsmith, Jack, 318
gold standard, 131, 136
Goldwater, Barry, 16, 71, 93, 94, 199, 200, 202, 205, 294, 311, 316, 322–23, 336
Gonzales, Alberto, 303
Goodell, Charles, 204, 206, 315
Goodwin, Doris Kerns, 59
Gorbachev, Mikhail, 74, 87
Gordon, Linda, 49, 54, 93
Gore, Albert, Jr., 84, 168, 186, 246, 253
Gore, Albert, Sr., 199, 204, 205
government: business in relation to, 110, 112; demand for services from, 108; nineteenth-century role of, 95–97; size of, 75–76, 100, 283–84, 292; trust in, 207, 234, 236, 239, 244. *See also* anti-statism; state-building
government expenditures, under Roosevelt, 127–47
government shutdown, 279–80
Graham, Daniel, 334, 337
Graham, Hugh, 27–28, 49, 52, 55–56, 354n49
Graham, Lindsey, 277, 278
Graham, Otis, Jr., 44, 45, 51
Grant, Hugh, 248
Great Society, 16, 20, 22, 76, 118–19, 313
Green, William, 128
Greenstein, Fred, 15–16
Griffith, Robert, 15
Guantánamo detention center, 304, 305
Gulf of Tonkin Resolution, 16, 317
Gulf Oil, 200
Gulf War (1991), 247, 309, 319
Gutman, Herbert, 47

Hacker, Jacob, 79–80, 99, 119–20
Haldeman, H. R., 316
Hamdan v. Rumsfeld (2004), 304
Hamilton, Shane, 70, 99
Harding, Warren, 233
hard power, 302–3
Harkin, Tom, 339
Harriman, Henry, 128
Harris, Fred, 315
Harris, Seymour, 200
Harrison, George L., 148
Hart, Gary, 84, 249

Hart, Jeffrey, 294
Hart, Philip, 207
Hartz, Louis, 13, 60, 61
Harvard Business School, 45, 46
Hastert, Dennis, 281
Hatfield, Mark, 316
Hawley, Ellis, 45, 48, 50, 60
Hays, Samuel, 27, 28, 57, 81
Hays, Wayne, 197, 211, 213, 217, 218, 242
Health Care Financing Administration, 182
Heard, Alexander, 199, 201, 205
Hebert, F. Edward, 242
Heclo, Hugh, 61, 63
Heller, Walter, 118
Helms, Jesse, 319, 327, 328, 331
Henderson, Leon, 146
Hennings, Thomas, 199
Heritage Foundation, 266, 327
Herring, G., 96
Hersh, Seymour, 296
Highway Trust Fund, 171
Hill, Anita, 248–49
historical institutionalism: and American conservatism, 76; and policy history, 49–50, 52, 58; and political time, 29–30
historiography. *See* new political history; political history
HI Trust Fund. *See* Hospital Insurance (HI) Trust Fund
Hochschild, Jennifer, 64
Hodgson, Godfrey, 17, 73, 266
Hoff, Joan, 21
Hoffman, Dustin, 241, 253
Hoffman, Paul, 200
Hofstadter, Richard, 1, 10, 14, 60, 81
Hoover, Herbert, 27, 114, 127–28
Hope, Bob, 322
Hopkins, Harry, 138, 142, 146
Hospital Insurance (HI) Trust Fund, 168, 170, 175, 179, 181–82, 185, 186
House Bank, 274–75
House Committee on Un-American Activities, 261
House Ethics Committee, 273–75, 283
House Intelligence Committee, 296
House Rules Committee, 261, 262, 273
House Ways and Means Committee, 158–64, 173, 176, 178, 185, 242, 259
Howard, Christopher, 56–57
Hughes, Philip, 215
Huitt, Ralph, 228
Human Events (magazine), 330
human rights: Carter and, 336, 338–39; Iran and, 344; Soviet Union and, 319, 325, 327, 329, 333
Human Rights Working Group of the Coalition for a New Foreign and Military Policy, 339
Humphrey, Hubert, 195, 214, 218, 229, 262
Huntington, Samuel, 14
Hussein, Saddam, 78, 319
Hyde, Henry, 252

Ickes, Harold, 133, 138, 139, 141, 142
Imperial Presidency, 12, 16–19, 290, 309
income taxes, 79–80, 107–8, 113–15
Independent Counsel Reorganization Act (1987), 299
independent prosecutors, 245, 250, 252, 253, 300, 301. *See also* Special Prosecutor's Office
inflation, 133
institutions: American Political Development and, 3, 23, 61–62; change in, 65–66; conservatism and, 75–77; constraints imposed by, 3–4, 24; policymaking and, 53–55; political history and, 5–6, 62, 65; reform discourse concerning, 226–28. *See also* historical institutionalism
Intelligence Oversight Board, 294, 295
interdisciplinarity, 9–10, 47
interest groups: conservative Republicans and, 282; criticisms of, 208–9; fiscal conservatism and, 137; importance of, 108
Intermediate-Range Nuclear Forces (INF) arms treaty, 74
Internal Revenue Service (IRS), 234, 235
International Olympic Committee, 347
international political economy, 64

Internet, 247
Iran-Contra affair, 245, 299, 302, 318. *See also* Nicaragua
Iran hostage crisis, 343, 344–45, 348
Iraq war (2003–), 79, 284, 319–20
isolationism, 15
Israel, 343

Jackson, Andrew, 233
Jackson, Henry "Scoop," 212, 325, 326–27, 333, 336, 342, 344
Jackson-Vanik amendment, 327
Jacobs, M., 98, 99, 100
Javits, Jacob, 314, 326
Jefferson, Thomas, 26
Jeffords, Jim, 83
Jews, in Soviet Union, 325, 327
John, Richard, 62, 96
John Paul II, Pope, 347
Johnson, Lyndon, 16–17, 20, 26, 31, 108, 118–19, 124, 170, 174–75, 201–2, 204–5, 238, 290, 294, 310–13, *312*
Jones, Charles, 25
Jones, Jerry, 330
Jones, Jesse, 148
Jones, Paula, 250
Jordan, Hamilton, 340
Jordan, Vernon, 251
journalism. *See* news media; newspapers
Journal of American History, 27, 41
Journal of Contemporary History, 84
Journal of Policy Analysis and Management, 46
Journal of Policy History, 42, 49, 50, 52, 58
Journal of Social History, 47

Katz, Michael, 54, 91
Katz, Milton, 200
Katznelson, Ira, 23, 61, 63, 97–98, 363n9
Kaye, Danny, 114
Kean, Robert, 160, 163
Keegan, George, 334
Keller, Morton, 45, 46, 57
Kelley, Robert, 43, 45, 48, 57
Kemp, Jack, 269, 272
Kennan, George F., 310
Kennedy, David, 125
Kennedy, Edward (Ted), 80, 206, 229, 238, 296, 315, 319, 346, 348
Kennedy, John, 16, 20, 118, 124, 201, 217, 236
Kennedy, Patrick, 238
Kennedy, Robert, 205
Kerry, John, 319
Kessler-Harris, A., 93
Key, V. O., 21
Keynes, John Maynard, 73, 146
Keynesianism, 146–48, 156
Khomeini, Ruhollah, 344–45
King, Larry, 247
King, Susan, 209
Kingdon, John, 23, 63
Kinnock, Neil, 249
Kirk, Grayson, 200
Kirkpatrick, Jeane, 334, 337
Kissinger, Henry, 295, 314–16, 322–26, 328–31, 336
Klein, J., 99
Kohn, Barbara Benson, 44
Kolko, Gabriel, 60, 110
Kopechne, Mary Joe, 238
Korean War, 15, 114, 115, 165
Kosovo, 56, 74, 301
Kousser, J. Morgan, 46
Kruse, Kevin, 69, 94
K Street Project, 282–84

labor, 80, 119–20, 199. *See also* unions
Ladd Taylor, Molly, 28, 49
Laird, Melvin, 315
Lamb, Brian, 229
Landon, Alfred, 134
Lassiter, Matthew, 69–70, 94
law, 30
Laxalt, Paul, 341
Leach, James, 300
Leach, Jim, 272
Leff, Mark, 125, 221
Lehman, John, 317

Leuchtenburg, William, 3, 13, 42, 110
Levin, Carl, 300
Levinson, Barry, 252
Lewinsky, Monica, 250–52, 280
Libby, Lewis "Scooter," 284, 303
liberalism: Clinton and, 83; and congressional power, 294–97; and congressional reform, 262–63; and fiscal conservatism, 124–25; grassroots, 84–85; and institutional reform, 227; McGovern and, 84; New Deal, 136, 149; new political history and, 100; persistence of, 81–87, 100, 264–65; political history and, 13–14, 110; and presidential power, 290; and Vietnam War, 313–14
Liddy, G. Gordon, 214
Lieberman, Robert, 64
Life (magazine), 226
Light, Paul, 24
Lincoln, Abraham, 304
Livingston, Robert, 252, 278
Long, Russell, 204, 215, 222, 236
Lott, Trent, 267, 273
Lowi, Theodore, 22–23
Lungren, Daniel, 268

MacArthur, Douglas, 309
MacAvoy, Paul, 45
MacDonald, Torbert, 207
Mack, Connie, 270
MacNeil/Lehrer News-Hour (television show), 274
Manley, John, 22
Mansfield, Mike, 314, 315, 317
Mao Zedong, *323*
Marmor, Theodore, 22, 170–71, 173
Mason, Noah, 160, 371n1
Mathias, Charles, 211
May, Ernest, 45, 47, 48–49, 56
Mayhew, David, 22, 25, 66
McAdoo, William, 127
McCarthy, Joseph, 15, 93, 235, 236, 272
McClellan, John, 199
McClory, Robert, 296
McCord, James, 240
McCraw, Thomas, 45, 46, 47
McDonnell Douglas, 200
McFarlane, Robert, 299
McGirr, Lisa, 70, 73, 94
McGovern, George, 83, 84, 214, 316, 336, 338, 347
McInnis, Scott, 259
McKee, Guian, 86
McNamara, Robert S., 313
Meany, George, 200
media. *See* news media
Medicaid, 83, 176
Medicare: conservatism and, 169; costs of, 122, 153, 173–78, 181–82; as earned benefit, 185; expansion of, 78; financing of, 83, 117–19, 167, 168–88, 272, 280; fiscal conservatism and, 169, 175, 185; formation of, 22; original financing design of, 172–78; Part A financing in, 172–75, 178–82; Part B financing in, 176–78, 182–86; parts of, 168, 184–86; popular support for, 114; post–1968 financing design of, 178–84; recent reform proposals for, 186–88; and Social Security, 119, 173–76; solvency of, 170–71, 178–82, 187; and taxation, 182, 380n5; welfare state scholarship and, 169–71
Medicare Act (1965), 182
Meese, Edwin, 298
Meiklejohn, Alexander, 206
Meyer, Frank, 72
Miami Herald (newspaper), 249
Michel, Robert, 269, 271
Michel, Sonya, 49
Milazzo, Paul, 98, 222
military-industrial complex, 307
Milken, Michael, 248
Milkis, Sidney, 24–25
Mills, C. Wright, 91
Mills, Wilbur, 22, 62, 154, 160–63, 165–78, 181–84, 186–88, 204, 205, 212, 214, 218, 222, 225, 242, 313, 357n91, 380n6
Mills v. Alabama (1966), 206
Milner, Helen, 63
Minchin, Timothy, 57
Miroff, Bruce, 84

Mitchell, John, 214
Mock, David, 48
Moley, Raymond, 131, 148
Mondale, Walter, 206, 346
monetary policy, 131, 133–34, 136
Montgomery, David, 92
Moore, Frank, 342
Moore, William Carlos, 273
Moos, Malcolm, 205
Morgenthau, Henry, Jr., 126, 135–49, 157
Morris, Dick, 250, 251
Morrison v. Olson (1988), 299
Moscow Olympics, 335, 347
Mossadegh, Muhammad, 344
Mozambique, 329
MSNBC, 247
MTV, 247
Mugwumps, 233
Murray, James, 221
Murray, William, 127
Muskie, Edmund, 214, 218
Mutch, Robert, 210, 381n3
Myers, Robert, 154, 158, 160–62, 164, 167, 174–77, 181

NAACP. *See* National Association for the Advancement of Colored People
Nader, Ralph, 80, 212, 229
Nash, George, 69, 72
National Academy of Political Science, 144–45
National Association for the Advancement of Colored People (NAACP), 262
National Association of Manufacturers, 199
National Bipartisan Commission on the Future of Medicare, 168
National Commitments Resolution (1969), 294
National Committee for an Effective Congress, 207, 209, 210, 212, 229
National Congressional Club, 331
National Conservative Political Action Committee, 265, 327
National Coordinating Committee for the Promotion of History, 43
National Council for Public History, 43
National Economic League, 127
National Endowment for the Humanities (NEH), 47
National Front for the Liberation of Angola (FNLA), 329
National Inquirer (tabloid), 249
National Intelligence Estimate on Soviet Strategic Objectives (NIE), 334, 337
National Organization of Women, 252
National Organization to Reduce Public Expenditures, 127
National Review (journal), 73
National Rifle Association, 327
national security: Carter and, 335–48; Congress and, 309–21; and détente, 321–34; Reagan and, 331–32, 348
National Security Agency, 296
National Security Council, 15, 245, 295, 299
National Union for Total Independence of Angola (UNITA), 329
NBC, 247
neoconservatives: and break from Democratic Party, 265, 321, 324–25, 348; policy positions of, 74–75, 79, 324–25, 327–28; and the state, 111
Neumann, Mark, 278
Neustadt, Richard, 14, 24, 47, 48–49, 56, 205
New Deal: coalition formed around, 75, 80, 119–20; financing, 113; and fiscal conservatism, 124–50, 171; and government, 88, 107; liberal historiography and, 13–14, 93, 110; liberalism of, 136, 149; presidential power and, 24–25; undermining of, 99
New Left: and policy history, 42; and political history, 1–2, 15, 60, 69, 91; and presidential power, 290
new political history: and American conservatism, 93–95; APD vs., 97–98; causal explanation in, 98; emergence of, 1–4, 90–93; future of, 99–101; on nineteenth-century government, 95–97; and political science, 61; political science and, 90–101; and state-building, 109; subject matter of, 19, 42; and taxation, 109

news media: and campaign finance, 210; and campaigns, 249; and Clinton scandals, 250–53; coverage by, 263; and entertainment, 237, 247, 252–53; Republican Party and, 271–72, 279; and scandals, 224–26, 234–38, 241, 247–49. *See also* television
newspapers, 248
New York Post (newspaper), 234
New York Times (newspaper), 128, 133, 240, 293
New York Times Co. v. Sullivan (1964), 206
Nicaragua, 245, 283, 299, 318, 343. *See also* Iran-Contra affair
Nightline (television show), 247
nineteenth-century politics, 95–97
Nitze, Paul, 325, 334, 337
Nixon, Richard, 12, 17–18, 20–21, 76, 120, 183, 203, 208, 210, 212–13, 215–19, 225, 232, 234, 239–40, 252, 265, 267, 274, 292–94, 297, 310, 311, 314–17, 321–27, 322, 323, 335, 336
Noble, Edward, 266
No Child Left Behind Act (2001), 77
Nol, Lon, 315
Noriega, Manuel, 319
Norquist, Grover, 269, 282–83
North, Oliver, 245, 299
North Atlantic Treaty Organization (NATO), 343
Novak, Robert, 331
Novak, W. J., 96
Novick, Peter, 44, 66
nuclear-freeze movement, 86
Nussle, James, 275

OASI. *See* Old Age and Survivors' Insurance
Obama, Barack, 77, 305, 320
Oberlander, Jonathan, 170–71, 179
Obey, David, 272
objectivity, 44, 236, 238
O'Brien, Lawrence, 175
O'Connor, Alice, 71, 94
Office of Government Ethics, 241
Office of Management and Budget, 18
Office of the Independent Counsel, 18, 297, 298
Office of War Information, 114
O'Hara, James, 215
Old Age and Survivors' Insurance (OASI), 156, 159–67
Old-Age Assistance, 155, 159–60, 164, 166
Old-Age Insurance and Unemployment Compensation, 155–56
Olympic Games, U.S. boycott of, 335, 347
O'Neill, Tip, 243, 269, 272, 342
Operation Desert Storm (1991), 78
Orfield, Gary, 22
organizational synthesis, 27–28, 45, 61, 91, 110
Organization of American Historians, 1
Orren, Gary, 207
Orren, Karen, 30, 50

Packwood, Robert, 246
PACs. *See* political action committees
Pahlavi, Shah, 344–45
Panama and Panama Canal, 319, 331, 340–41
Paris Peace Accords (1973), 317
particularity, 66
Pastore, John, 215
Patashnik, Eric, 24, 168
path dependence, 62, 64
Patman, Wright, 133, 137, 221, 242
Patterson, James, 31, 76
Pearson, Drew, 203, 226, 236
Pearson, James, 207, 211
Pell, Claiborne, 216
Penn State Press, 48, 49
Pentagon Papers, 240, 293
Penthouse (magazine), 295
Perkins, Frances, 129, 139
Perle, Richard, 334, 337
Perlstein, Rick, 71
Perot, Ross, 247
Peterson, Mark, 25
Phelps, Timothy, 249
Philadelphia Industrial Development Corporation, 86
Philadelphia Model Cities Administration, 86
Phillips, Howard, 340
Phillips-Fein, Kimberly, 71, 94–95, 99

Pierson, Paul, 24, 64–65, 76, 79–80, 88–89, 98, 99, 121
Pike, Otis, 295
Pipefitters v. United States (1972), 213
Pipes, Richard, 337
Pittman, Key, 133
Playboy (magazine), 295
Poage, W. R., 242
Podesta, John, 84
Poindexter, John, 245, 299
policy: alternatives to, 55–56; congressional role in, 22; conservatism and, 75–80; factors in formation of, 23; historical assumptions and analogies concerning, 56–57; historiography focused on, 4–5; implementation of, 22; institutional and cultural context for, 53–55; particularities of, 97–99; political science and, 12, 63; presidential role in, 23–24
policy analysis, 46–47, 51, 53, 61
policy communities, 5, 23
policy history: academic foundations of, 44–46; applications of, 46–47, 51–53, 59; arguments for value of, 48–49; categories of, 42, 53–58; definitions of, 45; development of, 42–53, 97–99; future of, 58–59; methodology of, 45–46; and policy analysis, 46–47, 51, 53, 61; and political time, 30–31; public history and, 42–44; since 1978, 41–59; status of, 41–42, 48, 50–53, 58–59
policy process, 58
political action committees (PACs), 197, 199, 202–3, 211, 213, 219–20, 283
political culture: and anti-statism, 111; defined, 57; and policy history, 57–58; and political time, 29
political economy, 64, 99
political history: and American conservatism, 68–89; "bottom up," 2, 19, 42, 61, 91; criticisms of, 1–2, 19; interdisciplinarity in, 9–10; liberal, 13–14, 110; and policy, 97–99; political science and, 60–67; and the presidential synthesis, 11–19; revival of, 1–4, 90–93; and social history, 221–22; value of, 65–66. *See also* new political history
political institutions. *See* institutions
political parties: and campaign finance, 198, 202–3; caucuses of, 262, 264, 273; in nineteenth century, 254–55; scandal as weapon of, 244, 254–55; strengthening of, 82; weakening of, 255
political process, and political time, 28–29
political regimes, 29–30
political science: and new political history, 90–101; and policymaking, 12, 63; political history and, 60–67; and the presidency, 21–26; and the presidential synthesis, 12, 14; and race, 64
political time: defined, 26; election cycles and, 308; reconceptualization of, 4, 13, 26–32; significance of, in scholarship, 64–65
Polsby, Nelson, 23
Popular Movement for the Liberation of Angola (MPLA), 329–30
Powe, Lucas, Jr., 30
Powell, Adam Clayton, 224, 225
Powell, Lewis, 213
power, hard vs. soft, 302–3
presidency: conservatism and, 290–306; leadership in, 25–26; limitations of, 21–26; political science critiques of, 21–26; popular opinion and, 25; power of, 11–19, 290–306, 309, 318; public opinion on, 304; scholarship on individuals in, 19–21. *See also* presidential synthesis
Presidential Campaign Fund, 204
presidential primaries, 82
presidential signing statements, 304
presidential studies, 24–25
presidential synthesis: criticisms of, 11–12, 91, 169–70; individual presidencies and, 19–21; liberal, 11–19; New Left and, 15, 91; persistence of, 19
President's Club, 203
Pressman, Jeffrey, 22
primaries. *See* presidential primaries
privacy, 236, 244–45
Public Citizen, 212
The Public Historian (journal), 43, 46

public history movement, 42–44, 51
public interest, 237–39
public interest groups, 81, 209, 227, 238–39
public opinion: on campaign finance, 203–4, 217; on executive branch, 304; on fiscal conservatism, 128; foreign policy as influence on, 308; on Olympic boycott, 347; on Panama Canal, 340; polls as gauge of, 366n49; on taxes, 108, 115; trust in government, 207, 234, 236, 239, 244; on Vietnam War, 314, 317; on Watergate, 240
public policy. *See* policy
Public Works Administration (PWA), 132–33

al Qaeda, 303
Quadagno, Jill, 54
quantitative analysis, 2, 42, 46, 51–52
Quayle, Dan, 74, 272
Quirk, Paul, 47

race: and anti-statism, 365n24; conservatism and, 69–70, 94; policy history and, 54; political science and, 64; and Social Security, 371n4; and suburbs, 69–70. *See also* African Americans
Rainey, Henry, 133
Rangel, Charles, 259
rational choice theory, 48, 50, 57, 61
Rauchway, E., 97
Rayburn, Sam, 161, 235, 261
Reagan, Ronald, 3, 18, 24, 69, 73, 74, 76–78, 80, 82, 86–87, 93, 100, 120, 121, 244–45, 268, 269, 272, 293, 297–300, 309, 322–23, 322, 330–34, 336, 337, 341, 343, 346, 348
realignment synthesis, 21–22, 30, 61
realism, 324
Reconstruction Finance Corporation (RFC), 141
Redford, Robert, 241
redistricting, 223
Reed, Ralph, 282
Rehnquist, William, 299
religion, 70, 77, 94, 265
Reno, Janet, 300
Republican Party: and American conservatism, 68, 69, 71, 73–77, 259–85; and campaign finance, 202, 210–15, 282–83; and Clinton, 74, 250–53, 276, 278–81, 300–302; conflicts within, 272; COS and, 270–72; and news media, 271–72, 279; power of, 276–85; in the South, 263, 274
Reuther, Walter, 200
Reynolds v. Sims (1946), 223
Rhode, David, 82
Ribicoff, Abraham, 326
Ribuffo, Leo, 68
Rice, Donna, 249
Richardson, Elliot, 240
Right. *See* American conservatism
Ripley, Randall, 22
Robinson, Kenneth, 296
Rockefeller Foundation, 43, 45
Rodgers, Daniel, 29, 89
Rollins, Ed, 274
Roncalio, Teno, 268
Roosevelt, Eleanor, 200
Roosevelt, Franklin, 12–14, 24, 26, 27, 110, 113, 125–49, 155, 171, 290, 291, 297, 304
Roosevelt, Theodore, 14, 44, 290
Rossiter, Clinton, 14
Rostenkowski, Dan, 245
Rostow, Eugene, 334, 337
Rothman, David, 47
Rove, Karl, 349
Ruml, Beardsley, 146
Rumsfeld, Donald, 294, 296, 328, 332
Rusk, Dean, 310
Russell Sage Foundation, 47
Russert, Tim, 247

Sadat, Anwar, 343
Sager, Ryan, 75
Salisbury, Harrison, 238
Salon (Internet magazine), 251
Sanders, Elizabeth, 61
Sandinista National Liberation Front, 343
Santorum, Rick, 282
Saturday Night Massacre, 240, 297

Savage, James, 125
savings and loan industry, 249
Scaife, Richard, 266
Scalia, Antonin, 299
scandals: barriers to, 235–37; in campaign finance, 199, 203, 214–18; Clinton's involvement in, 250–53; congressional, 224–26, 235, 242–43, 284; corruption, 233, 234, 239–41; democracy and, 233; historical instances of, 233; historiography of, 256; military, 246; news media and, 224–26, 234–38, 241, 247–49; non-political, 248; political use of, 243–46, 254–55; in postwar era, 234–37; prevalence of, 232–33; public interest and, 237–39; reform politics and, 234, 239–43; sex, 233, 236, 238, 246, 248–54, 284; television and, 234–38, 246–47. *See also* Iran-Contra affair; Watergate
Scanlon, Michael, 284
Scharansky, Anatoly, 339
Schattschneider, E. E., 21
Scheuer, Sidney, 210
Schickler, Eric, 98
Schlafly, Phyllis, 327
Schlesinger, Arthur, Jr., 1, 10, 12, 13, 15–18, 42, 60, 110, 290, 293
Schoenwald, Jonathan, 71
Schulman, Bruce, 16, 89, 221
Schultze, Charles, 118
Schumer, Charles, 232
Schweiker, Richard, 332
Scott, Hugh, 205, 211, 217
Sears, John, 332
Secretary of the Senate, 201, 208
Securities and Exchange Commission, 212, 235
Select Committee on Presidential Campaign Activities, 214
Senate Finance Committee, 185
Senate Intelligence Committee, 296
separation of powers, 17, 25, 298, 299
sex scandals, 233, 236, 238, 246, 248–54, 284
Shefter, Martin, 50
Shermer, Elizabeth, 71
Silbey, Joel, 28, 229
Silverberg, Helene, 56
Silver Purchase Act (1934), 133
Simpson, O. J., 248
Sirica, John, 240
60 Minutes (television show), 250
Skocpol, Theda, 3, 23–24, 48, 50, 55, 61, 62, 88–89
Skowronek, Stephen, 3, 13, 23–26, 49–50, 54, 61, 95
Smith, Howard, 267
Smith, J. S., 99
Smith, Rogers, 50, 64
Smith, Steven, 222
social historians and social history, 46–47, 221–22, 229
social insurance, 153–55, 157–59, 172. *See also* social welfare
Social Security: bureaucratic role in, 22; conservatism and, 30, 76, 78; costs of, 122, 153, 156, 297; design of, 138–39, 148, 154, 173; early questions concerning, 156–59; as earned benefit, 139, 153–55, 157, 160, 165; extension of, 156–57, 159–60, 162, 165–66; financing expansion of, 159–67, 292–93; fiscal conservatism and, 167; gender and, 371n4; and Medicare, 119, 173–76; popular support for, 114; race and, 371n4; self-supporting nature of, 155–56; taxation and, 113, 117, 138–39, 153–67; two tracks of, 154–55
Social Security Act (1935), 154–55, 372n6
Social Security Administration, 22, 156, 158–59, 167
Social Security Amendments (1939), 156–57
Social Security Amendments (1950), 148, 154, 164–66
Social Security Amendments (1954), 166
social welfare, 119–20, 122, 159. *See also* social insurance; welfare state
soft power, 302–3
Solzhenitsyn, Aleksander, 328–29
Somalia, 309, 319, 340, 348
Somoza, Anastasio, 343
Sonnenfeldt, Helmut, 331

sound bites, 236
South Africa, 329
southern Democrats: anti-statism of, 111; and campaign reform, 202; conservatism of, 170, 261, 266; fiscal conservatism of, 125, 148; liberal Democrats vs., 224; power of, 223–24, 226, 237, 261, 263; and social welfare, 93, 139
Soviet Union, 21, 73, 74, 77–78, 87, 235, 265, 297, 316, 321–49
Sparling, Jim, 219
Sparrow, Bartholomew, 225
Speaker's Advisory Group (SAG), 277
Special Prosecutor's Office, 241
Stans, Maurice, 212, 214
Stark, Pete, 259
Starr, Kenneth, 251–52
state-building: conservatism and, 169; democracy and, 108, 110, 112; fiscal conservatism and, 125; fiscal problems of, 112–23; new political history and, 109; strategies for, 108–9; taxation and, 107–8, 112–23. *See also* anti-statism; government
Stearns, Peter, 43, 47
Steel, Ronald, 311
Steiner, Gilbert, 47
Steinmo, Sven, 54
Steiwer, Frederick, 291
Stern, Philip, 209
Steuerle, Eugene, 24
Steven, Robert, 47
Steven, Rosemary, 47
Stevenson, Adlai, 234, 313
St. Louis Pipefitters Local Union No. 562, 211–12
Stone, I. F., 236
Stone, Richard, 343–44
Strategic Arms Limitation Talks I (SALT I), 324
Strategic Arms Limitation Talks II (SALT II), 296, 330, 331, 332, 335, 339–45, 348
Strategic Defense Initiative ("Star Wars"), 86
Strauss, Robert, 210–11
Studds, Gerry, 248
Studies in American Political Development (journal), 50, 62
Study of Congress, 228
Subcommittee Bill of Rights (1973), 263, 277
Sugrue, Thomas, 31, 56, 70, 85
Sundquist, James, 22, 61
sunshine laws, 243
Supplementary Medical Insurance (SMI) Trust Fund, 168, 182, 185
Supreme Court: and campaign finance, 197, 198, 206, 211–13, 219, 241; and congressional elections, 223–24; and conservatism, 265; on drug testing, 244; on electoral process, 263; on executive privilege/power, 240, 250, 293, 299; interventionism of, 223; on military tribunals, 304; power of, 18; presidential power and, 13–14; scandals involving, 245–46, 248–49; on surveillance, 296; and 2000 presidential election, 254
surveillance, 295–96, 318
Symington, Stuart, 314

Taft, Robert, 221
Tailhook Association, 246
Tarr, Joel, 43
taxes and taxation: anti-statism and, 111, 123; attitudes toward, 107–8, 112–15, 120–21, 123; business and, 112, 118; conservatism and, 79–80, 120–21, 269, 275, 281; democracy and, 107–23; earmarked, 117, 154–56, 164–65, 167, 172, 372n6; income taxes, 79–80, 107–8, 113–15; loopholes, 115–16, 137–38; Medicare and, 182, 380n5; New Deal and, 113; new political history and, 109; Social Security and, 113, 117, 138–39, 153–67; state-building and, 107–8, 112–23; strategies for, 108–9
Taylor, Maxwell D., 310
Team B, 334, 337–38
Teapot Dome affair, 233
Teeter, Robert, 330
Teles, Steve, 71
television: and campaigns, 198, 202–3, 205, 207–8, 212, 249; politicians on, 236; Republican Party and, 271–72; and scandal, 234–38, 246–47. *See also* news media
Thatcher, Margaret, 76, 347

think tanks, 266, 278, 327
Thomas, Bill, 186, 259
Thomas, Clarence, 248–49
Thomas, Elmer, 133
Thompson, Frank, 206
Thurmond, Strom, 328
time. *See* political time
Time (magazine), 280
Today (television show), 251
Tomlins, Christopher, 30
Toobin, Jeffrey, 251
Totenberg, Nina, 249
Tower, John, 246
Townsendite movement, 156
Trade Reform Act (1974), 327
Tripp, Linda, 251
troop withdrawal, 314–20
Truman, David, 60
Truman, Harry, 15, 20, 25, 115, 116, 124, 148, 159, 165, 234, 309
Trump, Donald, 248
trust funds, 117, 171, 179
trust in government, 207, 234, 236, 239, 244
TRW, 213
Tuchman, Jessica, 339
Tuck, Stephen, 85, 100
Tugwell, Rexford, 138
Tunney, John, 329
Turner, Ted, 246
TV Guide (magazine), 276
Twentieth Century Fund, 210
Twenty One (television show), 236

Udall, Morris, 211, 215, 217
Undistributed Profits Tax, 138
Unemployment Compensation, 372n10. *See also* Old-Age Insurance and Unemployment Compensation
Uniform Code of Military Justice, 304
Union Carbide, 200
unions, 80, 199–200, 211–13. *See also* labor
University of California at Santa Barbara, 43
University of Houston, 46
University of the District of Columbia, 46
USA Today (newspaper), 248
U.S. Court of Appeals for the District of Columbia, 299
U.S. Olympic Committee, 347

Vance, Cyrus, 338, 343, 348
Vandenberg-Murray amendment (1944), 158, 160, 162, 164
Vanderbilt, William, 200, 201
Van Doren, Charles, 236
Vanik, Charles, 326
vendor payments, 164
Vietnam War, 16–17, 20, 70, 77, 81, 119, 225, 227, 238, 240, 294, 309–18, 328
Viguerie, Richard, 202, 265, 266, 327, 328
Village Voice (newspaper), 295
Vinovskis, Maris, 59
Vogel, David, 112
Voting Rights Act (1965), 224

Wagner, Robert, 22, 128
Wag the Dog (film), 252–53
Walker, Robert, 270
Wallace, George, 205
Wallace, Henry, 143
Wall Street Journal (newspaper), 145, 284, 300
Walsh, Lawrence, 245, 299, 300
Wamp, Zach, 283
War on Poverty, 16, 31, 54, 56, 108, 118–19, 227
war on terrorism, 303–4
War Powers Act (1973), 17, 293, 301, 317
Warren, Earl, 30, 223
Washington Post (newspaper), 214, 251
watchdog journalism, 225, 238
Watergate, 17, 20–21, 195, 196, 214–19, 232, 239–40, 267, 293, 326–27, 336
Waterhouse, Benjamin Cooper, 73
Wattenberg, Ben, 345
Waxman, Henry, 84, 229, 263, 277
Webber, Carolyn, 115
Weber, John Vincent (Vin), 267, 270
Wedtech Corporation, 298
Weinberger, Casper, 78, 185, 299
Weinstein, James, 60

Weir, Margaret, 50
welfare state, 54, 57, 76, 88, 92–93, 97, 99, 119–20, 140, 153, 163, 169, 171, 188, 270, 272, 293. *See also* social welfare
Wertheimer, Fred, 213
Wesberry v. Sanders (1964), 223
Weyrich, Paul, 266, 327
Wheeler, Burton, 133
Wheeler, Stanton, 47
Whitewater affair, 251, 300
Wiebe, Robert, 27
Wildavsky, Aaron, 22, 24, 115
Wildmon, Donald, 70, 94
Wilkie, Wendell, 134
Will, George, 290
Williams, Aubrey, 146
Williams, John, 203, 204, 206
Williams, William Appleman, 307
Williams, W. R., 161
Wilson, Bob, 296
Wilson, James Q., 45
Witcover, Jules, 332
Witte, John, 116
Wittner, Lawrence, 86
Wolfowitz, Paul, 337
Wooden, William, 136
Woods, Randall Bennett, 310
Woodward, Bob, 239–40, 241
Wright, James, 272–74
Wright, Susan Webber, 250

Yoo, John, 301, 303
Young, Neil J., 73
Young Americans for Freedom, 331, 341
Young America's Foundation, 330

Zaire, 329
Zeitz, Joshua, 85